HTML5 and

ILLUSTRATED – First Edition

Complete

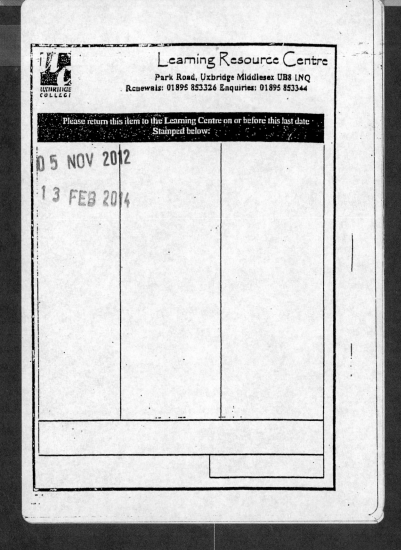

Sasha Vodnik

COURSE TECHNOLOGY
CENGAGE Learning

Australia • Brazil • Japan • Korea • Mexico • Singapore • Spain • United Kingdom • United States

COURSE TECHNOLOGY
CENGAGE Learning™

HTML5 and CSS3—Illustrated Complete, First Edition

Sasha Vodnik

Vice President, Publisher: Nicole Jones Pinard

Executive Editor: Marjorie Hunt

Associate Acquisitions Editor: Amanda Lyons

Senior Product Manager: Christina Kling Garrett

Associate Product Manager: Kim Klasner

Editorial Assistant: Brandelynn Perry

Director of Marketing: Elisa Roberts

Senior Marketing Manager: Ryan DeGrote

Developmental Editor: Marjorie Hopper

Content Project Manager: Matthew Hutchinson

Copy Editor: Troy Lilly

Proofreader: Foxxe Editorial

Indexer: BIM Indexing and Proofreading Services

QA Manuscript Reviewers: John Frietas, Jeff Schwartz, Danielle Shaw, Ashlee Welz Smith, Susan Whalen

Print Buyer: Fola Orekoya

Cover Designer: GEX Publishing Services

Cover Artist: Mark Hunt

Composition: GEX Publishing Services

For product information and technology assistance, contact us at
Cengage Learning Customer & Sales Support, 1-800-354-9706

For permission to use material from this text or product, submit all requests online at **www.cengage.com/permissions**
Further permissions questions can be emailed to
permissionrequest@cengage.com

Trademarks:

Some of the product names and company names used in this book have been used for identification purposes only and may be trademarks or registered trademarks of their respective manufacturers and sellers.

Library of Congress Control Number: 2011934600

ISBN-13: 978-1-111-52798-3
ISBN-10: 1-111-52798-9

Course Technology
20 Channel Center Street
Boston, MA 02210
USA

Cengage Learning is a leading provider of customized learning solutions with office locations around the globe, including Singapore, the United Kingdom, Australia, Mexico, Brazil, and Japan. Locate your local office at:
international.cengage.com/region

Cengage Learning products are represented in Canada by Nelson Education, Ltd.

To learn more about Course Technology, visit **www.cengage.com/coursetechnology**

To learn more about Cengage Learning, visit **www.cengage.com**

Purchase any of our products at your local college store or at our preferred online store **www.cengagebrain.com**

Printed in the United States of America

1 2 3 4 5 6 7 8 9 18 17 16 15 14 13 12 11

Brief Contents

Contents

Preface

Welcome to *HTML5 and CSS3—Illustrated Complete*, First Edition. If this is your first experience with the Illustrated series, you'll see that this book has a unique design: each skill is presented on two facing pages, with steps on the left and screens on the right. The layout makes it easy to learn a skill without having to read a lot of text and flip pages to see an illustration.

This book is an ideal learning tool for a wide range of learners—the "rookies" will find the clean design easy to follow and focused with only essential information presented, and the "hotshots" will appreciate being able to move quickly through the lessons to find the information they need without reading a lot of text. The design also makes this a great reference after the course is over! See the illustration on the right to learn more about the pedagogical and design elements of a typical lesson.

About This Book

This is a brand new book in the Illustrated Series—this is *not* a revision of *HTML Illustrated*, Third Edition by Cox, Reding and Wermers. This book takes a new, fresh approach to teaching HTML5 and CSS3 to develop Web pages and Web sites. Users learn to write and interpret HTML and CSS code using no more than a basic text editor and a browser. Encouraging users to see Web development as team process, sample projects include professionally-designed layouts and Web-ready text, allowing users to focus on building the skills needed to combine these elements into Web pages and Web sites. All code is tested on several widely-used browsers, and all steps can be completed by Windows or Mac users. In addition to basic HTML elements, units cover and incorporate new HTML5 semantic elements. CSS coverage includes downloadable fonts, multicolumn and fluid layouts, and semantically accurate table layouts using only CSS.

Each two-page spread focuses on a single skill.

Introduction briefly explains why the lesson skill is important.

A case scenario motivates the the steps and puts learning in context.

Tips and troubleshooting advice, right where you need it—next to the step itself.

Large screen shots keep students on track as they complete steps.

Brightly colored tabs indicate which section of the book you are in.

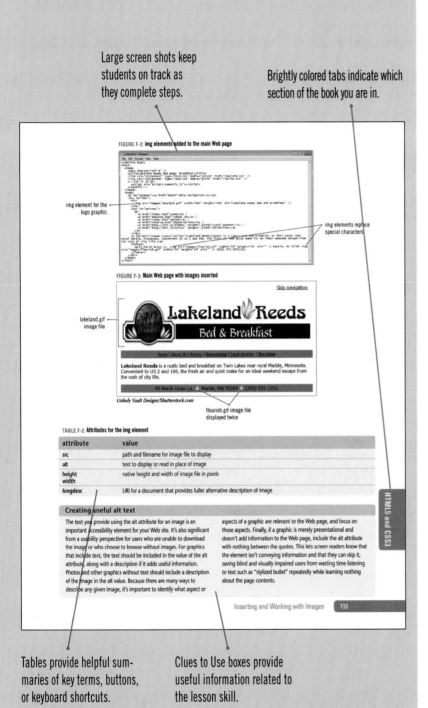

img element for the logo graphic

img elements replace special characters

lakeland.gif image file

flourish.gif image file displayed twice

Tables provide helpful summaries of key terms, buttons, or keyboard shortcuts.

Clues to Use boxes provide useful information related to the lesson skill.

Assignments

The lessons use Lakeland Reeds Bed and Breakfast, a fictional company, as the case study. The assignments on the light yellow pages at the end of each unit increase in difficulty. Assignments include:

- **Concepts Review** consist of multiple choice, matching, and screen identification questions.

- **Skills Reviews** are hands-on, step-by-step exercises that review the skills covered in each lesson in the unit.

- **Independent Challenges** are case projects requiring critical thinking and application of the unit skills. The Independent Challenges increase in difficulty, with the first one in each unit being the easiest. Independent Challenges 2 and 3 become increasingly open-ended, requiring more independent problem solving.

- **Real Life Independent Challenges** are practical exercises in which students create documents to help them with their every day lives.

- **Advanced Challenge Exercises** set within the Independent Challenges provide optional steps for more advanced students.

- **Visual Workshops** are practical, self-graded capstone projects that require independent problem solving.

Instructor Resources

The Instructor Resources CD is Course Technology's way of putting the resources and information needed to teach and learn effectively into your hands. With an integrated array of teaching and learning tools that offer you and your students a broad range of technology-based instructional options, we believe this CD represents the highest quality and most cutting edge resources available to instructors today. The resources available with this book are:

- **Instructor's Manual**—Available as an electronic file, the Instructor's Manual includes detailed lecture topics with teaching tips for each unit.

- **Sample Syllabus**—Prepare and customize your course easily using this sample course outline.

- **PowerPoint Presentations**—Each unit has a corresponding PowerPoint presentation that you can use in lecture, distribute to your students, or customize to suit your course.

- **Figure Files**—The figures in the text are provided on the Instructor Resources CD to help you illustrate key topics or concepts. You can create traditional overhead transparencies by printing the figure files. Or you can create electronic slide shows by using the figures in a presentation program such as PowerPoint.

- **Solutions to Exercises**—Solutions to Exercises contains every file students are asked to create or modify in the lessons and end-of-unit material. Also provided in this section, there is a document outlining the solutions for the end-of-unit Concepts Review, Skills Review, and Independent Challenges. An Annotated Solution File and Grading Rubric accompany each file and can be used together for quick and easy grading.

- **Data Files for Students**—To complete most of the units in this book, your students will need Data Files. You can post the Data Files on a file server for students to copy. The Data Files are available on the Instructor Resources CD-ROM, the Review Pack, and can also be downloaded from cengagebrain.com. For more information on how to download the Data Files, see page xvi.

Instruct students to use the Data Files List included on the Review Pack and the Instructor Resources CD. This list gives instructions on copying and organizing files.

- **ExamView**—ExamView is a powerful testing software package that allows you to create and administer printed, computer (LAN-based), and Internet exams. ExamView includes hundreds of questions that correspond to the topics covered in this text, enabling students to generate detailed study guides that include page references for further review. The computer-based and Internet testing components allow students to take exams at their computers, and also saves you time by grading each exam automatically.

Acknowledgements

Reviewers

Thank you to the reviewers who provided opinions and guided decisions during the creation of this book. They are as follows:

Dan Fergus, Brown College

Hazel Freeman, The University of Alabama

David Harden, Santa Rosa Junior College

Sherry Hopkins, Anne Arundel Community College

MaryAnn Kelly, Abby Kelley Foster Charter Public School

Jonathan Meersman, Milwaukee Area Technical College

Colleen Meyer, Cincinnati State Technical and Community College

Special Thanks

We are grateful to Jonathan Meersman, professor at Milwaukee Area Technical College, who provided the vision, inspiration, and initial impetus for creating this book.

Author Acknowledgements

Sasha Vodnik Creating this book has truly been a team effort. Thanks to the many people who helped shape and strengthen what I've written: Marj Hopper, whose feedback and guidance strongly influenced the final content of every page; Christina Kling-Garrett, who kept us focused and on schedule; John Freitas, Jeff Schwartz, Danielle Shaw, Ashlee Welz Smith, and Susan Whalen, whose careful reviews and thoughtful comments on each chapter removed many roadblocks for future users; Brandi Shailer, who set us on all on the path toward creating this book together; Matthew Hutchinson and the folks at GEX, Inc., who carefully transformed my words and pictures into usable, attractive layouts; John McKelvy, who created all the Web page layouts on which the sites created in this book are based; Ben Draisin, who imparted some of his insight into the finer points of JavaScript; and Anca Mosoiu, who shared her expertise in and passion for social media with me. Additional thanks go to my husband, Jason Bucy, who's helped me stay happy, healthy, and connected to life outside of HTML and CSS while I worked on this book.

Credits

All Web sites created in this book are based on designs by John McKelvy (www.mackjackstudio.com).

The images shown in some figures are used by permission from the following sources:

Elena Elisseeva/Shutterstock.com

Ron Rowan Photography/Shutterstock.com

Regien Paassen/Shutterstock.com

Unholy Vault Designs/Shutterstock.com

somchaij/Shutterstock.com

Weldon Schloneger/Shutterstock.com

Jessica Bethke/Shutterstock.com

Jim Gitzlaff/Shutterstock.com

Maxim Tupikov/Shutterstock.com

9507848116/Shutterstock.com

Lario Tus/Shutterstock.com

Jason Bucy

Faithe Wempen/sycamoreknoll.com

Read This Before You Begin

Frequently Asked Questions

What are Data Files?

A Data File is a partially completed file that you use to complete the steps in the units and exercises to create the final document that you submit to your instructor. Each unit opener page lists the Data Files that you need for that unit.

Where are the Data Files?

Your instructor will provide the Data Files to you or direct you to a location on a network drive from which you can download them. For information on how to download the Data Files from cengagebrain.com, see the inside back cover.

What software was used to write and test this book?

This book was written and tested using Notepad on a computer with a typical installation of Microsoft Windows 7 Home, and TextEdit on a computer with a typical installation of Macintosh OS 10.6. All Web pages were tested on the most recent versions of Firefox, Chrome, and Safari for Windows and Mac, as well as Internet Explorer 9, 8, 7, and 6 for Windows. Where Internet Explorer 6 provides quirky results, the text explains the issues and provides suggestions for further research and troubleshooting. File uploading instructions were written and tested using FileZilla on both Windows and Mac.

Do I need to be connected to the Internet to complete the steps and exercises in this book?

Some of the exercises in this book require that your computer be connected to the Internet. If you are not connected to the Internet, see your instructor for information on how to complete the exercises.

What do I do if my screen is different from the figures shown in this book?

This book was written and tested on computers with monitors set at a resolution of 1024 × 768. If your screen shows more or less information than the figures in the book, your monitor is probably set at a higher or lower resolution. If you don't see something on your screen, you might have to scroll down or up to see the object identified in the figures.

COURSECASTS Learning on the Go. Always Available...Always Relevant.

Our fast-paced world is driven by technology. You know because you are an active participant—always on the go, always keeping up with technological trends, and always learning new ways to embrace technology to power your life. Let CourseCasts, hosted by Ken Baldauf of Florida State University, be your guide into weekly updates in this ever-changing space. These timely, relevant podcasts are produced weekly and are available for download at http://coursecasts.course.com or directly from iTunes (search by CourseCasts). CourseCasts are a perfect solution to getting students (and even instructors) to learn on the go!

Preparing to Create a Web Site

People and organizations around the world share information using the **World Wide Web**, or Web for short. You can make your own information available on the Web by creating **Web pages**, which are documents formatted to be accessible on the Web, and then publishing them as **Web sites**, which are available to anyone with Web access. Many options are available for creating Web pages, but no matter which method you use, the first step involves a thoughtful planning process. 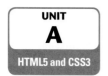 You have just been hired as a Web design intern by Great Northern Web Solutions. For your first project, the art director, Faduma Egal, has assigned you to create a new Web site for Lakeland Reeds Bed & Breakfast, one of Great Northern's clients. Before you start writing Lakeland's Web pages, you'll begin your work by creating a plan for the Web site, setting up a structure for the client's files, and considering the impact of usability, accessibility, and browser compatibility on the pages you'll be creating.

OBJECTIVES

Assemble a project plan

Create a storyboard

Implement Web accessibility standards

Evaluate Web site usability

Manage Web browser compatibility issues

Practice good file management

Configure your FTP client

Upload Web site files

Assembling a Project Plan

Whether you intend to make a single Web page or a large set of interrelated pages available, making information accessible on the Web starts with careful planning. This critical first step involves identifying the goals and objectives, as well as the target audience, of the Web site. Whether you're brainstorming for a personal site or meeting with a client regarding a site you've been hired to create, you sum up your work in this first step with a **project plan**, which is also known as a design document. You hold a planning meeting with Philip Blaine, owner of Lakeland Reeds B&B, to discuss the components he would like included in his new Web site. Figure A-1 shows the project plan you develop based on this meeting.

DETAILS

Important topics to consider in Web site planning include:

- **Identifying Web site goals and objectives**

  You want to ask a client a variety of questions to help understand goals and objectives for the site. For example, "What is the mission of the organization? Why do you want a Web site? What are the short-term goals of the Web site? What are the long-term goals of the Web site? What do you hope to gain by having a Web presence? Who is your target audience? Do your objectives support the needs of your target audience?" The more thorough you are in asking questions of the client, the better prepared you will be to design the Web site.

- **Identifying the target audience**

  It can be helpful to know the target audience for a Web site when choosing a layout and design. Web sites should look different based upon who will be visiting the site and why they are interested in the content. Some potential questions to ask about the target audience might be, "Who are the typical members of your audience? What is the mix of genders? What is the age range? What professions are they in? What is the average education level? Why will people visit this Web site? Will your visitors be using Microsoft Windows, Apple OS X, or another operating system? What size monitors are most common, and at what resolution will the site be viewed? Which Web browsers will they use to view the Web site?" While your client may not have ready answers to all of these questions, getting even a few answers can help prepare you for the design phase.

QUICK TIP

Listing exclusions in the project plan will help reduce the potential for scope creep, which is the expansion of a project beyond the original goals and objectives.

- **Identifying the type of Web site**

  Identifying the type of Web site the owner wants can help to focus the scope of the project. A Web site usually has one of a small number of main functions: a Web presence serving as an online informational brochure; providing important information for special interest groups and nonprofit organizations; showcasing examples of different types of works and designs commonly used by Web design individuals and agencies; providing multiple levels of information with page templates; extracting information from databases; or conducting the sale of products or services and other business transactions through the Internet. It is important to clearly define what the site will include, as well as what the site won't include.

- **Developing a budget**

  Every Web site design project should include a budget that is presented to the client prior to completing any work. The budget should be included in the project plan, which becomes part of the contract.

- **Creating a timeline**

  You should always provide the Web site owner with a timeline that includes the delivery date of the final Web site, along with various implementation milestones along the way. The timeline should always identify who is responsible for which tasks.

Great Northern Web Solutions

Project plan for Lakeland Reeds Bed and Breakfast

Objectives:

- Make general info about the facility and contact info available online
- Enable prospective guests to view the accommodations and grounds
- Allow prospective guests to book a stay online

Target audience:

- 35+
- Live in southern Canada and the upper Midwest U.S.
- Want to "get away from it all"
- Not sure about technical details of users; it's likely many will not be very experienced with the Web

Site type:

- Billboard (while the client wants some e-commerce functionality, they will accomplish this by linking to another site that takes reservations; thus, no advanced functionality is required for this site)

Budget:

- Hien is preparing a few detailed options for the client; this section will be updated when the budget is finalized and the contract is signed

Timeline:

Milestone	Date	Who's responsible
Design mockup submitted for approval	April 1, 2013	Project manager
Draft site published to testing server	April 15, 2013	Project manager
Feedback received from client	April 22, 2013	Phillip Blaine
Client feedback incorporated	May 1, 2013	Project manager
Final feedback from client	May 8, 2013	Phillip Blaine
Final feedback incorporated	May 22, 2013	Project manager
Final signoff from client	June 5, 2013	Phillip Blaine
Site goes live	June 5, 2013	Project manager

Client contact info:

Phillip Blaine

Lakeland Reeds Bed and Breakfast

45 Marsh Grass Ln.

Marble, MN 55764

(218) 555-5253

Deciding how much to charge

Estimating the amount of time a project will take can be difficult, especially for new Web designers. If you work for a Web design agency, the budget will typically be developed by your supervisors. If you are a freelance Web designer, you must place a value on your time that takes many things into consideration, such as the cost of computer equipment and software, supplying your own insurance, advertising, and other expenses. There really is no set hourly or project fee in this industry, as it varies dramatically depending upon the geographic market, competition, and experience level of the Web designer. New Web designers often barter, or trade, their skills for products or services offered by a Web site owner as a means of building a portfolio.

Creating a Storyboard

When you create a Web page or a Web site, it can be helpful to start by getting a clear idea of what you're trying to build. Web designers typically accomplish this by creating a **storyboard**, which is a sketch that outlines the components of each Web page and their places in the layout, as well as the links between the pages in a Web site. On a Web design team, often people responsible for art or design create the storyboard and hand it off to the developers to make into a Web page or Web site. You work with Karl Dixon, one of your colleagues in the art department, to create a storyboard for the Lakeland Reeds Web site based on the project plan you developed.

Storyboarding a Web site involves a few main steps:

- **Identify components to include**

  Before you start sketching, it's important to get a firm handle on all the elements that the Web site you're working on must include. A good place to start is your project plan, which should include a thorough inventory of items that must be part of the Web site; for instance, an existing logo and color scheme that a client already uses in all of their printed materials. You should augment this list with any other essential design elements based on your understanding of the site's target audience and functionality; for example, most multipage Web sites need a standardized navigation section that provides links to each of the pages.

- **Sketch possible layouts and then select one**

  The next step is to place the elements in a layout that's functional, usable, and, ideally, aesthetically pleasing. This step is often the job of a graphic designer; however, it's a skill that many Web developers without artistic backgrounds have built with study and practice. Whoever does this step, it often involves a series of sketches that either lay out a set of choices or progressively fine-tune a theme. For a simple Web site, a single layout should suffice for all the site's pages; however, if some pages have requirements that are best served by distinct layouts, these layouts need to be finalized in this step as well. Figure A-2 shows the layout for the pages of the Lakeland Reeds Web site.

- **Map the relationships between Web pages**

  Any time you're creating a Web site or a single Web page with links to other Web sites, it's helpful to map out the relationships between pages. This map is a crucial tool when you create the navigation system for the Web site. Figure A-3 lists the pages of the Lakeland Reeds Web site and illustrates the relationships between them, as well as links to external pages.

FIGURE A-2: Lakeland Reeds main Web page sketch

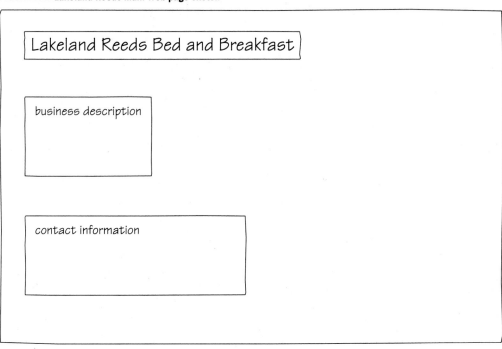

FIGURE A-3: Lakeland Reeds Web site relationships sketch

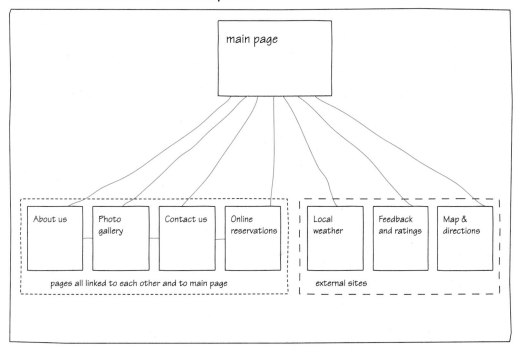

Creating a Web site from a template

An alternative to creating a layout for your Web site is to download a **template**, which is a generic layout that includes a color scheme and element positions, but which uses placeholder images and text. Some templates are available to download and use for free, while others must be purchased from the designer. A Web developer can simply replace the placeholder items with elements specific to the Web site being developed. While a template is not as specifically tailored to the companies or topics of the Web sites where it is used, it can save time in the Web development process and can be an invaluable tool when a site needs to be up right away.

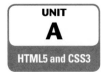

Implementing Web Accessibility Standards

Once you make a Web page publicly available on the Internet, users can access it using a wide variety of **user agents**, which are programs and devices that interpret Web documents. Many Web users view pages with the default settings in popular Web browsers such as Internet Explorer, Firefox, Chrome, and Safari. Some users with disabilities may use custom browser settings, or even specialized software or hardware, to access the Web. While laws in many countries spell out mandatory accessibility standards for government Web sites, building a high level of accessibility into any Web pages you create widens the potential audience for your work, as illustrated in Figure A-4. Thus, as a Web developer, it's important that you understand and implement Web accessibility standards as you create your Web pages in order to make them adaptable to the needs of different users and the capabilities of different user agents. A widely used reference for implementing Web accessibility is the **Web Content Accessibility Guidelines (WCAG)** maintained by the World Wide Web Consortium. To help ensure that the Lakeland Reeds B&B Web site is widely accessible, you review the main tenets of Web accessibility standards.

DETAILS

The WCAG describe techniques for helping your Web content meet the following goals as broadly as possible:

- **Perceivable**

  All of the contents of your Web pages need to be accessible in whatever format a given user is accessing it. This includes ensuring that any information that you convey visually is also available by non-visual means, such as text descriptions for images and videos. Many people with visual impairments access the Web using devices called **screen readers** that read aloud Web page text and descriptions that a user selects. In addition, any audio content should be accompanied by transcripts or written descriptions, which can substitute for many users with auditory impairments.

- **Operable**

  Users interface with computers in different ways. While many users scroll Web pages and click links using a mouse, ensuring that no elements of your Web pages rely on the use of a mouse makes your Web pages more accessible to people with some physical impairments. Web pages also need to allow users to explore and read them at their own paces, and should allow scrolling or self-updating features to be paused, stopped, or hidden. Designs should not include elements known to cause seizures, such as certain frequencies of flashing. Finally, navigation within the site and to external pages should be clearly indicated, easy to understand, and, ideally, redundant.

- **Understandable**

  The language that a Web page is written in should be indicated, and means should be included for users to understand any specialized vocabulary used. Links should not make unexpected drastic changes to the way a Web page is displayed; some warning should be given. When possible, forms that accept user input should include means for identifying common errors and allowing users to correct them.

- **Robust**

  Web pages should be coded according to Web standards, ensuring that they can be accessed by the widest possible variety of programs and devices.

FIGURE A-4: A Web page before and after an accessibility redesign

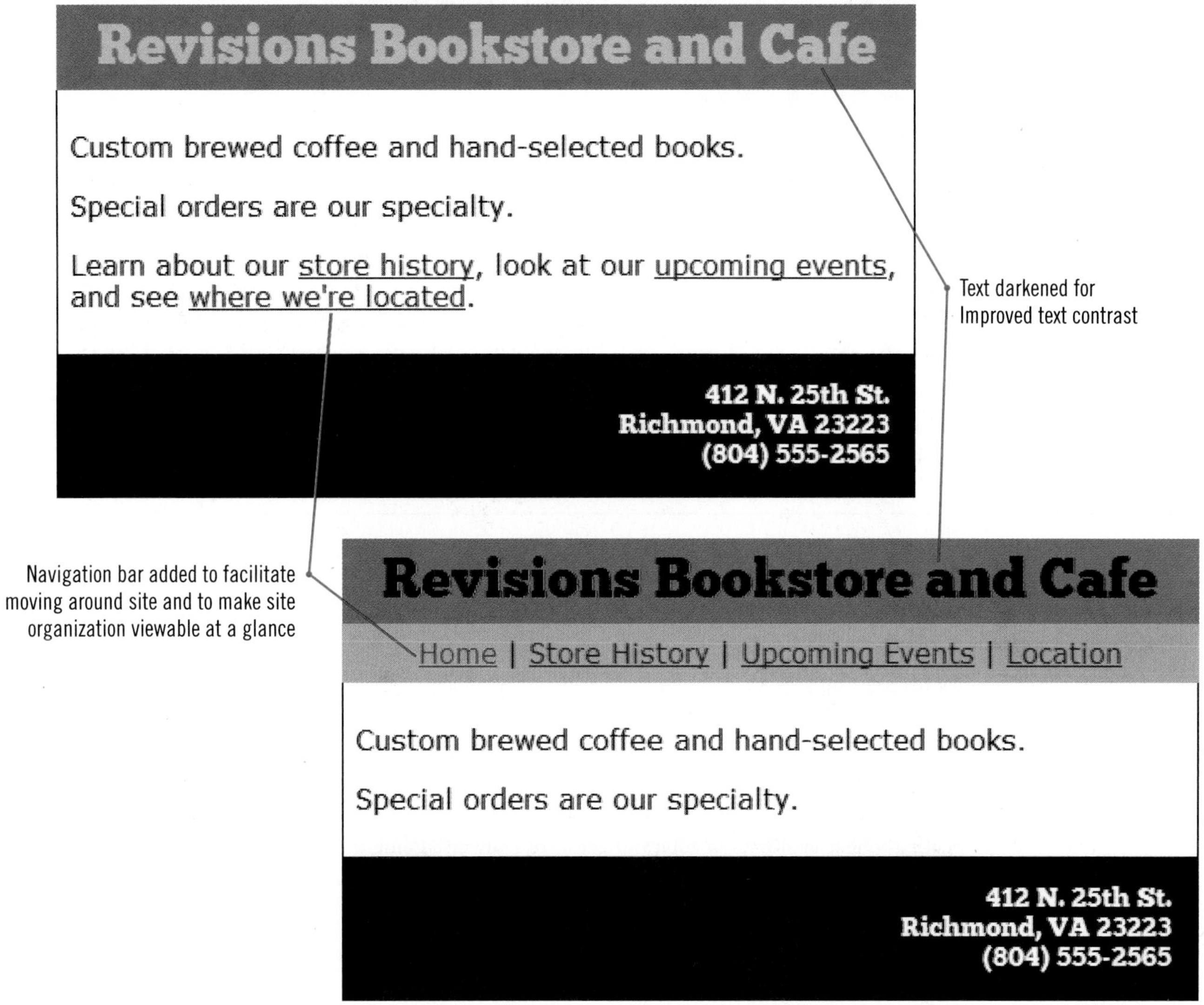

Revisions Bookstore and Cafe

Custom brewed coffee and hand-selected books.

Special orders are our specialty.

Learn about our <u>store history</u>, look at our <u>upcoming events</u>, and see <u>where we're located</u>.

412 N. 25th St.
Richmond, VA 23223
(804) 555-2565

Text darkened for
Improved text contrast

Navigation bar added to facilitate
moving around site and to make site
organization viewable at a glance

Revisions Bookstore and Cafe

<u>Home</u> | <u>Store History</u> | <u>Upcoming Events</u> | <u>Location</u>

Custom brewed coffee and hand-selected books.

Special orders are our specialty.

412 N. 25th St.
Richmond, VA 23223
(804) 555-2565

Web accessibility is a team effort

In addition to Web developers' work creating a site, other factors significantly influence Web accessibility. The developers of user agents make decisions that affect how their software and devices interact with Web content, which impacts whether users can access content in specific ways. In addition, some Web content is produced using software that automates the Web development process, and the accessibility choices of the makers of these packages affects the accessibility of the content produced using them. Thus, while Web developers have a crucial role to play in building and maintaining a Web that's available to everyone, it can be useful to see your role as part of a larger team and to recognize when you run against a limitation that you can't realistically fix.

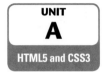
Evaluating Web Site Usability

Even among Web sites on similar topics or in a common area, there's often wide variety in how easy it is for users to accomplish their goals in visiting, whether accessing information or making purchases. It can be tempting to ignore evaluating a Web site's ease of use, known as **usability**, among the many tasks necessary to create and maintain it. However, usability is critically important in determining whether your users are satisfied or frustrated when they leave your Web site, whether the users make return visits, and whether they recommend the site to friends and colleagues. In addition, designing a usable Web site from the beginning is often much easier than improving the usability of an existing Web site. Thinking about who will use your site and what they'll want from it is an important starting point in creating a usable Web resource. As you prepare to work on the Lakeland Reeds Web site, you review Web usability guidelines.

DETAILS

The most usable Web sites share the following attributes, which are highlighted in Figure A-5:

- **Consistent and cohesive**

   All the pages on a Web site should be visually similar enough that users can tell that they're on the same site. Visual design, including a color scheme and logo, plays an important role. In addition, page elements, such as site navigation links, should appear in a consistent place on every page. Your Web site designs should also make use of elements that are standard on most other Web sites, making your Web site instantly familiar to even first-time visitors. Thus, an important part of creating a new Web design is exploring other Web sites sharing similar audiences or topics to get a clear understanding of the standard elements that users may expect to see.

- **Navigable**

   Users often have a specific goal when they visit most Web sites. It's important that your site's opening page makes it clear how users can accomplish the task before them, whether the user wants to find information on a specific topic, buy a product, or make a reservation. In addition, each page should include links that make it clear to users how to move to other areas of the site.

- **Understandable**

   The contents of your Web pages need to make sense to your users. Write text in as simple and straightforward a manner as possible, avoiding technical jargon unless your site targets a specific audience that understands it. Limit your Web page designs to the elements you need; overloading a page with too many options and too much information can overwhelm users and prevent them from getting what they need from your site.

FIGURE A-5: Usability features across a single Web site

Colors, logo, and layout are the same for all pages, so it's obvious at a glance that they're part of the same site

Pages share consistent navigation features, and the user's current location on the site is marked

Each page is narrowly focused and contains simple relevant text and graphics

Unholy Vault Designs/Shutterstock.com
Faithe Wempen/sycamoreknoll.com
Jason Bucy

Testing usability

Even when you create a Web site with usability in mind, it's easy to overlook some of your users' needs and quirks. Especially for larger Web sites, a crucial part of improving a site's usability is **usability testing**, in which a developer sits down with potential or actual users of the site, asks them to accomplish a task, notes how they go about it and whether they are successful, and asks for their feedback. Often observation of users can point out blind spots that developers have overlooked. Users' feedback may also suggest features that would add a lot of value for your site's visitors.

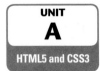
Managing Web Browser Compatibility Issues

Although everyone who views a given Web page is accessing the same document, different Web browsers translate and display the code differently. In addition to specialized hardware and software such as screen readers, several main Web browsers are in wide use, including Internet Explorer, Firefox, Chrome, and Safari on desktops, notebooks, and tablets, and a number of platform-specific browsers on handheld devices. In addition, each user may be accessing your Web page with an older or newer version of a given browser, and using Windows, OS X, Android, iOS, or another operating system; this multiplies the potential differences in how your page may be presented. While it may be impossible for your Web site to look identical in all versions of all user agents, you can take steps to ensure it looks as close to your original design as possible in many common configurations. **You prepare for your work on the Lakeland Reeds site by brushing up on development practices for maximizing the consistency of your Web pages across different user agents.

Tips for maximizing browser compatibility:

- **Practice good coding habits**

  While most Web browsers ignore minor coding errors, not all browsers are as forgiving with all errors. Therefore, as you learn Web page code and begin to practice working with it, it is important to stick to good coding habits.

- **Test your Web site with different user agents**

  Because different user agents may render the same code differently, the only way to experience potential discrepancies is to test your Web site in different user agents. While only the largest companies and Web design studios generally own the hardware necessary for exhaustive testing, you should research the user agent configurations that visitors to your site are most likely to be running and make sure you have the hardware and software to test these setups. In addition, software and Web services such as the one shown in Figure A-6 allow you to simulate the user experience in different Web browsers; these can be invaluable in maximizing the visual compatibility of your pages.

- **Validate your HTML and CSS code**

  Sometimes a Web page can display as expected in a user agent in spite of code that doesn't conform to specifications. In this case, it can be useful to put your code through an automated comparison against Web coding standards, a process known as **validation**. Several reputable Web sites offer validation services free of charge. In addition to double-checking code that seems error-free, validation can also help to identify the specific source of an error in your code if the error is difficult to track down.

FIGURE A-6: Gallery of browser previews generated by a Web site

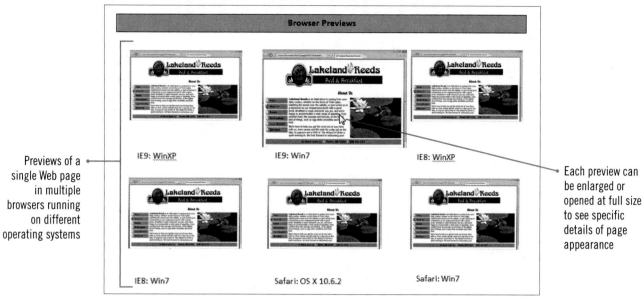

Previews of a single Web page in multiple browsers running on different operating systems

Each preview can be enlarged or opened at full size to see specific details of page appearance

Browser Previews

IE9: WinXP

IE9: Win7

IE8: WinXP

IE8: Win7

Safari: OS X 10.6.2

Safari: Win7

Unholy Vault Designs/Shutterstock.com
Jason Bucy

Practicing Good File Management

Another important step in preparing to create a Web site is to set up a folder and document structure for your Web site on your computer. It's important to keep all the files for your Web site in a common location so you can easily locate them when you want to make changes. In addition, as your Web site becomes larger, the number of individual files will likely mushroom, making organization a must. The main directory on the computer, USB drive, or shared network drive where you will save all of the files for your Web site is known as the **local root folder**. Using this folder only for files that are ready to be published helps you avoid erroneously publishing old or unfinished files. Faduma has supplied you with an automatically generated placeholder Web page for Lakeland Reeds. You create a local root folder for the site and move the provided files into it in preparation for publishing them to the Web.

STEPS

1. **Open your file manager, navigate to the drive and folder where you store your Data Files, open the Unit A folder, then open the Unit folder**

2. **Create a new folder inside the Unit folder**

3. **Rename the new folder wwwroot**

   You'll use the wwwroot folder to store the folders and files for the Lakeland Reeds Web site that are ready to be published to the Web.

4. **Move the index.html file to the wwwroot folder, then move the gnlogo.png file to the wwwroot folder**

   As shown in Figure A-7, the only file left in the Unit folder is htma-1.rtf, which contains your project plan for the Web site. While this file is related to your work on the Web site, you will not publish it to the Web, so it does not go in the wwwroot folder.

5. **Open the wwwroot folder**

   As Figure A-8 shows, the index.html and gnlogo.png files appear in the wwwroot folder.

FIGURE A-7: The wwwroot folder

Your location may be different

Folder created and renamed

Project plan file will not be published to the Web

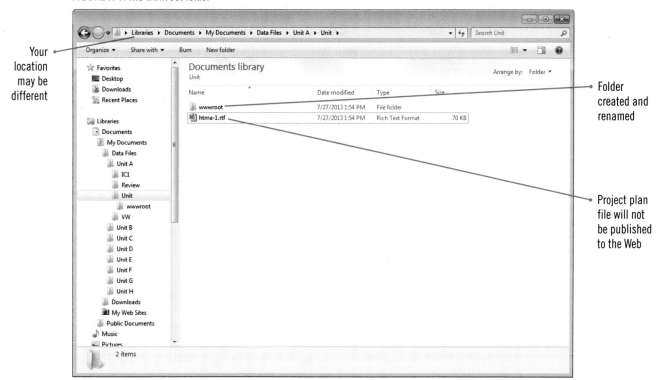

FIGURE A-8: Files to be published

Files ready to be published have been moved to the wwwroot folder

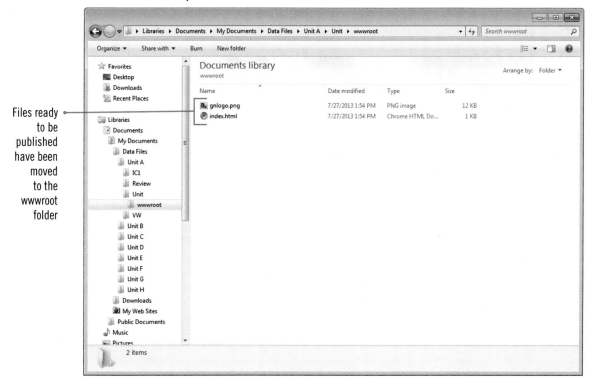

Configuring Your FTP Client

As you develop a Web site, you store your Web documents on your local computer. However, to make your site available to anyone with access to the Web, you need to copy the files to a **Web server**, which is a computer optimized to store and share Web documents and that has an extremely high-speed Internet connection. The most common method of transferring documents to a Web server is **File Transfer Protocol (FTP)**, which is a means of communication specifically created for moving files between two networked computers. While FTP capability is built into most popular operating systems, downloading and installing a dedicated FTP program makes the process much easier. Many such programs, known as **FTP clients**, are downloadable for free online. ▓▓▓▓ Before you begin work on the Lakeland Reeds Web site, you configure your FTP client to prepare for uploading your files to the Web.

STEPS

TROUBLE

These steps are for FileZilla, a free FTP client available at www.filezilla-project.org. If you are using a different FTP client, obtain configuration instructions from your instructor or technical support person, or from the documentation that came with the program.

1. **Open your FTP client**

2. **Click File, then click Site Manager**

   FileZilla opens the Site Manager dialog box, which provides options for setting up a new connection to a Web server.

3. **Click the New Site button, type a descriptive name for the Web server you are configuring, such as the name or abbreviation of your school or Web hosting company, then press [Enter]**

4. **Click the Host box, then type the FTP address provided by your instructor, technical support person, or Web host**

5. **Click the Logon Type list arrow, then click Ask for password**

6. **Click the User box, then type the user name provided by your instructor or technical support person**

   Figure A-9 shows the completed Site Manager dialog box.

TROUBLE

If you aren't able to connect to your Web server, ask your instructor or technical support person about other configuration options you might need to select.

7. **Click Connect, type your password, click the Remember password for this session check box to uncheck it, then click OK**

   FileZilla saves the new configuration and tests your connection to the FTP server. Figure A-10 shows a successful connection in FileZilla.

8. **Click the Close button ▨ to end your FTP connection and exit FileZilla**

FIGURE A-9: Site Manager dialog box

List of Web servers configured for this client

Descriptive name for the Web server

Saves configuration information and tests connection

Address of FTP server

"Normal" stores login information for this connection; "Ask for password" prompts for this information each time you connect

Login name for your Web server

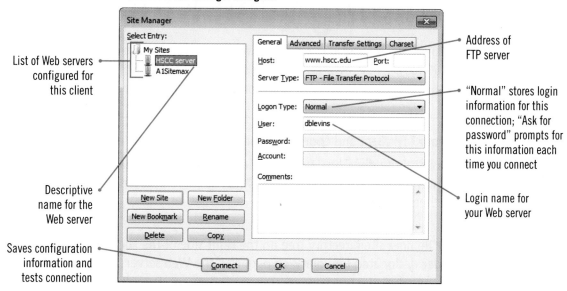

FIGURE A-10: View of connected Web server

Navigation area for directories on local computer

List of files and folders in current directory on local computer

Navigation area for directories on Web server

List of files and folders in current directory on Web server

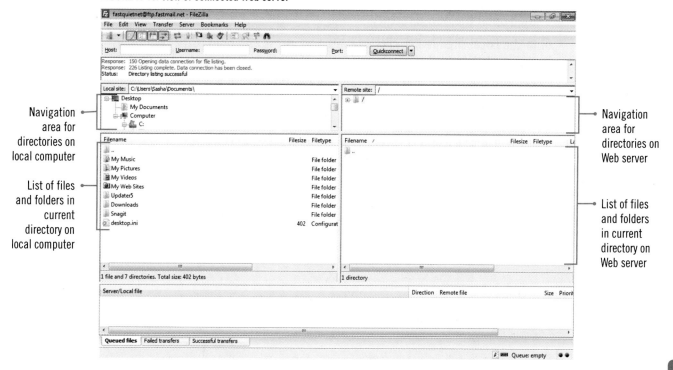

Configuring a testing server

As part of the Web development process, it's useful to upload your pages to your Web server for testing purposes before actually making them available to the public. The final upload location for pages on your Web server is not a good location for this purpose, because all pages you upload there are immediately available to the entire World Wide Web, even pages that still contain errors or don't display properly. Instead, Web developers often maintain a separate

testing server for their projects, which is a location available on a local network or on the Web that is non-publicized and may even require a password for access. When using an FTP client to access a testing server, you use the same local source folder as for final files. The target location, however, may be a different folder on the same Web server, or a different Web host altogether.

Uploading Web Site Files

Once your FTP client is configured to access your Web server, you can upload the files for your Web site and make them available via the Web. 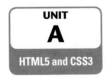 You upload the placeholder Web page for the Lakeland Reeds Web site to the Web host and verify that it was uploaded correctly.

STEPS

1. **Open your FTP client and connect to your Web server**

2. **Use the Local site directory tree on the left side of the FileZilla window to navigate to the drive and folder where you store your Data Files, open the Unit A folder, open the Unit folder, then open the wwwroot folder**
   The files you moved into the wwwroot folder appear in the Local site file list below the directory tree.

3. **Use the Remote site directory tree on the right side of the FileZilla window to Navigate to the folder designated for your Web pages on the Web server**
   Any Web documents that you copy to this directory are available on the Web.

4. **Right-click a blank area of the Remote site file list, click Create directory, type unit, press [Enter], then double-click the unit folder to open it**

5. **Repeat Step 4 to create a new directory named wwwroot, within the unit directory and then open the new directory**

6. **In the Local site file list, click gnlogo.png, press and hold [Ctrl] (Windows) or [command] (Mac), click index.html, release [Ctrl] or [command], then drag the selected files to the Remote site file list and release the mouse button**

7. **If necessary, enter your password, click the Remember password for this session check box to uncheck it, then click OK for each file**
   The files are copied to your Web server, as shown in Figure A-11.

8. **Click the Close button to end your FTP connection and exit FileZilla**

TROUBLE
If you do not see the Web page shown in Figure A-12, be sure you added the /unit/wwwroot directory path to the end of the default path to your Web documents.

9. **Open your Web browser, then navigate to the Web publishing address provided by your instructor or technical support person**
   The Lakeland Reeds placeholder page displays, as shown in Figure A-12.

10. **Close your Web browser**

FIGURE A-11: Web site files copied to Web server

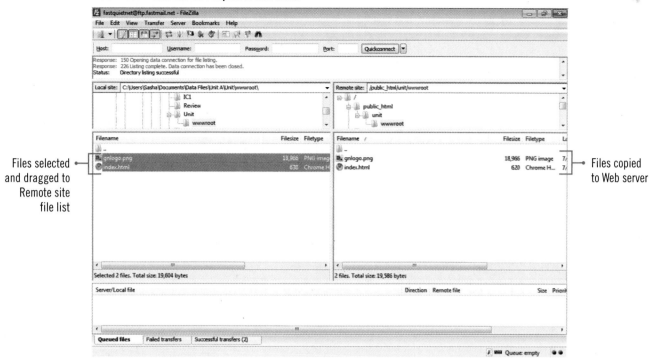

Files selected and dragged to Remote site file list

Files copied to Web server

FIGURE A-12: Lakeland Reeds placeholder Web page

Practice

For current SAM information, including versions and content details, visit SAM Central (http://www.cengage.com/samcentral). If you have a SAM user profile, you may have access to hands-on instruction, practice, and assessment of the skills covered in this unit. Since various versions of SAM are supported throughout the life of this text, check with your instructor for the correct instructions and URL/Web site for accessing assignments.

Concepts Review

Label each item in the FTP client dialog box shown in Figure A-13.

FIGURE A-13

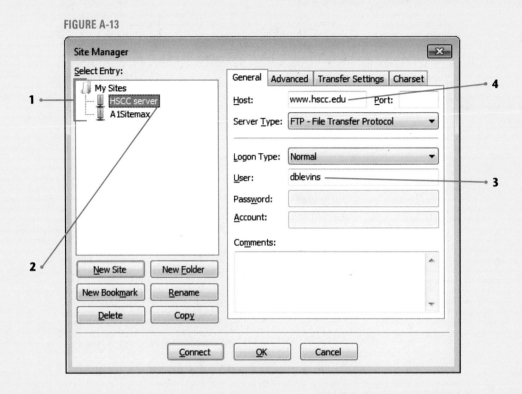

Match each term with the statement that best describes it.

5. **usability**
6. **local root folder**
7. **storyboard**
8. **File Transfer Protocol**
9. **validation**
10. **user agent**
11. **Web server**

a. an automated comparison of the code for a Web page against Web coding standards

b. a Web site's ease of use

c. a computer optimized to store and share Web documents, with an extremely high-speed Internet connection

d. a program or device that interprets Web documents

e. a means of communication specifically created for moving files between two networked computers

f. a sketch that outlines the components of each Web page and their places in the layout, as well as the links between the pages in a Web site

g. the main directory on the computer, USB drive, or shared network drive where you save all of the files for a Web site

Select the best answer from the list of choices.

12. The process of identifying the goals and objectives, as well as the target audience, of the Web site is summed up in the _____.

   a. Web server

   b. user agent

   c. project plan

   d. storyboard

13. On a Web design team, often people responsible for art or design create the _____ and hand it off to the developers to make into a Web page or Web site.

   a. storyboard

   b. validator

   c. FTP client

   d. user agent

14. What is one advantage of using a template to create a Web site?

   a. It is guaranteed to create an accessible site.

   b. It can save time in the development process.

   c. You can publish the resulting site without an FTP client.

   d. It doesn't require you to use multiple user agents to check the Web pages you create.

15. What is one advantage of building a high level of accessibility into any Web pages you create?

   a. It widens the potential audience for your work.

   b. It doesn't require you to use multiple user agents to check the Web pages you create.

   c. It eliminates the need to create a storyboard.

   d. You can publish the resulting site without an FTP client.

16. Making a Web site consistent, cohesive, navigable, and understandable helps improve its _____.

   a. project plan

   b. accessibility

   c. storyboard

   d. usability

17. A Web developer can get valuable feedback on a Web site by sitting down with potential or actual users and watching them attempt to accomplish a task, a process known as _____.

   a. storyboarding

   b. validation

   c. usability testing

   d. uploading

Skills Review

1. Practice good file management.

   a. Open your file manager.

   b. Navigate to the drive and folder where you store your Data Files, open the Unit A folder, then open the Review folder.

   c. Create an empty folder inside the Review folder and rename it **wwwroot**.

   d. Click and drag the index file to the wwwroot folder, then click and drag the gnlogo file to the wwwroot folder.

   e. View the contents of the wwwroot folder and compare your screen to Figure A-14.

2. Upload Web site files.

   a. Open your FTP client and connect to your Web server. If you are using an FTP client other than FileZilla, use the steps provided for your client instead of the steps below to upload the contents of the wwwroot folder to your Web server.

   b. In the Local site directory tree, navigate to the drive and folder where you store your Data Files, open the Unit A folder, open the Review folder, then open the wwwroot folder.

FIGURE A-14

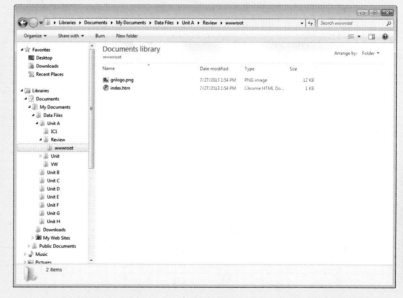

Skills Review (continued)

c. Use the Remote site directory tree on the right side of the FileZilla window to navigate to the folder designated for your Web pages on the Web server.

d. Right-click a blank area of the Remote site file list, create a new folder named **review**, then open the review folder.

e. Repeat Step d to create a new directory named **wwwroot** within the review directory, then open the new directory.

f. In the Local site file list, select the files gnlogo.png and index.html, then drag the files to the Remote site file list.

g. If necessary, enter your password, click the Remember password for this session check box to uncheck it, then click OK for each file.

h. Close your FTP connection and exit your FTP client.

i. Open your Web browser, then navigate to the Web publishing address provided by your instructor or technical support person to view the files you uploaded. Be sure to add the /review/wwwroot directory to the end of your default Web publishing address.

j. Close your Web browser.

Independent Challenge 1

Spotted Wren Garden Center, a local garden shop and plant store, has hired you to create a Web site for their business. Sarah Nguyen, the shop's owner and manager, would like you to create a Web presence as a new avenue of marketing, as well as a means to keep regular customers up to date on seasonal specials and new products. You start your work on the site by setting up a folder structure on your local machine for the Web site, copying the placeholder files that a colleague has created for you to the appropriate folder, creating the necessary folders on your Web server, and uploading and previewing the placeholder files.

a. In your file manager, navigate to the drive and folder where you store your Data Files, open the Unit A folder, then open the IC1 folder.

b. Create a new folder within the IC1 folder named **wwwroot**.

c. Move the index and birdhouse files to the wwwroot directory.

d. Open your FTP client and connect to your Web server.

e. In the Local site directory tree, navigate to the drive and folder where you store your Data Files, open the Unit A folder, open the IC1 folder, then open the wwwroot folder.

f. Use the Remote site directory tree on the right side of the FileZilla window to navigate to the folder designated for your Web pages on the Web server.

g. Create a new folder named **ic1** on the remote server, then open the ic1 folder and create a folder named **wwwroot** within it.

FIGURE A-15

Check back for the
Spotted Wren Garden Center

h. Drag the files index.html and birdhouse.jpg to the Remote site file list to upload them to the Web server, entering your password if necessary.

i. Close your FTP connection, exit your FTP client, then view the page you just uploaded in your Web browser, which should look like the one shown in Figure A-15. Be sure to include **/ic1/wwwroot** in the Web address.

j. Close your Web browser.

Independent Challenge 2

To help build your Web design skills, you have volunteered to create a Web site for the Murfreesboro Recreational Soccer League (MRSL). The league organizes recreational leagues every summer and fall for local, nonprofessional soccer players to get exercise and have fun. You start your work on the site by preparing directory structures on your local computer and your Web server, and researching potential accessibility and usability elements.

a. In your file manager, navigate to the drive and folder where you store your Data files, open the Unit A folder, then open the IC2 folder.

b. Create a new folder within the IC2 folder named **wwwroot**.

c. Open your FTP client and connect to your Web server.

d. Use the Remote site directory tree on the right side of the FileZilla window to navigate to the folder designated for your Web pages on the Web server.

e. Create a new folder named **ic2** on the remote server, then open the ic2 folder and create a folder named **wwwroot** within it. Your remote directory structure should resemble the one shown in Figure A-16.

f. Close your FTP connection, then exit your FTP client.

FIGURE A-16

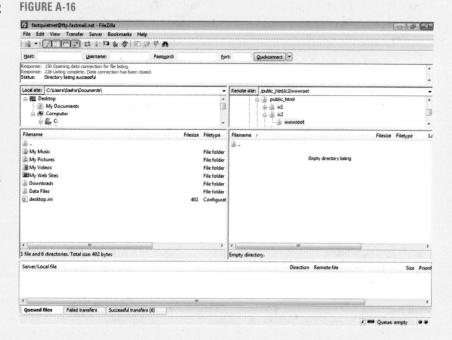

Advanced Challenge Exercise

- Open your Web browser, then use the search engine of your choice to find and explore at least two recreational sports Web sites.
- Using the "Implementing Web Accessibility" section of this unit as a guide, write a paragraph about each Web site that assesses the site's design in terms of accessibility. Specify at least three details of each Web site and explain why you feel they help or hinder the site's accessibility.
- Using the "Evaluating Web Site Usability" section of this unit as a guide, write a paragraph about each Web site that assesses the site's design in terms of usability. Specify at least three details of each Web site and explain why you feel they help or hinder the site's usability.

Independent Challenge 3

In your new job creating sites for a Web design firm, you've been assigned a new client, Hotel Natoma. The hotel's business manager, Diego Merckx, wants to use the Web to showcase the facility and its amenities. You start your work on the site by preparing directory structures on your local computer and your Web server, and researching potential browser compatibility issues to watch for by exploring similar Web sites.

a. In your file manager, navigate to the drive and folder where you store your Data files, open the Unit A folder, then open the IC3 folder. Create a **wwwroot** folder within the IC3 folder.

b. Open your FTP client, connect to your Web server, and use the Remote site directory tree on the right side of the FileZilla window to Navigate to the folder designated for your Web pages on the Web server.

Independent Challenge 3 (continued)

c. Create a new folder named **ic3** on the remote server, then create a folder named **wwwroot** within the ic3 folder. Your remote directory structure should resemble the one shown in Figure A-17.

d. Close your FTP connection, then exit your FTP client.

Advanced Challenge Exercise

- Open your Web browser, then use the search engine of your choice to find and explore at least two Web sites for small hotels.
- Using a search phrase such as "check browser compatibility," use the search engine of your choice to find a Web site that allows you to check a site's browser compatibility in multiple browsers for free.
- Use the browser compatibility site to use at least three browsers to compare the appearance of one of the hotel sites you explored. Save browser screenshots to the location where you store your Data Files and write a paragraph summarizing any differences in appearance that you notice.

FIGURE A-17

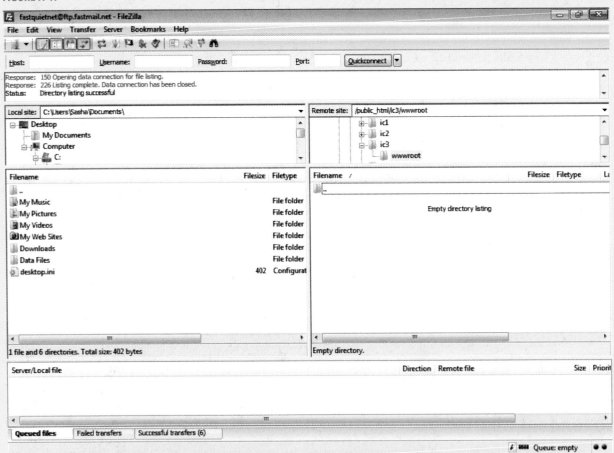

Real Life Independent Challenge

This Independent Challenge requires an Internet connection.

For this Independent Challenge, you will choose a topic or organization of personal interest and create a Web site for or about it. As a first step, you will create a project plan, survey other similar sites, and create a storyboard. Throughout this book, you will design and build the site.

This Real Life Independent Challenge will build from unit to unit, so you must complete the Real Life Independent Challenge in each unit to complete your Web site.

a. Create a project plan for your Web site using the components outlined in the "Assembling a Project Plan" section of this unit and the sample project plan in the htma-1.rtf data file. Include your name at the bottom of the project plan as the contact person. Your course syllabus may be helpful in creating a timeline of components to add to the site, as well as indicating a final publishing date.

b. Open your Web browser, then use the search engine of your choice to find and explore at least two other sites similar to the one you are planning. Write a summary of each site, noting the ways in which the site's focus is similar to and different from the one you are planning, and describing specific aspects of the site that you find less appealing or more appealing. Using the "Implementing Web Accessibility" and "Evaluating Web Site Usability" sections of this unit as a guide, assess the design of each Web site in terms of accessibility and usability.

c. Sketch a storyboard for your Web site, including at least one and no more than five Web pages. If you have a background in graphic design, or have a friend or colleague who's willing to help, sketch an arrangement of elements and include colors, graphics, and any other page elements the site should include.

d. Use your FTP client to connect to your Web server. Create a folder named **rlic**, then create a folder named **wwwroot** within the new folder.

Visual Workshop

Use your file manager and your FTP client to create the folder paths shown in Figure A-18.

FIGURE A-18

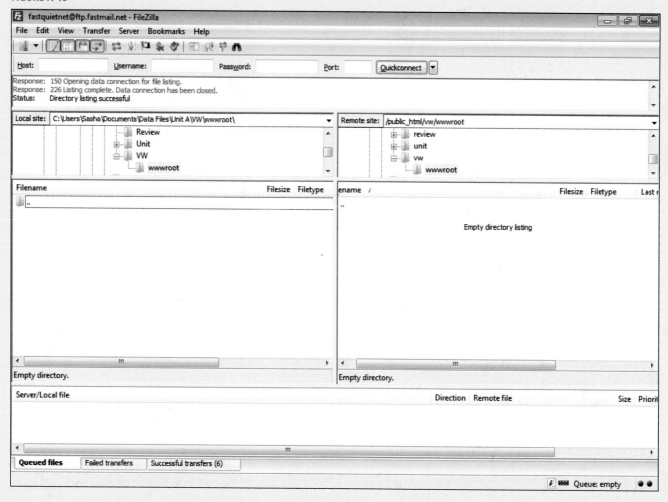

Preparing to Create a Web Site

Getting Started with HTML

After you plan out a Web site, you can begin to create it with nothing more than a basic text editor. Web pages are written in **Hypertext Markup Language (HTML)**, which is a standardized format for specifying the structure of a Web page. You can add HTML code to the text you want to be part of your Web pages in order to indicate the different types of content present. To test your pages and preview their appearance, you can open them in a Web browser or other user agent that interprets your HTML code and represents your Web page contents in a consistent way. Faduma Egal, the art director at Great Northern Web Solutions, has approved the plan you created for the Lakeland Reeds Bed & Breakfast Web site. She wants you to start work on the site by creating a home page containing basic information about the bed and breakfast, including contact information. In this unit, you'll learn more about HTML, and then create and test the main Lakeland Reeds B&B Web page.

OBJECTIVES

Assess the history of HTML

Compare HTML and XHTML

Create an HTML document

Set up the document head and body

Add Web page text

Preview your Web page

Implement one-sided tags

Validate your HTML code

Assessing the History of HTML

HTML was created in 1991 by Tim Berners-Lee. In the succeeding years, the language has undergone several major revisions, along with a couple periods of reinvention when the underlying purpose and direction of the language were reevaluated. Along the way, a few major themes emerged, all of which are important factors in understanding HTML today. You start your work on the Web site by exploring the history of HTML and the factors that have influenced the current version of the language, HTML5.

A few factors have heavily influenced the development of HTML:

- **Process and evolution**

  The first two versions of HTML were defined and published by the **Internet Engineering Task Force (IETF)**. In 1994, the **World Wide Web Consortium (W3C)** was founded to take on the responsibility of maintaining the language's standards, which it continues to do today. Although HTML has gone through several major versions (see Table B-1), in practice the language is constantly under transformation. Through ongoing proposals and debates, the W3C facilitates the process of clarifying and amending the existing specification to incorporate new features while keeping the language consistent. The W3C also maintains a vision for the next steps in the evolution of HTML in an attempt to clarify what developers and software companies want prioritized in future versions of the language.

- **Semantics vs. presentation**

  The publication of HTML 4 in 1997 marked a major turning point in the development of the language. Companies that created Web browser software had begun to anticipate the W3C standards by adding their own extensions to HTML that generally worked only on a particular brand of browser. Between these extensions and a mushrooming of overlapping features codified in previous versions of HTML, it was becoming clear that the language needed to narrow its focus. HTML 4 codified HTML as a **semantic** language, meaning its intended use was to indicate the meanings of elements such as headings and paragraphs in a Web page, but not to tell Web browsers how the elements should appear. The new version of HTML coincided with the rollout of a companion language, **Cascading Style Sheets (CSS)**. CSS is a presentational language, meaning that it's designed for describing the appearance of items.

  Many features of previous HTML versions were presentational rather than semantic and, thus, didn't fit the new model of HTML. However, because so many Web pages had already been written using these features, and existing Web browsers and other user agents supported them, the W3C designated these features as **deprecated**, meaning that, while these features could still be used, their use was no longer recommended, and alternatives to their use were available. This step gave Web designers time to learn new ways of coding and update their Web pages gradually while maintaining support for the current state of the Web.

- **Web application support**

  In the years since the HTML 4.01 specification was finalized, common uses of the Web have changed and grown in significant ways. The core updates that are part of HTML5 include integrated support for new features, such as embedding video, as well as enhancement of longstanding features, such as Web page forms.

TABLE B-1: The evolution of HTML

version	year	major changes
HTML 2.0 & 3.2	1995–97	Codified the current state of HTML
HTML 4 & 4.01	1997–99	Added support for CSS and several newly developed HTML features
HTML5	2008–present	Enriches semantic options, along with new features and enhancements

HTML and Web browser versions

In the early years of the Web, browser creators Microsoft and Netscape added to their browsers proprietary features that weren't supported by their competitors. This provided opportunities for Web developers to add new elements to their Web pages. However, it also meant that any Web page incorporating these features would be displayed differently depending on which browser was used to open it. This situation created difficulties for developers trying to reach the widest possible audience with their Web pages. Eventually, the major browser companies recognized that creating their own features would not be a major key to gaining or maintaining market share,

and they have joined with developers to support a largely standards-based Web.

On the flip side, recent updates to Web standards have not always been quickly or fully adopted by makers of browsers and other user agents. As a result, when considering whether to use a particular HTML feature in your Web pages, it's important to research which user agents support it and how widely the support-ing user agents are in use. In some cases, implementing new features will need to wait until your target audience has caught up with avail-able Web technologies.

Getting Started with HTML

Comparing HTML and XHTML

Efforts to enhance Web standards didn't stop with the publication of the HTML 4.01 specification in 2002. Instead, work began to make HTML interoperable with another markup language known as **Extensible Markup Language (XML)**. The result was a new specification known as **Extensible Hypertext Markup Language (XHTML)**, which for several years was seen as the successor to HTML. Today work continues on both HTML and XHTML, and each has similar, distinct applications. As you prepare to design Web pages, it's important to understand the differences between HTML and XHTML, and when each might be appropriate in your work.

HTML and XHTML both have distinct advantages:

- **XHTML is XML-compliant**

  In addition to HTML, many other markup languages exist for specialized applications. Many of these languages are subsets of XML. Like HTML, XML enables users to describe the structure of a document. However, because XML is a more generic language than HTML, it enables users to describe any kind of document, instead of only Web pages. XHTML grew out of work in the late '90s to make HTML comply with the rules of XML in order to facilitate the interoperation of Web pages with documents coded using other XML-based languages. The first phase of this work resulted in the XHTML 1.1 standard.

  Adapting existing HTML standards to adhere to XML syntax required that Web page authors change a few aspects of the way they write code, which are outlined in Table B-2. You'll see examples of these aspects as you begin to create Web pages.

- **HTML can handle coding errors and quirks**

  As HTML standards changed and grew during the '90s, flexibility became an important part of the language. Even if Web page authors made minor mistakes in writing code, user agents could often interpret the code loosely, rather than hewing unerringly to rules, and successfully display their best interpretations of what the authors intended. XML, however, does not tolerate errors. Thus, if a user agent encounters a coding error while attempting to display a Web page coded in XHTML, the user agent must display an error message rather than read the code more loosely.

  While work initially went forward to create XHTML 2.0 as a successor to XHTML 1.1, some members of the Web standards community dissented. The W3C's focus solely on XHTML as the path forward meant that Web pages containing coding errors would not be displayed correctly or at all. It also meant that any new features under consideration for the next version of XHTML would be unavailable in the billions of existing Web pages written in HTML unless their code was edited to comply with the rules of XHTML. Some community members saw this as an unnecessary barrier and instead began working together to build on the HTML 4.01 standard in order to create a specification that integrated markup features geared toward modern Web usage.

- **Moving forward: coexistence**

  Today, the W3C is improving and expanding both XHTML and HTML, seeing the two as parallel languages with their own reasons to exist. In this book, you'll learn how to create Web pages in both HTML and XHTML, so you can make your own decisions about which language is most appropriate for projects you work on in the future.

TABLE B-2: Differences between HTML and XHTML

aspect	HTML	XHTML
Tag nesting	Tags may be closed out of order	Tags must be closed in the order opened
Tag case	Tags may be written in upper or lower case	Tags must be written in lower case
Tag closure	Closing tags may be omitted for some elements	All opening tags must be matched with closing tags
Attribute-value pairs	Value may occur without attribute name	Attribute-value pair required
Empty elements	Empty elements do not need to be closed	Empty elements must be closed
Script and Style elements	Elements may be placed within HTML document	Elements must be in separate documents and linked to XHTML document
Attribute values	Values may be enclosed within quotes	Values must be enclosed within quotes
ID and Name attributes	Either attribute may be used	ID attribute may be used, but Name attribute prohibited
Character codes for special characters	Codes recommended	Codes required

The W3C and the WHATWG

After XHTML 1.1 was finalized, the W3C moved forward with adding new features to XHTML, and drafted a proposal for XHTML 2.0. However, a number of community members, including several major technology companies, felt that HTML, rather than XHTML, would better serve the future of the Web, and proposed that the W3C change course. When a W3C committee voted against this proposal, these companies formed the **Web Hypertext Application Technology Working Group (WHATWG)** to begin a process of creating a new HTML specification. Over time, the two organizations bridged their differences and agreed to collaborate in creating HTML5, with the W3C coordinating work on XHTML5.

Before finalizing the latest version of HTML, the two organizations are following a process of soliciting input and incorporating feedback from members of the Web community, including makers of user agents and other software and Web developers. As a result, the development process will likely continue for several years before all parties involved finalize a single standard. In the interim, however, different features of the developing specification may become available at different times.

Creating an HTML Document

An HTML document consists solely of text. As a result, you can create a Web page in a text editor such as Notepad, which is included with all current versions of Windows or TextEdit, which is part of Mac OS X. To create a Web page, you enter text that you want to display on the page along with HTML codes known as **tags**, which specify how a user agent should treat each item in the document. While most tags occur in pairs, some tags, known as **one-sided tags**, are used by themselves. ▨▨▨▨▨ You decide to use a text editor to create the home page for the Lakeland Reeds Bed and Breakfast.

STEPS

1. Start your text editor

A new, blank document opens, as shown in Figure B-1.

QUICK TIP
To read more about any HTML tag used in these steps, see Appendix A.

2. Type <!DOCTYPE html>, then press [Enter]

This one-sided tag creates an element known as the **DOCTYPE declaration**, which lets user agents know that the document contents are written in HTML.

3. Type <html>, press [Enter] twice, then type </html>

A tag pair assigns meaning to a Web page **element**, which is a specific component of the page, such as a paragraph or a heading. You place the **opening tag** at the start of the element you are marking and the **closing tag** at the end. HTML tags always start with an opening angle bracket (<) and end with a closing angle bracket (>). A closing tag is the same as its corresponding opening tag except that the opening angle bracket is followed by a slash (/). The text between the angle brackets specifies the HTML element type being applied to the selection. The html tag pair marks the beginning and the end of the Web page.

Your document should match the one shown in Figure B-2.

4. If you are using TextEdit on a Mac, click Format, then click Make Plain Text

5. Click File, then click Save

The Save As dialog box opens.

6. Navigate to the drive and folder where you store your Data Files, open the Unit B folder, then open the Unit folder

TROUBLE
If you are using TextEdit on a Mac, uncheck the Hide extension check box if necessary.

7. In the File name box (Windows) or Save As box (Mac), type index.html

The standard name for the main page of a Web site is "index." The .htm or .html extension signifies that a file is written in HTML.

8. If you are using Notepad in Windows, click the Save as type list arrow, then click All Files (*.*)

9. Click Save

The index.html file is saved to your storage location.

Other Web page creation software

Many other programs are available that allow you to create Web pages visually by clicking buttons and using drag-and-drop to place items on a page. However, creating your first Web pages by entering HTML directly—sometimes referred to as **hand-coding**—is one of the best ways to get familiar with HTML and the underlying structure of a Web page.

FIGURE B-1: **A blank document in Notepad**

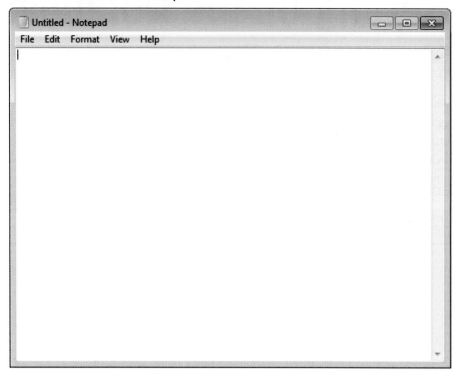

FIGURE B-2: **The basic structure of the Web page**

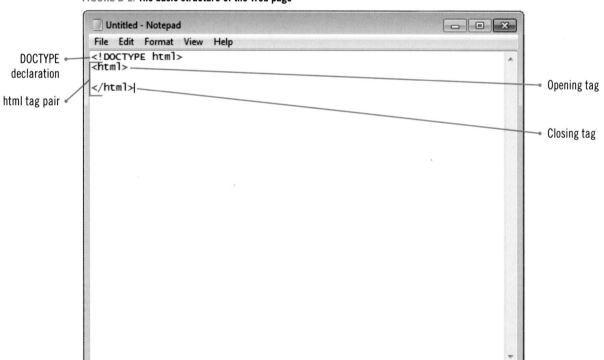

DOCTYPE declaration

html tag pair

Opening tag

Closing tag

HTML5 and CSS3

Setting Up the Document Head and Body

Within the html tag pair for a Web page, the document contents are divided into two sections. The head section contains elements that are not part of the main Web page, such as the page title that appears in a browser's title bar. The contents of the **body section** are visible in the main window of a Web browser and include elements like paragraphs and headings. Both the head and body tag pairs are located within the html tag pair. This situation is known as **nesting**, and most elements in the code for a Web page are nested within one or more other elements. ▓▓▓▓▓ As you continue creating the structure for the Lakeland Reeds Web page, you add the head and body sections to the page.

STEPS

1. **Click in the blank line between the opening and closing html tags, press [Spacebar] twice, then type** <head>

   Adding two spaces before a nested tag makes it appear indented. As your Web page code becomes longer and more complex, these indentations make it easier to identify the beginning and end of an element at a glance. Figure B-3 shows HTML code with several layers of nested tags that are formatted with indentations.

2. **Press [Enter] twice, press [Spacebar] twice, then type** </head>

3. **Press [Enter], press [Spacebar] twice, then type** <body>

4. **Press [Enter] twice, press [Spacebar] twice, then type** </body>

5. **Click in the blank line between the opening and closing head tags**

6. **Press [Spacebar] four times, type** <meta charset="utf-8" />, **then press [Enter]**

   The meta element enables you to pass information about a Web page to user agents that open it. The text following the name of the tag in the code you typed is an **attribute**, which you can use to provide additional information about an element. The charset attribute specifies the **character encoding**, which is the system user agents should employ to translate the electronic information representing the page into human-recognizable symbols, such as letters and numbers. Figure B-4 shows the completed Web page structure.

7. **Save your work**

> **QUICK TIP**
> To save your work without using the menus, you can press **[Ctrl]+[S]** (Windows) or **[command]+ [S]** (Mac).

Describing nested elements

An element nested within another element is called a **child element** of the enclosing element, and the enclosing element is known as the **parent element**. Two elements that are both children of the same element are known as **sibling elements**. In the code

```
<html>
  <head>
    <meta charset="utf-8" />
```

the head element is both a child of the html element and the parent of the meta element. In addition, here the html element is the **grandparent element** of the meta element, which can be referred to as a **grandchild element** of the html element.

Indentations
indicate
section of
code visually

```
comparisontable.html - Notepad
File  Edit  Format  View  Help
<!DOCTYPE html>
<html>
  <head>
    <meta charset="utf-8" />
    <title>Comparing HTML and XHTML</title>
  </head>
  <body>
    <p>HTML vs. XHTML</p>
    <table>
      <tr>
        <th>Aspect</th>
        <th>HTML</th>
        <th>XHTML</th>
      </tr>
      <tr>
        <td>Tag nesting</td>
        <td>Tags may be closed out of order</td>
        <td>Tags must be closed in the order opened</td>
      </tr>
      <tr>
        <td>Tag case</td>
        <td>Tags may be written in upper or lower case</td>
        <td>Tags must be written in lower case</td>
      </tr>
    </table>
  </body>
</html>
```

FIGURE B-4: **Completed Web page structure**

head section

body section

```
index.html - Notepad
File  Edit  Format  View  Help
<!DOCTYPE html>
<html>
  <head>
    <meta charset="utf-8" />
  </head>
  <body>
  </body>
</html>
```

meta tag
specifies
character
encoding

HTML5 and CSS3

HTML attributes

Many, but not all, HTML elements allow you to set attributes to specify details about a given element's properties. To use an attribute, you provide two pieces of information: an attribute name and the value you are assigning to the attribute. Together, these two pieces are known as an **attribute-value pair**. In the element <meta charset="utf-8" />, *charset* is the attribute name, and *utf-8* is the attribute value. In a tag pair, you specify any attributes in the opening tag, never in the closing one.

Adding Web Page Text

Because an HTML document is simply a plain text document that includes HTML codes, entering text for your Web pages is as simple as typing it. You then add the appropriate HTML tags to specify the element type for each text item on the page. ▨▨▨▨ Figure B-5 shows a sketch you created of a simplified initial version of the Lakeland Reeds Web page. You decide to enter the page title that will appear in the title bar of viewers' browsers, along with the basic information about Lakeland Reeds.

STEPS

QUICK TIP

This line is indented four spaces because it is nested within two elements: html and head.

1. **Click in the blank line above the closing head tag if necessary, press [Spacebar] four times, then type <title>Lakeland Reeds Bed and Breakfast</title>**

   The title element specifies text that appears in the title bar of the Web browser opening the page. This element is part of the document's head section because the text does not appear in the main browser window.

2. **Click in the blank line between the opening and closing body tags, press [Spacebar] four times, then type <h1>Lakeland Reeds Bed and Breakfast</h1>**

   The h1 element represents the highest-level heading on the page.

3. **Press [Enter], press [Spacebar] four times, then type <p>A country getaway perfect for fishing, boating, biking, or just watching the day go by.</p>**

   The p element marks a paragraph of text.

4. **Press [Enter], then type the following text, pressing [Spacebar] four times at the beginning of each line and pressing [Enter] at the end of each line except the last:**

   <p>Philip Blaine, Proprietor

   45 Marsh Grass Ln.

   Marble, MN 55764

   (218) 555-5253</p>

   Your document should look like the one shown in Figure B-6.

5. **Press [Enter], type <p>, type your first and last name, type a comma, then type HTML5 Unit B</p>**

6. **Save your work**

Adding comments to your HTML code

In addition to marking text that appears on your Web pages, you can create text elements in your Web page code that user agents ignore. These elements, known as **comments**, are not rendered by user agents and are viewable only by people who examine the HTML code of your Web pages. Comments can be especially helpful when you are creating or adding on to a large, complex Web document or Web site, or when other Web developers will be working with your code—now or in the future. Common uses for comments include explaining what a particular section of HTML does or pointing out the beginning and end of parts of a Web page containing numerous HTML elements. The comment tag pair begins with <!-- and ends with -->.

FIGURE B-5: Sketch of the Web page

Heading in browser title bar or tab → Lakeland Reeds Bed and Breakfast

Main page heading →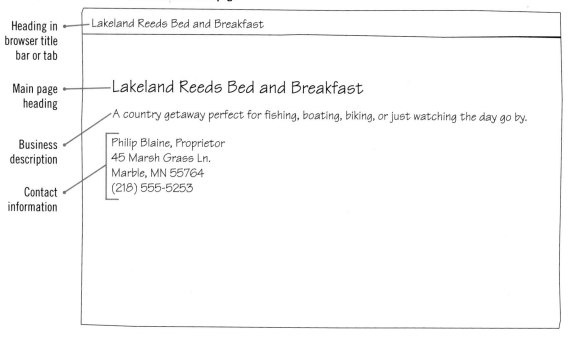

Lakeland Reeds Bed and Breakfast

Business description → A country getaway perfect for fishing, boating, biking, or just watching the day go by.

Contact information →
Philip Blaine, Proprietor
45 Marsh Grass Ln.
Marble, MN 55764
(218) 555-5253

FIGURE B-6: Title, h1, and p elements entered

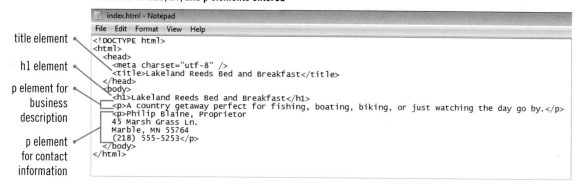

title element →
h1 element →
p element for business description →
p element for contact information →

```
index.html - Notepad
File  Edit  Format  View  Help
<!DOCTYPE html>
<html>
  <head>
    <meta charset="utf-8" />
    <title>Lakeland Reeds Bed and Breakfast</title>
  </head>
<body>
    <h1>Lakeland Reeds Bed and Breakfast</h1>
    <p>A country getaway perfect for fishing, boating, biking, or just watching the day go by.</p>
    <p>Philip Blaine, Proprietor
    45 Marsh Grass Ln.
    Marble, MN 55764
    (218) 555-5253</p>
</body>
</html>
```

Previewing Your Web Page

An important step in the process of creating a Web page is to **preview** it, which involves opening it in one or more user agents and examining the result. When a Web page isn't interpreted as expected by a user agent, you can research the problem and make corrections to the code before publishing the page. In addition, because different user agents can interpret the same page with slight differences, it's good practice to test your pages with multiple user agents. ▓▓▓▓ You decide to preview your Lakeland Reeds Web page in a browser.

STEPS

TROUBLE

If your Web page does not match Figure B-6, return to Notepad, compare your code to Figure B-7, edit as necessary, and save the file, then repeat Step 2 to preview your edited Web page.

1. **Using your file manager, navigate to the drive and folder where you store your Data Files, open the Unit B/Unit folder, then double-click index.html**

   The Web page opens in your system's default Web browser, as shown in Figure B-7. The address information runs together on a single line, rather than appearing on multiple lines as in the code.

2. **If multiple browsers are installed on your system, return to your file manager, right-click (Windows) or control-click (Mac) index.html, point to Open with, then click another browser name in the list**

   The Web page opens in a non-primary browser.

3. **If your Web page is open in two browsers, note any differences between them in the way the page is displayed**

   Often differences in the way each browser displays, or **renders**, a Web page are subtle, such as slight variations in the space between lines. Figure B-8 shows a Web page that is displayed differently in multiple browsers.

Why browsers display Web pages differently

The display of Web pages in HTML5 starts with the standards created by the W3C and the WHATWG. The standards list and describe all the available elements, along with parameters for how user agents should handle them. User agents are built around software known as **rendering engines** that translate Web page elements into visual, auditory, or tactile representations based on these standards. Because the standards require some interpretation, no two engines render the same HTML code in exactly the same way. In addition, the creators of rendering engines do not always implement all of the current standards in their software. Because the audience for your Web pages will almost always be using a number of different user agents, it's important to test your code in a variety of popular browsers and on multiple operating systems (such as Windows 7, Windows XP, and Mac OS X).

FIGURE B-7: Previewing the Web page

Contents of title element displayed in tab

Browser displays h1 element as a heading

Browser displays p elements as standard text

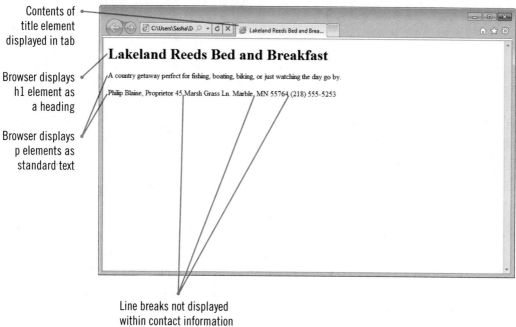

Line breaks not displayed within contact information

FIGURE B-8: Rendering differences between browsers

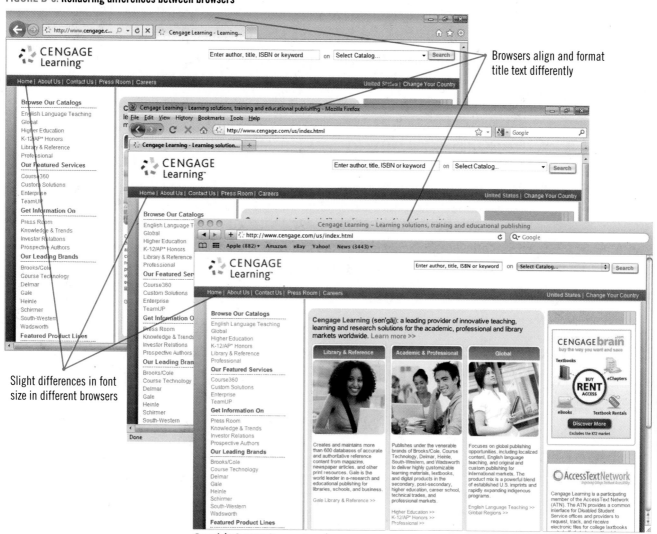

Browsers align and format title text differently

Slight differences in font size in different browsers

Copyright © 2010 Cengage Learning

Implementing One-Sided Tags

While you add most elements to a Web page using tag pairs, some elements require only a single tag. Instead of affecting text or other elements on the page, these one-sided elements generally represent a specific occurrence of an item or a behavior. You enter a one-sided element by typing a single tag. ▰▰▰▰ Although pressing [Enter] to insert line breaks in your HTML code is useful for making your code easier to understand, user agents ignore line breaks inserted this way when processing HTML code. To make the Lakeland Reeds address and phone number appear on multiple lines, you decide to add HTML line break codes that browsers will incorporate into the page layout.

STEPS

1. **In your text editor, click at the beginning of the line that reads 45 Marsh Grass Ln., then use ➙ and ◂ if necessary to position the insertion point immediately to the left of the 4**

QUICK TIP
Be sure to type a space between the r and the /.

2. **Press [Backspace] (Windows) or [delete] (Mac) five times to remove the indentation and move the street address to the end of the previous line, then type
**
   The br element inserts a line break. As a result, the text "45 Marsh Grass Ln." will be displayed on a new line when a user opens the document in a browser. Table B-3 summarizes the Web page elements you have implemented in your Web page.

3. **Click at the beginning of the line that reads Marble, MN 55764, then use ➙ and ◂ if necessary to position the insertion point immediately to the left of the first M**

4. **Press [Backspace] (Windows) or [delete] (Mac) five times, then type
**

5. **Click at the beginning of the line that reads (218) 555-5253</p>, then use ➙ and ◂ if necessary to position the insertion point immediately to the left of the (**

6. **Press [Backspace] (Windows) or [delete] (Mac) five times, then type
**
   Your document should look like the one shown in Figure B-9.

7. **Press [Ctrl][S] (Windows) or [command][s] (Mac)**
   Your changes are saved.

8. **Return to your primary Web browser, then click your browser's Refresh or Reload button**
   The browser loads the updated version of the Web page. The address and phone number now appear on multiple lines, as shown in Figure B-10.

9. **If you previously opened index.html in a second browser, refresh or reload the page to see the changes in that browser as well**

```
index.html - Notepad
File  Edit  Format  View  Help
<!DOCTYPE html>
<html>
  <head>
    <meta charset="utf-8" />
    <title>Lakeland Reeds Bed and Breakfast</title>
  </head>
  <body>
    <h1>Lakeland Reeds Bed and Breakfast</h1>
    <p>A country getaway perfect for fishing, boating, biking, or just watching the day go by.</p>
    <p>Philip Blaine, Proprietor<br />45 Marsh Grass Ln.<br />Marble, MN 55764<br />(218) 555-5253</p>
  </body>
</html>
```

Line break elements inserted to
break up contact information onto
multiple lines in browsers

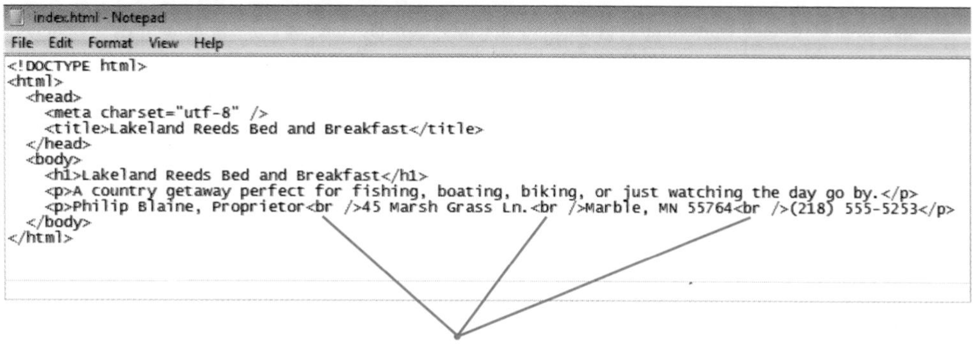

FIGURE B-10: **Web page displaying line breaks**

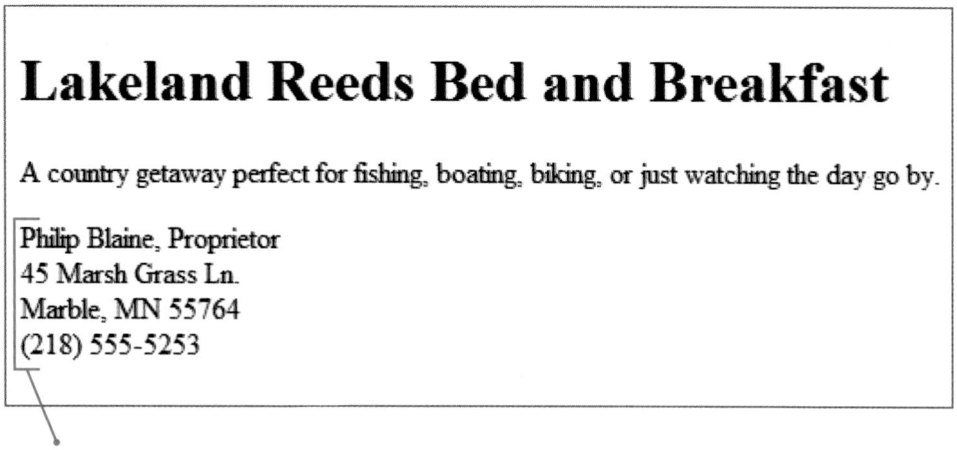

Lakeland Reeds Bed and Breakfast

A country getaway perfect for fishing, boating, biking, or just watching the day go by.

Philip Blaine, Proprietor
45 Marsh Grass Ln.
Marble, MN 55764
(218) 555-5253

Line break elements divide
up contact information onto
multiple lines

TABLE B-3: **Basic Web page elements**

element	function	code sample

html	marks the beginning and the end of the Web page	`<html>`
		  web page contents
		`</html>`

head	contains elements that are not part of the main Web page	`<head>`
		  head contents, such as title and meta elements
		`</head>`

body	includes contents that are visible in the main window of a Web browser	`<body>`
		  body contents, such as p and h1 elements
		`</body>`

meta	enables you to pass information about a Web page to user agents that open it	`<meta charset="utf-8" />`
title	specifies text that appears in the title bar of the Web browser opening the page	`<title>Lakeland Reeds</title>`
p	marks a paragraph of text	`<p>Escape to the lake!</p>`
h1	represents the highest-level heading on the page	`<h1>Lakeland Reeds</h1>`
br	inserts a line break	`45 Marsh Grass Ln. Marble, MN 55764`

HTML5 and CSS3

Validating Your HTML Code

You've seen that previewing your Web pages can be useful for spotting problems with your code and making sure that your Web pages display as expected for your users. Another tool is validation, which is an automated process of comparing code you've written against the HTML5 coding standards. When previewing a page reveals an error in your code that's difficult to track down, validation can sometimes be useful in identifying the specific source of the problem. In addition, sometimes a user agent can interpret a Web page as expected in spite of code that doesn't conform to specifications. In this case, validating your code and correcting errors can help to ensure that your code will continue to work with future versions of both user agents and HTML standards, which may not continue to deal seamlessly with erroneous coding. ▨▨▨▨ Faduma has given you the Web address of an online code validator and asks you to give her a validation report of the page you've created.

STEPS

1. **Open your Web browser, click in the Address Bar, type http://validator.w3.org/, then press [Enter]**

   The Web page opens for the validation service provided by the W3C, as shown in Figure B-11.

2. **Click the Validate by File Upload tab**

   Because your page is not yet published on the Internet, you'll upload your file directly to the w3.org Web site for validation.

3. **Click Browse or Choose File, navigate to the drive and folder where you store your Data Files, open the Unit B/Unit folder, then double-click index.html**

4. **Click Check**

   The browser uploads your document to the w3.org Web site and the result page opens, as shown in Figure B-12.

5. **Scroll down to read the validation results, including any Notes or Warnings**

6. **If you have space on a Web server for publishing your documents, create a local root folder within the Unit folder, move index.html to the local root folder, upload the file to your Web publishing location, then open index.html in your browser from the published location to verify that the upload was successful**

7. **Close any open browsers, then close your text editor.**

FIGURE B-11: W3C Validator Web page

Click for
options to
upload your
html file

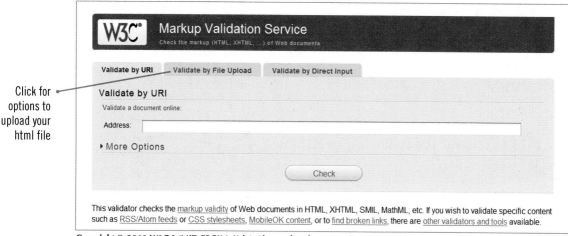

FIGURE B-12: Validation results Web page

Successful
validation
means the
index.htm
code meets
the guidelines
set out in
the HTML5
specification

Character
encoding
recognized in
the meta tag
you entered

Doctype
detected
from your
DOCTYPE
declaration

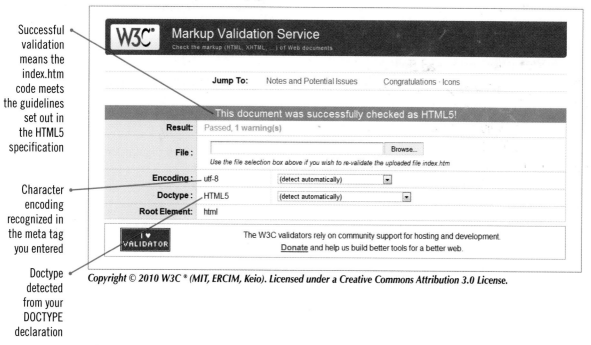

HTML5 and CSS3

Practice

For current SAM information, including versions and content details, visit SAM Central (http://www.cengage.com/samcentral). If you have a SAM user profile, you may have access to hands-on instruction, practice, and assessment of the skills covered in this unit. Since various versions of SAM are supported throughout the life of this text, check with your instructor for the correct instructions and URL/Web site for accessing assignments.

Concepts Review

Refer to Figure B-13 to answer the following questions.

FIGURE B-13

```
index.html - Notepad
File  Edit  Format  View  Help
<!DOCTYPE html>
<html>
   <head>
      <meta charset="utf-8" />
      <title>Lakeland Reeds Bed and Breakfast</title>
   </head>
   <body>
      <h1>Lakeland Reeds Bed and Breakfast</h1>
      <p>A country getaway perfect for fishing, boating, biking, or just watching the day go by.</p>
      <p>Philip Blaine, Proprietor<br />45 Marsh Grass Ln. <br />Marble, MN 55764<br />(218) 555-5253</p>
   </body>
</html>
```

a b c d e f g

1. Which tag marks the beginning of a paragraph?
2. Which tag marks the beginning of the highest-level heading?
3. Which tag marks the beginning of text that appears in the title bar of a Web browser?
4. Which tag creates a line break?
5. Which tag marks the beginning of page contents that are visible in the main window of a Web browser?
6. Which tag marks the beginning of a Web page?
7. Which tag marks the beginning of code that does not appear in the main browser window?

Match each HTML term with the statement that best describes it.

8. Hypertext Markup Language
9. World Wide Web Consortium
10. Extensible Markup Language
11. Extensible Hypertext Markup Language
12. Web Hypertext Application Technology Working Group

a. a generic language that enables users to describe the structure of any kind of document
b. a version of HTML that complies with the rules of XML
c. a standardized format for specifying the structure of a Web page
d. group responsible along with the W3C for the development of HTML5
e. organization founded to take on the responsibility of maintaining the standards of HTML

Select the best answer from the list of choices.

13. Which type of language is HTML?
- **a.** presentational
- **b.** deprecated
- **c.** semantic
- **d.** one-sided

14. Which is the companion language to HTML used to describe the appearance of elements?
- **a.** WHATWG
- **b.** CSS
- **c.** XHTML
- **d.** XML

15. Which element lets user agents know that the document contents are written in HTML?
- **a.** title
- **b.** html
- **c.** body
- **d.** DOCTYPE declaration

16. Which type of tag do you place at the end of an element you are marking?
- **a.** deprecated
- **b.** closing
- **c.** one-sided
- **d.** opening

17. What is the term for opening a Web page in one or more Web browsers and examining the result?
- **a.** tagging
- **b.** hand-coding
- **c.** validation
- **d.** previewing

Skills Review

1. Create an HTML document.
- **a.** Open a new document in your text editor.
- **b.** Type **<!DOCTYPE html>**, then press [Enter].
- **c.** Type **<html>**, press [Enter] twice, then type **</html>**.
- **d.** If you are using TextEdit on a Mac, click Format, then click Make Plain Text.
- **e.** Click File, then click Save.
- **f.** Navigate to the drive and folder where you store your Data Files, open the Unit B folder, then open the Review folder.
- **g.** In the File name box (Windows) or Save As box (Mac), type **index.html**.
- **h.** If you are using Notepad in Windows, click the Save as type list arrow, then click All Files (*.*).
- **i.** Click Save.

2. Set up the document head and body.
- **a.** Click in the blank line between the opening and closing html tags, press [Spacebar] twice, then type **<head>**.
- **b.** Press [Enter] twice, press [Spacebar] twice, then type **</head>**.
- **c.** Press [Enter], press [Spacebar] twice, then type **<body>**.
- **d.** Press [Enter] twice, press [Spacebar] twice, then type **</body>**.
- **e.** Click in the blank line between the opening and closing head tags, press [Spacebar] four times, type **<meta charset="utf-8" />**, then press [Enter].
- **f.** Save your work.

3. Add Web page text and one-sided tags.
- **a.** Click in the blank line above the closing head tag if necessary, press [Spacebar] four times, then type **<title>Big J's Deep Dish Pizza</title>**.
- **b.** Click in the blank line between the opening and closing body tags, press [Spacebar] four times, then type **<h1>Big J's Deep Dish Pizza</h1>**.
- **c.** Press [Enter], press [Spacebar] four times, then type **<p>Authentic Chicago-style deep dish pizza—eat in, carry out, or call for delivery.</p>**.
- **d.** Press [Enter], insert four spaces, then type the following text:
  **<p>150 St. Joseph St.
Toronto, ON M5S 2C3
(416) 555-3337</p>**
- **e.** Press [Enter], type **<p>**, type your first and last name, type a comma, then type **HTML5 Unit B, Skills Review</p>**.
- **f.** Save your work.

Skills Review (continued)

4. Preview your Web page.

a. Using your file manager, navigate to the drive and folder where you store your Data Files, open the Review folder, double-click index.html, then compare your screen to Figure B-14.

b. If multiple browsers are installed on your system, return to your file manager, right-click (Windows) or control-click index.html, point to Open with, then click another browser name in the list.

c. If your Web page is open in multiple browsers, note any differences between them in the way the page is displayed.

5. Validate your HTML code.

a. Open your Web browser, click in the Address Bar, type **http://validator.w3.org/**, then press [Enter].

b. Click the Validate by File Upload tab.

c. Click Browse or Choose File, navigate to the drive and folder where you store your Data Files, open the Unit B/Review folder, then double-click index.html.

d. Click Check.

e. Scroll down to read the validation results, including any Notes or Warnings.

f. If requested by your instructor, save or print the validation results.

g. If you have space on a Web server for publishing your documents, create a local root folder within the Review folder, move index.html to the local root folder, upload index.html to your Web publishing location, then open index.html in your browser from the published location to verify that the upload was successful.

h. Close any open browsers, then close your text editor.

Big J's Deep Dish Pizza

Authentic Chicago-style deep dish pizza--eat in, carry out, or call for delivery.

150 St. Joseph St.
Toronto, ON M5S 2C3
(416) 555-3337

Independent Challenge 1

Spotted Wren Garden Center, a local garden shop and plant store, has hired you to create a Web site for their business. Sarah Nguyen, the shop's owner and manager, would like you to create a Web presence as a new avenue of marketing, as well as a means to keep regular customers up to date on seasonal specials and new products.

a. Open a new document in your text editor, type **<!DOCTYPE html>**, then press [Enter].

b. Type **<html>**, press [Enter], press [Spacebar] twice, type <head>, then press [Enter].

c. Press [Spacebar] four times, type **<meta charset="utf-8" />**, then press [Enter] twice.

d. Press [Spacebar] twice, type **</head>**, then press [Enter].

e. Press [Spacebar] twice, type **<body>**, then press [Enter] twice.

f. Press [Spacebar] twice, type **</body>**, press [Enter], then type **</html>**.

g. Click File, click Save, navigate to the drive and folder where you store your Data Files, open the Unit B folder, then open the IC1 folder.

h. Click the File name box (Windows) or Save As box (Mac), then type **index.html**.

i. Click the Save as type list arrow and click All Files (*.*) (Windows), or click the File Format list arrow and click HTML (Mac), then click Save.

j. Click in the blank line above the closing head tag, press [Spacebar] four times, then type **<title>Spotted Wren Garden Center</title>**.

k. Click in the blank line between the opening and closing body tags, press [Spacebar] four times, then type **<h1>Spotted Wren Garden Center</h1>**.

Independent Challenge 1 (continued)

l. Press [Enter], press [Spacebar] four times, then type **<p>For your year-round garden and yard needs, with a focus on the unusual and hard to find.</p>**.

m. Press [Enter], insert four spaces, then type the following text:
   **<p>548 N. 58th St.
Omaha, NE 68132
(402) 555-9736</p>**

n. Press [Enter], type **<p>**, type your first and last name, type a comma, then type **HTML5 Unit B, Independent Challenge 1</p>**.

o. Save your work.

p. Use your file manager to navigate to the drive and folder where you store your Data Files, then open the Unit B/IC1 folder. Double-click index.html to view the Web page in your default browser and compare your screen to Figure B-15.

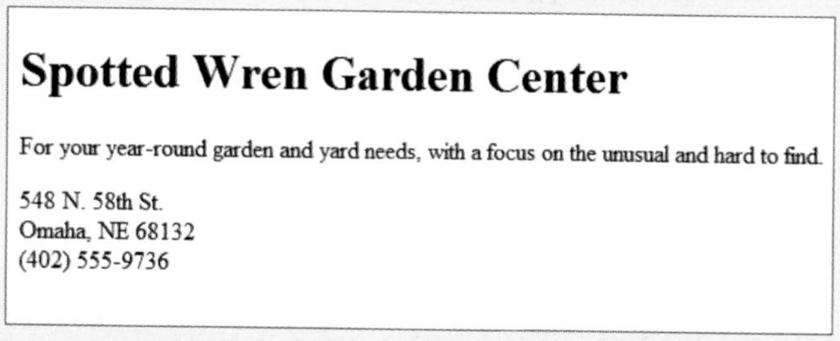

q. If multiple browsers are installed on your system, return to your file manager, right-click (Windows) or control-click (Mac) index.html, point to Open with, then click another browser name in the list, noting any differences between the browsers in the way the page is displayed.

r. In your Web browser, open http://validator.w3.org/, then click the Validate by File Upload tab.

s. Click Browse or Choose File, navigate to the drive and folder where you store your Data Files, open the IC1 folder, then double-click index.html.

t. Click Check, then scroll down to read the validation results, including any Notes or Warnings.

u. If requested by your instructor, save or print the validation results.

v. If you have space on a Web server for publishing your documents, create a local root folder within the IC1 folder, move index.html to the local root folder, upload index.html to your Web publishing location, then open index.html in your browser from the published location to verify that the upload was successful.

w. Close any open browsers, then close your text editor.

FIGURE B-15

Spotted Wren Garden Center

For your year-round garden and yard needs, with a focus on the unusual and hard to find.

548 N. 58th St.
Omaha, NE 68132
(402) 555-9736

Independent Challenge 2

To help build your Web design skills, you have volunteered to create a Web site for the Murfreesboro Recreational Soccer League (MRSL). The league organizes recreational leagues every summer and fall for local, nonprofessional soccer players to get exercise and have fun. You decide to start by creating a Web page with a basic description of the league along with contact information.

a. Open a new document in your text editor, type **<!DOCTYPE html>**, then press [Enter].

b. Enter the opening and closing html, head, and body tags. Be sure to indent the head and body tags two spaces.

c. On an empty line between the opening and closing head tags, press [Spacebar] four times, then type **<meta charset="utf-8" />**.

d. Click File, click Save, navigate to the drive and folder where you store your Data Files, open the Unit B folder, then open the IC2 folder. Click the File name box (Windows) or Save As box (Mac), then type **index.html**. Click the Save as type list arrow and click All Files (*.*) (Windows), or click the File Format list arrow and click HTML (Mac), then click Save.

e. Add a blank line in the head section, press [Spacebar] four times, then type **<title>Murfreesboro Regional Soccer League</title>**.

f. Add a blank line in the body section, press [Spacebar] four times, then type **<h1>Murfreesboro Regional Soccer League</h1>**.

Independent Challenge 2 (continued)

Advanced Challenge Exercise

- Beneath the h1 element, add a blank line, press [Spacebar] four times, then type **<h2> Part of the North American Recreational Soccer Association</h2>** to create a second-level heading.

g. Add a blank line in the body section, press [Spacebar] four times, then type **<p>Get exercise, have fun, and build your soccer skills playing with us. Teams for beginners as well as experienced players.</p>**.

h. Below the paragraph you just entered, enter four spaces, then add the following text:
**<p>c/o Davies Sporting Goods
418 N. Sartoris St.
Murfreesboro, TN 37130
(615) 555-2255</p>**

i. Press [Enter], type **<p>**, type your first and last name, type a comma, then type **HTML5 Unit B, Independent Challenge 2</p>**.

j. Save your work.

k. Using your file manager, navigate to the drive and folder where you store your Data Files, open the Unit B/IC2 folder, then double-click index.html to view the Web page in your default browser and compare your screen to Figure B-16.

FIGURE B-16

> ### Murfreesboro Regional Soccer League
>
> **Part of the North American Recreational Soccer Association**
>
> Get exercise, have fun, and build your soccer skills playing with us. Teams for beginners as well as experienced players.
>
> c/o Davies Sporting Goods
> 418 N. Sartoris St.
> Murfreesboro, TN 37130
> (615) 555-2255

l. If multiple browsers are installed on your system, return to your file manager, right-click (Windows) or control-click (Mac) index.html, point to Open with, then click another browser name in the list and note any differences between the browsers in the way the page is displayed.

m. In your Web browser, open http://validator.w3.org/, then click the Validate by File Upload tab.

n. Click Browse or Choose File, navigate to the drive and folder where you store your Data Files, open the Unit B/IC2 folder, then double-click index.html.

o. Click Check, then scroll down to read the validation results, including any Notes or Warnings.

p. If requested by your instructor, save or print the validation results.

q. If you have space on a Web server for publishing your documents, create a local root folder within the IC2 folder, move index.html to the local root folder, upload index.html to your Web publishing location, then open index.html in your browser from the published location to verify that the upload was successful.

r. Close any open browsers, then close your text editor.

Independent Challenge 3

In your new job creating sites for a Web design firm, you've been assigned a new client, Hotel Natoma. The hotel's business manager, Diego Merckx, wants to use the Web to showcase the facility and its amenities.

a. Open a new document in your text editor and enter a DOCTYPE declaration.

b. Enter the opening and closing html, head, and body tags. Be sure to indent the head and body tags.

c. In the head section, add a meta tag to specify the document's character encoding.

d. Save your file as **index.html** to the Unit B/IC3 folder on the drive and folder where you store your Data Files. Be sure to Click the Save as type list arrow and click All Files (*.*) (Windows), or click the File Format list arrow and click HTML (Mac), before you click Save.

e. In the head section, add a title element that displays the text **Hotel Natoma**.

f. In the body section, add a heading 1 element that displays the text **Hotel Natoma**.

Independent Challenge 3 (continued)

g. Add a paragraph element to the body section that displays the text **A low-impact, Earth-friendly home base in the center of everything San Francisco has to offer**.

h. Below the paragraph you just entered, add a paragraph element with line breaks to display the following contact information:

568 Natoma St.
San Francisco, CA 94103
(415) 555-8378

i. Press [Enter], type **<p>,** type your first and last name, type a comma, then type **HTML5 Unit B, Independent Challenge 3</p>**.

j. Save your work, then preview your page in your default Web browser. If multiple browsers are installed on your system, open your page in a secondary browser and note any differences between the two browsers in the way the page is displayed. Compare your screen to Figure B-17.

FIGURE B-17

> ## Hotel Natoma
>
> A low-impact, Earth-friendly home base in the center of everything San Francisco has to offer.
>
> 568 Natoma St.
> San Francisco, CA 94103
> (415) 555-8378

k. If you have space on a Web server for publishing your documents, create a local root folder within the IC3 folder, move index.html to the local root folder, upload index.html to your Web publishing location, then open index.html in your browser from the published location to verify that the upload was successful.

l. In your Web browser, open http://validator.w3.org/.

Advanced Challenge Exercise

- If you published your Web page, enter the Web address to open your Web page in the Address box, then click Check.

m. If you did not publish your Web page in Step j, click the Validate by File Upload tab.

n. Navigate to the location of the file you created, click Check, then scroll down to read the validation results.

o. If requested by your instructor, save or print the validation results.

p. Close any open browsers, then close your text editor.

Real Life Independent Challenge

This assignment builds on the personal Web site you started planning in Unit A. In this project, you will create the basic structure of your main Web page and add text to the page.

a. In your text editor, create the structuring tags for your Web site, including a DOCTYPE statement, a character encoding statement, and html, head, and body sections. Save the file as **index.html** to the Unit B/RLIC folder on the drive and folder where you store your Data Files.

b. Add a title element and a heading element. If you choose, the heading text may be different than the title text.

c. Create paragraph elements containing any text shown on your Web site sketch. Include a paragraph element containing your first and last name, and the text **HTML5 Unit B, Real Life Independent Challenge**.

d. Save your work, preview the page, and make any changes to the code that may be necessary.

e. Validate your code using the validator at w3.org.

Visual Workshop

Use a text editor to create the Web page shown in Figure B-18. Include a paragraph element after the content shown that contains your first and last name and the text **HTML5 Unit B, Visual Workshop**. When you are finished, save your work as **index.html** to the Unit B/VW folder on the drive and folder where you store your Data Files. Preview the Web page in your default Web browser, validate your code using the online validator at w3.org, then close your browser and your text editor.

Revisions Bookstore and Cafe

Custom brewed coffee and hand-selected books. Special orders are our specialty.

412 N. 25th St.
Richmond, VA 23223
(804) 555-2565

Getting Started with CSS

Files You Will Need:

To view a list of files needed for this unit, see the Data Files Grid in the back of the book.

Early versions of HTML included both semantic and presentational elements; for example, you could use the i element to format text as italic or the center element to center another element horizontally on the page. Presentational tags such as these made Web page code dense and complex, made changing the appearance of a Web page a significant undertaking because of the many individual tags to be edited, and had to be repeated on every page of a Web site to create a common layout and appearance. Early Web developers recognized that another solution was needed, and through the W3C, helped create Cascading Style Sheets (CSS) as a separate, complementary language for presentation. CSS code can be included in an HTML document, but CSS follows its own syntax rules. ▓▓▓▓ As you continue your work on the Lakeland Reeds Bed & Breakfast Web site, your supervisor, Faduma Egal, has asked you to add some layout features to the site. In this unit, you'll learn about CSS and integrate CSS formatting into your Web documents.

OBJECTIVES

Assess style rules
Create an embedded style sheet
Implement an id selector
Implement the div element
Implement a class selector
Create an external style sheet
Link to an external style sheet
Validate your CSS code

Assessing Style Rules

Rather than adding formatting elements to a Web page as in previous versions of HTML, CSS adds style information to elements defined in the HTML code for a Web page. You add CSS to an HTML document by inserting **style rules**, which are lines or blocks of CSS code that specify the presentation of Web page elements. Version 2.1 of the CSS standard has been in wide use for years, but recent additions and enhancements to the language have given rise to CSS3. ▅▅▅▅ As you prepare to integrate CSS into the Lakeland Reeds Web site, you review style rule structure and syntax.

CSS code builds on a few basic concepts:

- **Style rule syntax**

    A style rule is composed of two main parts. The rule starts with one or more **selectors**, which identify the HTML element or elements to which the style rule applies. One or more **name-value pairs** follow the selector(s); each pair specifies a CSS **property** to apply to the selector(s) and the value to assign to the property. Each name-value pair ends with a semicolon, and all of the name-value pairs declared for a selector are enclosed in a single set of curly braces. For instance, the style rule

    ```
    h1 {
       text-align: center;
       width: 40em;
       }
    ```

    centers the text of any h1 heading in a Web document and sets its width to 40 ems.

- **Kinds of selectors**

    CSS allows several selector types. The most general selectors are the names of HTML elements, such as h1 or p, which are known as **type selectors**. These selectors apply associated name/value pairs to every instance of the specified element in the associated Web document. For instance, the style rule in the previous paragraph centers the text and sets the width of any h1 heading in the HTML document, even if there is more than one. Likewise, a style rule using a p selector would apply the properties it specifies to all of a document's p elements.

- **Types of name-value pairs**

    CSS supports properties for many aspects of Web page presentation, including fonts, text, tables, lists, background, borders, and positioning. Multiple properties are defined for each area, enabling control over specific details of presentation. Table C-1 lists the properties you will use in this unit. Allowable values are specific to each property and vary widely, including keywords such as "centered," numerical values expressed in percentages or units of measurement, and relative measurements such as "smaller." If you're unsure of the allowable values for a property, you can look them up in online CSS references such as the one at www.w3c.org.

QUICK TIP

Appendix B lists the most commonly used properties from CSS versions 1 and 2, along with some of the most widely supported CSS3 properties.

TABLE C-1: CSS properties and values

group	affects	properties	allowable values	notes
Text alignment	the horizontal alignment of text.	text-align	**left**, **right**, **center**, **justify**, **inherit** (same value as enclosing element)	
Dimensions	the dimensions of an element, excluding border, padding, and margins.	width, height, max-width, max-height, min-width, min-height	**value** in em, pixels, or another supported unit, **percent** of the enclosing element, **inherit** (same value as enclosing element), **auto** (default)	
Border	the properties of the border around an element.	border-width, border-top-width, border-right-width, border-bottom-width, border-left-width	**thin**, **medium**, **thick**, **value** in em, pixels, or another supported unit	Specify width for all borders with border-width property, or use individual properties for specific sides.
		border-style, border-top-style, border-right-style, border-bottom-style, border-left-style	**dotted**, **dashed**, **solid**, **double**, **groove**, **ridge**, **inset**, **outset**	Specify style for all borders with border-style property, or use individual properties for specific sides.
		border-color, border-top-color, border-right-color, border-bottom-color, border-left-color	color as a **name** from cross-browser compatibility list, **rgb code** in the format rgb (*rrr,ggg,bbb*), or **hexadecimal code** in the format #*rrggbb*, **transparent**, **inherit** (value of enclosing element)	Specify color for all borders with border-color property, or use individual properties for specific sides.
		border	**width style color**	Shorthand property combining width, style, and color into a single declaration.
Padding	the space between element contents and border.	padding, padding-top, padding-right, padding-bottom, padding-left	**value** in em, pixels, or another supported unit, **percent** of the enclosing element.	Specify padding for all borders with padding property, or use individual properties for specific sides.
Margins	the space outside of the element border.	margin, margin-top, margin-right, margin-bottom, margin-left	**value** in em, pixels, or another supported unit, **percent** of the enclosing element, **auto** (default)	Specify margins for all borders with margins property, or use individual properties for specific sides.

Spacing your CSS code

Web page rendering engines recognize name-value pairs after a selector as starting after an opening curly brace { and ending with the closing curly brace }. As long as a semicolon follows each value, any number of spaces, tabs, and new lines can occur within a set of name-value pairs. As a result, the appearance of CSS code can vary widely. Some developers prefer to keep all name-value pairs on the same line as the selector, as shown at the top of Figure C-1, to keep their code compact and make it obvious which pairs are associated with which selector. Others prefer to give each name-value pair its own line, often indented beneath its selector, as shown at the bottom of Figure C-1, to make the code easier to read and parse. While the code shown in this book uses the latter format, don't be surprised to see the former—as well as other variations—in other examples of CSS that you may encounter. While you may be required to follow a given code format by an employer or client, such formatting is most often a matter of personal taste.

FIGURE C-1: Two alternative ways of entering CSS code

```
<style type="text/css">
    h1 {text-align: center;}
    #contact {text-align:right; padding-right:15px;}
    #box {border-width:3px; border-style:solid; border-color:black; width:800px; margin-left:auto; margin-right:auto;}
    .maintext {text-align:left; width:60%; margin-left:auto; margin-right:auto;}
</style>
```

```
<style type="text/css">
    h1 {
        text-align: center;
        }
    #contact {
        text-align: right;
        padding-right: 15px;
        }
    #box {
        border-width: 3px;
        border-style: solid;
        border-color: black;
        width: 800px;
        margin-left: auto;
        margin-right: auto;
        }
    .maintext {
        text-align: center;
        width: 60%;
        margin-left: auto;
        margin-right: auto;
        }
</style>
```

Creating an Embedded Style Sheet

While there are a few different ways to apply CSS styles to Web page elements, creating an embedded style sheet is the most straightforward solution for affecting the presentation of a single Web page. An **embedded style sheet** is a section of CSS code entered in the head element of an HTML document. You insert CSS code in a style element with an attribute specifying that the contents are written in CSS. You have created basic Web documents for each of the pages in the Lakeland Reeds B&B Web site. In addition, the art department at Great Northern Web Solutions has provided you a sketch of a visual layout for the site. You start your work with CSS by creating a style rule to center the main heading text.

STEPS

1. **Start your text editor, click File, click Open (or choose the appropriate options in your program for selecting a file), then navigate to the Unit C/Unit folder on the drive and folder where you store your Data Files**

2. **Select the file HTM C-1.html, then click Open (or choose the appropriate program-specific option to open the file)**

3. **Insert a blank line before the closing body tag, insert a paragraph element containing your first and last name and the text HTML5 Unit C, then save the file as index.html**

4. **Open index.html in your browser**
   In addition to your personal info, the Web page contains a level 1 heading, a level 2 heading, and two additional paragraphs.

5. **Return to your text editor, click at the end of the line containing the title element, then press [Enter]**

6. **Press [Spacebar] four times, type <style type="text/css">, press [Enter] twice, press [Spacebar] four times, then type </style>**
   You will enter your CSS code between the opening and closing style tags. The attribute "type" and value "text/css" in the opening tag specify that the code within the style element follows the rules of CSS.

7. **Click in the blank line between the opening and closing style tags, press [Spacebar] six times, type h1 {, press [Enter], press [Spacebar] eight times, type text-align: center;, press [Enter], press [Spacebar] eight times, then type }**
   The text-align property determines the horizontal alignment of text. This style rule center-aligns all text within h1 elements. Compare your document to Figure C-2.

8. **Save your document, return to your default browser, then click the Refresh or Reload button to view changes to your Web document**
   As Figure C-3 shows, the first line of text, which is an h1 element, is centered horizontally in the browser window.

FIGURE C-2: **Type style rule**

index.html - Notepad
File Edit Format View Help
<!DOCTYPE html>
<html>
<head>
<meta charset="utf-8" />
<title>Lakeland Reeds Bed and Breakfast</title>
<style type="text/css">
h1 {
text-align: center;
}
</style>
</head>
<body>
<h1>Lakeland Reeds Bed and Breakfast</h1>
<h2>A country getaway perfect for fishing, boating, biking, or just watching the day go by.</h2>
<p>Lakeland Reeds is a rustic bed and breakfast on Twin Lakes near rural Marble, Minnesota. Convenient to US 2 and 169, the fresh air and quiet make for an ideal weekend escape from the rush of city life.</p>
<p id="contact">Philip Blaine, Proprietor
45 Marsh Grass Ln.
Marble, MN 55764
(218) 555-5253</p>
</body>
</html>

Embedded stylesheet

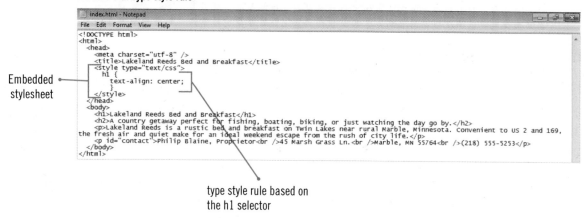

type style rule based on the h1 selector

FIGURE C-3: **Type style rule implemented Web page text styled by style rule**

Lakeland Reeds Bed and Breakfast
A country getaway perfect for fishing, boating, biking, or just watching the day go by.
Lakeland Reeds is a rustic bed and breakfast on Twin Lakes near rural Marble, Minnesota. Convenient to US 2 and 169, the fresh air and quiet make for an ideal weekend escape from the rush of city life.
Philip Blaine, Proprietor
45 Marsh Grass Ln.
Marble, MN 55764
(218) 555-5253

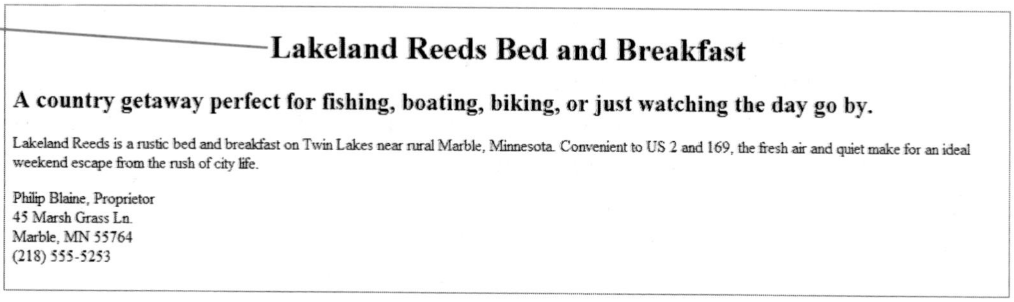

h1 heading text centered horizontally on the Web page

Implementing an id Selector

Sometimes instead of affecting the presentation of all the elements of a certain type, you want to make changes that affect only a single element. For instance, maybe a certain p element requires a different alignment or size from all the other p elements in a document. HTML allows you to add the id attribute to the opening tag for an element to give the element a name. You can then create a special type of selector known as an **id selector** to create CSS code that applies to that element alone. An id selector is simply a pound sign (#) followed by the id value for the element. Any name-value pairs following this selector apply only to the element with the specified id attribute value. ████████ The main Lakeland Reeds Web page contains several paragraph elements. The visual style for the page has one of them, the contact information, right-aligned. You use an id attribute and id selector to change the appearance of the contact information.

STEPS

1. **In your text editor, scroll down if necessary to the paragraph that begins <p>Philip Blaine, Proprietor**

QUICK TIP

Only one element in an HTML document can have a given id attribute value.

2. **In the opening <p> tag, click to position the insertion point between the p and the >, then press [Spacebar]**

3. **Type id="contact"**
   The paragraph containing the contact information is assigned the unique id value "contact".

4. **If necessary, scroll up to view the embedded style sheet, click after the closing brace for the h1 style rule, press [Enter], then press [Spacebar] six times**

5. **Type #contact { then press [Enter]**

6. **Press [Spacebar] eight times, type text-align: right;, then press [Enter]**
   The default value of text-align is "left", which aligns the left edges of each line of text in an element. Specifying a value of "right" lines up the right edges of the text instead and aligns the right edge of the element with the right edge of the enclosing element.

7. **Press [Spacebar] eight times, then type }**
   Compare your completed code to Figure C-4.

8. **Save your document, return to your default browser, then click the Refresh or Reload button to view changes to your Web document**
   As Figure C-5 shows, the contact information at the bottom of the page is right-aligned.

FIGURE C-4: Style rule using id selector

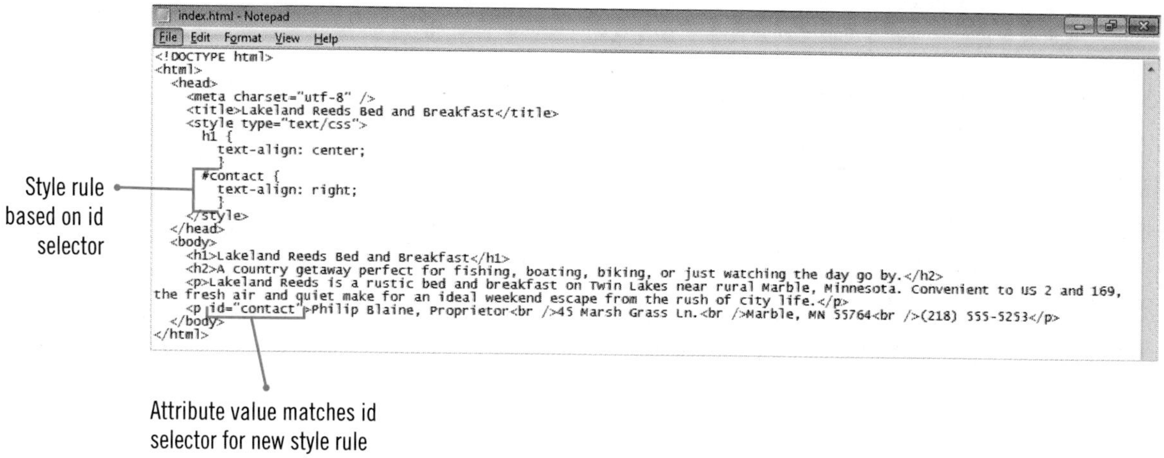

```
index.html - Notepad
File  Edit  Format  View  Help
<!DOCTYPE html>
<html>
  <head>
    <meta charset="utf-8" />
    <title>Lakeland Reeds Bed and Breakfast</title>
    <style type="text/css">
      h1 {
        text-align: center;
      }
      #contact {
        text-align: right;
      }
    </style>
  </head>
  <body>
    <h1>Lakeland Reeds Bed and Breakfast</h1>
    <h2>A country getaway perfect for fishing, boating, biking, or just watching the day go by.</h2>
    <p>Lakeland Reeds is a rustic bed and breakfast on Twin Lakes near rural Marble, Minnesota. Convenient to US 2 and 169,
the fresh air and quiet make for an ideal weekend escape from the rush of city life.</p>
    <p id="contact">Philip Blaine, Proprietor<br />45 Marsh Grass Ln.<br />Marble, MN 55764<br />(218) 555-5253</p>
  </body>
</html>
```

Style rule based on id selector

Attribute value matches id selector for new style rule

FIGURE C-5: Results of style rule based on id selector

Lakeland Reeds Bed and Breakfast

A country getaway perfect for fishing, boating, biking, or just watching the day go by.

Lakeland Reeds is a rustic bed and breakfast on Twin Lakes near rural Marble, Minnesota. Convenient to US 2 and 169, the fresh air and quiet make for an ideal weekend escape from the rush of city life.

Philip Blaine, Proprietor
45 Marsh Grass Ln.
Marble, MN 55764
(218) 555-5253

Contact information is right-aligned

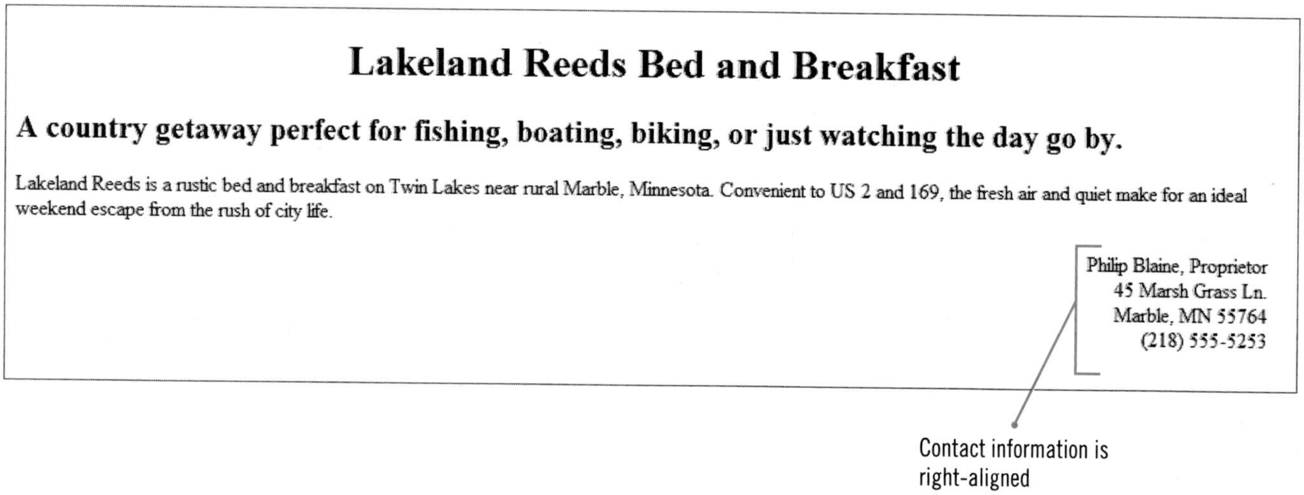

Implementing a style rule with multiple selectors

Sometimes you want to assign the same presentation properties to multiple types of elements. While you could create a style rule and duplicate it for each type selector, an easier way is to add multiple type selectors to a single rule. To do this, simply type the selectors with a comma after each one except the last. Adding a space after each comma is optional, but it helps make the code easier to read. After the final selector, type an opening curly brace and enter name-value pairs as you would for any other style rule. For example, you could create a style rule to center-align both the

h1 element and the element with the id "stores" using the following code:

```
h1, #stores {
text-align: center;
}
```

There's no limit to the number of element types that you can include in a single rule. In fact, many Web developers start their style sheets with a rule for 10–20 element types to apply a collection of global settings.

Implementing the div Element

Sometimes you want to affect the presentation of a section of a Web document that's not itself a single element. One strategy to accomplish this is to enclose the relevant code in another element and then specify styles for the enclosing element. Even though you can apply whatever changes you want to the contents of an element, many HTML elements describe their contents semantically; for example, the contents of an h1 element are assumed to be the highest level heading, while creating a p element implies that it contains a paragraph of text. However, HTML includes a generic element free of semantic meaning for cases where the section isn't a single element: the div element. Thus, you can assign CSS styles to a section of a Web document by enclosing the relevant block of HTML code in a div element, using the tag pair <div></div>. The visual design for the Lakeland Reeds Web page encloses the page content in a black box with a fixed width. You enclose the page contents in a div element and add the CSS code to change the visual layout of its contents.

STEPS

1. **In your text editor, click after the opening <body> tag, then press [Enter]**

2. **Press [Spacebar] four times, then type <div id="box">**

3. **At the bottom of the document, click after the closing </p> tag for the element containing the contact information, press [Enter], press [Spacebar] four times, then type </div>**

   The div element contains all the elements between the opening and closing tags.

4. **At the top of the body section, click before the opening <h1> tag, then press [Spacebar] two times**

   Because you are adding another element to your code, you need to increase the indentation of tags that occur within the new tag pair.

5. **Repeat Step 4 to add two spaces before the opening <h2> tag and before both of the opening <p> tags, as shown in Figure C-6, and also before the opening <p> tag for your name**

6. **If necessary, scroll up to view the embedded style sheet, click after the closing brace for the #contact style rule, press [Enter], press [Spacebar] six times, type #box { , then press [Enter]**

7. **Press [Spacebar] eight times, type border-width: 0.25em;, press [Enter], then add the remaining name-value pairs shown in Figure C-6**

   The specification "em" is a relative unit of measure that represents the current font size. If a user customizes font sizes for a browser, elements specified in em resize as well, preserving your Web page layout. The padding property creates blank space between the div element and elements nested inside it.

8. **If necessary, press [Enter] to create a blank line, press [Spacebar] eight times, then type }**

   Compare your completed code to Figure C-6.

9. **Save your document, return to your default browser, then click the Refresh or Reload button to view the changes to your Web document**

   The page contents are now surrounded by a black border that is horizontally centered on the screen, as shown in Figure C-7.

FIGURE C-6: div element added

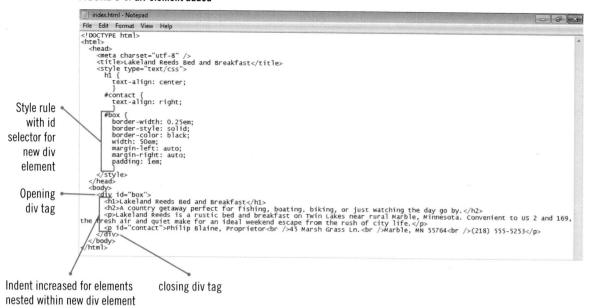

Style rule with id selector for new div element

Opening div tag

Indent increased for elements nested within new div element

closing div tag

FIGURE C-7: Results of new div element and style rule

Lakeland Reeds Bed and Breakfast

A country getaway perfect for fishing, boating, biking, or just watching the day go by.

Lakeland Reeds is a rustic bed and breakfast on Twin Lakes near rural Marble, Minnesota. Convenient to US 2 and 169, the fresh air and quiet make for an ideal weekend escape from the rush of city life.

Philip Blaine, Proprietor
45 Marsh Grass Ln.
Marble, MN 55764
(218) 555-5253

Contents of div element surrounded by 0.25-em-thick, solid black box

Box centered in browser window

Using HTML5 semantic elements

The div element is a useful tool for applying styles to elements or groups of elements that don't fit semantically into common HTML tags. However, the added semantic value of more specific tags can enhance the interpretation of your Web pages by user agents and increase the value of the information indexed by search engines. To bridge this gap, HTML5 defines a set of elements that serve the same function as the div element, but that include semantic value. These

elements include *section*, *article*, *header*, and *footer*. Some extra coding is required to make these elements work in older versions of Internet Explorer, so you should make sure you understand how to implement them, and be sure to test any pages that use them in affected browsers. However, whenever practical, implementing these semantic elements in your Web pages adds an extra level of information and can help you create a richer experience for your users.

Implementing a class Selector

Sometimes you want to apply a style rule to multiple elements in a Web document without adding an additional layer of HTML code. While the id attribute limits a given value to a single instance in a Web page, you can create a selector that applies to any number of elements on a page using the HTML class attribute, which does not have this limit. A **class selector** creates a style rule based on values assigned to elements using the HTML class attribute. This allows you to apply a style rule to an unlimited number of separate elements. A class selector consists of a period followed by a class attribute value. Your final step in implementing the visual design for the Lakeland Reeds Web page is to change the width and alignment of the two paragraphs that appear before the contact information. You add a class attribute to the two elements containing these paragraphs and then add a style rule to modify their presentation.

STEPS

1. **In your text editor, scroll down if necessary to the opening tag for the h2 element, click to position the insertion point between the 2 and the >, press [Spacebar], then type** class="maintext"

2. **In the opening <p> tag for the paragraph that begins "Lakeland Reeds is a rustic bed and breakfast", click to position the insertion point between the p and the >, press [Spacebar], then type** class="maintext"

   The h2 element and the first p element are both assigned the class value *maintext*.

3. **If necessary, scroll up to view the embedded style sheet, click after the closing brace for the #box style rule, press [Enter], then press [Spacebar] six times**

4. **Type .maintext { then press [Enter]**

5. **Press [Spacebar] eight times, type** text-align: center;, **then press [Enter]**

6. **Add the remaining name-value pairs shown in Figure C-8**

   Using a percentage value with the width property resizes an element relative to the size of the element enclosing it—in this case, the div element that creates the border. Setting the margin-left and margin-right properties to auto centers a non-text element within the element enclosing it.

7. **If necessary, press [Enter] to create a blank line after the last name-value pair, press [Spacebar] eight times, then type }**

   Compare your completed code to Figure C-8.

8. **Save your document, return to your default browser, then click the Refresh or Reload button to view changes to your Web document**

   As Figure C-9 shows, the h2 element and the p element that follows it are narrower than the surrounding border and centered within the border.

FIGURE C-8: **Style rule implemented using class selector**

```
        width: 50em;
        margin-left: auto;
        margin-right: auto;
        padding: 1em;
        }
      .maintext {
        text-align: center;
        width: 60%;
        margin-left: auto;
        margin-right: auto;
        }
    </style>
  </head>
  <body>
    <div id="box">
      <h1>Lakeland Reeds Bed and Breakfast</h1>
      <h2 class="maintext">A country getaway perfect for fishing, boating, biking, or just watching the day go by.</h2>
      <p class="maintext">Lakeland Reeds is a rustic bed and breakfast on Twin Lakes near rural Marble, Minnesota. Convenient
to US 2 and 169, the fresh air and quiet make for an ideal weekend escape from the rush of city life.</p>
      <p id="contact">Philip Blaine, Proprietor<br />45 Marsh Grass Ln.<br />Marble, MN 55764<br />(218) 555-5253</p>
    </div>
  </body>
</html>
```

Identical class values
applied to two elements

Style rule for
maintext class

FIGURE C-9: **Results of style rule based on class selector**

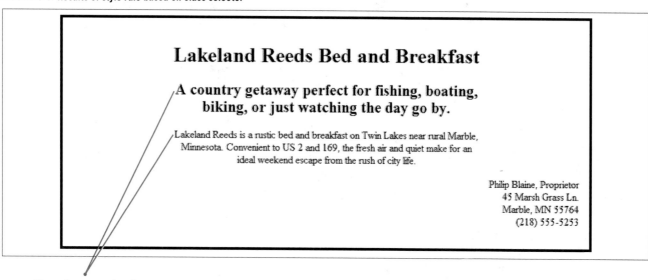

Elements narrowed and
centered within box

Inserting multiple attributes

There is no limit to the number of attributes you can include in a single HTML element. Thus, you can apply multiple style rules to a single element using any combination of a single id attribute and one or more class attributes. For example, you might assign a class to every paragraph in a given section of a Web page, along with an id for the first paragraph in the section to add extra elements to its style. The code for the opening tag might look as follows:

```
<p class="point1" id="opener1">
```

If multiple rules applied to the same element specify values for the same attribute, the value from the last rule in the style sheet is applied. This means it's important to take care with the order of rules in your style sheets. If your pages do not appear as you expect, verify that the order of rules is correct.

Creating an External Style Sheet

An embedded style sheet works well for a stand-alone Web page. However, as your Web presence grows into multiple pages, it becomes impractical to implement a given style change on every page; it also becomes challenging to keep embedded style sheets consistent between multiple pages. Instead, it's helpful to transition a growing Web site to an **external style sheet**, which is a separate file containing style information that multiple Web pages can link to. ▓▓▓▓▓ As you prepare to create more pages for the Lakeland Reeds Web site, you move the style information for the current page to an external style sheet in order to make the appearance of the site easier to modify as the site grows.

1. **In your text editor, scroll up if necessary to view the embedded style sheet, select all the code between the opening and closing style tags, click Edit, then click Cut**

   The contents of the embedded style sheet are removed from the Web document and placed on the clipboard.

2. **Save index.html, click File, click New, then in the new document that opens, type /* Lakeland Reeds Bed and Breakfast */ and press [Enter]**

   In CSS code, any text between /* and */ is treated as a comment and ignored by user agents. Comments are useful for describing the contents of your documents for other Web developers who may need to make changes to them in the future.

3. **Click Edit, click Paste, press [Enter], then add a comment including your first and last name along with the text HTML5 Unit C**

   The embedded style sheet code is pasted into the new document, as shown in Figure C-10.

4. **If you are using TextEdit on a Mac, click Format, then, if necessary, click Make Plain Text**

5. **Click File, click Save, navigate to the Unit C/Unit directory on the drive and folder where you store your Data Files, type lakeland.css, click the Encoding list arrow if necessary and click UTF-8, then click Save**

   Your external style sheet is saved with the filename "lakeland.css".

6. **Close lakeland.css, then if necessary, reopen index.html in your text editor**

7. **Select the lines containing the opening and closing <style> tags along with any blank lines between them, then press Delete**

8. **If necessary, click after the closing </title> tag, then press [Enter] to insert a blank line**

9. **Press [Spacebar] four times, then type <link rel="stylesheet" type="text/css" href="lakeland.css" />**

   Figure C-11 shows the Web page code with the external style sheet reference inserted. The link element makes the contents of an external file available in the HTML document. The values for the rel and type attributes specify that user agents should read the external document as a style sheet written in CSS. The href attribute specifies the filename of the external style sheet.

10. **Save your document, return to your default browser, then click the Refresh or Reload button**

    Your Web page appears just as it did when you were using an embedded style sheet. Even though you removed the style rules previously defined in the HTML document, you added a reference to the external document containing the rules. As a result, your browser still has access to the same style information and renders the Web page according to the same guidelines.

FIGURE C-10: **External style sheet**

CSS comment

Style rules moved from embedded style sheet

```
Untitled - Notepad
File  Edit  Format  View  Help
/* Lakeland Reeds Bed and Breakfast */
    h1 {
        text-align: center;
    }
    #contact {
        text-align: right;
    }
    #box {
        border-width: 0.25em;
        border-style: solid;
        border-color: black;
        width: 50em;
        margin-left: auto;
        margin-right: auto;
        padding: 1em;
    }
    .maintext {
        text-align: center;
        width: 60%;
        margin-left: auto;
        margin-right: auto;
    }
```

FIGURE C-11: **Web page linked to external style sheet**

link element loads contents of external css document

```
index.html - Notepad
File  Edit  Format  View  Help
<!DOCTYPE html>
<html>
  <head>
    <meta charset="utf-8" />
    <title>Lakeland Reeds Bed and Breakfast</title>
    <link rel="stylesheet" type="text/css" href="lakeland.css" />
  </head>
  <body>
    <div id="box">
      <h1>Lakeland Reeds Bed and Breakfast</h1>
      <h2 class="maintext">A country getaway perfect for fishing, boating, biking, or just watching the day go by.</h2>
      <p class="maintext">Lakeland Reeds is a rustic bed and breakfast on Twin Lakes near rural Marble, Minnesota. Convenient
to US 2 and 169, the fresh air and quiet make for an ideal weekend escape from the rush of city life.</p>
      <p id="contact">Philip Blaine, Proprietor<br />45 Marsh Grass Ln.<br />Marble, MN 55764<br />(218) 555-5253</p>
    </div>
  </body>
</html>
```

Filename of external style sheet

Implementing Inline styles

In addition to embedded and external style sheets, you can also incorporate CSS properties into an HTML document using inline styles. An **inline style** is a style rule inserted into the opening tag of an element using the style attribute. Figure C-12 shows an example of an inline style. Inline styles do not offer many of the benefits provided by other methods of applying styles. For instance, changing a style applied inline requires locating the style within HTML code, rather than simply looking at an embedded or external style sheet. Because of this and other drawbacks, many Web developers avoid using inline styles.

FIGURE C-12: **An inline style**

```
<h1 style="text-align: center;">Lakeland Reeds Bed and Breakfast</h1>
```

Linking to an External Style Sheet

Once you create an external style sheet for a Web site, you can apply the style rules it contains to every page on the site simply by adding to each HTML document a link element referencing the style sheet file. If you later decide to make changes to the layout of your Web site, any change you make to the external style sheet is reflected immediately on all the pages that link to it. ▓▓▓▓ You have created a second page for the Lakeland Reeds Web site and added to it the same class and id attributes that you used on the main Web page. You add a link in the new Web document to the external style sheet file you created in order to implement on the new page the same style rules you already created.

1. **In your text editor, open the file HTM C-2.html from the Unit C/Unit folder on the drive and folder where you store your Data Files, then save it as aboutus.html**

   As Figure C-13 shows, the file contains an element with an id value of "contact", a div element with an id value of "box", and multiple elements with the class value of "maintext".

2. **Insert a blank line before the closing body tag, then insert a paragraph element containing your first and last name and the text HTML5 Unit C**

3. **Open aboutus.html in your browser**

   All the page elements are left-aligned, and the page resembles the main Lakeland Reeds page at the beginning of the unit.

4. **Return to your text editor, click at the end of the line containing the title element, then press [Enter]**

5. **Press [Spacebar] four times, then type <link rel="stylesheet" type="text/css" href="lakeland .css" />**

   This is the same link code you inserted into index.html. Figure C-13 shows the completed code for the Web document.

6. **Save your document, return to your default browser, then click the Refresh or Reload button to view the changes to the About Us page**

   The browser now renders the Web page with a layout similar to the main page of the Web site.

7. **Reopen lakeland.css in your text editor, then in the .maintext style rule, change the value for text-align from center to left**

8. **Save your document, close your text editor, return to your default browser, then click the Refresh or Reload button to view the changes to the About Us page**

   As Figure C-14 shows, the h2 heading and the paragraphs below it are now left-aligned rather than center-aligned.

9. **Reopen index.html in your default browser**

   As shown in Figure C-14, the changes in the main page match the changes in the About Us page because the presentation of both documents is based on the external style sheet in lakeland.css.

FIGURE C-13: About Us page with link to external style sheet

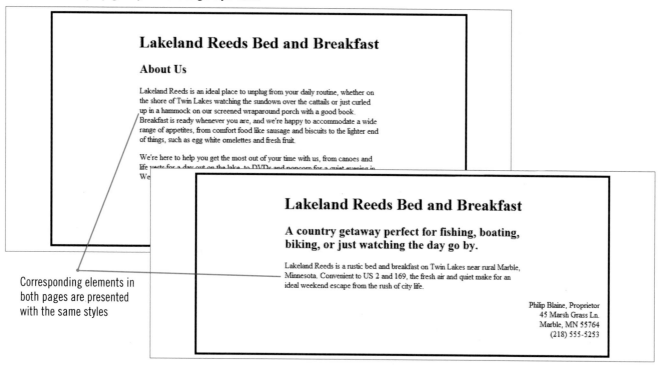

```
aboutus.html - Notepad
File  Edit  Format  View  Help
<!DOCTYPE html>
<html>
   <head>
      <meta charset="utf-8" />
      <title>Lakeland Reeds Bed and Breakfast - About Us</title>
      <link rel="stylesheet" type="text/css" href="lakeland.css" />
   </head>
   <body>
      <div id="box">
         <h1>Lakeland Reeds Bed and Breakfast</h1>
         <h2 class="maintext">About Us</h2>
         <p class="maintext">Lakeland Reeds is an ideal place to unplug from your daily routine, whether on the shore of Twin
Lakes watching the sundown over the cattails or just curled up in a hammock on our screened wraparound porch with a good
book.  Breakfast is ready whenever you are, and we're happy to accommodate a wide range of appetites, from comfort food like
sausage and biscuits to the lighter end of things, such as egg white omelettes and fresh fruit.</p>
         <p class="maintext">We're here to help you get the most out of your time with us, from canoes and life vests for a day
out on the lake, to DVDs and popcorn for a quiet evening in. We look forward to welcoming you!</p>
         <p id="contact">Philip Blaine, Proprietor<br />45 Marsh Grass Ln.<br />Marble, MN 55764<br />(218) 555-5253</p>
      </div>
   </body>
</html>
```

Every document linking to an external style sheet uses the same code for the link element

FIGURE C-14: Multiple pages styled with a single style sheet

Lakeland Reeds Bed and Breakfast

About Us

Lakeland Reeds is an ideal place to unplug from your daily routine, whether on the shore of Twin Lakes watching the sundown over the cattails or just curled up in a hammock on our screened wraparound porch with a good book. Breakfast is ready whenever you are, and we're happy to accommodate a wide range of appetites, from comfort food like sausage and biscuits to the lighter end of things, such as egg white omelettes and fresh fruit.

We're here to help you get the most out of your time with us, from canoes and life vests for a day out on the lake, to DVDs and popcorn for a quiet evening in. We...

Lakeland Reeds Bed and Breakfast

A country getaway perfect for fishing, boating, biking, or just watching the day go by.

Lakeland Reeds is a rustic bed and breakfast on Twin Lakes near rural Marble, Minnesota. Convenient to US 2 and 169, the fresh air and quiet make for an ideal weekend escape from the rush of city life.

Philip Blaine, Proprietor
45 Marsh Grass Ln.
Marble, MN 55764
(218) 555-5253

Corresponding elements in both pages are presented with the same styles

Combining embedded and external style sheets

Sometimes a Web page on a Web site you're developing might require styling that the site's other pages don't need. You can include style rules that apply only to one page in an external style sheet. However, as your Web site grows larger, you want to minimize the size of an external style sheet to avoid increasing the download time for your Web site and thereby delaying users who want to view your pages. In fact, it's fairly common to combine both embedded and external styles in the same Web site.

Because styles can be applied based on external or embedded style sheets, inline styles, or a browser's default settings, an element may be subject to multiple contradictory values for a given property. To resolve such conflicts, CSS includes rules of precedence for

determining which style rule to follow in a conflict: inline styles have the highest priority, followed by embedded styles, external styles, and finally browser settings. This process of determining precedence is known as **cascading** and results in all available styles coalescing into a single virtual style sheet for the user agent's reference in rendering content.

For some user agents, the order of embedded and external style sheets in your code changes the default order of precedence. To ensure that your Web pages follow standard cascading order when using both kinds of style sheets, be sure to always place the link element to an external style sheet before the style element for an embedded style sheet.

Validating Your CSS Code

Even when your CSS code works in your browser testing, it's important to validate it against CSS rules. Validation helps ensure the compatibility of your code with user agents other than those you test on, and goes a long way toward ensuring that your code remains usable through the continual enhancement and expansion of the CSS specification. There are several reputable online validators available that allow you to either copy and paste code from an embedded style sheet or upload a .css file for checking. ▰▰▰▰▰ You upload your external style sheet to a CSS validator on the W3C Web site to verify that it complies with the rules of CSS.

STEPS

QUICK TIP

You can find alternative validators by searching on the phrase **CSS validator** in a search engine.

1. **Open your Web browser, click in the Address Bar, type http://jigsaw.w3.org/css-validator/, then press [Enter]**
   The Web page opens for the CSS validation service provided by the W3C, as shown in Figure C-15.

2. **Click the By file upload tab**
   Because your Web site is not yet published on the Internet, you'll upload your file directly to the w3.org Web site for validation.

3. **Click Browse or Choose File, navigate to the drive and folder where you store your Data Files, open the Unit C/Unit folder, then double-click lakeland.css**

4. **Click More Options, if necessary click the Profile list arrow and click CSS Level 3, then click Check**
   The browser uploads your style sheet to the w3.org Web site and the result page opens, as shown in Figure C-16.

5. **Scroll down to read the validation results, including any notes or warnings**

6. **If you have space on a Web server for publishing your documents, create a local root folder within the Unit folder, move index.html, aboutus.html, and lakeland.css to the local root folder, then upload the files to your Web publishing location**

7. **Open index.htm in your browser from the published location to verify that the upload was successful, then open aboutus.html from the published location**

8. **Close any open browsers, then close your text editor**

Click to
display
options for
uploading
your file

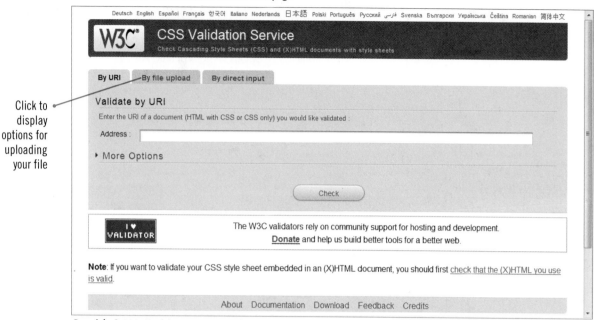

Copyright © 2010 W3C ® (MIT, ERCIM, Keio). Licensed under a Creative Commons Attribution 3.0 License.

FIGURE C-16: W3C CSS Validator results for lakeland.css

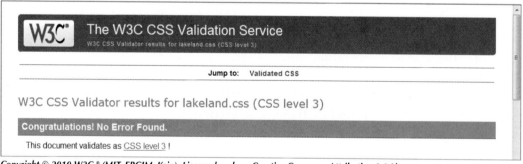

Copyright © 2010 W3C ® (MIT, ERCIM, Keio). Licensed under a Creative Commons Attribution 3.0 License.

Practice

For current SAM information, including versions and content details, visit SAM Central (http://www.cengage.com/samcentral). If you have a SAM user profile, you may have access to hands-on instruction, practice, and assessment of the skills covered in this unit. Since various versions of SAM are supported throughout the life of this text, check with your instructor for the correct instructions and URL/Web site for accessing assignments.

Concepts Review

Refer to Figure C-17.

FIGURE C-17

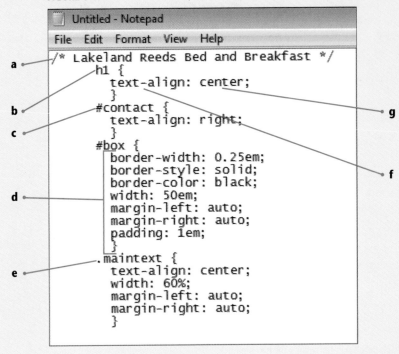

1. Which item is the value assigned to a CSS property?
2. Which item is ignored by a user agent?
3. Which item specifies a set of presentation rules?
4. Which item is a CSS property?
5. Which selector is based on the value of an HTML id attribute?
6. Which selector is based on the value of an HTML class attribute?
7. Which selector is based on the name of an HTML element?

Match each term with the statement that best describes it.

8. style rule
9. name-value pair
10. embedded style sheet
11. external style sheet
12. type selector
13. id selector
14. class selector

a. a selector that applies the specified name-value pairs only to the element with the specified id

b. a line or block of CSS code that specifies the presentation of Web page elements

c. a selector that creates a style rule based on values assigned to elements using the HTML class attribute

d. the most general type of selector, which is the name of an HTML element

e. a separate file containing style information that multiple Web pages can link to

f. a section of CSS code that specifies a CSS property to apply to the selector(s) and the value to assign to the property

g. a section of CSS code entered in the head element of an HTML document

Select the best answer from the list of choices.

15. Which part of a style rule identifies the HTML element or elements to which the style rule applies?

a. selector

b. property

c. value

d. the code between the opening and closing braces

16. A style rule ends with which of the following?

a. */

b. </style>

c. ;

d. }

17. A CSS comment ends with which of the following?

a. */

b. :

c. ;

d. </style>

18. A name-value pair ends with which of the following?

a. :

b. </style>

c. ;

d. }

19. An embedded style sheet ends with which of the following?

a. */

b. </style>

c. ;

d. :

20. Which is the most straightforward solution for affecting the presentation of single Web page?

a. inline styles

b. embedded style sheet

c. external style sheet

d. div element

21. Which of the following enables you to modify the presentation of multiple Web pages with a single change?

a. inline styles

b. embedded style sheet

c. external style sheet

d. div element

22. Which of the following is a class selector?

a. text-align: right

b. #lilac

c. .ideas

d. p

Skills Review

1. Create an embedded style sheet.

  a. Open the file HTM C-3.html in your text editor from the Unit C/Review folder on the drive and folder where you store your Data Files, then save it to the same folder as **index.html**.

  b. Preview index.html in your browser.

  c. Return to your text editor, then add a new line below the line containing the title element.

  d. Insert four spaces, type an opening style tag that specifies a data type of **text/css**, add two new lines, insert four spaces, then type a closing style tag.

  e. Click in the blank line between the opening and closing style tags, insert six spaces, insert a type selector for the h1 element followed by an opening curly brace, add a new line, insert eight spaces, add a name-value pair that left-aligns text, add a new line, insert eight spaces, then insert a closing curly brace.

  f. Save your document.

2. Implement an id selector.

  a. In your text editor, scroll down if necessary to the paragraph that begins with <p>150 St. Joseph St.

  b. In the opening <p> tag, click to position the insertion point between the p and the >, then insert a space.

  c. Insert an id attribute with a value of **contact**.

  d. If necessary, scroll up to view the embedded style sheet, insert a new line below the closing brace for the h1 style rule, then insert six spaces.

  e. Insert an id selector for the value "contact", then type an opening curly brace.

  f. Add a new line, insert eight spaces, then insert a name-value pair that right-aligns text.

  g. Add a new line, insert eight spaces, then insert a closing curly brace.

  h. Save your document, then return to your default browser and refresh the Web page to view your changes.

Skills Review (continued)

3. Implement the div element.

  a. In your text editor, add a blank line below the opening \<body\> tag.

  b. Insert four spaces, then insert a div tag with the id value of **box**.

  c. Add a blank line below the closing \</p\> tag for the element containing the contact information, insert four spaces, then insert a closing div tag.

  d. Add two spaces before the opening tag for the h1 element, then repeat for the h2 element and all three p elements.

  e. Add a new line beneath the contact style rule, insert six spaces, add an id selector for the value "box", then type an opening curly brace.

  f. Insert a name-value pair that sets each of the following on its own line, indented eight spaces:

- border width to **0.5em**.
- border style to **solid**.
- border color to **red**.
- element width to **30em**.
- left margin to **auto**.
- right margin to **auto**.
- padding to **1em**.

  g. Add a new line, insert eight spaces, then insert a closing curly brace.

  h. Save your document, then return to your default browser and refresh the Web page to view your changes.

4. Implement a class selector.

  a. In the opening h2 tag, click to position the insertion point between the 2 and the \>, then insert a space

  b. Insert a class attribute with a value of **maintext**.

  c. Repeat Steps a and b for the opening p tags for the paragraphs that begin "Eat in" and "Voted".

  d. Add a new line below the closing brace for the box style rule.

  e. Insert six spaces, add a class selector for the value "maintext", then type an opening curly brace.

  f. Add a new line, insert eight spaces, then insert a name-value pair that left-aligns text.

  g. Add a new line, insert eight spaces, then type a closing curly brace.

  h. Save your document, then return to your default browser and refresh the Web page to view your changes. Compare your Web page to Figure C-18.

5. Create an external style sheet.

  a. In the embedded style sheet, cut all the code between the opening and closing style tags.

  b. Save index.html, open a new file, then create a CSS comment containing the text **Big J's Deep Dish Pizza**.

  c. Add a new line, then paste the contents of the embedded style sheet.

  d. Add a comment containing your first and last name and the text **HTML5 Unit C, Skills Review**.

  e. If you are using TextEdit on a Mac, click Format, then click Make Plain Text.

  f. Save your work as **bigj.css** to the Unit C/Review directory on the drive and folder where you store your Data Files.

  g. Close the file, then reopen index.html in your text editor from the same directory.

  h. Delete the lines containing the opening and closing \<style\> tags along with any blank lines between them.

  i. Add a blank line below the line containing the title element, insert four spaces, then insert a link element that points to bigj.css.

FIGURE C-18

Big J's Deep Dish Pizza

Authentic Chicago-style pies

Eat in, carry out, or call for delivery.

Voted "Best Pizza Joint" by the Toronto Times!

150 St. Joseph St.
Toronto, ON M5S 2C3
(416) 555-3337

Skills Review (continued)

    j. Insert a blank line before the closing body tag, then insert a paragraph element containing your first and last name and the text **HTML5 Unit C, Skills Review**.

    k. Save your document, then return to your default browser and refresh the Web page to view your changes.

6. Link to an external style sheet.

    a. In your text editor, open the file HTM C-4.html from the Unit C/Review folder on the drive and folder where you store your Data Files, then save it as **history.html**.

    b. Preview history.html in your browser.

    c. In your text editor, add a blank line beneath the line containing the title element, insert four spaces, then insert a link element that points to the bigj.css style sheet.

    d. Insert a blank line before the closing body tag, then insert a paragraph element containing your first and last name and the text **HTML5 Unit C, Skills Review**.

    e. Save the document, then reload history.html in your default browser.

    f. Reopen bigj.css in your text editor, then in the maintext style rule, change the value for text alignment from center to left.

    g. Save your document, close your text editor, then refresh history.html in your default browser. Compare your Web page to Figure C-19.

    h. Refresh index.html in your default browser.

7. Validate your CSS code.

    a. Open **http://jigsaw.w3.org/css-validator/** in your Web browser.

    b. Click the By file upload tab.

    c. Click Browse or Choose File, then select bigj.css from the Unit C/Review folder in the drive and folder where you store your Data Files.

    d. Use the More Options link to set the Profile to CSS Level 3, then click Check.

    e. Scroll down to read the validation results, including any notes or warnings.

    f. If you have space on a Web server for publishing your documents, create a local root folder within the Review folder, move index.html, history.html, and bigj.css to the local root folder, then upload the files to your Web publishing location.

    g. Open index.html in your browser from the published location to verify that the upload was successful, then open history.html from the published location.

    h. Close any open browsers, then close your text editor.

FIGURE C-19

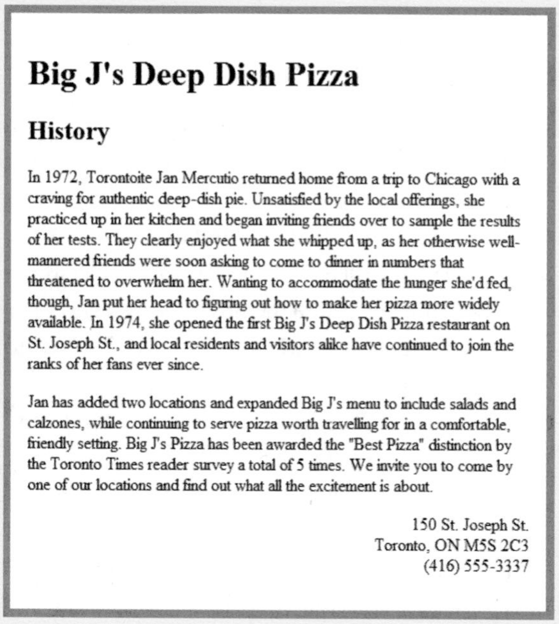

Big J's Deep Dish Pizza

History

In 1972, Torontoite Jan Mercutio returned home from a trip to Chicago with a craving for authentic deep-dish pie. Unsatisfied by the local offerings, she practiced up in her kitchen and began inviting friends over to sample the results of her tests. They clearly enjoyed what she whipped up, as her otherwise well-mannered friends were soon asking to come to dinner in numbers that threatened to overwhelm her. Wanting to accommodate the hunger she'd fed, though, Jan put her head to figuring out how to make her pizza more widely available. In 1974, she opened the first Big J's Deep Dish Pizza restaurant on St. Joseph St., and local residents and visitors alike have continued to join the ranks of her fans ever since.

Jan has added two locations and expanded Big J's menu to include salads and calzones, while continuing to serve pizza worth travelling for in a comfortable, friendly setting. Big J's Pizza has been awarded the "Best Pizza" distinction by the Toronto Times reader survey a total of 5 times. We invite you to come by one of our locations and find out what all the excitement is about.

150 St. Joseph St.
Toronto, ON M5S 2C3
(416) 555-3337

Independent Challenge 1

Sarah Nguyen, the owner and manager of the Spotted Wren Garden Center, is happy with your work so far on the company's Web site. She'd like you to add some presentation elements to the Web page you created, so you incorporate some CSS style rules.

    a. Open the file HTM C-5.html in your text editor from the Unit C/IC1 folder on the drive and folder where you store your Data Files, then save it to the same folder as **index.html**.

    b. In the head section, add opening and closing style tags, then insert a blank line between them.

    c. Create a style rule that uses a class selector to center the text of the h1 and h2 headings and the paragraph containing the contact information.

    d. Create a style rule that uses an id selector to left-align the text of the first paragraph element.

Independent Challenge 1 (continued)

e. Create a style rule that uses an id selector to right-align the text of the second paragraph element.

f. Insert a div element that contains the headings and the first two paragraph elements. Create a style rule that uses an id selector to style the div element with a width of **30em**, padding of **1em**, a **0.25em solid green** border, and left and right margins set to **auto**.

g. Insert a blank line before the closing body tag, then insert a paragraph element containing your first and last name and the text **HTML5 Unit C, Independent Challenge 1**.

h. Save your work, then preview your Web page in a browser. Compare your screen to Figure C-20. If necessary, make corrections to your code.

i. Validate your CSS code using the validator at **http://jigsaw.w3.org/css-validator/**.

j. If you have space on a Web server for publishing your documents, create a local root folder within the IC1 folder, move index.html to the local root folder, upload the file to your Web publishing location, then open the file in your browser from the published location.

k. Close your browser and your text editor.

FIGURE C-20

Spotted Wren Garden Center

For your year-round garden and yard needs

Looking for something unusual or hard to find?

Ask us!

548 N. 58th St. :: Omaha, NE 68132 :: (402) 555-9736

Independent Challenge 2

As you continue developing the Web site for the Murfreesboro Regional Soccer League, you decide to add presentation features to the Web pages. You've created two Web pages for the site, so you create an external style sheet.

a. Open the file HTM C-6.html in your text editor from the Unit C/IC2 folder on the drive and folder where you store your Data Files, then save it to the same folder as **index.html**. Open HTM C-7.html, then save it as **started.html**. Insert a blank line before the closing body tag in each document, then insert a paragraph element containing your first and last name and the text **HTML5 Unit C, Independent Challenge 2**. Save your work and preview both files in a Web browser.

b. Open a new document, enter a CSS comment containing the name of the organization, then save the document with the name **mrsl.css**.

c. Create a style rule that uses a type selector to center the text of h1 elements. Create a duplicate rule to style h2 elements.

d. Create a style rule for the main page content that uses a class selector to left-align text.

e. Create a style rule for the contact information that uses an id selector to right-align text.

f. Create a style rule to create a box that uses an id selector to set a width of **40em**, padding of **1em**, a **0.5em solid black** border, and left and right margins to **auto**.

Advanced Challenge Exercise

■ Combine the style rules for h1 and h2 elements into a single style rule.

■ Combine the style rules for the border width, style, and color into a single rule. Use the property **border**, inserting the values for width, style, and color with spaces between them and a semicolon only after the color value. Be sure to delete the border-width, border-style, and border-color properties.

g. In index.html, add an id attribute to the element containing the contact information that references the style rule you created in Step e, then add class attributes that reference the style rule you created in Step d to all elements in the body section except the headings and contact information.

h. In index.html, insert a div element that contains all the contents of the body section except the contact information. Give the element an id value that matches the selector for the style rule you created in Step f.

i. At the bottom of your external style sheet document, insert a comment containing your first and last name and the text **HTML5 Unit C, Independent Challenge 2**.

Independent Challenge 2 (continued)

j. Save your work, add link elements that reference your external style sheet to index.html and started.html, then save these files.

k. Preview index.html and started.html in a Web browser. Compare your documents to Figure C-21 and Figure C-22. If necessary, make corrections to your code.

FIGURE C-21

Murfreesboro Regional Soccer League

Part of the North American Recreational Soccer Association

Get exercise, have fun, and build your soccer skills playing with us.

Teams for beginners as well as experienced players.

MRSL
c/o Davies Sporting Goods
418 N. Sartoris St.
Murfreesboro, TN 37130
(615) 555-2255

FIGURE C-22

Murfreesboro Regional Soccer League

Part of the North American Recreational Soccer Association

The MRSL is open to players of all levels who want to play soccer in a relaxed, friendly environment. Even if you've never played soccer before, the MRSL is a great place to start.

To get a feel for our league, we recommend you call us at the number below or stop by Davies Sporting Goods to talk to one or our coordinators and get the details on our next all-team practice or workshop day. Then come kick around the ball with us and meet other players in the league.

If you're interested in joining up, you'll need to complete some paperwork and pay $65 for a seasonal membership ($40 for seniors and students).

We look forward to seeing you on the field!

MRSL
c/o Davies Sporting Goods
418 N. Sartoris St.
Murfreesboro, TN 37130
(615) 555-2255

l. Validate your CSS code using the validator at http://jigsaw.w3.org/css-validator/.

m. If you have space on a Web server for publishing your documents, create a local root folder within the IC2 folder, move index.html, started.html, and mrsl.css to the local root folder, upload the files to your Web publishing location, then open the Web pages in your browser from the published location.

n. Close your browser and your text editor.

Independent Challenge 3

As you continue your work on the Web site for Hotel Natoma, you incorporate a color scheme and basic text alignment using CSS.

a. Open the file HTM C-8.html in your text editor from the Unit C/IC3 folder on the drive and folder where you store your Data Files, then save it to the same folder as **index.html**. Open HTM C-9.html, then save it as **nearby.html**. Insert a blank line before the closing body tag in each document, then insert a paragraph element containing your first and last name and the text **HTML5 Unit C, Independent Challenge 3**. Save your work and preview both files in a Web browser.

b. Open a new document, enter a CSS comment containing the name of the organization, then save the document with the name **natoma.css**.

c. Create style rules to apply the following presentation details, adding HTML attributes to both Web documents when necessary:
- center the text of h1 elements
- right-align the contact information
- left-align the remaining text

Advanced Challenge Exercise

- Add CSS code to the external style sheet to create a **0.25em solid** border. Use the name **darkgreen** for the border color. Set the left and right margins to **auto**, set the padding to **1em**, and set the width to **30em**. Add HTML code as needed to both index.html and nearby.html to apply this style so it surrounds all of the page contents.
- Combine the style rules for the border width, style, and color into a single rule. Use the property **border**, inserting the values for width, style, and color with spaces between them and a semicolon only after the color value. Be sure to delete the border-width, border-style, and border-color properties.

Independent Challenge 3 (continued)

- Add CSS code to the external style sheet to create a **0.25em solid** border Use the name **darkblue** for the border color, and use a single rule to style the border. Set the left and right margins to **auto**, set the padding to **1em**, and set the width to **27em**. Add HTML code as needed to both index.html and nearby.html to apply this style so it that surrounds only the heading, as shown in Figure C-23 and Figure C-24. (*Hint*: This border is nested within the border surrounding the page contents, so the HTML element you use to create it should also be nested within the element used to create the border for the page.)

FIGURE C-23

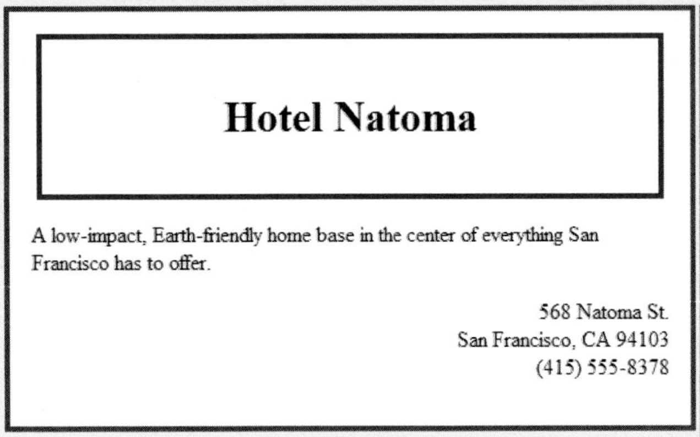

FIGURE C-24

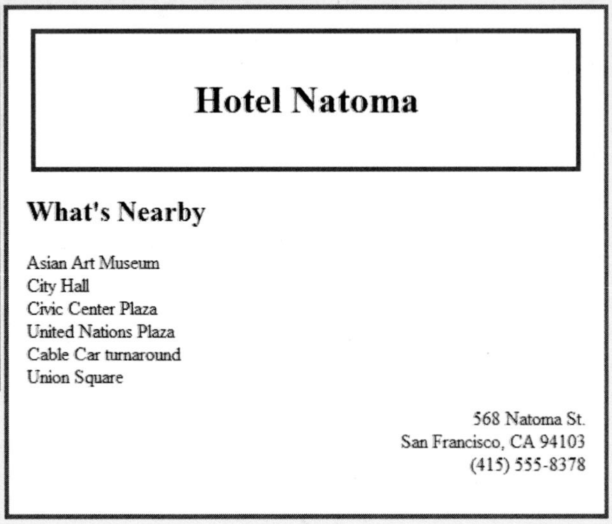

d. Save your work, add link elements that reference your external style sheet to index.html and nearby.html, then save these files.

e. Preview index.html and nearby.html in a Web browser. Compare your documents to Figure C-23 and Figure C-24. If necessary, make corrections to your code.

f. Validate your CSS code using the validator at **http://jigsaw.w3.org/css-validator/**.

g. If you have space on a Web server for publishing your documents, create a local root folder within the IC3 folder, move index.html, nearby.html, and natoma.css to the local root folder, upload the files to your Web publishing location, then open the Web pages in your browser from the published location.

h. Close your browser and your text editor.

Real Life Independent Challenge

This assignment builds on the personal Web site you have worked on in previous units. You will create one or more additional Web pages and specify presentational aspects for your Web site.

a. Copy any files you created in Unit B from the Unit B/RLIC folder to Unit C/RLIC.

b. Referring to the storyboard you created in Unit A, create any Web pages you didn't create in Unit B. Include a paragraph element at the bottom of each document containing your first and last names and the text **HTML5 Unit C, Real Life Independent Challenge**.

c. Using either the layout you sketched in Unit A, or drawing ideas from one or more Web pages similar to yours and whose design you like, plan style enhancements to add to your site. Include at least one text alignment property and at least one div element. Implement at least one of each of the following:

- type selector
- id selector
- class selector

d. Add the style rules, HTML attributes, and HTML elements necessary to implement the style enhancements from Step c. If your site contains only one page, use an embedded style sheet; otherwise, create an external style sheet and link to it from each Web page.

e. Preview each of your Web pages. Make any necessary edits to the HTML or CSS.

f. Validate your CSS code using the validator at **http://jigsaw.w3.org/css-validator/**.

g. If you have space on a Web server for publishing your documents, create a local root folder within the RLIC folder, move all of your Web documents and external style sheets to the local root folder, upload the files to your Web publishing location, then open the Web pages in your browser from the published location.

Visual Workshop

In your text editor, open the file HTM C-10.html from the /Unit C/VW directory on the drive and folder where you store your Data Files. Save the file as **index.html**, then preview it in a browser. Use your text editor to add the necessary presentational code to make your Web page match the one shown in Figure C-25. Use the color **royalblue** for the top border and **lightblue** for the bottom one. After the content shown, include a paragraph element that contains your first and last name and the text **HTML5 Unit C, Visual Workshop**. Validate your CSS using the online validator at **http://jigsaw.w3.org/css-validator/**. If you have space on a Web server, create a local root folder within the VW folder, move index.html to the local root folder, upload the file to your Web publishing location, then open the Web page in your browser from the published location. Close your browser and text editor.

FIGURE C-25

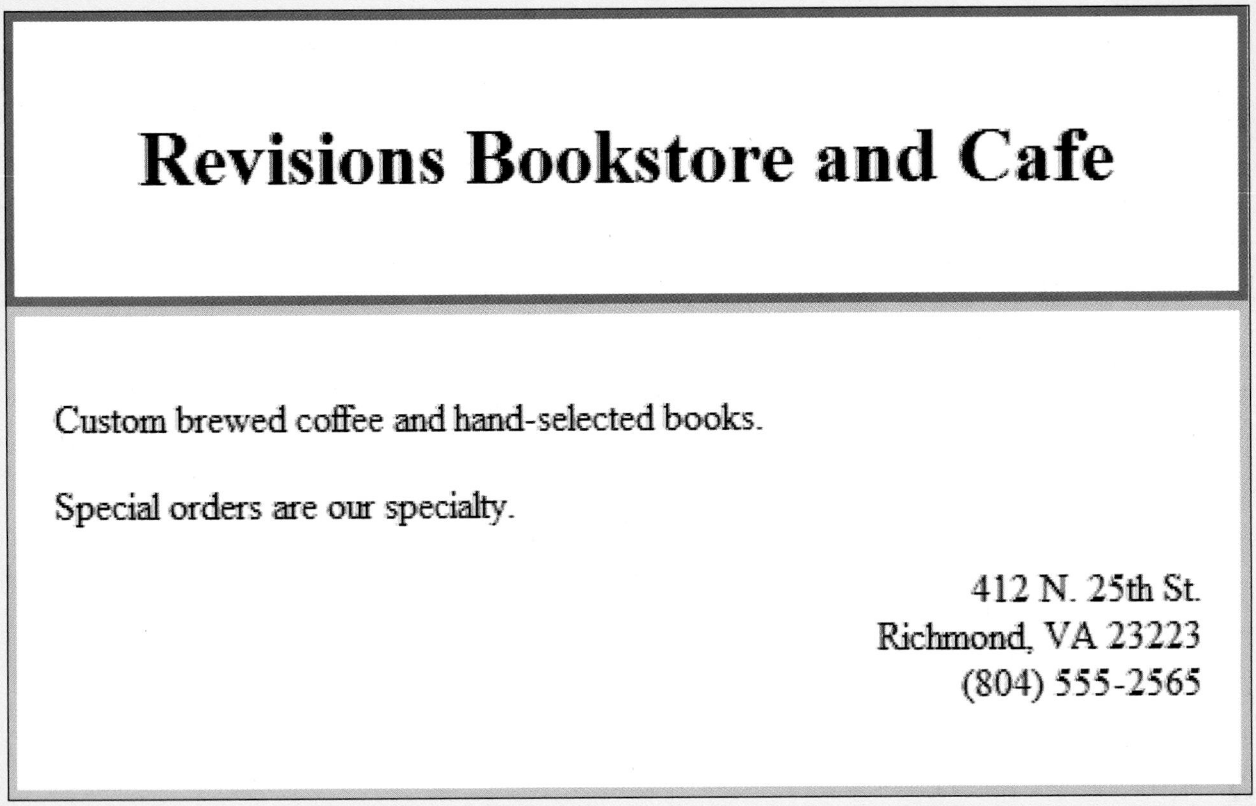

Revisions Bookstore and Cafe

Custom brewed coffee and hand-selected books.

Special orders are our specialty.

412 N. 25th St.
Richmond, VA 23223
(804) 555-2565

Formatting Text with CSS

Files You Will Need:

To view a list of files needed for this unit, see the Data Files Grid in the back of the book.

CSS and HTML support many properties and elements that let you customize the appearance of text in your Web pages. You can use styles to change the font, size, and color of text, and you can style text with bold, italic, and other variations.  As you continue your work on the Lakeland Reeds Bed and Breakfast Web site, you begin to implement the text formatting specified in the site design.

OBJECTIVES

Assess Web fonts

Declare a font family

Declare font sizes

Implement bold and italics

Change font colors

Change background colors

Use special characters

Provide alternative style sheets

Assessing Web Fonts

When you create a document in a word processing program, you can format text with any font installed on your computer. You can likewise format Web page text with different fonts, but you are limited by the fonts available on your *users'* machines. This limitation makes it a challenge to ensure that your Web pages appear consistently on different computers. Karl Dixon, one of your colleagues in the art department at Great Northern Web Solutions, has created a mock-up of the main Lakeland Reeds B&B Web page with text formatting. As you prepare to incorporate the fonts and other text characteristics into the Web page, you review strategies for working with fonts in Web pages.

DETAILS

A few strategies have evolved for implementing fonts consistently on the Web:

*   **Specifying multiple font families**

    You specify the font family for the text of an element using the CSS font-family property. The value consists of names of one or more **font families**, which are collections of single typefaces and their variants. For example, the Arial font family contains characters in the standard Arial typeface, including italic and bold versions of those characters. While you can specify a single font family as the property value, doing so is usually not a good idea. Every operating system has some font families installed by default, but different operating systems often have different fonts installed, meaning that not every browser or user agent will have a given font available for rendering. To bridge this discrepancy, CSS enables you to use a font stack as the value of the font-family property. A **font stack** is a list of font families in order of preference, separated by commas. For example, the CSS name-value pair

    ```
    font-family: tahoma, arial;
    ```

    specifies that a user agent should display the text of associated elements in Tahoma font, but if that's not available, the user agent should use Arial instead. Figure D-1 shows text using the above style rule in a browser with Tahoma and a browser without that font.

*   **Specifying a generic font family**

    CSS also defines five **generic font families**, which are groupings of font families according to shared characteristics. Two generic font families are based on whether a font incorporates **serifs**, which are small finishing strokes at the ends of lines making up each character. A font that uses these strokes is known as a **serif font**, while a font without these strokes is called a **sans-serif font**. Table D-1 shows examples of all five generic font families.

    You can add the name of a generic font family to the end of a font stack to provide guidance to user agents when your other font family choices are not available. For example,

    ```
    font-family: tahoma, arial, sans-serif;
    ```

    instructs user agents without access to either Tahoma or Arial to instead use the default sans-serif font on the user's system. You surround any font family name or generic font family name containing more than one word with quotes (for instance, "times new roman").

*   **Implementing downloadable fonts**

    Recent user agents can also download and apply fonts that are not installed on a user's computer. To implement such fonts, you upload one or more files containing elements of a font family you want to use to your Web publishing location or reference a licensed downloadable font available on a public server. You also add an **@font-face rule** to your style sheet, which is a variation of a style rule that indicates the font name and the location of the necessary files. You can then refer to the font by name in font-family value lists. Because not all user agents implement the @font-face rule, you should continue to name alternative font families for user agents that don't support downloadable fonts.

Lakeland Reeds Bed and Breakfast

About Us

Lakeland Reeds is an ideal place to unplug from your daily routine, whether on the shore of Twin Lakes watching the sunset over the cattails, or just curled up in a hammock on our wraparound porch with a good book. Breakfast is ready whenever you are, and we're happy to accommodate a wide range of appetites, from comfort food, like sausage and biscuits, to the lighter end of things, such as egg white omelettes and fresh fruit.

We're here to help you get the most out of your time w for a day out on the lake, to popcorn and a DVD of *The in. We look forward to welcoming you!

Text displayed in Arial

Lakeland Reeds Bed and Breakfast

About Us

Lakeland Reeds is an ideal place to unplug from your daily routine, whether on the shore of Twin Lakes watching the sunset over the cattails, or just curled up in a hammock on our wraparound porch with a good book. Breakfast is ready whenever you are, and we're happy to accommodate a wide range of appetites, from comfort food, like sausage and biscuits, to the lighter end of things, such as egg white omelettes and fresh fruit.

We're here to help you get the most out of your time with us, from canoes and life vests for a day out on the lake, to popcorn and a DVD of *The Wizard of Oz* for a quiet evening in. We look forward to welcoming you!

Philip Blaine, Proprietor
45 Marsh Grass Ln.
Marble, MN 55764
(218) 555-5253

Text displayed in Tahoma

TABLE D-1: Generic font families

generic font family	examples	characteristics	best for
Serif	Times New Roman Georgia	Finishing strokes at the end of each line making up a character	Headings on computer screens and other backlit displays
Sans-serif	Arial Tahoma	Lack of serifs ("sans" is French for "without")	Paragraphs of text on computer screens and other backlit displays
Monospace	Courier New Lucida Console	Each character uses the same amount of horizontal space	Code samples
Cursive	*Monotype Corsiva* Comic Sans	Flowing strokes that simulate handwritten text	Decorative purposes only, not main Web page text, as font families in these groups can be difficult to read
Fantasy	Papyrus **Impact**	Exaggerated style	

Choosing a downloadable font format

While the most common user agents support @font-face rules, several formats exist for downloadable fonts. While the Web Open Font Format (WOFF) is in line to become a standard, supporting older browsers and other user agents requires that you make each font available in multiple formats and that you specify the location of each file in your code. Table D-2 describes the most common downloadable font formats.

TABLE D-2: Common downloadable font formats

abbreviation	name	works with
TTF	TrueType Font	Most browsers except Internet Explorer and iPhone
EOT	Embedded OpenType	Internet Explorer
SVG	Scalable Vector Graphics	iPhone and iPad
WOFF	Web Open Font Format	Recent versions of all major browsers

Declaring a Font Family

To specify fonts in your CSS code, you use the font-family property. The property value is a font stack that includes one or more font family names and ends with a generic font family name. To customize the Web site and enhance the readability of text, you create style rules to change the fonts for heading and body text for the Lakeland Reeds B&B Web site.

STEPS

1. **Start your text editor then open the file HTM D-1.html from the Unit D/Unit folder on the drive and folder where you store your Data Files**

2. **Insert a blank line before the closing body tag, insert a paragraph element containing your first and last name and the text HTML5 Unit D, then save the file as aboutus.html**

3. **Open HTM D-2.css in your text editor, add a new comment containing your first and last name and the text HTML5 Unit D beneath the existing comment, then save the file as lakeland.css**

4. **Open aboutus.html in your browser**

   Figure D-2 shows the current appearance of the About Us Web page.

QUICK TIP

Tahoma was developed for enhanced readability on computer screens, and is installed on almost every Windows and Mac system.

5. **Return to lakeland.css in your text editor, insert a blank line above the closing curly brace for the #box style rule, press [Spacebar] twice, then type font-family: tahoma, arial, helvetica, sans-serif;**

   This style rule specifies the font for all text within the element with the id "box". User agents without access to the first choice, tahoma, should look next for arial, then, if necessary, for helvetica. If none of these are available, the text should be displayed in the user agent's default sans-serif font.

6. **Open stylesheet.css in your text editor, select all the code below the opening comment, click Edit, click Copy, then close stylesheet.css**

   Downloadable fonts often include a CSS @font-face rule containing descriptors optimized to work with a wide range of user agents. Table D-3 outlines the most commonly used descriptors in an @font-face rule.

7. **In lakeland.css, insert a blank line below the opening comment, click Edit, then click Paste**

   The code you copied is pasted into the style sheet, as shown in Figure D-3. An @font-face rule provides user agents the font name, file names, and file locations for a downloadable font.

QUICK TIP

"times new roman" is enclosed in quotes because the font name is more than one word.

8. **Insert a blank line above the closing curly brace for the h1, h2 style rule, press [Spacebar] twice, then type font-family: CuprumFFURegular, georgia, "times new roman", times, serif;**

   This name-value pair specifies CuprumFFURegular, the downloadable font you referenced with the @font-face rule, as the first choice for h1 and h2 elements. Figure D-3 shows the completed code.

TROUBLE

If the Tahoma font is not installed on your computer, the body text of your Web page may differ from Figure D-4.

9. **Save your work, then refresh aboutus.html in your browser**

   As Figure D-4 shows, the default heading and body text are replaced with the fonts you specified.

Linking to externally hosted fonts

Instead of using fonts located on your Web server in your Web pages, many companies that create and license fonts enable you to link to fonts on their Web servers. To do so, you add an additional link element to your HTML file using a Web address provided by the host as the value for the href attribute. The address links to a font-specific style sheet on a Web server run by the font provider, making it unnecessary for you to add an @font-face rule to your own style sheet document.

FIGURE D-2: The About Us Web page

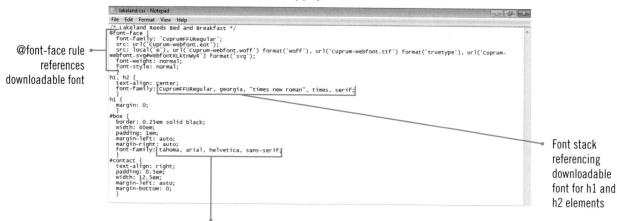

FIGURE D-3: @font-face rule and font-family properties added

@font-face rule references downloadable font

Font stack referencing downloadable font for h1 and h2 elements

Font stack for element with id "box"

FIGURE D-4: New fonts implemented

Headings styled with CuprumFFURegular font

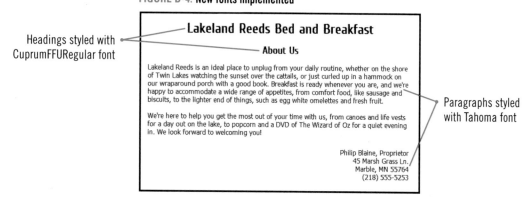

Paragraphs styled with Tahoma font

TABLE D-3: common @font-face descriptors

descriptor	value	purpose
font-family	*family-name*	Creates the name you use to reference the font in all of your CSS code.
src	local(*name*), url(*url*), format(*format*), where *name* is the name of an installed font family, *url* is the remote location of the font, and *format* is the format	Provides parameters for user agents to locate the font family and understand its formatting. Different formats require different combinations of local, url, and format, and Internet Explorer 6 compatibility requires specific formatting.
font-weight	normal, bold, 100, 200, 300, 400, 500, 600, 700, 800, or 900	Specify the font-weight, font-style, and font-stretch values for which the font family should be used. Using these descriptors, you can import several variants of the same font family, use the same font-family name for all of them, and enable user agents to apply bold, italic, condensed, or expanded versions where appropriate.
font-style	normal, italic, or oblique	
font-stretch	normal, ultra-condensed, extra-condensed, condensed, semi-condensed, semi-expanded, expanded, extra-expanded, ultra-expanded	

Declaring Font Sizes

You can specify the font size of an element using the CSS font-size property. This property changes the font size of any Web page element that includes text. You can specify font-size values in many different units, but the most widely supported are percent and em. ▰▰▰▰ The Lakeland Reeds B&B Web site incorporates both h1 and h2 elements. While you can plan on an h1 heading appearing larger than an h2 heading, different browsers may assign different font sizes to a given heading level. For this reason, it's useful to specify font sizes for headings in your style sheets in order to standardize the visual display of headings in different browsers. You specify the font sizes for the h1 and h2 elements in your style sheet.

STEPS

1. **In lakeland.css, insert a blank line above the closing curly brace for the h1 style rule, press [Spacebar] twice, then type** font-size: 2em;
   You specify the font size in em to ensure that it can scale up or down in different user agents and remain proportional to the rest of the Web page.

2. **Insert a blank line after the closing curly brace for the h1 style rule, type** h2 {, **then press [Enter]**

3. **Press [Spacebar] twice, type** font-size: 1.5em;, **then press [Enter]**

4. **Press [Spacebar] twice, then type** }
   Your style sheet should match the one shown in Figure D-5.

5. **Save your work, then refresh** aboutus.html **in your browser**
   Compare your Web page to Figure D-6. Because the font sizes you specified match the defaults for many Web browsers, you may notice no difference in the appearance of your Web page.

Working with headings

In addition to the h1 element, which specifies a top-level heading, HTML supports additional heading elements for lower-level headings from h2 through h6. Browsers commonly display headings in bold with the default serif font using a spectrum of font sizes, with h1 as the largest heading and h6 as the smallest, as shown in Table D-4. You could achieve the visual formatting of a heading using the div element; however, using elements that specify the functions of their content—in this case, headers—creates additional possibilities for how different user agents interpret and render the elements. In addition, incorporating such semantic elements offers more opportunities for page layout features using more advanced Web development techniques. For example, you could include code that automatically generates an outline at the top of a Web page based on the heading elements in the page.

TABLE D-4: Relative font sizes for heading elements

element	sample formatting
h1	**Heading text**
h2	**Heading text**
h3	**Heading text**
h4	**Heading text**
h5	**Heading text**
h6	**Heading text**

FIGURE D-5: Font size properties incorporated into style sheet

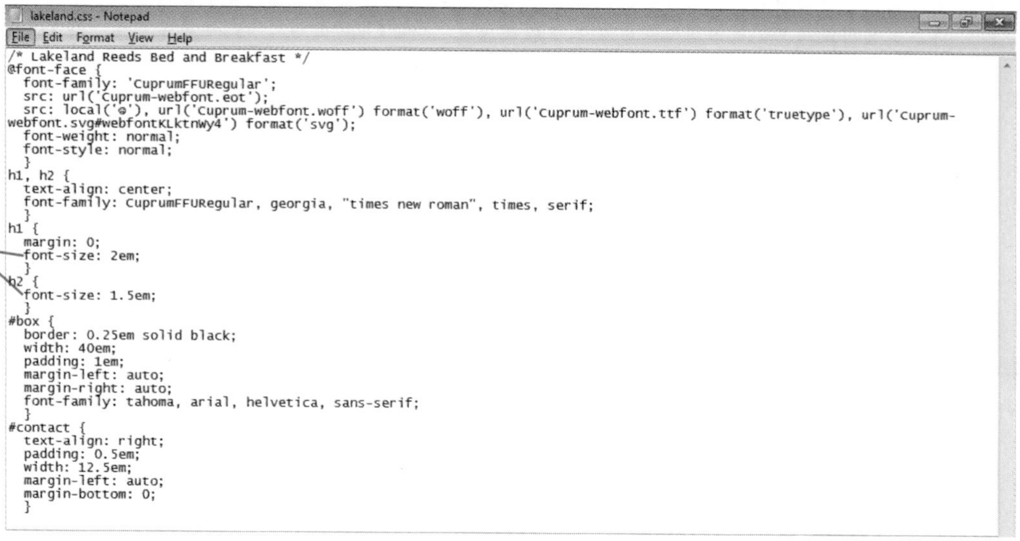

Font sizes styled for headings

```
lakeland.css - Notepad
File  Edit  Format  View  Help
/* Lakeland Reeds Bed and Breakfast */
@font-face {
    font-family: 'CuprumFFURegular';
    src: url('Cuprum-webfont.eot');
    src: local('☺'), url('Cuprum-webfont.woff') format('woff'), url('Cuprum-webfont.ttf') format('truetype'), url('Cuprum-
webfont.svg#webfontKLktnwy4') format('svg');
    font-weight: normal;
    font-style: normal;
    }
h1, h2 {
    text-align: center;
    font-family: CuprumFFURegular, georgia, "times new roman", times, serif;
    }
h1 {
    margin: 0;
    font-size: 2em;
    }
h2 {
    font-size: 1.5em;
    }
#box {
    border: 0.25em solid black;
    width: 40em;
    padding: 1em;
    margin-left: auto;
    margin-right: auto;
    font-family: tahoma, arial, helvetica, sans-serif;
    }
#contact {
    text-align: right;
    padding: 0.5em;
    width: 12.5em;
    margin-left: auto;
    margin-bottom: 0;
    }
```

FIGURE D-6: Web page displaying updated font sizes

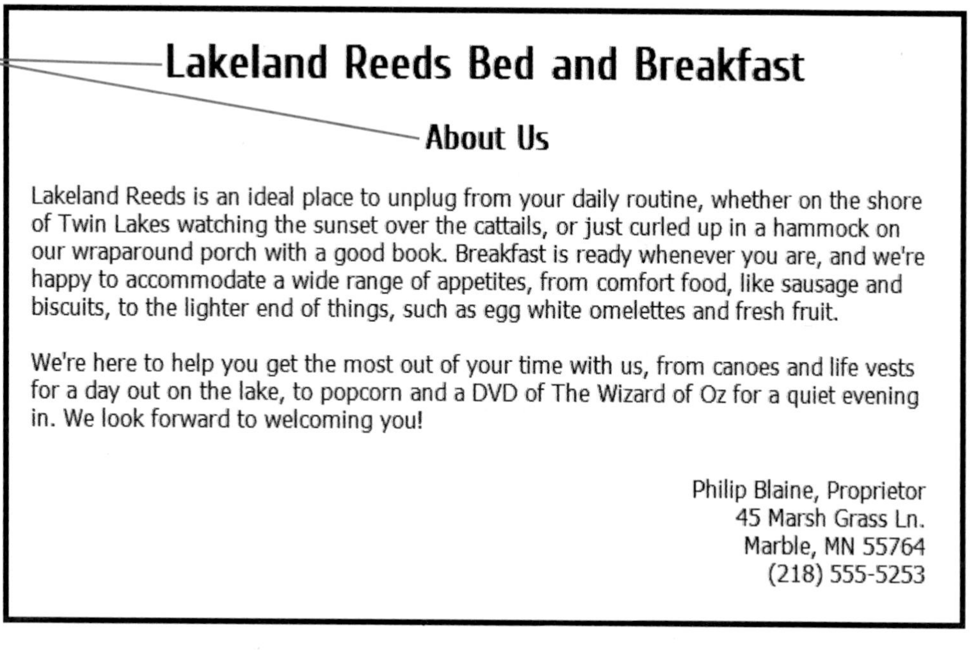

Headings reflect font sizes set in style sheet

Lakeland Reeds Bed and Breakfast

About Us

Lakeland Reeds is an ideal place to unplug from your daily routine, whether on the shore of Twin Lakes watching the sunset over the cattails, or just curled up in a hammock on our wraparound porch with a good book. Breakfast is ready whenever you are, and we're happy to accommodate a wide range of appetites, from comfort food, like sausage and biscuits, to the lighter end of things, such as egg white omelettes and fresh fruit.

We're here to help you get the most out of your time with us, from canoes and life vests for a day out on the lake, to popcorn and a DVD of The Wizard of Oz for a quiet evening in. We look forward to welcoming you!

Philip Blaine, Proprietor
45 Marsh Grass Ln.
Marble, MN 55764
(218) 555-5253

Implementing Bold and Italics

CSS enables you to modify Web page text in a number of ways. Two of the most common are making text bold and italic. You can make text bold using the font-weight property, while the font-style property allows you to add italics. Bold and italic styles are often applied to words or phrases, rather than to entire paragraphs or pages. Thus, you often need a way to indicate the section of a paragraph to format. You can use the span element for this purpose. The **span element** is a generic element, like div; however, it allows you to isolate a specific section of a larger element. ⬛⬛ You use the font-weight property to apply bold to the name of the B&B at the start of the first paragraph. You also use the font-style property to italicize the title of the DVD in the second paragraph.

STEPS

1. **Return to aboutus.html in your text editor, place the insertion point just to the left of the L in the name Lakeland Reeds at the start of the first p element, then type <span id="callout">**

2. **Place the insertion point just to the right of the s at the end of the word Reeds, then type </span>**

   Figure D-7 shows the code for the span element. The span element transforms the text it contains into an object on the Web page to which you can apply styles. Including an id attribute allows you to create a style rule that affects only the contents of this span element.

3. **Return to lakeland.css in your text editor, insert a blank line at the end of the document, type #callout {, press [Enter], press [Spacebar] twice, type font-weight: bold;, press [Enter], press [Spacebar] twice, then type }**

   Figure D-8 shows the #callout style rule in the style sheet.

4. **Return to aboutus.html in your text editor, place the insertion point just to the left of the T at the start of the name The Wizard of Oz near the end of the second p element, then type <span id="title">**

5. **Place the insertion point just to the right of the z at the end of the word Oz, then type </span>**

   Your completed Web page code should match Figure D-7.

6. **Save your work, return to lakeland.css in your text editor, insert a blank line at the end of the document, type #title {, press [Enter], press [Spacebar] twice, type font-style: italic;, press [Enter], press [Spacebar] twice, then type }**

   Your completed style sheet should match Figure D-8.

7. **Save your work, then refresh aboutus.html in your browser**

   As shown in Figure D-9, the name Lakeland Reeds in the first paragraph appears in bold, and the movie title The Wizard of Oz is displayed in italics.

Comparing block-level and inline elements

The W3C separates HTML elements into two types: block-level and inline. **Block-level elements** are the larger chunks that structure a Web page, such as headings and paragraphs. **Inline elements** are more fine-grained elements that appear within block-level elements; a word or phrase within a paragraph is one example of an inline element. In general, a block-level element starts on a new line, while an inline element continues on the same line as the previous element. The div and span elements share a common purpose, as generic elements that enable you to style sections of Web page text without adding any default formatting. The only difference between the two is that div is a block-level element, while span is an inline element.

FIGURE D-7: HTML document incorporating span elements

```
aboutus.html - Notepad
File  Edit  Format  View  Help
<!DOCTYPE html>
<html>
  <head>
    <meta charset="utf-8" />
    <title>Lakeland Reeds Bed and Breakfast - About Us</title>
    <link rel="stylesheet" type="text/css" href="lakeland.css" />
  </head>
  <body>
    <div id="box">
      <h1>Lakeland Reeds Bed and Breakfast</h1>
      <h2>About Us</h2>
      <p><span id="callout">Lakeland Reeds</span> is an ideal place to unplug from your daily routine, whether on the shore
of Twin Lakes watching the sunset over the cattails, or just curled up in a hammock on our wraparound porch with a good book.
  Breakfast is ready whenever you are, and we're happy to accommodate a wide range of appetites, from comfort food, like
sausage and biscuits, to the lighter end of things, such as egg white omelettes and fresh fruit.</p>
        <p>We're here to help you get the most out of your time with us, from canoes and life vests for a day out on the lake,
to popcorn and a DVD of <span id="title">The Wizard of Oz</span> for a quiet evening in. We look forward to welcoming you!
</p>
        <p id="contact">Philip Blaine, Proprietor<br />45 Marsh Grass Ln.<br />Marble, MN 55764<br />(218) 555-5253</p>
    </div>
  </body>
</html>
```

Span elements added to enable you to
style sections of larger elements

FIGURE D-8: Style sheet with properties for bold and italic text

```
lakeland.css - Notepad
File  Edit  Format  View  Help
/* Lakeland Reeds Bed and Breakfast */
@font-face {
  font-family: 'CuprumFFURegular';
  src: url('Cuprum-webfont.eot');
  src: local('☺'), url('Cuprum-webfont.woff') format('woff'), url('Cuprum-webfont.ttf') format('truetype'), url('Cuprum-
webfont.svg#webfontKLktnwy4') format('svg');
  font-weight: normal;
  font-style: normal;
  }
h1, h2 {
  text-align: center;
  font-family: CuprumFFURegular, georgia, "times new roman", times, serif;
  }
h1 {
  margin: 0;
  font-size: 2em;
  }
h2 {
  font-size: 1.5em;
  }
#box {
  border: 0.25em solid black;
  width: 40em;
  padding: 1em;
  margin-left: auto;
  margin-right: auto;
  font-family: tahoma, arial, helvetica, sans-serif;
  }
#contact {
  text-align: right;
  padding: 0.5em;
  width: 12.5em;
  margin-left: auto;
  margin-bottom: 0;
  }
#callout {
  font-weight: bold;
  }
#title {
  font-style: italic;
  }
```

Use the font-weight property to style text as bold

Use the font-style property to
style text in italic

FIGURE D-9: Web page displaying bold and italic text

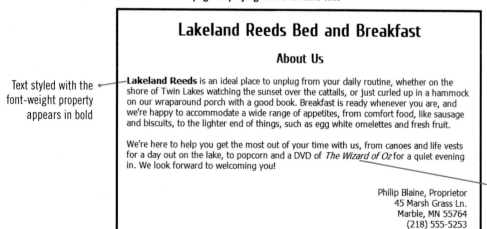

Text styled with the
font-weight property
appears in bold

Text styled with the
font-style property
appears in italics

Changing Font Colors

CSS allows you to specify the color of text and many other Web page elements by using the color property. You can specify a color in four different ways: as a name, in hexadecimal format, in rgb format, and in hsl format. Table D-5 provides an overview of these systems. Earlier versions of CSS supported 16-color names, and CSS3 enlarged that list to include a larger standardized list of 147 colors that all major browsers support. However, these names severely limit the range of colors available. The hexadecimal and rgb systems allow you to provide values for the amounts of red, green, and blue that create the color you want to use, resulting in over 16 million possibilities. Using the **hexadecimal system**, the value starts with a pound sign (#), followed by six digits, which may include the numbers 0–9 and the letters a–f. The first two digits specify the red value, the middle two digits indicate the green value, and the final pair of digits represents the blue value. With the **rgb system**, you provide a set of comma-separated values known as an **rgb triplet**. Each value ranges from 0–255 or 0–100%, which represent the amounts of red, green, and blue in the color. CSS3 added support for the **hsl system**, which enables you to create colors by specifying values or percentages for hue, saturation, and light. ▰▰▰▰▰ You format the name of the owner at the bottom of the Web page in dark green using an rgb triplet.

STEPS

1. **Return to aboutus.html in your text editor, place the insertion point just to the left of the P at the start of the name Philip Blaine near the bottom of the document, then type <span id="name">**

2. **Place the insertion point just to the right of the r at the end of the word Proprietor, then type </span>**

   Figure D-10 shows the code for the span element.

QUICK TIP

Many free Web-based utilities provide rgb values for a color you select. Try searching on the phrase **rgb selector** in a search engine to find some of these utilities.

3. **Save your work, then return to lakeland.css in your text editor**

4. **Insert a blank line at the end of the document, then enter the following style rule:**
   #name {

       color: rgb(0,82,0);

   }

   Figure D-11 shows the #name style rule in the style sheet.

5. **Save your work, then refresh aboutus.html in your browser**

   As shown in Figure D-12, the line "Philip Blaine, Proprietor" in the contact information at the bottom of the page appears in dark green.

TABLE D-5: CSS color systems

color system	format	advantages	disadvantages
name	*name* where *name* is CSS3 list of 147 colors	Names are easier to remember and harder to enter incorrectly.	Limited color selection
hexadecimal	#*rrggbb* or #*rgb* where *rr* (or *r*) is the red value, *gg* (or *g*) is the green value, and *bb* (or *b*) is the blue value in hexadecimal absolute value (00–FF or 0–F)	Can specify over 16 million colors	Format is not intuitive; values are not easy to remember and harder to proofread
rgb	rgb(*rrr,ggg,bbb*) where *rrr* is the red value, *ggg* is the green value, and *bbb* is the blue value in absolute value (0–255) or percent (0%–100%)	Can specify over 16 million colors; format more intuitive than hexadecimal; can create using graphic design software	Values are not easy to remember and harder to proofread
hsl	hsl(*hhh,sss,lll*) where hhh is the hue value in degrees (0–360), sss is the saturation value in percent (0%–100%), and lll is the light value in percent (0%–100%)	More intuitive than rgb-based systems; not based on the use of CRT monitors	Not widely supported by older browsers

FIGURE D-10: Span element added with id "name"

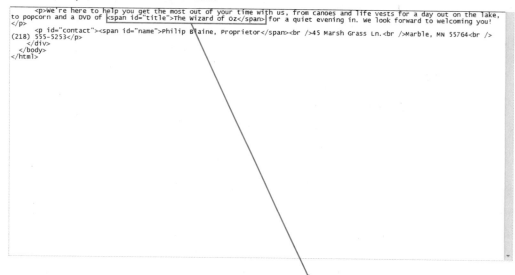

```
        <p>we're here to help you get the most out of your time with us, from canoes and life vests for a day out on the lake,
to popcorn and a DVD of <span id="title">The Wizard of Oz</span> for a quiet evening in. We look forward to welcoming you!
</p>
        <p id="contact"><span id="name">Philip Blaine, Proprietor</span><br />45 Marsh Grass Ln.<br />Marble, MN 55764<br />
(218) 555-5253</p>
      </div>
    </body>
</html>
```

Code for span element to enable you to style the first line of the contact information

FIGURE D-11: CSS code to style font color

```
#contact {
    text-align: right;
    padding: 0.5em;
    width: 12.5em;
    margin-left: auto;
    margin-bottom: 0;
    }
#callout {
    font-weight: bold;
    }
#title {
    font-style: italic;
    }
#name {
    color: rgb(0,82,0);
```

Style rule for span element encompassing first line of contact information

Font color styled using rgb color value

FIGURE D-12: Font color changed

Lakeland Reeds Bed and Breakfast

About Us

Lakeland Reeds is an ideal place to unplug from your daily routine, whether on the shore of Twin Lakes watching the sunset over the cattails, or just curled up in a hammock on our wraparound porch with a good book. Breakfast is ready whenever you are, and we're happy to accommodate a wide range of appetites, from comfort food, like sausage and biscuits, to the lighter end of things, such as egg white omelettes and fresh fruit.

We're here to help you get the most out of your time with us, from canoes and life vests for a day out on the lake, to popcorn and a DVD of *The Wizard of Oz* for a quiet evening in. We look forward to welcoming you!

Philip Blaine, Proprietor
45 Marsh Grass Ln.
Marble, MN 55764
(218) 555-5253

Font color within span element changed using color property

Using colors judiciously

Although rgb values make over 16 million colors available for use on your Web pages, it's best not to try to use all of them at once. In fact, some of the best visual designs use only two or three colors, with one or two of them reserved for small-scale applications with specific purposes.

Changing Background Colors

In addition to text, you can set color properties for other aspects of many Web page elements. The ability to modify background colors is particularly important when working with Web page text. For Web page usability, it's important that text contrasts with its background. The default white background for a Web page works fine with the default text color of black, as well as with other dark text colors. However, light-colored text is difficult or impossible to read without changes to the background color. You can change the background color for an entire Web page or for a specific element, allowing you to use different text colors for different elements. ████ You add a background color to the contact information at the bottom of the Web page. You also style the h1 element with text and background colors.

STEPS

1. **Return to lakeland.css in your text editor, insert a blank line above the closing curly brace for the h1 style rule, press [Spacebar] twice, type color: white;, press [Enter], press [Spacebar] twice, then type background: rgb(0,82,0);**

   You can use multiple ways of specifying colors in the same style sheet. The color name "white" is part of the CSS3 list of 147 color names. The code you entered sets the text of h1 elements to white and creates a dark green background for contrast.

2. **Insert a blank line above the closing curly brace for the #contact style rule, press [Spacebar] twice, then type background: rgb(218,165,32);**

   This name-value pair creates a goldenrod background behind the contact information at the bottom of the Web page.

   > **QUICK TIP**
   > You can set the background property for the body element to change the background color for the entire Web page.

3. **Insert a blank line above the closing curly brace for the #box style rule, press [Spacebar] twice, then type background: rgb(255,255,185);**

   The background property for the element with the id "box" sets the background color for the Web page text to a light yellow. Figure D-13 shows the new name-value pairs in the style sheet.

4. **Save your work, then refresh aboutus.html in your browser**

   The title "Lakeland Reeds Bed and Breakfast" appears in white with a dark green background, and the contact information is displayed with a goldenrod background.

5. **Return to lakeland.css in your text editor, insert a blank line above the closing curly brace for the h1 style rule, press [Spacebar] twice, then type padding: 0.25em;**

   Increasing the padding adds space between the edges of the text and the outer border of the heading element.

6. **Insert a blank line above the closing curly brace for the #name style rule, press [Spacebar] twice, then type font-weight: bold;**

   Figure D-13 shows the style sheet containing the new code.

7. **Save your work, then refresh aboutus.html in your browser**

   Figure D-14 shows your Web page with background colors and line height applied.

FIGURE D-13: Properties inserted to change font color and background colors

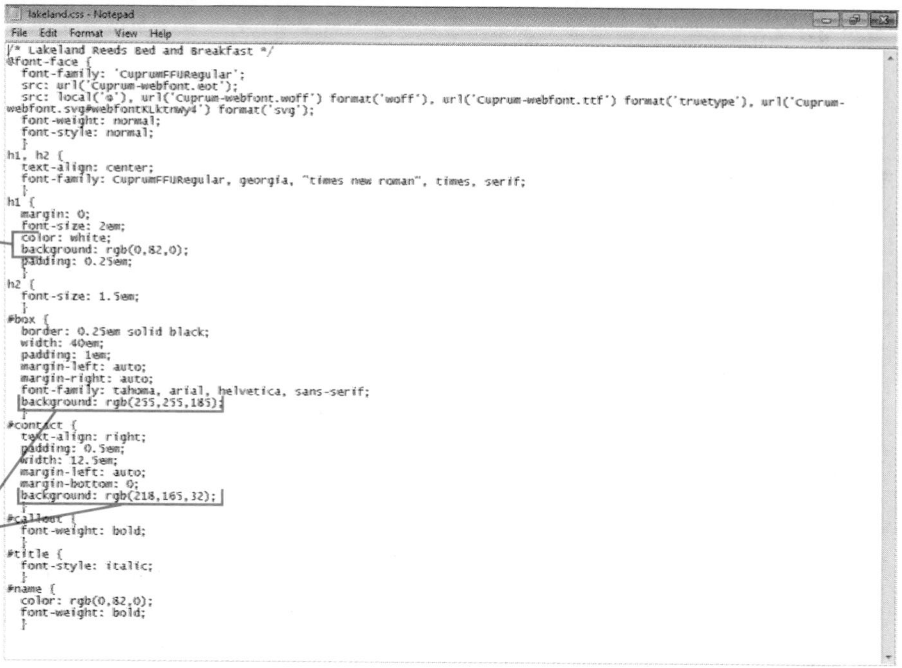

color and background properties implemented together to maintain contrast

background properties for individual screen elements

```
/* Lakeland Reeds Bed and Breakfast */
@font-face {
    font-family: 'CuprumFFURegular';
    src: url('Cuprum-webfont.eot');
    src: local('☺'), url('Cuprum-webfont.woff') format('woff'), url('Cuprum-webfont.ttf') format('truetype'), url('Cuprum-
webfont.svg#webfontKLktnwy4') format('svg');
    font-weight: normal;
    font-style: normal;
}
h1, h2 {
    text-align: center;
    font-family: CuprumFFURegular, georgia, "times new roman", times, serif;
}
h1 {
    margin: 0;
    font-size: 2em;
    color: white;
    background: rgb(0,82,0);
    padding: 0.25em;
}
h2 {
    font-size: 1.5em;
}
#box {
    border: 0.25em solid black;
    width: 40em;
    padding: 1em;
    margin-left: auto;
    margin-right: auto;
    font-family: tahoma, arial, helvetica, sans-serif;
    background: rgb(255,255,185);
}
#contact {
    text-align: right;
    padding: 0.5em;
    width: 12.5em;
    margin-left: auto;
    margin-bottom: 0;
    background: rgb(218,165,32);
}
#callout {
    font-weight: bold;
}
#title {
    font-style: italic;
}
#name {
    color: rgb(0,82,0);
    font-weight: bold;
}
```

FIGURE D-14: About Us page with styled background colors

Light font color contrasts with dark background for legibility

Background colors changed using background property

Lakeland Reeds Bed and Breakfast

About Us

Lakeland Reeds is an ideal place to unplug from your daily routine, whether on the shore of Twin Lakes watching the sunset over the cattails, or just curled up in a hammock on our wraparound porch with a good book. Breakfast is ready whenever you are, and we're happy to accommodate a wide range of appetites, from comfort food, like sausage and biscuits, to the lighter end of things, such as egg white omelettes and fresh fruit.

We're here to help you get the most out of your time with us, from canoes and life vests for a day out on the lake, to popcorn and a DVD of *The Wizard of Oz* for a quiet evening in. We look forward to welcoming you!

Philip Blaine, Proprietor
45 Marsh Grass Ln.
Marble, MN 55764
(218) 555-5253

Understanding hexadecimal values

The two rgb color systems—using a triplet of rgb values or using hexadecimal values—allow you to specify the same 16.7 million colors. Each value in an rgb triplet can range from 0 to 255, giving you 256 possible values (1–255, plus the value 0). Hexadecimal values provide the same range in only two digits. The standard decimal numbering system allows 10 possibilities for each digit: the numbers 0–9. Hexadecimal (from roots meaning "six" and "ten") offers 16 possibilities for each digit: the numbers 0–9 plus the letters A–F.

Many common colors are represented in hexadecimal notation with repeating pairs of digits (such as #00DDFF). CSS supports shortening these values to three digits, with the assumption that any three-digit hexadecimal value represents the color created by doubling each digit. Thus, a user agent would interpret the hexadecimal value #0DF as #00DDFF.

Using Special Characters

You add most text to your Web pages simply by typing it. However, there is a handful of common characters that run the risk of being misinterpreted by user agents as computer instructions rather than as plain text. To employ these characters in your Web pages, you represent them with **character references**, which are specially formatted codes that represent characters in the HTML document character set. Character references always begin with an ampersand (&) and end with a semicolon (;). The rest of the code consists of either a pound sign (#) followed by numbers or an English language abbreviation for the associated character name. Every character has a number code, but only a few commonly used characters also have an abbreviation-based alternative. Character references exist for any character you can type; however, the only characters for which it's important to use the codes are those listed in Table D-6. You replace the "and" in the name of the business with an ampersand symbol in both the main page heading and the title element to match the appearance of the organization name on signs and other branded materials.

STEPS

1. **Return to aboutus.html in your text editor, then locate the title element**

2. **Delete the word and in the name Lakeland Reeds Bed and Breakfast, type &, then, if necessary, insert a space before and after the character reference**

3. **Locate the h1 element**

4. **Delete the word and in the name Lakeland Reeds Bed and Breakfast, type &, then, if necessary, insert a space before and after the character reference**

   Figure D-15 shows the special characters inserted in the code for the Web page.

5. **Save your work, then refresh aboutus.html in your browser**

   As shown in Figure D-16, the word "and" in the browser title bar and in the main Web page heading is replace with the ampersand (&) symbol.

6. **Use a validator to check your documents for conformance with the HTML5 and CSS3 specifications, then make any edits necessary to resolve issues and revalidate until both documents pass**

Inserting characters not on the keyboard

In addition to inserting characters that shouldn't be typed directly into HTML code, you can use character references to add symbols to your Web pages that aren't visibly available on a keyboard. Such symbols may include bullet characters, accented letters, and international currency symbols. You can use a search engine to locate one of the many available online references and look up the character reference for any character you might want to use.

FIGURE D-15: **Codes for special characters inserted in Web page**

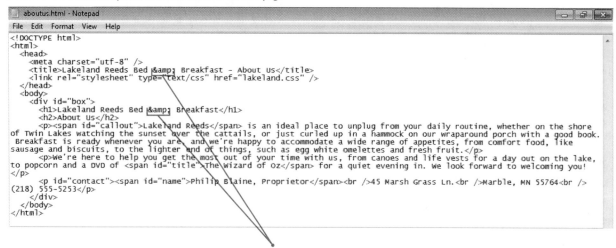

Character codes representing ampersands

FIGURE D-16: **About Us page incorporating special characters**

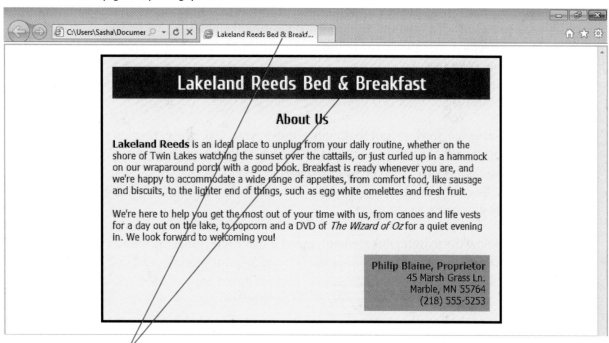

& character codes translated
by browser into ampersands

TABLE D-6: **Important character references**

character	character name	decimal numeric character reference	named character reference
&	ampersand	&#38;	&amp;
'	apostrophe	&#39;	' (does not work in Internet Explorer)
>	greater-than sign	&#62;	&gt;
<	less-than sign	&#60;	&lt;
"	quotation mark	&#34;	&quot;

Providing Alternative Style Sheets

Web pages can be accessed on computer screens, as printouts, and via a number of other types of user agents. Because these destinations can vary widely in factors like size, resolution, and contrast, styling created for one output is not always ideal on others. To accommodate these differences, HTML allows you to link to multiple style sheets in the same Web document, using the media attribute of the link element to specify which type of device should use each style sheet. Table D-7 describes the available values for the media attribute. ▨▨▨▨ You want to make sure the Lakeland Reeds Web pages are legible when printed, so you create and link a second style sheet for printed output.

STEPS

1. **Return to lakeland.css in your text editor, then save a copy of the document as llprint.css**

QUICK TIP

Some Web browsers automatically change printed output to black and white, but using a print style sheet ensures that this formatting is available for users of all browsers.

2. **In the h1 style rule, delete the color and background properties and their values**
    This change reverts the format for the main heading to black text on a white background.

3. **In the #box style rule, remove the background and border name-value pairs, in the #contact style rule, remove the background pair, then, in the #name style rule, remove the color pair**
    Removing these pairs removes the border and the font and background colors from the page contents in printed output. Figure D-17 shows the completed style sheet.

QUICK TIP

You can also add the media attribute to style elements in the head section of an HTML document to specify alternative embedded style sheets.

4. **Save your work, return to aboutus.html in your text editor, then, in the link element, position the insertion point just to the left of the word href, press [Spacebar], type media="screen", then press [Spacebar]**
    The "screen" value for the media attribute specifies that the lakeland.css style sheet is optimized for viewing on a standard computer screen.

5. **Below the existing link element, insert a blank line, press [Spacebar] four times, then type <link rel="stylesheet" type="text/css" media="print" href="llprint.css" />**
    The new element links to the new style sheet you created and specifies that it should be used for printed output. Figure D-18 shows the code for the completed Web page.

6. **Save your work, then refresh aboutus.html in your browser**
    The browser continues to apply the lakeland.css style sheet, so the appearance doesn't change.

7. **If available in your browser, view a print preview of the current page**
    As shown in Figure D-19, the text appears in black with a white background and no border.

8. **Close the print preview, validate llprint.css, then, if you have space on a Web server for publishing your documents, create a local root folder within the Unit folder. Move all the files in the Unit folder to the local root folder, upload the files to your Web publishing location, then open aboutus.htm in your browser from the published location to verify that the upload was successful**

9. **Close your browser, then close your text editor**

FIGURE D-17: Style sheet for printed versions of the Web site

```
llprint.css - Notepad
File  Edit  Format  View  Help
/* Lakeland Reeds Bed and Breakfast */
@font-face {
    font-family: 'CuprumFFURegular';
    src: url('Cuprum-webfont.eot');
    src: local('☺'), url('Cuprum-webfont.woff') format('woff'), url('Cuprum-webfont.ttf') format('truetype'), url('Cuprum-
webfont.svg#webfontKLktnwy4') format('svg');
    font-weight: normal;
    font-style: normal;
}
h1, h2 {
    text-align: center;
    font-family: CuprumFFURegular, georgia, "times new roman", times, serif;
}
h1 {
    margin: 0;
    font-size: 2em;
    padding: 0.25em;
}
h2 {
    font-size: 1.5em;
}
#box {
    width: 40em;
    padding: 1em;
    margin-left: auto;
    margin-right: auto;
    font-family: tahoma, arial, helvetica, sans-serif;
}
#contact {
    text-align: right;
    padding: 0.5em;
    width: 12.5em;
    margin-left: auto;
    margin-bottom: 0;
}
#callout {
    font-weight: bold;
}
#title {
    font-style: italic;
}
#name {
    font-weight: bold;
}
```

FIGURE D-18: Link elements for multiple style sheets

link element added for new style sheet with media value of "print"

media attribute added to original link element with value set to "screen"

```
aboutus.html - Notepad
File  Edit  Format  View  Help
<!DOCTYPE html>
<html>
    <head>
        <meta charset="utf-8" />
        <title>Lakeland Reeds Bed &amp; Breakfast - About Us</title>
        <link rel="stylesheet" type="text/css" media="screen" href="lakeland.css" />
        <link rel="stylesheet" type="text/css" media="print" href="llprint.css" />  </head>
    <body>
        <div id="box">
            <h1>Lakeland Reeds Bed &amp; Breakfast</h1>
```

FIGURE D-19: Print preview of About Us Web page

Border does not appear around Web page contents

Content displayed without font colors and background colors

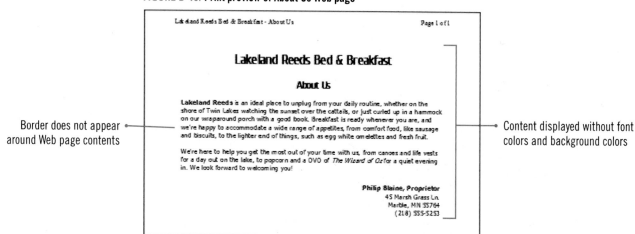

Lakeland Reeds Bed & Breakfast - About Us   Page 1 of 1

Lakeland Reeds Bed & Breakfast

About Us

Lakeland Reeds is an ideal place to unplug from your daily routine, whether on the shore of Twin Lakes watching the sunset over the cattails, or just curled up in a hammock on our wraparound porch with a good book. Breakfast is ready whenever you are, and we're happy to accommodate a wide range of appetites, from comfort food, like sausage and biscuits, to the lighter end of things, such as egg white omelettes and fresh fruit.

We're here to help you get the most out of your time with us, from canoes and life vests for a day out on the lake, to popcorn and a DVD of *The Wizard of Oz* for a quiet evening in. We look forward to welcoming you!

Philip Blaine, Proprietor
45 Marsh Grass Ln.
Marble, MN 55764
(218) 555-5253

TABLE D-7: Values for link element media attribute

media type	intended use
all	All devices
aural	Screen reader
braille	Tactile feedback device
handheld	Device with a small screen
print	Printed output and print preview on a screen
projection	Projection device
screen	Computer screen
tty	Teletype or similar terminal
tv	Low-resolution display with limited colors, like a non-high-definition television

Practice

For current SAM information, including versions and content details, visit SAM Central (http://www.cengage.com/samcentral). If you have a SAM user profile, you may have access to hands-on instruction, practice, and assessment of the skills covered in this unit. Since various versions of SAM are supported throughout the life of this text, check with your instructor for the correct instructions and URL/Web site for accessing assignments.

Concepts Review

Refer to Figure D-20.

FIGURE D-20

```
lakeland.css - Notepad
File Edit Format View Help
/* Lakeland Reeds Bed and Breakfast */
@font-face {
    font-family: 'CuprumFFURegular';
    src: url('Cuprum-webfont.eot');
    src: local('☺'), url('Cuprum-webfont.woff') format('woff'), url('Cuprum-webfont.ttf') format('truetype'), url('Cuprum-
webfont.svg#webfontKLktnwy4') format('svg');
    font-weight: normal;
    font-style: normal;
}
h1, h2 {
    text-align: center;
    font-family: CuprumFFURegular, georgia, "times new roman", times, serif;
}
h1 {
    margin: 0;
    font-size: 2em;
    color: white;
    background: rgb(0,82,0);
    padding: 0.25em;
}
h2 {
    font-size: 1.5em;
}
#box {
    border: 0.25em solid black;
    width: 40em;
    padding: 1em;
    margin-left: auto;
    margin-right: auto;
    font-family: tahoma, arial, helvetica, sans-serif;
    background: rgb(255,255,185);
}
#contact {
    text-align: right;
    padding: 0.5em;
    width: 12.5em;
    margin-left: auto;
    margin-bottom: 0;
    background: rgb(218,165,32);
}
#callout {
    font-weight: bold;
}
#title {
    font-style: italic;
}
#name {
    color: rgb(0,82,0);
    font-weight: bold;
}
```

a, b, c, d, e, f, g

1. Which item makes text bold?
2. Which item changes the color of an element's text?
3. Which item lets user agents know where to find a downloadable font?
4. Which item changes the color of an element's background?
5. Which item makes text italic?
6. Which item changes the size of an element's text?
7. Which item specifies a font family to apply to an element's text?

Match each term with the statement that best describes it.

8. block-level element
9. character reference
10. rgb system
11. inline element
12. generic font family
13. hexadecimal system
14. font stack

a. a system for specifying color on a Web page in which you provide red, green, and blue values represented with numbers 0–9 and letters a–f

b. a fine-grained element, such as a word or phrase within a paragraph

c. a system for specifying color on a Web page in which you provide red, green, and blue values represented as one-, two-, or three-digit numbers

d. a grouping of font families according to shared characteristics

e. a specially formatted string of characters that represents a character in the HTML document character set

f. a list of font families in order of preference, separated by commas

g. one of the larger chunks that structures a Web page, such as a heading or a paragraph

Select the best answer from the list of choices.

15. You specify the font family for the text of an element using the CSS _____ property.
    - **a.** font-weight
    - **b.** font-family
    - **c.** font-style
    - **d.** font-color

16. You format Web page text as bold using the CSS _____ property.
    - **a.** font-weight
    - **b.** font-family
    - **c.** font-style
    - **d.** font-size

17. You specify the size of Web page text using the CSS _____ property.
    - **a.** font-weight
    - **b.** font-color
    - **c.** font-family
    - **d.** font-size

18. You format Web page text as italic using the CSS _____ property.
    - **a.** font-style
    - **b.** font-color
    - **c.** font-family
    - **d.** font-size

19. The _____ element is a generic element that allows you to isolate a specific section of a larger element.
    - **a.** div
    - **b.** span
    - **c.** p
    - **d.** h1

20. Sans-serif is an example of a(n) _____ .
    - **a.** font stack
    - **b.** inline element
    - **c.** font family
    - **d.** generic font family

21. When is it important to use a character reference to add a character to a Web page?
    - **a.** for any character you enter in a Web document
    - **b.** in place of any numerical digit
    - **c.** in place of a few special characters that run the risk of being misinterpreted by user agents as computer instructions
    - **d.** to insert any non-English-language character

22. Which attribute of the link element lets you specify the intended use of an external style sheet?
    - **a.** media
    - **b.** type
    - **c.** rel
    - **d.** href

Skills Review

1. **Declare a font family.**
   a. Start your text editor then open the file HTM D-3.html from the Unit D/Review folder on the drive and folder where you store your Data Files.
   b. Insert a blank line before the closing body tag, insert a paragraph element containing your first and last name and the text **HTML5 Unit D, Skills Review**, then save the file as **history.html**.
   c. Open HTM D-4.css in your text editor, add a new comment containing your first and last name and the text **HTML5 Unit D, Skills Review** beneath the existing comment, then save the file as **bigj.css**.
   d. Preview history.html in your browser.
   e. Return to bigj.css in your text editor, insert a blank line above the closing curly brace for the #box style rule, then add a name-value pair styling the text with the font stack **tahoma, verdana, arial, helvetica, sans-serif**.
   f. Open stylesheet.css in your text editor, copy all the code below the opening comment to the clipboard, then close stylesheet.css.
   g. In bigj.css, paste the copied code into a blank line below the opening comment.
   h. Create a style rule that styles the h1 and h2 elements with the font stack **MolengoRegular, arial, helvetica, sans-serif**.
   i. Save your work then refresh history.html in your browser.

Skills Review (continued)

2. Declare font sizes.

  a. In bigj.css, add a name-value pair to the h1 style rule that sets the font size to **2em**.

  b. Add a name-value pair to the h2 style rule that sets the font size to **1.5em**.

  c. Save your work then refresh history.html in your browser.

3. Implement bold and italic.

  a. Return to history.html in your text editor, then create a span element with the id **title** containing the text **Toronto Times** in the second to last paragraph.

  b. Return to bigj.css in your text editor, then add a style rule to the bottom of the document that styles the text of the element with the id **title** in italics.

  c. Return to history.html in your text editor, then create a span element with the id **phone** containing the phone number near the bottom of the document.

  d. Save your work, return to bigj.css in your text editor, then add a style rule to the bottom of the document that styles the text of the element with the id **phone** in bold.

  e. Insert a blank line above the closing curly brace for the #words style rule, then add a name-value pair that styles the text in bold.

  f. Save your work then refresh history.html in your browser.

4. Change font and background colors.

  a. Return to bigj.css in your text editor, insert a blank line above the closing curly brace for the #words style rule, then add a name-value pair changing the font color to **red**.

  b. Save your work, then refresh history.html in your browser.

  c. Return to bigj.css in your text editor, insert a blank line above the closing curly brace for the #words style rule, then add a name-value pair changing the background color to **black**.

  d. Add name-value pairs changing the background colors of the h1, h2, and contact elements to **rgb(255,204,102)**.

  e. Save your work, then refresh history.html in your browser.

5. Use special characters.

  a. Return to history.html in your text editor.

  b. In the title element, replace the apostrophe in the name "Big J's Deep Dish Pizza" with the code **'**.

  c. Repeat Step b for the h1 element.

  d. Save your work, then refresh history.html in your browser. Compare your screen to Figure D-21.

  e. Use a validator to check your documents for conformance with the HTML5 and CSS3 specifications, then make any edits necessary to resolve issues and revalidate until both documents pass.

6. Provide alternative style sheets.

  a. Return to bigj.css in your text editor, then save a copy of the document as **bjprint.css**.

  b. Remove the name-value pairs that set the background color for the h1, h2, #contact, and #words elements.

  c. In the #box style rule, remove the border name-value pair, then in the #words style rule, remove the name-pair that styles the font color.

  d. Save your work, return to history.html in your text editor, then in the link element, add a media attribute with a value of **screen**.

  e. Below the existing link element, insert a new link element that duplicates the existing element, change the value for the href attribute to **bjprint.css**, then change the value of the media attribute to **print**.

  f. Save your work, then refresh history.html in your browser.

  g. If available in your browser, view a print preview of the current page. Compare your screen to Figure D-22.

FIGURE D-21

FIGURE D-22

Skills Review (continued)

h. Close the print preview, use a validator to check bjprint.css for conformance with the CSS3 specification, then make any edits necessary to resolve issues and revalidate until the document passes.

i. If you have space on a Web server for publishing your documents, create a local root folder within the Review folder, move all the files in the Review folder to the local root folder, upload the files to your Web publishing location, then open history.html in your browser from the published location to verify that the upload was successful.

j. Close your browser, then close your text editor.

Independent Challenge 1

Sarah Nguyen, the owner and manager of the Spotted Wren Garden Center, is happy with your work so far on the company's Web site. She'd like you to begin to personalize the site by incorporating fonts and colors.

a. Open HTM D-5.html in your text editor from the Unit D/IC1 folder and save a copy as **hours.html**. Open HTM D-6.css in your text editor and save a copy as **spotwren.css**. Before the closing body tag in hours.html insert a paragraph element containing your first and last name and the text **HTML5 Unit D, Independent Challenge 1**. Add the same information as a new comment beneath the existing one in spotwren.css.

b. Copy both @font-face rules from stylesheet.css into spotwren.css. Add name-value pairs to style font families for the following elements:
- body: **verdana**, with **arial** and **helvetica** as backup font families, and **sans-serif** as the generic font family
- h1: **LatinModernSans10Bold**, with **arial** and **helvetica** as backup font families, and **sans-serif** as the generic font family
- h2 and tagline id: **LatinModernSans10Regular**, with **arial** and **helvetica** as backup font families, and **sans-serif** as the generic font family

c. Create a style rule to set the font size of the h1 element to **2em**. Create a second rule to set the font size of the h2 element to **1.5em**.

d. In hours.html, add a span element to contain each day of the week, for a total of seven new elements. Set the class of each element to "day". In spotwren.css, add a style rule that bolds the text of all elements that are part of the "day" class.

e. Set the font color of the h2 element to the color with the following rgb values: red: **51**, green: **102**, blue: **0**.

f. Set the background color of the box class to the color with the following rgb values: red: **255**, green: **238**, blue: **68**.

g. In the last p element, replace each occurrence of **::** with a bullet using the character code **•**.

h. Save your work then save a copy of your external style sheet with the name **swprint.css**. Remove the name-value pairs that style text color and background color. In the style rule for the box class, change the border color from **green** to **black**, then save your work.

i. In hours.html, add an attribute to the link element to specify its use for computer screens. Insert a second link element referencing swprint.css and specifying its use for printouts. Save your work.

j. Preview your Web page in a browser and compare your screen to Figure D-23. Open a print preview if available and compare your screen to Figure D-24. Validate both your HTML and CSS documents.

k. If you have space on a Web server for publishing your documents, create a local root folder within the IC1 folder, move all the files in the IC1 folder to the local root folder, upload the files to your Web publishing location, then open hours.html in your browser from the published location to verify that the upload was successful.

l. Close your browser, then close your text editor.

FIGURE D-23

FIGURE D-24

Independent Challenge 2

As you continue developing the Web site for the Murfreesboro Regional Soccer League, you incorporate font styling and colors into the site.

a. Open HTM D-7.html in your text editor from the Unit D/IC2 folder and save a copy as **started.html**. Open HTM D-8.css in your text editor and save a copy as **mrsl.css**. Before the closing body tag in started.html, insert a paragraph element containing your first and last name and the text **HTML5 Unit D, Independent Challenge 2**. Add the same information as a new comment beneath the existing one in mrsl.css.

Advanced Challenge Exercise

- Create and implement a sans-serif font stack for the body text. Include at least two font families and one generic font family. (*Hint:* The sans-serif font family shown in Figure D-25 is Tahoma.)
- Create and implement a serif font stack for the h1 text and for the element with the id value "narsa". Include at least two font families and one generic font family. (*Hint:* The serif font family shown in Figure D-25 is Georgia.)

b. Set the font size of the h1 element to **2em**. Set the font size of the element with the id "narsa" to **1.25em**.

c. Use a span element with an id attribute to bold the text "MRSL" near the bottom of the Web page.

d. Set the font color of the element with the id "contact" to **white** and set the background color to **black**.

e. Set the background color of the element with the id "head" to the color with the following rgb values: red: **140**, green: **198**, blue: **63**.

f. Save your work, then save a copy of your external style sheet with the name **mrsprint.css**. Remove the name-value pairs that style text color, background color, and borders, then save your work.

g. In started.html, add an attribute to the link element to specify its use for computer screens. Insert a second link element referencing mrsprint.css and specifying its use for printouts. Save your work.

h. Preview your Web page in a browser and compare your screen to Figure D-25. Open a print preview if available and compare your screen to Figure D-26. Validate both your HTML and CSS documents.

i. If you have space on a Web server for publishing your documents, create a local root folder within the IC2 folder, move all the files in the IC2 folder to the local root folder, upload the files to your Web publishing location, then open started.html in your browser from the published location to verify that the upload was successful.

j. Close your browser, then close your text editor.

FIGURE D-25

Murfreesboro Regional Soccer League
Part of the North American Recreational Soccer Association

The MRSL is open to players of all levels who want to play soccer in a relaxed, friendly environment. Even if you've never played soccer before, the MRSL is a great place to start.

To get a feel for our league, we recommend you call us at the number below or stop by Davies Sporting Goods to talk to one or our coordinators and get the details on our next all-team practice or workshop day. Then come kick around the ball with us and meet other players in the league.

If you're interested in joining up, you'll need to complete some paperwork and pay $65 for a seasonal membership ($40 for seniors and students).

We look forward to seeing you on the field!

MRSL
c/o Davies Sporting Goods
418 N. Sartoris St.
Murfreesboro, TN 37130
(615) 555-2255

FIGURE D-26

Murfreesboro Regional Soccer League - Getting Started   Page 1 of 1

Murfreesboro Regional Soccer League
Part of the North American Recreational Soccer Association

The MRSL is open to players of all levels who want to play soccer in a relaxed, friendly environment. Even if you've never played soccer before, the MRSL is a great place to start.

To get a feel for our league, we recommend you call us at the number below or stop by Davies Sporting Goods to talk to one or our coordinators and get the details on our next all-team practice or workshop day. Then come kick around the ball with us and meet other players in the league.

If you're interested in joining up, you'll need to complete some paperwork and pay $65 for a seasonal membership ($40 for seniors and students).

We look forward to seeing you on the field!

MRSL
c/o Davies Sporting Goods
418 N. Sartoris St.
Murfreesboro, TN 37130
(615) 555-2255

file://webcore/Documents/Work/Cengage/HTML 5 Illustrated/Unit D/Solution Files/IC2/...   8/31/2010

Independent Challenge 3

As you continue your work on the Web site for Hotel Natoma, you incorporate fonts and colors using CSS.

a. Open HTM D-9.html in your text editor from the Unit D/IC3 folder and save a copy as **nearby.html**. Open HTM D-10.css in your text editor and save a copy as **natoma.css**. Before the closing body tag in nearby.html, insert a paragraph element containing your first and last name and the text **HTML5 Unit D, Independent Challenge 3**. Add the same information as a new comment beneath the existing one in natoma.css.

b. Copy the @font-face rule from stylesheet.css and paste it into natoma.css. Add code to style the h1 element with the font face you imported, and supply at least one serif font family and a generic font family as fallback options. Add a name-value pair to style the h1 element as normal, rather than bold, text. Change the font color to **white** and the background color to the color with the following rgb values: red: **8**, green: **32**, blue: **8**.

c. Style text in the body element in a sans-serif font and supply at least one sans-serif font family and a generic font family as fallback options.

d. Style the element with the id "box" with the background color with the following rgb values: red: **147**, green: **173**, blue: **120**. Style the element with the id "contact" with a background color of white.

Advanced Challenge Exercise

This Advanced Challenge Exercise requires an Internet connection.

- Use your Web browser and a search engine to find a list of HTML character references.
- Explore the special characters available and find one that seems appropriate for separating sections of text, such as a bullet.
- Copy the numeric character reference to the clipboard, return to nearby.html in your browser, and replace each pipe character in the contact information at the bottom of the document with the character reference you chose. Be sure to include a space before and after each character reference.
- View the Web page in your browser. If the character does not appear as you expected, return to the list in your Web browser, select a different character, and repeat the previous step as necessary until you are satisfied with the result.

e. Save your work in natoma.css, then save a copy with another name and edit the new style sheet to remove font and background colors.

f. In nearby.html, specify that the referenced external style sheet is intended for use on a monitor. Add a reference to the new style sheet you created and specify that it is intended for printed use.

g. Open HTM D-11.html in your text editor and save a copy as **index.html**. Edit the existing style sheet reference and add a new one as described in Step f. If you completed the Advanced Challenge Exercise above, copy the contact information containing the character references you selected from nearby.html and paste it into index.html to replace the corresponding paragraph.

Independent Challenge 3 (continued)

h. Preview both Web pages in a browser. The appearance of nearby.html should resemble Figure D-27. For each document, open a print preview if available. Your preview of nearby.html should look similar to Figure D-28. Validate all of your HTML and CSS documents.

i. If you have space on a Web server for publishing your documents, create a local root folder within the IC3 folder, move all the files in the IC3 folder to the local root folder, upload the files to your Web publishing location, then open nearby.html and index.html in your browser from the published location to verify that the upload was successful.

j. Close your browser, then close your text editor.

FIGURE D-27

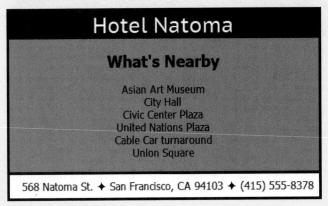

FIGURE D-28

Real Life Independent Challenge

This assignment builds on the personal Web site you have worked on in previous units. You will add font styling and color to your Web site.

a. Copy your Web site files to the Unit D/RLIC folder on the drive and folder where you store your Data Files.

b. Referring to your storyboard and any other design documents, decide which sections of the page will use serif fonts and which will use sans-serif fonts. Decide which font families you'd like to use. If you'd like to use a downloadable font, enter a phrase such as "@font-face free download" in your search engine and explore the fonts you find.

c. In your external style sheet, add font stacks for the fonts you've chosen. Be sure to include at least one backup font family and one generic font family in each stack. If you're implementing a downloadable font, add the **@font-face** rule to the style sheet.

d. Using your design documents, decide which sections of text, if any, you'd like to style with font colors, and decide where you'd like to add background colors. Enter a phrase such as "HTML color picker" in your search engine to find a resource for picking colors that provides the associated rgb or hexadecimal value and use these colors to style your Web site. (*Hint*: If the borders of a background color don't appear as you expect, try setting the padding and margin for the element to **0**, or changing your existing values.)

e. If any of your Web pages need bold or italic formatting, add the necessary span elements and style rules to apply these styles.

f. Apply any character codes necessary to replace potentially confusing characters for browsers. If you want to implement other characters that aren't available on your keyboard, enter a phrase such as "HTML character references" in your Web browser and explore the results to find the code for the character(s) you need.

g. Save your style sheet document, create a copy with a different name, and customize it for printed output. Change the existing link elements in all of your Web pages to designated the original style sheet document for screen output. Add another link element to each Web page referencing your new style sheet and designating it for printed output.

h. Preview your Web pages in at least two browsers and make any edits necessary for them to appear as you expected. If available, open a print preview of each document and verify that the printed version is free of color. Validate all of your HTML and CSS documents and make any edits necessary to address any issues.

i. If you have space on a Web server for publishing your documents, create a local root folder within the RLIC folder, move all the files in the RLIC folder to the local root folder, upload the files to your Web publishing location, then open each Web page in your browser from the published location to verify that the upload was successful.

j. Close your browser, then close your text editor.

Visual Workshop

In your text editor, open the file HTM D-12.html from the Unit D/VW directory on the drive and folder where you store your Data Files. Save the file as **index.html**, then preview it in a browser. Use your text editor to style the Web page to match the one shown in Figure D-29. Specify a font stack starting with Verdana as the default font family for the body element. Use the downloadable font ChunkFiveRegular with a font stack for the main heading and for the contact information, copying the @font-face rule from the stylesheet.css file. For the main heading, use the rgb triplet **189,204,212** for the background, specify that the font should not appear in bold, and specify a font size. Add a paragraph element after the content shown that contains your first and last name and the text **HTML5 Unit D, Visual Workshop**. Validate your HTML and CSS code. If you have space on a Web server, create a local root folder within the VW folder, move **index.html** to the local root folder, upload the file to your Web publishing location, then open the Web page in your browser from the published location. Close your browser and text editor.

Revisions Bookstore and Cafe

Custom brewed coffee and hand-selected books.

Special orders are our specialty.

412 N. 25th St.
Richmond, VA 23223
(804) 555-2565

Inserting and Working with Links

Files You Will Need:

To view a list of files needed for this unit, see the Data Files Grid in the back of the book.

While a Web site is made up of a collection of Web pages, another important element sets apart a Web site from a simple group of pages: linking. A **hyperlink**, more commonly known as a **link**, is text or another Web page element that users can select to open another document containing related content. Links let you widen the scope of a Web page from a standalone source of information to an integral part of a set of options available on a Web site. In turn, links enable you to integrate the contents of a Web site with anything available on the Web. Now that you have created a basic set of Web pages for Lakeland Reeds B&B, you integrate them into a Web site by creating links between the pages. You also include links to related documents and to relevant information available on other Web sites.

OBJECTIVES

Understand links

Create relative links

Create absolute links

Style links with CSS pseudo-classes

Open links in new windows or tabs

Link to anchors

Create a link to a document

Increase navigational accessibility

Understanding Links

The World Wide Web was initially built on the concept of **hypertext**, which refers to links in and between text-only documents. Today, you can create links on any visible Web page element, but the underlying power remains the same: the ability to present options for more information to users while displaying only a small subset on the screen at a time. ▓▓▓ As you prepare to incorporate links into the Lakeland Reeds B&B Web site, you review how to create and organize Web page links.

Use the following techniques to implement links effectively:

- **Creating links**

  To create a link, you enclose the text or other element you want to serve as a link within an **a element** using the <a></a> tag pair. You use the href attribute to specify the name of the Web page or other document to link to, which is known as the **target document**. Table E-1 explains the most common values for the href attribute. When a user agent encounters an a element, it enables users to interact with the element to open the linked document; for example, in a browser, users most commonly click linked text or images to follow links.

  Visual browsers apply colors to linked text to indicate that it is a link and to convey a user's interactions with the link at a glance. By convention, an unclicked link is blue, a link that a user is in the process of clicking is red, and a link to a Web page or document that a user has already viewed is purple. Because CSS allows you to customize these colors, it's uncommon to see this color combination on the Web today.

- **Organizing links**

  Virtually every Web site includes a set of links for moving between Web pages in the site. This design element is known as a **navigation bar** or **nav bar**, and usually occurs near the top of a Web page, as shown in Figure E-1, or along one of the sides. A navigation bar should maintain the same location and appearance on every page in a Web site in order to give users a reliable way to move between pages. Some larger Web sites include a second set of links at the bottom of each page for information that most users may need only occasionally, such as the site's privacy policy or contact information for a company or organization.

  While the contents of a Web page should ideally not be much bigger than an average user's screen, longer Web pages make sense for some applications. In these situations, it can be useful to create an additional navigation bar that scrolls the user's screen to a section of the current page.

QUICK TIP

While several other protocols are in use on the Internet, the Web uses only http and https.

- **Referencing Web resources**

  Every Web page and other document available on the Web can be referred to using a **uniform resource identifier (URI)**, also known as a **Web address**, which is a standard format for specifying how and where to access a resource on the Internet. As shown in Figure E-2, a URI consists of three parts: the scheme, the server name, and the path. The **scheme** is the way that computers ask for and communicate about the requested document. Web servers make documents available using the **Hypertext Transfer Protocol (http)** or **Hypertext Transfer Protocol Secure (https)** schemes. The **server name**, such as course.com or mail.google.com, identifies the general location of the target document on the Web. The **path** is the sequence of folders in which the target document is stored on the server. A path may end with a filename such as index.html, which is the name of the document a user agent should open in response to a user selecting the link. However, some URIs, such as the one shown in Figure E-2, terminate instead with a series of variable names and values that a program on the Web server uses to generate content dynamically. For instance, a link to a specific location on a map Web site includes information in the URI that enables the Web site to show the desired spot.

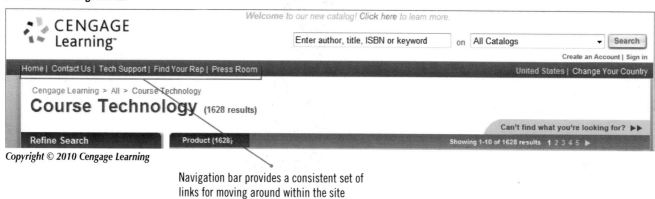

Navigation bar provides a consistent set of
links for moving around within the site

FIGURE E-2: **A uniform resource identifier (URI)**

$$\texttt{https://mail.google.com/mail/?shva=1\#inbox}$$

Scheme   Server name   Path

TABLE E-1: **Possible values for the href attribute**

value	description	example
filename	the filename of a Web page or other document located in the same directory as the current page	`history.html`
	the path and filename of a Web page in a different location on the same server	`/docs/register.pdf`
URI	scheme, server name, and, optionally, path for a resource located on another server	`https://mail.google.com/mail/?shva=1#inbox`
anchor	named location within the current Web document, preceded by a pound sign (#); can also be appended to a filename or URI	`#section3`

HTML5 and CSS3

Creating Relative Links

You can link to other documents in an a element in two basic ways. When you enter a URI, you're creating an **absolute link**, which is the full and complete address for the target document on the Web. In some situations, however, it makes more sense to create a **relative link**, which gives only the path and filename information necessary to locate the target document based on the location of the current Web page. Because Web pages on a small Web site almost always share the same folder on a Web server, it's most efficient to create relative links when creating a nav bar. You start adding links to the Lakeland Reeds B&B Web site by creating a nav bar at the top of each Web page.

STEPS

1. **In your text editor, open** HTM E-1.html **from the** Unit E/Unit folder **on the drive and folder where you store your Data Files, save it as** index.html, **then repeat to save** HTM E-2.html **as** aboutus.html, HTM E-3.html **as** rooms.html, HTM E-4.html **as** reserve.html, **and** HTM E-5.css **as** lakeland.css

2. **In** index.html, **create a new line beneath the h1 element, indent the same number of spaces and type** <div>, **press** [Enter], **indent two additional spaces, type** <p id="mainnav">, **then press** [Enter]

QUICK TIP
The pipe (|) key is located just above the [Enter] or [Return] key on most keyboards.

3. **Indent two additional spaces, type** Home, **press** [Spacebar], **type a pipe symbol (|), then press** [Enter]

4. **Repeat Step 3 to add the following lines of code at the same indent level:**
   About Us |

   Rooms |

   Reservations |

   Local Weather |

   Directions

   The pipe symbols create separations between the text for different links. Because only HTML elements and CSS code affect the appearance of text on the Web page, you can add line breaks to make the code easier to read without changing the layout in user agents.

5. **On a blank line, indent two fewer spaces than previously, type** </p>, **press** [Enter], **indent two fewer spaces than previously, then type** </div>

QUICK TIP
If a user selects a link to the current page, the user agent simply reloads the page. It's important to include this link in the nav bar for use on other pages in the Web site.

6. **Place the insertion point just to the left of the word** Home, **type** <a href="index.html">, **move the insertion point just after the word** Home, **then type** </a>
   The href value "index.html" is a relative link to the main page of the Web site.

7. **Repeat Step 6 to add a elements to the text for the following three links:**
   <a href="aboutus.html">**About Us**</a>

   <a href="rooms.html">**Rooms**</a>

   <a href="reserve.html">**Reservations**</a>

   Figure E-3 shows the completed code for the links.

8. **Save your work, then open** index.html **in your browser**
   Figure E-4 shows the main Web page containing the nav bar. The alignment and background color are styled by a rule in lakeland.css using the #mainnav selector.

9. **Click** About Us **in the nav bar**
   The "About Us" Web page opens.

FIGURE E-3: Navigation bar code with relative links

Code for nav bar with relative links to pages on the same site

```
<div id="box">
  <h1>Lakeland Reeds Bed &amp; Breakfast</h1>
  <div>
    <p id="mainnav">
      <a href="index.html">Home</a> |
      <a href="aboutus.html">About Us</a> |
      <a href="rooms.html">Rooms</a> |
      <a href="reserve.html">Reservations</a> |
      Local Weather |
      Directions
    </p>
  </div>
</div>
```

FIGURE E-4: Web page displaying nav bar

Navigation bar

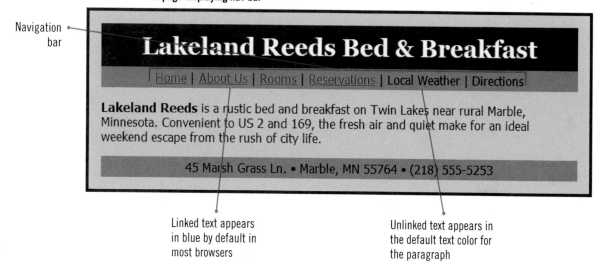

Linked text appears in blue by default in most browsers

Unlinked text appears in the default text color for the paragraph

HTML5 and CSS3

Creating effective link text

You can create a link on any text on a Web page. However, keeping a few rules in mind can enhance your site's accessibility and usability. Above all, link text should describe the target document. In a nav bar, a word or two that summarizes the content is usually sufficient. When you're inserting a link within a paragraph, a few words or a phrase may make more sense. For instance, instead of linking a phrase like "click here," creating a link on text like "read more about your local watershed" helps users verify they're accessing the information they want. Users of screen readers may also check the link text on a Web page as a means of scanning the page; using descriptive text increases accessibility in this instance.

Creating Absolute Links

Providing entire URIs in a elements isn't necessary for links to other pages in a small Web site. However, when you want to link to information on another Web site, you must use absolute links. ████ Philip Blaine, the owner of Lakeland Reeds B&B, wants to include a link to an online weather forecast for the town where the B&B is located. He'd also like the page to incorporate a link that enables users to easily generate customized driving directions to the establishment. You add absolute links targeting external Web sites to the last two items on the nav bar.

STEPS

1. **In your browser, open a site that provides current weather conditions, such as wunderground.com or weather.com, type Marble, MN in the location search box, then press [Enter]**
   The Web site displays current weather conditions in Marble, MN, along with a forecast.

QUICK TIP

If the URI you paste contains the & symbol, replace each occurrence with & to ensure your code validates.

2. **Click in the browser address box to select the address, then copy it to the Clipboard**

3. **Return to index.html in your text editor, place the insertion point just to the left of the phrase Local Weather, type <a href=", paste the contents of the Clipboard, type ">, place the insertion point just after the phrase Local Weather, type </a>, then save your work**
   The href value is an absolute link consisting of the entire URI for the target Web page.

QUICK TIP

If the URI in the address bar contains no text after the server name, explore the page for a way to create a link containing the information you've entered, such as the "link" link on maps.google.com, and verify that the link text begins with http.

4. **Return to your Web browser, open a site that provides driving directions, such as maps.google.com or mapquest.com, then click the Directions or Get Directions link**

5. **In the End or Destination section of the form that opens, enter Marble, MN, leaving any other fields blank, then click the Get Directions button**
   A Web page opens with a destination of Marble, MN, selected. If your home address doesn't appear automatically, you may be prompted to enter a starting point.

6. **Click in the browser address box to select the address, then copy it to the Clipboard**

QUICK TIP

If the URI you paste contains the & symbol, replace each occurrence with & to ensure your code validates.

7. **Return to index.html in your text editor, place the insertion point just to the left of the phrase Directions, type <a href=", paste the contents of the Clipboard, type ">, place the insertion point just after the phrase Directions, then type </a>**
   Figure E-5 shows the completed code for the two external links.

8. **Save your work, open index.html in your Web browser, then test the Local Weather and Directions links**
   Figure E-6 shows the completed nav bar.

9. **Return to index.html in your text editor, select the entire code for the nav bar, including the opening and closing div tags, copy the code to the Clipboard, paste it below the h1 element in aboutus.html, rooms.html, and reserve.html, then save your work on each document**

10. **In your Web browser, use the links on the index.html nav bar to open the other pages in the Web site, then verify that all the links work on each page**

FIGURE E-5: Navigation bar code with absolute links

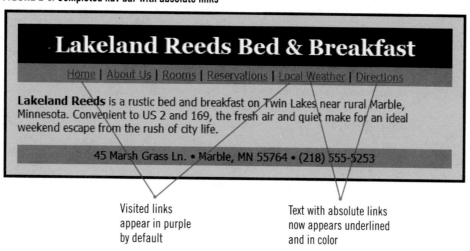

Code to create absolute links for weather and directions

```
index.html - Notepad
File  Edit  Format  View  Help
<!DOCTYPE html>
<html>
  <head>
    <meta charset="utf-8" />
    <title>Lakeland Reeds Bed &amp; Breakfast</title>
    <link rel="stylesheet" type="text/css" media="screen" href="lakeland.css" />
    <link rel="stylesheet" type="text/css" media="print" href="llprint.css" />
  </head>
  <body>
    <div id="box">
      <h1>Lakeland Reeds Bed &amp; Breakfast</h1>
      <div>
        <p id="mainnav">
          <a href="index.html">Home</a> |
          <a href="aboutus.html">About Us</a> |
          <a href="rooms.html">Rooms</a> |
          <a href="reserve.html">Reservations</a> |
          <a href="http://www.wunderground.com/cgi-bin/findweather/getForecast?query=marble,%20mn&amp;wuSelect=WEATHER">Local
weather</a> |
          <a href="http://maps.google.com/maps?f=q&amp;source=s_q&amp;hl=en&amp;geocode=&amp;q=marble,+mn&amp;sll=37.0625,-
95.677068&amp;sspn=34.534108,55.634766&amp;ie=UTF8&amp;hq=&amp;hnear=Marble,+Itasca,+Minnesota&amp;z=13">Directions</a>
        </p>
      </div>
      <p><span class="callout">Lakeland Reeds</span> is a rustic bed and breakfast on Twin Lakes near rural Marble,
Minnesota. Convenient to US 2 and 169, the fresh air and quiet make for an ideal weekend escape from the rush of city
life.</p>
      <p id="footer">45 Marsh Grass Ln. &#8226; Marble, MN 55764 &#8226; (218) 555-5253</p>
    </div>
  </body>
</html>
```

Your URIs may be different

FIGURE E-6: Completed nav bar with absolute links

Lakeland Reeds Bed & Breakfast

Home | About Us | Rooms | Reservations | Local Weather | Directions

Lakeland Reeds is a rustic bed and breakfast on Twin Lakes near rural Marble, Minnesota. Convenient to US 2 and 169, the fresh air and quiet make for an ideal weekend escape from the rush of city life.

45 Marsh Grass Ln. • Marble, MN 55764 • (218) 555-5253

Visited links appear in purple by default

Text with absolute links now appears underlined and in color

Understanding mailto links

In addition to creating links that target Web pages and other documents, you can construct a link that creates a new email to a specified recipient. Instead of beginning with http://, these links start with mailto: and are often referred to as **mailto links**. Despite their usefulness, mailto links present both usability and security issues and are not widely used. When a mailto link is activated, it's up to the user agent to identify which program should complete the request. This program is known as the default mail client. On some systems, the default mail client is a program; other systems default to a Web-based email system. Especially on a shared computer, this situation can mean that accessing the link creates unpredictable results, including failure to create the email, accompanied by an error message. In addition, because a mailto link includes a real email address and is publicly available on the Internet, these links are prime targets for programs known as **email harvesters**, which continually explore Web pages looking for email addresses that in turn receive spam emails.

If communication from your users is important, a few alternatives have replaced mailto links. Using more advanced HTML elements, you can create a form where users can enter comments and contact information, and then submit it to you without your email address being exposed on the Web. You can also create a personal or organizational social network feed and make it available on your Web site, inviting users to direct feedback or questions to you through that network instead of via email.

Styling Links with CSS Pseudo-Classes

Just as with any other Web page element, you can use CSS to style links. However, unlike unlinked text and other Web page elements, linked elements have four different possible states, as detailed in Table E-2. Using CSS pseudo-classes, you can create CSS styles to change the format of a link depending on which state it is in. A **pseudo-class** is a categorization of a Web page element, but it is based on a relationship or condition of the element at a given moment, rather than on a static property value. You create pseudo-classes for the Lakeland Reeds B&B nav bar to maximize contrast within the site's color scheme.

STEPS

1. **Return to lakeland.css in your text editor, then insert a new line at the bottom**

2. **Type #mainnav a:link {, press [Enter], indent two spaces, type color: black;, press [Enter], indent two spaces, then type }**

   #mainnav is the id value for the p element that contains the nav bar text. The a:link pseudo-class applies only when the other three do not. The #mainnav a:link selector specifies any a element in the link pseudo-class that's within the element with the id "mainnav".

QUICK TIP

The a:active style rule must follow the a:hover style rule to be effective. Likewise, the a:hover style rule must follow both the a:link and a:visited style rules.

3. **Press [Enter], then add the code for the remaining three pseudo-classes shown in Figure E-7**

   Figure E-7 shows the completed code for the pseudo-classes in the style sheet. The a:visited and a:active rules style links in dark brown when they have been visited or are being clicked. The a:hover rule makes text white when a user's mouse pointer is over it but not clicking it; the resulting mouse interaction is known as a **rollover effect**.

4. **Save your work, return to your Web browser, then, if possible, clear your browsing history**

   The method for clearing browsing history varies among browsers but is commonly listed under privacy or safety settings.

5. **Reload index.html in your browser, then move your mouse pointer over the About Us link in the nav bar**

   As Figure E-8 shows, the link text appears white when the mouse pointer is over it.

6. **Press and hold the mouse button**

   The link text changes to dark brown.

QUICK TIP

While it's common to change font color for links using pseudo-classes, you can change other element styles as well, including background.

7. **Release the mouse button, then let the target page load**

   As Figure E-9 shows, the Home and About Us links appears dark brown, indicating that you've visited those pages.

TABLE E-2: pseudo-class states for linked elements

pseudo-class	applies to
a:link	link that has not been visited, does not currently have the mouse pointer over it, and is not being clicked
a:visited	link to a document that has already been viewed
a:hover	link that the mouse pointer is currently over
a:active	link that is currently being clicked

```
#mainnav a:link {
    color: black;
    }
#mainnav a:visited {
    color: #422100;
    }
#mainnav a:hover {
    color: white;
    }
#mainnav a:active {
    color: #422100;
    }
```

FIGURE E-8: Nav bar styled using pseudo-classes

a:hover pseudo-class changes link text to white when mouse pointer is over it

Link text changed to black for unfollowed links

FIGURE E-9: Visited links styled using pseudo-classes

a:visited pseudo-class changes link text to dark brown for visited pages

Implementing descendant selectors

In addition to creating selectors based on element type, id, and class, you can combine multiple selectors to target elements based on their nesting. This type of selector, known as a **descendant selector**, can serve as a shorthand notation that in many cases lets you avoid adding additional class values to your HTML code. To create a descendant selector, you enter the parent element, followed by a space and the child element. For instance, a style rule starting with the selector #box p would apply to any p element within the element with the id "box". The parent or child in a descendant selector can be an element type, id, class, or pseudo-class.

Opening Links in New Windows or Tabs

By default, a link opens a new Web page in the same window and tab as the source page. This avoids overwhelming users with windows and tabs and enables users to revisit previous pages using the back buttons in their browsers. In certain situations, however, you want to be able to open a Web page in a new window or tab. For instance, some Web sites spawn target pages for links to external sites in new windows or tabs so users can have both sites open at once. Opening a link in a new window or tab from a Web page containing a lot of information allows a user to easily return to their place on the original page when they're done with the linked information. You can control where a link target opens by including the target attribute of the a element with a value of "_blank". In consultation with Philip and the designers in the art department, you've decided that the Local Weather and Directions link targets should open in new windows. You add the target attribute to these links.

STEPS

1. **Return to index.html in your text editor, then locate the code for the nav bar**

2. **Position the insertion point before the closing > in the opening <a> tag for the** Local Weather **link**

3. **Press [Spacebar], then type** target="_blank"

4. **Position the insertion point before the closing > in the opening <a> tag for the** Directions **link**

5. **Press [Spacebar], then type** target="_blank"
   Figure E-10 shows the Web page code with the target attributes added.

6. **Save your work, then refresh** index.html **in your Web browser**

7. **Click the** Local Weather **link**
   The Web page displaying the current weather opens in a new tab or new browser window, depending on the settings and capabilities of your browser.

Shortening links

Especially long external links can clutter your Web page code. To make your code easier to read, you can use a **link shortener** such as bit.ly or tinyurl.com, which are Web-based services that transform large, unwieldy links into manageable URIs. To use these services, you start by copying the full URI of the Web page you want to link to, then navigating to the Web site of whichever link shortener you choose. Next you paste your long link into the text box for that purpose, then click the associated button, which is often labeled "shorten" or something similar. The Web page processes your link and returns a new link that starts with the link shortener's name.

You then copy the new link to the Clipboard and paste it into your Web page.

One drawback of using shortened links in your Web site is that users are unable to tell from inspecting the URI what domain the link targets, which could be unsettling to some people. Shortened links make more sense on Web sites for large, well-established businesses and organizations and for Web sites that target people likely to have experience using such links. You may want to consider avoiding using shortened links on a Web site for a person or organization that's not well known, or on a site that targets more security-focused users.

```
index.html - Notepad
File  Edit  Format  View  Help
<!DOCTYPE html>
<html>
  <head>
    <meta charset="utf-8" />
    <title>Lakeland Reeds Bed &amp; Breakfast</title>
    <link rel="stylesheet" type="text/css" media="screen" href="lakeland.css" />
    <link rel="stylesheet" type="text/css" media="print" href="llprint.css" />
  </head>
  <body>
    <div id="box">
      <h1>Lakeland Reeds Bed &amp; Breakfast</h1>
      <div>
        <p id="mainnav">
          <a href="index.html">Home</a> |
          <a href="aboutus.html">About Us</a> |
          <a href="rooms.html">Rooms</a> |
          <a href="reserve.html">Reservations</a> |
          <a href="http://www.wunderground.com/cgi-bin/findweather/getForecast?query=marble,%20mn&amp;wuSelect=WEATHER"
target="_blank">Local
weather</a> |
          <a href="http://maps.google.com/maps?f=q&amp;source=s_q&amp;hl=en&amp;geocode=&amp;q=marble,+mn&amp;sll=37.0625,-
95.677068&amp;sspn=34.534108,55.634766&amp;ie=UTF8&amp;hq=&amp;hnear=Marble,+Itasca,+Minnesota&amp;z=13"
target="_blank">Directions</a>
        </p>
      </div>
      <p><span class="callout">Lakeland Reeds</span> is a rustic bed and breakfast on Twin Lakes near rural Marble,
Minnesota. Convenient to US 2 and 169, the fresh air and quiet make for an ideal weekend escape from the rush of city
life.</p>
      <p id="footer">45 Marsh Grass Ln. &#8226; Marble, MN 55764 &#8226; (218) 555-5253</p>
    </div>
  </body>
</html>
```

target attribute set to _blank
for both links to external sites

Linking to Anchors

In addition to linking to other Web pages in your own Web site or an external one, sometimes it's useful to link to locations within the current Web page. These links use the same elements and attributes as other links you've created, but instead of linking to URIs or filenames, you link to named locations, known as **anchors**, within the current document. You create anchors by assigning unique names to elements in your Web page using the HTML id attribute. To reference an anchor with the href attribute of the a element, you simply precede it with a pound sign (#). ███████ The Rooms Web page on the Lakeland Reeds B&B Web site contains descriptions of the four different rooms that guests can reserve. You add anchors to the room descriptions, then add a second nav bar containing a link to each description.

1. **Return to rooms.html in your text editor**

2. **Locate the h3 element containing the text Sun Room, then add an id attribute with the value sun to the opening tag**

3. **Repeat Step 2 to add an id attribute with the value reed to the h3 element containing the text Reed Room, an id attribute with the value tree to the h3 element containing the text Treehouse, and an id attribute with the value garden to the h3 element containing the text Garden Room**

4. **Insert a blank line above the h3 element with the id reed, indent and enter the code <p class="toplink"><a href="#box">Back to top</a></p>, then repeat to add code above the h3 elements with the ids tree and garden and above the p element with the id footer**
   The topmost visible element on the Web page is the outline created by style rules applied to the div element with the id "box". Thus, you can use the target name #box to link to the top of the Web page. Figure E-11 shows the completed code for the anchor values and the Back to top links.

5. **Add a blank line before the h3 element containing the text Sun Room, indent and type <div>, press [Enter], indent two additional spaces, type <p id="pagenav">, then press [Enter]**

6. **Indent two additional spaces, type <a href="#sun">Sun Room</a> |, press [Enter], then enter the remaining three lines of code for the nav bar from Figure E-12**

7. **On a blank line, indent two fewer spaces than previously, type </p>, press [Enter], indent two fewer spaces than previously, then type </div>**
   Figure E-12 shows the completed code for the nav bar for links within the page.

8. **Save your work, then open lakeland.css in your text editor**

9. **Add a blank line above the style rules for the #mainnav pseudo-classes, then enter the code for the pseudo-classes shown in Figure E-13**
   As Figure E-13 shows, you enter two sets of pseudo-classes. The #pagenav style rules style the second nav bar you inserted, while the generic a: style rules apply to the Back to Top links, which are not covered by the other sets of style rules.

QUICK TIP
Most Web browsers attempt to scroll the page to place the target anchor at the top of the window. However, if the Web page is not long enough to make this possible, the target may remain in the middle or at the bottom of the window.

10. **Save your work, open rooms.html in your Web browser, then click each of the links in the new nav bar and each of the Back to top links**
    The alignment and background color for the new nav bar are styled by a rule in lakeland.css using the #pagenav selector.

FIGURE E-11: **Code containing anchor values and Back to top links**

```
      <h3 id="sun">Sun Room</h3>
      <p class="desc">With windows on three sides, the sunlight in this second-floor room supports a large selection of
houseplants.</p>
      <p class="beds">1 queen bed.</p>
      <p class="toplink"><a href="#box">Back to top</a></p>
      <h3 id="reed">Reed Room</h3>
      <p class="desc">This first-floor room looks out over the reeds on the edge of the lake and the water beyond.</p>
      <p class="beds">1 queen bed and 1 twin bed.</p>
      <p class="toplink"><a href="#box">Back to top</a></p>
      <h3 id="tree">Treehouse</h3>
      <p class="desc">A winding staircase takes you to your own private getaway at the top of the house, with view of the
surrounding trees and meadows and the lake.</p>
      <p class="beds">1 queen bed.</p>
      <p class="toplink"><a href="#box">Back to top</a></p>
      <h3 id="garden">Garden Room</h3>
      <p class="desc">This room's French doors open onto our stone patio and flower garden.</p>
      <p class="beds">1 queen bed and 2 twin beds.</p>
      <p class="toplink"><a href="#box">Back to top</a></p>
      <p id="footer">45 Marsh Grass Ln. &#8226; Marble, MN 55764 &#8226; (218) 555-5253<br /></p>
```

FIGURE E-12: **Completed code for new nav bar**

```
<div>
  <p id="pagenav">
    <a href="#sun">Sun Room</a> |
    <a href="#reed">Reed Room</a> |
    <a href="#tree">Treehouse</a> |
    <a href="#garden">Garden Room</a>
  </p>
</div>
```

FIGURE E-13: **Style rules for generic link text and for new nav bar**

```
a:link {
  color: #422100;
  }
a:visited {
  color: #422100;
  }
a:hover {
  color: black;
  }
a:active {
  color: #422100;
  }
#pagenav a:link {
  color: white;
  }
#pagenav a:visited {
  color: #D7C39C;
  }
#pagenav a:hover {
  color: #C6A971;
  }
#pagenav a:active {
  color: white;
  }
```

Style rules for links not covered by id-specific selectors

Style rules for links in new nav bar

Linking to anchors in other documents

You can combine a relative or absolute link with an anchor to link to a specific element in a different document. Simply enter the URI or filename for the target document, add a pound sign (#) to the end, then add the anchor name. When the target page opens in a user's browser, the page scrolls to the specified anchor.

Creating a Link to a Document

Most Web page links are to other Web pages. However, sometimes it's useful to create a link to another type of document, such as formatted text in a PDF file or data in CSV format. You can specify any type of computer-readable document as the value for an href attribute. 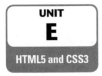 Philip has created a form for reserving the entire grounds of Lakeland Reeds B&B for special events, and he's saved the form as a PDF file. You add a link to this file on the Reservations page. You also create an updated version of the version of the style sheet for printed output.

STEPS

1. **Return to reserve.html in your text editor**

2. **Locate the text Read about reserving Lakeland Reeds for a wedding or other special event. below the h2 element, then position the insertion point to the left of the word Read**

3. **Type <a href="weddings.pdf">**

4. **Position the insertion point to the right of the period after the word event, type </a>, then save your work**

   Figure E-14 shows the completed code for the link.

5. **Open reserve.html in your Web browser, then click the link Read about reserving Lakeland Reeds for a wedding or other special event**

   If your computer has a PDF reader installed, the document opens, as shown in Figure E-15.

6. **If the PDF file opened in a program other than your Web browser, close the program displaying the file**

7. **Return to lakeland.css in your text editor, save your work, then save a copy as llprint.css**

8. **Remove all name-value pairs that specify color, including the border name-value pair in the #box rule, change all the colors in style rules based on pseudo-classes to black, then save your work**

   Because the background color for printed output will be white, changing all link colors to black increases legibility in printed formats.

Avoiding confusion in target documents

Although you can link to documents in most any format from your Web pages, it's important to keep in mind that HTML documents are the ones that your users are guaranteed to be able to access. To be able to access documents in other formats, users' computers must have programs installed that interpret these files. The PDF format has become an unofficial Web standard for documents that require a specific printed format, such as forms that must be filled out by hand and/or signed, and you can rely on most of your users having the capability to view and print PDFs. Make documents in other formats available based on the likely computer configurations

of your target audience. For instance, on a Web site by and for users of a highly specialized type of software, you'd be safe in making files in that software format available; however, on a site for the general public, it's unlikely that most users would be able to access such files.

Keep in mind that Web-focused formats such as HTML and PDF minimize file sizes as much as possible, meaning that documents usually download quickly. If you are making a document available in another format, pay attention to the file size and take any steps available to reduce the size.

```
<h2>Reservations</h2>
<p>We're happy to take reservations up to a year in advance by phone, fax, or email.</p>
<p>Feel free to contact us with any queries about Lakeland Reeds, or about planning your trip.</p>
<p><a href="weddings.pdf">Read about reserving Lakeland Reeds for a wedding or other special event.</a> (PDF)</p>
<div id="contact">
    <p><span id="name">Philip Blaine, Proprietor</span><br />45 Marsh Grass Ln.<br />Marble, MN 55764</p>
    <p>
        <span class="callout">Phone</span>: (218) 555-5253<br />
        <span class="callout">Fax</span>: (218) 555-0413<br />
        <span class="callout">Email</span>: lrbb [at] example [dot] com
    </p>
</div>
```

Value of href attribute is the name of a PDF file

Closing tag

FIGURE E-15: Target PDF file in PDF reader

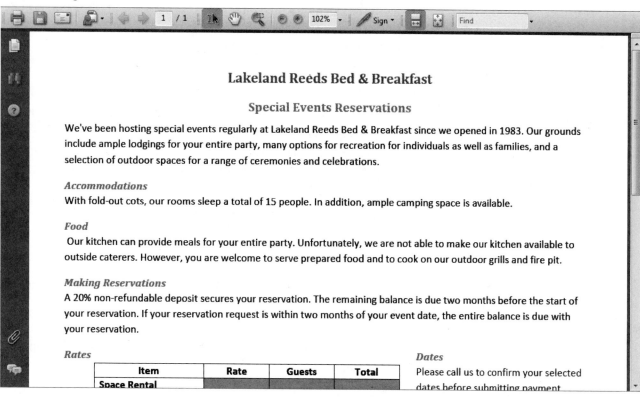

Lakeland Reeds Bed & Breakfast

Special Events Reservations

We've been hosting special events regularly at Lakeland Reeds Bed & Breakfast since we opened in 1983. Our grounds include ample lodgings for your entire party, many options for recreation for individuals as well as families, and a selection of outdoor spaces for a range of ceremonies and celebrations.

Accommodations
With fold-out cots, our rooms sleep a total of 15 people. In addition, ample camping space is available.

Food
Our kitchen can provide meals for your entire party. Unfortunately, we are not able to make our kitchen available to outside caterers. However, you are welcome to serve prepared food and to cook on our outdoor grills and fire pit.

Making Reservations
A 20% non-refundable deposit secures your reservation. The remaining balance is due two months before the start of your reservation. If your reservation request is within two months of your event date, the entire balance is due with your reservation.

Rates

Item	Rate	Guests	Total
Space Rental			

Dates
Please call us to confirm your selected dates before submitting payment.

HTML5 and CSS3

Inserting and Working with Links

Increasing Navigational Accessibility

Nav bars can present accessibility challenges for users with limited or no sight. Users of screen readers, for instance, often experience a Web page element-by-element in sequence from top to bottom, meaning that a screen reader would read the heading followed by each link in a nav bar before getting to the main content of the page. To provide more navigation options, it's good practice to include a **skip link** at the top of each Web page, which targets an anchor at the start of the main page content and allows users to bypass navigation. In addition, HTML5 introduced nav, a semantic element, to mark the main elements of site and page navigation. The nav element is expected to replace the need for skip links because assistive software will be able to offer users the option of bypassing it. For now, you can make your Web pages most accessible by incorporating both of these options. ▓▓▓▓ You add a skip link to each Web page in the Lakeland Reeds B&B site, and you make the site navigation and page navigation sections into nav elements.

STEPS

1. **Return to index.html in your text editor, locate the opening <p> tag for the first paragraph of Web page text, and add the attribute id="main"**

2. **Add a blank line beneath the opening <body> tag, indent to align with the div tag that follows, then type <p id="skipnav"><a href="#main">Skip navigation</a></p>**
   Figure E-16 shows the code for the target anchor and the skip link.

> **TROUBLE**
> Be sure not to delete the </div> tag at the end of the document just before the </body> tag, which is the closing tag for a different element.

3. **Below the h1 element, delete the tag <div>, type <nav>, then above the p element with the id value main, delete </div>, then type </nav>**

4. **Add a blank line above the closing tag for the head element near the top of the document, then enter the three lines of code shown in Figure E-16**
   Because recent versions of Internet Explorer interpret semantic elements in unexpected ways, you can ensure compatibility by including a **script**, which is more complex Web page code written in another programming language. This element is surrounded by comments and instructions so all user agents except the affected versions of Internet Explorer will ignore it.

> **TROUBLE**
> If your browser displays an error message about scripts, choose the appropriate option to allow the script on the current page to run.

5. **Save your work, then refresh index.html in your browser**
   As Figure E-17 shows, the skip link appears at the top of the browser window. Replacing the div element with the nav element does not change the page's appearance.

6. **Drag the bottom border of your browser up so only the skip link and the h1 heading are visible, then click Skip navigation**
   The browser displays the beginning of the main page content.

> **TROUBLE**
> If you do not see the main page content after clicking the skip link, double-check the code you entered in Steps 1 and 2 for errors.

7. **Repeat Steps 1–6 for aboutus.html and reserve.html, adding the id attribute in Step 1 to the h2 element in each document**

8. **Repeat Steps 1–7 for rooms.html, adding the id attribute in Step 1 to the h2 element, then replace the <div> and </div> tags for the internal page nav bar with <nav> and </nav>, then change the Back to top href values to #skipnav**
   Because the box element is no longer the first element on the page, you change the "Back to top" link targets to #skipnav so the links take users all the way to the top of the browser window.

9. **Validate the code for all your Web pages and style sheets, then make any necessary changes**

10. **If you have space on a Web server, publish your files to your Web publishing location, open index.html in your browser from the published location, then use the links to verify that all the pages display as expected**

FIGURE E-16: Skip link code

Script reference for compatibility with Internet Explorer

Code for skip link

div element replaced with nav to indicate content and function

Anchor at start of main page content serves as target for skip link

FIGURE E-17: Web page with skip link

Skip navigation —— Skip link to move to main page content

Lakeland Reeds Bed & Breakfast

Home | About Us | Rooms | Reservations | Local Weather | Directions

Lakeland Reeds is a rustic bed and breakfast on Twin Lakes near rural Marble, Minnesota. Convenient to US 2 and 169, the fresh air and quiet make for an ideal weekend escape from the rush of city life.

45 Marsh Grass Ln. • Marble, MN 55764 • (218) 555-5253

Implementing additional semantic elements

In addition to nav, HTML5 introduced several other semantic elements intended to indicate the contents and function of Web page elements that were previously created using div elements. The rich semantic information that all of these elements offer opens the door for Web pages that adapt more readily and creatively to different types of devices' user agents, from touch pads and smart phones to screen readers and other assistive devices. Table E-3 details several of these elements.

Like the nav element, these other semantic elements require the inclusion of a script to work properly with versions of Internet Explorer earlier than version 9. In addition, any CSS style rule for an HTML5 semantic element should include the name-value pair display: block; to maximize browser compatibility. It's unnecessary to specify this style for semantic elements without other associated CSS, however.

TABLE E-3: Additional HTML5 semantic elements

element	intended use
article	standalone piece of work, such as a single entry in a blog
aside	part of a page that's tangential to the main page content; in a book, this might lend itself to a sidebar or pull quote
footer	information about a section or document that usually appears at the end, such as attributions and/or footnotes
header	information about a section or document that usually appears at the beginning, such as a heading, logo, and/or table of contents
hgroup	group of related elements that include a heading; enables user agents to recognize content such as a tagline as related to a heading
section	section of content focused on a common theme, such as a chapter of a larger work

Practice

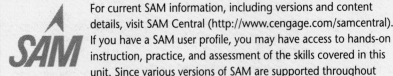

For current SAM information, including versions and content details, visit SAM Central (http://www.cengage.com/samcentral). If you have a SAM user profile, you may have access to hands-on instruction, practice, and assessment of the skills covered in this unit. Since various versions of SAM are supported throughout the life of this text, check with your instructor for the correct instructions and URL/Web site for accessing assignments.

Concepts Review

Refer to Figure E-18.

FIGURE E-18

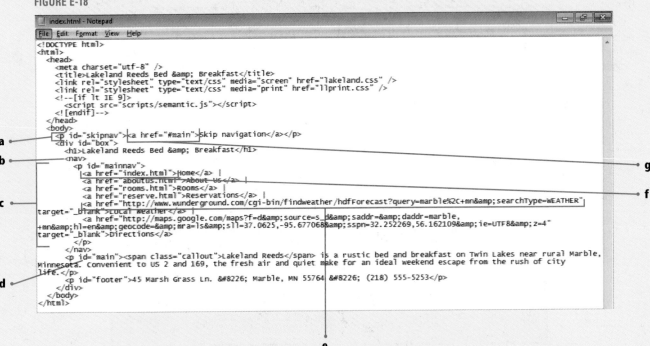

1. Which item is the code for a nav bar?
2. Which item is an absolute link?
3. Which item is a relative link?
4. Which item is an anchor?
5. Which item links to an anchor?
6. Which item is a semantic element for navigational content?
7. Which item creates a skip link?

Match each term with the statement that best describes it.

8. Uniform resource identifier (URI)
9. Relative link
10. Anchor
11. Nav bar
12. Absolute link
13. Skip link
14. Pseudo-class

a. A set of links for moving between Web pages in a Web site

b. A categorization of a Web page element based on a relationship or condition of the element at a given moment

c. A type of link that specifies the full and complete address for the target document on the Web

d. A standard format for specifying how and where to access a resource on the Internet

e. A link that targets an anchor at the start of the main page content and allows users to bypass navigation

f. A named location within a document

g. A link that gives only the path and filename information necessary to locate the target document based on the location of the current Web page

Select the best answer from the list of choices.

15. When creating a link, the Web page or other document you link to is known as the _____.
    - **a.** relative link
    - **b.** target
    - **c.** absolute link
    - **d.** hypertext

16. Which type of Web reference contains a scheme, a server name, and a path?
    - **a.** URI
    - **b.** relative link
    - **c.** anchor
    - **d.** nav element

17. Web servers make documents available using which protocol?
    - **a.** ftp
    - **b.** http
    - **c.** mailto
    - **d.** telnet

18. What does the value "#section3" for the href attribute target?
    - **a.** a URI
    - **b.** a PDF file
    - **c.** a filename
    - **d.** an anchor

19. When you enter a URI, which of the following are you creating?
    - **a.** an anchor
    - **b.** a skip link
    - **c.** an absolute link
    - **d.** a relative link

20. Because Web pages on a small Web site almost always share the same folder on a Web server, it's most efficient to create which type of links when creating a nav bar?
    - **a.** absolute
    - **b.** relative
    - **c.** anchor
    - **d.** skip

21. Which pseudo-class is active when a user's mouse pointer is over the affected link?
    - **a.** a:link
    - **b.** a:visited
    - **c.** a:hover
    - **d.** a:active

22. You create anchors by assigning unique names to elements in your Web page using which attribute?
    - **a.** id
    - **b.** class
    - **c.** href
    - **d.** target

Skills Review

1. **Create relative links.**
   a. In your text editor, open HTM E-6.html from the Unit E/Review folder on the drive and folder where you store your Data Files, save it as **index.html**, then repeat to save HTM E-7.html as **history.html**, HTM E-8.html as **location.html**, and HTM E-9.css as **bigj.css**.
   b. In index.html, enter an opening div tag beneath the h1 element, then below it, indent two additional spaces and add an opening p tag with an id value of **mainnav.**
   c. Insert a new line below the code you just added, indent two additional spaces, type **Home**, add a space, then type a pipe symbol.
   d. Repeat Step c to add the following lines of code at the same indent level:
   History |
   Menu |
   Locations
   e. Insert a new line below the code you just added, indent two fewer spaces than previously, insert a closing p tag, insert another new line, indent two fewer spaces than previously, then insert a closing div tag.
   f. Create a link on the word Home that opens the page index.html, then repeat to add links to the text History to open the page **history.html**, and Locations to open **location.html**.
   g. Save your work, open index.html in your browser, then click the **Locations** link to test it.

2. **Create absolute links.**
   a. Copy the full address of the first location from the Locations Web page to the Clipboard, open a Web site that provides maps, such as maps.google.com or mapquest.com, paste the contents of the Clipboard into the location box on the Web page, then press [Enter].

Skills Review (continued)

b. Click in the browser address box to select the URI, then copy it to the Clipboard. If the URI in the address bar contains no text after the server name, explore the page for a way to create a link containing the information you've entered, such as the Link link on maps.google.com, verify that the link text begins with http, then copy it to the Clipboard.

c. Return to location.html in your text editor, then add an absolute link on the word Map at the end of the first address, pasting the URI from the Clipboard as the href value. Be sure to add the closing tag for the a element. If the URI you paste contains the ampersand (&) symbol, replace each occurrence with & to ensure your code validates.

d. Repeat Steps a–c for the remaining two locations, save your work, then open location.html in your Web browser and test each of the Map links.

3. Style links with CSS pseudo-classes.

a. Return to bigj.css in your text editor, then insert a new line at the bottom.

b. Add a style rule using a pseudo-class that formats the font color of a default link in the element with the id "mainnav" as **red**. Repeat to add rules to format the font colors of visited links within the element with the id "mainnav" as **#ffcc66**, links with the mouse pointer over them as **white**, and active links as **#ffcc66**. Ensure that the rules appear in your style sheet in the above order.

c. Save your work, return to your Web browser, then if possible, clear your browsing history.

d. Reload index.html in your browser, then verify that the font color changes for links in the nav bar when the mouse pointer is over them, when they are being clicked, and when the target pages have been viewed.

4. Open links in new windows or tabs.

a. Return to location.html in your text editor, locate the end of the opening a tag for the first Map link, insert a space after the closing quote around the URI, then add an attribute-value pair that opens the link in a new browser window or tab. Repeat for the remaining two Map links.

b. Save your work, reload location.html in your browser, then test each Map link.

5. Link to anchors.

a. Return to location.html in your text editor.

b. Locate the h3 element containing the text Queen's Park, then add an id attribute with the value **queen** to the opening tag.

c. Repeat Step b to add an id attribute with the value **stclair** to the h3 element containing the text St. Clair, and an id attribute with the value **dundas** to the h3 element containing the text Dundas.

d. Insert a blank line above the h3 element with the id stclair, then indent and insert a p element with the class **toplink**. Within the p element, insert the text **Back to top**, then link the text to the anchor with the id box.

e. Repeat Step d to add the same code above the h3 element with the id dundas and above the p element with the id contact.

f. Add a blank line before the h3 element containing the text Queen's Park, indent and enter an opening div tag, add another blank line beneath the code you just entered, indent two additional spaces, then add a p tag with the id **pagenav**.

g. Add a blank line beneath the code you just entered, indent two additional spaces, insert the text Queen's Park followed by a space and a pipe symbol, then create a link on the text **Queen's Park** that moves to the element with the id queen. Repeat to add the text **St. Clair**, followed by a space and a pipe symbol. Link the text St. Clair to the element with the id stclair and add the text **Dundas** and link it to the element with the id dundas.

h. Beneath the code you just entered, add closing tags for the p and div elements, reducing the indentation as necessary to match the opening tags.

i. Save your work, then open bigj.css in your text editor.

j. Add a blank line above the style rules for the #mainnav pseudo-classes, then enter a style rule using a pseudo-class that formats the font color of a default link as **#663300**. Repeat to add rules to format the font colors of visited links as **#754719**, links with the mouse pointer over them as **black**, and active links as **#754719**. Ensure that the rules appear in your style sheet in the above order.

Skills Review (continued)

k. Add a blank line above the style rules for the #mainnav pseudo-classes, then enter a style rule using a pseudo-class that formats the font color of a default link in the element with the id "pagenav" as **black**. Repeat to add rules to format the font colors of visited links within the element with the id "pagenav" as **#754719**, links with the mouse pointer over them as **#663300**, and active links as **#754719**. Ensure that the rules appear in your style sheet in the above order.

l. Save your work, open location.html in your Web browser, then click each of the links in the new nav bar and each of the Back to top links.

6. Create a link to a document.

a. Return to index.html in your text editor.

b. In the code for the nav bar, add a link on the text Menu that opens bigjmenu.pdf.

c. Open index.html in your Web browser, then click the Menu link to test it. If the PDF file opened in a program other than your Web browser, close the program displaying the file.

d. Return to index.html in your text editor, select the entire code for the nav bar including the opening and closing div tags, copy the code to the Clipboard, paste it below the h1 element in history.html and location.html, then save your work on each document.

e. In your Web browser, use the links on the index.html nav bar to open the other pages in the Web site, then verify that all the links work on each page.

f. Return to bigj.css in your text editor, save your work, then save a copy as **bjprint.css**.

g. Remove all name-value pairs that specify color, including any border name-value pairs, change all the colors in style rules based on pseudo-classes to **black**, then save your work.

7. Increase navigational accessibility.

a. Return to index.html in your text editor, locate the opening <p> tag for the first paragraph of the Web page text, and add an id attribute with the value "main".

b. Add a blank line beneath the opening <body> tag, add a p element with the id **skipnav** containing the text **Skip navigation**, then add a link to the text Skip navigation that moves to the anchor with the id **main**.

c. Below the h1 element, replace the opening div tag with an opening nav tag. Above the p element with the id value "main", replace the closing div tag with a closing nav tag.

d. Add a blank line above the closing tag for the head element near the top of the document, then enter the following three lines of code with appropriate indentation:

```
<!--[if lt IE 9]>
   <script src="scripts/semantic.js"></script>
<![endif]-->
```

e. Save your work, then refresh index.html in your browser. If your browser displays an error message about scripts, choose the appropriate option to allow the script on the current page to run. Figure E-19 shows the final appearance of index.html.

f. Drag the bottom border of your browser up so only the skip link and the h1 heading are visible, then click Skip navigation.

g. Repeat Steps a–f for history.html, adding the id attribute in Step a to the h2 element.

FIGURE E-19

Skip navigation

Big J's Deep Dish Pizza

Home | History | Menu | Locations

Authentic Chicago-style pies

Eat in, carry out, or call for delivery.

Voted "Best Pizza Joint" by the *Toronto Times*

150 St. Joseph St.
Toronto, ON M5S 2C3
(416) 555-3337

Skills Review (continued)

h. Repeat Steps a–f for location.html, adding the id attribute in Step a to the h2 element, then replace the opening and closing div tags for the internal page nav bar with opening and closing nav tags. Change the "Back to top" href values to **#skipnav**. Figure E-20 shows the final appearance of location.html.

i. Validate the code for all your Web pages and style sheets.

Independent Challenge 1

As you continue your work on the Web site for the Spotted Wren Garden Center, you add a nav bar and links to gardening resources, along with navigational accessibility features.

a. Open HTM E-10.html in your text editor from the Unit E/IC1 folder. Insert a blank line before the closing body tag, then insert a paragraph element containing your first and last name and the text **HTML5 Unit E, Independent Challenge 1**. Save the file as **index.html**, then repeat to save HTM E-11.html as **hours.html** and HTM E-12.html as **resource.html**. Open HTM E-13.css. Below the existing comment at the top of the document, add another comment containing your first and last name and the text **HTML5 Unit E, Independent Challenge 1**. Save the file as **spotwren.css**.

b. In index.html, insert a div element beneath the opening tag for the "content" div element. Add a p element with the id **mainnav**, then add the text and separating characters for a nav bar, using the link text **Home**, **Hours**, **Location**, and **Gardening Resources**.

FIGURE E-20

Skip navigation

Big J's Deep Dish Pizza

Home | History | Menu | Locations

Locations

Queen's Park/UT | St. Clair | Dundas

Queen's Park/UT

150 St. Joseph St., Toronto, ON M5S 2C3 [Map]
(416) 555-3337

    Mon-Thu: 11am - 10pm
    Fri-Sat: 11am - 11pm
    Sun: Noon - 10pm

Back to top

St. Clair

783 St. Clair Ave. W, Toronto, ON M6G 3P7 [Map]
(416) 555-2047

    Mon-Thu: 11am - 9:30pm
    Fri-Sat: 11am - 11pm
    Sun: Noon - 9:30pm

Back to top

Dundas

360 Dundas St. W, Toronto, ON M5T 1G4 [Map]
(416) 555-1011

    Mon-Thu: 11am - 11pm
    Fri-Sat: 11am - Midnight
    Sun: Noon - 11pm

Back to top

150 St. Joseph St.
Toronto, ON M5S 2C3
(416) 555-3337

c. Link the word Home to index.html, Hours to hours.html, and Gardening Resources to resource.html. Save your work, then open index.html in your browser and verify that the links you entered open the appropriate pages.

d. Copy the business street address from the Web page, open the Web page for a map provider, such as maps.google.com or mapquest.com, then open a map showing the business location. Copy the URI in your browser's address box, or if the URI in the address bar contains no text after the server name, explore the page for a way to create a link containing the information you've entered, such as the Link link on maps.google.com, verify that the link text begins with http, then copy it.

e. Return to index.html in your text editor, then add an absolute link to the word Location in the nav bar using the map URI you copied. Convert any occurrence of an ampersand symbol (&) to **&amp**; and add code to specify that the target should open in a new window. Save your work. Reload index.html in your browser, then verify that the new link works correctly.

f. Copy the code for the nav bar from index.html and paste it into the other two html documents at the top of the "content" div element.

g. Return to spotwren.css in your text editor, then add four style rules using pseudo-classes to format the font color of a default link in the element with the id "mainnav" as **white**, a visited link as **#d6d6c2**, a link with the mouse pointer over it as **#ffff00**, and an active link as **#ffcc00**. Ensure that the rules appear in your style sheet in the order specified.

h. Save your work, return to your browser and clear your browser history if possible, reload index.html, and verify that the default font color is white, that the font color changes on rollovers and clicks, and that links that have been followed appear in a different color than unfollowed links.

i. Return to resource.html in your text editor. On the text Lawn and Garden Care Tip Sheet, add a link that opens tipsheet.pdf.

Independent Challenge 1 (continued)

j. Use a search engine to identify a site that provides weather forecasts for gardeners, using a search phrase such as **gardening weather forecast**. Navigate to the gardening forecast for Omaha, NE, copy the URI, then return to resource.html in your text editor and add a link to the URI you copied on the phrase Gardening weather forecast. Save your work.

k. Return to spotwren.css in your text editor, then above the existing pseudo-class rules, add four style rules using pseudo-classes to format the font color of a default link as **#993300**, a visited link as **#999966**, a link with the mouse pointer over it as **black**, and an active link as **#999966**. Ensure that the rules appear in your style sheet in the order specified. Open resource.html in your browser, verify that the link colors change in response to rollovers and clicks, then test all the links on the page.

l. Return to index.html in your text editor. Add an anchor with the name **main** to the first p element beneath the nav bar. Create a skip navigation link beneath the opening body tag that moves to the "main" anchor. Repeat for hours.html and resource. html, adding the anchor to the h2 element in each document. Save your work on each file, then reload each file in your browser and test the skip navigation link. Figure E-21 shows resource.html.

m. Return to index.html in your text editor, replace the div element enclosing the nav bar with a nav element, then add the following three lines of code immediately before the closing head tag:

FIGURE E-21

```
<!--[if lt IE 9]>
  <script src="scripts/semantic.js"></script>
<![endif]-->
```

n. Repeat Step m for resource.html and hours.html.

o. Return to spotwren.css in your text editor, remove all name-value pairs that reference colors, change all colors in rules based on pseudo-classes to black, then save a copy of the file as **swprint.css**.

p. Validate all your HTML and CSS documents.

q. If you have space on a Web server for publishing your documents, create a local root folder within the IC1 folder, move all the files and folders in the IC1 folder to the local root folder, upload the files to your Web publishing location, then open index.html in your browser from the published location and test the links.

r. Close your browser, then close your text editor.

Independent Challenge 2

As you continue developing the Web site for the Murfreesboro Regional Soccer League, you create links between pages as well as links to anchors. You also incorporate features to make the site navigation more accessible.

a. Open HTM E-14.html in your text editor from the Unit E/IC2 folder. Insert a blank line before the closing body tag, then insert a paragraph element containing your first and last name and the text **HTML5 Unit E, Independent Challenge 2**. Save the file as **index.html**, then repeat to save HTM E-15.html as **started.html** and HTM E-16. html as **schedule.html**. Open HTM E-17.css, then below the existing comment at the top of the document, add another comment containing your first and last name and the text **HTML5 Unit E, Independent Challenge 2**. Save the file as **mrsl.css**.

b. In index.html, insert a div element above the opening tag for the "maintext" div element. Add a p element with the id **mainnav**, then add the text and separating characters for a nav bar, using the link text **Home**, **Getting Started**, **Schedules**, and **Field Location**.

c. Link the word Home to index.html, Getting Started to started.html, and Schedules to schedule.html. Save your work, then open index.html in your browser and verify that the links you entered open the appropriate pages.

Independent Challenge 2 (continued)

d. In your browser, open a Web site that provides maps, such as maps.google.com or mapquest.com, then display a map that shows the address **515 Cherry Ln., Murfreesboro, TN**. Copy the URI in your browser's address box, or if the URI in the address bar contains no text after the server name, explore the page for a way to create a link containing the information you've entered, such as the Link link on maps.google.com, verify that the link text begins with http, then copy it.

e. Return to index.html in your text editor, then add an absolute link to the phrase Field Location in the nav bar using the URI you copied. Add code to specify that the target should open in a new window, then save your work. Reload index.html in your browser, then verify that the Field Location link works correctly.

f. Copy the code for the nav bar from index.html and paste it into the other two html documents above the opening tags for the "maintext" div elements.

g. Return to mrsl.css in your text editor, then add four style rules using pseudo-classes to format the font color of a default link in the element with the id "mainnav" as **white**, a visited link as **#8CC63F**, a link with the mouse pointer over it as **red**, and an active link as **#8CC63F**. Ensure that the rules appear in your style sheet in the order specified.

h. Save your work, return to your browser and clear your browser history if possible, reload index.html, and verify that the default font color is white, that the font color changes on rollovers and clicks, and that links that have been followed appear in a different color than unfollowed links.

i. Return to schedule.html in your text editor. Above the h3 element containing the text Red, add a p element with the id "**pagenav**", then add the text and separating characters for a nav bar, using the link text **Red**, **Blue**, **Green**, and **Yellow**.

j. Add an anchor to each of the four h3 elements on the page with an anchor name matching the displayed text. Link each of the four words on the page nav bar you created in the previous step to the anchor for the corresponding h3 element.

k. Beneath the paragraph containing schedule information for the Red team, add a p element with a class value of **toplink** containing the text **Back to top**. Link the text to the "maintext" anchor. Copy the code you created and paste it beneath the schedule paragraphs for the remaining three teams, then save your work.

l. Return to mrsl.css in your text editor, then add four style rules using pseudo-classes to format the font color of a default link in the element with the id "pagenav" as **black**, a visited link as #754719, a link with the mouse pointer over it as **red**, and an active link as #754719. Ensure that the rules appear in your style sheet in the order specified, save your work, open schedule.html in your browser, verify that the link colors change in response to rollovers and clicks, then test all the links on the page nav bar and all the Back to top links.

m. Return to index.html in your text editor. Add an anchor with the name **main** to the first p element beneath the nav bar. Create a skip navigation link beneath the opening body tag that moves to the "main" anchor. Repeat for started.html and schedule.html, adding the anchor to the h2 element in each document. In schedule.html, change the link targets for the four Back to top links to the skipnav anchor. Save your work on each file.

n. Return to mrsl.css in your text editor, then above the existing pseudo-class rules add four style rules using pseudo-classes to format the font color of a default link as #663300, a visited link as #663300, a link with the mouse pointer over it as **black**, and an active link as #663300. Ensure that the rules appear in your style sheet in the order specified. Save your work, then then reload each HTML file in your browser and test the skip navigation links. Figure E-22 shows schedule.html.

o. Return to index.html in your text editor, replace the div element enclosing the nav bar with a nav element, then add the following three lines of code immediately before the closing head tag:

```
<!--[if lt IE 9]>
   <script src="scripts/semantic.js"></script>
<![endif]-->
```

FIGURE E-22

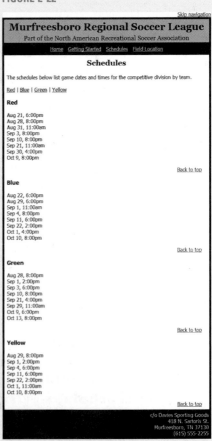

Independent Challenge 2 (continued)

p. Repeat Step o for started.html and schedule.html. In schedule.html, enclose the p element containing the page nav bar in a nav element, increasing the indentation for the existing code.

Advanced Challenge Exercise

- Return to index.html in your text editor. Replace the div element that has the id **headings** with the semantic **header** element, using the opening tag **<header>** with no attributes and the closing tag **</header>**.
- Near the bottom of the document, enclose the p element that has the id contact in a semantic footer element, using the opening tag **<footer>** with no attributes and the closing tag **</footer>**.
- Save your work, then repeat the previous two steps for started.html and schedule.html.
- Return to mrsl.css in your text editor. Locate the #headings style rule and change the selector to a type selector based on the "header" element. Add a name-value pair to the style rule that sets the display of the element to **block**. Save your work, open index.html in your browser, then verify that the appearance of all three Web pages is unchanged.

q. Return to mrsl.css in your text editor, remove all name-value pairs that reference colors, change the colors for all rules based on pseudo-classes to **black**, then save a copy of the file as **mrsprint.css**.

r. Validate all your HTML and CSS documents.

s. If you have space on a Web server for publishing your documents, create a local root folder within the IC2 folder, move all the files and folders in the IC2 folder to the local root folder, upload the files to your Web publishing location, then open index.html in your browser from the published location and test the links.

t. Close your browser, then close your text editor.

Independent Challenge 3

This Independent Challenge requires an Internet connection.

As you continue your work on the Web site for Hotel Natoma, you incorporate links between pages as well as to external Web sites, and incorporate navigational accessibility features.

a. Open HTM E-18.html in your text editor from the Unit E/IC3 folder. Insert a blank line before the closing body tag, then insert a paragraph element containing your first and last name and the text **HTML5 Unit E, Independent Challenge 3**. Save the file as **index.html**, then repeat to save HTM E-19.html as **nearby.html**. Open HTM E-20.css, then below the existing comment at the top of the document, add another comment containing your first and last name and the text **HTML5 Unit E, Independent Challenge 3**. Save the file as **natoma.css**.

b. In nearby.html, insert a nav bar beneath the h1 element. Enclose your code in a div element and lay out the navigation bar text using a paragraph element with with id **mainnav**. Add the link text **Home, What's Nearby**, and **Location**. Link the word Home to index.html and What's Nearby to nearby.html. Save your work, then open nearby.html in your browser and verify that the links you entered open the appropriate pages.

c. In your browser, open a Web site that provides maps, such as maps.google.com or mapquest.com, then display a map that shows the address **568 Natoma St., San Francisco, CA**. Copy the URI in your browser's address box, or if the URI in the address bar contains no text after the server name, explore the page for a way to create a link containing the information you've entered, such as the Link link on maps.google.com. Verify that the link text begins with http, then copy it.

d. Add an absolute link to the phrase "Location" in the nav bar using the URI you copied. If necessary, replace any occurences of ampersand (&) with the appropriate character reference. Add code to specify that the target should open in a new window, then save your work. Reload nearby.html in your browser.

e. Use a search engine to locate a Web page related to each of the topics in the What's Nearby list, then link the corresponding text to the site you identified. Save your work, then open nearby.html in your browser and check all the links.

Independent Challenge 3 (continued)

Advanced Challenge Exercise

- Open a Web site that provides a link shortening service, such as bit.ly or tinyurl.com. Paste the location URI you copied above into the appropriate box on the Web page, then click the associated button to generate the shortened URI.
- Copy the shortened URI, return to nearby.html in your text editor, then replace the href value for the link you created on the phrase "Location" in the nav bar with the shortened URI you copied. Save your work, reload nearby.html in your browser, then verify that the Location link works correctly.
- Repeat the process above to shorten the link on each topic in the What's Nearby list. Save your work, then open nearby.html in your browser and check all the links.

f. Copy the code for the nav bar from nearby.html, then paste it into index.html beneath the h1 element.

g. Return to natoma.css in your text editor, then add four style rules using pseudo-classes to format the font color of a default link in the element with the id "mainnav" as **#213621**, a visited link as **#394D39**, a link with the mouse pointer over it as **black**, and an active link as **#394D39**. Ensure that the rules appear in your style sheet in the order specified.

h. Above the pseudo-class rules you just entered, add four style rules using pseudo-classes to format the font color of a default link as **#213621**, a visited link as **#526352**, a link with the mouse pointer over it as **black**, and an active link as **#526352**. Ensure that the rules appear in your style sheet in the order specified.

i. Save your work, return to your browser and clear your browser history if possible, reload index.html, and verify that the default font color is **white**, that the font color changes on rollovers and clicks, and that links that have been followed appear in a different color than unfollowed links.

j. Return to index.html in your text editor. Add an anchor with the name **main** to the first p element beneath the nav bar. Create a skip navigation link beneath the opening body tag that moves to the "main" anchor. Repeat for nearby.html, adding the anchor to the h2 element. Save your work on each file.

k. Reload each HTML file in your browser and test the skip navigation links. Figure E-23 shows nearby.html.

l. Return to index.html in your text editor, replace the div element enclosing the nav bar with a nav element, then add the following three lines of code immediately before the closing head tag:

FIGURE E-23

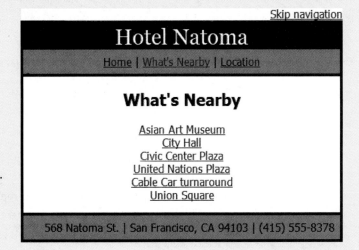

```
<!--[if lt IE 9]>
  <script src="scripts/semantic.js"></script>
<![endif]-->
```

m. Repeat the previous step for nearby.html.

n. Return to natoma.css in your text editor, remove all name-value pairs that reference colors, change the colors for all rules based on pseudo-classes to **black**, then save a copy of the file as **hnprint.css**.

o. Validate all your HTML and CSS documents.

p. If you have space on a Web server for publishing your documents, create a local root folder within the IC3 folder, move all the files and folders in the IC3 folder to the local root folder, upload the files to your Web publishing location, then open index.html in your browser from the published location and test the links.

q. Close your browser, then close your text editor.

Real Life Independent Challenge

This assignment builds on the personal Web site you have worked on in previous units. You will add links between the pages of your Web site, along with features to increase the accessibility of your navigation.

a. Copy your Web site files to the Unit E/RLIC folder on the drive and folder where you store your Data Files.

b. On your main Web page, create a nav bar including links to all the pages on your Web site, along with links to any relevant documents and external Web pages. If appropriate, designate one or more links to open in new windows or tabs. Copy the nav bar to the rest of the pages in your site.

c. Create pseudo-classes to set the font color of links in all four states.

d. For each of your Web pages that contains multiple sections, create a nav bar for moving within the page. Include a link at the end of each section that moves back to the top of the page. Add pseudo-classes for links in the page nav bar.

e. Add a skip link at the top of each page that moves to an anchor below the main nav bar. If you created page navigation anywhere on your site, update the links to move back to the top of the page to target the skip link. Add a third set of pseudo-classes to your style sheet above the ones you already created to format links that aren't children of the elements specified in the other pseudo-class rules.

f. Copy the scripts directory from the Unit E/Unit folder to the Unit E/RLIC folder, then add the script reference from Figure E-16 to the code of your all your Web pages. Enclose all your nav bars in nav elements.

g. Save changes to your style sheet document, save a copy using the name of your print style sheet, then take out name-value pairs that set color and change all colors in rules based on pseudo-classes to black.

h. Preview your Web pages in at least two browsers, then make any edits necessary for them to appear as you expected.

i. Validate all of your HTML and CSS documents and make any edits necessary to resolve any issues.

j. If you have space on a Web server for publishing your documents, create a local root folder within the RLIC folder, move all the files in the RLIC folder to the local root folder, upload the files to your Web publishing location, then open each Web page in your browser from the published location to verify that the upload was successful.

k. Close your browser, then close your text editor.

Visual Workshop

In your text editor, open the file HTM D-21.html from the Unit E/VW directory on the drive and folder where you store your Data Files and save it as **index.html**. Open HTM D-22.css, then save it as **revision.css**. Use your text editor to style the Web page to match the one shown in Figure E-24. Use the id **mainnav** for the nav bar. Link the text Location to a map showing the location listed at the bottom of the page. The target pages for the other links may be nonexistent pages. Use pseudo-classes to format all four states for the nav bar links and the skip link. Add the script reference from Figure E-16 to the head section of your Web page, then enclose the nav bar in a nav element. Add a paragraph element after the content shown that contains your first and last name and the text **HTML5 Unit E, Visual Workshop**. Validate your HTML and CSS code. If you have space on a Web server, create a local root folder within the VW folder, move both files to the local root folder, upload the file to your Web publishing location, then open the Web page in your browser from the published location. Close your browser and text editor.

FIGURE E-24

Inserting and Working with Images

Files You Will Need:

To view a list of files needed for this unit, see the Data Files Grid in the back of the book.

Just as in print media, images are integral in conveying information on the Web. You can use HTML to incorporate images into your Web pages and specify CSS properties to affect the way user agents display the images. Your design colleagues at Great Northern Sites have provided a logo image and several other graphics for the Lakeland Reeds B&B Web site. In this unit, you add the layout and presentational codes to add these images to the site.

OBJECTIVES

Evaluate image file types

Insert images

Align images

Control page flow

Insert a background image

Associate images with related text

Use images as links

Insert a favicon

Evaluating Image File Types

You can include many types of images, from company logos to photographs, on a Web page. Just as you can link to an external style sheet, you add an image to a Web page by linking to a separate file. While you may not be responsible for providing the image files themselves for inclusion on a Web page, designers who create the art may look to you as a Web developer for advice on aspects such as file format, size, and resolution. ▓▓▓▓▓ As you prepare to incorporate graphics into the Web site for Lakeland Reeds B&B, you review the basics of images in HTML documents.

DETAILS

To create optimal graphics for the Web, it's important to understand a few concepts:

- **File types**

  Images can currently be represented electronically in two ways: as bitmaps or as vectors. A **bitmap image** represents an image as a grid of dots and specifies the color of each dot. A **vector graphic** instead encodes the appearance of a graphic as geometric shapes. Many file formats are available that render bitmap or vector representations in different ways. The three most widely used formats on the Web are all different types of bitmap encoding. The **JPEG** or **JPG** format, named for the Joint Photographic Experts Group that created it, is optimized for images that contain many colors, such as photographs. **GIF**, an abbreviation for graphics interchange format, works best for art that contains limited numbers of colors and areas with defined borders between areas. As an added benefit, the GIF file type supports transparent pixels, allowing the page background or other elements to show through parts of an image.

  JPEG and GIF have been the standard Web formats for photos and drawn art, respectively, for years. Recently, though, user agent support has been increasing for two newer formats that offer their own advantages. **PNG**, short for Portable Network Graphics, was originally designed as a free alternative to GIF when GIF usage required licensing fees. While the patents on GIF have expired, PNG has won fans with its addition of an **alpha channel**, which allows graphics creators to specify the level of opacity for areas of a graphic, from totally transparent to totally opaque, or anywhere in between. More recently, the **Scalable Vector Graphics (SVG)** format has seen wider support in browsers. SVG is optimal for encoding line art; however, unlike the GIF or JPEG formats, which use bitmaps to encode graphics at specific dimensions, an SVG file can be displayed at different dimensions with no decrease in quality. Table F-1 summarizes support for the four main image formats in some of the most widely used Web browsers.

- **Resolution and size**

  When using any bitmap file formats, including JPEG, GIF, and PNG, it's important that an image is created and formatted with its use on the Web site in mind. All bitmap images are created to be displayed at a set resolution and size. **Resolution**, measured in **dots per inch (dpi)**, specifies how close the dots in the bitmap should appear on the output. While the standard for display on a monitor is 72 dpi, other media have different standards: for example, many home and office printers can print at 2400 dpi or greater. While a higher dpi image provides more detail, it also creates a file with a greater file size and takes up extra room on a Web page. Thus, it's important to save an image specifically for use on the Web to minimize download time and to ensure that the image fits in the page layout.

  The size of a bitmap image is measured in **pixels**, which are the individual dots that make up the image. Every bitmap image is created with a specific length and width. While a vector graphic can be scaled larger or smaller with no change in quality, bitmap graphics display optimally only at their original, or **native**, length and width, as shown in Figure F-1. Scaling an image to a smaller size than its native resolution negatively impacts the way the image is displayed; in addition, since a smaller bitmap is generally a smaller file size, displaying a file below its native resolution unnecessarily increases the amount of data users have to download. While scaling an image to a larger size than its native resolution decreases the amount of data that users have to download compared to the image's native size, it also results in markedly poor image quality. Thus, in addition to creating graphics with the correct resolution for the Web, it's important that designers generate them at the precise dimensions required for the layout.

FIGURE F-1: Scaling bitmaps

Image displayed larger than its native size

Image displayed smaller than its native size

Image displayed at its native size

Photo/Sasha Vodnik

TABLE F-1: Support for image formats in recent browser versions

format	Internet Explorer (IE)			Firefox	Chrome	Safari	Opera
	IE6 and earlier	IE7 and IE8	IE9 and later				
GIF	full	full	full	full	full	full	full	full
JPEG	full	full	full	full	full	full	full	full
PNG	limited; no alpha	limited	full	full	full	full	full	full
SVG	low	low	medium	medium	medium	high	high	high

Assessing the future of SVG

The most widely supported graphics formats—GIF, JPEG, and PNG—require external files created with image editors. SVG graphics, however, are written in a markup language similar to XML. As support for the format grows, you will be able to create simple graphics like you create style sheets: by creating external documents in a text editor and linking them to your Web pages. Browser makers are also beginning to incorporate support for SVG code within HTML documents, meaning that eventually you will have the option to embed graphics like you embed CSS.

Inserting Images

You add an image to an HTML document using the one-sided img element. The element must include two attributes: src, whose value is the path and filename of the image file to display, and alt, which specifies text to display in case the image is unavailable or needs to be read in user agents by software such as screen readers. Table F-2 details all available attributes for the img element. Like span and br, img elements are inline elements by default. You can wrap an img element in its own block element, such as a div element, and align it horizontally using standard block-level alignment techniques. For an image occurring within a paragraph of text, the bottom of an image is aligned with the bottom of the text, which is known as the **baseline**. You add the Lakeland Reeds B&B logo in place of the heading at the top of the page in the Web site. You also replace the bullets separating the sections of the contact information with decorative graphics.

STEPS

1. **In your text editor, open HTM F-1.html from the Unit F/Unit folder on the drive and folder where you store your Data Files, insert a blank line before the closing body tag, insert a paragraph element containing your first and last name and the text HTML5 Unit F, save it as index.html, repeat to save HTM F-2.html as rooms.html then use a CSS comment to add the same information to HTM F-3.css and save it as lakeland.css**

QUICK TIP
Be sure to type a space before the closing /.

2. **In index.html, locate the h1 element, delete the text Lakeland Reeds Bed & Breakfast, leaving the <h1> and </h1> tags, move the </h1> tag to a separate line at the same indent level, then on a blank line between the h1 tags, indent two additional spaces and type <img src="images/lakeland.gif" width="664" height="180" alt="Lakeland Reeds Bed and Breakfast" />**

   While the width and height attributes are not required, it's highly recommended that you use them to specify the native dimensions of the image. This ensures that if a visual user agent is unable for any reason to display the referenced image, it can maintain a corresponding amount of blank space, preserving the layout of your Web page. Width and height attributes are always in pixels, so it's not necessary to specify units. Figure F-2 shows the code for the img element.

3. **In the paragraph element at the bottom of the page containing contact information, replace the first occurrence of the character code • with <img src="images/flourish.gif" width="16" height="16" alt="" />, then repeat to replace the second occurrence of the character code with the same HTML code**

   Figure F-2 shows the completed code for adding images to the main Web page.

4. **Save your work, then return to lakeland.css in your text editor**

QUICK TIP
Don't make changes to the h1, h2, nav style rule.

5. **In the h1 style rule, remove all name–value pairs except font-size, then add the code margin: 0;**

6. **Save your work, then open index.html in your default browser**

   Figure F-3 shows index.html with images in a browser.

7. **Repeat Steps 2 through 4 to add the logo and decorative graphic to the corresponding elements in rooms.html, then preview your changes**

img element for the logo graphic

img elements replace special characters

```
index.html - Notepad
File  Edit  Format  View  Help
<!DOCTYPE html>
<html>
  <head>
    <meta charset="utf-8" />
    <title>Lakeland Reeds Bed &amp; Breakfast</title>
    <link rel="stylesheet" type="text/css" media="screen" href="lakeland.css" />
    <link rel="stylesheet" type="text/css" media="print" href="llprint.css" />
    <!--[if lt IE 9]>
    <script src="scripts/semantic.js"></script>
    <![endif]-->
  </head>
  <body>
    <p id="skipnav"><a href="#main">Skip navigation</a></p>
    <div id="box">
      <h1>
        <img src="images/lakeland.gif" width="664" height="180" alt="Lakeland Reeds Bed and Breakfast" />
      </h1>
      <nav id="mainnav">
        <p>
          <a href="index.html">Home</a> |
          <a href="aboutus.html">About Us</a> |
          <a href="rooms.html">Rooms</a> |
          <a href="reserve.html">Reservations</a> |
          <a href="http://bit.ly/dl8xGc" target="_blank">Local Weather</a> |
          <a href="http://bit.ly/cO7vcs" target="_blank">Directions</a>
        </p>
      </nav>
      <p id="main"><span class="callout">Lakeland Reeds</span> is a rustic bed and breakfast on Twin Lakes near
rural Marble, Minnesota. Convenient to US 2 and 169, the fresh air and quiet make for an ideal weekend escape from
the rush of city life.</p>
      <footer>
        <p>45 Marsh Grass Ln. <img src="images/flourish.gif" width="16" height="16" alt="" /> Marble, MN 55764 <img
src="images/flourish.gif" width="16" height="16" alt="" /> (218) 555-5253</p>
      </footer>
    </div>
  </body>
</html>
```

FIGURE F-3: Main Web page with images inserted

lakeland.gif image file

flourish.gif image file displayed twice

Unholy Vault Designs/Shutterstock.com

TABLE F-2: Attributes for the img element

attribute	value
src	path and filename for image file to display
alt	text to display or read in place of image
height width	native height and width of image file in pixels
longdesc	URI for a document that provides fuller alternative description of image

Creating useful alt text

The text you provide using the alt attribute for an image is an important accessibility element for your Web site. It's also significant from a usability perspective for users who are unable to download the image or who choose to browse without images. For graphics that include text, the text should be included in the value of the alt attribute, along with a description if it adds useful information. Photos and other graphics without text should include a description of the image in the alt value. Because there are many ways to describe any given image, it's important to identify what aspect or aspects of a graphic are relevant to the Web page, and focus on those aspects. Finally, if a graphic is merely presentational and doesn't add information to the Web page, include the alt attribute with nothing between the quotes. This lets screen readers know that the element isn't conveying information and that they can skip it, saving blind and visually impaired users from wasting time listening to text such as "stylized bullet" repeatedly while learning nothing about the page contents.

Aligning Images

HTML5 includes the semantic figure element to mark images that add information to a Web page. A user agent should be able to link the contents of a figure element and move them to another location (similar to an appendix in a book) without affecting the information conveyed by the Web page. Thus, a logo image would not be marked as a figure, because it's integral to stating the overall subject of each Web page. A picture, chart, or map illustrating the topic of a paragraph of text, however, would be marked as a figure. When integrating larger figures and other images with Web page contents, you can use the CSS float property to enable text or other Web page elements to flow around the figure. The left and right values of the float property align the top of the element with the top of the next element, and align the image horizontally with the left or right edge of the parent element, respectively. You add a photo of one of the rooms to complement the text on the main page and use the float property to flow the text around it. You also add figure elements containing images of each of the rooms on the Rooms page.

1. **In index.html below the nav element for the main nav bar, insert a new line and indent to match the nav element, type <figure id="main">, press [Enter] twice, indent to match the opening tag, type </figure>, then delete the attribute–value pair id="main" from the following p element**

2. **Move the insertion point to the blank line between the figure tags, indent two spaces more than the figure tags, then type <img src="images/sun.jpg" width="369" height="268" alt=" "/>**

   Because the image is decorative on this page rather than adding important information, you include an empty alt attribute to indicate that screen readers can ignore it, and that no substitute text needs to be displayed in a browser in case the image is unavailable.

3. **Save your changes, then reload the Web page in your browser**

   Because Web page elements are displayed sequentially from top to bottom by default, the browser displays sun.jpg aligned with the left side of the screen above the paragraph of text.

QUICK TIP
To make them easier to locate, the style rules in the style sheet have been grouped by selector type.

4. **Return to lakeland.css in your text editor, create a new style rule based on the figure selector, then add the name–value pairs display: block, float:right, margin: 0 0 0.5em 1em, and padding: 0**

   The value of "right" for the float property aligns the right edge of the image with the right edge of the parent element. Figure F-4 shows the completed code.

5. **Save your work, then reload the Web page in your browser**

   As Figure F-5 shows, the image is right-aligned, and the paragraph text flows around it, starting at the top of the image. Because the image is higher than the text of both elements that follow it, the contact information flows around the image as well.

6. **Return to rooms.html in your text editor, then insert the code for the four figure elements shown in Figure F-6 beneath the h3 headings**

TROUBLE
The Web page text may no longer match up with the images. You'll fix this in the next lesson.

7. **Save your work, open rooms.html in your browser, then scroll through the document to view the images**

   The style rule you created above based on the figure selector right-aligns these elements as well and flows the text that follows around them.

```
        font-family: tahoma, arial, helvetica, sans-serif;
    }
    figure {
        display: block;
        float: right;
        margin: 0 0 0.5em 1em;
        padding: 0;
    }
    footer {
```

float property takes element out of top-to-bottom flow of page and allows other page elements to appear next to it

FIGURE F-5: **Web page with image aligned**

Paragraphs below image flow to left

float: right name–value pair aligns element with right side of parent element and lets elements below it flow around it

Faithe Wempen/sycamoreknoll.com

FIGURE F-6: **Code for inserting images on Rooms Web page**

```
        </nav>
        <h3 id="sun">Sun Room</h3>
        <figure>
            <img src="images/sun.jpg" width="369" height="268" alt="a bedroom with large windows and a desk, dresser, and queen bed" />
        </figure>
        <p class="desc">with windows on three sides, the sunlight in this second-floor room supports a large selection of houseplants.</p>
        <p class="beds">1 queen bed.</p>
        <p class="toplink"><a href="#skipnav">Back to top</a></p>
        <h3 id="reed">Reed Room</h3>
        <figure>
            <img src="images/reed.jpg" width="370" height="277" alt="a bedroom with a tall window, a dresser with mirror, and a queen bed" />
        </figure>
        <p class="desc">This first-floor room looks out over the reeds on the edge of the lake and the water beyond.</p>
        <p class="beds">1 queen bed and 1 twin bed.</p>
        <p class="toplink"><a href="#skipnav">Back to top</a></p>
        <h3 id="tree">Treehouse</h3>
        <figure>
            <img src="images/tree.jpg" width="370" height="277" alt="a low-ceilinged bedroom with a woodgrain wall and a queen bed" />
        </figure>
        <p class="desc">A winding staircase takes you to your own private getaway at the top of the house, with view of the surrounding trees and meadows and
the lake.</p>
        <p class="beds">1 queen bed.</p>
        <p class="toplink"><a href="#skipnav">Back to top</a></p>
        <h3 id="garden">Garden Room</h3>
        <figure>
            <img src="images/garden.jpg" width="370" height="277" alt="a bedroom with ornate wood moldings and a magnifying lens perched above a fireplace" />
        </figure>
        <p class="desc">This room's French doors open onto our stone patio and flower garden.</p>
        <p class="beds">1 queen bed and 2 twin beds.</p>
        <p class="toplink"><a href="#skipnav">Back to top</a></p>
```

figure elements for four images

Floating figure elements in IE6

While recent versions of all major browsers can float elements without major issues, this is not the case for older browsers. Of particular note is Internet Explorer 6 (IE6), which is still in wide use in some large organizations and in some parts of the world. A bug in IE6 causes some floated elements to take up extra space on the page, changing the layout. It's important to know the browser preferences of the audience for any Web site you develop. If your audience included a large percentage of IE6 users, it would be important to understand this issue and implement methods that work around it. You can research this issue further by using a Web browser to search on "ie6 double margin bug".

Controlling Page Flow

The CSS float property enables a lot of possibilities for basic image alignment. However, in some situations, using float is not enough to create the layout you want. For instance, sometimes you want to ensure that text or another object follows a floated element, rather than running alongside it. You can control the flow of Web page elements more precisely with the CSS clear property, which prevents floated elements from being displayed to the left, right, or on either side of another element. **EXECUTE** You add the clear property to the paragraph containing contact information to make it appear beneath the image you added, as well as to the links that return users to the top of the page on the Rooms page.

STEPS

1. **Return to lakeland.css in your text editor**

2. **Locate the footer style rule, insert a new line before the closing curly brace, indent two spaces, then type clear: right;**

   Specifying the value "right" for the clear property prevents a floated element from being displayed to the right of the current element. Because the bed.jpg image currently is displayed to the right, this name–value pair will move the contact information below the image. Figure F-7 shows the clear property inserted in the style sheet.

3. **Save your work, then reload index.html in your browser**

   As Figure F-8 shows, the contact information is displayed below the image.

4. **Return to lakeland.css in your text editor**

5. **Insert a blank line before the closing } for the .toplink style rule, indent two spaces, then type clear:right;**

   Elements with the "toplink" class are the final elements in the room descriptions on the Rooms Web page. Adding a clear value to them ensures that they are displayed consistently at the right edge of the page content, and that the room descriptions are spaced equally.

6. **Save your work, then reload rooms.html in your browser**

   As Figure F-9 shows, the Back to top links are displayed below the figure elements for the rooms.

Obtaining permission for image use

Although it's possible to find and copy images from the Web for use on your own Web pages, it's important to make sure you have permission to use a given image before incorporating it into your designs. In addition to avoiding potential legal action for unauthorized use of someone else's work, it's a show of respect to photographers and designers to ask for permission to use their work.

For small projects, a photographer or designer may allow use in return for credit and a link to their site; larger professional sites usually need to pay a use fee and agree on terms of use. If you're hiring a designer to create artwork for your Web site, make sure your agreement specifies how long and in what context you or your organization may use the work.

```
footer {
  display: block;
  background: #B8944D;
  padding: 0.25em;
  margin: 0;
  clear: right;
}
```

clear property added
to style rule for
footer element

FIGURE F-8: Web page with clear property added

clear property causes footer
element to be displayed without
floated elements to its right

Unholy Vault Designs/Shutterstock.com
Faithe Wempen/sycamoreknoll.com

FIGURE F-9: Back to top links styled with clear property

Unholy Vault Designs/Shutterstock.com
Faithe Wempen/sycamoreknoll.com

Inserting a Background Image

In addition to specifying a color as the background for a Web page or Web page element, you can provide a path and filename for a background image using the background-image property. As with background colors, it's important to choose a background image that provides contrast with other Web page elements, especially text. Because user agents may display the same Web page in windows of different sizes, a given background image may not fill the entire window. In addition, it's best to minimize the sizes of background images to minimize download time for a Web page. User agents address both of these issues through the default behavior of **tiling** small background images, meaning that, like tiles on a floor or wall, the images are displayed repeatedly both across and down a page to fill up the browser window. The designers have provided you with a background image for the Lakeland Reeds B&B Web site. You will preserve a background color behind the current contents so the image shows only at the edges of the page, maintaining readability.

STEPS

1. **In your browser, open the file lake.jpg from the Unit F/Unit/images folder**
   The image is tall and narrow.

2. **Return to lakeland.css in your text editor**

3. **In the body style rule, insert a blank line before the closing }, indent two spaces, then type background: url("images/lake.jpg");**
   The value for the background property always starts with the text "url". The relative path, if necessary, and the filename for the background image are enclosed in parentheses and either single or double quotes.

QUICK TIP

The page contents are within a div element with the id "box" that has a background color of "white"; this prevents the background image from appearing behind the text.

4. **Insert a blank line above the code you just entered, indent two spaces, then type background: #6e93c8;**
   You specify a background color for user agents that don't display images, or for situations where the background image file is unavailable. The background color you specified matches the light blue at the top of the image, preserving both the contrast for the skip link and the overall color scheme of the Web site. When name–value pairs conflict, the one that occurs later in the rule takes precedence; you specify the background color first and the image second to ensure the image is displayed if it's available, and that the color value is present as a backup. Figure F-10 shows the code for the background color and image.

5. **Beneath the closing } for the a:active style rule, add style rules to change the colors for #skipnav a:link to white, #skipnav a:visited to white, #skipnav a:hover to #ff9, and #skipnav a:active to white**
   Because the background for the skip link is changing from a light to dark color, you change the text color to preserve contrast.

6. **Save your work, then reload index.html in your browser**
   As Figure F-11 shows, the background image appears as the background for the Web page. The image is repeated from left to right to fill the entire width of the browser window.

```
/* Lakeland Reeds Bed and Breakfast */
@font-face {
  font-family: 'CuprumFFURegular';
  src: url('fonts/Cuprum-webfont.eot');
  src: local('☺'), url('fonts/Cuprum-webfont.woff') format('woff'), url('fonts/(
webfont.svg#webfontKLktnWy4') format('svg');
  font-weight: normal;
  font-style: normal;
  }
body {
  padding: 0;
  margin: 0;
  font-family: tahoma, arial, helvetica, sans-serif;
  background: #6e93c8;
  background: url("images/lake.jpg");
  }
figure {
  display: block;
```

Background color and image
added using background property

FIGURE F-11: Main Web page with background image

Tall, narrow
background
image is
tiled to fill
the entire
screen

Unholy Vault Designs/Shutterstock.com
Faithe Wempen/sycamoreknoll.com
Photo/Sasha Vodnik

Styling an image with opacity

Recent versions of all major browsers support opacity values for images. By changing the opacity of an image, you can increase its contrast with other page elements or make it more closely match a site's design. The standard CSS3 syntax uses the "opacity" property with a decimal value from 0 (fully transparent) to 1 (fully opaque). For instance, to set 50% opacity, you could use the code

```
opacity: 0.5;
```

Older versions of Internet Explorer don't support this syntax, however, and require an additional name–value pair using a Microsoft-specific property:

```
filter: alpha(opacity=number);
```

where *number* is a percentage from 0 (fully transparent) to 100 (fully opaque).

Associating Images with Related Text

In addition to specifying alternative text for an image with the alt attribute, you can associate other types of text with an image. Many images benefit from a text caption that provides context, explanation, or credit. To associate caption text with an img element, you place the text in a figcaption element that is nested within the figure element for the image. You can also specify additional information using the title attribute, which is supported by the img element as well as most other HTML elements. Most visual user agents display the value of this attribute as floating text when a user moves the mouse pointer over the associated element. When no title attribute is specified, some browsers display the alt text as a floating tooltip instead. Because the images on the Rooms Web page are already explained by the surrounding content, you decide not to add captions to them. However, you add a caption to the image on the main page of the Web site. You also create title attributes with empty values for images with alt text to prevent the alt text from being displayed as tooltips.

STEPS

1. **Return to index.html in your text editor, insert a new line beneath the img tag for the file sun.jpg, indent the same number of spaces as the img element, then type**
   <figcaption>The Sun Room</figcaption>
   The figcaption element marks the text it contains as a caption for the associated image within the figure element.

2. **Save your work, return to lakeland.css in your text editor, then add a name–value pair to the figure style rule to set text-align to center**

QUICK TIP
The display property lets you change the behavior of an element from inline to block or vice versa.

3. **Create a new style rule using the figcaption selector that sets the margin and the padding to 0, then add the name–value pair display: block;**

4. **Save your work, then refresh index.html in your Web browser**
   The text "The Sun Room" is displayed beneath the image in the middle of the Web page.

5. **Return to index.html in your text editor, position the insertion point just before the word The in the caption you created, type <a href="rooms.html#sun">, position the insertion point just after the word Room, then type </a>**
   Because users who see the photo might want to know more about the room shown, you format the caption as a link to the description of the room on the rooms.html Web page. Figure F-12 shows the completed code for the figcaption element.

6. **Save your work, reload index.html in your Web browser, then click the text The Sun Room and verify that that Sun Room section of rooms.html opens**
   Figure F-13 shows the index.html page containing the caption.

7. **Return to index.html in your text editor, position the insertion point after the final " in the img element for lakeland.gif, press [Spacebar], type title="", then save your work**

8. **Repeat Step 7 in rooms.html for the logo and for the img elements for sun.jpg, reed.jpg, tree.jpg, and garden.jpg**
   Figure F-14 shows the completed code for each img element.

9. **Reload rooms.html in your Web browser, then verify that no floating text appears when you move your mouse pointer over the images**

figcaption element
associates text with an
image in a figure

```
<figure id="main">
    <img src="images/sun.jpg" width="369" height="268" alt="" />
<figcaption><a href="rooms.html#sun">The Sun Room</a></figcaption>
</figure>
```

FIGURE F-13: **Figure caption in Web page**

Unholy Vault Designs/Shutterstock.com
Faithe Wempen/sycamoreknoll.com
Photo/Sasha Vodnik

Figure caption is linked
to Web page providing
more details about the
pictured room

FIGURE F-14: **Code with title attributes added**

logo image
for all files

Rooms:
sun.jpg,
reed.jpg, tree.
jpg, and
garden.jpg

```
<h1>
    <img src="images/lakeland.gif" width="664" height="180" alt="Lakeland Reeds Bed and Breakfast" title="" />
</h1>
```

```
<h3 id="sun">Sun Room</h3>
<figure>
    <img src="images/sun.jpg" width="369" height="268" alt="a bedroom with large windows and a desk, dresser,
and queen bed" title="" />
</figure>
    <p class="desc">With windows on three sides, the sunlight in this second-floor room supports a large
selection of houseplants.</p>
    <p class="beds">1 queen bed.</p>
    <p class="toplink"><a href="#skipnav">Back to top</a></p>
<h3 id="reed">Reed Room</h3>
<figure>
    <img src="images/reed.jpg" width="370" height="277" alt="a bedroom with a tall window, a dresser with
mirror, and a queen bed" title="" />
</figure>
    <p class="desc">This first-floor room looks out over the reeds on the edge of the lake and the water
beyond.</p>
    <p class="beds">1 queen bed and 1 twin bed.</p>
    <p class="toplink"><a href="#skipnav">Back to top</a></p>
<h3 id="tree">Treehouse</h3>
<figure>
    <img src="images/tree.jpg" width="370" height="277" alt="a low-ceilinged bedroom with a woodgrain wall and
a queen bed" title="" />
</figure>
    <p class="desc">A winding staircase takes you to your own private getaway at the top of the house, with view
of the surrounding trees and meadows and the lake.</p>
    <p class="beds">1 queen bed.</p>
    <p class="toplink"><a href="#skipnav">Back to top</a></p>
<h3 id="garden">Garden Room</h3>
<figure>
    <img src="images/garden.jpg" width="370" height="277" alt="a bedroom with ornate wood moldings and a
magnifying lens perched above a fireplace" title="" />
</figure>
    <p class="desc">This room's French doors open onto our stone patio and flower garden.</p>
    <p class="beds">1 queen bed and 2 twin beds.</p>
    <p class="toplink"><a href="#skipnav">Back to top</a></p>
```

Using Images as Links

You can add a link to an image in an HTML document by enclosing the img element in an a element. By default, many visual user agents add a colored border around a linked image to display the color associated with its link state. As with text links, you can use pseudo-classes to modify the colors, or you can use CSS to remove the border altogether. Many Web sites add links to the logo image on each page to return to the main page of the site. You link the logo image on each page back to index.html to provide an extra shortcut for visitors to the site.

STEPS

1. **Return to rooms.html in your text editor**

2. **Position the insertion point before the opening < of the img tag for the lakeland.gif image near the top of the document, then type <a href="index.html">**

3. **Position the insertion point after the closing > of the img tag, type </a>, then save your work**

   Figure F-15 shows the final link code.

4. **Return to lakeland.css in your text editor, then insert a new style rule using the img selector that sets the border value to 0**

   This rule prevents a colored border from being displayed around linked images. Figure F-16 shows the style rule.

5. **Save your work, refresh rooms.html in your browser, then click the logo image at the top of the Web page**

   The main page of the Lakeland Reeds B&B Web site opens.

FIGURE F-15: a element enclosing img element

```
    <div id="box">
      <h1>
        <a href="index.html"><img src="images/lakeland.gif" width="664" height="180" alt="Lakeland Reeds Bed and
Breakfast" title="" /></a>
      </h1>
      <nav id="mainnav">
```

Opening and closing a tags surround img element

FIGURE F-16: New style rule based on img selector

```
img {
   border: 0;
   }
```


Inserting preformatted code for linked images

Many Web sites, such as social networks, make images containing their logos available for use on personal or organizational Web sites to facilitate linking. Often these sites provide HTML code that you can copy and paste directly into your Web page code. In many cases this code is nothing more than an img element with an href attribute referencing a publicly available graphic hosted on the target site, along with an a element linking to a specific page on the site. Thus, as long as the site's user agreement allows it, you can use any of the styles and techniques that you'd use for other images and links to style this code to fit your site.

Inserting a Favicon

Many user agents allow Web page authors to specify the icon associated with a Web page in the address bar and on the bookmark or favorites menu and bar. This custom icon, known as a **favicon**, is a graphic file 16 pixels in width by 16 pixels in height, saved in the .ico format, and named favicon.ico. You can specify a favicon for all the pages on a Web site by placing the favicon.ico in the root folder for the Web site. You can also specify a different favicon on an individual page using the link element to reference the appropriate .ico file. Because user agents don't always recognize the file in the root folder, it's best to add link elements as well to ensure that your favicon is accessible to users of as many user agents as possible. The art department has created a favicon, which you add to the Lakeland Reeds B&B Web site.

STEPS

1. **In your file manager, navigate to the Unit F/Unit folder on the drive and folder where you store your Data Files**

2. **Make a copy of the file HTM F-4.ico, then rename the copy favicon.ico**

3. **Return to index.html in your text editor, then insert a blank line beneath the link element for the second external style sheet**

4. **Indent four spaces, type <link rel="shortcut icon" href="favicon.ico" />, then save your work**

   Figure F-17 shows the code for the link element inserted in the document.

5. **Reload index.html in your Web browser, then examine the address bar and the browser title bar or tab for the Lakeland Reeds favicon, which resembles the icon you inserted in the contact information at the bottom of the page**

   Figure F-18 shows the favicon in a browser. However, some browsers show favicons only for Web sites accessed over the Internet and don't look for the icons for local files.

6. **Repeat Steps 3 and 4 for rooms.html**

7. **Return to lakeland.css in your text editor, save your work, save a copy as llprint.css, remove all name–value pairs that specify color as well as the pair that specifies the background image, change all the colors in style rules based on pseudo-classes to black, then save your work**

8. **Validate the code for your Web pages and your style sheet, then make changes as necessary to fix any errors**

9. **If you have space on a Web server for publishing your documents, create a local root folder within the Unit folder, move all the files in the Unit folder to the local root folder, then upload the files to your Web publishing location**

10. **Open index.html in your browser from the published location to verify that the upload was successful, check the address bar and the browser title bar or tab for the Lakeland Reeds favicon, then navigate to the rooms.html to verify the upload and the favicon**

```
index.html - Notepad
File  Edit  Format  View  Help
<!DOCTYPE html>
<html>
  <head>
    <meta charset="utf-8" />
    <title>Lakeland Reeds Bed &amp; Breakfast</title>
    <link rel="stylesheet" type="text/css" media="screen" href="lakeland.css" />
    <link rel="stylesheet" type="text/css" media="print" href="llprint.css" />
    <link rel="shortcut icon" href="favicon.ico" />
    <!--[if lt IE 9]>
      <script src="scripts/semantic.js"></script>
    <![endif]-->
  </head>
```

link element associates favicon
with Web page in browsers that
don't support the other method

FIGURE F-18:

Customized
favicon for the
Lakeland Reeds
B&B Web site

Unholy Vault Designs/Shutterstock.com
Photo/Sasha Vodnik

HTML5 and CSS3

Labeling text appropriately

Optimizing your use of the figcaption element and the alt and title attributes of the image tag requires examining the purpose of any image-related text you want to add to your Web pages. As a general rule, alt text should describe an image without adding additional information, as this text is intended to be able to substitute for the image. A caption can add information not provided by surrounding page content. The title attribute is generally used to provide explanation or additional information if a user seeks it out. While increasing the resources available to your site's users is often helpful, remember that in some instances, excluding one or more of these types of associated text can actually increase your sites usability or accessibility.

Practice

For current SAM information, including versions and content details, visit SAM Central (http://www.cengage.com/samcentral). If you have a SAM user profile, you may have access to hands-on instruction, practice, and assessment of the skills covered in this unit. Since various versions of SAM are supported throughout the life of this text, check with your instructor for the correct instructions and URL/Web site for accessing assignments.

Concepts Review

Refer to Figure F-19.

FIGURE F-19

Unholy Vault Designs/Shutterstock.com
Faithe Wempen/sycamoreknoll.com
Photo/Sasha Vodnik

1. **Which item is styled by providing a url value for the background property?**
2. **Which item is created using the figcaption element?**
3. **Which item is styled using the float property?**
4. **Which item is styled using the clear property?**
5. **Which item is an inline image?**
6. **Which item is created using the link element?**

Match each term with the statement that best describes it.

7. **native**
8. **baseline**
9. **resolution**
10. **pixel**
11. **alpha channel**

a. specifies how close the dots in a bitmap should appear on the output
b. one of the dots that make up a bitmap image
c. another term for the original dimensions of a bitmap image
d. allows graphics creators to specify the level of opacity for areas of a graphic
e. the bottom of a line of text

Select the best answer from the list of choices.

12. **Which type of image is represented as a grid of dots and their colors?**
    - **a.** SVG
    - **b.** bitmap
    - **c.** vector
    - **d.** native

13. **Which type of image encodes the appearance of a graphic as geometric shapes?**
    - **a.** bitmap
    - **b.** GIF
    - **c.** vector
    - **d.** JPEG

14. **Which image type is best for photographs?**
    - **a.** GIF
    - **b.** JPEG
    - **c.** PNG
    - **d.** SVG

15. **Which is the most widely supported format for images with limited colors and defined borders between areas?**
    - **a.** GIF
    - **b.** JPEG
    - **c.** PNG
    - **d.** SVG

16. **Which attribute do you use to specify text to display in case an image is unavailable or to be read in user agents by programs such as screen readers?**
    - **a.** figcaption
    - **b.** href
    - **c.** title
    - **d.** alt

17. **Which property enables text or other Web page elements to flow around an element?**
    - **a.** float
    - **b.** clear
    - **c.** alt
    - **d.** title

18. **Which property prevents floated elements from being displayed to the left, right, or on both sides of an element?**
    - **a.** float
    - **b.** clear
    - **c.** alt
    - **d.** title

Skills Review

1. **Insert images.**
   a. In your text editor, open HTM F-5.html from the Unit F/Review folder on the drive and folder where you store your Data Files. Insert a blank line before the closing body tag, then insert a paragraph element containing your first and last name and the text **HTML5 Unit F, Skills Review**. Save the file as **index.html**, then repeat to save HTM F-6.html as **history.html** and HTM F-7.html as **location.html**. In HTM F-8.css add a comment containing your first and last name and the text **HTML5 Unit F, Skills Review**, then save the file as **bigj.css**.
   b. In index.html, insert opening and closing div tags with the id **logo** just before the h1 element at the same indent level on separate lines, then on a blank line between the div tags, indent two additional spaces and add an img element that references the file **images/bigjs.gif**. Specify a height and a width of **225**, then add **Big J's Deep Dish Pizza** as alt text.
   c. Save your work, then open index.html in your default browser.
   d. Repeat Step b to add the logo element and graphic to the corresponding location in history.html and location.html, then preview your changes.

Skills Review (continued)

2. Align images.

   a. Return to bigj.css in your text editor.

   b. Create a new style rule based on the logo id selector, then add the name–value pair **float: right;**.

   c. Save your work, then reload index.html in your browser.

   d. Return to history.html in your text editor, locate the p element that begins "Jan has added two locations"… then insert the following code above it:

```
<figure>
  <img src="images/slices.jpg" width="350" height="228" alt="A red banner reading Pizza next to a
neon sign with the words Fresh Hot Slices" />
</figure>
```

   e. Return to bigj.css in your text editor.

   f. Create a new style rule based on the figure selector, then set the display value to **block**, the float value to **left**, the padding to **0 0.5em 0.25em 0.5em**, the margin to **0**, and text-align to **center**.

   g. Create a new style rule for img elements within figure elements, then set the margin and padding to **0**.

   h. Save your work, reload history.html in your browser, then scroll down to verify that the figure you inserted is left-aligned with text flowing along the right side.

3. Control page flow.

   a. Return to bigj.css in your text editor.

   b. Locate the #awards style rule, then add the clear property with a value that prevents a floated element from being displayed to the right.

   c. Save your work, then reload index.html in your browser.

4. Insert a background image.

   a. In your browser, open the file brick.jpg from the Unit F/Review/images folder.

   b. Return to bigj.css in your text editor.

   c. In the body style rule, insert a name–value pair that sets **brick.jpg** as the background image for the site.

   d. Insert a blank line above the code you just entered, then add a name–value pair to set the background color to **white**.

   e. Using the #skiplink selector, add a new rule style rule that sets the background to **white** and adds **0.25em** of padding to all sides.

   f. Save your work, then reload index.html in your browser.

5. Associate images with related text.

   a. Return to history.html in your text editor, then beneath the img tag for the file slices.jpg, type **\<figcaption\> Big J's famous neon sign\</figcaption\>**.

   b. Save your work, then return to bigj.css in your text editor.

   c. Using the figcaption selector, create a new style rule that sets the margin and the padding to **0**, font-weight to **bold**, and display to **block**.

   d. Save your work, then refresh history.html in your Web browser.

   e. Return to index.html in your text editor, add the title attribute to the img tag for bigjs.gif with a null value (""), then save your work.

   f. Repeat Step e for the logo images in history.html and location.html, and for the slices.jpg image in history.html, then save your work.

   g. Reload index.html in your Web browser, verify that no tooltip appears when you move your mouse pointer over the logo image, then repeat to test the images in history.html and location.html.

Skills Review (continued)

6. **Use images as links.**

   a. Return to history.html in your text editor.

   b. Add a link to the bigjs.gif img element that opens index.html, then save your work.

   c. In bigj.css, add a style rule based on the img selector that sets the border property to 0.

   d. Refresh history.html in your browser, then click the logo image at the top of the Web page to test the link.

   e. Repeat Steps b and c to add a link to the img element for the logo graphic in location.html.

7. **Insert a favicon.**

   a. In your file manager, navigate to the Unit F/Review folder on the drive and folder where you store your Data Files, then rename the file HTM F-9.ico as **favicon.ico**.

   b. Return to index.html in your text editor, then below the existing link elements add a new link element that links to favicon.ico as a shortcut icon.

   c. Reload index.html in your Web browser, then examine the address bar and the browser title bar or tab for the Big J's favicon, which resembles the red J in the logo graphic, as shown in Figure F-20. (You may not see the icon unless you view your Web site through an Internet connection.)

   d. Repeat Steps b and c for history.html and location.html. Figure F-21 shows history.html.

   e. Return to bigj.css in your text editor, save your work, save a copy as **bjprint.css**, remove all name–value pairs that specify color as well as the pair that specifies the background image, change all the colors in style rules based on pseudo-classes to black, then save your work.

   f. Validate the code for all your Web pages and your style sheet, then make changes as necessary to fix any errors.

   g. If you have space on a Web server for publishing your documents, create a local root folder within the Review folder, move all the files and folders in the Review folder to the local root folder, then upload the files and folders to your Web publishing location.

   h. Open index.html in your browser from the published location to verify that the upload was successful, check the address bar and the browser title bar or tab for the Big J's favicon, then navigate to the remaining pages to verify the uploads and the favicon.

FIGURE F-20

Xtremer/Shutterstock.com

FIGURE F-21

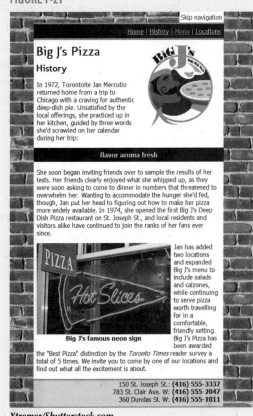

Xtremer/Shutterstock.com
Photo/Sasha Vodnik

Independent Challenge 1

Sarah Nguyen, the owner of the Spotted Wren Garden Center, has provided you with a version of the company logo for the Web site, as well as related photos and a favicon. You add these images to the company's Web site.

   a. Open HTM F-10.html from the Unit F/IC1 folder in your text editor. Insert a blank line before the closing body tag, then insert a paragraph element containing your first and last name and the text **HTML5 Unit F, Independent Challenge 1**. Save the file as **index.html**, then repeat to save HTM F-11.html as **hours.html** and HTM F-12.html as **resource.html**. Open HTM F-13.css, below the existing comment at the top of the document, add another comment with your first and last name and the text **HTML5 Unit F, Independent Challenge 1**. Save the file as **spotwren.css**.

Independent Challenge 1 (continued)

b. In index.html, replace the contents of the h1 element with an img element referencing the file **images/spotwren.gif**. Specify a width of **864** and a height of **184**, and add **Spotted Wren Garden Center** as the alt text. Repeat for hours.html and resource.html, then save your work.

c. In spotwren.css, create a rule based on the "h1 img" selector that specifies the value **block** for the display property. Save your work, then preview all three Web pages in your browser.

d. In index.html, below the closing tag for the nav element, add a figure element. Add an id attribute with the value **main**, then delete the identical attribute–value pair from the p element below. Within the figure element, add an image element that references the file **images/quince.jpg**. Specify a width of **350** and a height of **233**, and enter a **small red flower** as alt text. Save your work, then refresh the page in your browser.

e. Return to spotwren.css, then add a style rule based on the figure selector that specifies a display value of block, and a margin and a padding of **0**. Add a second style rule based on the figure img selector that sets margin and padding to **0** and specifies a float value of right. Add a property to the footer style rule that prevents the element from being displayed with a floated element to its right.

f. Return to hours.html, then repeat Step d to add an img element that references **images/cone.jpg** and specifies a width of **232**, a height of **350**, and **a monarch butterfly perched on a purple coneflower** as alt text. Repeat for resource.html to reference **images/flowers.jpg**, specifying a width of **150**, a height of **225**, and **a cluster of purple coneflowers** as alt text.

g. Return to spotwren.css in your text editor, then add a background property to the body style rule that sets the image file located at **images/grass.jpg** as the background. Insert a name–value pair before the one you just inserted that sets the background color to **green** in case the background image is unavailable. Add a property to the #box style rule to set the background color of the element to **white**. Save your work, then refresh each Web page in your browser.

h. Return to spotwren.css in your text editor, then add the same name–value pairs you added to the body style rule in Step g to the #skipnav style rule. Add a name–value pair to the #skiplink style rule that sets the background to **white**. Save your work, then reload index.html in your browser to verify that the skip link is easily readable.

i. Add the title attribute with an empty value to the img elements on all three Web pages, then save your work.

j. In your file manager, navigate to the Unit F/IC1 folder, make a copy of the file HTM F-14.ico, then rename the copy **favicon.ico**. Return to index.html in your text editor, then add a link element that references favicon.ico as a favicon. Repeat for hours.html and resource.html. Save your work, then preview the files in your Web browser. Figure F-22 shows the main Web page.

k. Return to spotwren.css in your text editor, remove all name–value pairs that reference colors, change all colors in rules based on pseudo-classes to **black**, then save a copy of the file as **swprint.css**.

l. Validate all your HTML and CSS documents.

m. If you have space on a Web server for publishing your documents, create a local root folder within the IC1 folder, move all the files and folders in the IC1 folder to the local root folder, upload the files to your Web publishing location, then open all three Web pages in your browser from the published location.

n. Close your browser, then close your text editor.

FIGURE F-22

For your year-round garden and yard needs

Looking for something unusual or hard to find?

Ask us!

548 N. 58th St. • Omaha, NE 68132 • (402) 555-9736

Weldon Schloneger/Shutterstock.com
Maxim Tupikov/Shutterstock.com
Xtremer/Shutterstock.com

Independent Challenge 2

You incorporate the logo for the Murfreesboro Recreational Soccer League into the organizational Web site that you are creating. You also add images from some of the groups events.

a. Open HTM F-15.html from the Unit F/IC2 folder in your text editor. Insert a blank line before the closing body tag, then insert a paragraph element containing your first and last name and the text **HTML5 Unit F, Independent Challenge 2**. Save the file as **index.html**, then repeat to save HTM F-16.html as **started.html** and HTM F-17.html as **schedule.html**. Open HTM F-18.css, below the existing comment at the top of the document, add another comment your first and last name and the text **HTML5 Unit F, Independent Challenge 2**. Save the file as **mrsl.css**.

Advanced Challenge Exercise

- In your file manager, navigate to the Unit F/IC2/images folder. Click jump.jpg, then in a blank document in your text editor or on a sheet of paper, note the height and width displayed. If necessary, in Windows right-click the file and click Properties, or on a Mac, control-click the file and click Get Info to view the dimensions.
- Close the properties or info window if necessary, then double-click jump.jpg to open it in your default image viewer. Study the image, then write a description of less than 15 words in your text document or on your sheet of paper. Close the image.
- Repeat the previous two bullets for kick.jpg and mrsl.gif, being sure to include any text in an image in your description.

b. In index.html, beneath the nav element insert a div element with the id **logo** containing an img element that references the file **mrsl.gif** in the images folder. Specify height, width, and alt values based on the information you recorded above, or use the following values: height: **376**; width: **198**; and alt: **Murfreesboro Recreational Soccer League**.

c. In mrsl.css, create a rule based on the **#logo** img selector that specifies the value **block** for the **display** property and floats the image on the left side of the parent element. Save your work, then preview the Web page in your browser.

d. In started.html, beneath the h2 element insert a figure element containing an img element that references the file **kick.jpg** in the images folder. Specify height, width, and alt values based on the information you recorded above, or use the following values: height: **350**; width: **233**; and alt: **a soccer player about to kick a ball**. Repeat for schedule.html, placing the figure element above the element with id pagenav and referencing the file **jump.jpg.**, using the values you determined or the following: height: **350**; width: **526**; and alt: **two soccer players vying for control of a ball**.

e. Return to mrsl.css, then add a style rule based on the **figure** selector that sets display to **block**, floats the element on the right, and specifies margin of **0** and padding of **1em 0 0.25em 0.5em**. Create a second style rule based on the **footer** selector that prevents the element from being displayed with a floated element to its left. Save your work, then preview all three Web pages.

f. Return to mrsl.css in your text editor, then add a background property to the body style rule that sets the image file located at **images/grass.jpg** as the background. Insert a name–value pair before the one you just inserted that sets the background color to **green** in case the background image is unavailable. Add a property to the #box style rule to set the background color of the element to **white**. Save your work, then refresh each Web page in your browser.

g. Return to mrsl.css in your text editor, then add the same name–value pairs you added to the body style rule in Step f to the #skipnav style rule. Add a name–value pair to the #skiplink style rule that sets the background to **black**. At the bottom of the style sheet, create style rules for the #skipnav element based on the four link pseudo-classes, setting the link color to **white** in each state. Save your work, then reload index.html in your browser to verify that the skip link is easily readable.

h. Add the title attribute with an empty value to the img elements on all three Web pages, then save your work.

HTML5 and CSS3

Independent Challenge 2 (continued)

i. In your file manager, navigate to the Unit F/IC2 folder, make a copy of the file HTM F-19.ico, then rename the copy **favicon.ico**. Return to index.html in your text editor, then add a link element that references favicon.ico as a favicon. Repeat for started.html and schedule.html. Save your work, then preview the files in your Web browser. Figure F-23 shows the main Web page, and Figure F-24 shows the Getting Started page.

j. Return to mrsl.css in your text editor, remove all name–value pairs that reference colors, change all colors in rules based on pseudo-classes to **black**, then save a copy of the file as **mrsprint.css**.

k. Validate all your HTML and CSS documents.

l. If you have space on a Web server for publishing your documents, create a local root folder within the IC2 folder, move all the files and folders in the IC2 folder to the local root folder, upload the files to your Web publishing location, then open all three Web pages in your browser from the published location.

m. Close your browser, then close your text editor.

FIGURE F-23

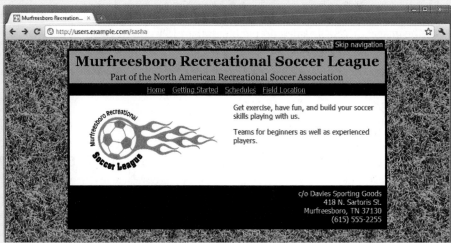

Xtremer/Shutterstock.com

FIGURE F-24

Lario Tus/Shutterstock.com
Xtremer/Shutterstock.com

Inserting and Working with Images

Independent Challenge 3

Diego Merckx, the manager of Hotel Natoma, has provided you with a Web-ready version of the facility's logo as well as photos of a few local attractions. You incorporate these into the hotel's Web site.

a. Open HTM F-20.html from the Unit F/IC3 folder in your text editor. Insert a blank line before the closing body tag, then insert a paragraph element containing your first and last name and the text **HTML5 Unit F, Independent Challenge 3**. Save the file as **index.html**, then repeat to save HTM F-21.html as **nearby.html**. Open HTM F-22.css, below the existing comment at the top of the document, add another comment with your first and last name and the text **HTML5 Unit F, Independent Challenge 3**. Save the file as **natoma.css**.

b. In index.html, replace the contents of the h1 element with an img element that references **images/natoma.gif**. Specify a width of **368**, a height of **65**, and alt text of **Hotel Natoma**. Repeat for nearby.html. Add a style rule to the style sheet to style img elements within h1 elements, setting the display to **block**, the padding to **0**, and the margin to **0 auto**.

c. In index.html, above the p element containing contact information, add a figure element containing an img element referencing **images/bridge.jpg**. Specify a width of **350**, a height of **232**, and the **Golden Gate Bridge** as alt text. Add a property to make the figure part of the center class, then add a style rule for the center class to the style sheet, setting the padding to **0** and the margin to **0 auto**. Create a second rule to style any img element within an element in the center class, setting the padding to **0 0 2em 0** and the margin to **0**. Create a third rule for figure elements to set the display property to **block**.

Advanced Challenge Exercise

- In nearby.html, add a figure element containing an img element that references **images/asian_sm.jpg**, specifying a width of **150**, height of **89**, and **front facade of the Asian Art Museum** as alt text. Add a figcaption element before the closing figure tag containing the text **Asian Art Museum**. Repeat to create a second figure element referencing **images/cable_sm.jpg**, with the same dimensions, a cable car as alt text, and **Cable Cars** as the content of the figcaption element.

- Specify a class of **right** for both figure elements added in the previous step, then add a rule to the style sheet using the **right** class selector, setting the margin to **0 1em 0 0**, padding to **0**, float to **right**, and **clear** to right. Create another rule that applies to images within an element in the right class, setting the display to **block** and padding and margin to **0**. Create another rule based on the figcaption element that centers text and sets the margin and padding to **0**.

- Add a link to the asian_sm.jpg image with a target of **images/asian_lg.jpg**. Add the same link to the text within the figcaption element for this image. Repeat for the cable_sm.jpg image, linking the image and the figcaption text to **images/cable_lg.jpg**. (*Note*: the link to the text should go within the figcaption element, not outside of it.)

- Add a title attribute to each image with a value of **Click to enlarge**.

- Save your work, open nearby.html in your browser, move the pointer over one of the images you inserted to verify that the text **Click to enlarge** appears, then click the first image to verify a larger version of the image opens in the browser. Return to the nearby.html page, then repeat to test the link on the caption and both links for the second image.

d. Add the title attribute with an empty value to the logo img elements on both Web pages and to the bridge image on the main page, then save your work.

Independent Challenge 3 (continued)

e. In your file manager, navigate to the Unit F/IC3 folder, make a copy of the file HTM F-23.ico, then rename the copy **favicon.ico**. Return to index.html in your text editor, then add a link element that references favicon.ico as a favicon. Repeat for nearby.html. Save your work, then preview the files in your Web browser. Figure F-25 shows the main Web page, and Figure F-26 shows the What's Nearby page.

f. Return to natoma.css in your text editor, remove all name–value pairs that reference colors, change all colors in rules based on pseudo-classes to **black**, then save a copy of the file as **hnprint.css**.

g. Validate all your HTML and CSS documents.

h. If you have space on a Web server for publishing your documents, create a local root folder within the IC3 folder, move all the files and folders in the IC3 folder to the local root folder, upload the files to your Web publishing location, then open both Web pages in your browser from the published location.

i. Close your browser, then close your text editor.

FIGURE F-25

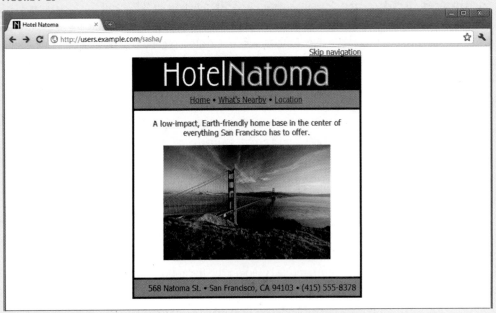

somchaij/Shutterstock.com

FIGURE F-26

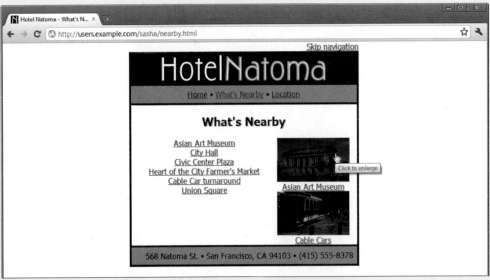

Photos/Sasha Vodnik

Real Life Independent Challenge

This assignment builds on the personal Web site you have worked on in previous units. You identify and add images to your Web site.

a. Copy your Web site files to the Unit F/RLIC folder on the drive and folder where you store your Data Files.

b. Review your storyboard and any other design documents to identify locations and sources for images on your Web pages. If your original designs did not include images, create a revised sketch that incorporates one or more images, including logos, photos, and/or background images.

c. Identify sources for your images—which may include a designer who works with your organization, your own photo collection, and/or friends with design skills—and collect them. Verify that you have permission to use the images you collect for your Web site.

d. Incorporate the images you collected into your Web site. Be sure to specify height, width, and alt attributes for each img element. Use the figure element where appropriate and add captions with the figcaption element. Specify values for padding and margin to create the desired amount of space between adjacent elements. Use the float and clear elements at least once each.

e. Save changes to your style sheet document, save a copy using the name of your print style sheet, then take out name–value pairs that set color and change all colors in rules based on pseudo-classes to **black**.

f. Preview your Web pages in at least two browsers and make any edits necessary for them to appear as you expected.

g. Validate all of your HTML and CSS documents and make any edits necessary to address any issues.

h. If you have space on a Web server for publishing your documents, create a local root folder within the RLIC folder, move all the files in the RLIC folder to the local root folder, upload the files to your Web publishing location, then open each Web page in your browser from the published location to verify that the upload was successful.

i. Close your browser, then close your text editor.

Visual Workshop

In your text editor, open the file HTM F-24.html from the Unit F/VW directory on the drive and folder where you store your Data Files, add a paragraph before the closing body tag that contains your first and last name and the text **HTML5 Unit F, Visual Workshop**, then save the file as **index.html**. Open HTM F-25.css, add a comment containing the same information, then save it as **revision.css**. Use your text editor along with the files in the images folder to style the Web page to match the one shown in Figure F-27. The logo graphic is revision.gif, and the background image is books.jpg. Save a copy of HTM F-26.ico as **favicon.ico** and specify this image as the favicon for the page. Save a copy of your style sheet with the name **revprint.css**, then make any necessary changes for print formatting. When you are finished, validate your HTML and CSS code. If you have space on a Web server, create a local root folder within the VW folder, move both files to the local root folder, upload the file to your Web publishing location, then open the Web page in your browser from the published location. Close your browser and text editor.

FIGURE F-27

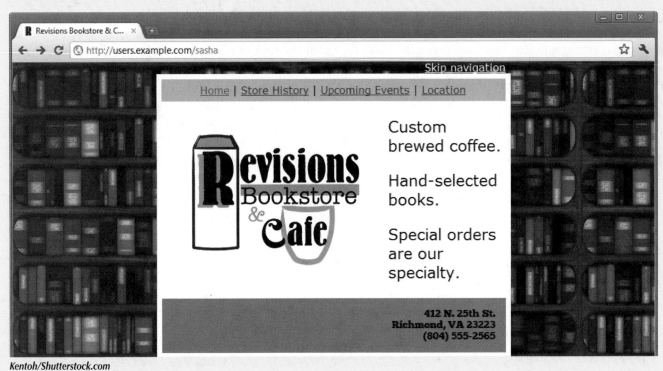

Kentoh/Shutterstock.com

Organizing Content with Lists and Tables

Files You Will Need:

To view a list of files needed for this unit, see the Data Files Grid in the back of the book.

While standard paragraphs are appropriate for many types of Web page content, some information is easier to present and understand in more specific formats. HTML includes elements that enable you to present information as lists or tables. In addition to changing the display of information in a browser, these elements convey semantic data about their contents, facilitating access by many types of user agents. As you continue your work on the Web site for the Lakeland Reeds Bed & Breakfast, you add lists and tabular content. You also use list elements to add semantic value to existing Web site content.

OBJECTIVES

Create an ordered list

Create an unordered list

Create a description list

Create a navigation bar using a list

Insert a table

Span columns and rows

Format a table with CSS

Apply a table-like structure to other elements

Creating an Ordered List

You use the HTML ol element to create a list in which items are numbered or lettered sequentially. This type of list is known as an **ordered list**, because the order in which the items are listed is important. You create each item in an ordered list with the li element. All the li elements for a list are nested within the opening and closing ol tags. The default marker for each list item is determined by the user agent rendering the Web page but is most often an Arabic numeral (1, 2, 3, . . .). You can use the values of the CSS list-style-type property shown in Table G-1 to change the markers to letters or to a different numbering style. ▓▓▓ Philip Blaine, the owner of Lakeland Reeds B&B, has provided additional information that he'd like you to incorporate into the Reservations Web page. You start by adding a list of the most popular weekends at the B&B.

STEPS

1. **In your text editor, open HTM G-1.html from the Unit G/Unit folder on the drive and folder where you store your Data Files, insert a blank line before the closing body tag, insert a paragraph element containing your first and last name and the text HTML5 Unit G, save it as index.html, repeat to save HTM G-2.html as aboutus.html, HTM G-3. html as rooms.html, and HTM G-4.html as reserve.html, then use a CSS comment to add the same information to HTM G-5.css and save it as lakeland.css**

QUICK TIP
Each h3 heading is grouped with its related elements using the semantic section element, which helps user agents identify units of content that share a common theme.

2. **In reserve.html, insert a blank line beneath the paragraph Our most sought-after weekends, indent to the same level as the paragraph, type <ol>, add another blank line, indent to the same level, then type </ol>**

   All items in an ordered list are contained between the opening and closing tags for the ol element.

3. **Insert a blank line beneath <ol>, indent two additional spaces, then type <li>Independence Day</li>**

   The content of each list item is contained between the opening and closing tags for the li element.

4. **Insert a blank line beneath the code you just entered, indent to the same level, then type <li>Memorial Day</li>**

5. **Insert a blank line beneath the code you just entered, indent to the same level, then type <li>Labor Day</li>**

   Figure G-1 shows the completed code for the ordered list.

6. **Save your work, then open reserve.html in your browser**

   As Figure G-2 shows, the list is displayed using the default style, with each list item numbered sequentially starting at the number 1.

TABLE G-1: Widely supported values for the CSS list-style-type property for the ol element

value	result
decimal	1. first item 2. second item
lower-roman	i. first item ii. second item
upper-roman	I. first item II. second item
lower-alpha	a. first item b. second item
upper-alpha	A. first item B. second item
none	first item second item

FIGURE G-1: HTML code for ordered list

ol element
contains
list items

li elements mark
list item content

FIGURE G-2: Ordered list in Reservations Web page

Sequential
numbers
displayed
before
list items

Photos/Sasha Vodnik

Specifying additional values for list-style-type

In addition to the widely supported values for list-style-type listed in Table G-1, browser support is growing for list enumerators in other numbering and lettering systems. With the exception of Internet Explorer 6, all commonly used browsers support the values "armenian", "georgian", and "lower-greek". Support for many other languages is increasing among user agents as well. To find the latest status on other languages, search on "list-style-type languages" in a search engine.

Organizing Content with Lists and Tables　　**159**

Creating an Unordered List

HTML also enables you to create a list in which the order of list items doesn't matter. You create this type of list, known as an **unordered list**, using the ul element. You mark list item content with the same li element that you use for an ordered list. List items are displayed with a bullet at the start of each line. The default bullet character is a solid circle, but you can use the CSS list-style-type property with the values shown in Table G-2 to specify a different bullet shape. ░░░░░ Philip created a list of special events for which visitors might want to reserve the entire bed-and-breakfast facility. You add the list to the Reservations Web page as an unordered list.

STEPS

1. **In reserve.html, insert a blank line beneath the paragraph that begins** Lakeland Reeds is also available, **indent to the same level as the paragraph, type** <ul>, **add another blank line, indent to the same level, then type** </ul>

   All items in an ordered list are contained between the opening and closing tags for the ul element.

2. **Insert a blank line beneath** <ul>, **indent two additional spaces, then type** <li>Weddings</li>

   While the containing element is specific to the type of list you're creating, you use the li element for list items when creating either ordered or unordered lists.

3. **Insert a blank line beneath the code you just entered, indent to the same level, then type** <li>Birthdays</li>

4. **Insert a blank line beneath the code you just entered, indent to the same level, then type** <li>Family Reunions</li>

   Figure G-3 shows the completed code for the ordered list.

5. **Save your work, then reload** reserve.html **in your browser**

   As Figure G-4 shows, the unordered list is displayed using the default style with a solid circular bullet next to each list item.

6. **Return to** lakeland.css **in your text editor, create a style rule using the** ul **type selector, then add the name–value pair** list-style-type: square;

7. **Save your work, then reload** reserve.html **in your browser**

   As Figure G-5 shows, the bullet characters are now displayed as solid squares.

TABLE G-2: Values for the CSS list-style-type property for the ul element

property	description	example
circle	unfilled circle	○ list item
disc	filled circle (default)	● list item
square	filled square	■ list item
none	no character	list item

Specifying custom bullets

In addition to choosing from the standard selection of bullet characters using the list-style-type property, you can instead choose to specify an image to display as the bullet character using the list-style-image property. The syntax is the same as that for specifying a background image: the text *url* followed by the path and filename of the image file, enclosed in quotes and parentheses. For instance, the code

```
ul {
    list-style-image:url("images/browntri.gif");
    }
```

specifies the file browntri.gif, located in the images folder, as the bullet character for unordered lists.

FIGURE G-3: Code for unordered list

ul element
contains
list items

li elements mark
list item content

```
<section>
   <h3>Rates</h3>
</section>
<section>
   <h3>Special Events</h3>
   <p>Lakeland Reeds is also available for booking group special events, including</p>
   <ul>
      <li>Weddings</li>
      <li>Birthdays</li>
      <li>Family Reunions</li>
   </ul>
   <p><a href="weddings.pdf">Guidelines and reservation form for a special event at Lakeland Reeds.</a> (PDF)</p>
</section>
```

FIGURE G-4: Unordered list in Web page

Default
bullet
character
displayed
before each
list item

Special Events

Lakeland Reeds is also available for booking group special events, including

- Weddings
- Birthdays
- Family Reunions

Guidelines and reservation form for a special event at Lakeland Reeds. (PDF)

Photo/Sasha Vodnik

FIGURE G-5: Unordered list with customized bullets

Bullet
character
changed to
square

Special Events

Lakeland Reeds is also available for booking group special events, including

- Weddings
- Birthdays
- Family Reunions

Guidelines and reservation form for a special event at Lakeland Reeds. (PDF)

Photo/Sasha Vodnik

Creating a Description List

In addition to ol and ul, HTML includes an element that marks content as a third type of list. The dl element creates a **description list**, which enables you to specify a name–value pair for each list item. A description list was known in previous versions of HTML as a **definition list**, because it was originally intended for listing terms and their definitions. However, in HTML5, dl is recommended as a semantic marker for any content that includes items and descriptions. Unlike ol and ul, dl does not use the li element to specify list items. Instead, each list item is composed of two elements: dt marks the term or item being described, and dd indicates the description. The contact information for Philip Blaine on the Reservations page is a set of name–value pairs. You change the markup for this section to a definition list to add semantic information to the data and to increase your options for visual presentation.

QUICK TIP

Adding a class enables you to style this list and others like it in your Web site without specifying default formatting for every description list on your site.

1. Return to reserve.html in your text editor, locate the <p> tag immediately before the span element containing the text Philip Blaine, Proprietor, then replace it with <dl class="contact">

2. Delete the code <span id="name">, type <dt>Proprietor</dt>, then press [Enter]

3. Indent to match the previous line, type <dd>, delete everything after the word Blaine, then at the end of the line type </dd>

4. On the next line, indent to match the previous line, replace the code <span class="callout"> with <dt>, replace </span> with </dt>, then press [Enter]

5. Indent to match the previous line, replace the colon and space with <dd>, then replace <br /> with </dd>

TROUBLE

Because there's no <br /> element after the email information, just insert </dd> after the word **com**.

6. Repeat Steps 4 and 5 to convert the fax and email information to list items

7. Beneath the final dd element, replace </p> with </dl>
   Figure G-6 shows the completed code.

8. Save your work, return to lakeland.css in your text editor, locate the style rule that sets the font-family value for a group of type selectors to a font stack starting with CuprumFFURegular, then add dt to the list of type selectors

9. Add a style rule that sets the font-weight to bold for each dt element within the contact class
   Figure G-7 shows the completed style sheet code.

10. Save your work, then reload reserve.html in your browser
    As Figure G-8 shows, the list items are displayed in the default layout with the second line indented beneath the first and additional space between each item–description pair.

dl element marks start and end of description list

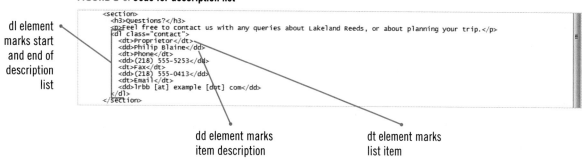

```
<section>
  <h3>Questions?</h3>
  <p>Feel free to contact us with any queries about Lakeland Reeds, or about planning your trip.</p>
  <dl class="contact">
    <dt>Proprietor</dt>
    <dd>Philip Blaine</dd>
    <dt>Phone</dt>
    <dd>(218) 555-5253</dd>
    <dt>Fax</dt>
    <dd>(218) 555-0413</dd>
    <dt>Email</dt>
    <dd>lrbb [at] example [dot] com</dd>
  </dl>
</section>
```

dd element marks item description

dt element marks list item

FIGURE G-7: **Style sheet containing styles for dt elements**

```
dt, h1, h2, h3, nav, footer {
  font-family: CuprumFFURegular, georgia, "times new roman", times, serif;
}
h1, h2, nav, footer {
```

```
.contact dt {
  font-weight: bold;
}
```

FIGURE G-8: **Web page with description list**

dt elements are left-aligned

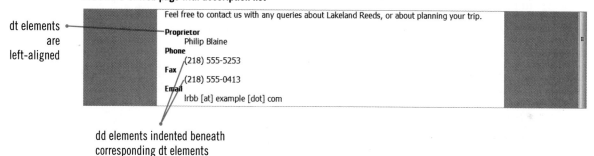

Feel free to contact us with any queries about Lakeland Reeds, or about planning your trip.

Proprietor
    Philip Blaine
Phone
    (218) 555-5253
Fax
    (218) 555-0413
Email
    lrbb [at] example [dot] com

dd elements indented beneath corresponding dt elements

Creating nested lists

Sometimes nesting a list within another list is the clearest way to present information. It's easy to nest lists in HTML: you simply insert valid code for a list within the content of an li element.

For instance, Figure G-9 shows the appearance in a browser of the nested lists created by the following code:

```
<ol>
  <li>
    Fruits
    <ul>
      <li>apples</li>
      <li>pomegranates</li>
    </ul>
  </li>
  <li>
    Vegetables
    <ul>
      <li>carrots</li>
      <li>beets</li>
    </ul>
  </li>
</ol>
```

FIGURE G-9

1. Fruits
   - apples
   - pomegranates
2. Vegetables
   - carrots
   - beets

HTML5 and CSS3

Creating a Navigation Bar Using a List

Some common Web page content that at first glance may not appear to be a list may nevertheless benefit from being marked up using list elements. One common example is a navigation bar, which is fundamentally a list of related links. By marking up a navigation bar using the ul and li elements, you add semantic information that helps user agents more accurately render it. In addition, list elements give you greater layout flexibility using fewer HTML tags, making your code easier for yourself and other developers to read. You convert the main navigation bar to an ordered list.

STEPS

1. Return to reserve.html in your text editor, locate the opening <nav> tag for the main nav bar, then in the line below it, replace the p with ul, leaving the id attribute–value pair unchanged

2. Position the insertion point just to the left of the opening <a> tag for the Home link, type <li>, position the insertion point at the end of the line, delete | and the space before it, then type </li>

3. Repeat Step 2 to enclose the remaining links in li elements

4. In the line beneath the Directions link, replace </p> with </ul>

   Your code should match Figure G-10.

5. Save your work, return to lakeland.css in your text editor, create a new style rule based on the #mainnav li selector, then add the following name–value pairs:

   ```
   display: inline;

   list-style-type: none;

   padding: 0.25em;
   ```

   Setting the value of display to inline keeps all the elements on the same line, rather than displaying them on separate lines, which is the default. Setting list-style-type to none prevents bullet characters from displaying next to each item. The padding value creates space between the links, as well as between the nav bar and the elements above and below it.

6. Save your work, then reload reserve.html in your browser

   As Figure G-11 shows, there is very little change in the appearance of the nav bar. However, the nav bar code now semantically indicates that it's a list of related items.

7. Return to reserve.html in your text editor, then copy all the code between the opening and closing nav tags to the Clipboard

8. Switch to index.html in your text editor, select the code between the opening and closing nav tags, paste the contents of the Clipboard to replace the selection, save your work, then repeat for aboutus.html and rooms.html

9. Return to reserve.html in your Web browser, then use the nav bar to navigate to the other pages in the Web site and ensure the new nav bar is displayed consistently across the pages

An li
element
contains
each link in
the nav bar

```
<nav>
    <ul id="mainnav">
        <li><a href="index.html">Home</a></li>
        <li><a href="aboutus.html">About Us</a></li>
        <li><a href="rooms.html">Rooms</a></li>
        <li><a href="reserve.html">Reservations</a></li>
        <li><a href="http://bit.ly/dl8xGc" target="_blank">Local Weather</a></li>
        <li><a href="http://bit.ly/co7vcs" target="_blank">Directions</a></li>
    </ul>
</nav>
```

FIGURE G-11: Modified nav bar in browser

Extra space
between links
replaces pipe
characters,
but nav
bar styling
remains
unchanged

Unholy Vault Designs/Shutterstock.com
Photo/Sasha Vodnik

HTML5 and CSS3

Inserting a Table

In addition to a simple list of items or items and descriptions, HTML enables you to present a larger set of information as a table. As Figure G-14 shows, a table organizes data in horizontal **rows** and vertical **columns**. Each item of data in a table is displayed in a **cell**, which is the intersection of a row and a column. To create a table in HTML, you use four main elements: table marks the start and end of the table, th marks the content of a header cell, td marks the content of a data cell, and tr groups cells into rows. You can also add semantic information to a table by using the thead element to mark the header rows of the table, tbody to mark the rows that make up the body, and tfoot to mark footer rows. Table G-3 provides an overview of structuring elements for tables. ████ Philip would like the Web site to include a breakdown of rates for rooms at Lakeland Reeds B&B during different times of the year. You add this information to the Reservations page as a table.

STEPS

1. **Return to reserve.html in your text editor, insert a blank line beneath the opening h3 tag for the heading Rates, indent to match the previous line, type <table>, press [Enter], indent to match the previous line, then type </table>**

2. **Insert a blank line beneath the <table> tag, indent two spaces more than the previous line, type <thead>, press [Enter], indent to match the previous line, then type </thead>**

3. **Press [Enter], indent to match the previous line, type <tbody>, press [Enter], indent to match the previous line, then type </tbody>**

   The basic structuring tags you've entered for the table should match Figure G-12.

4. **Insert a blank line beneath the <thead> tag, indent two spaces more than the previous line, type <tr>, press [Enter], indent to match the previous line, type </tr>, then repeat to add two tr elements in the tbody section**

5. **Insert a blank line beneath the first <tr> tag in the thead section, indent two spaces more than the previous line, type <th>Period</th>, press [Enter], then enter the remaining five lines of code shown in Figure G-13**

6. **Insert the two sets of td elements shown in Figure G-13**

   Your code should match Figure G-13.

7. **Insert a blank line beneath the closing table tag, indent to match the previous line, then type <p>* High Season includes Memorial Day weekend through Labor Day weekend</p>**

8. **Save your work, return to lakeland.css in your text editor, then add the following style rule:**

   ```
   td, th {
      border: 1px solid black;
   }
   ```

9. **Save your work, then reload reserve.html in your browser**

   As Figure G-14 shows, the table content you entered is displayed in a grid, with a border around each cell. The content of each th element and td element occupies an individual cell, and the cells are grouped in rows based on the tr elements you entered. The number of cells in each row is sufficient for a browser to calculate the number of columns; therefore, no element is required to specify the number or arrangement of columns.

FIGURE G-12: Basic table structuring tags

```
<table>
   <thead>
   </thead>
   <tbody>
   </tbody>
</table>
```

FIGURE G-13: Code for complete table

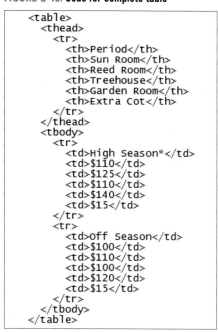

```
<table>
   <thead>
     <tr>
       <th>Period</th>
       <th>Sun Room</th>
       <th>Reed Room</th>
       <th>Treehouse</th>
       <th>Garden Room</th>
       <th>Extra Cot</th>
     </tr>
   </thead>
   <tbody>
     <tr>
       <td>High Season*</td>
       <td>$110</td>
       <td>$125</td>
       <td>$110</td>
       <td>$140</td>
       <td>$15</td>
     </tr>
     <tr>
       <td>Off Season</td>
       <td>$100</td>
       <td>$110</td>
       <td>$100</td>
       <td>$120</td>
       <td>$15</td>
     </tr>
   </tbody>
</table>
```

FIGURE G-14: Table in browser

Table column consists of a vertical series of cells

Header cell content is centered and displayed in bold

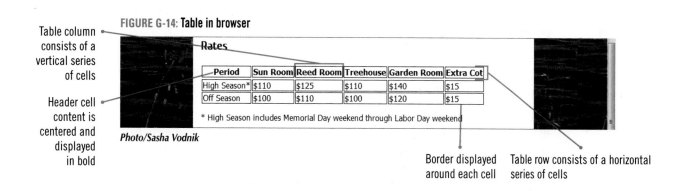

Rates

Period	Sun Room	Reed Room	Treehouse	Garden Room	Extra Cot
High Season*	$110	$125	$110	$140	$15
Off Season	$100	$110	$100	$120	$15

* High Season includes Memorial Day weekend through Labor Day weekend

Photo/Sasha Vodnik

Border displayed around each cell

Table row consists of a horizontal series of cells

TABLE G-3: HTML Table Structuring Elements

element	marks
table	start and end of table content
thead	group of one or more rows that contain column headers; when a long table is printed, these are displayed at the top of each page
tbody	group of one or more rows that contain main body of table
tfoot	group of one or more rows that contain column footers; when a long table is printed, these are displayed at the bottom of each page
tr	start and end of a row
th	content of a table header cell; content is centered by default in most browsers
td	content of a standard table cell

Organizing Content with Lists and Tables

Spanning Columns and Rows

When a table contains cells that repeat the same content across a row or down a column, you can improve usability by removing all but one occurrence of the content formatting the cell to be displayed across multiple columns or rows. To merge a cell across multiple columns in an HTML table, you use the colspan attribute in the opening th or td tag for the cell to specify the number of columns in which it should be displayed. Likewise, you use the rowspan attribute to specify the number of rows for cell content to span. ▰▰▰▰▰ You add colspan and rowspan attributes to make the Rates table easier to read.

STEPS

1. **Return to reserve.html in your text editor, insert a new line beneath the <thead> tag, indent two additional spaces, type <tr>, press [Enter], indent to match the previous line, then type </tr>**

2. **Between the opening and closing tr tags you just entered, indent two additional spaces and add the following code:**

    ```
    <th>Period</th>
    <th colspan="4">Room</th>
    <th>Extra Cot</th>
    ```

    Although the new header row includes only three cells, the colspan attribute marks the second cell to be displayed in the second, third, fourth, and fifth columns, meaning that the row occupies the same number of columns as the other rows in the table.

3. **Save your work, then reload reserve.html in your browser**

    As Figure G-15 shows, the text "Room" now appears just once in the table, and the cell that contains it spans four columns. However, the headings "Period" and "Extra Cot" are now duplicated in the two heading rows.

4. **Return to reserve.html in your text editor, in the code for the first table row, click before the closing > in the opening tag for the th element containing the text Period, press [Spacebar], then type rowspan="2"**

5. **In the code for the same row, click before the closing > in the opening tag for the th element containing the text Extra Cot, press [Spacebar], then type rowspan="2"**

6. **Delete the th element in the second heading row containing the text Period, then delete the th element in the second heading row containing the text Extra Cot**

    Even though the second heading row contains code for only four cells, the two cells that use the rowspan attribute in the previous row provide content for the two additional cells.

7. **In the first tr element in the tbody section, click before the closing > in the opening tag for the td element containing the text $15, press [Spacebar], then type rowspan="2"**

8. **In the second tr element in the tbody section, delete the td element containing the text $15**

    Figure G-16 shows the completed code for the table.

9. **Save your work, then refresh reserve.html in your browser**

    As Figure G-17 shows, the cells containing the text "Period", "Extra Cot", and "$15" all span two rows.

FIGURE G-15: Heading cell spanning multiple columns

colspan attribute causes cell contents to be displayed across four columns

Rates					
Period	Room				Extra Cot
Period	Sun Room	Reed Room	Treehouse	Garden Room	Extra Cot
High Season*	$110	$125	$110	$140	$15
Off Season	$100	$110	$100	$120	$15

* High Season includes Memorial Day weekend through Labor Day weekend

Photo/Sasha Vodnik

FIGURE G-16: Code containing colspan and rowspan attributes

colspan attribute added to display cell content in multiple columns

```
<table>
  <thead>
    <tr>
      <th rowspan="2">Period</th>
      <th colspan="4">Room</th>
      <th rowspan="2">Extra Cot</th>
    </tr>
    <tr>
      <th>Sun Room</th>
      <th>Reed Room</th>
      <th>Treehouse</th>
      <th>Garden Room</th>
    </tr>
  </thead>
  <tbody>
    <tr>
      <td>High Season*</td>
      <td>$110</td>
      <td>$125</td>
      <td>$110</td>
      <td>$140</td>
      <td rowspan="2">$15</td>
    </tr>
    <tr>
      <td>Off Season</td>
      <td>$100</td>
      <td>$110</td>
      <td>$100</td>
      <td>$120</td>
    </tr>
  </tbody>
</table>
```

rowspan attributes added to display cell content in multiple rows

FIGURE G-17: Table cells spanning multiple rows

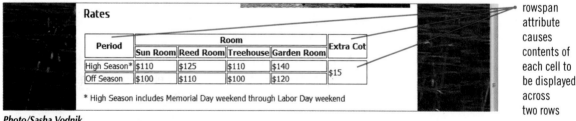

Rates					
Period	Room				Extra Cot
	Sun Room	Reed Room	Treehouse	Garden Room	
High Season*	$110	$125	$110	$140	$15
Off Season	$100	$110	$100	$120	

* High Season includes Memorial Day weekend through Labor Day weekend

Photo/Sasha Vodnik

rowspan attribute causes contents of each cell to be displayed across two rows

Calculating table columns

In a table that doesn't use colspan or rowspan attributes, you can verify that each row includes content for every column by ensuring that each row contains the same number of th or td elements. When you use colspan and rowspan attributes, you still need to confirm that your content fits the table dimensions. To do so, start by adding the values for all colspan attributes used in the row. Next, add the number of th or td elements in the row without colspan attributes. Finally, add the number of th or td cells in earlier rows whose content is part of the current row due to rowspan values. In short: **current row colspan total + cells in current row without colspan + cells spanning from previous rows = total columns**

Running this calculation on any row of your table should produce the same value.

If one or more rows appear to be shorter or longer than the surrounding rows, it can be helpful to preview your Web page in a browser and inspect the table to identify the cell where the contents of one row are no longer related to the contents in adjacent rows. You may simply need to adjust a rowspan or colspan value, or add or remove a cell.

Organizing Content with Lists and Tables

Formatting a Table with CSS

CSS enables you to style many aspects of a Web page table. In addition to controlling font faces and font and background colors, you can style the borders between cells. Table G-4 describes the CSS properties and values that affect table borders. You can style an entire table, a table section (such as thead or tbody) or individual rows or cells. In addition, you can use the HTML colgroup and col elements to assign styles to a single column or to a group of columns. ▬▬▬ You style the borders and add background colors to different sections of your table to make it easier for users to read and understand.

STEPS

1. **Return to lakeland.css in your text editor, delete the style rule based on the td, th selector, then add the style rules shown in Figure G-18**

2. **Save your work, then reload reserve.html in your browser**
   As Figure G-19 shows, the border-collapse property merges adjacent borders into a single line. The width property for the table element controls the overall width of the table. Setting only the border-bottom value for th elements creates a single line rather than a grid for column headings.

3. **Return to reserve.html in your text editor, insert a blank line beneath the opening table tag, indent two additional spaces, then add the following code:**

```
<colgroup>
   <col class="firstcol" />
   <col class="roomcols" span="4" />
   <col class="cotcol" />
</colgroup>
```

   By default, each col element applies to a single column, starting from the left side of the table. However, you can group consecutive columns into a single col element by specifying the number of columns to include as the value of the span attribute. The col elements you entered divide the six columns of your table into three units to which you can apply styles: the "firstcol" class applies to the first column; the "roomcols" group, with a span value of "4", includes the next four columns; and the "cotcol" class applies to the last column. All col elements must be contained in a colgroup element.

4. **In the tbody section, locate the td element containing the text High Season, add the code class="season" to the opening tag, locate the td element containing the text Off Season, then add the code class="season" to the opening tag**
   You can add a class or id attribute to any cell to style it specifically.

5. **In the opening tag for the p element below the closing table tag, click before the >, press [Spacebar], then type class="tablenote"**

6. **Save your work, return to lakeland.css in your text editor, then add the style rules shown in Figure G-20**

7. **In the th style rule, add the name–value pair background: #B8944D;**

8. **Near the top of the style sheet, locate the style rule that sets the font-family value for a group of type selectors to a font stack starting with CuprumFFURegular, then add th to the list of type selectors**
   Figure G-20 shows the completed code for the style sheet.

9. **Save your work, then reload reserve.html in your browser**
   As Figure G-21 shows, different background colors are applied to the columns based on the styling of the corresponding col and colgroup elements.

```
table {
  width: 90%;
  margin: 0 auto;
  padding: 0;
  border-collapse: collapse;
  }
td {
  border: 1px solid black;
  padding: 0.25em;
  }
th {
  border-bottom: 1px solid black;
  padding: 0.25em;
  }
```

FIGURE G-19: **Table with styles applied**

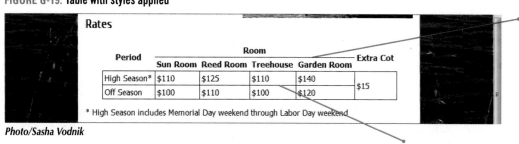

border-bottom attribute creates an underline beneath header cell content

border-collapse attribute merges cell borders of adjacent cells into a single line

Photo/Sasha Vodnik

FIGURE G-20: **Completed style rules for table elements**

```
dt, h1, h2, h3, nav, footer, th {
  font-family: CuprumFFURegular, georgia, "times new roman", times, serif;
  }
h1, h2, nav, footer {
```

th selector added to style rule for font family

```
th {
  border-bottom: 1px solid black;
  padding: 0.25em;
  background: #B8944D;
  }
```

background attribute-value pair added to th style rule

Code to add in Step 6

```
.cotcol {
  background: #9daecd;
  width: 15%;
  }
.desc {
  padding: 0;
  margin: 1em 0 0 2em;
  }
.firstcol {
  background: #f1eace;
  width: 25%;
  }
.rates td {
  text-align: center;
  }
.rates td.season {
  text-align: left;
  }
.roomcols {
  background: #aecdf4;
  width: 15%;
  }
.tablenote {
  width: 90%;
  margin: 0.25em auto;
  }
.toplink {
```

FIGURE G-21: **Table with background and font styling applied**

Background color styling for th elements takes cascading precedence over styling for column groups

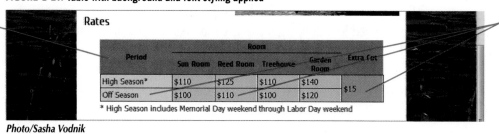

Background colors applied using style rules based on column groups

Photo/Sasha Vodnik

Organizing Content with Lists and Tables

Applying a Table-Like Structure to Other Elements

Sometimes you may be tempted to use HTML table markup to arrange Web page elements that don't otherwise belong in a table so they appear visually in a grid. While table and related elements should be used only to mark data whose relationships are best understood as a table, CSS lets you specify that you want elements treated as components of a table, but without marking them semantically as tabular data. To implement this layout, you use block-level elements, such as divs, to create a structure that parallels the arrangement of table, tr, and td elements in an HTML table. ▰▰▰ You convert the description list containing contact information for making reservations to a table-like layout using CSS.

STEPS

1. **Return to reserve.html in your text editor, scroll down to the Questions? section, then in the opening and closing tags for the description list, replace the dl with div, leaving the id attribute–value pair unchanged**

2. **Add a new line containing <div class="row"> before each dt element at the same indent level, add a new line containing </div> after each dd element, then increase the indentation for each dt and dd element by two spaces**

   The div elements group content similar to the way a tr element does in an HTML table.

3. **Replace each <dt> tag with <div class="category">, each <dd> tag with <div>, and each </dt> and </dd> tag with </div>**

   The div elements that replace the dt and dd elements mark the contents of each cell. Figure G-22 shows the completed Web page code for approximating a table layout.

4. **Save your work, return to lakeland.css in your text editor, change the selector for the .contact dt rule to .category, then enter the style rules shown in Figure G-23**

   The .contact rule sets the display property to table for the description list. The .row rule styles the next level of div elements to behave as table rows. The .row div rule specifies that the next level of div elements behave as table cells, and specifies values for vertical and horizontal padding.

5. **Save your work, refresh reserve.html in your browser, then scroll down to the Questions? section**

   As Figure G-24 shows, the contact information is arranged in a grid without borders.

QUICK TIP
Do not delete the border name–value pairs for table elements because they make printed output easier to read.

6. **Return to lakeland.css in your text editor, save your work, save a copy as llprint.css, remove all name–value pairs that specify color as well as the pair that specifies the background image, change all the colors in style rules based on pseudo-classes to black, then save your work**

7. **Validate the code for all your Web pages and your style sheets, and make changes as necessary to fix any errors**

8. **If you have space on a Web server for publishing your documents, create a local root folder within the Unit folder, move all the files in the Unit folder to the local root folder, upload the files to your Web publishing location, open index.html in your browser from the published location, then use the nav bar to open the remaining Web page and verify that the upload was successful**

```
<div class="contact">
  <div class="row">
    <div class="category">Proprietor</div>
    <div>Philip Blaine</div>
  </div>
  <div class="row">
    <div class="category">Phone</div>
    <div>(218) 555-5253</div>
  </div>
  <div class="row">
    <div class="category">Fax</div>
    <div>(218) 555-0413</div>
  </div>
  <div class="row">
    <div class="category">Email</div>
    <div>lrbb [at] example [dot] com</div>
  </div>
</div>
```

FIGURE G-23: **CSS code to display contact information in table-like layout**

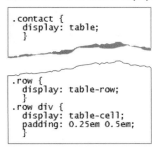

```
.contact {
  display: table;
}
```

```
.row {
  display: table-row;
}
.row div {
  display: table-cell;
  padding: 0.25em 0.5em;
}
```

FIGURE G-24: **Contact information displayed in table-like layout**

Photo/Sasha Vodnik

Resisting the temptation to use tables for layout

You can style table borders with all the properties that are available for other Web page elements, including removing borders completely. In the early days of the Web, many developers combined spanned rows and columns with invisible borders to enable the positioning of text, images, and other elements side by side, and in specific areas of a Web page. However, as CSS grew and user agent support for it matured, CSS placement properties, which you'll learn in an upcoming unit, became the preferred method for positioning HTML elements. While you can place elements in arbitrary locations by manipulating the number and sizes of rows and columns in a table, doing so erroneously assigns semantic meaning to your Web page content; this suggests that user agents should attempt to understand it as a table of related data. In addition, this use of a table creates particularly strong challenges for non-visual user agents such as screen readers in conveying the relationships between Web page elements. For these reasons, you should restrict your use of tables only to data whose meaning can be better understood in a grid layout.

Organizing Content with Lists and Tables

Practice

Concepts Review

For current SAM information, including versions and content details, visit SAM Central (http://www.cengage.com/samcentral). If you have a SAM user profile, you may have access to hands-on instruction, practice, and assessment of the skills covered in this unit. Since various versions of SAM are supported throughout the life of this text, check with your instructor for the correct instructions and URL/Web site for accessing assignments.

Refer to Figure G-25.

FIGURE G-25

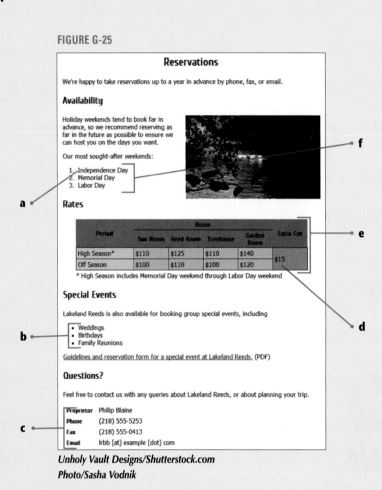

Unholy Vault Designs/Shutterstock.com
Photo/Sasha Vodnik

1. **Which item is created using the table element?**
2. **Which item is created using the li element?**
3. **Which item is created using the td element?**
4. **Which item is created using the ul element?**
5. **Which item is created using the ol element?**
6. **Which item is created using only div elements?**

Match each term with the statement that best describes it.

7. **ordered list**	**a.** a group of table contents arranged vertically
8. **unordered list**	**b.** a list that enables you to specify a name–value pair for each list item
9. **description list**	**c.** a list in which the order of list items doesn't matter
10. **row**	**d.** a table component that displays a single item of data
11. **column**	**e.** a list in which items are numbered or lettered sequentially
12. **cell**	**f.** a group of table contents arranged horizontally

Select the best answer from the list of choices.

13. Which element do you use to create a list in which items are numbered or lettered sequentially?
    - **a.** ol
    - **b.** ul
    - **c.** dl
    - **d.** dd

14. Which element do you use to create a list that is usually displayed with bullet characters?
    - **a.** ol
    - **b.** ul
    - **c.** dl
    - **d.** dd

15. Which element do you use to create a list that enables you to specify a name–value pair for each list item?
    - **a.** li
    - **b.** ol
    - **c.** ul
    - **d.** dl

16. Which element marks the term being described in a description list?
    - **a.** li
    - **b.** dt
    - **c.** dd
    - **d.** td

17. Which element marks the description of an item in a description list?
    - **a.** li
    - **b.** dt
    - **c.** dd
    - **d.** td

18. Which element marks the content of a table header cell?
    - **a.** thead
    - **b.** tbody
    - **c.** th
    - **d.** td

19. Which element marks the content of a table body cell?
    - **a.** thead
    - **b.** tbody
    - **c.** th
    - **d.** td

20. Which element marks the rows that make up the head section of a table?
    - **a.** thead
    - **b.** tbody
    - **c.** th
    - **d.** td

21. Which element marks the rows that make up the body section of a table?
    - **a.** thead
    - **b.** tbody
    - **c.** th
    - **d.** td

Skills Review

1. **Create an ordered list.**
   a. In your text editor, open HTM G-6.html from the Unit G/Review folder on the drive and folder where you store your Data Files, insert a blank line before the closing body tag, then insert a paragraph element containing your first and last name and the text **HTML5 Unit G, Skills Review**. Save it as **index.html**, then repeat to save HTM G-7.html as **history.html** and HTM G-8.html as **location.html**. Use a CSS comment to add the same information to HTM G-9.css and save it as **bigj.css**.
   b. In index.html, beneath the p element containing the text "Enjoy award winning pizza in your home in just three steps:", insert a blank line, then insert starting and ending tags for an ordered list on separate lines at the same indent level as the preceding p element.
   c. On a new line between the tags you just entered, indent two additional spaces, then add a list item element containing the text **Call the location nearest you**.
   d. Repeat Step c to insert two additional list items containing the text **Place your order and listen for your doorbell** and **Open the box and dig in!**
   e. Save your work, then open index.html in your browser.

2. **Create an unordered list.**
   a. In history.html, locate the p element with the id "words", then edit the opening and closing tags for the element to make it an unordered list with the same id.
   b. Move each of the words "flavor", "aroma", and "fresh" onto its own line, then mark each as a list item.

Skills Review (continued)

   c. Save your work, return to bigj.css in your text editor, then create a style rule for list item elements within the element with the id words that makes the list items display without bullets. (*Hint*: Use the value **none** for the list-style-type property.)

   d. Save your work, then open history.html in your browser.

3. Create a description list.

   a. Return to index.html in your text editor, locate the p element with the id "contact", then edit the opening and closing tags for the element to make it a div element with the same id.

   b. Insert a line beneath the opening contact div tag, indent two additional spaces, then add an opening tag for a description list. Repeat to add the closing description list tag above the closing div tag. Increase the indent by two spaces for each line of code within the description list element.

   c. Mark the address "150 St. Joseph St." as a description list term, delete the colon and space that follow it, move the rest of the current line of code onto its own line at the same indent level, delete the line break tag at the end of the line, then mark the contents of the new line as a description list description. (*Hint*: Include the span element within the code for the description item.) Repeat for the contact information for the remaining two locations.

   d. Save your work, then reload index.html in your browser.

4. Create a navigation bar using a list.

   a. Return to index.html in your text editor, locate the p element with the id "mainnav", then edit the opening and closing tags for the element to make it an unordered list with the same id.

   b. Delete the space and the pipe character following the code for the first nav bar link, mark the entire line of code as a list item, then repeat for the remaining three links.

   c. Save your work, return to bigj.css in your text editor, create a new style rule based for list items within the element with the id mainnav, then add name–value pairs styling display as **inline**, making no bullet character appear before each item, and setting padding to **0.25em** on all sides.

   d. Save your work, reload index.html in your browser, then verify that the nav bar appears as shown in Figure G-26 and that all links work correctly.

   e. Return to index.html in your text editor, then copy all the code between the opening and closing nav tags to the Clipboard.

   f. Switch to history.html in your text editor, select the code between the opening and closing nav tags, paste the contents of the Clipboard to replace the selection, save your work, then repeat for location.html.

   g. Return to index.html in your Web browser, then use the nav bar to navigate to the other pages in the Web site and ensure the new nav bar is displayed consistently across all pages.

5. Insert a table.

   a. Return to location.html in your text editor, locate the h3 heading containing the text "Queen's Park/UT", insert a blank line beneath the p element containing address information, indent to match the previous line, then insert opening and closing tags for a table element on separate lines at the same indent level.

FIGURE G-26

   b. Between the opening and closing tags you just entered, add opening and closing tags for table head and table body sections with each tag on its own line and indented two spaces more than the table tags.

   c. Within the table head tags, add opening and closing tags for a table row, with each tag on its own line and indented two spaces more than the thead tags. Repeat to add opening and closing tags for three table rows in the table body section.

Skills Review (continued)

d. Within the table row element for the table head section, add table head cell elements containing the text **Days**, **Open**, and **Close** on separate lines, indented two spaces more than the opening table row tag. Repeat to add the following contents to table data cell elements in the three table body rows:

Row 1: **Mon-Thu, 11am, 10pm**

Row 2: **Fri-Sat, 11am, 11pm**

Row 3: **Sun, Noon, 10pm**

e. Delete the p element with the class hours immediately beneath the table you just created.

f. Repeat Steps a–e to insert two more tables:

h3 heading "St. Clair":

Row 1: **Mon-Thu, 11am, 9:30pm**

Row 2: **Fri-Sat, 11am, 11pm**

Row 3: **Sun, Noon, 9:30pm**

h3 heading "Dundas":

Row 1: **Mon-Thu, 11am, 11pm**

Row 2: **Fri-Sat, 11am, Midnight**

Row 3: **Sun, Noon, 11pm**

g. Save your work, then return to bigj.css in your text editor. Add a style rule for table head cell and table data cell elements that sets borders to **1px solid black**.

h. Save your work, then reload location.html in your browser.

6. **Span columns and rows.**

a. Return to location.html in your text editor, locate the table you inserted beneath the h3 heading "Queen's Park/UT", then insert opening and closing tags for a new row element just beneath the opening tag for the table head section. Add a table head cell element that spans two rows containing the text **Day**. Add a second table head cell that spans two columns containing the text **Hours**.

b. In the code for the second table row in the table head section, delete the code for the cell containing the text "Days".

c. Repeat Steps a and b for the remaining two tables in the document. Save your work, then reload location.html in your browser.

7. **Format a table with CSS.**

a. Return to bigj.css in your text editor, then delete the style rule based on the td, th selector. Add a style rule that is based on the table type selector and sets margins to **1em**, padding to **0**, and collapses borders. Add a style rule that is based on the td type selector and sets borders to **1px solid black** and padding to **0.25em**. Add a style rule that is based on the th type selector and sets borders to **1px solid black**, padding to **0.25em**, and background to **#fc6**.

b. Save your work, then reload location.html in your browser.

c. Return to location.html in your text editor, insert a blank line beneath the opening table tag for the first table you created, indent two additional spaces, then add a container element for column groups. Within the container element, add an element that applies the class **daycol** to the first column, then add another element that is without a class value and spans the last two columns. Repeat for the other two tables.

d. In the table body section of each table, add the class **days** to the first table data element in each table row.

e. Save your work, then return to bigj.css in your text editor. Add a style rule for the class **days** that sets the font weight to **bold**. Add a style rule for the class **daycol** that sets the background to **#e0e0e0**.

f. Save your work, then reload location.html in your browser.

8. **Apply a table-like structure to other elements.**

a. Return to index.html in your text editor, then locate the dl element near the bottom of the document. Replace the opening <dl> tag with **<div id="contact">**. Replace the closing </dl> tag with **</div>**. Before each dt element, at the same indent level, add a new line containing an opening div tag with a class value of **row**. Add a new line containing a closing div tag after each dd element, then increase the indentation for each dt and dd element by two spaces.

Skills Review (continued)

b. Replace each <dt> and <dd> tag with **<div>** and each </dt> and </dd> tag with **</div>**.

c. Save your work, then return to bigj.css in your text editor. Create a style rule for the id **contact**, then add name–value pairs to set the display to **table** and the padding and margin to **0**. Create a style rule for the class **row**, then add an name–value pair to set the display to **table-row**. Create a style rule for div elements within elements with the class **row**, then add name–value pairs to set the display to **table-cell** and set the padding to **0.1em 0.5em**.

d. Save your work, copy the contact div element along with its contents to the Clipboard, then paste it into history.html and location.html to replace the existing contact element in each document. Save your work, refresh location.html in your browser, verify that the contact information at the bottom of the page matches that shown in Figure G-27, then use the nav bar to open the main page and the History page and verify that the contact information appears consistently across the site.

e. Return to bigj.css in your text editor, save your work, save a copy as **bjprint.css**, remove all name–value pairs that specify color as well as the pair that specifies the background image, change all the colors in style rules based on pseudo-classes to **black**, then save your work.

f. Validate the code for all your Web pages and your style sheets, and make changes as necessary to fix any errors.

g. If you have space on a Web server for publishing your documents, create a local root folder within the Review folder, move all the files in the Review folder to the local root folder, upload the files to your Web publishing location, open index.html in your browser from the published location, then use the nav bar to open the remaining Web page and verify that the upload was successful.

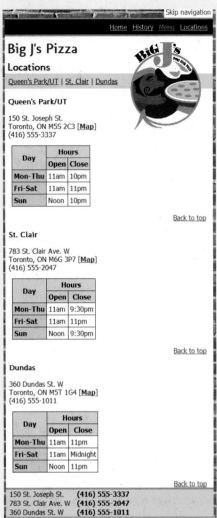

FIGURE G-27

Independent Challenge 1

Sarah Nguyen, the owner of the Spotted Wren Garden Center, has given you additional content to add to the Web site you've been creating for her. You add this information using lists and tables.

a. Open HTM G-10.html from the Unit G/IC1 folder in your text editor. Insert a blank line before the closing body tag, then insert a paragraph element containing your first and last name and the text **HTML5 Unit G, Independent Challenge 1**. Save the file as **index.html**, then repeat to save HTM G-11.html as **hours.html**, and HTM G-12.html as **resource.html**. Open HTM G-13.css, below the existing comment at the top of the document, add another comment with your first and last name and the text **HTML5 Unit G, Independent Challenge 1**. Save the file as **spotwren.css**.

b. In resource.html, change the four paragraph elements beneath the h2 heading "Resources" to an unordered list by replacing the opening and closing p tags with opening and closing **li** tags and then enclosing all four elements in a **ul** element. Save your work, then view resource.html in your Web browser to verify that the four paragraphs are displayed as an unordered list.

c. Return to resource.html in your text editor. Beneath the text "Omaha area plant hardiness zone information", insert the following table. (*Hint*: Use rowspan attributes for the cells containing the text **Zone**, **Last frost**, **First frost**, **May 1**, and **Oct 15**. Use a colspan attribute for the cell containing the text **Average annual minimum temp**. The HTML character code for the degree symbol is **°**).

| Zone | Average annual minimum temp | | Last frost | First frost |
	Fahrenheit	Celsius		
4b	-25°F to -20°F	-28.9°C to -31.6°C		
5a	-20°F to -15°F	-26.2°C to -28.8°C	May 1	Oct 15
5b	-15°F to -10°F	-23.4°C to -26.1°C		

d. Delete the closing list item tag after the text "Omaha area plant hardiness zone information" above the table, add a blank line beneath the closing tag for the table, indent two fewer spaces, then add the closing list item tag. Save your work, then return to spotwren.css in your text editor. Add a style rule for table elements that sets the margin to **1em 0**, the padding to **0**, and collapses borders. Add a style rule for table data cell elements that sets borders to **1px solid black** and padding to **0.25em**. Add a style rule for table header cell elements that sets borders to **1px solid black**, padding to **0.25em**, and the background to **#e0e0e0**. Save your work, then reload resource.html in your browser and verify that the table appears as shown in Figure G-28.

e. Return to resource.html in your text editor. Mark up the list of plant names as a description list with the common names as terms and the Latin names that follow as descriptions. Delete the closing list item tag for the text "Recommended drought-tolerant perennials" above the list, then delete the closing unordered list tag below that line. Add a blank line beneath the closing tag for the description list, indent two fewer spaces, then type a closing list item tag for an unordered list. Add another blank line beneath the current line, indent two fewer spaces, then type a closing tag for an unordered list. Save your work, then return to spotwren.css in your text editor. Add a style rule to style the contents of all description elements in a description list in italic. Save your work, then reload resource.html in your browser. Verify that definition list matches the one shown in Figure G-28.

f. Return to resource.html in your text editor. Convert the code for the nav bar to an unordered list by changing the p element that encloses the links to a **ul** element, then enclosing the code for each link in an **li** element. Delete the space and pipe character (|) after each link. Save your work, then return to spotwren.css in your text editor. Create a style rule that applies only to list item elements within the element with the id "mainnav". Set the display property to **inline** and the padding to **0.25em**, then set the list to display without a bullet character. Save your work, reload resource.html in your browser, then verify that the appearance of the nav bar matches Figure G-28. Return to resource.html in your text editor, copy the new nav bar code to the Clipboard, then use it to replace the existing nav bar code in index.html and hours.html. Save your work, then view index.html and hours.html in your browser to verify that the nav bar is displayed as expected.

g. Return to hours.html in your text editor. Indent each line of code containing store hours information by four additional spaces. Beneath the h2 heading, insert a new line containing a div element with the class **table** at the same indent level as the previous line. Add a closing tag for the div element after the last line of store hours information. Enclose each line of code containing store hours information in a div element that belongs to the class **row**, then delete the opening and closing p tags from each line. Change the opening and closing span tags enclosing each day of the week to div tags. Click before the opening time on the first line, press **[Enter]**, indent to match the previous line, then enclose the hour information in a **div** element. Repeat for the remaining days.

FIGURE G-28

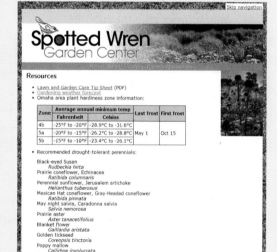

Jim Gitzlaff/Shutterstock.com
Maxim Tupikov/Shutterstock.com
Xtremer/Shutterstock.com

Independent Challenge 1 (continued)

h. Return to spotwren.css in your text editor. Add a style rule to style elements of the class row to display like table rows. Add a style rule to style div elements within elements of the class row to display like table cells with padding set to **0.1em 0.5em**. Add a style rule to style elements of the class table to display like tables with a margin and padding value of **0**. Save your work, then reload hours.html in your browser. Verify that the list of hours matches the one shown in Figure G-29.

i. Return to spotwren.css in your text editor, remove all name–value pairs that reference colors as well as the pair that specifies the background image, change all colors in rules based on pseudo-classes to **black**, then save a copy of the file as **swprint.css**.

j. Validate all your HTML and CSS documents.

k. If you have space on a Web server for publishing your documents, create a local root folder within the IC1 folder, move all the files and folders in the IC1 folder to the local root folder, upload the files to your Web publishing location, then open all three Web pages in your browser from the published location.

l. Close your browser, then close your text editor.

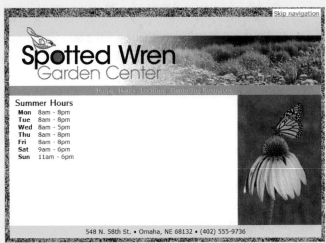
Independent Challenge 2

You incorporate the logo for the Murfreesboro Recreational Soccer League into the organizational Web site that you are creating. You also add images from some of the group's events.

a. Open HTM G-14.html from the Unit G/IC2 folder in your text editor. Insert a blank line before the closing body tag, then insert a paragraph element containing your first and last name and the text **HTML5 Unit G, Independent Challenge 2**. Save the file as **index.html**, then repeat to save HTM G-15.html as **started. html** and HTM G-16.html as **schedule.html**. Open HTM G-17.css, then below the existing comment at the top of the document, add another comment containing your first and last name and the text **HTML5 Unit G, Independent Challenge 2**. Save the file as **mrsl.css**.

b. In started.html, locate the paragraph that begins "If you're interested in joining up". Mark the text "complete some paperwork" as a list item for an unordered list. Delete the word "and" following the text you just marked, then mark the remainder of the sentence as a second list item. Enclose the two list items within an element that marks an unordered list and indent all elements appropriately. Move the closing paragraph tag after the word "to" just before the start of the list.

Advanced Challenge Exercise

■ Position the insertion point before the closing list item tag for the second list item, press **[Enter]** twice, then indent to match the first list item. On the blank line you created, insert opening and closing tags for a second unordered list, which will be nested within the first list. Add a list item containing the text **$65 (standard)** and a second list item containing the text **$40 (seniors and students)**. Edit the second list item in the previous list to read **pay for a seasonal membership**. Save your work.

■ In mrsl.css, add a style rule that applies to all unordered lists. Set the property list-style-image to **url("images/ soccer.gif")** to specify a soccer ball icon as the unordered list bullet. Save your work, open started.html in your browser, then verify the page matches Figure G-30.

Independent Challenge 2 (continued)

c. Return to started.html in your text editor. Convert the code for the nav bar to an unordered list by changing the p element that encloses the links to an element that marks an unordered list, then enclosing the code for each link in a list item element. Delete the space and pipe character (|) after each link. Save your work, then return to mrsl.css in your text editor. Create a style rule that applies only to list item elements within the element with the id "mainnav". Set the display property to **inline** and the padding to **0.25em**, and set the list to display without a bullet character. Save your work, reload started.html in your browser, then verify that the appearance of the nav bar matches Figure G-30. Return to started.html in your text editor, copy the new nav bar code to the Clipboard, then use it to replace the existing nav bar code in index.html and schedule.html. Save your work, then view index.html and schedule.html in your browser to verify that the nav bar is displayed as expected.

d. In schedule.html, convert the four lists of game dates and times into tables. Create a heading row for each table with heading cells containing the text **Date** and **Time**. Split the information for each game into two cells, the first containing the date and the second containing the start time. Save your work, then return to mrsl.css in your text editor. Add a style rule for table elements that sets the margin to **1em 0**, the padding to **0**, and collapses borders. Add a style rule for table data cell elements that sets borders to **1px solid black** and padding to **0.25em**. Add a style rule for table header cell elements that sets borders to **1px solid black**, padding to **0.25em**, and the background to **#e0e0e0**. Save your work, then preview schedule.html in your browser. Verify that all four tables are displayed correctly.

e. Using Figure G-31 as a guide, add a third column to each table that displays the field letter where each game will be played. (*Hint*: To add a column, add a new cell at the end of each row element.) Save your work, reload schedule.html in your browser, then verify that your tables match those shown in Figure G-31.

f. Return to mrsl.css in your text editor, remove all name–value pairs that reference colors as well as the pairs that specify background images, change all colors in rules based on pseudo-classes to black, then save a copy of the file as **mrsprint.css**.

g. Validate all your HTML and CSS documents.

h. If you have space on a Web server for publishing your documents, create a local root folder within the IC2 folder, move all the files and folders in the IC2 folder to the local root folder, upload the files to your Web publishing location, then open all three Web pages in your browser from the published location.

i. Close your browser, then close your text editor.

FIGURE G-30

Lario Tus/Shutterstock.com

Xtremer/Shutterstock.com

FIGURE G-31

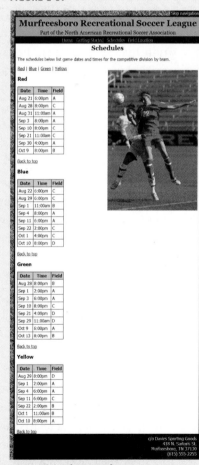

9507848116 /Shutterstock.com

Xtremer/Shutterstock.com

Independent Challenge 3

As you continue your work on the Web site for Hotel Natoma, you incorporate additional information about the hotel and local attractions using some of the techniques for organizing content that you learned in this unit.

a. Open HTM G-18.html from the Unit G/IC3 folder in your text editor. Insert a blank line before the closing body tag, then insert a paragraph element containing your first and last name and the text **HTML5 Unit G, Independent Challenge 3**. Save the file as **index.html**, then repeat to save HTM G-19.html as **nearby. html** and HTM G-20.html as **greensf.html**. Open HTM G-21.css, then below the existing comment at the top of the document, add another comment containing your first and last name and the text **HTML5 Unit G, Independent Challenge 3**. Save the file as **natoma.css**.

b. In nearby.html, mark the list of nearby locations as an unordered list. Save your work, then preview the page in your browser and compare it to Figure G-33.

c. In greensf.html, mark the list of green destinations as an ordered list. Save your work, then preview the page in your browser.

Advanced Challenge Exercise

■ In natoma.css, add a style rule to style ordered lists using lowercase Roman numerals. (*Hint*: Use the **lower-roman** value for the list-style-type property.) Save your work, then preview the page in your browser and compare it to Figure G-32.

d. In greensf.html, convert the markup for the main nav bar to use an unordered list and remove the bullets between links. Save your work, then add a style rule to natoma.css that sets the display of list items in the element with the id mainnav to **inline**, removes bullet characters, and sets padding to **0.25em**. Preview the Web page in your browser and compare it to Figure G-32. (*Note*: If you did not complete the Advanced Challenge Exercise, your ordered list will be displayed with standard numbers rather than Roman numerals.)

e. Copy the revised code for the nav bar to the Clipboard, then use it to replace the existing code for the nav bars in index.html and nearby.html. Save your work, then preview each file in your browser to ensure the nav bar is displayed consistently across the site.

f. Return to natoma.css in your text editor, change all border colors to black. remove all other name–value pairs that reference colors, change all colors in rules based on pseudo-classes to black, then save a copy of the file as **hnprint.css**.

g. Validate all your HTML and CSS documents.

h. If you have space on a Web server for publishing your documents, create a local root folder within the IC3 folder, move all the files and folders in the IC3 folder to the local root folder, upload the files to your Web publishing location, then open both Web pages in your browser from the published location.

i. Close your browser, then close your text editor.

FIGURE G-32

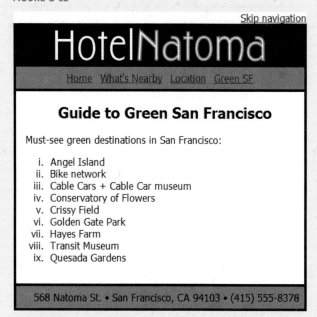

FIGURE G-33

Photos/Sasha Vodnik

Real Life Independent Challenge

This assignment builds on the personal Web site you have worked on in previous units. As you continue to organize and add content to your Web site, you make use of the elements you learned in this unit.

a. Copy your Web site files to the Unit G/RLIC folder on the drive and folder where you store your Data Files.

b. Review your existing Web pages for any content that would be easier to read or would be better marked semantically as a list or as a table. Review your storyboard and any other design documents to identify any additional planned content that should be organized using one of these methods.

c. For each list you are adding to your Web site, decide which list type makes the most sense. If you are adding an ordered or unordered list, choose a bullet character or ordering system as appropriate. Add the lists to your Web site on the appropriate Web pages. Save your work and preview all affected Web pages in a browser.

d. Convert the code for the nav bar on your Web site to use an unordered list. Add appropropriate styles to your style sheet to preserve the appearance of your nav bar. Copy the code you created to all the Web pages in your site. Save your work and preview all Web pages in a browser.

e. For each table you are adding to your Web site, start by sketching the table on a sheet of paper. Decide which rows will be table head rows and which will be table body rows. Identify any cells that will span multiple columns or multiple rows. Count the total columns in the table. Add each table at the appropriate location in your Web site, then save each page and preview it in a browser. If a table does not display as expected, refer to your code and your sketch to identify discrepancies.

f. Save changes to your style sheet document, save a copy using the name of your print style sheet, then take out name–value pairs that set color and background images and change all colors in rules based on pseudo-classes to black.

g. Preview your Web pages in at least two browsers and make any edits necessary for them to appear as you expected.

h. Validate all of your HTML and CSS documents and make any edits necessary to address any issues.

i. If you have space on a Web server for publishing your documents, create a local root folder within the RLIC folder, move all the files in the RLIC folder to the local root folder, upload the files to your Web publishing location, then open each Web page in your browser from the published location to verify that the upload was successful.

j. Close your browser, then close your text editor.

Visual Workshop

In your text editor, open the file HTM G-22.html from the /Unit G/VW directory on the drive and folder where you store your Data Files, before the closing body tag add a paragraph that contains your first and last name and the text **HTML5 Unit G, Visual Workshop**, then save the file as **upcoming.html**. Open HTM G-23.css, add a comment containing the same information, then save it as **revision.css**. Use your text editor to add the table shown in Figure G-34. (*Hint*: Use the **title** class to italicize the book title.) Convert the nav bar layout to use an unordered list. Save your work, save a copy of your style sheet with the name **revprint.css**, then make any necessary changes for print formatting. When you are finished, validate your HTML and CSS code. If you have space on a Web server, create a local root folder within the VW folder, move both files to the local root folder, upload the file to your Web publishing location, then open the Web page in your browser from the published location. Close your browser and text editor.

FIGURE G-34

Kentoh/Shutterstock.com

Implementing Page Layout with HTML and CSS

Combining HTML elements with basic CSS attributes offers some flexibility in the arrangement and appearance of Web page elements. You can use more advanced CSS to create even more complex layouts and to exercise more detailed control over the layout of your Web pages. 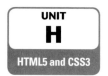 You prepare to add new layout features to the Lakeland Reeds B&B Web site.

OBJECTIVES

Assess the CSS box model

Construct a multicolumn layout with float

Implement relative positioning

Implement absolute positioning

Stack elements

Create a multicolumn layout using positioning

Create a fluid layout

Control the visibility of elements

Assessing the CSS Box Model

Creating and modifying page layouts in CSS involves specifying size and position information for Web page elements. CSS represents the characteristics of every Web page element using the box model, which treats each element as a rectangular box having several global properties. Figure H-1 shows the relationship between the CSS padding, border, and margin properties in the box model. ░░░░░ As you prepare to apply more complex layout features to the Web site for Lakeland Reeds B&B, you familiarize yourself with the CSS box model.

DETAILS

A few concepts are important for using box model properties effectively:

- **Distinguishing between padding, border, and margin**

  The padding, border, and margin properties all create space around the contents of a Web page element, but it's important to understand the relationship of these elements to each other in order to create the results you want. Of the three properties, border, formatted with the width, style, and color that you specify, is the only one that can be seen in a Web browser. However, a name-value pair of border: 0; means that the border for the affected element is not visible and takes up no space. Whether a border is visible or not, it serves as a reference point for the other two properties, as illustrated in Figure H-1. Padding is the space inside a border between the border and the element content, while margin is the space outside the border between the border and adjacent or parent elements.

QUICK TIP
You can set the CSS3 box-sizing property to "border-box" to change how box sizing is calculated, fitting the border and padding along with the content within the dimensions specified by "width" and "height"; however, the property is not globally supported.

- **Calculating box size**

  The size of the padding, border, and margin all increase the amount of space on a Web page that an element occupies or influences. However, the dimensions of these properties are generally not included in the calculated width or height of an element. By default, when you specify dimensions for an element using the width and height properties, the values you specify apply only to the element content. Any values you specify for padding, border, or margin are added to the height or width value you specify. Especially when you're fitting an element into a limited amount of space, you need to subtract the additional area occupied by padding, border, and margin to arrive at the appropriate width or height value, as Figure H-2 illustrates. For instance, when the width of an element must fit into a limited space, you have to subtract both the left and right values for padding, border, and margin to arrive at the appropriate width value for your style sheet. Similarly, to calculate a height value, you need to subtract all three values for the top and bottom of the element.

  There is one exception to this rule: when the bottom margin of one element is adjacent to the top margin of another element, the margins combine, or **collapse**, into a single margin equal to the greater of the two values.

- **Combining properties**

  As you create more complex layouts, setting specific widths for the padding and margin of specific sides of elements becomes more important. The box model supports a separate property for each side for both padding and margin, such as padding-top or margin-left. However, you can save time while coding and simplify your code by combining properties. When you want to set a common value for all four sides of an element, you can use generic properties with single values. For instance, padding: 0; sets padding on all four sides of an element to 0, while margin: 1em; sets the margin to 1 em all around an element. These properties also support more detailed shorthand values. As Table H-1 illustrates, if you provide four values for the margin or padding property, browsers apply the first value to the top and continue in a clockwise direction with the second value applied to the right, the third value to the bottom, and the final value to the left. For a name-value pair with three values, the first value applies to the top, the second to both the left and right, and the final value to the bottom. If you provide two values for either of these properties, browsers apply the first value to the top and bottom, and the second value to the left and right sides.

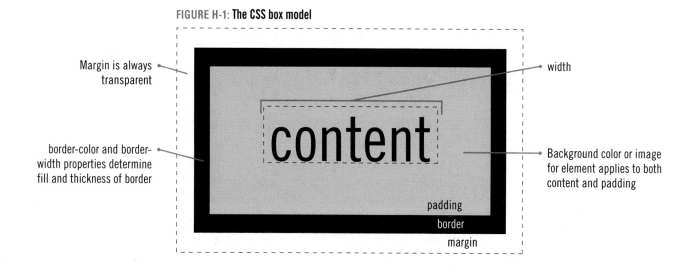

FIGURE H-1: **The CSS box model**

Margin is always transparent

width

border-color and border-width properties determine fill and thickness of border

Background color or image for element applies to both content and padding

content

padding
border
margin

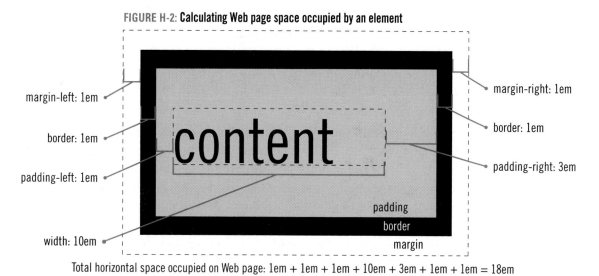

FIGURE H-2: **Calculating Web page space occupied by an element**

margin-left: 1em

margin-right: 1em

border: 1em

border: 1em

padding-left: 1em

content

padding-right: 3em

padding
border
margin

width: 10em

Total horizontal space occupied on Web page: 1em + 1em + 1em + 10em + 3em + 1em + 1em = 18em

TABLE H-1: **Box model shorthand properties**

property	# of values	values apply to	shorthand examples	equivalent to	
padding margin	four	top, right, bottom, left	margin: 0 1em 1em 0; padding: 0 1em 1em 0;	margin-top: 0; margin-right: 1em; margin-bottom: 1em; margin-left: 0;	padding-top: 0; padding-right: 1em; padding-bottom: 1em; padding-left: 0;
	three	top, left/right, bottom	margin: 0 2em 1em; padding: 0 2em 1em;	margin-top: 0; margin-right: 2em; margin-bottom: 1em; margin-left: 2em;	padding-top: 0; padding-right: 2em; padding-bottom: 1em; padding-left: 2em;
	two	top/bottom, left/right	margin: 0 1em; padding: 0 1em;	margin-top: 0; margin-right: 1em; margin-bottom: 0; margin-left: 1em;	padding-top: 0; padding-right: 1em; padding-bottom: 0; padding-left: 1em;
	one	top/left/bottom/right	margin: 1em; padding: 1em;	margin-top: 1em; margin-right: 1em; margin-bottom: 1em; margin-left: 1em;	padding-top: 1em; padding-right: 1em; padding-bottom: 1em; padding-left: 1em;
border	three	width, style, color	border: 3px solid red;	border-width: 3px; border-style: solid; border-color: red;	

Constructing a Multicolumn Layout with Float

Because user agents render HTML documents from top to bottom, it's relatively straightforward to create layouts that stack styled elements vertically. However, some of the most widely used layouts in print media involve columns of text and graphics running parallel to each other down the page. You can use the float and clear properties to create a basic version of this arrangement, known as a multicolumn layout, to unlock new possibilities for the arrangement of elements on your Web pages.  The design modifications that you created with the art department involve transforming the nav bar into a stacked set of links running down the left side of the page, with the main body of the page displayed to the right. You add styles to create this layout.

STEPS

1. **In your text editor, open HTM H-1.html from the Unit H/Unit folder where you store your Data Files, insert a blank line before the closing body tag, insert a paragraph element containing your first and last name and the text HTML5 Unit H, save it as aboutus.html, then use a CSS comment to add the same information to HTM H-2.css and save it as lakeland.css**

QUICK TIP
The margin and padding settings for your other style rules have already been adjusted to account for this new style rule.

2. **In lakeland.css, beneath the @font-face rule, insert a style rule that is based on the selectors article, body, dd, div, dl, dt, figcaption, figure, footer, h1, h2, h3, li, nav, ol, p, section, table, th, td, and ul and that sets both margin and padding to 0**

   Setting the margin and padding to 0 for commonly used elements helps you ensure that you are specifying precise values for all of your page elements, rather than relying on default browser styles, which can vary between user agents.

3. **Examine the other rules in the style sheet, locate the #mainnav li style rule, then delete the name–value pair display: inline;**

   By removing the value *inline* for display, you cause the links to return to the default arrangement of list items: as block elements stacked one on top of the next.

QUICK TIP
While most current browsers enable users to resize text specified in pixels rather than em, IE6 does not. If IE6 support is not crucial for your target audience, using pixels can simplify sizing.

4. **Locate the #mainnav style rule, add the name–value pairs float:left; and width: 7em;, then remove the background name–value pair**

   Setting the float property styles the main content that follows the nav bar to be displayed next to it. Removing the background color emphasizes the space between the nav bar list items with whitespace, creating the appearance of a set of separate buttons.

5. **Below the #mainnav style rule, create a new style rule based on the #mainnav a selector, then set the text-decoration property to none**

   This rule removes the underline from the nav bar link text, reinforcing the appearance of buttons.

6. **In the #content style rule, set the float property to right, then set the width to 32em**

   The combination of float and width properties for both the mainnav and content elements creates the appearance of two columns. Figure H-3 shows the completed style sheet code.

7. **Save your work, then open aboutus.html in your browser**

   As Figure H-4 shows, the nav bar links are displayed in a vertical stack along the left side of the screen, and the remaining page content is displayed in a second column to the right.

FIGURE H-3: Style sheet code for multicolumn layout

margin and padding set to 0 for commonly used elements

Style rules for content and child elements

Style rules for mainnav and child elements

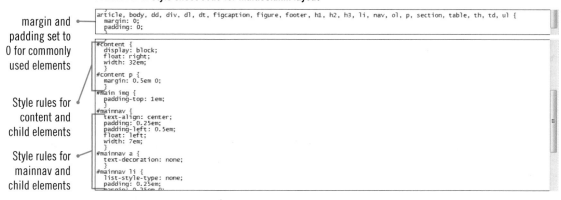

```
article, body, dd, div, dl, dt, figcaption, figure, footer, h1, h2, h3, li, nav, ol, p, section, table, th, td, ul {
    margin: 0;
    padding: 0;
}
#content {
    display: block;
    float: right;
    width: 32em;
}
#content p {
    margin: 0.5em 0;
}
#main img {
    padding-top: 1em;
}
#mainnav {
    text-align: center;
    padding: 0.25em;
    padding-left: 0.5em;
    float: left;
    width: 7em;
}
#mainnav a {
    text-decoration: none;
}
#mainnav li {
    list-style-type: none;
    padding: 0.25em;
    margin: 0.25em 0;
```

FIGURE H-4: Two-column layout in browser

Nav bar floated as left column

content element floated as right column

Unholy Vault Designs/Shutterstock.com
Jason Bucy

Adding additional columns

In addition to two-column layouts like the one shown in Figure H-4, multicolumn layouts including three columns are common on the Web. You can use the method outlined in this lesson to create a three-column layout by creating three content sections in your document and floating the first two on the left and the right. As long as the widths of the three sections (including padding, borders, and margins on both sides) total less than the total width of the parent element, the three sections are displayed side by side as columns when you open the page in a browser.

You'll explore advanced tools for creating layouts with more than three columns later in this unit.

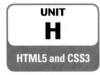

Implementing Relative Positioning

So far, your layouts have been limited to Web page elements being displayed based on the order they appear in your HTML documents, known as the **page flow**, or by moving elements outside the page flow to the left or right using the float property. CSS also lets you specify the exact position of an element on a Web page using the position property. You can make adjustments to the default position of an element while preserving the space allotted to the element in the default page flow. You implement this technique, known as **relative positioning**, by setting the position property to "relative". You style the exact location of the element using the top and left properties, as detailed in Table H-2. Figure H-5 illustrates how relative positioning affects the flow of elements in a Web page. You'd like the top of the nav bar to be even with the first paragraph of text in the second column, rather than with the header, so you use relative positioning to move it down while maintaining its position on the left side of the Web page.

STEPS

1. **Return to lakeland.css, in your text editor**

QUICK TIP
You can determine top and left positioning values by calculating the amount of space you need to move an element, or by simple trial and error.

2. **At the bottom of the #mainnav ul selector, add the name–value pairs position: relative; and top: 2em;**
   This code moves the list containing the nav bar elements down the page 2em while preserving its position in the left column. Figure H-6 shows the inserted code.

3. **Save your work, then refresh aboutus.html in your browser**
   As Figure H-7 shows, the top of the nav bar is now below the h2 heading and even with the top of the main text in the right column.

TABLE H-2: CSS properties and values for relative positioning

property	value	note
position	**relative**	Moves the element relative to its original position but preserves the space reserved for the element in its original position
top	**value** in em, pixels, or another supported unit, or **percent** of the height of the parent element	Moves the element the specified distance from the top edge of the closest ancestor element that is also positioned; the default value, 0, leaves the element in its original vertical position
left	**value** in em, pixels, or another supported unit, or percent of the width of the **parent** element	Moves the element the specified distance from the left edge of the closest ancestor element that is also positioned; the default value, 0, leaves the element in its original horizontal position

Maintaining accessibility with positioning

When you alter the layout of your Web pages using positioning, it's important to plan for non-visual user agents, as well as devices with smaller screens, to make sure your page content still flows logically. User agents that don't process positioning continue to render all content from top to bottom in the document. Thus, your HTML code should contain elements in the order users will encounter them. In addition, you can help all user agents understand the content of your pages and present it appropriately by using semantic elements to indicate the content of different columns; for instance, nav for the nav bar, aside for a sidebar, and article for main page content.

FIGURE H-5: Relative positioning and page flow

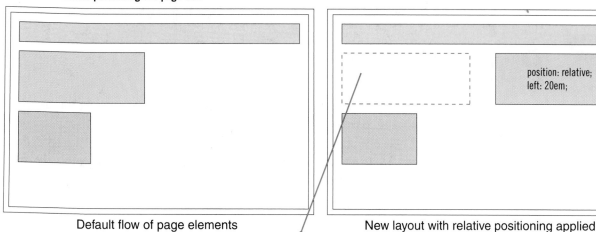

Default flow of page elements

New layout with relative positioning applied

Other page elements do not reflow into originally occupied space after relative positioning

FIGURE H-6: Code to relatively position nav bar

```
#mainnav ul {
  margin: 0;
  padding: 0;
  position: relative;
  top: 2em;
}
```

position and top properties added to move nav bar down

FIGURE H-7: Nav bar relatively positioned

Nav bar moved down 2em from original location in page flow

Unholy Vault Designs/Shutterstock.com
Jason Bucy

Implementing Absolute Positioning

An alternative to relative positioning is **absolute positioning**, which takes an element out of the page flow entirely and allows other elements to flow into the space it would have occupied. As with relative positioning, you can specify the new location of an absolutely positioned element relative to the closest ancestor element that is itself positioned. In addition to the top and left properties, you can use the right and bottom properties as well, causing the effects detailed in Table H-3. Figure H-8 illustrates how absolute positioning affects the flow of elements in a Web page. ██████ You want to add a decorative icon next to each nav bar button. You insert the images within the list items for the nav bar buttons and use absolute positioning to take them out of the list item block elements and specify their new locations.

STEPS

1. **Return to aboutus.html in your text editor, then after the opening <li> tag for the list item containing the text About Us, enter the following tag:**

   `<img src="images/fl_dark.gif" width="45" height="45" alt="" title="" />`

   This code inserts a shaded icon to mark the current page in the nav bar.

QUICK TIP

When the remaining Web pages are modified for the vertical nav bar, the fl_dark. gif image will be inserted to the left of the link for the current page, and the fl_light.gif image will be added next to each of the other links.

2. **Insert the following after the opening <li> for each remaining nav bar button:**

   `<img src="images/fl_light.gif" width="45" height="45" alt="" title="" />`

   A matching icon with different shading marks each of the remaining nav bar icons.

3. **Save your work, then reload aboutus.html in your browser**

   An icon appears to the left of the text for each button and increases the button height.

4. **Return to lakeland.css in your text editor, then in the #mainnav style rule, change the value for the padding-left property to 1em, the value for the text-align property to left, and the value for the width property to 6em**

   This code narrows the nav bar buttons and inserts space for the icons to the left of the nav bar.

5. **Beneath the img style rule, add a style rule that is based on the li img selector and sets position to absolute, left to -40px, and top to -8px**

   A negative value for left moves the left border of the element to the left, rather than to the right. Similarly, a negative value for top moves the element up.

6. **In the #mainnav li style rule, add a name–value pair that sets position to relative**

   The location of an absolutely positioned element is calculated based on the closest ancestor element that has a position applied to it. You set the position of list items in the nav bar to relative without changing the position in order to simplify positioning the image for each nav bar button. Figure H-9 shows the style sheet containing your additions and changes.

QUICK TIP

Internet Explorer 6 renders some positioned elements inaccurately. If you need to position elements for a Web page that needs to be IE6 compatible, search on the phrase "ie6 positioning bug" for workaround tips.

7. **Save your work, then refresh aboutus.html in your browser**

   As Figure H-10 shows, the nav bar icons are displayed to the left of the buttons.

FIGURE H-8: Absolute positioning and page flow

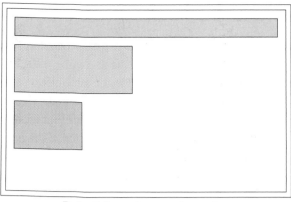

Default flow of page elements

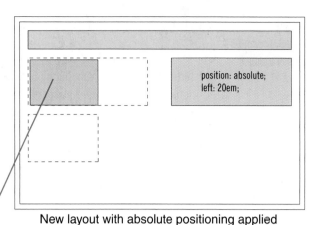

```
position: absolute;
left: 20em;
```

New layout with absolute positioning applied

Page elements following absolutely positioned
element reflow to occupy its space

FIGURE H-9: Code to absolutely position images

```
li img {
    position: absolute;
    left: -40px;
    top: -8px;
}
```

```
#mainnav {
    text-align: left;
    padding: 0.25em;
    padding-left: 1em;
    float: left;
    width: 6em;
}
#mainnav a {
    text-decoration: none;
}
#mainnav li {
    list-style-type: none;
    padding: 0.25em;
    margin: 0.25em 0;
    background: #B8944D;
    position: relative;
}
```

FIGURE H-10: Images absolutely positioned

Icon images
moved outside
of nav bar
buttons using
absolute
positioning

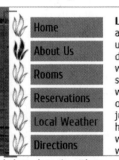

Unholy Vault Designs/Shutterstock.com

Jason Bucy

TABLE H-3: CSS properties and values for absolute positioning

property	value	result
position	**absolute**	Moves the element relative to its original position and allows other elements to flow into the space that the absolutely positioned element would have otherwise occupied
top bottom	**value** in em, pixels, or another supported unit, or **percent** of the height of the parent element	Moves the element the specified distance from the top, bottom, left, or right edge of the closest ancestor element that is also positioned
left right	**value** in em, pixels, or another supported unit, or **percent** of the width of the parent element	

Stacking Elements

One of the additional effects of using positioning in your layouts is the possibility of two elements occupying the same space on a Web page. Both relatively and absolutely positioned elements can be moved to positions occupied by other elements, or two positioned elements can be moved to the same place. While it requires careful planning to ensure that a positioned element doesn't unintentionally obscure the view of another element, the ability to overlap, or **stack**, elements introduces additional possibilities for creative layouts. A positioned element is placed in a new **layer**, which is a new level displayed on top of the basic flow of elements on the Web page. As Figure H-11 illustrates, the arrangement of layers is similar to placing clear sheets of plastic over a page in a book. You can control the stacking order of positioned elements by assigning values for the z-index property to each element. Numbers can be positive or negative, and an element with a larger z-index value is displayed on top of an element with a smaller value. You want to modify the nav bar so the icon for each button overlaps the edge of the button. You also want to incorporate a green bar into the background of the nav bar for contrast. You reposition the nav bar icons, and you add the background box using the z-image property to set the stacking order.

STEPS

1. **Return to lakeland.css in your text editor, then in the #mainnav style rule, change the value for padding-left to 0.5em and the value for width to 7em**

QUICK TIP
You can apply a z-index value only to an element for which you've declared a value for the position property.

2. **In the #mainnav li style rule, change the value for padding to 0.25em 0.25em 0.25em 1em**

3. **In the li img style rule, change the value for left to -22px**

4. **Save your work, then reload aboutus.html in your browser**
   Each icon now overlaps the end of its corresponding button.

5. **Return to aboutus.html in your text editor, then below the closing </ul> tag for the list containing the nav bar buttons, insert opening and closing tags for a div element with no content and the id navaccent**

6. **Save your work, return to lakeland.css in your text editor, then above the #pagenav style rule, add a style rule the for the element with the id navaccent that sets the width to 1.5em, the height to 12.25em, the background to #4D8103, the position to relative, top to -10em, and left to -0.75em**

QUICK TIP
Values for the z-index property can be any number, including a negative number. Stacking order is based solely on which element has a larger z-index value, not on the actual value.

7. **Save your work, then reload aboutus.html in your browser**
   The green box you created is positioned in front of the buttons and icons instead of behind them.

8. **Return to lakeland.css in your text editor, in the #navaccent style rule add the name–value pair z-index: 1, then in the #mainnav ul style rule, add the name–value pair z-index: 2**
   Figure H-12 shows the completed code for the style sheet.

9. **Save your work, then reload aboutus.html in your browser**
   As Figure H-13 shows, the green bar is now displayed behind the nav bar buttons.

Implementing fixed position

In addition to relative and absolute, the position property supports a third value: fixed. An element with **fixed positioning** behaves just like an element with absolute positioning except that it is displayed at the top of the stacking order and it is positioned relative to the browser window rather than to a Web page element. As a result, fixed positioning causes an element to remain in the same location in a browser window as a user scrolls through the Web page. This styling can be useful for information or tools that users may need at any point on a long Web page. However, keep in mind that Internet Explorer 6 and browsers on most mobile devices don't support this value.

FIGURE H-11: Stacking positioned elements

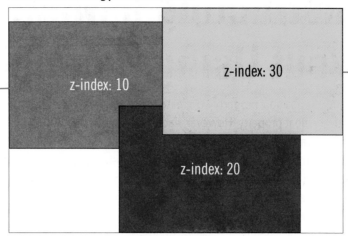

Element with the lowest z-index value is stacked below other positioned elements

z-index: 10

z-index: 30

z-index: 20

Element with the highest z-index value is stacked on top of other positioned elements

FIGURE H-12: Style sheet code for stacked items in nav bar

```
li img {
   position: absolute;
   left: -22px;
   top: -8px;
   }
```

```
#mainnav {
   text-align: left;
   padding: 0.25em;
   padding-left: 0.5em;
   float: left;
   width: 7em;
   }
#mainnav a {
   text-decoration: none;
   }
#mainnav li {
   list-style-type: none;
   padding: 0.25em 0.25em 0.25em 1em;
   margin: 0.25em 0;
   background: #B8944D;
   position: relative;
   }
#mainnav ul {
   margin: 0;
   padding: 0;
   position: relative;
   top: 2em;
   z-index: 2;
   }
#name {
   font-weight: bold;
   }
#navaccent {
   width: 1.5em;
   height: 12.25em;
   background: #4D8103;
   position: relative;
   top: -10em;
   left: -0.75em;
   z-index: 1;
   }
```

FIGURE H-13: Nav bar elements ordered using z-index values

z-index values used to reorder nav accent div behind list element containing buttons

Unholy Vault Designs/Shutterstock.com

Jason Bucy

Implementing Page Layout with HTML and CSS

Constructing a Multicolumn Layout Using Positioning

You can use the position property to create multicolumn layouts that look and behave just like those created with the float property. However, each method can be useful in specific situations. Positioning can enable you to create three-column layouts with more flexibility and allows for four-column layouts as well. Figure H-14 illustrates different methods for creating a multicolumn layout. In the new Lakeland Reeds B&B Web site layout, the width of the main page content can widen and narrow depending on the size of the browser window. To start the process of making this change, you switch from float-based to position-based columns.

STEPS

1. **Return to lakeland.css in your text editor, then in the #mainnav style rule, delete the name–value pair float: left;**

2. **At the end of the #mainnav style rule, add the name-value pairs position: absolute; and left: 15px;**

   Instead of floating the nav bar on the left side of the page, you give it an absolute position.

3. **In the #box style rule, add the code position: relative;**

   Giving the box element a relative position without left or top values leaves it in the same place on the page while positioning the mainnav element relative to it.

4. **In the #content style rule, delete the name–value pairs float: right; and width: 32em;**

5. **At the end of the #content style rule, add the code margin-left: 10em;**

   You remove the float property from the main page content. If you were creating a fixed-width page using positioning, you could position this element as well. However, because you want the element width to change based on the width of the browser window, you leave the content in the page flow and add a left margin that leaves space for the nav bar. Figure H-15 shows the updated code for the style sheet.

6. **Save your work, then reload aboutus.html in your browser.**

   As Figure H-16 shows that, even though you changed the styling of the nav bar and the main page content, the page layout is unchanged.

Understanding IE6 and positioning

Internet Explorer 6 includes a few bugs in the way it renders positioned elements. While this unit focuses on positioning techniques for browsers without such bugs, you may find yourself designing or maintaining Web pages for an audience with significant IE6 use. In this case, it's important to continually test your pages in IE6 as your design them. Because the IE6 bugs have been around for several years, many workarounds have been developed for these bugs. To research a particular rendering error you may be encountering, search on the terms "ie6 positioning bug" in a Web search engine.

FIGURE H-14: Comparing multicolumn layout methods

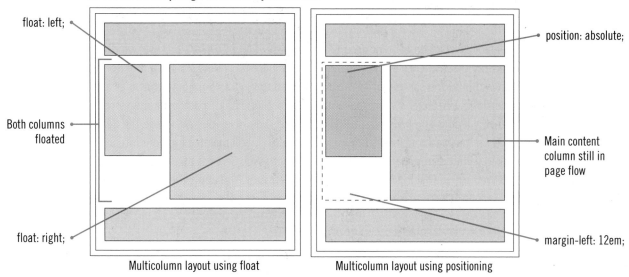

float: left;

Both columns floated

float: right;

position: absolute;

Main content column still in page flow

margin-left: 12em;

Multicolumn layout using float

Multicolumn layout using positioning

FIGURE H-15: Style sheet code for positioned column layout

margin-left value increased to create space for nav bar

Nav bar removed from page flow with absolute positioning

```
#content {
  display: block;
  margin-left: 10em;
  }
#content p {
  margin: 0.5em 0;
  }
#main img {
  padding-top: 1em;
  }
#mainnav {
  text-align: left;
  padding: 0.25em;
  padding-left: 0.5em;
  width: 7em;
  position: absolute;
  left: 15px;
  }
```

FIGURE H-16: Multicolumn layout using positioning

Unholy Vault Designs/Shutterstock.com
Jason Bucy

Creating a Fluid Layout

By default, Web page content occupies the entire width of a user's browser window. One simple technique for ensuring consistency of the visual design in different window sizes and monitor resolutions is to specify a fixed width for the content of a Web page, creating what's commonly known as a **fixed layout**. However, some designers prefer to take advantage of the additional space on larger screens. By creating a **fluid layout**, which is also known as a **liquid layout**, you give your Web page the flexibility to adjust its width based on the width of a user's browser window while still maintaining your intended layout. You've worked with the art department at Great Northern Web Services to adapt the design for the Lakeland Reeds B&B Web site so that it adjusts to different screen sizes. You apply those changes now.

STEPS

1. **Return to lakeland.css in your text editor**

2. **In the body style rule, change the width property name to min-width, then insert a new line and add the name–value pair max-width: 60em;**

   Figure H-17 shows the changed code. The min-width property sets the minimum width for an element. By changing the width property for body to min-width, you're keeping the Web page at least as wide as its previous fixed width. The max-width property sets the maximum width of an element, allowing your Web page content to widen a limited amount to fit a larger browser window.

3. **Save your changes, then reload aboutus.html in your browser**

   Depending on the size of your browser window, the Web page may be displayed wider than before, or may look exactly the same.

> **TROUBLE**
> If your computer monitor is smaller or displays a lower resolution, you may not be able to widen your browser window enough to cause the page elements to reflow.

4. **If your browser window is maximized, click the Restore Down button 🔲, then drag the right side of your browser window to the left and the right and notice any changes in the locations of text and other elements on the page**

   As Figure H-18 shows, the browser changes the locations of elements on the Web page to occupy the additional space, a process known as **reflowing**.

Determining page widths

When planning the design of a Web site, it's important to start by understanding the screen resolution of most of your expected users. While the numbers of pixels that different monitors can display varies widely, 1024 pixels in width by 768 pixels in height is a widely accepted lowest common denominator for computers. However, even a Web site that's 1024 pixels wide would be cut off on such displays because a few other factors are involved. Most importantly, browsers themselves use some pixels on both sides for the scroll bar and window borders. As a result, many designers use a standard width of 960 pixels for Web sites created with a general audience in mind.

Designing Web pages for mobile devices such as phones and tablets requires planning for much smaller displays. When designing for mobile users, some Web designers create a second Web site that's optimized for small screens, while other designers create a single Web site that looks good on small devices and scales up to large screens as well. Creating a Web site that's usable for mobile users requires careful planning and testing.

FIGURE H-17: Style sheet code for fluid layout

min-width property sets the minimum width for the element

max-width property sets the maximum width for the element

```
body {
    min-width: 44em;
    max-width: 60em;
    margin: 0 auto;
    font-family: tahoma, arial, helvetica, sans-serif;
    background: #6e93c8;
    background: url("images/lake.jpg");
}
```

FIGURE H-18: Web page at minimum and maximum widths

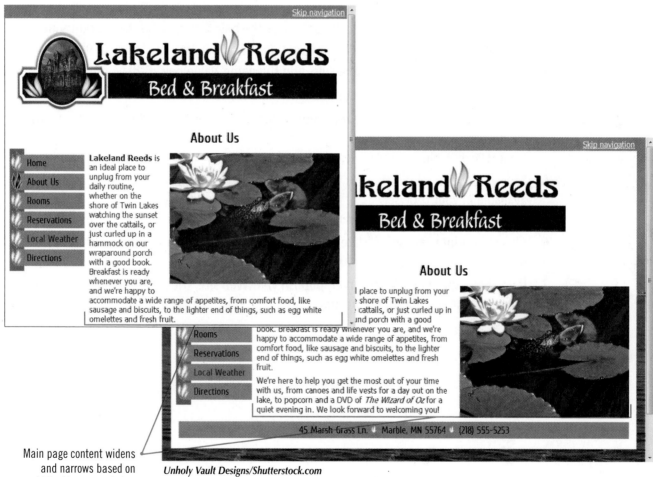

Main page content widens and narrows based on width of browser window

Unholy Vault Designs/Shutterstock.com
Jason Bucy
Photo/Sasha Vodnik

Controlling the Visibility of Elements

In addition to specifying where elements should be displayed in a Web page, you can use CSS properties to style whether an element is displayed at all. CSS includes two properties for this purpose. When you set the visibility property to "hidden", the contents of an element are no longer visible on the Web page. However, the element is still part of the page flow, meaning that it still takes up space on the page. As an alternative, you can set the display property to "none". In addition to not being visible, an element styled with this value is removed from the page flow, allowing other elements to occupy the space where it would have been displayed. Figure H-19 illustrates the difference between these two styles. The vertical nav bar takes up space on the Web page but is not necessary for printed output. You update the print style sheet for the Web site and use the display style to remove the nav bar when the page is printed.

STEPS

1. Return to lakeland.css in your text editor, save a copy as llprint.css, remove all name–value pairs that specify color as well as the pair that specifies the background image, then change all the colors in style rules based on pseudo-classes to black

2. At the end of the #mainnav style rule, add the name–value pair display: none;

3. In the #content style rule, delete the code margin-left: 10em;

> **QUICK TIP**
> Removing the margin and the width settings allows the main content to reflow across the entire printed page.

4. In the body style rule, remove the name–value pairs for the min-width and max-width properties

   Figure H-20 shows the final code for your style sheet.

5. Save your work, reload aboutus.html in your browser, then display a print preview if available in your browser

   As Figure H-21 shows, the nav bar is removed from the print layout.

6. Close the print preview, validate the code for aboutus.html and your style sheets, then make changes as necessary to fix any errors

7. If you have space on a Web server, publish your Web site, then open aboutus.html in your browser from the published location

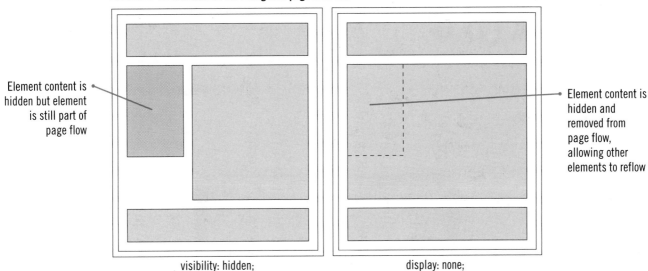

Element content is hidden but element is still part of page flow

Element content is hidden and removed from page flow, allowing other elements to reflow

visibility: hidden;   display: none;

FIGURE H-20: **Style sheet code to hide nav bar in printed output**

Margin property removed from #content style rule

```
#content {
    display: block;
    }
#content p {
    margin: 0.5em 0;
    }
#main img {
    padding-top: 1em;
    }
#mainnav {
    text-align: left;
    padding: 0.25em;
    padding-left: 0.5em;
    width: 7em;
    position: absolute;
    left: 15px;
    display: none;
    }
```

display: none hides the #mainnav element and removes it from the page flow

FIGURE H-21: **Nav bar removed from printed output**

Nav bar hidden and removed from page flow, allowing main content to occupy entire width of printed page

Unholy Vault Designs/Shutterstock.com
Jason Bucy

Practice

For current SAM information, including versions and content details, visit SAM Central (http://www.cengage.com/samcentral). If you have a SAM user profile, you may have access to hands-on instruction, practice, and assessment of the skills covered in this unit. Since various versions of SAM are supported throughout the life of this text, check with your instructor for the correct instructions and URL/Web site for accessing assignments.

Concepts Review

Refer to Figure H-22.

FIGURE H-22

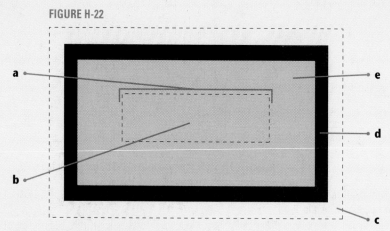

1. Which item represents the element margin?
2. Which item represents the element padding?
3. Which item represents the element content?
4. Which item represents the element border?
5. Which item represents the element width?

Match each term with the statement that best describes it.

6. **multicolumn layout**
7. **relative positioning**
8. **absolute positioning**
9. **fixed layout**
10. **fluid layout**
11. **layer**

a. a new level of content displayed on top of the basic flow of elements on the Web page

b. a layout that specifies a fixed width for the content of a Web page

c. a layout involving columns of text and graphics running parallel to each other down the page

d. lets you make adjustments to the default position of an element while preserving the space allotted to the element in the default page flow

e. a layout with the flexibility to adjust its width based on the width of a user's browser window

f. takes an element out of the page flow entirely and allows other elements to flow into the space it would have occupied

Select the best answer from the list of choices.

12. **Which does CSS use to represent the characteristics of every Web page element?**
   a. absolute positioning
   b. multicolumn layout
   c. box model
   d. fluid layout
13. **Which property is NOT useful in creating a multicolumn layout?**
   a. width
   b. background
   c. float
   d. position
14. **Which name-value pair takes an element out of the page flow entirely and allows other elements to flow into the space it would have occupied?**
   a. display: none
   b. position: relative
   c. position: absolute
   d. visibility: hidden

15. **Which name-value pair makes the contents of an element no longer visible on the Web page but leaves the element in the page flow?**

    a. position: relative   **c.** position: none

    b. display: none   **d.** visibility: hidden

16. **Which property enables you to change the stacking order of layers?**

    a. visibility   **c.** display

    b. z-index   **d.** position

Skills Review

1. **Construct a multicolumn layout with float.**

   a. In your text editor, open HTM H-3.html from the Unit H/Review folder where you store your Data Files, insert a blank line before the closing body tag, insert a paragraph element containing your first and last name and the text **HTML5 Unit H, Skills Review**, save it as **index.html**, then use a CSS comment to add the same information to HTM H-4.css and save it as **bigj.css**.

   b. Open index.html in your browser, then examine the Web page elements for the redesigned page.

   c. Return to index.html in your text editor, locate the footer element, then add the id values **foot1**, **foot2**, and **foot3** to the three div elements within the footer. Save your work.

   d. In bigj.css, beneath the @font-face rule, insert a style rule based on the selectors article, body, dd, div, dl, dt, figcaption, figure, footer, h1, h2, h3, li, nav, ol, p, section, table, th, td, and ul that sets both **margin** and **padding** to **0**.

   e. Create a style rule based on the foot1 id selector that floats the element to the **left** and sets its width to **320px**, a rule based on the **foot2** id selector that floats the element to the **right** and sets its width to **320px**, and a style rule based on the **foot3** id selector that sets the margins of the element to **0 auto** and sets its width to **320px**.

   f. Save your work, reload index.html in your browser, then verify that the addresses in the footer are displayed in three columns.

2. **Implement relative and absolute positioning.**

   a. Return to index.html in your text editor. In the li elements within the unordered list containing the nav bar links, add the id values **navlink1**, **navlink2**, **navlink3**, and **navlink4**. Save your work.

   b. In bigj.css, create a style rule for the id values you just created. Set background to **red**, then specify a background image of **images/redflag.png**. Also specify position as **absolute**, and width and height values of **150px**.

   c. In the "#mainnav li a" style rule, delete the name-value pair **background: red**.

   d. Create a style rule based just on the navlink1 id selector and specify a left value of **0**. Repeat for navlink2 to set a left value of **150px**, navlink3 to set a right value of **150px**, and navlink4 to set a right value of **0**.

   e. In the "#mainnav li a" style rule, delete **display: block**. Set position to **relative** and top to **20px**.

   f. In the #box style rule, set the position to **relative**.

   g. Save your work, refresh index.htm, then verify that the navigation bar links are displayed on red triangles along the top.

3. **Stack elements.**

   a. In index.html above the footer element, insert an empty div element with a class value of **center**. Save your work.

   b. In bigj.css, add a style rule based on the center class selector. Set the background to **white**, the width to **100%**, the height to **80px**, font-size to **1.5em**, padding to **2em**, position to **absolute**, and top to **200px**.

   c. Save your work, then reload index.html in your browser and observe the stacking order of the logo image and the box.

   d. Return to bigj.css in your text editor, then in the .center style rule, add code to set the z-index to **1**.

   e. Create a style rule based on the **logo** id selector, then set the position to **relative** and the z-index to **2**.

   f. In the "#mainnav li" style rule, set the z-index to **3**.

   g. Save your work, reload index.html in your browser, then verify that the white rectangle is displayed behind the logo.

4. **Construct a multicolumn layout using positioning.**

   a. Return to index.html in your text editor, locate the two aside elements above the div element you added earlier, add the class value **right** to the first aside element, then add the class value **left** to the second. Save your work.

   b. In bigj.css, create a style rule that applies to both of the classes you just applied. Add code to set width to **200px**, height to **80px**, font-size to **1.5em**, text-align to **center**, padding to **2em**, position to **absolute**, top to **200px**, z-index to **2**, and background to **none**.

Skills Review (continued)

c. Create a style rule based just on the left class selector and specify a border-left value of **5px solid black**. Repeat for right to set a right value of **0px** and a border-right value of **5px solid black**.

d. Save your work, then reload index.html in your browser and verify that a column of text appears on either side of the logo image, as shown in Figure H-23.

5. Create a fluid layout.

a. Return to bigj.css in your text editor.

b. In the #box style rule, change the width property name to **min-width**, then add code to set the max-width to **1060px**. Repeat for the #skipnav style rule.

c. Save your changes, then reload index.html in your browser.

d. If your browser window is maximized, click the Restore Down button.

e. Drag the right side of your browser window to the left and to the right and observe any reflowing.

6. Control the visibility of elements.

a. Return to bigj.css in your text editor, then save a copy as **bjprint.css**. Remove the name-value pairs that set color in the article, footer, and .strong style rules. Remove the name-value pairs that set borders for the .left and .right style rules.

b. At the end of the "#mainnav li a" style rule, add code to set display to **none**. Repeat for the #skipnav style rule.

c. In the #box style rule, remove the name-value pairs for the min-width and max-width properties. Repeat for the #skipnav style rule.

d. Save your work, reload index.html in your browser, then display a print preview if available in your browser. Verify that the "Skip navigation" link and the nav bar links are not displayed, as shown in Figure H-24.

e. Close the print preview, validate the code for index.html and your style sheets, then make changes as necessary to fix any errors.

f. If you have space on a Web server, publish your Web site, then open index.html in your browser from the published location.

FIGURE H-23

FIGURE H-24

Independent Challenge 1

Sarah Nguyen, the owner of the Spotted Wren Garden Center, has asked you to make a few layout changes to the store's Web site. She also had a graphic designer split the logo into two separate images in order to reduce the total size of the files: the text is a gif file, while the photo is a jpg. You implement the new features on the home page.

a. In your text editor, open HTM H-5.html from the Unit H/IC1 folder. Insert a blank line before the closing body tag, then insert a paragraph element containing your first and last name and the text **HTML5 Unit H, Independent Challenge 1**. Save the file as **index.html**, then repeat to add the same information as a CSS comment in HTM H-6.css, saving the file as **spotwren.css**.

b. In index.html, locate the img element containing the logo image within the h1 element near the top of the page. Change the value for the src attribute to **images/swlogo_l.gif** and the width to **468**.

c. Just above the h1 element, insert a div element with an id of **logobg**. Within the div element, add an img element with a src value of **images/swlogo_r.jpg**, width of **578**, height of **184**, and an alt value of **grasses and flowers in bloom**. Save your work.

d. Return to spotwren.css in your text editor, then in the #box style rule, set position to **relative**. Create a style rule based on the "#logo img" selector. Set display to **block** and position to **relative**. Add another style rule based on the "#logobg img" selector. Set position to **absolute** and specify a right value that keeps the element in its original location. Set z-index values for the "#logo img" and the "#logobg img" elements so "#logo img" is stacked on top of "#logobg img". Save your work, then open index.html in your browser and verify that the appearance of the two stacked images for the logo graphic matches the appearance of the original logo graphic.

e. Return to spotwren.css in your text editor, then delete the #skiplink style rule. In the #skipnav style rule, delete the two background name-value pairs. Set position to **absolute**, specify a value for right that aligns the right edge of the element with the right edge of the parent element, and specify a z-index value that stacks the element on top of the "#logo img" element. Save your work.

Independent Challenge 1 (continued)

f. Return to index.html in your text editor. Delete the opening and closing span tags enclosing the text "Skip navigation", but leave the text. Save your work, then reload index.html in your browser and verify that the text "Skip navigation" is now displayed over the yellow border of the logo graphic and that the graphic is flush with the top of the browser window.

g. Return to spotwren.css in your text editor. In the aside style rule, set position to **relative**, width to **250px**, and create a right border that's **10px** wide, solid, and the same color as the background of the nav bar. In the article style rule, set position to **absolute**; a left value that leaves room for the aside element, including margin, padding, and border; and a width value that occupies the remaining width specified in the #box element. Save your work, reload index.html in your browser, then verify that the specials are displayed on the left side of the page and the main page content on the right side of the page, with a border the same color as the nav bar between them. See Figure H-25.

FIGURE H-25

h. Return to spotwren.css in your text editor, change the border color for the aside element to **black**, remove the name-value pairs that specify the background image and background color for the body element, remove all non-border name-value pairs that specify color, change all colors in rules based on pseudo-classes to **black**, then save a copy of the file as **swprint.css**.

i. Validate your HTML and CSS documents.

j. If you have space on a Web server, publish your Web site, then open **index.html** in your browser from the published location.

k. Close your browser, then close your text editor.

Weldon Schloneger/Shutterstock.com, Maxim Tupikov/ Shutterstock.com, Xtremer/Shutterstock.com

Independent Challenge 2

You incorporate the logo for the Murfreesboro Recreational Soccer League into the organizational Web site that you are creating. You also add images from some of the group's events.

a. In your text editor, open HTM H-7.html from the Unit H/IC2 folder. Insert a blank line before the closing body tag, then insert a paragraph element containing your first and last name and the text **HTML5 Unit H, Independent Challenge 2**. Save the file as **index.html**, then repeat to add the same information as a CSS comment in HTM H-8.css, saving the file as **mrsl.css**.

b. In index.html, locate the two img elements near the top of the page. Assign a unique id value to the div element containing each img, then save your work. Return to mrsl.css, then add code to the #box style rule to set the position to **relative**. Create a style rule that is based on the id selector you specified for the first img element and that takes it out of the flow of the page and positions its left margin flush with the left margin of the parent element. Repeat for the second img element, positioning its right margin flush with the right margin of the parent element. Save your work, open index.html in your browser, then verify that the images appear at both edges of the top of the body section.

c. Return to index.html in your text editor. In the h1 element below the images you styled, add a line break element after each word except the last. Enclose each word within a span element and assign each a unique id. Save your work. Return to mrsl.css, then add style rules that position all four word elements while retaining their space in the page flow. Using calculations and/or trial and error, position the first word so its left edge is just to the left of the first logo image. Position each remaining word farther to the right so the words are staggered, as shown in Figure H-26. Save your work and refresh index.html in your browser as many times as necessary until you are satisfied with the appearance of the words.

FIGURE H-26

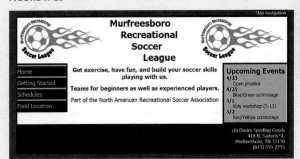

Independent Challenge 2 (continued)

d. Return to mrsl.css in your text editor. Edit the "#mainnav li" style rule to change the display of the unordered list containing the nav bar links from inline to the default layout. Change the background of the #mainnav element from black to **#8CC63F**. Delete the #mainnav name–value pairs for padding. Set the alignment of all text within the nav bar to **left**. Set the width of the nav bar to **175px** and float it to the left of the page content that follows it. Set top, right, and bottom borders that are **5px solid black**. Add a right margin of **10px**. In the "#mainnav li" style rule, add padding of **0.25em** to the top and bottom and a top margin of **0.25em**. Save your work, reload index.html in your browser, then verify that the nav bar links are stacked vertically and that the nav bar is displayed on the left edge of the page.

e. Create a style rule based on the aside selector. Set the element to float to the right of content that follows it, set padding to **8px**, top, left, and bottom borders that are **5px solid black**, a background of **#8CC63F**, and a left margin of **10px**. Save your work, reload **index.html** in your browser, then verify that the "Upcoming Events" list is displayed on the right edge of the page.

Advanced Challenge Exercise

- Return to mrsl.css in your text editor, then for the #mainnav and aside elements set the height to **250px**.
- Add bottom padding of **16px** to the #mainnav element. Remove the bottom borders from the #mainnav and aside elements.
- Save your work, reload index.html in your browser, then verify that the bottoms of the nav bar and sidebar are flush with the footer box at the bottom of the page.

f. Return to mrsl.css in your text editor, remove all name–value pairs that reference colors and background images, then change all colors in rules based on pseudo-classes to **black**. Add code to the #mainnav and #skipnav style rules to prevent the elements from displaying and to remove them from the page flow. Save a copy of the file as **mrsprint.css**.

g. Reload index.html in your browser, then display a print preview if available in your browser. Verify that the "Skip navigation" link and the nav bar are not displayed, as shown in Figure H-27.

h. Validate your HTML and CSS documents.

i. If you have space on a Web server, publish your Web site, then open index.html in your browser from the published location.

j. Close your browser, then close your text editor.

FIGURE H-27

> Murfreesboro Recreational Soccer League
>
> Get exercise, have fun, and build your soccer skills playing with us.
>
> Teams for beginners as well as experienced players.
>
> Part of the North American Recreational Soccer Association
>
> **Upcoming Events**
> 4/23
>   Open practice
> 4/25
>   Blue/Green scrimmage
> 5/1
>   Kids workshop (5-13)
> 5/2
>   Red/Yellow scrimmage
>
> c/o Davies Sporting Goods
> 418 N. Sartoris St.
> Murfreesboro, TN 37130
> (615) 555-2255

Independent Challenge 3

You've been working with Diego Merckx, the manager of Hotel Natoma, to develop a new multicolumn layout for the Web site. You style a page of museum listings with the new layout.

a. In your text editor, open HTM H-9.html from the Unit H/IC3 folder. Insert a blank line before the closing body tag, then insert a paragraph element containing your first and last name and the text **HTML5 Unit H, Independent Challenge 3**. Save the file as **museums.html**, then repeat to add the same information to HTM H-10.css, saving the file as **natoma.css**.

b. In natoma.css, set the position for the element with the id box to **relative**. Set the position for the element with the id skipnav to remove it from the page flow, then place it **10px** from the right edge of the parent element and **5px** from the top of the parent element. Save your work, open museums.html in your browser, then verify that the "Skip navigation" link is displayed in front of the green block surrounding the logo image.

Independent Challenge 3 (continued)

c. In natoma.css, modify the style rule for the #mainnav element and its child elements to convert it from a horizontal to a vertical navigation bar. Set the position for the #mainnav element to remove it from the page flow and position it as shown in Figure H-28. Add a margin to the article element in order to create adequate room for the nav bar along the left side of the page. Save your work and reload museums.html in your browser.

FIGURE H-28

Advanced Challenge Exercise

- In natoma.css, style the footer element with a position value of **fixed** and a bottom value of **0** to keep the footer always visible at the bottom of the Web page. Save your work, then reload museums.html in your browser.
- Add sufficient padding to the bottom of the box element so the last list item, "Zeum," is visible above the footer when you scroll to the bottom of the page in your browser.
- If necessary, add the width property to the style rule for the footer element so the footer width matches the width of the rest of the page content, then save your work and reload the page in your browser.
- If necessary, expand the border property for the footer element to cover all sides of the element, then save your work and reload the page in your browser.

d. Return to natoma.css in your text editor, change all border colors to **black**, remove all other name-value pairs that reference colors, then change all colors in rules based on pseudo-classes to **black**. Add code to the #mainnav style rule to prevent the element from displaying and to remove it from the page flow. Repeat for the #skipnav style rule. Save a copy of the file as **hnprint.css**.

e. Reload museums.html in your browser, then display a print preview if available in your browser. Verify that the "Skip navigation" link and the nav bar are not displayed, as shown in Figure H-29.

f. Validate all your HTML and CSS documents.

g. If you have space on a Web server, publish your Web site, then open museums.html in your browser from the published location.

h. Close your browser, then close your text editor.

Real Life Independent Challenge

FIGURE H-29

This assignment builds on the personal Web site you have worked on in previous units. You'll implement positioning and layout features that you learned in this unit.

a. Copy your Web site files to the Unit H/RLIC folder on the drive and folder where you store your Data Files.

b. Navigate through the pages of your Web site. Sketch the basic site layout on a sheet of paper, then create one or more sketches of an alternative layout using features you learned in this unit. Incorporate at least three features from the following list: multicolumn layout, relative positioning, absolute positioning, stacked elements, fluid layout.

c. Implement the new features from your sketch, saving and reloading your Web pages regularly during the process to ensure your code is creating the desired effects.

d. When your new layout is complete, save changes to your style sheet document, save a copy using the name of your print style sheet, then make the necessary alterations to the style sheet code for a print style sheet. If appropriate, add code to suppress the display of specific page elements in printed output.

e. Preview your Web pages in at least two browsers and make any edits necessary for them to appear as you expected.

f. Validate all of your HTML and CSS documents and make any edits necessary to address any issues.

g. If you have space on a Web server, publish your Web site, then open each page from the published location.

h. Close your browser, then close your text editor.

Visual Workshop

In your text editor, open the file HTM H-11.html from the Unit H/VW directory on the drive and folder where you store your Data Files, add a paragraph before the closing body tag that contains your first and last name and the text **HTML5 Unit H, Visual Workshop**, then save the file as **upcoming.html**. Open HTM H-12.css, add a comment containing the same information, then save it as **revision.css**. Use your text editor to create the layout shown in Figure H-30. Save your work, save a copy of your style sheet with the name **revprint.css**, then make any necessary changes for print formatting. When you are finished, validate your HTML and CSS code. If you have space on a Web server, publish your files, then open the Web page in your browser from the published location. Close your browser and text editor.

FIGURE H-30

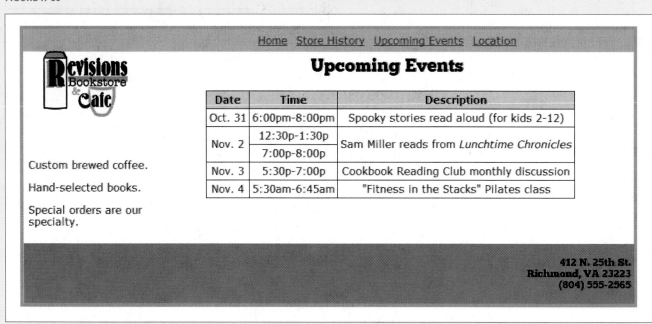

Implementing Page Layout with HTML and CSS

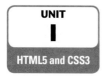

UNIT

I

HTML5 and CSS3

Applying Advanced CSS Styling

Files You Will Need:

To view a list of files needed for this unit, see the Data Files Grid in the back of the book.

Recent versions of CSS have increased the aspects of Web pages that CSS can style. While using the newest CSS features requires careful planning, many of these effects can significantly decrease the time you spend developing a Web site. In this unit, you'll implement new CSS styles to enhance the layout of the Lakeland Reeds B&B Web site.

OBJECTIVES

Assess advanced CSS styles

Implement pseudo-elements

Add generated content

Integrate opacity

Create rounded corners

Create text shadows

Add box shadows

Test browser capabilities with Modernizr

Assessing Advanced CSS Styles

In addition to basic effects like text formatting and element positioning, CSS can style many different aspects of your Web pages. Many of the CSS properties proposed as part of the development of CSS3 enable browsers to create effects that until recently were only available by integrating images. As with the newest HTML features, the specifications from the W3C are only one aspect of using the most recently developed CSS properties. In fact one of the most important factors in deciding what code to include in a Web site is considering which features are supported by different browsers and how they are supported. You've collaborated with the design team and planned a few tweaks to the design of the Lakeland Reeds B&B Web site. As you prepare to incorporate the new properties, you review a few guidelines for working with more recently developed CSS properties.

Best practices for using newer features consistently and predictably include

- **Progressive enhancement and graceful degradation**

  Different browsers handle a given CSS property differently depending on a number of factors. An older browser generally won't support features developed after the browser was released. In addition, the specifications for some CSS features are modified over time, and older browsers support only earlier versions of CSS features. Even though a few main browsers are used for most Web viewing, many versions of each are still in use. Web developers use two main practices to plan Web sites that are usable across this spectrum of capabilities. The main content and capabilities of a Web site should be available for users of the least-featured browsers employed by a significant share of your users. Rather than making advanced features crucial to the layout of a Web site, you add additional features as enhancements only for browsers that can render them, a practice known as **progressive enhancement**. A complementary practice, **graceful degradation**, involves ensuring that the appearance and usability of a Web site doesn't depend on any advanced features; the site should degrade gracefully, meaning that when viewed in browsers that don't support some features, Web page elements that use those features should nevertheless be displayed in a usable way. Figure I-1 shows the same Web page code in browsers with different levels of feature support. You've already implemented both of these concepts in your Web development work for more widely supported features; for instance, when specifying an image as a Web page background, you also specified a color as a fallback. However, these practices are especially important when working with new features that aren't necessarily widely supported.

- **Shims and patches**

  In addition to building backward-compatible sites by specifying alternative code, another useful tool is a script written specifically to bridge the gap between browsers with reduced feature sets and more fully featured browsers. Many of these scripts, known as **shims** or **patches**, are available for use by anyone free of charge. Some address only a single issue; the script that makes HTML5 semantic elements available in recent versions of Internet Explorer, which you've included in your Web pages in previous units, is one such shim. Other tools package many shims together into a library of scripts; later in this unit, you'll implement one such tool, known as Modernizr.

FIGURE I-1: Graceful degradation

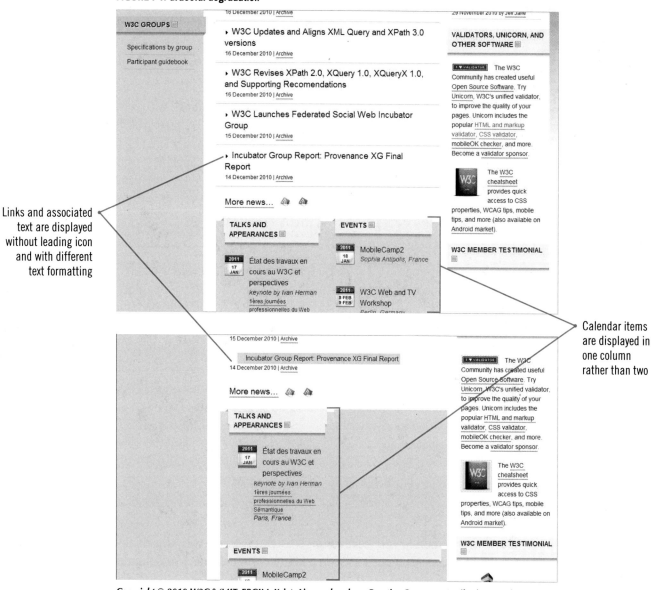

Links and associated text are displayed without leading icon and with different text formatting

Calendar items are displayed in one column rather than two

Working with browser-specific styles

Sometimes the creators of browser rendering engines include support for CSS properties whose functions and syntax haven't yet reached consensus in the W3C development process. To support these properties while ensuring that the browsers won't misinterpret future standards, a few groups incorporate browser-specific prefixes into the property names that they implement. For instance, early implementations of the border-radius property used the property name -webkit-border-radius for browsers that use the WebKit rendering engine (including Chrome and Safari) and -moz-border-radius for browsers using the Mozilla rendering engine (including Firefox). Some properties also have variants with an -o- prefix for the Opera browser.

When you specify code for one of these properties, you should always specify name-value pairs for each of the browser-specific variants first and conclude the code for the style with the code for the generic style; in this example, you'd finish with the border-radius property. Because a later name-value pair in a style rule supersedes an earlier one that duplicates it, newer browsers that support the final specification for a property and its generic name-value pair will use the final line of code, while older browsers will use the relevant browser-specific code and ignore the generic property name.

Implementing Pseudo-elements

Beginning in version 2 of the language, CSS has included **pseudo-elements**, which are selectors that enable you to isolate a piece of a larger element for styling. Like a pseudo-class, a pseudo-element is preceded by a colon (:). In recent browsers, you can precede a pseudo-element with two colons (::) to differentiate it visually from a pseudo-class; however, because older versions of Internet Explorer don't recognize this format, it's best to use double colons only for CSS3 pseudo-elements, which these browsers don't recognize anyway. Table I-1 describes five commonly used CSS pseudo-elements. You explore how the first-letter and first-line pseudo-elements affect the presentation of text on the home page.

STEPS

1. **In your text editor, open HTM I-1.html from the Unit I/Unit folder where you store your Data Files, insert a blank line before the closing body tag, insert a paragraph element containing your first and last name and the text HTML5 Unit I, save it as index.html, repeat to save HTM I-2.html as aboutus.html, HTM I-3.html as rooms.html, and HTM I-4.html as reserve.html, then use a CSS comment to add the same information to HTM I-5.css and save it as lakeland.css**

2. **Return to aboutus.html in your text editor and examine the code**

    In addition to the conditional comment you added to include a script in an earlier unit, another comment adds an embedded style sheet for certain browsers. In the code [if lt IE 7], *lt* stands for *less than*. The code specifies that installations of Internet Explorer with version numbers less than 7 should use the embedded styles; all other browsers ignore it. The styles correct for rendering errors in IE6 and earlier versions.

3. **Open index.html in your browser**

    The first two words of the main paragraph of text are displayed in bold as a result of styles applied to a span element.

4. **Return to lakeland.css in your text editor, create a style rule with the #maintext:first-line selector, add a name-value pair to style text in bold, save your work, then reload index.html in your browser**

    As Figure I-2 shows, the entire first line is displayed in bold.

> **QUICK TIP**
> Selecting the most appropriate line-height value for a drop cap often requires trial and error.

5. **Return to lakeland.css in your text editor, delete the #maintext:first-line style rule, create a style rule with the #maintext:first-letter selector, then add name-value pairs to set font size to 3em, float the element on the left, and set line-height to 0.8em**

    The :first-letter selector allows you to create a **drop cap**, a common visual effect in print media in which the first letter of a paragraph or section is enlarged and drops below the first line of text. You use the float property to make the text that follows the enlarged letter flow around it. Setting the line height for a drop cap is commonly necessary to integrate the letter optimally with the remaining paragraph text.

6. **Save your work, then reload index.html in your browser**

    As Figure I-3 shows, the first letter of Lakeland Reeds is enlarged, and multiple lines of text run to its right.

FIGURE I-2: :first-line pseudo-element applied to paragraph

Font weight for entire first line set to bold

Unholy Vault Designs/Shutterstock.com
Faithe Wempen/sycamoreknoll.com
Photo/Sasha Vodnik

FIGURE I-3: :first-letter pseudo-element applied to paragraph

First letter styled as a drop cap

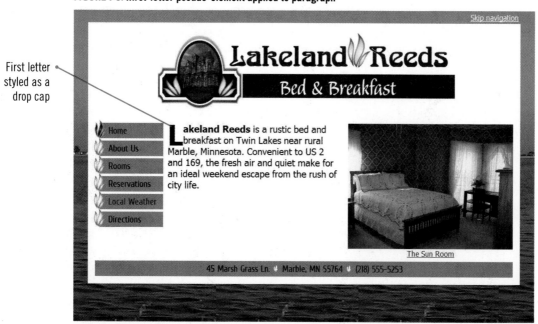

Unholy Vault Designs/Shutterstock.com
Faithe Wempen/sycamoreknoll.com
Photo/Sasha Vodnik

TABLE I-1: CSS pseudo-elements

pseudo-element	effect	CSS version
:first-line	styles the first line of text in the current element	2.1
:first-letter	styles the first letter of text in the current element	2.1
:before	inserts specified content before the current element	2.1
:after	inserts specified content after the current element	2.1
::selection	styles Web page content selected by user	3

Adding Generated Content

Unlike the other pseudo-elements, which simply select parts of existing Web page elements, the :before and :after pseudo-elements enable you to insert content into Web pages using style rules. You can use these selectors to add repeating text or icons to all elements of a given class, for instance, or to specify beginning or ending indicators for each page in a Web site. Each description on the Rooms page includes a section listing the number and size of beds. You use the :before pseudo-element to add an icon before the bed details for each room.

STEPS

1. **Open rooms.html in your browser, then scroll down to view the room descriptions**

   The code for each bed detail paragraph is part of the beds class.

2. **Return to lakeland.css in your text editor**

3. **Below the .beds style rule, create a style rule based on the .beds:before selector**

   This selector creates and selects an element before each element in the class beds.

4. **Within the style rule you created, add the following name-value pair:**

   ```
   content: url("images/bedicon.png");
   ```

   Figure I-4 shows the completed rule. Style rules based on the :before or :after pseudo-elements must specify a value for the content property, which can be either text or the path and name for an image file. Table I-2 shows the syntax for the most common values of the content property.

5. **Save your work, reload rooms.html in your browser, then scroll down to view the room descriptions**

   As Figure I-5 shows, an icon depicting a bed is displayed at the start of each paragraph that describes beds.

FIGURE I-4: **Style rule using the :before pseudo-element**

```
.beds {
   padding: 0;
   margin: 1em 0 0 2em;
   font-weight: bold;
   }
.beds:before {
   content: url("images/bedicon.png");
   }
.callout {
   font-weight: bold;
   }
```

Value of content property will be displayed before each element in the beds class

FIGURE I-5: **:before pseudo-element applied to beds class**

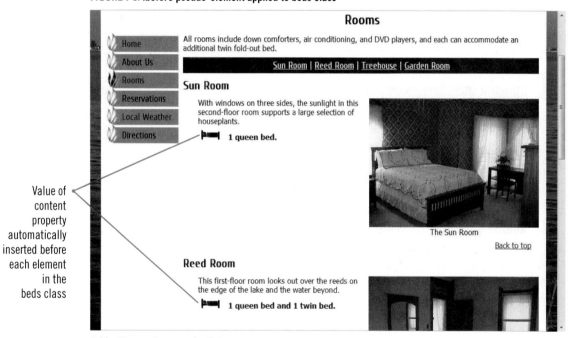

Value of content property automatically inserted before each element in the beds class

Faithe Wempen/sycamoreknoll.com
Photo/Sasha Vodnik

HTML5 and CSS3

TABLE I-2: **Common values for the content property**

content type	syntax	example
text	"*text*"	content: "Chapter: ";
image	url("*path/image*")	content: url("images/bed.png");

Integrating Opacity

CSS enables you to specify the color numerically for a Web page element using the hexadecimal, rgb (red green blue), and hsl (hue saturation light) systems. While all three systems provide you access to a similar range of colors, CSS3 made both rgb and hsl more flexible by adding an alpha channel. The resulting systems are known as rgba and hsla; in each system, the earlier triplet of values becomes a set of four, with the final value representing the level of opacity as a decimal value from 0 (fully transparent) to 1 (totally opaque). Because many browsers in current use don't support the rgba property, it's important to use it along with a corresponding rgb name-value pair as a backup. Older browsers do not support either the hsl or hsla properties, so adding an rgb triplet is a useful tool for graceful degradation for these properties as well. On the main page and the rooms page, you want to position the figure captions over the corresponding images with a background to make them more noticeable. You specify a semi-transparent white background with a solid white background as a backup.

1. **Return to lakeland.css in your text editor**

2. **In the figcaption style rule, add name-value pairs to set the position to absolute, left and bottom to 0, padding to 0.5em 0, margin to 0, and width to 100%**

3. **Add a name-value pair that sets the background property to rgb(255, 255, 255)**

   This code provides a backup rgb value for browsers that don't support rgba, allowing your Web pages to degrade gracefully.

4. **Beneath the name-value pair you inserted in Step 3, add a name-value pair that sets the background property to rgba(255, 255, 255, 0.6)**

   The value for this property includes an alpha value that sets the background to 60% opaque. Figure I-6 shows the completed code for the figcaption style rule.

5. **Save your work, then reload index.html in your browser**

   As Figure I-7 shows, the caption is overlaid at the bottom of the image, with a semi-transparent background in newer browsers and a solid white background in browsers that don't support rgba.

6. **Reload rooms.html in your browser, then scroll down to verify that the captions are overlaid on the room images with semi-transparent backgrounds**

FIGURE I-6: **Code to create translucent figure captions**

```
figcaption {
   display: block;
   position: absolute;
   bottom: 0;
   left: 0;
   padding: 0.5em 0;
   margin: 0;
   width: 100%;
   background: rgb(255, 255, 255);
   background: rgba(255, 255, 255, 0.6);
   }
```

FIGURE I-7: **rgba value applied to figcaption element**

Alpha value of 0.6 makes white background transparent

Unholy Vault Designs/Shutterstock.com
Faithe Wempen/sycamoreknoll.com
Photo/Sasha Vodnik

Creating Rounded Corners

CSS3 enables a number of functions using style rules that previously required a good deal more work to implement. One of these, transforming the corners of an element from a square to a rounded appearance, required creating and positioning image files simulating a rounded edge in one or more of the corners of an element. To create this effect in recent browsers, you instead use the CSS3 border-radius property along with –moz and –webkit styles for versions of some browsers created during the development of this property. Values for this property are expressed in pixels, with 0 creating a standard square border and larger numbers increasing the curve of the rounded area. The border-radius property sets values for all four corners of an element at once, while you can use specific properties for individual corners. Table I-3 lists properties for specific corners for different rendering engines. The layout you created with the design team includes rounded corners on the right corners of each button, the bottom corners of the footer, and all four corners of the container element for the page content. You add these rounded corners using CSS.

STEPS

QUICK TIP

You can specify two values for any border-radius property to create more oblong corners; the first value is the horizontal radius and the second is the vertical radius.

1. **Return to lakeland.css in your text editor, then after the last name-value pair in the #mainnav li style rule, add the six lines of code shown in Figure I-8**

   The first two name-value pairs set the upper-right and lower-right radii using WebKit-specific properties. The next two lines repeat these settings using Mozilla-specific code. The final two lines again repeat the settings using generic properties; any browser that supports this standard code will ignore the previous browser-specific settings.

2. **Save your work, then reload index.html in your browser**

   As Figure I-8 shows, the upper- and lower-right corners of each button are rounded in most browsers. In this case, the original square corners that are displayed in older browsers don't affect the layout, so the feature degrades gracefully without any additional code.

3. **Return to lakeland.css in your text editor, then after the last name-value pair in the footer p style rule, add the six lines of code shown in Figure I-9**

   Similar to the code for the nav bar buttons, these properties set radii for the lower-left and lower- right corners of the footer using the WebKit, Mozilla, and generic properties.

QUICK TIP

You can also use the border-radius property as a shorthand property, specifying 2, 3, or 4 values to set different border radii for different corners with a single name-value pair.

4. **In the #box style rule, add the following code after the final name-value pair:**

   ```
   -webkit-border-radius: 10px;
   -moz-border-radius: 10px;
   border-radius: 10px;
   ```

   These name-value pairs set the same border radius for all four corners of the #box element using the WebKit, Mozilla, and generic properties.

5. **Save your work, then reload index.html in your browser**

   As Figure I-9 shows, the two lower corners of the footer, as well as all four corners of the white box containing the page content, are rounded.

6. **Use the nav bar links to open the other pages of the Web site**

   Because you applied these properties to existing elements and ids, the new styles are applied to all the pages on your site.

FIGURE I-8: Code for rounded corners and resulting nav bar appearance

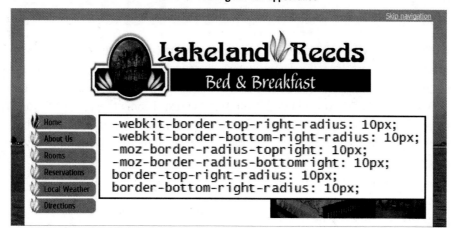

```
-webkit-border-top-right-radius: 10px;
-webkit-border-bottom-right-radius: 10px;
-moz-border-radius-topright: 10px;
-moz-border-radius-bottomright: 10px;
border-top-right-radius: 10px;
border-bottom-right-radius: 10px;
```

Unholy Vault Designs/Shutterstock.com
Faithe Wempen/sycamoreknoll.com
Photo/Sasha Vodnik

FIGURE I-9: Code for rounded corners and resulting footer and box appearance

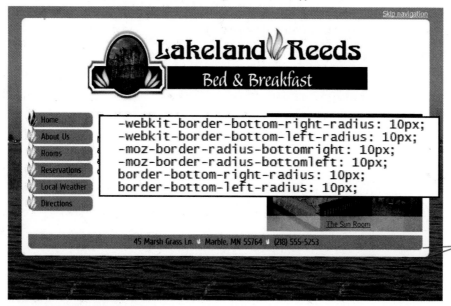

```
-webkit-border-bottom-right-radius: 10px;
-webkit-border-bottom-left-radius: 10px;
-moz-border-radius-bottomright: 10px;
-moz-border-radius-bottomleft: 10px;
border-bottom-right-radius: 10px;
border-bottom-left-radius: 10px;
```

Rounded corners applied to lower-left and lower-right corners of footer, and to all four corners of the box element

Unholy Vault Designs/Shutterstock.com
Faithe Wempen/sycamoreknoll.com
Photo/Sasha Vodnik

TABLE I-3: Browser-specific border radius properties

rendering engine	corner-specific properties	apply to
WebKit	-webkit-border-top-left-radius -webkit-border-top-right-radius -webkit-border-bottom-left-radius -webkit-border-bottom-right-radius	Safari 4 and earlier
Mozilla	-moz-border-radius-topleft -moz-border-radius-topright -moz-border-radius-bottomleft -moz-border-radius-bottomright	Firefox 3.6 and earlier
generic	border-top-left-radius border-top-right-radius border-bottom-left-radius border-bottom-right-radius	Chrome Firefox 4 and later Safari 5 and later Internet Explorer 9 and later Opera 10.5 and later

Creating Text Shadows

Another effect used in some print layouts is a text shadow, which creates the appearance of a shadow on a surface behind each letter. Traditionally, text shadows have been brought to Web pages by creating the effects in image manipulation software and then linking to a graphic showing the text in the HTML code. CSS3 enables you to add shadows to text using the text-shadow property. The property takes four values: horizontal offset, vertical offset, blur, and shadow color. Table I-4 and Figure I-10 detail how each property affects the appearance of a text shadow. ⬛⬛⬛ You enhance the rollover effect of the nav bar text by adding a text shadow to the a:hover rule for main nav bar text.

STEPS

QUICK TIP
Because you have other hover effects in place for nav bar text, this feature already degrades gracefully in your Web pages.

1. **Return to lakeland.css in your text editor**

2. **At the end of the #mainnav a:hover style rule, add the code text-shadow: 1px 1px 1px black;**

   This code creates a text shadow with a horizontal offset, vertical offset, and blur of 1px, and a shadow color of black.

3. **Save your work, then reload index.html in your browser**

   The appearance of the nav bar text is unchanged.

4. **Move the mouse pointer over the links in the nav bar**

   As Figure I-11 shows, most browsers add a shadow to nav bar text when the mouse pointer is over it.

FIGURE I-10: **Values for the text-shadow property**

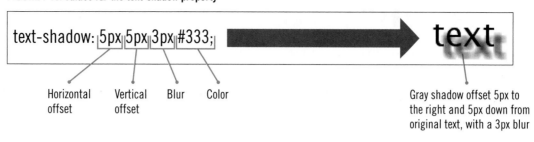

Horizontal offset   Vertical offset   Blur   Color

Gray shadow offset 5px to the right and 5px down from original text, with a 3px blur

FIGURE I-11: **Text shadow on a Web page**

Shadow is displayed 1px below and 1px to the right of the original text, with a 1px blur

Black shadow added to nav bar text when pointer is over it

Unholy Vault Designs/Shutterstock.com
Faithe Wempen/sycamoreknoll.com
Photo/Sasha Vodnik

TABLE I-4: **Values for the text-shadow property**

value	affects	notes
horizontal offset	location of shadow horizontally behind text	Required value; may be negative; must be first number in list
vertical offset	location of shadow vertically behind text	Required value; may be negative; must be second number in list
blur	width and lightness of shadow	Optional value; must be positive; must be third number in list
color	color of shadow behind text	Optional value; may appear before or after numerical settings

Adding Box Shadows

Design in print media doesn't limit shadows to text; shadows are also used on entire units of page content. The CSS3 box-shadow property allows you to apply a shadow to many Web page elements as well. The box-shadow property uses the same values as the text-shadow property: horizontal offset, vertical offset, blur, and shadow color. Unlike text-shadow, however, box-shadow also has –webkit and –moz variants.  You add a box shadow to each link button in the nav bar.

STEPS

1. **Return to lakeland.css in your text editor**

2. **In the #mainnav li style rule, add the following code at the bottom:**
   ```
   -webkit-box-shadow: 1px 1px 4px black;
   -moz-box-shadow: 1px 1px 4px black;
   box-shadow: 1px 1px 4px black;
   ```

3. **Save your changes, then reload index.html in your browser**

   As Figure I-12 shows, browsers that support box shadows display a shadow around the white box containing each nav bar link.

4. **Return to lakeland.css in your text editor, then change each 1px value in the code you just entered to 2px**

   Increasing the horizontal and vertical offsets moves the shadow farther away from the main box. Figure I-13 shows the completed code.

5. **Save your changes, then reload index.html in your browser**

   Figure I-14 shows the changes in the appearance of the box shadows.

FIGURE I-12: Box shadows applied to nav bar buttons

Unholy Vault Designs/Shutterstock.com
Faithe Wempen/sycamoreknoll.com
Photo/Sasha Vodnik

Edges of box shadows are 1px
to the right and 1px down from
edges of original elements

FIGURE I-13: Code for bigger box shadow

```
-webkit-box-shadow: 2px 2px 4px black;
-moz-box-shadow: 2px 2px 4px black;
box-shadow: 2px 2px 4px black;
```

FIGURE I-14: Box shadows with increased horizontal and vertical offsets

Unholy Vault Designs/Shutterstock.com
Faithe Wempen/sycamoreknoll.com
Photo/Sasha Vodnik

Edges of box shadows are now
2px to the right and 2px down
from edges of original elements

Testing Browser Capabilities with Modernizr

Some styles can neatly fall back to other CSS properties, such as an rgb color value substituting when an rgba value isn't recognized. Others, however, require you to provide an entirely different set of styles for graceful degradation. One popular tool for enabling such alternative code is Modernizr, a free script library created by Faruk Ateş and Paul Irish. Once Modernizr is linked to a Web page, it tests each user's browser to detect which properties are supported. Based on the results, Modernizr generates a set of CSS classes. You can write alternative code for different browsers and use these classes to ensure that only the code relevant to a specific browser is rendered. For browsers that don't support any box-shadow properties, you want to simulate a box shadow by creating borders in shades of gray on two sides of an element. You link Modernizr to the main Web page and then specify the alternative code.

STEPS

QUICK TIP

The Modernizr library includes the script you've been using to make HTML5 elements available for styling in Internet Explorer.

1. **Return to aboutus.html in your text editor, delete the three-line comment just before the closing </head> tag, insert a blank line in the same location, then indent and enter the following element:**
   ```
   <script src="scripts/modernizr-1.6.min.js"></script>
   ```
   This script element links to an external script file containing the Modernizr library.

2. **In the opening <html> tag, add the attribute-value pair class="no-js"**
   This class is required for Modernizr to work. Figure I-15 shows the completed HTML code.

QUICK TIP

The class names that correspond to each feature are listed in the online documentation for Modernizr.

3. **Return to lakeland.css in your text editor, create a new style rule based on the .boxshadow #mainnav li selector, then use the cut-and-paste functions of your text editor to remove the three box shadow name-value pairs from the #mainnav li style rule and insert them into the new rule you created**
   For each feature for which Modernizr finds support in a user's browser, it adds a class value to the html element. For the box-shadow properties, the class name created after a successful test is .boxshadow. If this class exists, the browser supports the style, and this rule is implemented; if box shadow support isn't present, the class isn't created, and the browser ignores this style rule.

4. **At the bottom of the #mainnav li style rule, add the following code:**
   ```
   border-bottom: 2px solid #666;
   border-right: 2px solid #777;
   ```
   This code adds bottom and right borders in different shades of gray to the nav bar buttons.

5. **Above the first name-value pair in the .boxshadow #mainnav li style rule, add the code border: none**
   This code removes the gray borders only in browsers that can create the CSS box shadow effect.

6. **Save your work, then reload aboutus.html in your browser**
   Figure I-16 shows the shadow effect in a browser that doesn't support CSS box shadows.

TROUBLE

Because they are not part of official CSS specifications, all browser-specific properties trigger validation errors, and you may also receive an erroneous error for your rgba value. You can safely ignore all these errors.

7. **Convert lakeland.css to a print style sheet with the name Iprint.css, validate the code for your Web pages and your style sheets, then make changes as necessary to fix any errors**

8. **If you have space on a Web server, publish your Web site, then open your Web pages in your browser from the published location**

FIGURE I-15: Web page code incorporating Modernizr script

```
<!DOCTYPE html>
<html class="no-js">
  <head>
    <meta charset="utf-8" />
    <title>Lakeland Reeds Bed &amp; Breakfast - About Us</title>
    <link rel="stylesheet" type="text/css" media="screen" href="lakeland.css" />
    <link rel="stylesheet" type="text/css" media="print" href="llprint.css" />
    <!--[if lt IE 7]>
      <style type="text/css">
        #mainnav {left: 0px;}
        li img {left: -42px;}
      </style>
    <![endif]-->
    <script src="scripts/modernizr-1.6.min.js"></script>
  </head>
```

Previous script element replaced with reference to external file containing Modernizr script

Class added to apply results of Modernizr scripts to Web page

FIGURE I-16: Alternative box shadow code in browser without box-shadow property support

Unholy Vault Designs/Shutterstock.com
Jason Bucy
Photo/Sasha Vodnik

Modernizr applies shadow-like gray borders only in browsers that don't support the box-shadow property

Browser sniffing vs. feature detection

Ensuring cross-browser compatibility has been an important task in Web development since early in the Web's existence. For much of that time, Web developers tried to identify the brand and version of each user's browser by using a script to ask the browser to identify itself, a technique known as **browser sniffing**, While you may encounter browser sniffing scripts in your work on existing Web sites, the technique has an important drawback; browsers may not always identify themselves accurately. Modernizr instead approaches the problem by running a series of tests and using the results to decide which features a user's browser supports, a process known as **feature detection**. Feature detection is more reliable than browser sniffing and also provides a more detailed picture of the capabilities of a user's browser.

Practice

Concepts Review

For current SAM information, including versions and content details, visit SAM Central (http://www.cengage.com/samcentral). If you have a SAM user profile, you may have access to hands-on instruction, practice, and assessment of the skills covered in this unit. Since various versions of SAM are supported throughout the life of this text, check with your instructor for the correct instructions and URL/Web site for accessing assignments.

Refer to Figure I-17.

FIGURE I-17

Unholy Vault Designs/Shutterstock.com
Faithe Wempen/sycamoreknoll.com
Photo/Sasha Vodnik

1. Which feature is created with an rgba color value?
2. Which feature is created with the text-shadow property?
3. Which feature is created with the box-shadow property?
4. Which feature is created with the :first-letter pseudo-element?
5. Which feature is created with the border-radius property?

Match each term with the statement that best describes it.

6. **progressive enhancement**
7. **graceful degradation**
8. **shim**
9. **pseudo-element**
10. **drop cap**

a. a script written specifically to bridge the gap between browsers with reduced feature sets and more fully featured browsers

b. a selector that enables you to isolate a piece of a larger element for styling

c. adding additional features to a Web page as enhancements only for browsers that can render them

d. a common visual effect in print media in which the first letter of a paragraph or section is enlarged

e. ensuring that the appearance and usability of a Web site doesn't depend on any advanced features

Select the best answer from the list of choices.

11. Specifying a fallback color for a background image is an example of _____.

    a. a shim
          c. a patch

    b. a pseudo-element
      d. graceful degradation

12. Which is an example of a shim or patch?

    a. Internet Explorer
      c. CSS

    b. Modernizr
         d. the meta element

13. If you were using the -moz-border-radius property in a style rule, which additional property should you include as the last property in the code for that feature?

    a. -webkit-border-radius
     c. border-radius

    b. -o-border-radius
         d. background

14. To support users of older versions of Internet Explorer, you should precede non-CSS3 pseudo-elements with _____.

    a. :
            c. -ie

    b. ::
           d. a space

15. Which is a CSS3 pseudo-element?

    a. first-line
        c. before

    b. first-letter
      d. selection

16. Which pseudo-element enables you to insert content into Web pages using style rules?

    a. first-line
        c. before

    b. first-letter
      d. selection

17. Which of the values the rgba set (255,100,178,0.5) represents opacity?

    a. 255
          c. 178

    b. 100
          d. 0.5

18. The browser prefix -moz targets which rendering engine?

    a. WebKit
       c. Opera

    b. Mozilla
      d. all of them

Skills Review

1. Implement pseudo-elements.

    a. In your text editor, open HTM I-6.html from the Unit I/Review folder where you store your Data Files, insert a blank line before the closing body tag, insert a paragraph element containing your first and last name and the text **HTML5 Unit I, Skills Review**, save it as **history.html**, then use a CSS comment to add the same information to HTM I-7.css and save it as **bigj.css**.

    b. In bigj.css, create a style rule with the **.content .maintext:first-letter** selector, then add name-value pairs to set font size to **3em**, float the element on the **left**, and set line height to **0.8em**.

    c. Save your work, open history.html in your browser, then verify that each of the three paragraphs telling the history of the restaurant begins with a drop cap.

2. Add generated content.

    a. Return to bigj.css in your text editor.

    b. Below the footer style rule, create a style rule based on the **footer .callout:before** selector.

    c. Within the style rule you created, add a name-value pair that specifies the file **phone.png** located in the **images** directory as the content of the specified pseudo-element.

    d. Save your work, reload history.html in your browser, scroll down to the footer, then verify that a phone icon is displayed before each phone number.

Skills Review (continued)

3. Integrate opacity.

   a. Return to bigj.css in your text editor, then locate the figcaption style rule.

   b. Add name-value pairs to set the position to **absolute**, left and bottom to **0**, padding to **0.5em 0**, and width to **100%**.

   c. Add a name-value pair that sets the background property to an rgb value of **255, 255, 255**.

   d. Beneath the name-value pair you inserted in Step c, add a name-value pair that sets the background to an rgba value of **255, 255, 255, 0.6**.

   e. Save your work, reload history.html in your browser, then verify that the figure caption has a translucent background and is overlaid on the image of the pizza sign.

4. Create rounded corners.

   a. Return to bigj.css in your text editor, then locate the #words style rule.

   b. Add name-value pairs to set the width to **40%** and margin to **0 auto**.

   c. Add name-value pairs for the -webkit and -moz browser-specific properties to create rounded corners, setting the values to **15px**, then add the generic property set to the same value.

   d. Save your work, reload history.html in your browser, then verify that the black box containing the list of words is narrower than the rest of the page content and is displayed with rounded corners.

5. Create text shadows.

   a. Return to bigj.css in your text editor.

   b. At the end of the #mainnav a:hover style rule, add code to create a text shadow using the values **1px 1px 1px black**.

   c. Save your work, then reload history.html in your browser.

   d. Move the mouse pointer over the links in the nav bar and verify that a text shadow is displayed when the mouse pointer is over each link.

6. Add box shadows.

   a. Return to bigj.css in your text editor

   b. In the figure style rule, add name-value pairs for the -webkit and -moz browser-specific properties to create box shadows, setting the values to **2px 2px 4px red**, then add the generic property set to the same value.

   c. Save your changes, reload history.html in your browser, then verify that a red box shadow is displayed on the right and bottom edges of the image of the pizza sign, as shown in Figure I-18.

7. Test browser capabilities.

   a. Return to history.html in your text editor, delete the three-line comment just before the closing </head> tag, insert a blank line in the same location, then indent and enter the element **<script src="scripts/modernizr-1.6.min.js"></script>**.

   b. Add the **no-js** class to the opening <html> tag, then save your work.

   c. Return to bigj.css in your text editor, create a new style rule based on the **.boxshadow figure** selector, then cut and paste the three box shadow name-value pairs from the figure style rule to the new rule you created.

FIGURE I-18

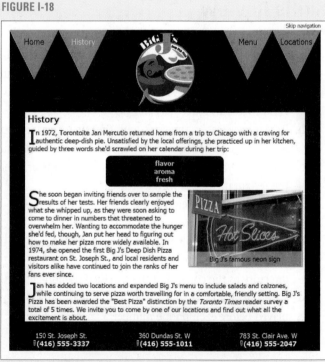

Photo/Sasha Vodnik

Skills Review (continued)

d. At the bottom of the figure style rule, add code to set the bottom and right borders to **2px solid red**.

e. Above the first name-value pair in the **.boxshadow figure** style rule, add code to set all borders to **none**.

f. Save your work, reload history.html in your browser. Verify that recent browser versions continue to display a box shadow on the image of the pizza sign, while older browsers display red lines along the right and bottom of the image to approximate a box shadow.

g. Convert bigj.css to a print style sheet with the name **bjprint.css**, validate the code for your Web pages and your style sheets, then make changes as necessary to fix any errors.

h. If you have space on a Web server, publish your Web site, then open history.html in your browser from the published location.

Independent Challenge 1

As you continue your work on the Web site of the Spotted Wren Garden Center, you continue adjusting the layout by incorporating advanced CSS styles.

a. Open HTM I-8.html from the Unit I/IC1 folder in your text editor. Insert a blank line before the closing body tag, insert a paragraph element containing your first and last name and the text **HTML5 Unit I, Independent Challenge 1**, save it as **resource.html**, then use a CSS comment to add the same information to HTM I-9.css, saving the file as **spotwren.css**.

b. In spotwren.css, create a style rule that applies to the first line of li elements within article elements. Set the font weight to **bold**. Save your work, then open resource.html in your browser and verify that only the first line of each list item is displayed in bold.

c. Add CSS code to overlay figure captions over the associated figure content by positioning them absolutely with zero offset from the bottom left. Add a background rgb color of **(221, 221, 221)** followed by the same value as an rgba value. Determine an appropriate alpha value through trial and error. Save your work, then reload resource.html in your browser and verify the "Prairie Coneflower" figure caption is legible.

d. Create a purple text shadow for figure captions using the values **1px 1px 1px #909** for the text-shadow property. Save your work and preview resource.html in your browser.

e. Add a green text shadow to footer text using the values text-shadow: **1px 1px 2px green** for the text-shadow property. Save your work, preview resource.html in your browser, and compare the page to Figure I-19.

FIGURE I-19

Resources

- Lawn and Garden Care Tip Sheet (PDF)
- Gardening weather forecast
- Omaha area plant hardiness zone information:

Prairie Coneflower

| Zone | Average annual minimum temp | | Last frost | First frost |
	Fahrenheit	Celsius		
4b	-25°F to -20°F	-28.9°C to -31.6°C		
5a	-20°F to -15°F	-26.2°C to -28.8°C	May 1	Oct 15
5b	-15°F to -10°F	-23.4°C to -26.1°C		

- **Recommended drought-tolerant perennials:**
  Black-eyed Susan
   Rudbeckia hirta
  Prairie coneflower, Echinacea
   Ratibida columnaris
  Perennial sunflower, Jerusalem artichoke
   Helianthus tuberosus
  Mexican Hat coneflower, Gray-Headed coneflower
   Ratibida pinnata
  May night salvia, Caradonna salvia
   Salvia nemorosa
  Prairie aster
   Aster tanacetifolius
  Blanket flower
   Gaillardia aristata
  Golden tickseed
   Coreopsis tinctoria
  Poppy mallow
   Callirhoe involucrata
  Cranesbill geranium
   Geranium maculatum
  Spike gayfeather
   Liatris spicata
  Butterfly milkweed
   Asclepias tuberosa

548 N. 58th St. • Omaha, NE 68132 • (402) 555-9736

Jim Gitzlaff/Shutterstock.com

Maxim Tupikov/Shutterstock.com

Xtremer/Shutterstock.com

Independent Challenge 1 (continued)

f. Return to spotwren.css in your text editor, change the border color for the aside element to black, remove the name-value pairs that specify the background image and background color for the body element, remove the second background name-value pair for figcaption, and remove all non-border name-value pairs that specify color for other elements. Remove text shadows and in all other rules based on pseudo-classes, change all colors to black. Save a copy of the file as **swprint.css**.

g. Validate your HTML and CSS documents.

h. If you have space on a Web server, publish your Web site, then open resource.html in your browser from the published location.

i. Close your browser, then close your text editor.

Independent Challenge 2

As you continue your work on the Murfreesboro Recreational Soccer League Web site, you integrate rounded corners into the design to evoke the center circle on a soccer field. You also incorporate some advanced CSS styles to enhance existing elements.

a. Open HTM I-10.html from the Unit I/IC2 folder in your text editor. Insert a blank line before the closing body tag, insert a paragraph element containing your first and last name and the text **HTML5 Unit I, Independent Challenge 2**, save the file as **schedule.html**, then use a CSS comment to add the same information to HTM I-11.css and save it as **mrsl.css**.

b. In mrsl.css, locate the h1 #affiliation style rule. Add a second name-value pair for background after the existing background property. Specify an rgba value for the new property, copying the existing rgb value and experimenting to find an alpha value that enables you to see the texture of the grass but keeps the text highly legible. Save your work and preview schedule.html in your browser. Your main heading and subheading should match those shown in Figure I-20.

c. Add code to the style rule for list items in the #mainnav element that sets the border radius to **20px**. Specify all necessary browser-specific properties as well as the generic property. Save your work, then reload schedule.html in your browser. Your nav bar links should match those shown in Figure I-20.

d. Add code to the style rule for the #skiplink element that sets the bottom-left border radius to **20px**. Specify all necessary browser-specific properties as well as the generic property. Save your work, then reload schedule.html in your browser. Your skip link should match the one shown in Figure I-20.

FIGURE I-20

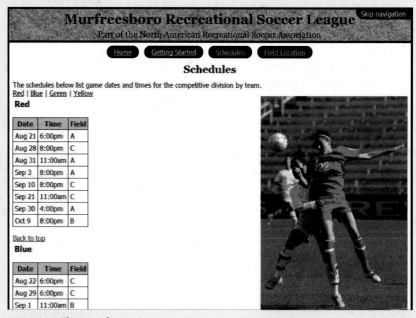

9507848116/Shutterstock.com
Xtremer/Shutterstock.com

Independent Challenge 2 (continued)

Advanced Challenge Exercise

- Using a pseudo-element, create a style rule that inserts a space followed by the word "Team" after each h3 element within an article element. (*Hint*: To create the space, insert a space after the opening quote for the value but before the first letter of the text to insert.)

- Create a box shadow around all four sides of every img element within a figure element. Set both the x and y offsets to **0px**, and use a high value, such as **20px**, for the blur. Use **#ffd700** for the shadow color. Specify all necessary browser-specific properties as well as the generic property. Save your work, then reload schedule.html in your browser. Your headings and figure should match those shown in Figure I-21.

e. Return to mrsl.css in your text editor, remove all attribute-value pairs that reference colors as well as the pairs that specify background images, then change all colors in rules based on pseudo-classes to black. Save a copy of the file as **mrsprint.css**.

f. Validate your HTML and CSS documents.

g. If you have space on a Web server, publish your Web site, then open schedule.html in your browser from the published location.

h. Close your browser, then close your text editor.

Independent Challenge 3

As you continue to work with Diego Merckx to refine the design of the Hotel Natoma Web site, you implement a few advanced CSS features.

FIGURE I-21

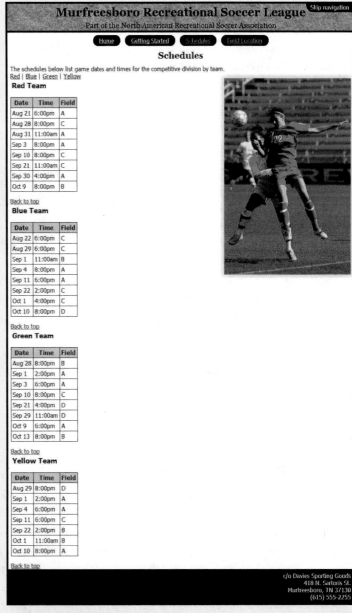

9507848116/Shutterstock.com
Xtremer/Shutterstock.com

a. Open HTM I-12.html from the Unit I/IC3 folder in your text editor. Insert a blank line before the closing body tag, then insert a paragraph element containing your first and last name and the text **HTML5 Unit I, Independent Challenge 3**. Save the file as **nearby .html**. Open HTM I-13.css, below the existing comment at the top of the document, add another comment containing your first and last name and the text **HTML5 Unit I, Independent Challenge 3**. Save the file as **natoma.css**.

b. In natoma.css, add CSS code to overlay figure captions over the associated figure content by positioning them absolutely with 0 offset from the bottom left. Add an appropriate rgba value for the background and precede it with an appropriate rgb color as a backup. Save your work, then reload nearby.html in your browser and verify that the figure captions are clearly legible.

Independent Challenge 3 (continued)

c. Add rounded corners to the top left and bottom right of the Web page. Start by adding properties to round the top left and bottom right corners of the #box element with a **40px** radius. Next add properties for the h1 element to round the top left corner with a radius of **35px**, and for the footer element to round the bottom right corner with a radius of **35px**. Ensure that you specify both browser-specific and generic properties for each corner. Save your work, then reload nearby.html in your browser and verify that both corners are rounded, as shown in Figure I-22.

d. Add rounded corners to the top left and bottom right corner of each list item in the main nav bar, with a radius of **20px**. Ensure that you specify both browser-specific and generic properties for each corner. Save your work, then reload nearby.html in your browser and verify that both corners are rounded, as shown in Figure I-22.

FIGURE I-22

Photos/Sasha Vodnik

Advanced Challenge Exercise

- Replace the existing script reference in nearby.html with a reference to the Modernizr script in the scripts folder. If necessary, refer to the "Testing Browser Capabilities with Modernizr" lesson in this unit for the script element code. In addition, add a class attribute to the html element with a value of **"no-js"**.

- Create a new style rule based on the ".borderradius #mainnav li" selector, then move all the border-radius properties from the "#mainnav li" style rule to the new rule.

- In the "#mainnav li" style rule, set the background to the file **buttonbg.png**, which is located in the images folder. Add another name-value pair to set the width to **102px**.

- Copy the name-value pair in the "#mainnav li" style rule that specifies a background color and add it to the ".borderradius #mainnav li" rule. Add a name-value pair to the ".borderradius #mainnav li" rule that sets width to **auto**.

- Save your work, then if you have access to Internet Explorer version 8 or earlier, or an older version of another browser, open nearby.html in your older browser. The nav bar buttons should be displayed with rounded corners, but each button should be the same width, which indicates that the backup rule based on the Modernizr testing is applying an image for the button backgrounds to simulate rounded corners.

e. In natoma.css, change all border colors to **black**, change all colors in rules based on pseudo-classes to **black**, remove the second background attribute for the figcaption element, then remove all other attribute-value pairs that reference colors. Save a copy of the file as **hnprint.css**.

f. Validate all your HTML and CSS documents.

g. If you have space on a Web server, publish your Web site, then open nearby.html in your browser from the published location.

h. Close your browser, then close your text editor.

Real Life Independent Challenge

This assignment builds on the personal Web site you have worked on in previous units. You'll implement advanced CSS features that you learned in this unit.

a. Copy your Web site files to the Unit I/RLIC folder on the drive and folder where you store your Data Files.

b. Navigate through the pages of your Web site. Identify at least three features you learned in this unit that you want to make use of in your site, and decide on which page or pages you'd like to implement each one.

c. Implement the new features, saving and reloading your Web pages regularly during the process to ensure your Web pages are displayed with the desired effects.

d. When you finish implementing each feature, test the relevant page or pages in multiple browsers, including older browser versions if available, to ensure that your pages degrade gracefully.

e. When your code is complete, save changes to your style sheet document, then save a copy using the name of your print style sheet and make the necessary alterations to the style sheet code for a print style sheet.

f. Validate all of your HTML and CSS documents and make any edits necessary to address any issues.

g. If you have space on a Web server, publish your Web site, then open each page in your browser from the published location.

h. Close your browser, then close your text editor.

Visual Workshop

In your text editor, open the file HTM I-14.html from the Unit I/VW directory on the drive and folder where you store your Data Files, add a paragraph before the closing body tag that contains your first and last name and the text **HTML5 Unit I, Visual Workshop**, then save the file as **upcoming.html**. Open HTM I-15.css, add a comment containing the same information, then save it as **revision.css**. Open upcoming.html in your browser, then use your text editor to add advanced features to make your Web page match Figure I-23. Add code to test browser capabilities for the box shadow, then add backup styling for older browsers. Save your work, save a copy of your style sheet with the name **revprint.css**, then remove any styles for text shadow and make any other changes necessary for print formatting, leaving the styles that create box shadows unchanged. When you are finished, validate your HTML and CSS code. If you have space on a Web server, publish your files, then open the Web page in your browser from the published location. Close your browser and text editor.

FIGURE I-23

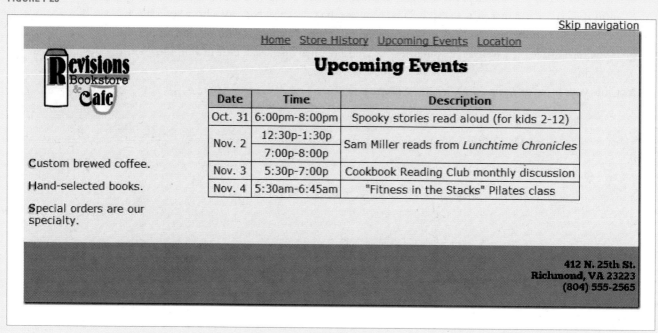

Creating and Processing Web Forms

Files You Will Need:

To view a list of files needed for this unit, see the Data Files Grid in the back of the book.

While Web sites are really useful for communicating information to an audience, sometimes you want to invite communications from users as well. HTML enables you to receive user input by creating **forms**, which are groups of elements that let users type text, select from lists, check boxes, and/or click buttons to provide information, and then submit that information. 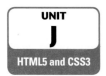 Phillip Blaine, the owner of Lakeland Reeds B&B, reports that customers have found his Web site useful and informative. He commonly hears that visitors would like to be able to make reservations and ask questions on the site directly. To meet this need, you design and create a feedback form.

OBJECTIVES

Design a form

Create a form

Create text fields

Customize text fields

Create check boxes

Create option buttons

Create a drop-down menu

Enable form submission

Designing a Form

Like many other parts of a Web site, it's useful to plan out a form before coding it. Understanding what information you need to collect, identifying the type of data required for each item, and ensuring that your form is logically organized and includes adequate explanations can increase usability as well as improve the accuracy and relevance of information that users provide.  You met with Phillip Blaine to create a plan for the feedback form that he wants to integrate into the Lakeland Reeds B&B Web site. Figure J-1 shows a sketch of the form that you created based on the meeting. Before you finalize the form, you review some important steps in designing a form.

A few tasks are particularly important in designing a usable form:

- **Identify the types of information you need to collect**

  Especially in larger organizations, form data can be used in many ways; for instance, the data can generate address information for sending a catalog, or the data could be used to create an account and login name for a user in an online system. Users provide most information in a form though input elements, which support different types of user interaction depending on the value of the type attribute. Table J-1 lists and describes the most commonly used values. Form elements in which users enter or select data are also known as **fields**.

  To make the data a user submits as useful as possible, it's important to ask for information in distinct pieces. For instance, if your Web form included a single field into which users entered their first and last names, you would not easily be able to sort the resulting information by last name. Providing separate input elements instead for first name and last name would enable sorting resulting records by last name. While almost every piece of information could be further broken down, it's important to clarify what you're likely to need to do with the information; thus, while you could collect street address information with separate fields for house number and street name, for most purposes, a single field for the whole address is sufficient.

- **Create a logical flow**

  A form should display related fields near each other; for example, if you were collecting name and mailing address information, you'd want to display the fields in the order that users are accustomed to specifying an address: first name, last name, street, city, etc. In addition, when you want users to complete the fields in a specific order, place the first field at the top and subsequent fields below it. Many forms end with a field where users can enter a question or additional information. Placing such a field at the end of a form invites users to first enter information in specific fields where possible, then enter in the final field anything they haven't found another place to say.

- **Integrate labels and legends**

  Fields are displayed on Web pages as boxes to check, boxes in which to enter text, or lists of options. To make the significance of each field clear to users, it's important to associate each field with a **label**, which is an element containing descriptive text that is associated with a form element.

  In most forms, groups of fields form logical units; for example, in an order form, name and address information might make up one group, details on items to order another, and payment details a third. In a Web page form, these groups are known as **fieldsets**. By default, most browsers surround the fields in a fieldset with a box, creating a visual cue that the fields share a common subject. You can further increase the usability of your form by adding a descriptive title to each fieldset. Such a title is known as a **legend** and is created using the legend element.

FIGURE J-1: Sketch of Lakeland Reeds feedback form

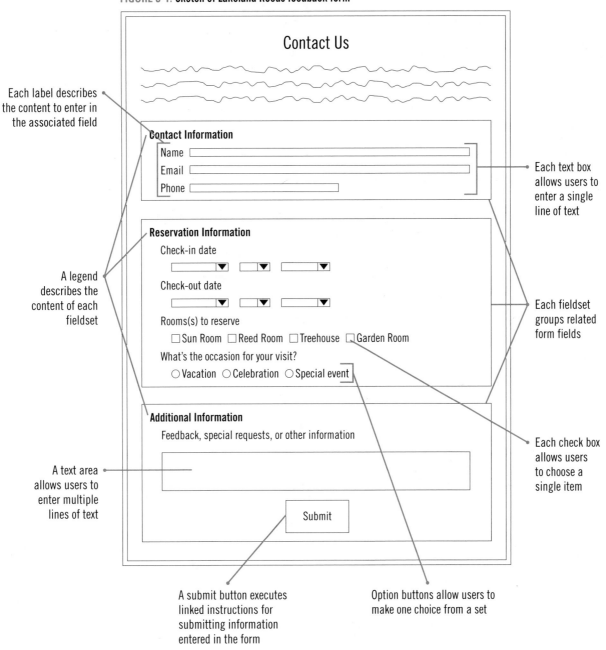

Each label describes the content to enter in the associated field

A legend describes the content of each fieldset

A text area allows users to enter multiple lines of text

Each text box allows users to enter a single line of text

Each fieldset groups related form fields

Each check box allows users to choose a single item

A submit button executes linked instructions for submitting information entered in the form

Option buttons allow users to make one choice from a set

TABLE J-1: Commonly used input type values

value	creates	example
checkbox	a check box, which allows users to select a single item	☐ Treehouse
radio	an option button, which lets users select one option from a set of choices	○ Celebration
submit	a submit button, which users can click to send the data they have provided to the server	Submit
text	a text box into which users can type a single line of text	Phone

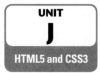

Creating a Form

Like a table, a Web page form contains a series of nested elements. You mark form contents with the form element. A fieldset element contains the elements in each section of the form, including a legend element describing the contents of the fieldset. Table J-2 details some of the most commonly used form elements. ██ ███ As you begin to create the Lakeland Reeds B&B contact form, you enter the basic structuring elements.

STEPS

1. In your text editor, open HTM J-1.html from the Unit J/Unit folder where you store your Data Files, insert a blank line before the closing body tag, insert a paragraph element containing your first and last name and the text HTML5 Unit J, save it as contact.html, then use CSS comments to add the same information to HTM J-2.css, saving it as lakeland.css, and to HTM J-3.css, saving it as llform.css

2. In contact.html, add a new line beneath the h2 element, indent to match the opening h2 tag, then insert opening and closing form tags on separate lines

3. Between the opening and closing form tags, add four sets of opening and closing fieldset tags on separate lines with the id values contactinfo, reserveinfo, additionalinfo, and submitbutton

QUICK TIP

The span elements are necessary for cross-browser styling you'll apply in a later step.

4. Within the contactinfo fieldset element, add the code <legend>Contact Information</legend>

5. Repeat Step 4 to add the legend Reservation Information to the reserveinfo fieldset and the legend Additional Information to the additionalinfo fieldset

6. Beneath the legend element in the reserveinfo fieldset, add four sets of opening and closing fieldset tags on separate lines with the id values checkin, checkout, roombox, and occasionbox

   Figure J-2 shows the completed form and fieldset tags.

7. Within the checkin fieldset, add the code <legend>Check-in date</legend>, then repeat to add the legends Check-out date to the checkout fieldset, Room(s) to reserve to the roombox fieldset, and What's the occasion for your visit? to the occasionbox fieldset

   Compare your code to Figure J-2.

TROUBLE

Browsers vary in the way they present fieldsets by default, so your browser may not match the figure exactly.

8. Save your work, then open contact.html in your browser

   As Figure J-3 shows, each fieldset is displayed with a border and the associated legend.

9. Return to contact.html in your text editor, copy the link element that references lakeland.css, insert a new line above the favicon link element, paste the code from the Clipboard, then change the href value in the pasted element to llform.css

   The llform.css file contains cross-browser styling that matches the rest of the Web site.

10. Save your work, then reload contact.html in your browser

    As Figure J-3 shows, the form is styled with fonts and colors that match the rest of the Web page.

```
<article id="content">
   <h2 id="main">Contact Us</h2>
   <form>
      <fieldset id="contactinfo">
         <legend><span>Contact Information</span></legend>
      </fieldset>
      <fieldset id="reserveinfo">
         <legend><span>Reservation Information</span></legend>
         <fieldset id="checkin">
            <legend>Check-in date</legend>
         </fieldset>
         <fieldset id="checkout">
            <legend>Check-out date</legend>
         </fieldset>
         <fieldset id="roombox">
            <legend>Room(s) to reserve</legend>
         </fieldset>
         <fieldset id="occasionbox">
            <legend>What's the occasion for your visit?</legend>
         </fieldset>
      </fieldset>
      <fieldset id="additionalinfo">
         <legend><span>Additional Information</span></legend>
      </fieldset>
      <fieldset id="submitbutton">
      </fieldset>
   </form>
</article>
```

fieldset elements nested within reserveinfo fieldset

FIGURE J-3: Form outline in browser before and after styling

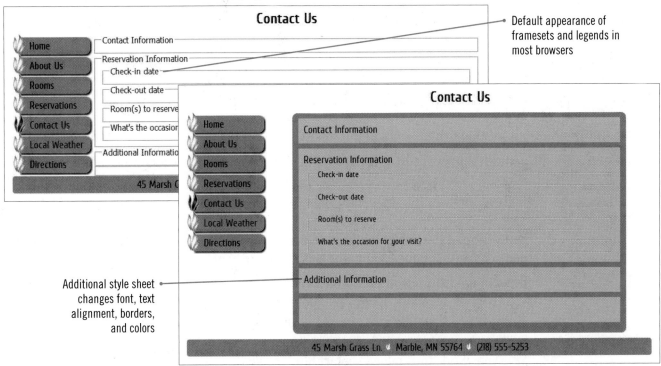

Default appearance of framesets and legends in most browsers

Additional style sheet changes font, text alignment, borders, and colors

TABLE J-2: HTML form elements

element	marks
fieldset	a group of related form fields and associated labels
form	all the elements that are part of a form
input	an individual item of data that users can enter
label	a heading describing the associated input element
legend	a heading describing the topic of the fieldset
optgroup	a group of option elements
option	a single entry in a drop-down list
select	a set of entries to display as a drop-down list
textarea	a multiline area where users can enter text

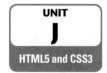
Creating Text Fields

You can use the input element to create many different types of fields that accept user input in your forms. Setting the type attribute to "text" creates a single-line text field known as a **text box**, in which users can type a small amount of text. HTML5 introduces a number of additional input values that create text boxes with specific semantic meanings; Table J-3 details the most common values. Some user agents provide additional functionality for some of these text boxes; for instance, in an email field, newer browsers check for the common elements that all email addresses must contain and alert users if their entries are not valid email addresses. You can also use the textarea element to create a **text area**, which is a field that allows users to enter multiple lines of text. You add general text boxes for name and phone number, a special-purpose text box to collect users' email addresses, and a text area, along with legends.

1. **Return to contact.html in your text editor**

2. **Within the contactinfo fieldset, beneath the legend element, enter opening and closing label tags on separate lines, then insert a new line between the tags and type Name**

   Text within the label element serves as the label for the associated field.

3. **Repeat Step 2 to create two more label elements below the one you just created, containing the text Email and Phone respectively, and an additional label element beneath the legend in the additionalinfo fieldset containing the text Feedback, special requests, or other information**

4. **Beneath the text Name in the first label element, enter the following tag:**
   ```
   <input type="text" name="name" id="nameinput" />
   ```
   Specifying the value "text" for the type attribute creates a generic text box.

5. **Beneath the text Email in the second label element, enter the following tag:**
   ```
   <input type="email" name="email" id="emailinput" />
   ```
   The value "email" for the type attribute creates a text box and enables any special features a user agent might apply to an email field.

6. **Repeat Step 4 to create a text input element with the name phone and the id phoneinput beneath the text Phone within the third label element**

7. **Beneath the label text in the additionalinfo fieldset, enter the code**
   ```
   <textarea id="feedback" name="feedback" rows="4" cols="55"></textarea>
   ```
   The rows attribute specifies how many rows of input are visible, while the cols attribute approximates how many characters in a monospace font should fit across the box. Figure J-4 shows the completed code.

8. **Save your work, then reload contact.html in your browser**

   As Figure J-5 shows, the text of each label is displayed along with a text box corresponding to each input element.

9. **Click in the first text box and type your first and last name, then click in the textarea box in the Additional Information section and type the text of this step to test the functionality of the box**

   As you reach the end of a line in the textarea box, the text wraps, beginning a new line.

FIGURE J-4: Text fields added to Web page

```
<form>
    <fieldset id="contactinfo">
        <legend><span>Contact Information</span></legend>
        <label>
            Name
            <input type="text" name="name" id="nameinput" />
        </label>
        <label>
            Email
            <input type="email" name="email" id="emailinput" />
        </label>
        <label>
            Phone
            <input type="text" name="phone" id="phoneinput" />
        </label>
    </fieldset>
    <fieldset id="reserveinfo">
        <legend><span>Reservation Information</span></legend>
        <fieldset id="checkin">
            <legend>Check-in date</legend>
        </fieldset>
        <fieldset id="checkout">
            <legend>Check-out date</legend>
        </fieldset>
        <fieldset id="roombox">
            <legend>Room(s) to reserve</legend>
        </fieldset>
        <fieldset id="occasionbox">
            <legend>What's the occasion for your visit?</legend>
        </fieldset>
    </fieldset>
    <fieldset id="additionalinfo">
        <legend><span>Additional Information</span></legend>
        <label>
            Feedback, special requests, or other information
            <textarea id="feedback" name="feedback" rows="4" cols="55"></textarea>
        </label>
    </fieldset>
    <fieldset id="submitbutton">
    </fieldset>
</form>
```

input and textarea elements nested within associated label elements

FIGURE J-5: Text fields and associated labels displayed in form

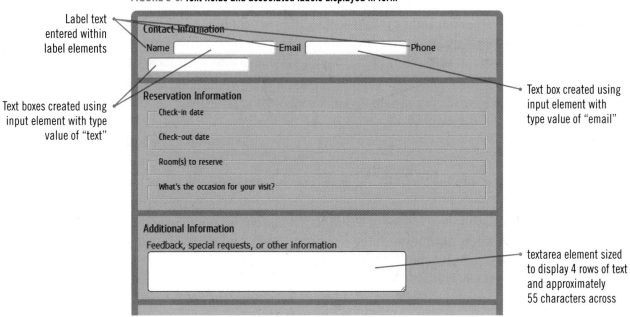

Label text entered within label elements

Text boxes created using input element with type value of "text"

Text box created using input element with type value of "email"

textarea element sized to display 4 rows of text and approximately 55 characters across

TABLE J-3: Input values for special data types

value	result
password	most browsers display text entered by users as bullets or asterisks rather than showing the actual characters
email	newer browsers may validate to ensure that entries are valid email addresses; touchscreen devices with on-screen keyboards may display customized buttons for email input, such as an @ key or a .com key
url	newer browsers may validate entries to ensure that they are valid Web addresses; touchscreen devices with on-screen keyboards may display customized buttons for input, such as a .com key
search	browsers may style input to match styling of search boxes in other parts of the user interface
tel	can be used in conjunction with style sheet or script code to verify that entries are valid telephone numbers

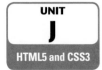

Customizing Text Fields

Labels and fields usually require styling to optimize usability. Good layout can transform a disorganized list of words and boxes into sets of labels and fields whose relationship is clear. In addition to specifying the position of label and input elements, you can control the width of text boxes and limit the number of characters users can enter in each one, as detailed in Table J-4. You can also insert attributes to input elements that add usability features in browsers that support them. ⬛⬛⬛⬛ You add styles to the style sheet to display the labels and text boxes in parallel columns. You also use an HTML attribute to add placeholder text to two of the fields in your form.

STEPS

1. **Return to llform.css in your text editor, create a style rule for label elements in the element with the id contactinfo, then set display to block, position to relative, and margin to 12px 0**

2. **Create a style rule for input elements in the element with the id contactinfo, then set position to absolute and left to 100px**

   The first rule you added causes each label element to start a new line and increases the space between lines. The second rule moves all the input elements a uniform distance to the right of their corresponding labels.

3. **Create a style rule for the elements with the ids nameinput and emailinput and set width to 30em, then create a style rule for the element with the id phoneinput and set width to 12em**

   Compare your code to Figure J-6.

4. **Save your work, then reload contact.html in your browser**

   As Figure J-8 shows, the fields associated with the Name and Email labels are displayed with the same length, while the Phone text box is shorter. In addition, the labels and input boxes are displayed in separate columns.

5. **Return to contact.html in your text editor, then in the input tag with the id nameinput add the name-value pair placeholder="First and last name"**

   Newer browsers display the value of the placeholder attribute as light-colored text in the associated text box and remove it when a user selects the box in preparation for text entry. Placeholder text can be useful in providing examples or formats for input or for describing what users should enter in a given text box.

6. **In the input tag with the id emailinput add the name-value pair placeholder="address@example.com"**

7. **Save your work, return to llform.css in your text editor, then add a style rule based on the input:focus and textarea:focus selectors that sets the background to #e3d5ba**

   The focus pseudo-class applies to an element that a user has selected. This rule changes the background color for the field a user is working with. Figure J-7 shows the completed code.

TROUBLE
Because some older browsers don't support the placeholder attribute, your browser may not match Figure J-8 exactly.

8. **Save your work, then reload contact.html in your browser**

   As Figure J-8 shows, placeholder text appears in gray in the first two text boxes.

9. **Click in the Name text box, type your name, then click in the Email text box**

   Once you click in a text box, the placeholder text is no longer displayed, and the background color changes.

```
#contactinfo label {
  display: block;
  position: relative;
  margin: 12px 0;
  }
#contactinfo input {
  position: absolute;
  left: 100px;
  }
#nameinput, #emailinput {
  width: 30em;
  }
#phoneinput {
  width: 12em;
  }
```

FIGURE J-7: Code to create placeholder text and hover color

```
<label>
  Name
  <input type="text" name="name" id="nameinput" placeholder="First and last name" />
</label>
<label>
  Email
  <input type="email" name="email" id="emailinput" placeholder="address@example.com" />
</label>
```

```
input:focus, textarea:focus {
  background: #e3d5ba;
  }
```

Values for placeholder attributes specify default text to display in text boxes

FIGURE J-8: Text boxes with positioning, size, and placeholder text applied

Contact Information

Name	First and last name
Email	address@example.com
Phone	

TABLE J-4: Sizing attributes for text boxes

attribute	supported values	effect
width	width in em, pixels, or another supported unit	sets the width of the text box
maxlength	number greater than 0	specifies the maximum number of characters a user can enter in the text box

Creating Check Boxes

Sometimes rather than allowing users to enter text, you want to present them with a predetermined set of choices. When you want users to be able to select one or more predefined choices independent of each other, a check box usually makes the most sense. A **check box** is a box that users can click to add or remove a check mark, enabling users to select or deselect it. A check box is ideal for allowing users to indicate whether a particular statement applies to them. Because a user may wish to reserve more than one room at Lakeland Reeds, you use check boxes for inputs in the "Room(s) to reserve" fieldset.

1. Return to contact.html in your text editor, then beneath the legend element in the roombox fieldset, enter four pairs of label tags on separate lines

2. In the opening tag for the first label element, add the name-value pair for="sun", then repeat for the remaining three label elements using the values reed, tree, and garden

QUICK TIP
A check box should always precede its label text for optimal usability.

3. Within the first label element, enter the tag <input type="checkbox" id="sun" value="Sun Room" />; then on a new line type Sun Room

   Because users do not enter text in a check box, you use the value attribute to specify text to be submitted with the form if the check box is selected.

4. Repeat Step 3 for the remaining label elements, creating input elements with the following attributes and label text:

   ```
   id="reed" value="Reed Room"        Reed Room
   id="tree" value="Treehouse"        Treehouse
   id="garden" value="Garden Room"    Garden Room
   ```

5. Add the name-value pair name="room" to each of the four input tags

   Figure J-9 shows the completed code for the check boxes and labels.

6. Save your work, then return to llform.css

7. Create a style rule for label elements within the element with the id roombox, then add a name-value pair to set the right margin to 25px

   This style adds space between each label and the check box that follows it.

8. Save your work, then reload contact.html in your browser

   Figure J-10 shows the check boxes in the Web page.

9. Click each check box to select it, then click each check box again to deselect it

   You can select as many or as few check boxes at once as you want.

```
<fieldset id="roombox">
  <legend>Room(s) to reserve</legend>
  <label for="sun">
    <input type="checkbox" id="sun" value="Sun Room" name="room" />
    Sun Room
  </label>
  <label for="reed">
    <input type="checkbox" id="reed" value="Reed Room" name="room" />
    Reed Room
  </label>
  <label for="tree">
    <input type="checkbox" id="tree" value="Treehouse" name="room" />
    Treehouse
  </label for="garden">
  <label>
    <input type="checkbox" id="garden" value="Garden Room" name="room" />
    Garden Room
  </label>
</fieldset>
```

type set to
"checkbox"

FIGURE J-10: **Text boxes displayed in form**

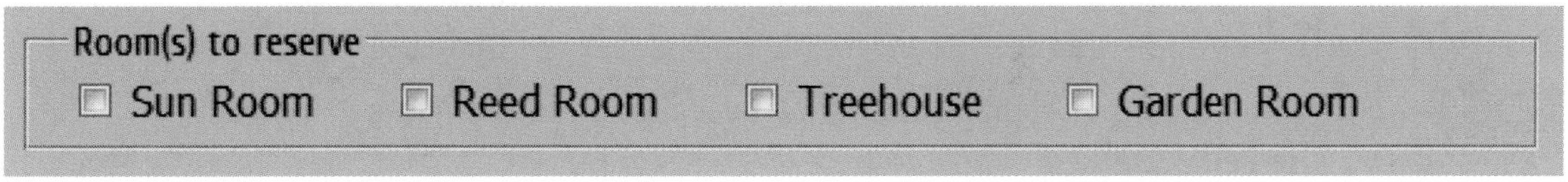

Room(s) to reserve
☐ Sun Room   ☐ Reed Room   ☐ Treehouse   ☐ Garden Room

HTML5 and CSS3

Marking fields as required

Often one or more fields on a Web form are marked as required. Many Web sites implement scripts to check if required fields are completed; if not, these scripts can prevent the submission of the form and display an error message. HTML5 introduced the *required* attribute, which can replace script-based verification in some user agents. You simply add the attribute *required* (or *required="required"* in XHTML-compliant documents) to any required field. You should also include a visual cue on your Web page for each required field, along with an explanation of what the cue means. The *required* attribute can't replace script-based validation for Web sites that must support older browsers, but if your site's users primarily or exclusively access your site using newer browsers, it can be a powerful shortcut.

Creating Option Buttons

Another type of input, the **option button**, presents users with a circular box for selecting one option from a set of choices. An option button is also known as a **radio button** and is best suited for prompting users to select only one item from a group, such as the age range that applies to users. When used appropriately, both option buttons and check boxes ensure that all user input for a particular element matches a standard list of options, preventing typographical errors and enabling you to precisely direct or sort responses that are submitted. Each input element in a set of option buttons must include the name attribute with a value identical to all other members of the set. You can also include the checked attribute for one option button in a set, causing browsers to display the button as selected by default. ▓▓▓ Phillip Blaine would like users to select only one answer for the survey question, so you use option buttons for the input elements. Because most visitors are on vacation, he'd like the vacation option to be selected by default when users open the Web page.

STEPS

1. **Return to** contact.html **in your text editor, then beneath the** legend **element in the** occasionbox **fieldset, enter three pairs of** label **tags on separate lines**

2. **In the opening tag for the first** label **element, add the name-value pair** for="vacation"**, then repeat for the remaining two** label **elements using the values** celebration **and** event

3. **Within the first** label **element, enter the tag** <input type="radio" name="occasion" id="vacation" value="Vacation" />**; then on a new line type** Vacation

   HTML5 allows the checked attribute with no value; for XHTML-compliant code, however, you must restate the attribute as the value to supply a full attribute-value pair.

QUICK TIP
Include the attribute-value pairs type="radio" and name="occasion" for all three input elements.

4. **Repeat Step 3 to complete the remaining** label **elements having input elements with the following attributes and label text:**
   ```
   id="celebration" value="Celebration"    Celebration
   id="event" value="Special Event"        Special Event
   ```

QUICK TIP
Check boxes also support the checked attribute.

5. **Within the** input **element with the id** vacation**, add the name-value pair** checked="checked"

   HTML5 allows the checked attribute with no value; for XHTML-compliant code, however, you must restate the attribute as the value to supply a full attribute-value pair. Figure J-11 shows the completed code for the option buttons and labels.

6. **Save your work, then return to** llform.css

7. **In the style rule for** label **elements within the element with the id** roombox**, add a selector for** label **elements within the element with the id** occasionbox

   This style adds space between each label and the option button that follows it.

8. **Save your work, reload** contact.html **in your browser**

   As Figure J-12 shows, the "Vacation" option button is automatically selected.

9. **Click the** Celebration **and** Special Event **option buttons to select them**

   As you click each button in the set, the previously selected button is deselected.

FIGURE J-11: Code for option buttons

```
<fieldset id="occasionbox">
    <legend>What's the occasion for your visit?</legend>
    <label for="vacation">
        <input type="radio" name="occasion" id="vacation" value="Vacation" checked="checked" />
        Vacation
    </label>
    <label for="celebration">
        <input type="radio" name="occasion" id="celebration" value="Celebration" />
        Celebration
    </label>
    <label for="event">
        <input type="radio" name="occasion" id="event" value="Special Event" />
        Special Event
    </label>
</fieldset>
```

type set to
"radio"

All input elements in the
set share the same value
for the name attribute

FIGURE J-12: Option buttons displayed in form

What's the occasion for your visit?
- ⦿ Vacation   ○ Celebration   ○ Special Event

Option selected by default
using the "selected" attribute

Implementing selection interfaces

HTML5 implemented several new input values that provide users with specific types of predefined options. Table J-5 details several of these values, along with the previously existing "file" value. All of these values create Web page features known as **selection interfaces**, which present users with allowable options visually or enable them to manipulate values without entering text. Before the HTML5 revision, a number of these interfaces were commonly created using scripts. While the HTML5 alternatives make the features easier to code, older browsers do not recognize or support these input values. Thus, if your Web page design relies on any of these input values, you'll likely need to include scripts or other field types that mimic their functions as backups in order for your pages to degrade gracefully.

TABLE J-5: Input values that may invoke selection interfaces

value(s)	description	browser implementations
number	enables you to specify a range of valid numbers that users can input	arrows that users can click to increase or decrease the value numeric virtual keyboards (touchscreen devices)
range	enables you to specify a range of valid numbers that users can input	a slider bar that enables users to increase or decrease the value by dragging a pointer along a line
date, month, week, time, datetime, datetime-local	accepts dates, times, and related values using a standard format	a calendar that users can scroll through and click on to select date-related values
color	supports hexadecimal color values	a color picker that visually represents colors and lets users click colors to select them
file	accepts the path and filename for a file to upload from a user's device	file navigation features that let users select a file from local storage

Creating a Drop-Down Menu

Another option for creating a list of options from which users can select is to create a **drop-down menu**, which browsers display as a small text box with a triangle next to it. Users can click the triangle to view the entire list of options; once a user clicks an option to select it, the list is hidden and the selected value is displayed in the text box. Drop-down menus are best suited to fields where you want to present a large number of options that would occupy a lot of space as option buttons. You use the select element to create a drop-down menu, with option elements nested within it to specify the list items. 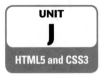 Phillip Blaine wants to give users who want to make reservations the option to specify arrival and departure dates. You create a drop-down menu for the date, month, and year for both dates.

STEPS

1. **In your text editor open the file htmj-4.txt, select all the contents, copy them to the Clipboard, then close the file**

2. **Return to contact.html in your text editor, add a new line beneath the legend element in the checkin fieldset, then paste the contents of the Clipboard**
   You'll use these lists of dates, months, and years to create your drop-down menus.

3. **Add opening and closing select tags around the list of months, specifying the value inmonth for the id and name attributes, repeat for the list of dates using the value indate, then repeat for the list of years using the value inyear**

4. **In the list of months, click before the word January, type <option value="01">, click after the word January, type </option>, then repeat to add option elements to the remaining months, assigning the value 02 to February, 03 to March, and so on**

5. **In the list of dates, click before the number 1, type <option value="01">, click after the number 1, type </option>, then repeat to add option elements to the remaining dates, assigning the value 02 to 2, 03 to 3, and so on**

6. **In the list of years, click before 2013, type <option value="2013">, click after 2013, type </option>, then repeat to add option elements to the remaining years, assigning a value attribute corresponding to each year**
   Figure J-13 shows the completed code for the check-in dates.

7. **Copy the three select elements to the Clipboard, insert a blank line below the legend element in the checkout fieldset, paste the contents of the Clipboard, then change the id and name values for the select elements you pasted to outmonth, outdate, and outyear, respectively**
   You'll offer the same date options to users for selecting a check-out date.

8. **Save your work, then reload contact.html in your browser**
   As Figure J-14 shows, the first option element within each select element is displayed as the default choice.

9. **Use the drop-down menus to select a check-in date of August 3, 2015 and a check-out date of August 6, 2015**

FIGURE J-13: **Code for check-in drop-down menus**

Each select element creates a drop-down menu

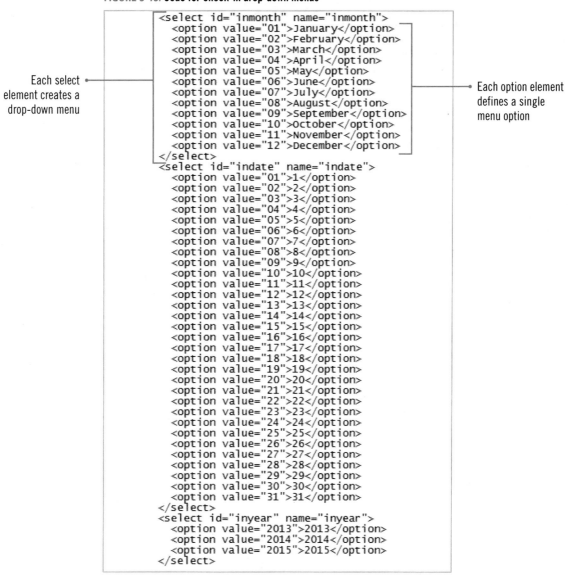

Each option element defines a single menu option

```
<select id="inmonth" name="inmonth">
   <option value="01">January</option>
   <option value="02">February</option>
   <option value="03">March</option>
   <option value="04">April</option>
   <option value="05">May</option>
   <option value="06">June</option>
   <option value="07">July</option>
   <option value="08">August</option>
   <option value="09">September</option>
   <option value="10">October</option>
   <option value="11">November</option>
   <option value="12">December</option>
</select>
<select id="indate" name="indate">
   <option value="01">1</option>
   <option value="02">2</option>
   <option value="03">3</option>
   <option value="04">4</option>
   <option value="05">5</option>
   <option value="06">6</option>
   <option value="07">7</option>
   <option value="08">8</option>
   <option value="09">9</option>
   <option value="10">10</option>
   <option value="11">11</option>
   <option value="12">12</option>
   <option value="13">13</option>
   <option value="14">14</option>
   <option value="15">15</option>
   <option value="16">16</option>
   <option value="17">17</option>
   <option value="18">18</option>
   <option value="19">19</option>
   <option value="20">20</option>
   <option value="21">21</option>
   <option value="22">22</option>
   <option value="23">23</option>
   <option value="24">24</option>
   <option value="25">25</option>
   <option value="26">26</option>
   <option value="27">27</option>
   <option value="28">28</option>
   <option value="29">29</option>
   <option value="30">30</option>
   <option value="31">31</option>
</select>
<select id="inyear" name="inyear">
   <option value="2013">2013</option>
   <option value="2014">2014</option>
   <option value="2015">2015</option>
</select>
```

FIGURE J-14: **Drop-down menus for check-in and check-out dates**

Drop-down menus fit long lists of choices into a small area of the Web page

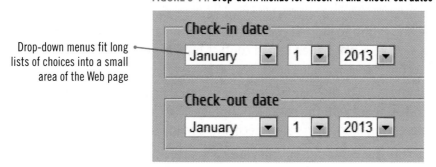

Check-in date

January ▾ | 1 ▾ | 2013 ▾

Check-out date

January ▾ | 1 ▾ | 2013 ▾

Creating option groups

Especially in a long set of options, it's sometimes helpful to group the options in a drop-down menu. For instance, if you were presenting users with a list of countries, grouping the countries by continent could help a user more quickly identify the part of the list where their country is located. To create an option group, you enclose a group of option elements within an *optgroup* element. You then use the *label* attribute to add heading text to the group. In most browsers, options are indented below the label for their group, creating a hierarchical list that can simplify navigation.

Creating and Processing Web Forms

Enabling Form Submission

UNIT J
HTML5 and CSS3

A form needs to include a **submit button**, which is a button that users can click to submit the data they've entered. You can use the "submit" input type to create a standard submit button. Table J-6 details two other input values that also create buttons. In the opening form tag, you add the "action" attribute to specify the name and location of a script on your Web server to accept the form data, and the "method" attribute to indicate the way the data should be submitted. User agents group the name attribute of each field with the value entered or selected by a user; thus, every field with information to be submitted must have a value for the name attribute. Figure J-15 shows an example of what submitted user data from the contact form might look like. ▨▨▨ You'll work later with other members of the Web site team to set up and test a server script to process the data. For now, you create a submit button.

STEPS

1. **Return to** contact.html **in your text editor**

2. **Within the** submitbutton **fieldset, enter the following code:**
   ```
   <input type="submit" id="submit" value="Submit" />
   ```
   The value attribute specifies the text displayed on the button.

3. **Save your work, then reload** contact.html **in your browser**
   The submit button is displayed at the bottom of the form. By default, form buttons are usually gray with black text and a subtle box shadow.

4. **Return to** contact.html **in your text editor, then just above the closing** </head> **tag, enter the following code:**
   ```
   <!--[if IE]>
     <style type="text/css">
       legend span {top: 0;}
       legend {color: black;}
       #submit {position: relative; left: -80px;}
     </style>
   <![endif]-->
   ```
   Internet Explorer lays out form elements differently than other browsers. This conditional comment creates an embedded style sheet for this Web page, but only if the browser opening the files identifies itself as IE.

5. **Save your work, return to** llform.css **in your text editor, add the two style rules shown in Figure J-16, save your work, then reload** contact.html **in your browser**
   As Figure J-17 shows, the submit button now matches the style of the rest of the form.

6. **Create a print version of the main style sheet with the name** llprint.css **and a print version of the form style sheet with the name** llformpr.css**, then in** contact.html**, add a link element referencing** llformpr.css **and specifying a media value of** print

7. **Validate the code for** contact.html **and your style sheets, then make changes as necessary to fix any errors**

8. **If you have space on a Web server, publish your Web site, then open** contact.html **in your browser from the published location**

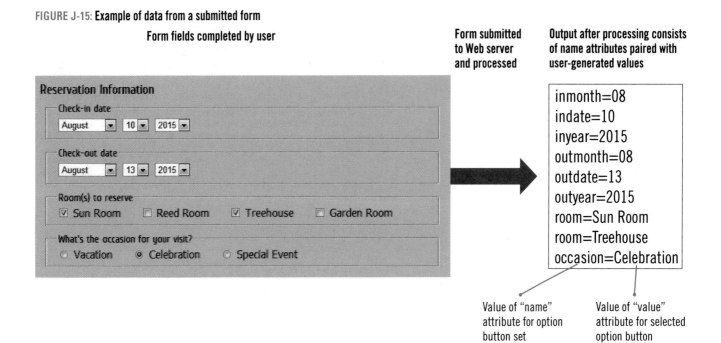

Form fields completed by user

Form submitted to Web server and processed

Output after processing consists of name attributes paired with user-generated values

```
inmonth=08
indate=10
inyear=2015
outmonth=08
outdate=13
outyear=2015
room=Sun Room
room=Treehouse
occasion=Celebration
```

Value of "name" attribute for option button set

Value of "value" attribute for selected option button

FIGURE J-16: **Code to style submit button**

```
#submit {
    background: #e3d5ba;
    font-size: 1.25em;
    }
#submitbutton {
    border: none;
    background: #6a91ca;
    padding: 0.5em 0 0 0;
    text-align: center;
    }
```

FIGURE J-17: **Completed contact form**

Submit button styled and centered

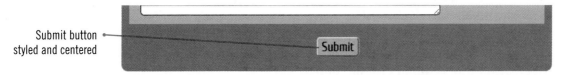

TABLE J-6: **Input values for buttons**

value	description	attributes
submit	creates a default submit button that submits user input based on form or button attributes	**value** specifies button text
image	creates a submit button using an image	**src** specifies the image file name and location **alt** provides alternative text for users of non-visual user agents
reset	clears all user input and resets fields to defaults; not used by some designers because users can confuse it with a submit button and lose all input	**value** specifies button text
button	creates a generic button that can be programmed using a script	value specifies button text

Practice

Concepts Review

For current SAM information, including versions and content details, visit SAM Central (http://www.cengage.com/samcentral). If you have a SAM user profile, you may have access to hands-on instruction, practice, and assessment of the skills covered in this unit. Since various versions of SAM are supported throughout the life of this text, check with your instructor for the correct instructions and URL/Web site for accessing assignments.

Refer to Figure J-18.

FIGURE J-18

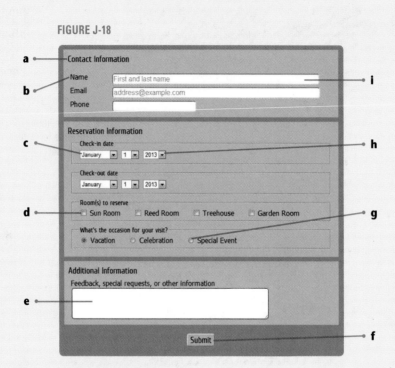

1. Which item is created with a select element?
2. Which item is created with an option element?
3. Which element is created using an input type of "checkbox"?
4. Which element is created using an input type of "radio"?
5. Which element is created using an input type of "text"?
6. Which item is created with a textarea element?
7. Which item is created with a legend element?
8. Which item is created with a label element?
9. Which element is created using an input type of "submit"?

Match each term with the statement that best describes it.

10. field
11. label
12. fieldset
13. legend
14. text box
15. check box
16. option button
17. text area
18. submit button

a. a single-line text field
b. a button that users can click to submit the data they've entered
c. a descriptive title for a fieldset
d. a form element in which users enter or select data
e. a box that users can click to add or remove a check mark
f. a group of fields that form a logical unit
g. descriptive text associated with a form element
h. a box for selecting one option from a set of choices
i. a field that allows users to enter multiple lines of text

Select the best answer from the list of choices.

19. Which is an example of asking users for information in distinct pieces?
   a. using a single text box for first and last name   **c.** separating date entry into month, date, and year fields
   b. using a text area for general questions   **d.** creating custom text for a submit button

20. Which element is used to explain the purpose of other form elements?
   a. input   **c.** option
   b. legend   **d.** textarea

21. Newer browsers display the value of the _____ attribute as light-colored text in the associated text box and remove it when a user selects the box in preparation for text entry.
   a. placeholder   **c.** legend
   b. type   **d.** label

22. Which pseudo-class applies to an element that a user has selected?
   a. hover   **c.** active
   b. focus   **d.** followed

23. Each input element in a set of option buttons must include the _____ attribute with a value identical to all other members of the set.
   a. selected   **c.** value
   b. id   **d.** name

24. Which element do you use to create a drop-down menu?
   a. fieldset   **c.** input
   b. textarea   **d.** select

25. When submitting a form, user agents group the _____ attribute of each field with the value entered or selected by a user.
   a. name   **c.** placeholder
   b. id   **d.** value

Skills Review

1. Create a form.

  a. In your text editor, open HTM J-5.html from the Unit J/Review folder where you store your Data Files, insert a blank line before the closing body tag, insert a paragraph element containing your first and last name and the text **HTML5 Unit J**, and save it as **order.html**, then use CSS comments to add the same information to HTM J-6.css, saving it as **bigj.css**, and to HTM J-7.css, saving it as **bigjform.css**.

  b. In order.html, add a new line beneath the h2 element, indent to match the opening h2 tag, then insert opening and closing form tags on separate lines.

  c. Between the opening and closing form tags, add four sets of opening and closing fieldset tags on separate lines with the id values **deliveryinfo**, **orderinfo**, **additionalinfo**, and **submitbutton**.

  d. Within the deliveryinfo fieldset element, add the text **Delivery Information** within a span element, then enclose the span element within a legend element. Repeat, including the span element, to add the legend **Order** to the orderinfo fieldset and the legend **Special Instructions** to the additionalinfo fieldset.

  e. Beneath the legend element in the orderinfo fieldset, add three sets of opening and closing fieldset tags on separate lines with the id values **crustbox**, **sizebox**, and **toppingbox**.

  f. Within the crustbox fieldset, add a legend element containing the text **Crust**, then repeat to add the legends **Size** to the sizebox fieldset and **Topping(s)** to the toppingbox fieldset. Save your work, then open order.html in your browser.

  g. Return to order.html in your text editor, copy the link element that references bigj.css, insert a new line above the favicon link element, paste the code from the Clipboard, then change the href value in the pasted element to **bigjform.css**. Save your work, then reload order.html in your browser.

Skills Review (continued)

2. Create text fields.

   a. Return to order.html in your text editor.

   b. Within the deliveryinfo fieldset, beneath the legend element, add a label element containing the text **Name**. Repeat to create four more label elements below the one you just created, containing the text **Street Address**, **City**, **Email**, and **Phone**, respectively, then add an additional label element beneath the legend in the additionalinfo fieldset containing the text **Special requests, delivery details**.

   c. Beneath the text Name in the first label element, enter an input tag for a text field with the name **name** and id **nameinput**, then add a name-value pair to the opening label tag associating it with the input element you created. Repeat to create a text field below the text Street Address with the name **address** and id **addrinput**, a text field below the text City with the name **city** and id **cityinput**, an email field below the text Email with the name **email** and id **emailinput**, and a text field below the text Phone with the name **phone** and id **phoneinput**.

   d. Beneath the label text in the additionalinfo fieldset, insert an element to create a text area with the name **instructions** and id **instructions** that displays **3** rows and **60** columns of input. Add a name-value pair to the opening label tag, associating it with the text area you created.

   e. Save your work, then reload order.html in your browser. Enter text in each of the fields you just created.

3. Customize text fields.

   a. Return to bigjform.css in your text editor, create a style rule for label elements in the element with the id deliveryinfo, then set the display to **block**, the position to **relative**, and the margin to **12px 0**.

   b. Create a style rule for input elements in the element with the id deliveryinfo, then set position to **absolute** and left to **120px**.

   c. Create a style rule for the elements with the ids nameinput, emailinput, and addrinput, and set the width to **30em**, then create a style rule for the elements with the ids cityinput and phoneinput, and set the width to **12em**.

   d. Save your work, then reload order.html in your browser.

   e. Return to order.html in your text editor, then in the input tag with the id nameinput, add **First and last name** as placeholder text. Repeat to add **Building number and street** to the input tag with the id addrinput and **address@example.com** to the input tag with the id emailinput. Save your work.

   f. Return to bigjform.css in your text editor, then add a style rule that sets the backgrounds of the input and textarea elements to **#f99** when users select them.

   g. Save your work, then reload order.html in your browser. Verify that the placeholder text is displayed in the fields where you added it, then click in each text field and verify that the background color changes.

4. Create check boxes.

   a. Return to order.html in your text editor, then beneath the legend element in the toppingbox fieldset, enter five pairs of label tags on separate lines.

   b. In the opening tag for the first label element, add an attribute-value pair to associate it with the element having the id **pepperoni**. Within the label element, enter code to create an input element for a check box with the id **pepperoni** and value **Pepperoni**. Add a new line beneath the input element and enter the text **Pepperoni**.

   c. Repeat Step b to complete the remaining label elements with input elements with the following attributes and label text:

id	value	label text
sausage	Sausage	Sausage
greenpep	Green Peppers	Green Peppers
onion	Onions	Onions
xcheese	Extra Cheese	Extra Cheese

   d. Add the name attribute with the value **toppings** to each of the five input tags.

   e. Save your work, then return to bigjform.css.

   f. Create a style rule for label elements within the element having the id **toppingbox**, then add a name-value pair to set the right margin to **25px**.

Skills Review (continued)

g. Save your work, then reload order.html in your browser. Click each check box to select it, then click each check box again to deselect it.

5. Create option buttons.

a. Return to order.html in your text editor, then beneath the legend element in the crustbox fieldset, enter two pairs of label tags on separate lines.

b. In the opening tag for the first label element, add an attribute-value pair to associate it with the element having the id **thin**. Within the label element, enter code to create an input element for an option button with the id **thin** and value **Thin**. Add a new line beneath the input element and enter the text **Thin Crust**.

c. Repeat Step b to associate the second label element with the element having the id **thick** and to create an input element for an option button with the id **thick**, value **Deep Dish**, and label text **Deep Dish**. Add an attribute to make this option selected by default. Save your work, then return to bigjform.css.

d. In the style rule for label elements within the element with the id toppingbox, add a selector for **label** elements within the element with the id **crustbox**.

e. Save your work, then reload order.html in your browser. Click the Thin Crust and Deep Dish option buttons to select them.

6. Create a drop-down menu.

a. Return to order.html in your text editor, add a new line beneath the legend element in the sizebox fieldset, then add opening and closing tags for a select element with the id and name **size**.

b. Add an option element with a value attribute set to **small** and the content **Small**. Repeat to create option elements with a value of **medium** and content **Medium**, a value of **large** and content **Large**, and a value of **XL** and content **Extra Large**.

c. Save your work, then reload order.html in your browser. Use the drop-down menu to select each of the size options.

7. Enable form submission.

a. Return to order.html in your text editor.

b. Within the submitbutton fieldset, enter code for an input element that creates a submit button with an id of **submit** and value of **Add to Cart**.

c. Save your work, then return to bigjform.css in your text editor. Add a style rule for the element with the id submit that sets the background to **red** and the font size to **1.25em**. Add another style rule for the element with the id submitbutton that removes the border, sets the background to **black**, sets padding to **0.5em 0 0 0**, and center-aligns text.

d. Save your work, then reload order.html in your browser. Compare your screen to Figure J-19.

e. Create a print version of the main style sheet with the name **bjprint.css** and a print version of the form style sheet with the name **bjformpr.css**, then in order.html, add a link element referencing **bjformpr.css** and specifying a media value of **print**.

f. Validate the code for order.html and your style sheets, then make changes as necessary to fix any errors.

g. If you have space on a Web server, publish your Web site, then open order.html in your browser from the published location.

FIGURE J-19

Independent Challenge 1

The Spotted Wren Garden Center has begun offering free landscaping consultations. Sarah Nguyen, the owner, would like to add a form to the Web site to enable users to request an appointment. You create and style the form.

a. Open HTM J-8.html from the Unit J/IC1 folder in your text editor. Insert a blank line before the closing body tag, insert a paragraph element containing your first and last name and the text **HTML5 Unit J, Independent Challenge 1**, and save it as **quote.html**, then use a CSS comment to add the same information to **HTM J-9.css**, saving the file as **spotwren.css**.

b. In quote.html, insert tags for a form element before the closing article tag. Within the form element, add tags for five fieldset elements with the id values **contactinfo**, **timinginfo**, **jobtype**, **additionalinfo**, and **submitbutton**. Save your work, then in spotwren.css, add a style rule for the form element to set the background color to **#6c6** and specify a padding of **20px** at the top of the element. Add a style rule for fieldset elements that sets the bottom margin to **12px**, the element width to **90%**, and the margins to **0 auto**.

c. In the fieldset with the id contactinfo, add the legend **Contact Info** followed by five label elements. Within the first label element, add the label text **Name**, then add code to create a text box with the id **nameinput** and the name **name**. Add an attribute to the opening label tag to associate it with the input element you created. Repeat for the remaining label elements, using the following values:

id	name	label text
addrinput	address	Street Address
zipinput	zip	Zip Code
emailinput	email	Email
phoneinput	phone	Phone

d. Edit the emailinput element to specify that the expected data is an email address. Add the placeholder text **First and last name** to the nameinput element and **address@example.com** to the emailinput element.

e. Save your work, then in spotwren.css, add a style rule that sets the font weight for legend elements to **bold**. Add another style rule that applies to label elements within the element with the id contactinfo, setting the display to **block**, the position to **relative**, and the margin to **12px 0**. Create a style rule that applies to input elements within the element having the id contactinfo, setting the position to **absolute** and **130px** to the left. Create another rule that sets the widths of the elements with the ids nameinput, emailinput, and addrinput to **30em**, and an additional rule that sets the widths of the elements with the ids zipinput and phoneinput to **12em**.

f. In the fieldset with the id timinginfo, add the legend **Best day(s) to schedule a visit** followed by seven label elements. Within the first label element, add code to create a check box with the id **monday**, the name **days**, and the value **Monday**, then add the label text **Monday**. Add an attribute to the opening label tag to associate it with the input element you created. Repeat for the remaining label elements to create check boxes for the other six days of the week in chronological order.

g. In the fieldset with the id jobtype, add the legend **Project Area** followed by four label elements. Within the first label element, add code to create an option button with the id **front**, the name **area**, and the value **House front**, then add the label text **Front of House**. Add an attribute to the opening label tag to associate it with the input element you created. Repeat for the remaining label elements, using the same name and the following additional values:

id	value	label text
border	Border	Border of Property
multiple	Multiple	Multiple Areas (please specify in Notes box below)
other	Other	Other (please specify in Notes box below)

Independent Challenge 1 (continued)

h. Save your work, then in spotwren.css, add a style rule for label elements in the element with the id jobtype that sets the display to **block**. Save your changes to spotwren.css.

i. In the fieldset with the id additionalinfo, add the legend **Additional Information** followed by a label element. Within the label element, add the label text **Notes**, then add code to create a text area with the id and name **notes**, displaying **4** rows and **60** columns of input. Add an attribute to the opening label tag to associate it with the text area element you created.

j. In the fieldset with the id submitbutton, add code to create a submit button with the id **submit** and the value **Submit Request**. Save your work. In spotwren.css, create a style rule that applies to the element with the id submitbutton and that removes the border, center-aligns the text, and removes the bottom margin. Save your changes to spotwren.css.

k. Add a style rule that applies to currently selected input and textarea elements, setting the background to **#ff0**. Save your work, preview quote.html in your browser, then compare your screen with Figure J-20.

l. Create a print version of the stylesheet, saving it with the name **swprint.css**, then validate your HTML and CSS documents. If you have space on a Web server, publish your Web site, then open resource.html in your browser from the published location.

m. Close your browser, then close your text editor.

FIGURE J-20

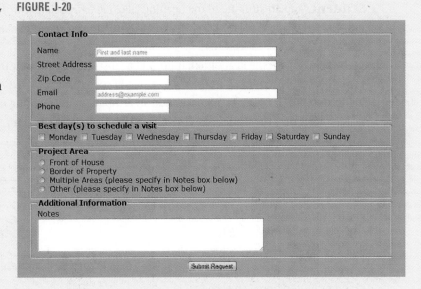

Independent Challenge 2

The coordinators of the Murfreesboro Recreational Soccer League would like to allow prospective new members to sign up on the Web site. You create a form to allow users to enter basic information.

a. Open HTM J-10.html from the Unit J/IC2 folder in your text editor. Insert a blank line before the closing body tag, insert a paragraph element containing your first and last name and the text **HTML5 Unit J, Independent Challenge 2**, save the file as **signup.html**, then use a CSS comment to add the same information to HTM J-11.css and save it as **mrsl.css**.

b. In signup.html, below the h2 element, add a form element containing five fieldsets. Add the following ids to the fieldsets: **contactinfo**, **agebox**, **membershipbox**, **additionalinfo**, **submitbutton**. Add legends to the first four fieldsets containing the text **Contact Information**, **Age Range**, **Special Memberships**, and **Additional Information**. Save your work, then in mrsl.css, add a style rule to set the width of the form to **60%** and the margin to **0 auto**. Add another style rule to set the fieldset borders to **2px solid black**, and a third to present the text of legends in **bold**. Save your changes to mrsl.css.

c. In the first fieldset, add four label elements. Add the label text **First Name**, **Last Name**, **Email**, and **Phone**. Add a text input field below the label text in the first label element, using the id **fnameinput** and the name **fname**. Add an attribute to the label tag to associate it with this element. Repeat to add a text input field to the second label element with the id **lnameinput** and the name **lname**, an email field to the third label element with the id **emailinput** and the name **email**, and a text input field to the fourth label element with the id **phoneinput** and the name **phone**. Specify **First name** as placeholder text for the first text field, **Last name** for the second, and **address@example.com** for the third. Save your work.

Independent Challenge 2 (continued)

d. In mrsl.css, add a style rule setting the background for input and textarea elements to **#f99** when users select them. Add a style rule for labels in the contactinfo element, setting the display to **block**, the position to **relative**, and the margin to **12px 0**. Create another style rule for input elements within the contactinfo element, setting position to **absolute** and **130px** to the left. Create style rules to set the widths of the emailinput element to **30em**, fnameinput and lnameinput elements to **20em**, and the phoneinput element to **12em**. Save your changes to mrsl.css.

e. In the fieldset with the id agebox, add a select element with the id and name **agerange**. Create eight options for the drop-down list, displaying the text **4-6**, **7-9**, **10-12**, **13-15**, **16-17**, **18-35**, **36-54**, and **55+**. Set the value for the first option to **D1**, the second to **D2**, and so on through the final element, which will have the value **D8**.

f. In the fieldset with the id membershipbox, add two label elements. Within the first label element, add code to create a check box with the id **student**, the name **memberships**, and the value **Student**, then add the label text **Student**. Add an attribute to the opening label tag to associate it with the input element you created. Repeat for the second label element to create a check box with the id **senior**, the name **memberships**, and the value **Senior**, then add the label text **Senior**.

g. In the fieldset with the id additionalinfo, add a label element. Within the label element, add the label text **Questions or special requests**, then add code to create a text area with the id and name **feedback**, displaying **7** rows and **50** columns of input. Add an attribute to the opening label tag to associate it with the text area element you created. Save your work, then in mrsl.css, add a style rule for the element with the id feedback and setting the display to **block**. Save your changes to mrsl.css.

h. In the fieldset with the id submitbutton, add code to create a submit button with the id **submit** and the value **Submit**. Save your work. In mrsl.css, create a style rule that applies to the element with the id submitbutton, removing the border and center-aligning text. Create a style rule for the element with the id submit, setting the background to **#090**, the font size to **1.5em**, and the font weight to **bold**. Save your changes to mrsl.css. Open signup.html in your Web browser and compare your screen to Figure J-21.

FIGURE J-21

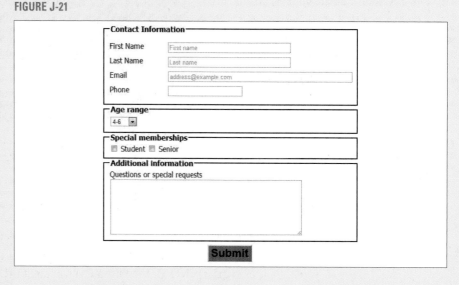

Advanced Challenge Exercise

- In the fnameinput and lnameinput elements, add the attribute-value pair **required=required**.
- Below the h2 element, insert a new line containing a paragraph element with the text **Fields marked with * are required.** Add the id **formexpl** to the opening paragraph tag.
- After the label text First name, type a space followed by *. Repeat for the label text Last name.
- In the paragraph element and the two labels, enclose the * with a span element having the class **req**. Save your work.
- In mrsl.css, add a style rule for the req class, setting the color to **red**. Add another style rule for the id formexpl, setting the width to **60%** and the margin to **0 auto**. Save your work.
- Preview the Web page in your browser, then click the Submit button without entering text in either of the name fields. (*Note:* Not all browsers check for required fields.)

Independent Challenge 2 (continued)

i. Create a print version of the style sheet, saving it with the name **mrsprint.css**, then validate your HTML and CSS documents.

j. If you have space on a Web server, publish your Web site, then open signup.html in your browser from the published location.

k. Close your browser, then close your text editor.

Independent Challenge 3

Diego Merckx, the manager of the Hotel Natoma, wants to allow guests to initiate reservations using the Web site. You create a Web page form based on the information he wants to collect from potential visitors.

a. Open HTM J-12.html from the Unit J/IC3 folder in your text editor. Insert a blank line before the closing body tag, then insert a paragraph element containing your first and last name and the text **HTML5 Unit J, Independent Challenge 3**. Save the file as **reserve.html**, then use CSS comments to add the same information to HTM J-13.css, saving it as **natoma.css**, and HTM J-14.css, saving it as **hnform.css**.

b. In reserve.html, add a form element below the h2 element, then add four fieldsets. Add the legend text **Contact Information**, **Reservation Information**, and **Additional Information** to the first three fieldsets. Add an appropriate id to each fieldset (the fourth fieldset will contain the Submit button). Within the fieldset having the legend Reservation Information, nest five additional fieldsets, add the legends **Party size**, **Bed preference**, **Check-in date**, **Check-out date**, and **Parking**, then add an appropriate id to each fieldset.

c. Save your work, then preview the Web page in a browser. In reserve.html, add a link element that references the file **hnform.css**, specifying a media type of **screen**. Save your work, then refresh the page in your browser.

d. In reserve.html, add three label elements to the first fieldset, containing the label text **Name**, **Email**, and **Phone**. Add code for a text box within each label element, using the relevant input types and appropriate name and id values. Add placeholder text if appropriate. Associate each label element with the enclosed text box. Save your work, then in hnform.css, add styles to set the display for the labels to **block**, the position to **relative**, and adding a **12px** margin to the left and right sides. Add styles to set the position for the text boxes in the first fieldset to **absolute** and specifying a left value that moves all the boxes to the right of the label text; add styles to set an appropriate width for each text box, then add styles to set the background color of selected input and textarea elements to **#e3d5ba**. Save your work, then reload the Web page in your browser.

e. In the fieldset with the legend Party size, add two label elements containing the label text **Number in your party** and **Number of rooms required**. Add code for a text box within each label element using appropriate name and id values. Associate each label element with the enclosed text box. Save your work, then in hnform.css, add styles to add a right margin of **20px** to both of the text boxes you created and specify a width of **3em** for both. Save your work, then reload the Web page in your browser.

f. In the fieldset with the legend Bed preference, add three label elements containing the label text **King/Queen**, **Twin**, and **Other/Mix (please specify in Additional Information section below)**. Add code for a check box before the label text within each label element, using appropriate name and id values. Associate each label element with the enclosed check box. Save your work, then in hnform.css, add styles to add a right margin of **25px** to each check box element. Save your work, then reload the Web page in your browser.

g. In the fieldset with the legend Check-in date, paste the contents of htmj-15.txt. Create three drop-down lists, using the pasted text as list items to create lists of months, dates, and years. Add appropriate ids and names to the lists. Copy the code for the three drop-down lists and paste it into the fieldset with the legend Check-out date, then change the ids and names for the pasted items to unique values. Save your work, then in hnform.css, add styles to make the Check-in date fieldset float to the **left** and the Check-out date fieldset float to the **right**, and to set the width of each element to **45%** of the parent. Save your work, then reload the Web page in your browser.

Independent Challenge 3 (continued)

h. In the fieldset with the legend Parking, add a label element containing the label text **I need parking for**. Add code for a text box within the label element using appropriate name and id values. Associate the label element with the enclosed text box. After the code for the text box, add the text **vehicles**. Save your work, then in hnform.css, add styles to set the width of the text box to **3em**. Save your work, then reload the Web page in your browser.

i. In the fieldset containing the legend text Additional Information, add a label element. Within the label element, add the label text **Feedback, special requests, or other information**, then add code to create a text area with an appropriate id and name, displaying **4** rows and **55** columns of input. Associate the label element with the text area element. Save your work, then in hnform.css, add styles to set the display for both the label and text area elements to **block**. Save your changes, then reload the Web page in your browser.

j. In the final fieldset, add code to create a submit button with an appropriate id and the value **Submit**. Save your work. In hnform.css, create a style rule that applies to the fieldset, removing the border and center-aligning text. Add styles setting the background of the submit button to **#e3d5ba**, font size to **1.25em**, and a **10px** border radius to the upper-left and lower-right corners. Save your work, then reload the Web page in your browser and compare your screen to Figure J-22.

FIGURE J-22

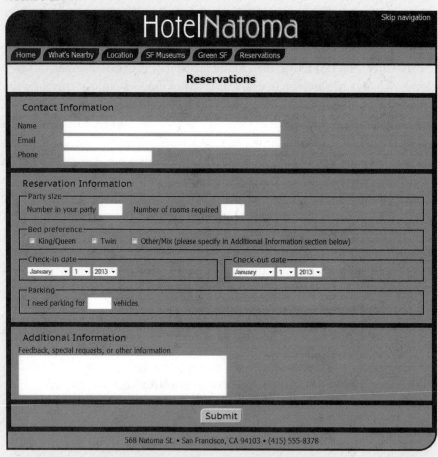

Creating and Processing Web Forms

Advanced Challenge Exercise

- Change the input type for the text boxes in the Party size and Parking fieldsets from text to **number**. In the input element with the label Number in your party, add the attribute-value pairs **min="1"** and **max="50"**. In the input element with the label Number of rooms required, add the attribute-value pairs **min="1"** and **max="38"**. In the input element beneath the legend Parking, add the attribute-value pairs **min="0"** and **max="22"**. Save your work, reload the Web page in your browser, and explore any formatting or tools the browser may have added to the number fields.

- In the opening tag for the form element, add a unique id value, then in hnform.css, change the selector for the form style rule to reflect the new id. Add a new form element below the nav element containing the main nav bar, assigning it a unique id. Add a label element to the form containing the text **Google**, then below it, add a text box using the input type **search**. Add appropriate name and id values and associate the label element with the search box. Below the label element, add code for a submit button with a value of **Search**.

- In the opening tag for the new form element, add the code **action="http://www.google.com/search" method="get"**. Save your work, then in hnform.css, add a style rule for the new form element, then add styles to give the form an **absolute** position **10px** from the right and **80px** from the top of the closest ancestor element with positioning. Add another style rule to set the width of the text box to **170px**. Save your work, then reload the Web page in your browser and note if your browser formats the search box at the top of the page differently than other text boxes. In the search box, type **HTML5**, then click the Search button.

k. Create print versions of the style sheets, saving them with the names **hnprint.css** and **hnfprint.css**, add a link element to reserve.html referencing hnfprint.css for printed output, save your work, then validate your HTML and CSS documents.

l. If you have space on a Web server, publish your Web site, then open reserve.html in your browser from the published location.

m. Close your browser, then close your text editor.

Real Life Independent Challenge

This assignment builds on the personal Web site you have worked on in previous units. You'll plan and add a form to your site.

a. Copy your Web site files to the Unit J/RLIC folder on the drive and folder where you store your Data Files.

b. On paper or in a new document in your text editor, list specific information you'd like users to be able to submit from your Web site. Break each piece of information down to an appropriate size to work with once it's submitted.

c. Group the information you've listed into categories. For each piece of information, identify the most appropriate form element to use in collecting it. Sketch the form you want to create, including fieldsets containing related fields.

d. If necessary, create a new Web page for the form and update the nav bar on each of the site's pages to include the new page.

e. Add a form element, followed by the fieldset elements necessary to structure your form. Next add fields and labels. Finally, add style rules to your style sheet document to optimize the form layout and increase usability. Implement placeholder text and/or background color for fields that users click. Save your work, then preview your form in a browser.

f. Create a print version of your style sheet, save your work, then validate all of your HTML and CSS documents and make any edits necessary to address any issues.

g. If you have space on a Web server, publish your Web site, then open the page containing your form in your browser from the published location.

h. Close your browser, then close your text editor.

Visual Workshop

In your text editor, open the file HTML J-16.html from the Unit J/VW directory on the drive and folder where you store your Data Files, add a paragraph before the closing body tag that contains your first and last name and the text **HTML5 Unit J, Visual Workshop**, save the file as **signup.html**, then use CSS comments to add the same information to **HTM J-17.css**, saving it as **revision.css**. Use your text editor to add a form to make your Web page match Figure J-23. Save your work, save a copy of your style sheet with the name **revprint.css**, then make any necessary changes for print formatting. When you are finished, validate your HTML and CSS code. If you have space on a Web server, publish your files, then open the Web page in your browser from the published location. Close your browser and text editor.

FIGURE J-23

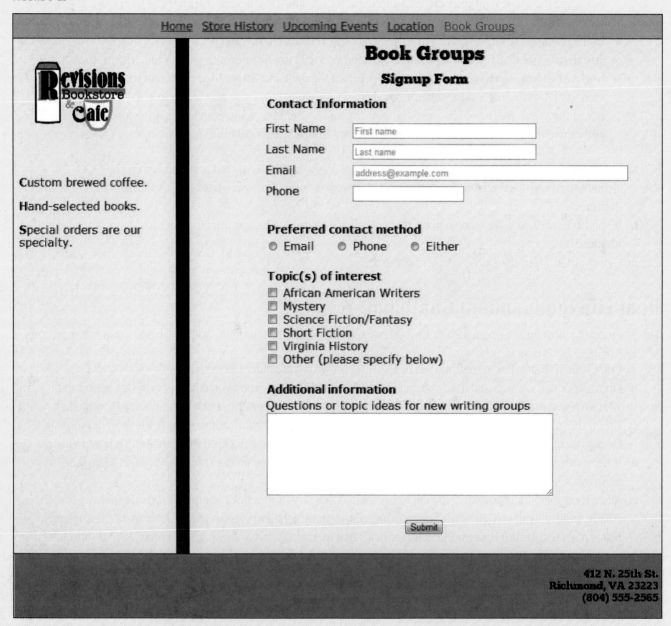

Creating and Processing Web Forms

Incorporating Video and Audio

Files You Will Need:

To view a list of files needed for this unit, see the Data Files Grid in the back of the book.

In addition to the text and graphics you've worked with so far, HTML also supports incorporating video and animated elements into Web pages. Used appropriately, these elements can contribute significant content and can complement the design of a Web site. Philip Blaine is thinking about adding an Events page to the Lakeland Reeds B&B Web site in order to describe local happenings at different times of year. He's provided you video and audio files associated with a couple of the events. In this unit, you'll add the video and audio to the Web site and explore other visual effects that enhance the presentation of content on the Web site.

OBJECTIVES

Understand Web video and audio

Use the video element

Incorporate the source element

Control playback

Add video support for older browsers

Provide a fallback image

Implement the audio element

Add audio support for older browsers

Understanding Web Video and Audio

Video and audio are widespread on the Web today, with tools available that let users manipulate and publish videos straight from cameras or phones, and upload podcasts and self-produced music. As a Web developer, you'll need to make choices about how you incorporate video and audio into your Web pages so as to accommodate the technologies that your intended audience uses as well as potential licensing issues for business clients. Thus, understanding the details of how video and audio are encoded, published, and viewed for the Web is crucial. ▓▓▓▓ As you prepare to work on adding the new content to the Lakeland Reeds B&B Web site, you review the nuts and bolts of online video and audio encoding and publishing.

Publishing video and audio on the Web relies on a few main concepts:

• **Encoding and containers**

The process of transforming a moving image and/or sound into a digital file is known as **encoding**. Video and audio can be encoded in many different ways, and research is always going on to create new ways to encode each that result in smaller file sizes and preserve image and sound quality. Each encoding method is known as a **codec**—short for coder/decoder. Three main video codecs are in wide use on the Web today: **H.264**, **Theora**, and **VP8**. Likewise, most audio on the Web is encoded as **AAC**, **MP3**, or **Vorbis**. Table K-1 describes these codecs.

For video, codecs are not the end of the story, however. Because video is most often accompanied by audio, an encoded set of video data, known as a **stream**, is packaged for distribution within a file known as a **container**. A container file may contain an accompanying audio stream as well. Several container formats are popular on the Web today, including **MPEG-4**, **Ogg**, **WebM**, and **Flash Video**. While most container formats can accommodate a variety of codecs, each container is commonly used with a particular audio codec and a particular video codec. Table K-2 describes the common container formats.

• **Helper programs**

Playing a video or audio file on a computer has traditionally required a program, known as a **helper program** or a **plugin**, that can both unpack the relevant container and decode the video and audio streams. Because not all programs have been able to deal with all containers or codecs, users have long needed to download and install multiple software packages to play Web video and audio from different sources. Clicking some links to media would open program windows outside the browser window, while others might open a new browser tab or window displaying the video or showing audio controls.

• **Browser support**

QUICK TIP
Search on the terms *browser video support* in a search engine to research which browsers currently support which containers natively.

Recent versions of major browsers have simplified Web video and audio somewhat by incorporating the ability to process media files and play Web video and audio within browser software itself. Combined with the video and audio elements introduced in HTML5, these new browser abilities provide Web developers with more control over how media is presented on a Web page as well as the options available to users for interacting with it. Figure K-1 shows a Web page containing a video with relevant controls along with the controls for an audio file.

At the time this book was written, not all browsers natively supported all containers or codecs. While a few combinations of containers and codecs are becoming especially popular, none has emerged as a universal standard, meaning that Web developers have to take extra steps when publishing media—especially video—to ensure the files are available to a wide spectrum of users. You'll explore some of these methods in this unit.

Controls for playing audio

Controls for viewing video

Video displayed in Web page

Video/Sasha Vodnik

TABLE K-1: Main Web video and audio codecs

name	developed by	licensing
H.264; also known as MPEG-4 Advanced Video Coding, or MPEG-4 part 10	the Moving Pictures Experts Group (MPEG)	commercial use requires licensing and payment of royalties through MPEG LA
Theora	the Xiph.org Foundation	use requires no licensing or royalty payments
VP8	On2; owned by Google	use requires no licensing or royalty payments
AAC	a consortium of companies; declared a standard by MPEG	use requires no licensing or royalty payments; makers of AAC codecs must pay licensing fees
MP3; also known as MPEG-1 or MPEG-2 Audio Layer 3 (or III)	MPEG	use requires no licensing or royalty payments; makers of programs or devices that encode or decode MP3 must pay licensing fees
Vorbis	the Xiph.org Foundation	use requires no licensing or royalty payments

TABLE K-2: Most popular container formats

name	extension	common video encoding	common audio encoding
MPEG-4	.mp4, .m4v	H.264 video	AAC audio
Ogg	.ogv	Theora video	Vorbis audio
WebM	.webm	VP8 video	Vorbis audio
Flash Video	.flv	various proprietary and public formats	various proprietary and public formats

HTML5 and CSS3

Using the video Element

To add video to a Web page, you use the video element, introduced in HTML5. Table K-3 details the attributes of the video element, which you use to indicate how video is presented to users of your Web page, as well as the type and location of the specific video file to play. You've been provided the same video in three different files having the .m4v, .ogv, and .webm extensions. You start by incorporating the .m4v file into the Web page.

STEPS

1. **In your text editor, open HTM K-1.html from the Unit K/Unit folder where you store your Data Files, insert a blank line before the closing body tag, insert a paragraph element containing your first and last name and the text HTML5 Unit K, then save it as events.html**

2. **In events.html, beneath the paragraph containing the text June and July, insert opening and closing video tags on separate lines**

3. **Within the opening video tag, add the attribute-value pairs src="media/bfly.m4v", width="320", and height="240"**

   Similar to their use in the img element, these attributes specify the video file to display and the dimensions of the video element within the Web page. The referenced video file is 320px × 240px, so you set the dimensions of the video element to match.

4. **Add the attribute-value pair type='video/mp4; codecs="avc1.42E01E, mp4a.40.2"'**

   The type attribute of the source element specifies the container format and codecs used to encode the file referenced by the src attribute. The entire value for the type attribute is surrounded by single quotes to avoid confusion with the double quotes that surround the codec values. The container format is expressed using the relevant **MIME types**, which are drawn from a standardized list of data types. Table K-4 lists type values for the container formats and codecs listed in Tables K-1 and K-2. Figure K-2 shows the completed code for the video element.

TROUBLE
At the time this book was written, only IE9+ and Safari 3+ supported MPEG-4 and H.264 natively. In the next lesson, you'll add support for additional containers and codecs.

5. **Save your work, then open events.html in your browser**

   If your browser displays a message saying that some Web page items are blocked, follow the steps provided to allow the blocked content. If your browser supports the MPEG-4 container and H.264/AAC codecs natively, the opening frame of the video is displayed as shown in Figure K-3.

6. **If the video is visible in your browser, right-click the opening frame, then if available, click Play**

   If the Play option is available, the video, which is just over 30 seconds long, plays through once.

TABLE K-3: Video element attributes

attribute	usage	value(s)
audio	enables control over audio channel	muted
autoplay	specifies that video should begin playing immediately when the page is loaded	autoplay / none
controls	requests that the browser display its default playback controls	controls / none
height	specifies the height of the element in pixels	n, where n is the height in pixels
loop	indicates that the browser should restart playback each time it reaches the end of the video	loop / none
poster	specifies a path and filename for an image to display before video playback starts	path/filename
preload	indicates whether the browser should download the video file when opening the Web page (auto), download only metadata related to the video file (metadata), or wait to download until the video is played (none)	auto / metadata / none
src	specifies the path and filename of the video file	path/filename
width	specifies the width of the element in pixels	n, where n is the width in pixels

FIGURE K-2: Web page code containing video element

Opening and closing video tags added

```
<article id="content">
    <h2 id="main">Events</h2>
    <p>Don't have a specific date in mind for your getaway? Explore seasonal experiences and special events you won't
want to miss!</p>
    <section>
        <h3>Butterfly Season</h3>
        <p class="eventdate">June and July</p>
        <video src="media/bfly.m4v" width="320" height="240" type="video/mp4; codecs="avc1.42E01E, mp4a.40.2"">
        </video>
        <p>Minnesota plays host to a variety of beautiful butterflies in high summer. As a result of our participation a
region-wide effort to increase butterfly habitat by planting more native bushes and shrubs, more butterflies visit Lakeland
Reeds' gardens each year. The video shows one of our butterfly-friendly bushes covered during a typical late June/early July
peak.</p>
    </section>
    <section>
        <h3>Accordion Rendezvous</h3>
        <p class="eventdate">last weekend in September</p>
        <p>Lovers of the squeezebox gather every year in the Twin Lakes area to share songs and play music together. Come
to play or just to listen. The audio clip below features a short, energetic tune by our own Phillip Blaine.</p>
    </section>
</article>
```

type value describes container format, video codec, and audio codec

FIGURE K-3: Video displayed on Web page

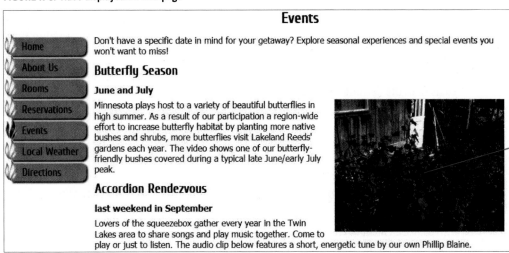

First frame of video displayed by default

Video/Sasha Vodnik

TABLE K-4: Video element type values

type	name	MIME type or codec
container format	MPEG-4	video/mp4
	Ogg	video/ogg
	WebM	video/webm
	Flash Video	video/x-flv
video codec	H.264 (baseline profile)	avc1.42E01E
	Theora	theora
	VP8	vp8

Incorporating the source Element

While many modern browsers can render video natively without requiring users to install additional programs, not all browsers support all containers. Thus, it's often necessary to reference multiple video files, each specifying the same video in different encoding and container formats, to accommodate the potential range of browser capabilities of your users. You can nest multiple instances of another HTML5 element, the source element, within a video element to specify the location and encoding of multiple files. You realize that a significant proportion of the audience for the Lakeland Reeds B&B Web site will be unable to view the video if you make only the MPEG-4/H.264/AAC file available. You use the source element to reference all three video formats you were provided.

STEPS

1. **Return to** events.html **in your text editor**

2. **Between the opening and closing** video **tags, add three one-sided** source **tags on separate lines**

> **QUICK TIP**
>
> Be sure to remove the space after the last value in the opening video tag after removing the src and type attributes.

3. **Within the first** source **tag, cut and paste the** src **and** type **attribute-value pairs from the opening** video **tag**

   Even though you're specifying three alternative source files, you continue to set the height and width of the element in the opening video tag.

4. **In the second** source **tag, add the attribute-value pairs** src="media/bfly.webm" **and** type='video/webm; codecs="vp8, vorbis"'

   This source element references a file containing the same video in a WebM container, encoded with the VP8 video codec and the Vorbis audio codec.

5. **In the third** source **tag, add the attribute-value pairs** src="media/bfly.ogv" **and** type='video/ogg; codecs="theora, vorbis"'

   This source element references a file containing the same video in an Ogg container, encoded with the Theora video codec and the Vorbis audio codec. Figure K-4 shows the completed code.

> **TROUBLE**
>
> At the time this book was written, only recent versions of Firefox, Chrome, and Opera supported WebM/VP8/Vorbis and Ogg/Theora/Vorbis natively. Later in this unit, you'll add support for most older browsers.

6. **Save your work, then reload** events.html **in your browser**

   If your browser supports MPEG-4/H.264/AAC, WebM/VP8/Vorbis, or Ogg/Theora/Vorbis natively, the opening frame of the video is displayed as shown in Figure K-5.

7. **If the video is visible in your browser, right-click the opening frame, then if available, click Play**

   If the Play option is available, the video, which is just over 30 seconds long, plays through once.

Encoding video in Web-ready formats

Especially if you're developing Web pages on your own, you may need to convert a single video file into multiple formats. Many tools are available to handle this conversion. While some software that simplifies and automates the process is available for purchase, some powerful tools are available free or on a donation basis as well. These free and low-cost alternatives are often just as powerful as their more expensive counterparts, but may require more configuration and may not be as well documented. If you're working on a well-funded project with a tight deadline, purchasing software may make the most sense; however, if you're working with a budget, it can be well worth your time to familiarize yourself with the free or low-cost tools. Try searching on "HTML5 video encoder" or "video encoder" plus the name of the container type to which you want to convert.

Whichever type of software you choose, be sure to download or purchase it from a company or organization that you're familiar with or that is recommended to you by someone you trust. Obtaining software from an untrusted source can expose your computer system to malware.

```
<article id="content">
    <h2 id="main">Events</h2>
    <p>Don't have a specific date in mind for your getaway? Explore seasonal experiences and special events you won't
want to miss!</p>
    <section>
        <h3>Butterfly Season</h3>
        <p class="eventdate">June and July</p>
        <video width="320" height="240">
            <source src="media/bfly.m4v" type='video/mp4; codecs="avc1.42E01E, mp4a.40.2"' />
            <source src="media/bfly.webm" type='video/webm; codecs="vp8, vorbis"' />
            <source src="media/bfly.ogv" type='video/ogg; codecs="theora, vorbis"' />
        </video>
        <p>Minnesota plays host to a variety of beautiful butterflies in high summer. As a result of our participation a
region-wide effort to increase butterfly habitat by planting more native bushes and shrubs, more butterflies visit Lakeland
Reeds' gardens each year. The video shows one of our butterfly-friendly bushes covered during a typical late June/early July
peak.</p>
    </section>
    <section>
        <h3>Accordion Rendezvous</h3>
        <p class="eventdate">last weekend in September</p>
        <p>Lovers of the squeezebox gather every year in the Twin Lakes area to share songs and play music together. Come
to play or just to listen. The audio clip below features a short, energetic tune by our own Phillip Blaine.</p>
    </section>
</article>
```

source elements added for three files in different container formats and encoded using different codecs

Events

Home
About Us
Rooms
Reservations
Events
Local Weather
Directions

Don't have a specific date in mind for your getaway? Explore seasonal experiences and special events you won't want to miss!

Butterfly Season

June and July

Minnesota plays host to a variety of beautiful butterflies in high summer. As a result of our participation a region-wide effort to increase butterfly habitat by planting more native bushes and shrubs, more butterflies visit Lakeland Reeds' gardens each year. The video shows one of our butterfly-friendly bushes covered during a typical late June/early July peak.

Accordion Rendezvous

last weekend in September

Lovers of the squeezebox gather every year in the Twin Lakes area to share songs and play music together. Come to play or just to listen. The audio clip below features a short, energetic tune by our own Phillip Blaine.

Video/Sasha Vodnik

First frame of video displayed in all browsers that support HTML5 video element and can decode at least one of the three source files specified

Controlling Playback

The video element supports several attributes that give you control over how the element is displayed and what types of interaction are available to users. The presence of the controls attribute instructs browsers to add their default controls to the video element; this enables user control over actions like playing and pausing content and adjusting audio volume. Likewise, the preload attribute indicates whether a browser should download the relevant video file before a user plays it, the loop attribute indicates that the browser should restart playback each time it reaches the end of the video, and the autoplay attribute tells browsers to start playback of the video immediately when the page is loaded. Table K-5 summarizes these attributes. While each one is relevant for specific situations, you'll most often use controls. While most of the playback attributes aren't relevant to the Lakeland Reeds Web page, you do want to provide users with the ability to more easily start and stop the video, so you decide to add playback controls to the video element.

STEPS

1. **Return to events.html in your text editor**

2. **In the video element, add the attribute-value pair controls="controls"**

   In a Web page written in HTML5, you can express this attribute as simply *controls*, without specifying a value. The code you entered is the XHTML-compatible version, which requires both an attribute and a value. Figure K-6 shows the completed code.

3. **Save your work, then reload events.html in your browser**

   As Figure K-7 shows, browsers that support the container formats and codecs you've specified display controls in conjunction with the video element. These controls typically include a start button, a slider for jumping to a position in the video, and one or more options for adjusting the audio level.

4. **If the video is displayed in your browser, click the Play button, which is usually a triangle pointing to the right**

   The video begins to play.

5. **Click the Pause button, which is typically indicated by two parallel lines that replace the Play button**

   The video pauses, and the frame where you paused it continues to be displayed.

> **QUICK TIP**
> The audio button is often marked by an icon resembling a speaker with concentric arcs of increasing size on one side.

6. **Click the Play button, drag the position slider back to the beginning, then click the Audio button twice to turn the sound off and on, and drag the slider up and down to adjust the audio level**

   As you drag the audio slider up, the volume increases, and as you drag it down, the level decreases. Not all browsers include an audio slider in the controls.

Including video from an external site

Uploading video to a video hosting site such as YouTube can be a shortcut to including it in your Web pages. Such sites generally provide links that automatically generate HTML code for any video you upload—and in some cases, for other videos they host as well. In some cases, you can select whether you'd like HTML5 video code, Flash object code, or both. This process can remove a lot of specialized technical work from the task of adding a video to a Web site, while preserving your control over the appearance of your Web pages.

```
        <article id="content">
          <h2 id="main">Events</h2>
          <p>Don't have a specific date in mind for your getaway? Explore seasonal experiences and special events you won't
want to miss!</p>
          <section>
            <h3>Butterfly Season</h3>
            <p class="eventdate">June and July</p>
            <video width="320" height="240" controls="controls">
              <source src="media/bfly.m4v" type='video/mp4; codecs="avc1.42E01E, mp4a.40.2"' />
              <source src="media/bfly.webm" type='video/webm; codecs="vp8, vorbis"' />
              <source src="media/bfly.ogv" type='video/ogg; codecs="theora, vorbis"' />
            </video>
            <p>Minnesota plays host to a variety of beautiful butterflies in high summer. As a result of our participation a
region-wide effort to increase butterfly habitat by planting more native bushes and shrubs, more butterflies visit Lakeland
Reeds' gardens each year. The video shows one of our butterfly-friendly bushes covered during a typical late June/early July
peak.</p>
          </section>
          <section>
            <h3>Accordion Rendezvous</h3>
            <p class="eventdate">last weekend in September</p>
            <p>Lovers of the squeezebox gather every year in the Twin Lakes area to share songs and play music together. Come
to play or just to listen. The audio clip below features a short, energetic tune by our own Phillip Blaine.</p>
          </section>
        </article>
```

XHTML-compatible attribute-value pair
for displaying video controls

FIGURE K-7: Default video controls in different browsers

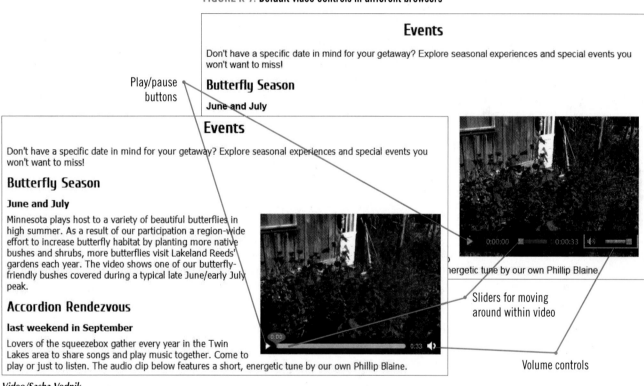

Play/pause
buttons

Sliders for moving
around within video

Volume controls

Video/Sasha Vodnik

TABLE K-5: Attributes for controlling playback

attribute	description
controls	instructs browsers to add their default controls to the video element
preload	indicates whether a browser should download the relevant video file before a user plays it
loop	indicates that the browser should restart playback each time it reaches the end of the video
autoplay	tells browsers to start playback of the video immediately when the page is loaded

Adding Video Support for Older Browsers

In spite of the promise of HTML5 video, the fact remains that many Web users are running older browsers that don't recognize HTML5 elements like video and source. Fortunately, HTML5 enables you to incorporate support for video that works for users of older browsers, while maintaining the benefits of HTML5 video for browsers that support it. Older browsers rely on additional software to play videos, and many such programs are available. Adobe Flash is the most widely installed program, and thus a common choice for supporting a wide array of older browsers. To make a Flash video available to older browsers, you use the object and param elements, which are detailed in Table K-6. These elements specify the file type and location, along with other settings.  A colleague has encoded the movie for you in the appropriate format for the Flash player. You'll add this version as a fallback option to maximize the number of users that will be able to view the movie.

STEPS

1. **Return to events.html in your text editor, then above the closing video tag, enter opening and closing object tags on separate lines**

2. **In the opening object tag, add the attribute-value pairs type="application/x-shockwave-flash", data="media/bfly.swf", width="320", and height="240"**

   Older browsers that aren't HTML5 compatible will ignore the video and source tags; thus, you need to specify the width and height again. Just as for the HTML5 elements, the value for the type attribute is a MIME type. The data attribute specifies the Flash file in which the video is encoded.

   > **QUICK TIP**
   > A Flash file may itself include some preset parameter behaviors, meaning that changing param settings may not always have the expected effect.

3. **Between the opening and closing object tags, enter the following param elements on separate lines:**

   ```
   <param name="movie" value="media/bfly.swf" />

   <param name="wmode" value="opaque" />

   <param name="loop" value="false" />

   <param name="play" value="false" />
   ```

   In the past, different browsers have implemented the object element in different ways. Thus, even though you specified the path to the video file with the data attribute of the object element, you specify it again in the first param element to maximize cross-browser compatibility. Different types of content make use of their own customized parameter names and values. Table K-7 explains the parameters used in this code. Figure K-8 shows the completed code.

   > **QUICK TIP**
   > If you have access to an older browser, such as Internet Explorer 8 or earlier, use it to open the file in this step.

4. **Save your work, then reload events.html in your browser**

   If your browser doesn't support the HTML5 video element, it ignores the video and source tags and renders the object element instead. In this case, the Flash player is displayed, as shown in Figure K-9.

5. **Use the controls indicated in Figure K-9 to start and stop the video, move forward and backward within it, and adjust the audio level**

TABLE K-6: The object and param elements

element	description	attributes
object	includes the content of an external resource in the current Web page	data="path/filename" type="MIME_type" width="width" height="height"
param	defines one or more parameters related to the external resource in the containing object element	name="parameter_name" vale="parameter value"

FIGURE K-8: Code to incorporate the Flash version of the video

object and param elements specify attributes and settings for Flash Player

```
<article id="content">
    <h2 id="main">Events</h2>
    <p>Don't have a specific date in mind for your getaway? Explore seasonal experiences and special events you won't
want to miss!</p>
    <section>
        <h3>Butterfly Season</h3>
        <p class="eventdate">June and July</p>
        <video width="320" height="240" controls="controls">
            <source src="media/bfly.m4v" type='video/mp4; codecs="avc1.42E01E, mp4a.40.2"' />
            <source src="media/bfly.webm" type='video/webm; codecs="vp8, vorbis"' />
            <source src="media/bfly.ogv" type='video/ogg; codecs="theora, vorbis"' />
            <object type="application/x-shockwave-flash" data="media/bfly.swf" width="320" height="240">
                <param name="movie" value="media/bfly.swf" />
                <param name="wmode" value="opaque" />
                <param name="loop" value="false" />
                <param name="play" value="false" />
            </object>
        </video>
        <p>Minnesota plays host to a variety of beautiful butterflies in high summer. As a result of our participation a
region-wide effort to increase butterfly habitat by planting more native bushes and shrubs, more butterflies visit Lakeland
Reeds' gardens each year. The video shows one of our butterfly-friendly bushes covered during a typical late June/early July
peak.</p>
    </section>
    <section>
        <h3>Accordion Rendezvous</h3>
        <p class="eventdate">last weekend in September</p>
        <p>Lovers of the squeezebox gather every year in the Twin Lakes area to share songs and play music together. Come
to play or just to listen. The audio clip below features a short, energetic tune by our own Phillip Blaine.</p>
    </section>
</article>
```

FIGURE K-9: Video displayed in Flash Player

Events

Don't have a specific date in mind for your getaway? Explore seasonal experiences and special events you won't want to miss!

Home

About Us

Rooms

Reservations

Events

Local Weather

Directions

Butterfly Season

June and July

Minnesota plays host to a variety of beautiful butterflies in high summer. As a result of our participation a region-wide effort to increase butterfly habitat by planting more native bushes and shrubs, more butterflies visit Lakeland Reeds' gardens each year. The video shows one of our butterfly-friendly bushes covered during a typical late June/early July peak.

Accordion Rendezvous

last weekend in September

Lovers of the squeezebox gather every year in the Twin Lakes area to share songs and play music together. Come to play or just to listen. The audio clip below features a short,

00.00/00.00

Video/Sasha Vodnik

Controls are embedded within Flash Player video and are displayed the same way across browsers

TABLE K-7: Adobe Flash parameters

name	description	values
movie	points to the file containing the content to be played	*path/filename*
wmode	indicates how Flash content should be displayed relative to surrounding Web page content	**window** (default): Flash content is displayed in its own window on the page **opaque**: Flash content blocks any Web page elements below it based on z-index values **transparent**: Any transparent areas of Flash content show any Web page elements below
loop	indicates whether content should restart upon reaching the end	**true** (default) **false**
play	indicates whether content should begin playing immediately upon loading, without waiting for user interaction	**true** (default) **false**

Providing a Fallback Image

Despite your best efforts, it's likely that some potential users of any given Web page will be unable to view video content. This can result from a variety of factors, including the use of an obscure or highly specialized browser, or a decision on the user's part not to devote the system resources necessary for decoding and viewing video. To preserve the layout of your Web pages for such users and to give them a taste of the content in the video, both the video and object elements enable you to specify a fallback image. In browsers that understand the video element, the image is displayed only if a browser can render none of the specified video formats; other browsers display the image only if the content specified in the object element is unavailable or cannot be rendered. ███████ Phillip Blaine has provided you an image file that consists of a single frame of the butterfly video. You'll add this image as a fallback for both the video and object elements.

STEPS

QUICK TIP

Version 3 of iOS, the operating system for Apple mobile devices, contained a bug that prevented video content from being rendered if the poster attribute is also present; you should omit this attribute when targeting users of this version.

1. **Return to** events.html **in your text editor**

2. **In the opening** video **tag, add the attribute-value pair** poster="images/bfly.png"
   The poster attribute specifies a fallback image for the video element.

3. **Above the closing** object **tag, insert a new line, enter an** img **tag, then add attribute-value pairs to specify the** source **as** images/bfly.png, **alternative text of** a bush with purple flowers covered in dark butterflies, **width of** 320, **height of** 240, **and** title **of** Unfortunately, your browser isn't able to play this video.
   Figure K-10 shows the completed code for the fallback image.

QUICK TIP

If you have access to a browser that doesn't recognize HTML5 elements and doesn't have Flash installed, use it to open the file in this step.

4. **Save your work, then reload** events.html **in your browser**
   If your browser supports HTML5 but not one of the video formats in the source files, or if your browser supports neither HTML5 elements nor Flash, the image is displayed, as shown in Figure K-11.

Making videos accessible

Unlike the img element, the video element does not support an alt attribute. Instead, work is underway to create a standard for incorporating captions and other supplementary material within the container, along with the encoded video and audio streams. Ideally, users would be able to explore the available material and decide, for example, to display captions of any speech over the video itself (for deaf users or users who are hard of hearing), or to turn on an extra audio track that describes the video content (for blind users or users with low sight). Some Web sites use scripts to put a system like this in place. Other developers have taken to including a paragraph containing fallback text after all other elements within a video element; if a user's browser can't render any video, the user is presented with links for downloading the video file as well as a text transcript.

```
            <article id="content">
              <h2 id="main">Events</h2>
              <p>Don't have a specific date in mind for your getaway? Explore seasonal experiences and special events you won't
            want to miss!</p>
              <section>
                <h3>Butterfly Season</h3>
                <p class="eventdate">June and July</p>
                <video width="320" height="240" controls="controls" poster="images/bfly.png">
                  <source src="media/bfly.m4v" type='video/mp4; codecs="avc1.42E01E, mp4a.40.2"' />
                  <source src="media/bfly.webm" type='video/webm; codecs="vp8, vorbis"' />
                  <source src="media/bfly.ogv" type='video/ogg; codecs="theora, vorbis"' />
                  <object type="application/x-shockwave-flash" data="media/bfly.swf" width="320" height="240">
                    <param name="movie" value="media/bfly.swf" />
                    <param name="wmode" value="opaque" />
                    <param name="loop" value="false" />
                    <param name="play" value="false" />
                    <img src="images/bfly.png" alt="a bush with purple flowers covered in dark butterflies" width="320"
            height="240" title="unfortunately, your browser isn't able to play this video." />
                  </object>
                </video>
                <p>Minnesota plays host to a variety of beautiful butterflies in high summer. As a result of our participation a
            region-wide effort to increase butterfly habitat by planting more native bushes and shrubs, more butterflies visit Lakeland
            Reeds' gardens each year. The video shows one of our butterfly-friendly bushes covered during a typical late June/early July
            peak.</p>
              </section>
              <section>
                <h3>Accordion Rendezvous</h3>
                <p class="eventdate">last weekend in September</p>
                <p>Lovers of the squeezebox gather every year in the Twin Lakes area to share songs and play music together. Come
            to play or just to listen. The audio clip below features a short, energetic tune by our own Phillip Blaine.</p>
              </section>
            </article>
```

Embedded
img element
specifies
fallback image
for browsers
that don't
support the
video element

poster attribute specifies
fallback image for
browsers that support the
video element

Events

Home

About Us

Rooms

Reservations

Events

Local Weather

Directions

Don't have a specific date in mind for your getaway? Explore seasonal experiences and special events you won't want to miss!

Butterfly Season

June and July

Minnesota plays host to a variety of beautiful butterflies in high summer. As a result of our participation a region-wide effort to increase butterfly habitat by planting more native bushes and shrubs, more butterflies visit Lakeland Reeds' gardens each year. The video shows one of our butterfly-friendly bushes covered during a typical late June/early July peak.

Accordion Rendezvous

last weekend in September

Lovers of the squeezebox gather every year in the Twin Lakes area to share songs and play music together. Come to play or just to listen. The audio clip below features a short, energetic tune by our own Phillip Blaine.

Video/Sasha Vodnik

Fallback image displays
a frame of the video

Implementing the audio Element

In addition to the video element, HTML5 also introduced an audio element for linking audio files to a Web page and enabling users to control playback. The audio element makes use of the same attributes as the video element and accepts nested source elements for source files in multiple formats. Table K-8 details the MIME types for two of the most common audio file formats for the Web. Phillip would like you to add the option for users to play a recording of a short song in the Accordion Festival section of the Events page. You'll add the file in two formats, mp3 and Ogg; one or both of these formats are supported by most current browsers.

STEPS

1. **Return to events.html in your text editor**

2. **Just above the closing section tag for the Accordion Rendezvous section, insert opening and closing audio tags on separate lines**

3. **In the opening audio tag, add the attribute-value pair controls="controls"**
   Because an audio element contains no visual content, it's invisible on a Web page unless controls are displayed. Therefore, it's almost always a good idea to include controls.

4. **Within the audio element, add a source element containing the attribute-value pairs src="media/bonfire.mp3" and type="audio/mpeg"**

5. **Beneath the code you just entered, add a second source element containing the attribute-value pairs src="media/bonfire.ogg" and type='audio/ogg; codecs="vorbis"'**
   Figure K-12 shows the completed code.

6. **Save your work, then reload events.html in your browser**
   If your browser recognizes the audio element and supports the mp3 or Ogg formats, the audio controls are displayed beneath the text describing the accordion festival, as shown in Figure K-13.

7. **If the audio controls are displayed in your browser, use them to start and stop the song, move forward and backward within it, and, if possible, adjust the volume**

```
      <article id="content">
        <h2 id="main">Events</h2>
        <p>Don't have a specific date in mind for your getaway? Explore seasonal experiences and special events you won't
want to miss!</p>
        <section>
          <h3>Butterfly Season</h3>
          <p class="eventdate">June and July</p>
          <video width="320" height="240" controls="controls" poster="images/bfly.png">
            <source src="media/bfly.m4v" type='video/mp4; codecs="avc1.42E01E, mp4a.40.2"' />
            <source src="media/bfly.webm" type='video/webm; codecs="vp8, vorbis"' />
            <source src="media/bfly.ogv" type='video/ogg; codecs="theora, vorbis"' />
            <object type="application/x-shockwave-flash" data="media/bfly.swf" width="320" height="240">
              <param name="movie" value="media/bfly.swf" />
              <param name="wmode" value="opaque" />
              <param name="loop" value="false" />
              <param name="play" value="false" />
              <img src="images/bfly.png" alt="a bush with purple flowers covered in dark butterflies" width="320"
height="240" title="Unfortunately, your browser isn't able to play this video." />
            </object>
          </video>
          <p>Minnesota plays host to a variety of beautiful butterflies in high summer. As a result of our participation a
region-wide effort to increase butterfly habitat by planting more native bushes and shrubs, more butterflies visit Lakeland
Reeds' gardens each year. The video shows one of our butterfly-friendly bushes covered during a typical late June/early July
peak.</p>
        </section>
        <section>
          <h3>Accordion Rendezvous</h3>
          <p class="eventdate">last weekend in September</p>
          <p>Lovers of the squeezebox gather every year in the Twin Lakes area to share songs and play music together. Come
to play or just to listen. The audio clip below features a short, energetic tune by our own Phillip Blaine.</p>
          <audio controls="controls">
            <source src="media/bonfire.mp3" type="audio/mpeg" />
            <source src="media/bonfire.ogg" type='audio/ogg; codecs="vorbis"' />
          </audio>
        </section>
      </article>
```

audio and
source
elements
specify settings
and source
files

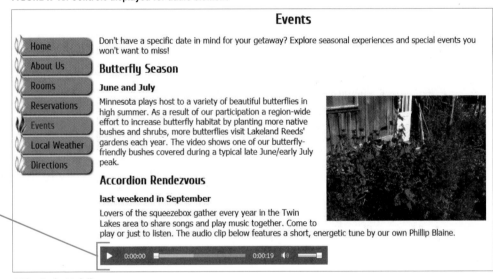

Audio controls
match functions
and appearance
of video controls

Video/Sasha Vodnik

TABLE K-8: MIME types for common audio formats

name	MIME type
mp3	audio/mpeg
Ogg	audio/ogg

HTML5 and CSS3

Adding Audio Support for Older Browsers

As with embedded video, not all older browsers recognize the HTML5 audio tag. You can specify fallback content using an object element, just as you would for a video. Phillip has provided a file that contains the same song you added in the previous lesson and that is in a format that Flash can play. You'll add an object element referencing this new file to provide a fallback option for users of older browsers.

STEPS

1. **Return to events.html in your text editor, then above the closing audio tag, enter opening and closing object tags on separate lines**

2. **In the opening object tag, add the attribute-value pairs type="application/ x-shockwave-flash", data="media/bonfire.swf", width="320", and height="30"**

3. **Between the opening and closing object tags, enter the following param elements on separate lines:**

   ```
   <param name="movie" value="media/bonfire.swf" />

   <param name="wmode" value="opaque" />

   <param name="loop" value="false" />

   <param name="play" value="false" />
   ```

   Even though the file contains no video, you still indicate its location with the movie parameter. Figure K-14 shows the completed code.

QUICK TIP
If you have access to an older browser, such as Internet Explorer 8 or earlier, use it to open the file in this step.

4. **Save your work, then reload events.html in your browser**

   If your browser doesn't support the HTML5 audio element, the Flash player displays playback controls for the song, as shown in Figure K-15.

5. **Use the controls to start and stop the song, move forward and backward within it, and adjust the volume**

6. **Validate the code for events.html, then make changes as necessary to fix any errors**

7. **If you have space on a Web server, publish your Web site, then open events.html in your browser from the published location and test the video and audio elements**

FIGURE K-14: Code to incorporate the Flash version of the song

object and
param elements
specify
attributes and
settings for
Flash Player

```
<section>
    <h3>Accordion Rendezvous</h3>
    <p class="eventdate">last weekend in September</p>
    <p>Lovers of the squeezebox gather every year in the Twin Lakes area to share songs and play music together. Come
to play or just to listen. The audio clip below features a short, energetic tune by our own Phillip Blaine.</p>
    <audio controls="controls">
        <source src="media/bonfire.mp3" type="audio/mpeg" />
        <source src="media/bonfire.ogg" type="audio/ogg; codecs="vorbis"' />
        <object type="application/x-shockwave-flash" data="media/bonfire.swf" width="320" height="30">
            <param name="movie" value="media/bonfire.swf" />
            <param name="wmode" value="opaque" />
            <param name="loop" value="false" />
            <param name="play" value="false" />
        </object>
    </audio>
</section>
```

FIGURE K-15: Audio controls displayed in Flash Player

Events

Don't have a specific date in mind for your getaway? Explore seasonal experiences and special events you won't want to miss!

Butterfly Season

June and July

Minnesota plays host to a variety of beautiful butterflies in high summer. As a result of our participation a region-wide effort to increase butterfly habitat by planting more native bushes and shrubs, more butterflies visit Lakeland Reeds' gardens each year. The video shows one of our butterfly-friendly bushes covered during a typical late June/early July peak.

Accordion Rendezvous

last weekend in September

Lovers of the squeezebox gather every year in the Twin Lakes area to share songs and play music together. Come to play or just to listen. The audio clip below features a short, energetic tune by our own Phillip Blaine.

Video/Sasha Vodnik

Controls are embedded within Flash
Player audio file and are displayed
the same way across browsers

Evaluating the advantages and drawbacks of Flash

In its role as an important Web plugin and format, Adobe Flash elicits strong feelings from some Web developers, browser makers, standards organizations, and user advocates. Because Flash is installed on the computers of so many Web users, it offers developers the ability to create Web content—including videos, animations, and even entire Web pages—that are displayed predictably in different browsers and under different operating systems. However, some members of the Web community see danger in relying on Flash, arguing that Flash player software uses a disproportionate amount of system resources, that the Web should be based on free and unpatented technologies rather than proprietary ones like Flash, and that browsers themselves should, without requiring a plugin, support the types of content that Flash is often used to publish. While standards like HTML5 video and audio may challenge the dominant position of Flash in some types of content delivery, Flash is not likely to disappear as a force on the Web for the time being.

Practice

Concepts Review

Refer to Figure K-16.

FIGURE K-16

1. **Which item specifies a fallback image for browsers that recognize the video element?**
2. **Which item embeds audio for HTML5-compatible browsers?**
3. **Which item specifies a fallback Flash file for browsers that don't recognize HTML5 elements?**
4. **Which item specifies a fallback image for browsers that don't recognize HTML5 elements?**
5. **Which item embeds video for HTML5-compatible browsers?**
6. **Which item specifies a parameter for Flash Player?**
7. **Which item specifies that browsers should display controls for interacting with the related element?**

Match each term with the statement that best describes it.

8. **plugin**
9. **container**
10. **codec**
11. **type**
12. **stream**
13. **encoding**

a. a file in which video and/or audio is packaged for distribution

b. a standardized data type that describes a container format

c. the process of transforming a moving image and/or sound into a digital file

d. a specific encoding method; short for coder/decoder

e. an encoded set of video or audio data

f. a program that can both unpack a video or audio container and decode the video and audio streams

Select the best answer from the list of choices.

14. H.264, Theora, and VP8 are examples of popular _____ on the Web today.

  a. container formats

  b. plugins

  c. codecs

  d. MIME types

15. Which of the following is a codec used to encode audio?

  a. AAC

  b. Ogg

  c. VP8

  d. m4v

16. Which of the following is a codec used to encode video?

  a. AAC

  b. Ogg

  c. VP8

  d. m4v

17. Which of the following is a container format?

  a. H.264

  b. Vorbis

  c. MP3

  d. WebM

18. Which of the following is Flash Player an example of?

  a. a container format

  b. a plugin

  c. a codec

  d. an HTML5 element

19. Which attribute lets you specify a fallback image for the video element?

  a. poster

  b. loop

  c. controls

  d. preload

20. Which element do you use to provide video for older browsers?

  a. video

  b. source

  c. object

  d. audio

Skills Review

1. Use the video element.

  a. In your text editor, open HTM K-2.html from the Unit K/Review folder where you store your Data Files, insert a blank line before the closing body tag, insert a paragraph element containing your first and last name and the text **HTML5 Unit K, Skills Review**, then save it as **news.html**.

  b. In events.html, just before the closing section tag for the first section, insert opening and closing video tags on separate lines.

  c. Within the opening video tag, add attribute-value pairs to set the source to **media/market.m4v**, the width to **480**, the height to **390**, and the type to **'video/mp4; codecs="avc1.42E01E, mp4a.40.2"'**.

  d. Save your work, then open news.html in your browser. If the video is visible in your browser, right-click the opening frame, then click the Play button if available.

2. Incorporate the source element.

  a. Return to news.html in your text editor, then between the opening and closing video tags, add three one-sided source tags on separate lines.

  b. Within the first source tag, cut and paste the src and type attribute-value pairs from the opening video tag.

  c. In the second source tag, add attribute-value pairs to set the source to **media/market.webm** and the type to **'video/webm; codecs="vp8, vorbis"'**. In the third source tag, add attribute-value pairs to set the source to **media/market.ogv** and the type to **'video/ogg; codecs="theora, vorbis"'**.

  d. Save your work, then reload news.html in your browser. If the video is visible in your browser, right-click the opening frame, then click the Play button.

3. Control playback.

  a. Return to news.html in your text editor, then in the video element, add an attribute-value pair to indicate that browsers should display controls for the video.

  b. Save your work, then reload news.html in your browser.

  c. If the video is displayed in your browser, use the controls to navigate through the video and, if possible, adjust the volume.

Skills Review (continued)

4. Add video support for older browsers.

a. Return to news.html in your text editor, then above the closing video tag, enter opening and closing object tags on separate lines.

b. In the opening object tag, add attribute-value pairs to set the type to **application/x-shockwave-flash**, the data to **media/market.swf**, the width to **480**, and the height to **390**.

c. Between the opening and closing object tags, add elements to set the following parameters:

name	value
movie	media/market.swf
wmode	opaque
loop	false
play	false

d. Save your work, then reload news.html in your browser.

e. If the Flash player is displayed in your browser, use the controls to navigate through the video and adjust the volume.

5. Provide a fallback image.

a. Return to news.html in your text editor, then in the opening video tag, add an attribute-value pair to specify **images/market.png** as a fallback image.

b. Above the closing object tag, add an element to specify a backup image for browsers that don't recognize the video element, specifying **images/market.png** as the source, alternative text of **Big J's Pizza**, width of **480**, height of **360**, and title of **Unfortunately, your browser isn't able to play this video**.

c. Save your work, then if you have access to a browser that doesn't support HTML5 elements or Flash, open news.html in that browser.

6. Implement the audio element.

a. Return to news.html in your text editor, then just above the closing section tag for the second section, insert opening and closing audio tags on separate lines.

b. In the opening audio tag, add an attribute-value pair to indicate that browsers should display controls for the element.

c. Within the audio element, add a source element specifying a source of **media/dance.mp3** and a type of **audio/mpeg**. Add a second source element specifying a source of **media/dance.ogg** and a type of **'audio/ogg; codecs="vorbis"'**.

d. Save your work, then reload news.html in your browser. If the audio controls are displayed in your browser, use them to start and stop the song, move forward and backward within it, and, if possible, adjust the volume. Figure K-17 shows the display of the video and audio elements in one browser.

7. Add audio support for older browsers.

a. Return to news.html in your text editor, then above the closing audio tag, enter opening and closing object tags on separate lines

FIGURE K-17

Video/Sasha Vodnik

Skills Review (continued)

b. In the opening object tag, add attribute-value pairs to set the type to **application/x-shockwave-flash**, the data to **media/dance.swf**, the width to **320**, and the height to **30**.

c. Between the opening and closing object tags, add elements to set the following parameters:

name	value
movie	media/dance.swf
wmode	opaque
loop	false
play	false

d. Save your work, then reload news.html in your browser. If the Flash player is displayed in your browser, use the controls to start and stop the song, move forward and backward within it, and adjust the volume.

e. Validate the code for news.html, then make changes as necessary to fix any errors.

f. If you have space on a Web server, publish your Web site, then open news.html in your browser from the published location and test the video and audio elements.

Independent Challenge 1

The Spotted Wren Garden Center is adding videos of gardens and landscaping projects to their Web site to give current and potential customers ideas that they might want to implement for their own homes and businesses. Sarah Nguyen, the manager, has provided you a set of files containing the first project to be spotlighted. You'll add it to a new page on the Web site.

a. Open HTM K-3.html from the Unit K/IC1 folder in your text editor. Insert a blank line before the closing body tag, insert a paragraph element containing your first and last name and the text **HTML5 Unit K, Independent Challenge 1**, then save it as **great.html**.

b. In great.html, within the figure element beneath the h3 heading, add code to incorporate a video for browsers that recognize HTML5 elements. Specify a width of **480** and a height of **272**, and indicate that browsers should display video controls. Add references to the following three source files:

source	MIME type	codecs
media/gardens.m4v	video/mp4	avc1.42E01E, mp4a.40.2
media/gardens.webm	video/webm	vp8, vorbis
media/gardens.ogv	video/ogg	theora, vorbis

c. Save your work. If you have access to an HTML5-compatible browser, open great.html and verify that the video plays. Figure K-18 shows the Web page displaying an HTML5 video.

d. Add code for a Flash version of the video to the Web page. Specify the file **media/gardens.swf** as the source, a width of **480**, and a height of **302**. Add code to set the following parameters:

name	value
movie	media/gardens.swf
wmode	opaque
loop	false
play	false

e. Save your work. If you have access to a browser that does not recognize HTML5 elements and that has the Flash Player plugin installed, open great.html and verify that the video plays.

f. Add the file **images/gardens.png** as a fallback image for both the HTML5 and Flash code. Specify a width of **480** and a height of **272**, and provide appropriate alternative and title text for the Flash fallback code.

Independent Challenge 1 (continued)

g. Save your work. If you have access to a browser that does not recognize HTML5 elements and does not have the Flash Player plugin installed, open great.html and verify that the fallback image is displayed.

h. Validate great.html. If you have space on a Web server, publish your Web site, then open great.html in your browser from the published location.

i. Close your browser, then close your text editor.

FIGURE K-18

Video/Diana Vodnik, Xtremer/Shutterstock.com

Independent Challenge 2

The coordinators of the Murfreesboro Recreational Soccer League would like to add some footage from a soccer game to the Web site in place of one of the static images. They've provided you a video in several formats and asked you to incorporate it into the site.

a. Open HTM K-4.html from the Unit K/IC2 folder in your text editor. Insert a blank line before the closing body tag, insert a paragraph element containing your first and last name and the text **HTML5 Unit K, Independent Challenge 2**, then save the file as **schedule.html**.

b. Within the figure element near the top of the article element, delete the img element. Add code to incorporate a video for browsers that recognize HTML5 elements. Specify a width of **320** and a height of **240**, and indicate that browsers should display video controls. Add references to the following three source files:

source	MIME type	codecs
media/match.m4v	video/mp4	avc1.42E01E, mp4a.40.2
media/match.webm	video/webm	vp8, vorbis
media/match.ogv	video/ogg	theora, vorbis

Independent Challenge 2 (continued)

c. Save your work. If you have access to an HTML5-compatible browser, open schedule.html and verify that the video plays. Figure K-19 shows the Web page displaying an HTML5 video.

d. Add code for a Flash version of the video to the Web page. Specify the file **media/match.swf** as the source, a width of **320**, and a height of **270**. Add code to set the following parameters:

name	value
movie	media/match.swf
wmode	opaque
loop	false
play	false

e. Save your work. If you have access to a browser that does not recognize HTML5 elements and that has the Flash Player plugin installed, open schedule.html and verify that the video plays.

f. Add the file **images/match.png** as a fallback image for both the HTML5 and Flash code. Specify a width of **320** and a height of **240**, and provide appropriate alternative and title text for the Flash fallback code.

g. Save your work. If you have access to a browser that does not recognize HTML5 elements and does not have the Flash Player plugin installed, open schedule.html and verify that the fallback image is displayed.

Advanced Challenge Exercise

- Edit the HTML5-compatible code to make the video play automatically when the Web page is loaded. Add code to make the video automatically repeat from the beginning each time it reaches the end.
- Save your work, reload the page in a browser that recognizes HTML5 elements, then verify that the video starts automatically and restarts automatically when reaching the end.
- Edit the code for the Flash version of the video to make the video play automatically when the Web page is loaded and to make the video repeat automatically from the beginning each time it reaches the end. (*Hint*: Change the values of relevant parameters from *false* to *true*.)
- Save your work, reload the page in a browser that does not recognize HTML5 elements and has the Flash Player plugin installed, then verify that the video starts automatically and restarts automatically when reaching the end.

h. Validate schedule.html. If you have space on a Web server, publish your Web site, then open schedule.html in your browser from the published location.

i. Close your browser, then close your text editor.

FIGURE K-19

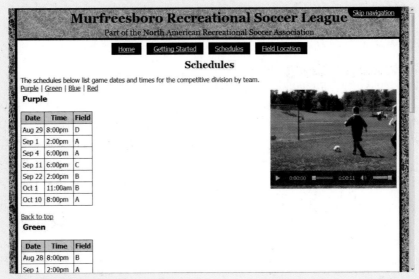

Video/Kim Davis, Xtremer/Shutterstock.com

Independent Challenge 3

Diego Merckx, the manager of the Hotel Natoma, would like to add videos of local attractions within walking distance of the hotel to help potential guests visualize its great location. To start, he's given you multiple versions of a video of a cable car being turned around at the terminus on Powell Street. You'll add this video to the Web site.

a. Open HTM K-5.html from the Unit K/IC3 folder in your text editor. Insert a blank line before the closing body tag, then insert a paragraph element containing your first and last name and the text **HTML5 Unit K, Independent Challenge 3**, then save the file as **nearby.html**.

b. Within the figure element beneath the h2 heading, add code to incorporate a video for browsers that recognize HTML5 elements. Specify a width of **480** and a height of **272**, and indicate that browsers should display video controls. Add references to the following three source files:

source	MIME type	codecs
media/cablecar.m4v	video/mp4	avc1.42E01E, mp4a.40.2
media/cablecar.webm	video/webm	vp8, vorbis
media/cablecar.ogv	video/ogg	theora, vorbis

c. Save your work. If you have access to an HTML5-compatible browser, open schedule.html and verify that the video plays. Figure K-20 shows the Web page displaying an HTML5 video.

d. Add code for a Flash version of the video to the Web page. Specify the file **media/cablecar.swf** as the source, a width of **480**, and a height of **302**. Add code to set the following parameters:

name	value
movie	media/cablecar.swf
wmode	opaque
loop	false
play	false

e. Save your work. If you have access to a browser that does not recognize HTML5 elements and that has the Flash Player plugin installed, open nearby.html and verify that the video plays.

f. Add the file **images/cablecar.png** as a fallback image for both the HTML5 and Flash code. Specify a width of **480** and a height of **272**, and provide appropriate alternative and title text for the Flash fallback code.

g. Save your work. If you have access to a browser that does not recognize HTML5 elements and does not have the Flash Player plugin installed, open nearby.html and verify that the fallback image is displayed.

Advanced Challenge Exercise

- If you have an account on YouTube or another video sharing service, upload cablecar.m4v to the site.
- When the video is uploaded, copy the automatically generated code to embed it on a Web page. (*Hint*: If you don't see the code, consult the site's Help or Support section.)
- Use the code to replace the corresponding code in your Web page—if the code provided uses HTML5, use it to replace the HTML5 code you already added; if the code does not use HTML5 elements, use it to replace your code for Flash Player. If the site offers you both options, use the provided code to replace all of the code you created.
- Save your work, then reload your Web page in one or more browsers that enable you to see the effect of the code you added.

Independent Challenge 3 (continued)

h. Validate nearby.html. If you have space on a Web server, publish your Web site, then open nearby.html in your browser from the published location.

i. Close your browser, then close your text editor.

FIGURE K-20

Video/Sasha Vodnik

Real Life Independent Challenge

This assignment builds on the personal Web site you have worked on in previous units. You'll add video and/or audio to your site.

a. Copy your Web site files to the Unit K/RLIC folder on the drive and folder where you store your Data Files.

b. Identify a video or audio clip that you'd like to add to your Web site. Page through the site and locate the most appropriate place for it, or plan a new page for it.

c. Research tools for converting your video into H.264, Ogg, and WebM containers, and your audio into MP3 and Ogg containers. If necessary, consult your technical support person for guidance.

d. Convert the files, then add them to your Web site. Make any necessary changes to the style sheet to preserve or enhance the layout.

e. If you have access to software for creating Flash video and audio and have experience in doing so, convert your clip to a Flash-compatible format and add code to the document to present this content as a fallback. Alternatively, upload your content to a video sharing site such as YouTube and paste the automatically generated Flash-compatible code from the site into your Web page.

f. If you added a video to your site, create and incorporate a fallback image.

g. Validate all of your HTML and CSS documents and make any edits necessary to address any issues.

h. If you have space on a Web server, publish your Web site, then open the page containing your clip in your browser from the published location.

i. Close your browser, then close your text editor.

Visual Workshop

In your text editor, open the file HTM K-6.html from the Unit K/VW directory on the drive and folder where you store your Data Files, add a paragraph before the closing body tag that contains your first and last name and the text **HTML5 Unit K, Visual Workshop**, then save the file as **readers.html**. Use your text editor to add the audio clips rumi.mp3, rumi.ogg, and rumi.swf from the media folder. When you're finished, your Web page should match Figure K-21. Save your work, then validate your HTML code. If you have space on a Web server, publish your files, then open the Web page in your browser from the published location. Close your browser and text editor.

FIGURE K-21

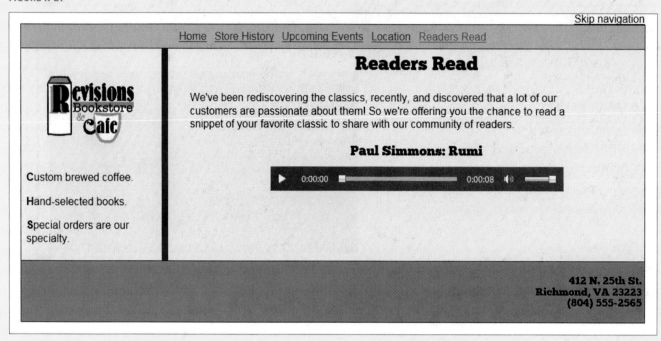

Incorporating Video and Audio

Programming Web Pages with JavaScript

HTML and CSS enable you to create and manipulate a limited set of Web page elements and properties. You can increase the range of actions you can perform on Web page elements by writing and including scripts with your Web pages. The most widely supported scripting language among modern Web browsers is **JavaScript**. Philip Blaine, the owner of Lakeland Reeds Bed & Breakfast, would like the feedback form on his Web site to confirm when a user's information has been submitted. He'd also like you to add support for older browsers for some of the HTML5-only features you incorporated. You'll create code for these changes using JavaScript.

OBJECTIVES

Explore the Document Object Model

Add content using a script

Trigger a script using an event handler

Create a function

Store and compare data in variables

Generate Web page content dynamically

Script fallback options with Modernizr

Integrate an existing script

Exploring the Document Object Model

All of the enhancements that JavaScript can bring to your Web pages are rooted in looking up, and in some cases changing, data associated with parts of HTML documents. Writing code to accomplish this requires a standardized way of referring to the parts of a Web page; this system is known as the **Document Object Model (DOM)**. You can think of the DOM as a hierarchical arrangement of the content of an HTML document into a tree-like structure, which is known as **DOM tree**. Figure L-1 shows the code for a sample Web page along with the corresponding DOM tree. In the DOM, each part of an HTML document—including elements, attributes, and text content—is represented by a node. ▉▉▉▉ You review the underlying concepts of the DOM in preparation for working with JavaScript.

DETAILS

You create code by combining several types of information associated with a node:

- **Objects**

  In the DOM, each HTML element is considered an **object**. To retrieve data from or make changes to a Web page element requires first writing code that identifies the specific object you want to work with. One of the most straightforward ways to reference an object is by looking up the value of its id attribute. For an element without an id value, JavaScript instead allows you to specify where in the DOM tree the object is located by using parent-child or other relationships.

- **Properties**

  Each DOM node is associated with a standard set of information; each piece of information is known as a **property**. Standard properties for objects include the text content associated with an object, the name of the object, and the name of an associated attribute. Each attribute represents its own node and is associated with its own properties, including its value. Table L-1 lists a few commonly used properties.

- **Methods**

  The DOM also defines **methods**, which are actions that can be performed for each node. For instance, your scripts can access data associated with any HTML element with an id attribute by using the getElementById() method. Most method names are followed by parentheses between which you specify information specific to the method; for the getElementById() method, you identify the id value of the desired element within the parentheses. Thus, to access information for an element with the id *logo*, you could use the code getElementById("logo"). Table L-2 lists a few commonly used methods.

QUICK TIP

JavaScript also supports an alternative notation known as square bracket notation, which is useful in creating more advanced scripts.

- **Combining objects, properties, and methods**

  You use a combination of objects, properties, and methods to specify an item in the DOM that you want to access. You specify these elements in order from most general to most specific. Any reference to a DOM node begins with the *document* object, which is the node at the top of the DOM tree. Next you specify one or more methods or objects to move to a specific place in the DOM; for instance, if you wanted to retrieve the value of the element with the id "logo", you could next use the method getElementById("logo") to identify the node within the DOM where the information you want is located. Often you want to retrieve or set the value of a node; one of the most common ways to do so is by including the innerHTML property at the end of your code.

  To identify a specific item within the DOM, you list the appropriate objects, properties, and methods in order, separated by periods. This syntax, known as **dot notation**, connects all the parts of your statement into a single string of characters. Thus, using dot notation, you could reference the value of the element with the id "logo" using the following code: document.getElementById("logo").innerHTML.

FIGURE L-1: A DOM tree

HTML code

```
<html>
  <head>
    <title>
      Lakeland Reeds Bed &amp; Breakfast
    </title>
  </head>
  <body>
    <h1>
      <img src="images/logo.gif" />
    </h1>
    <p id="addr">
      45 Marsh Grass Ln. • Marble, MN 55764 • (218) 555-5253
    </p>
  </body>
</html>
```

DOM tree

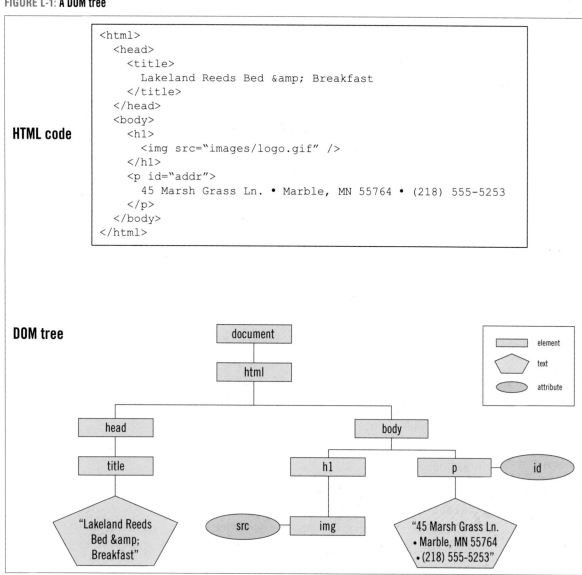

TABLE L-1: Commonly used properties

property	refers to	example
innerHTML	the content of an object	the text in a paragraph element
value	the current value of another property	the value of the href property for an a element

TABLE L-2: Commonly used methods

method	associated action
write	add text content and/or HTML code to a Web page document
getElementById	locate an element with a given id value within the DOM tree
alert	opens a small alert box that displays a customized message

Adding Content Using a Script

JavaScript enables you to change or enhance your Web pages in a variety of ways. One of the simplest is to use a script to add content to a page. You can specify any element in the DOM using the getElementById method. You can use the innerHTML property to look up or specify a value for a given element. Code for a single instruction in a script is known as a **statement**. While complex scripts can include hundreds or thousands of statements, you can achieve some goals with a script that contains only a single statement. ▄▄▄ Phillip would like a message that thanks the user and is displayed above the form after the contents are submitted. You start by adding a script to add the text for a thank-you message to the page contents.

1. In your text editor, open HTM L-1.html from the Unit L/Unit folder where you store your Data Files, insert a blank line before the closing body tag, insert a paragraph element containing your first and last name and the text HTML5 Unit L, then save it as contact.html

2. Beneath the h2 element near the top of the body section, insert a blank line and indent, then enter the code <p id="message"></p>

3. Below the code you just entered, insert a blank line and indent, then enter the tag <script>

4. Beneath the opening script tag you just entered, insert a blank line and indent, then enter </script>

> **QUICK TIP**
>
> JavaScript interprets the end of a line as the end of a state-ment; however, end-ing every statement with a semicolon makes code easier for developers to interpret.

5. Between the opening and closing script tags, indent and enter the following code on a single line:

```
document.getElementById("message").innerHTML=("Thanks for contacting Lakeland Reeds Bed & Breakfast!");
```

As in CSS, JavaScript ignores spaces outside of quoted text; thus, you can add or exclude spaces surrounding an equals sign, for instance, without affecting the validity of the code. Figure L-2 shows the completed code.

6. Save your work, then open contact.html in your browser

As Figure L-3 shows, the script you entered adds the thank-you message to the Web page.

> **TROUBLE**
>
> The Inspect Element feature is available only in Chrome, Safari (must be enabled), and using the FireBug exten-sion for Firefox.

7. Right-click the thank-you message, click Inspect Element, then examine the source code for the paragraph with the id message

Note that the browser has inserted the text of the thank-you message within the opening and closing para-graph tags.

FIGURE L-2: **Web page code containing script**

```
<article id="content">
  <h2 id="main">Contact Us</h2>
  <p id="message"></p>
  <script>
    document.getElementById("message").innerHTML=("Thanks for contacting Lakeland Reeds Bed & Breakfast!");
  </script>
  <form name="contact" id="contact">
```

FIGURE L-3: **Web page displaying text inserted by script**

Unholy Vault Designs/Shutterstock.com

Text inserted into
Web page by script

Preserving accessibility for users agents that don't support scripting

A small number of Web users access pages with browsers or devices that are unable to interpret JavaScript or that can't access the full range of JavaScript code. Such users may be using older browsers, may have JavaScript disabled in their browsers for security reasons, or may be using assistive devices. A number of strategies enable you to broaden the accessibility of your Web pages that contain scripts. As with other Web page features, you should ensure that any content or functionality added to your Web pages with a script is also available by other means. While some pages degrade gracefully without any additional code, it's sometimes useful to add fallback content within the HTML noscript element, whose contents are rendered only when JavaScript isn't available. You should also avoid using event handlers that are device specific, such as *onKeyDown*, which requires a keyboard, or *onMouseOver*, which requires a mouse or other pointing device. If it isn't possible to make a scripted page accessible, another option is to create an alternative page that is displayed for users without JavaScript access. Search on the phrase *JavaScript accessibility* for more details on creating accessible scripts.

HTML5 and CSS3

Triggering a Script Using an Event Handler

Using a script to add content to a Web page when it opens is something that you can do more easily with simple HTML. However, you can make this type of script much more flexible and powerful by linking it with a user action. A number of actions, known as **events**, are defined for Web pages. You can indicate code to execute in response to a specific event on a specific element by using an **event handler**, which is an HTML attribute that specifies a type of user action. Table L-3 lists event handlers supported by HTML and JavaScript. Event handlers are composed of multiple words strung together, and the first letter of each word after the first word is generally capitalized for clarity. By adding an event handler as an attribute for an element with which a user can interact, such as a link or button, and specifying JavaScript code to execute as the value of the attribute, you can program the content of a Web page to change in response to user activities. ▰▰▱▱ Because you want the thank-you message to be displayed after the form is submitted, you add the code to an event handler in the Submit button element.

1. **Return to contact.html in your text editor**

2. **Locate the script element you entered in the previous lesson, then delete the opening and closing script tags and the text between them**

3. **Near the end of the form element, locate the input element with the id submit**

QUICK TIP
For XHTML compatibility, event handlers must be entered as all lowercase.

4. **Click just before the closing /> in the input tag, then type the following code without any line breaks:**

   ```
   onclick='document.getElementById("message").innerHTML=("Thanks for
   contacting Lakeland Reeds Bed & Breakfast!");'
   ```

   The value for the onClick event handler begins with the same script code you entered in the previous lesson. Because the JavaScript code contains some values enclosed in double quotes, the entire value is enclosed in single quotes to avoid confusion in parsing. Figure L-4 shows the completed code.

5. **Add a space after the code you entered, save your work, then reload contact.html in your browser**

   The thank-you message is no longer displayed beneath the "Contact Us" heading.

QUICK TIP
Screen readers and other devices for Web accessibility generally support the onclick handler when used with a clickable element such as a link or button.

6. **Scroll to the bottom of the page, click the Submit button, then if necessary scroll to the top of the page**

   As Figure L-5 shows, the thank-you message is displayed beneath the "Contact Us" heading in response to the button click.

FIGURE L-4: Event handler in Web page code

```
                </fieldset>
                <fieldset id="submitbutton">
                    <input type="button" id="submit" value="Submit" onclick='document.getElementById("message").innerHTML=("Thanks
for contacting Lakeland Reeds Bed & Breakfast!");' />
                </fieldset>
            </form>
```

Event handler and code
to run added to input tag

FIGURE L-5: Text added to Web page based on event

Unholy Vault Designs/Shutterstock.com

Confirmation text displayed in response
to clicking the Submit button

TABLE L-3: Basic events and event handlers

event	event handler	description
click	onClick	the main mouse button is clicked and released
focus	onFocus	an element is selected
blur	onBlur	an element is no longer selected
mouseover	onMouseOver	the mouse pointer moves over an element
mouseout	onMouseOut	the mouse pointer moves off an element
keydown	onKeyDown	a key on the keyboard is pressed
keyup	onKeyUp	a key on the keyboard is released
submit	onSubmit	form contents are submitted
reset	onReset	form fields are reset to their defaults

Creating a Function

As your JavaScript code becomes more complex, it's useful to be able to group multiple lines of code and call them as a single unit. JavaScript enables you to do this by creating a **function**, which is a chunk of code with a name assigned to it. The first line of a function begins with the word "function," followed by its name and a pair of parentheses. The punctuation for a function parallels that of a CSS style rule: an opening curly brace ({) goes at the beginning; each line of code within the function ends with a semicolon; and the entire function ends with a closing curly brace (}). To simplify the HTML for the submit button, you move the code that writes the thank-you text to an external script file, convert it to a function, and reference the function in the submit button element.

STEPS

1. **Return to** contact.html **in your text editor**

2. **In the input element for the** Submit button, **select the entire value of the onclick attribute, excluding the beginning and ending single quotes, then use the** Cut **command in your text editor to move the selected code to the Clipboard**

TROUBLE
The file HTM L-2.js should be empty when you open it.

3. **Save your work, in your text editor open the file** HTM L-2.js **from the** Unit L/Unit/scripts **folder, type** //, **enter your first and last name and the text** HTML5 Unit L, **press** [Enter] **twice, then save the file in the same location with the name** form.js
   In JavaScript, any characters after // in a line are treated as a comment.

4. **Type** function writeTy() {, **then press** [Enter]

5. **Indent two spaces, then use the** Paste **command in your text editor to paste the contents of the Clipboard into the file**

6. **Click after the semicolon, press** [Enter], **indent two spaces, then type** }
   Figure L-6 shows the completed code for the function.

7. **Save your work, return to** contact.html, **then after the text** onclick= **in the** input **tag for the Submit button, between the two single quotes, type** writeTy()
   Figure L-7 shows the new value for the event handler.

8. **Scroll to the top of** contact.html, **insert a blank line beneath the existing script element, then indent and type** <script src="scripts/form.js"></script>
   This script element references the form.js file, making the function you just created available in the contact. html Web page. Figure L-7 shows the new script element inserted in the code.

9. **Save your work, reload** contact.html **in your browser, then click the** Submit button
   Once again, the thank-you message is displayed beneath the *Contact Us* heading in response to the button click, this time using the function you created in the external form.js file.

FIGURE L-6: **Function added to external file**

```
function writeTy() {
    document.getElementById("message").innerHTML=("Thanks for contacting Lakeland Reeds Bed & Breakfast!");
    }
```

FIGURE L-7: **Web page code referencing external script file and function**

```
          <script src="scripts/modernizr-1.6.min.js"></script>
          <script src="scripts/form.js"></script>
          <!--[if lt IE 7]>
```

script element references
external file containing
writeTy function

```
          </fieldset>
          <fieldset id="submitbutton">
            <input type="button" id="submit" value="Submit" onclick='writeTy()' />
          </fieldset>
        </form>
```

onclick value references
writeTy function

HTML5 and CSS3

Implementing jQuery and other libraries

Web developers using JavaScript for more complex applications often find that they need to use the same sets of code repeatedly in different contexts to create the same effects. In response to this common situation, developers group reusable code in collections known as **libraries**. By attaching a single script file containing a library to a Web page document, developers instantly have access to all the functions stored in the file. Many freely distributable libraries are available online; currently, jQuery is one of the most popular libraries in use. Web sites that use jQuery or other libraries are still creating scripts with JavaScript, but are using libraries to simplify the process of writing complex scripts.

Storing and Comparing Data in Variables

JavaScript supports the use of symbols known as **operators** to compare or change the values of multiple objects or properties. You've already used the **assignment operator** (=), which enables you to assign a value. In addition, JavaScript lets you analyze and manipulate values in more complex ways. You can compare values of different elements using **comparison operators**, which let you determine whether two values are the same, and **logical operators**, which allow you to logically connect multiple values in a comparison (see Table L-4). It can be useful to store the results of JavaScript commands, whether the value of a Web page element retrieved with the innerHTML method or the result of an equation using operators; you can do this in JavaScript by creating a **variable**. A common application of stored values and calculations is a **conditional statement**, in which the result of a comparison in values determines which one of multiple options is executed by a script.  Before the Web page contents are submitted, Phillip would like to be sure that each user enters a name. You create a function using a conditional statement to perform this validation.

STEPS

1. **Return to form.js in your text editor, click after the closing } at the end of the writeTy() function, then press [Enter] twice**

2. **Type function checkReqFields() {, then press [Enter]**

3. **Indent two spaces, then type**

   ```
   var name=document.getElementById('nameinput').value;
   ```
   This code creates a variable called *name*. It then navigates the DOM tree to look up the value of the *nameinput* element and assigns this as the value of the *name* variable.

4. **Press [Enter], indent two spaces, then type the code shown in Figure L-8**

   The first line starts a conditional statement that checks if the value of the *name* variable is null, meaning that it has no value, or if the *name* variable is empty. If so, the script uses the alert method to display a pop-up box containing the text *First name must be filled out*, and then halts execution of the function with the statement *return false*.

5. **Press [Enter], indent two spaces, type writeTy();, then press [Enter]**

   If the function hasn't been halted earlier, the writeTy() function, which writes the thank-you message to the Web page, is triggered.

6. **Indent two spaces, type document.forms('contact').reset();, press [Enter], indent two spaces, then type }**

   This statement calls a method that clears all user input. Figure L-8 shows the completed code.

7. **Save your work, return to contact.html in your text editor, then in the input element for the submit button, change the value of the onclick attribute to 'checkReqFields() ', as shown in Figure L-8**

8. **Save your work, reload contact.html, then click the Submit button**

   As Figure L-9 shows, a pop-up box opens, displaying the alert message.

9. **Click OK, type your name in the Name box, then click the Submit button**

   Because the Name field is not empty, the thank-you message is displayed and the form is cleared.

FIGURE L-8: **New function and event handler reference**

Code to add
in Step 4

```
function checkReqFields() {
  var name=document.getElementById('nameinput').value;
  if (name==null || name=="") {
    alert("First name must be filled out");
    return false;
  }
  writeTy();
  document.forms('contact').reset();
}
```

```
<fieldset id="submitbutton">
  <input type="button" id="submit" value="Submit" onclick='checkReqFields()' />
</fieldset>
```

New function triggered
by click event

FIGURE L-9: **Alert box triggered by form validation function**

Appearance of
text box and
title text
varies among
browsers

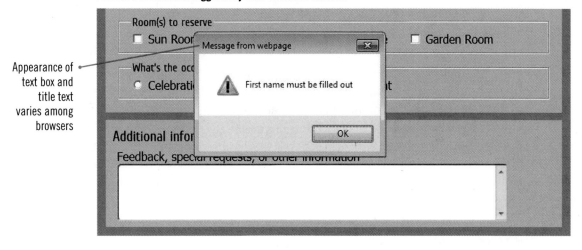

TABLE L-4: **Operators**

operator type	operator	description	example
comparison	==	is equal to	if (a == b)
	!=	is not equal to	if (a != b)
logical	&&	and	if (a == b && c == d)
	||	or	if (a == b || a == c)
	!	not	if (a == b || !(a == c))
assignment	=	assigns a value	var name = "Faduma"

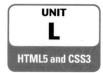

Generating Web Page Content Dynamically

You can combine different JavaScript tools to create powerful features for your Web pages. By accessing, storing, manipulating, and writing values that are based on user input, you can reconfigure parts of a Web page based on user activities or input. These are the basic tools used to create scripts that create interactive menus, where submenus are displayed in response to the mouse pointer hovering over a menu option. Likewise, these tools can enable you to customize a Web page in response to user input, preferences, or actions. You personalize the thank-you message by incorporating the name entered by the user. Also, to enhance the accessibility of your Web page, you move the message from the text of the Web page to an alert box.

STEPS

1. **Return to form.js in your text editor**

2. **Near the bottom of the checkReqFields function, click between the parentheses in the code writeTy();, then type name**
   When a function is called, the value of any variable between the parentheses is passed to the function.

3. **In the first line of the writeTy function at the top of the document, click between the parentheses, then type person**
   In the code that creates a function, any value between the parentheses specifies the name assigned within the function to any value passed to the function when it's called. In this case, the checkReqFields function is passing the value of its *name* variable, and the writeTy function will work with this value using the name *person*.

4. **In the second line of the writeTy function, move the insertion point just to the left of the exclamation mark, type a comma, insert a space, type "+person+", then type another space**
   Figure L-10 shows the completed code. When assigning a value, any literal text, such as the text you inserted earlier, is added within quotes in order to indicate that the characters are to be rendered literally. Any variable values, however, must be added outside of the quotes. The + signs, known in this context as **concatenation operators**, serve to unite the literal and variable values into a single string to be assigned to the specified Web page element.

5. **Save your work, reload contact.html in your browser, type your name in the Name box, then click the Submit button**
   As Figure L-11 shows, the name you entered in the Name box is incorporated into the thank-you message.

6. **Return to form.js in your text editor, then in the second line of the writeTy function, delete the text document.getElementById("message").innerHTML= and type alert**
   You removed the code that identifies the *message* element in the Web page and specifies that you want to replace its text content. In its place, you added the *alert* method, which instead creates an alert box that displays the text that follows. Figure L-12 shows the revised code.

7. **Save your work, reload contact.html in your browser, type your name in the Name box, then click the Submit button**
   The same confirmation message is displayed in an alert box.

8. **Click OK to close the alert box**

FIGURE L-10: **Code to create text customized based on user input**

```
function writeTy(person) {
  document.getElementById("message").innerHTML=("Thanks for contacting Lakeland Reeds Bed & Breakfast, "+person+" !");
  }

function checkReqFields() {
  var name=document.getElementById('nameinput').value;
  if (name==null || name=="") {
    alert("First name must be filled out");
    return false;
    }
  writeTy(name);
  document.forms('contact').reset();
  }
```

Name of variable whose
value will be passed to
this function

Name assigned to variable
value passed to the function

Value of person variable added to
personalize thank you message

FIGURE L-11: **Customized thank-you message**

Unholy Vault Designs/Shutterstock.com

Name entered by user added
to end of thank-you message

FIGURE L-12: **Code to display thank-you message in an alert box**

alert method
replaces
innerHTML

```
function writeTy(person) {
  alert("Thanks for contacting Lakeland Reeds Bed & Breakfast, "+person+" !");
  }

function checkReqFields() {
  var name=document.getElementById('nameinput').value;
  if (name==null || name=="") {
    alert("First name must be filled out");
    return false;
    }
  writeTy(name);
  document.forms('contact').reset();
  }
```

Including quotes in generated text

JavaScript enables you to dynamically generate text and page elements by specifying text and HTML code within pairs of single or double quotes. However, what do you do when you want generated text to include a single or double quote? If you type a quote as part of a text string, JavaScript will parse it as the beginning or end of a pair, rather than as a character that you want to use literally. To change the way JavaScript deals with a quote, or with any character that has special meaning to JavaScript, however, you simply precede the character with a backslash (\ ). Thus, to display the text *Everyone here says, "Hi!"* in an alert box, for example, you'd use the code `alert('Everyone here says, \"Hi!\"');`.

Scripting Fallback Options with Modernizr

In a previous unit, you incorporated the modernizr.js file into a Web page and used its property support testing to provide alternative styles for older browsers. Some newer CSS and HTML features can't be duplicated with styles, though. You can provide fallback options for some of them with JavaScript code, however. Older browsers that don't support the placeholder attribute for the input element don't display the hints you've specified to users. You add a basic script to your Web site that uses the results of the Modernizr test for placeholder support to add the placeholder text as default content for the corresponding input elements so it shows up in the browser.

STEPS

1. **Return to form.js in your text editor, click at the end of the last line of code, then press [Enter] twice**

2. **Type function addPlaceholders() {, then press [Enter]**

3. **Indent two spaces, then type if (!Modernizr.input.placeholder) {**

   The *if* statement marks the start of a conditional statement that tests whether the value within parentheses is true. *Modernizr.input.placeholder* is an element added to the DOM by the Modernizr script only if the current browser supports the placeholder attribute for the input element. The exclamation mark means "not". Thus, this conditional statement tests whether the Modernizr.input.placeholder element is missing; if this is the case, the code that follows will be executed.

4. **Press [Enter], indent four spaces, then type the two lines of code shown in Figure L-13**

   The first line of code sets the value of the *nameinput* element—the Name box—to "First and last name". This means that this code will appear in the box as if the user entered it. The second line of code performs the same action for the *emailinput* element, setting the value to "address@example.com".

5. **Press [Enter], indent four spaces, type }, press [Enter], indent two spaces, type }, then press [Enter] twice**

6. **Type window.onload=function() {, press [Enter], indent two spaces, type addPlaceholders();, press [Enter], indent two spaces, then type }**

   This code is automatically executed when the script is processed by a browser, and automatically runs the addPlaceholders function you created above. Figure L-13 shows the final code.

7. **Save your work, then if you have access to a browser that doesn't support the placeholder attribute, open contact.html in that browser**

   As Figure L-14 shows, the text you specified for the Name and Email boxes is displayed, providing user prompts in browsers that don't support the placeholder attribute.

QUICK TIP
Because users would need to delete this text before entering their own, more advanced scripts clear the placeholder content when users click a field.

FIGURE L-13: New code to generate placeholder text for older browsers

```
function addPlaceholders() {
   if (!Modernizr.input.placeholder) {
      document.getElementById('nameinput').value="First and last name";
      document.getElementById('emailinput').value="address@example.com";
   }
}

window.onload=function() {
   addPlaceholders();
}
```

Code to add
in Step 4

Code to run addPlaceholders
function automatically when
the Web page opens

FIGURE L-14: Script-generated placeholder text in an older browser

Unholy Vault Designs/Shutterstock.com

Placeholder text added as default
contents of Name and Email boxes

Scripting the canvas element

Among the many new elements introduced by HTML5 is the canvas element, which functions like an area of blank canvas on a Web page onto which you can place a combination of text, images, color, gradient fills, and other visual effects. However, while canvas itself is an HTML element, you add content to a canvas instance using JavaScript. Canvas has its own set of JavaScript properties and methods; for instance, the fillStyle and strokeStyle properties set the color, pattern, or other style of an area or a line, respectively, while the fillRect, strokeRect, and clearRect methods draw filled or outlined rectangles or clear the pixels from a rectangular area, respectively. While additional libraries are required to support canvas in older versions of Internet Explorer, the element opens the door to vast possibilities in visual design for Web pages.

Integrating an Existing Script

Because JavaScript has been in use on the Web for quite a while, other developers have already written code to accomplish most common tasks. Many developers maintain Web sites where they make their code available for download and reuse, and where they explain how the code works. Thus, it's often possible to download an existing script for a task you're trying to accomplish and then customize the script as necessary for your purposes.  Phillip would like the Web page to apply some of the same features to the fallback placeholder text that modern browsers apply to HTML5 placeholder text. In particular, he thinks it's important that placeholder text is cleared automatically when a user clicks the Name or Email box. He has provided you a JavaScript file containing a generic script to accomplish this task. You integrate the new script into the Contact Us page.

STEPS

1. **Open html-3.txt in your text editor**

2. **Press [Ctrl][A] or use the appropriate command in your text editor to select all the contents of the file, copy the selection to the Clipboard, then close the file**

3. **Return to form.js in your text editor**

4. **Add a blank line before the text function addPlaceholders();, type /*, add a blank line after the last line of the addPlaceholders function, then type */**

   You create a multi-line comment in JavaScript the same way you do in CSS: by typing /* at the start and */ at the end. Because the new code you're inserting duplicates the functionality of the addPlaceholders function you created, you'll mark the existing code as a comment to preserve it but prevent it from being executed.

5. **Press [Enter] twice, then paste the contents of the Clipboard into your document**

   The inserted code contains properties, methods, and operators you haven't worked with before. However, since the code comes from a trusted source and you know what it does, you can integrate it into your Web site and use its functionality. Figure L-15 shows the completed form.js file.

6. **Save your work, then if you have access to a browser that doesn't support the placeholder attribute, open contact.html in that browser**

   The values of the placeholder attributes for the Name and Email boxes are inserted as contents in the corresponding boxes, mirroring the fallback script you created in the last lesson.

7. **Click in the Name box, type your name, then click the Email box**

   As Figure L-16 shows, the contents of each field are removed after you click the field. In addition, when you enter text in a field and then leave the field, the text you entered is not replaced by the placeholder text.

8. **Validate the code for contact.html, then make changes if necessary to fix any errors**

9. **If you have space on a Web server, publish your Web site, open contact.html in your browser from the published location, then test the form**

FIGURE L-15: addPlaceholders function replaced

```
/*
function addPlaceholders() {
  if (!Modernizr.input.placeholder) {
    document.getElementById('nameinput').value="First and last name";
    document.getElementById('emailinput').value="address@example.com";
  }
}
*/

function addPlaceholders() {
  if (!Modernizr.input.placeholder) {
    var inputs = document.getElementsByTagName("input");
    for (var i=0;i<inputs.length;i++) {
      if (inputs[i].getAttribute("type") == "text" || "email") {
        if (inputs[i].getAttribute("placeholder") && inputs[i].getAttribute("placeholder").length > 0) {
          inputs[i].value = inputs[i].getAttribute("placeholder");
          inputs[i].onclick = function() {
            if (this.value == this.getAttribute("placeholder")) {
              this.value = "";
            }
            return false;
          }
          inputs[i].onblur = function() {
            if (this.value.length < 1) {
              this.value = this.getAttribute("placeholder");
            }
          }
        }
      }
    }
  }
}
window.onload=function() {
  addPlaceholders();
}
```

New addPlaceholders
function inserted

Comment tags added to prevent
old addPlaceholders function
from being executed

FIGURE L-16: New placeholder text features created by inserted script

Unholy Vault Designs/Shutterstock.com

Placeholder text is removed from
each text box when you click it

Debugging a script

As with HTML and CSS code, sometimes the JavaScript code that you write doesn't produce the results you expect. In such cases, however, a few simple troubleshooting steps can help you identify and fix most errors. First, check capitalization. Because JavaScript is case-sensitive, references to properties, methods, objects, or variables with inconsistent capitalization can produce unpredictable results. Next, check punctuation. While semicolons aren't strictly required at the ends of statements, single and double quotes, parentheses, brackets ([ ]), and braces ({ }) must occur in matched sets.

Missing closing quotes or braces are common coding errors. As you write more complex scripts, it can be worthwhile to obtain and use software designed for coding, which can automatically add punctuation in matched sets and alert you if a closing mark is missing. Finally, some browsers enable you to view error messages generated when scripts don't work. These error messages often include line numbers in scripts, indicating the point of failure, and providing you a place to start your research into possible errors when an error isn't obvious.

Practice

Concepts Review

For current SAM information, including versions and content details, visit SAM Central (http://www.cengage.com/samcentral). If you have a SAM user profile, you may have access to hands-on instruction, practice, and assessment of the skills covered in this unit. Since various versions of SAM are supported throughout the life of this text, check with your instructor for the correct instructions and URL/Web site for accessing assignments.

Refer to Figure L-17.

FIGURE L-17

```
a  function writeTy() {
      document.getElementById("message").innerHTML=("Thanks for contacting Lakeland Reeds Bed & Breakfast!");
   }

   function checkReqFields() {
b     var name=document.getElementById('nameinput').value;
      if (name==null || name=="") {
         alert("First name must be filled out");
         return false;
c     }
      writeTy();
d     document.forms('contact').reset();
   }
```

d   e   f

```
         <fieldset id="submitbutton">
            <input type="button" id="submit" value="Submit" onclick='checkReqFields()' />
         </fieldset>
```

g

1. Which item is an event handler?
2. Which item creates a variable?
3. Which item is an object?
4. Which item creates a function?
5. Which item is an operator?
6. Which item specifies a method?
7. Which item specifies a property?

Match each term with the statement that best describes it.

8. DOM
9. DOM tree
10. node
11. dot notation
12. event
13. conditional statement

a. the syntax used in JavaScript for identifying a specific item within the DOM by listing the appropriate objects, properties, and methods in order, separated by periods

b. a way of envisioning the a hierarchical arrangement of the content of an HTML document as a tree-like structure

c. code in which the result of a comparison in values determines which one of multiple options is executed by a script

d. a user action that can be used to start the execution of JavaScript code

e. a standardized system for referring to the parts of a Web page

f. the representation of a single part of an HTML document such as an element, attribute, or text content in the DOM

Select the best answer from the list of choices.

14. In the DOM, each HTML element is considered _____.
- **a.** a property
- **b.** an object
- **c.** a method
- **d.** a value

15. Each piece of information associated with a DOM node is known as _____.
- **a.** a property
- **b.** an object
- **c.** a method
- **d.** a value

16. Actions that can be performed on DOM nodes are known as _____.
- **a.** properties
- **b.** statements
- **c.** methods
- **d.** values

17. You can indicate code to execute in response to a specific event on a specific element by using _____.
- **a.** a value
- **b.** a statement
- **c.** a method
- **d.** an event handler

18. Which operator type allows you to compare values of different elements?
- **a.** the assignment operator
- **b.** a logical operator
- **c.** a comparison operator
- **d.** the concatenation operator

19. Which operator type allows you to logically connect multiple values in a comparison?
- **a.** the assignment operator
- **b.** a logical operator
- **c.** a comparison operator
- **d.** the concatenation operator

20. You can store the results of JavaScript commands by creating _____.
- **a.** a variable
- **b.** an event handler
- **c.** a DOM
- **d.** a method

Skills Review

1. Add content using a script.
- **a.** In your text editor, open HTM L-4.html from the Unit L/Review folder where you store your Data Files, insert a blank line before the closing body tag, insert a paragraph element containing your first and last name and the text **HTML5 Unit L, Skills Review**, then save it as **order.html**.
- **b.** Beneath the h2 element near the top of the body section, insert a blank div element with the id **message**.
- **c.** Below the code you just entered, insert a **script** element. Between the opening and closing tags, add JavaScript code referencing the **innerHTML** of the element with the id **message**, then setting the value to the text string **This pizza has been added to your cart**.
- **d.** Save your work, then open **order.html** in your browser. Right click the text generated by the script you entered in the previous step, click **Inspect Element**, then examine the code for the paragraph with the id **message**.

2. Trigger a script using an event handler.
- **a.** Return to order.html in your text editor.
- **b.** Delete the script element you entered in Step 1c, including its content.
- **c.** Near the end of the form element, locate the input element with the id **submit**.
- **d.** Just before the closing /> in the input tag, enter an event handler that responds to a user clicking the mouse button, then set the value of this attribute to a statement that sets the value of the innerHTML for the element with the id **message** to the text string **This pizza has been added to your cart**. Ensure that the entire statement is surrounded by quotes, and that a different kind of quote is used where needed within the statement. Also ensure that the input tag contains a space before the closing /.
- **e.** Save your work, then reload order.html in your browser.
- **f.** Scroll to the bottom of the page, click the Add to Cart button, if necessary scroll to the top of the page, then verify that the confirmation statement is displayed in the same location below the heading.

Skills Review (continued)

3. Create a function.

a. Return to order.html in your text editor.

b. In the input element for the Add to Cart button, select the entire statement you used for the value of the event handler attribute, excluding the beginning and ending quotes, then use the Cut command in your text editor to move the selected code to the Clipboard.

c. Save your work, then in your text editor, open the file HTM L-5.js from the scripts folder, add a comment containing your first and last name and the text **HTML5 Unit L, Skills Review**, then save the file in the same location with the name **order.js**.

d. In the order.js file, create a function named **writeConf**, pasting the contents of the Clipboard as the contents of the function.

e. Save your work, return to order.html, then after the event handler attribute in the input tag for the Add to Cart button, add a reference to the function so that it runs when a user clicks the button.

f. In the document head section, add a script element that loads the **order.js** file.

g. Save your work, reload order.html in your browser, then click the Add to Cart button to verify that the confirmation statement appears as it has previously.

4. Store and compare data in variables.

a. Return to order.js in your text editor, then create a new function called **validateReq**. Add a statement that creates a variable named **name** and assigns it the value of the element with the id **nameinput**. Repeat to add variables with the names **address**, **city**, and **phone** and to assign them the values of the elements with the ids **addrinput**, **cityinput**, and **phoneinput**, respectively.

b. Create a conditional statement that tests if the values of any of the four variables you created in Step a are either null or empty strings. If any of these conditions is met, the statement should generate an alert box containing the text **Name**, **Street Address**, **City**, and **Phone** must be filled out, and then return **false**.

c. After the conditional statement, add code to trigger the writeConf function.

d. Add a statement that resets the form with the name order, then if necessary add the appropriate character to close the function.

e. Save your work, return to order.html in your text editor, then in the input element for the Add to Cart button, change the value of the event handler attribute so it runs the function you just created.

f. Save your work, reload order.html, click the Add to Cart button, then verify that an alert box opens prompting you to complete all required fields.

g. Click OK, complete the Name, Address, City, and Phone boxes, click the Add to Cart button, then verify that the confirmation statement appears as it has previously.

5. Generate Web page content dynamically.

a. Return to order.js in your text editor.

b. Near the bottom of the validateReq function, locate the statement that triggers the writeConf function, then edit the code so it passes the **city** variable to the function.

c. Edit the writeConf function at the top of the document so it assigns the name **place** to any variable passed to it.

d. Edit the second line of the writeConf function to add the words **for delivery** to at the end of the confirmation message, followed by a space, the value of the **place** variable, and a period.

e. Save your work, reload order.html in your browser, complete the Name, Address, City, and Phone boxes, click the Add to Cart button, then verify that the city you entered in the City box is displayed as part of the confirmation message.

f. Return to order.js in your text editor, then in the writeConf function, edit the statement that displays the confirmation message to show it in an alert box instead of as part of the Web page.

Skills Review (continued)

g. Save your work, reload contact.html in your browser, complete the Name, Address, City, and Phone boxes, click the Add to Cart button, then verify that the confirmation message is displayed in an alert box as shown in Figure L-18.

h. Click OK.

6. Script fallback options with Modernizr.

a. Return to order.js in your text editor, then add a new function called **insertPlaceholders**.

b. Add code to the function to create a conditional that tests if the **Modernizr.input.placeholder** element is missing from the DOM. If the element is missing, the function should assign the value **First and last name** to the element with the id **nameinput**, **Building number and street** to the element with the id **addrinput**, and **address@example.com** to the element with the id **emailinput**.

FIGURE L-18

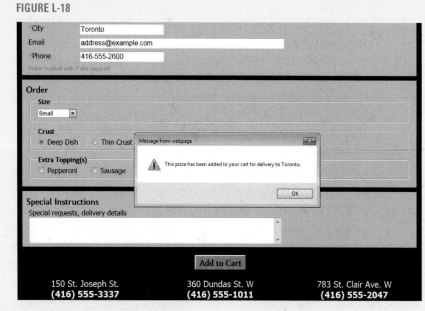

c. If necessary, add the appropriate characters to close the conditional statement and the function.

d. After the function you just created, add code that executes when the Web page loads that triggers the **insertPlaceholders** function to run.

e. Save your work, then if you have access to a browser that doesn't support the placeholder attribute, open order.html in that browser and verify that the placeholder text is displayed.

7. Integrate an existing script.

a. Open html-6.js in your text editor. Select all the contents of the file, copy the selection to the Clipboard, then close the file.

b. In order.js, mark the existing insertPlaceholders function as a comment, then paste the contents of the Clipboard below it.

c. Save your work, then if you have access to a browser that doesn't support the placeholder attribute, open order.html in that browser.

d. Click in the Name box, type your name, click the Email box, then verify that that placeholder text behaves like placeholder text in browsers that support the placeholder attribute.

e. Validate the code for order.html, then make changes if necessary to fix any errors.

f. If you have space on a Web server, publish your Web site, open **order.html** in your browser from the published location, then test the form.

Independent Challenge 1

Sarah Nguyen, the manager of the Spotted Wren Garden Center, would like you to add a couple features to the form on the company's Web site. She'd like the specified placeholder text to be displayed no matter what browser a user opens the site on. In addition, she'd like boilerplate text automatically inserted in the Additional Information section if users select certain options in the Project Area section. You'll incorporate scripts into the Web site to add the requested features.

Independent Challenge 1 (continued)

a. Open HTM L-7.html from the Unit L/IC1 folder in your text editor. Insert a blank line before the closing body tag, insert a paragraph element containing your first and last name and the text **HTML5 Unit L, Independent Challenge 1**, then save it as **quote.html**. Open **HTM L-8.js** from the scripts folder, add a JavaScript comment at the top of the file containing the same information as in the HTML file, then save the file in the same location as **quote.js**.

b. Open quote.html in a Web browser that doesn't recognize the placeholder attribute and verify that no placeholder text is displayed in the form.

c. In quote.html, add an element that loads the contents of the **quote.js** file. Save your work, then reload quote.html in your browser and verify that the placeholder text is displayed.

d. In quote.js, create a function named **multipleBP**. Within the function, create a variable named **mult** and set its value to the element with the id **multiple**. Next create a conditional statement that tests if the **checked** attribute exists for the element referenced by the variable **mult**. If the condition is true, the conditional statement should add the text **List of all project areas:** as the value of the element with the id **notes**.

e. Create a function named **otherBP**. Within the function, create a variable named **other** and set its value to the element with the id **other**. Next create a conditional statement that tests if the **checked** attribute exists for the element referenced by the variable **other**. If the condition is true, the conditional statement should add the text **Description of project area:** as the value of the element with the id **notes**.

f. In quote.html, add an event handler to the input element with the id **multiple** that triggers the **multipleBP** function when a user clicks the element. Add an event handler to the input element with the id **other** that triggers the **otherBP** function when a user clicks the element.

g. Reload quote.html in your Web browser. Click the Multiple Areas option button and verify that the text List of all project areas: is displayed in the textarea element near the bottom of the form, as shown in Figure L-19. Click the Other option button and verify that the text Description of project area: is displayed in the textarea element.

h. Validate quote.html. If you have space on a Web server, publish your Web site, then open great.html in your browser from the published location.

i. Close your browser, then close your text editor.

FIGURE L-19

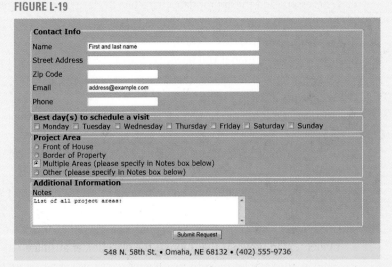

548 N. 58th St. • Omaha, NE 68132 • (402) 555-9736

Independent Challenge 2

As you continue to develop the Web site for the Murfreesboro Recreational Soccer League, you decide to compact the contents of the Schedules page and make the content interactive using scripts. You'll implement an accordion effect, which enables users to display and hide sections of the Web page by clicking links.

a. Open HTM L-9.html from the Unit L/IC2 folder in your text editor. Insert a blank line before the closing body tag, insert a paragraph element containing your first and last name and the text **HTML5 Unit L, Independent Challenge 2**, then save the file as **schedule.html**. Repeat to add a CSS comment with the same information to HTM L-10.css and save it as **mrsl.css**. Open **HTM L-11.js** from the scripts folder, add a JavaScript comment at the top of the file containing the same information as in the HTML file, then save the file in the same location as **accordion.js**.

b. In accordion.js, create a variable named **openAccordion** no value (*Hint*: to set an empty value, use a pair of single or double quote marks with nothing in between.).

c. Create a function named **runAccordion**, assigning the variable name **index** to a value passed to the function. Within the function, do the following:

- Create a variable named **nID** with a value equal to the text **Accordion** plus the value of the variable **index** plus the text **Content**. The variable value should include no spaces.
- Create a conditional statement that tests whether the value of **openAccordion** is equal to the value of **nID**; if so, set the value of **nID** to an **empty value**.
- Create a variable named **opening** and set its value to the following code:
  (nID == '') ? null : document.getElementById(nID);
  (*Note*: This is code for a conditional statement that assigns a value to the variable based on the result of the condition in parentheses. The conditional statement includes two single quotes, not a double quote.)
- Create a variable named **closing** and use the following conditional statement as its value:
  (openAccordion == '') ? null : document.getElementById(openAccordion);
- Create a standard conditional statement that checks if the value of the **opening** variable is **not null**; if this statement is correct, the statement should set **opening.style.height** to **300px** and set **opening.style.display** to **block**.
- Create a standard conditional statement that checks if the value of the **closing** variable is **not null**; if this statement is correct, the statement should set **closing.style.height** to **0px** and set **closing.style.display** to **none**.
- Add a statement that sets the value of **openAccordion** to the value of **nID**.

d. In schedule.html, add code that loads the contents of the **accordion.js** file. Delete the paragraph element with the id pagenav, along with its contents.

e. Add code to all four h3 elements on the page specifying a **class** of **AccordionTitle**. Mark the text within each h3 element with an **a** element, setting the href value to **#**. Add an **event handler** to each a element that's triggered when the element is **clicked**; set the value of the first to **runAccordion(1)**, the second to **runAccordion(2)**, and so on. Also add the **onselectstart** event handler attribute to each a element with a value of **return false**.

f. For the div elements immediately following the h3 elements, specify a **class** value of **AccordionContent**. Add an **id** value to the first div element of **Accordion1Content**, an **id** value for the second of **Accordion2Content**, and so on. Change the text of the instructions below the h2 heading to **Click a competitive division team name below for the schedule of game dates and times.**

g. In mrsl.css, add a style rule for the **AccordionTitle** class that sets **position** to **relative**, **text indent** to **20px**, **background** to **#f2ebde**, **padding** to **0.5em 0**, and **margin** to **0.2em 0**. Add a style rule for the **AccordionContent** class that sets **position** to **relative**, **height** to **0px**, and **display** to **none**.

h. Open **schedule.html** in a browser, then click one of the **team name links**. The corresponding schedule should be displayed, as shown in Figure L-20. If necessary, use the debugging steps described in this unit to track down and repair any errors in your code until the Web page behaves as described.

i. Create a print version of your style sheet that sets **display** to **block** for the AccordionContent class.

FIGURE L-20

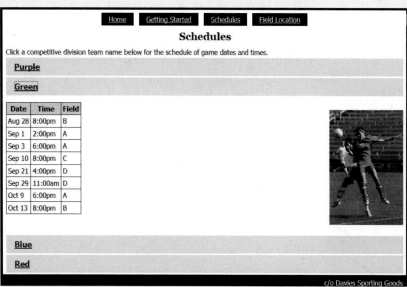

9507848116/Shutterstock.com

Independent Challenge 2 (continued)

Advanced Challenge Exercise

- On a piece of paper or in a blank document in a Word processor, add your first and last name and the text **HTML5, Independent Challenge 2 – ACE**, then answer the following questions:
- What was the effect of changing the opening.style.height property?
- What was the effect of changing the opening.style.display property?
- How did the numbers that the event handlers passed along to the function affect the results generated by the function?
- What was the effect of setting display to block in the print version of the style sheet?

j. Validate schedule.html and your style sheets. (*Note*: The onselectstart event handler is Internet Explorer-specific and necessary for the widest possible browser compatibility for this code. Although each occurrence of this event handler will trigger a validator error, you can safely ignore all four of these error messages.) If you have space on a Web server, publish your Web site, then open schedule.html in your browser from the published location and test the accordion effect.

k. Close your browser, then close your text editor.

Independent Challenge 3

Diego Merckx, the manager of the Hotel Natoma, would to make the list of local attractions on the hotel's Web site interactive. When a user's mouse pointer is over a link to an attraction, he'd like the Web page to display an image of the attraction. He also wants to make sure this dynamic behavior works for users navigating the page with a keyboard rather than a mouse. You create and incorporate a JavaScript function into the Web site to add this functionality.

a. Open **HTM L-12.html** from the Unit L/IC3 folder in your text editor. Insert a blank line before the closing body tag, then insert a paragraph element containing your first and last name and the text **HTML5 Unit L, Independent Challenge 3**, then save the file as **nearby.html**. Open **HTM L-13.js** from the scripts folder, add a JavaScript comment at the top of the file containing the same information as in the HTML file, then save the file in the same location as **gallery.js**.

b. In gallery.js, create a function named **switchPix**, and assign the names file and desc to values passed to the function.

c. Add a statement to the function that sets the value of the HTML code for the element with the id **pix** to the text **<img src="images/**, followed by the value of the **file** attribute, followed by **.jpg" width="480" height="270" alt=**", followed by the value of the **desc** attribute, followed by " **/>**. (*Hint*: Remember to use the \ character before any quote character that should appear in the HTML code.)

d. In nearby.html, add code that loads the contents of the **gallery.js** file. Add an event handler to the **a** element for the text Asian Art Museum that responds to the mouse pointer moving over the element to call the switchPix function, passing the values **'asian','Asian Art Museum'**. Add a second event handler that responds to the link being selected to call the same function with the same values. (*Note*: The second event handler enables users navigating the Web page with a keyboard to trigger the images to change.)

e. Repeat Step d to add event handlers to the remaining three links to call the **switchPix** function, passing the following values:

link text	values
City Hall	'cityhall','San Francisco City Hall'
Heart of the City Farmer's Market	'market','Civic Center Farmers Market'
Cable Car turnaround	'cablecar','Cable Car turnaround'

Independent Challenge 3 (continued)

f. Open nearby.html in your browser, then move your mouse pointer over the list of links and verify that the image on the right side of the page changes depending on which link you're pointing to, as shown in Figure L-21. If necessary, research the keyboard shortcut for your browser that allows moving through the links in a Web page, then use the shortcut to navigate through the links and verify that the same image switch takes place based on the link selected.

FIGURE L-21

Photo/Sasha Vodnik

Advanced Challenge Exercise

- On a piece of paper or in a blank document in a Word processor, answer the following questions:
- How does the statement you created within the switchPix function change the HTML of the Web page?
- What roles are played in the function by the two values passed when calling the function with the event handlers in the Web page?
- Why would the first event handler you added not by itself result in an accessible Web page for people navigating the Web page with a keyboard?

g. Validate nearby.html. If you have space on a Web server, publish your Web site, then open nearby.html in your browser from the published location and verify that the gallery effect works.

h. Close your browser, then close your text editor.

Real Life Independent Challenge

This assignment builds on the personal Web site you have worked on in previous units. You'll add a feature created with JavaScript to your site.

a. Copy your Web site files to the Unit L/RLIC folder on the drive and folder where you store your Data Files.

b. Identify a feature you'd like to add to your Web site that requires a script. Common possibilities include fallback options for CSS3 features or features you've seen on other Web sites.

c. Create the code for your new feature in an external JavaScript file. If you're using code obtained from another source, ensure that you have permission to use the code. Save the file with an appropriate name.

d. Add a link to the external script file within the Web page or pages that will use the feature.

e. Add one or more event handlers if necessary to run your script. Ensure that the code can be triggered using either a keyboard or a mouse.

f. Open your Web page in a browser and test your feature. If the code doesn't work as you expect, review the debugging tips in this unit and make any necessary changes to the code. If you're using code from another source, ensure that you understand what the code is doing, and verify that any code in your HTML document used to trigger the script is providing the script with input it expects.

g. Validate your HTML document(s) and make any edits necessary to address any issues.

h. If you have space on a Web server, publish your Web site, then open one of the pages containing your scripted feature in your browser from the published location.

i. Close your browser, then close your text editor.

Visual Workshop

In your text editor, open the file HTM L-14.html from the Unit L/VW directory on the drive and folder where you store your Data Files, add a paragraph before the closing body tag that contains your first and last name and the text **HTML5 Unit L, Visual Workshop**, then save the file as **signup.html**. Open HTM L-15.js from the scripts folder, add a JavaScript comment at the top of the file containing the same information as in the HTML file, then save the file in the same location as form.js. Add a link within signup.html to form.js, then verify that placeholder text is displayed in a browser that doesn't support the placeholder attribute. In form.js, add a function that displays a confirmation message when the form validates correctly, and incorporate the first name of the user in the message, as shown in Figure L-22. Add another function that verifies that the First Name and Last Name boxes aren't empty, and displays an appropriate alert box if one or both of them are. The function should also clear the form after the confirmation message is displayed. Add an onclick event handler to the submit button that triggers the validation function. Save your work, then validate your HTML code. If you have space on a Web server, publish your files, then open the Web page in your browser from the published location. Close your browser and text editor.

FIGURE L-22

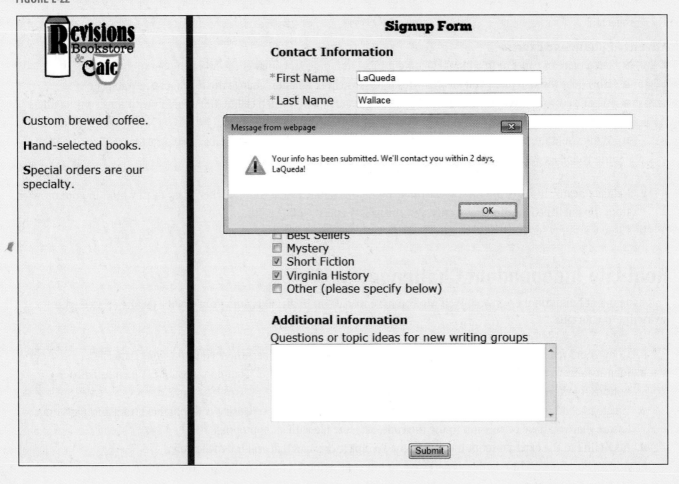

Programming Web Pages with JavaScript

Integrating Social Media Tools

For businesses and organizations, effective use of the Web involves more than the creation and maintenance of a Web page or Web site. Providing users, customers, and community members with methods for sharing online content and integrating their own comments is at the heart of **social media**. Used correctly, social media can enhance your Web presence by enabling people who frequent your business or support your cause to spread the word to their own networks of friends and colleagues. Phillip Blaine would like your help understanding social media and integrating social media tools into the Lakeland Reeds B&B Web site. In this unit, you'll incorporate some of these tools into the company's Web site.

OBJECTIVES

Understand social networking

Integrate a Facebook account with a Web site

Integrate a Twitter account feed

Add a Twitter hash tag feed

Participate in social bookmarking

Create a blog

Embed a YouTube video

Link to an RSS feed

Understanding Social Media

Aside from a feedback or order form, a basic Web site generally allows little opportunity for user feedback. One of the key characteristics of social media is to facilitate two-way communication. Users can create content that other users see on your Web site; in addition, you can incorporate tools that aid users with telling other people about your business or organization. As you prepare to show Phillip different options for social media tools on the Lakeland Reeds Web site, you review some of the main types of social media.

While many types of social media Web sites exist, a few are especially popular:

- **Social networking sites**

    A **social networking site** is a Web site such as Facebook or LinkedIn that enables people to share information about common interests, news, and events with friends, colleagues, and any other people they choose. While membership in a social networking site is generally open to most anyone, users generally restrict access to their information and news only to other users whom they actually know or with whom they share a common interest: members of their **social networks**. Figure M-1 illustrates a few of the common features of social networking sites. Many social networking sites offer prewritten HTML or JavaScript code to make it easy for users to show some social networking information in their own Web pages. The items created by this code, known as widgets, can add a variety of content, such as displaying your recent updates on the social networking site or providing a formatted link for Web site users to connect with you or your business on the social networking site.

- **Blogs and microblogs**

    A **blog** is a special-purpose Web site that enables one person or a small number of people to post news or updates, usually focused on a narrow topic. While some individuals use the format as a public journal of significant events in their lives, blogs have found many other uses; for instance, journalists may maintain blogs providing additional information about topics in articles they write, or a bookstore may share new arrivals or dates of readings as soon as they're scheduled. Twitter, a site that shares aspects with both social networking sites and blogs, is sometimes referred to as a **microblog**, as it limits user updates to 140 characters.

- **Video hosts**

    Video hosting sites such as YouTube enable most anyone with a computer or mobile phone and an Internet connection to create video and distribute it widely. In conjunction with social networking sites and blogs, video hosts provide a visually powerful way to connect with an audience. Video in social media sites can range from shots of a baby's first steps to professionally produced documentaries and music videos; the user posting a video can choose to allow viewers to post comments and rate the video. While video hosting sites are the starting point for making videos widely available, social networks can be particularly effective for spreading the word about them.

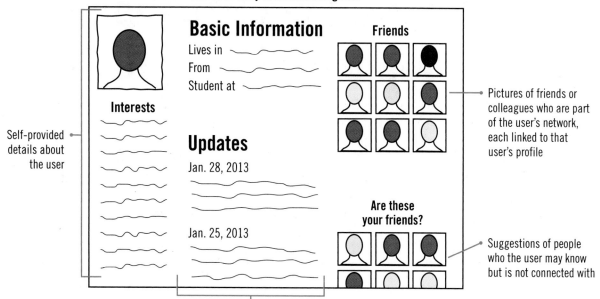

Self-provided details about the user

News, questions, links, or other thoughts posted by the user, which can generally be viewed only by people who are part of the user's network

Pictures of friends or colleagues who are part of the user's network, each linked to that user's profile

Suggestions of people who the user may know but is not connected with

Integrating a Facebook Account with a Web Site

When potential customers view the Web page for a business or organization, it's a great opportunity to let them know about your social media presence and to invite them to become part of your network on one or more social networking sites. While each social networking site enables you to integrate it into your own Web site in unique ways, using one of the provided widgets is generally a quick, effective way to create a bridge to your social network. Many of Phillip's past guests at the B&B are Facebook users, so Phillip would like to see what a Facebook widget would look like on the Lakeland Reeds home page. Because he hasn't yet created a Facebook page for the B&B, you'll add a widget using sample data from another organization.

STEPS

1. **In your text editor, open HTM M-1.html from the Unit M/Unit folder where you store your Data Files, insert a blank line before the closing body tag, insert a paragraph element containing your first and last name and the text HTML5 Unit M, then save it as index.html**

QUICK TIP

If entering this URL doesn't open the Social Plugins page, use a search engine to search on the terms *Facebook social plugins* and follow the top search result from facebook.com.

2. **In your browser, open http://developers.facebook.com/docs/plugins, explore the page that opens, then click the Like Box link**

   A Facebook page that lists Social Plugins opens.

3. **In the Facebook Page URL box, type facebook.com/cengagebrain, uncheck the Show stream box, if necessary check the Show faces box, click the Get Code button, select the contents of the iframe box, copy it to the Clipboard, then click Okay**

4. **In index.html, delete the contents of the figure element, then paste the copied code within the opening and closing figure tags**

   Figure M-2 shows the inserted code with space and tabs added to make it easier to read. Like many widgets, this code uses the HTML iframe element. This element creates an **inline frame**, which acts as a self-contained Web page within the HTML document where it's located. Inline frames are commonly used to present content from other Web sites while preserving formatting and presentation that may look quite different from the surrounding Web page. The src attribute for the iframe element specifies the URI of the content to be displayed.

TROUBLE

If your widget doesn't include the organization name or faces shown in Figure M-3, wait an additional minute to allow it to load, then if necessary, press and hold [Shift] while you click your browser's **Refresh** or **Reload button**.

5. **Save your work, then open index.html in your browser**

   As Figure M-3 shows, the widget is displayed at the right side of the page beneath the nav bar. If Lakeland Reeds B&B had a Facebook account, this widget could be configured to show a list of Facebook users who are already connected with Lakeland Reeds B&B on Facebook. If no faces are displayed, change the height values within the src and style attributes in the iframe element to 350, then save your work and reload the page in your browser.

6. **Repeat Steps 2 and 3, unchecking the Show Faces box and ensuring that the Show stream box is checked**

TROUBLE

If the widget contents don't change, press and hold [Shift] while you click your browser's **Refresh** or **Reload button**.

7. **In index.html, delete the contents of the figure element, then paste the copied code within the opening and closing figure tags**

8. **Save your work, then reload index.html in your browser**

   As Figure M-4 shows, this widget shows a **feed**, which is the most recent set of updates created by the organization, from the specified Facebook page. Because social networking sites lend themselves to user updates much more frequently than a static Web page, a widget showing a feed can be a useful Web site addition.

Code for
Facebook
widget pasted
within figure
element

```
<article id="content">
    <figure class="clearright">
        <iframe src="http://www.facebook.com/plugins/likebox.php?href=facebook.com
%2Fcengagebrain&amp;width=292&amp;colorscheme=light&amp;show_faces=true&amp;stream=false&amp;header=true&amp;height=427"
scrolling="no" frameborder="0" style="border:none; overflow:hidden; width:292px; height:427px;"
allowTransparency="true"></iframe>
    </figure>
    <p id="maintext"><span class="callout">Lakeland Reeds</span> is a rustic bed and breakfast on Twin Lakes near rural
Marble, Minnesota. Convenient to US 2 and 169, the fresh air and quiet make for an ideal weekend escape from the rush of city
life.</p>
</article>
```

FIGURE M-3: **Web page displaying Facebook widget**

A selection of Facebook
users who like the linked
sample page

Widget content
displayed within
iframe element

Unholy Vault Designs/Shutterstock.com
Photos/Sasha Vodnik

FIGURE M-4: **Facebook user feed displayed in Web page**

Recent updates from
the linked profile

Different parameters
provided in widget
code to display
different information

Unholy Vault Designs/Shutterstock.com

Choosing an appropriate social networking site for your audience

While a few social networking sites are widely known across much of the world, many such sites exist. Because different sites are prevalent in different countries or regions or with different groups of people, it's important to consider which site might best suit your needs when planning to integrate social media into your Web site. If the geographic focus of your business or organization is limited, you should familiarize yourself with the most popular sites for the relevant area. It's also crucial to consider which sites the people you want to connect with are likely to be using; for instance, at the time of this writing, in North America, Facebook was a popular general-purpose site, while LinkedIn users focused mainly on business and professional networking. Keep in mind as well that while you may already use one or more social networking sites personally, it may make sense to choose an entirely different site for networking for your business or organization.

Integrating a Twitter Account Feed

In addition to using Twitter to communicate about specials or provide coupon codes, some businesses are using the site to listen to what people are saying about them in order to quickly respond to customers' concerns. Like Facebook, Twitter makes code available for widgets that you can embed in your own Web pages. For organizations that use Twitter instead of or in addition to Facebook or another social network, it may make sense to add your Twitter feed to your Web site. You can add a Twitter feed to your Web site to display your own most recent Twitter postings—known as **tweets**—as well as to show tweets from your favorite Twitter users, a limited selection of tweets that you have marked as favorites, or tweets with **specific keywords**. Phillip would like to see how a Twitter feed on the Lakeland Reeds Web site would differ from a Facebook feed. As you did with Facebook, you'll add a demonstration widget using sample data from another organization.

STEPS

1. **Return to** index.html **in your text editor**

2. **In your browser, open** twitter.com/about/resources/widgets, **then click the** My Website link

3. **Read the descriptions of the listed widgets, then click the** Profile Widget link

4. **In the** Username box, **type** cengagebrain, **then press** [Enter]
   The Web page displays a preview of the widget.

5. **Click the** Preferences, Appearance, **and** Dimensions links **and explore the available settings**

6. **Click** Finish & Grab Code, **select all the code in the code box, then copy it to the Clipboard**

7. **In** index.html, **delete the contents of the figure element, then paste the copied code within the opening and closing figure tags**
   Rather than using an inline frame, this code references a JavaScript file on a remote Web site, adding code to customize and run the remote script to create the feed. Figure M-5 shows the pasted code.

8. **Save your work, then open** index.html **in your browser**
   As Figure M-6 shows, the widget shares some similarities with the Facebook widget but has a unique appearance.

JavaScript code for Twitter widget

```
<article id="content">
  <figure class="clearright">
    <script src="http://widgets.twimg.com/j/2/widget.js"></script>
    <script>
      new TWTR.Widget({
        version: 2,
        type: 'profile',
        rpp: 4,
        interval: 6000,
        width: 250,
        height: 300,
        theme: {
          shell: {
            background: '#333333',
            color: '#ffffff'
          },
          tweets: {
            background: '#000000',
            color: '#ffffff',
            links: '#4aed05'
          }
        },
        features: {
          scrollbar: false,
          loop: false,
          live: false,
          hashtags: true,
          timestamp: true,
          avatars: false,
          behavior: 'all'
        }
      }).render().setuser('cengagebrain').start();
    </script>
  </figure>
  <p id="maintext"><span class="callout">Lakeland Reeds</span> is a rustic bed and breakfast on Twin Lakes near rural
Marble, Minnesota. Convenient to US 2 and 169, the fresh air and quiet make for an ideal weekend escape from the rush of city
life.</p>
</article>
```

FIGURE M-6: Web page incorporating Twitter user feed

Unholy Vault Designs/Shutterstock.com

Obtaining code for widgets

Many large social networking sites make widget code available on their Web sites. While different sites may label this code differently, you can usually find what you need by searching on the term *widget* along with the name of the Web site in a search engine. The sites

generally provide interfaces that let you configure the options you'd like to show and hide for a given widget, and then generate the code for you based on your selections.

Adding a Twitter Hash Tag Feed

Even though many social media sites share common features, sometimes it can be advantageous to use a particular site because of an available feature. While many social media sites enable users to post short updates, Twitter was among the first to popularize the inclusion of searchable codes known as **hash tags** that allow users to find postings on a given topic. A hash tag begins with the hash or pound symbol (#), giving the tag its name. While you can add a widget to a Web site to display your personal or organizational Twitter feed, other widgets enable you to incorporate posts from all Twitter users on a certain topic. If you encourage your customers or clients to incorporate a specific hash tag into their postings about your business or organization, you can easily display the most recent comments about your business right on your Web site.  Phillip would like you to show him an example of a feed based on a hash tag, so you add the relevant widget to the Lakeland Reeds B&B home page.

STEPS

1. **Return to** index.html **in your text editor**

2. **In your browser, open** twitter.com/about/resources/widgets, **then click the** My Website link

3. **Read the descriptions of the listed widgets, then click the** Search Widget link

4. **In the** Search Query box **type** #minnesota, **in the** Title box **type** Lakeland Reeds Bed & Breakfast, **in the** Caption box **type** Minnesota Goings-on, **then click the** Test settings button
   The Web page displays a preview of the widget.

5. **Click the** Preferences, Appearance, **and** Dimensions links **and explore the available settings**

6. **Click** Finish & Grab Code, **select all the code in the code box, then copy it to the Clipboard**

7. **In** index.html, **delete the contents of the figure element, then paste the code you copied within the opening and closing figure tags**
   As Figure M-7 shows, the replacement code uses the same script from Twitter to search for and display recent updates based on the #minnesota hash tag.

8. **Save your work, then open** index.html **in your browser**
   Figure M-8 shows the #minnesota hash tag feed in the Twitter widget.

Script variables
changed to
search on
#minnesota
hash tag

```
<article id="content">
    <figure class="clearright">
        <script src="http://widgets.twimg.com/j/2/widget.js"></script>
        <script>
          new TWTR.Widget({
            version: 2,
            type: 'search',
            search: '#minnesota',
            interval: 6000,
            title: 'Lakeland Reeds Bed &amp; Breakfast',
            subject: 'Minnesota Goings-on',
            width: 250,
            height: 300,
            theme: {
              shell: {
                background: '#8ec1da',
                color: '#ffffff'
              },
              tweets: {
                background: '#ffffff',
                color: '#444444',
                links: '#1985b5'
              }
            },
            features: {
              scrollbar: false,
              loop: true,
              live: true,
              hashtags: true,
              timestamp: true,
              avatars: true,
              toptweets: true,
              behavior: 'default'
            }
          }).render().start();
        </script>
    </figure>
    <p id="maintext"><span class="callout">Lakeland Reeds</span> is a rustic bed and breakfast on Twin Lakes near rural
Marble, Minnesota. Convenient to US 2 and 169, the fresh air and quiet make for an ideal weekend escape from the rush of city
life.</p>
</article>
```

Custom values
for widget title
and subject

Head and
subhead
customized
in script

All entries
shown include
the #minnesota
hash tag

Unholy Vault Designs/Shutterstock.com

Participating in Social Bookmarking

Adding social media widgets to your Web site can provide users a window to your social media presence. You can more fully engage with current and potential customers, though, by inviting them to connect with you on social media sites. The process of making such connections is known as **social bookmarking**. In addition to widgets, popular social networking sites also provide code to insert in your Web pages to create a button that users can click to join your network on that site. Phillip is considering creating Facebook and Twitter accounts, and would like to see what the main Web page for Lakeland Reeds B&B would look like with social bookmarking buttons for these two sites. You add code to insert these buttons.

STEPS

1. **Return to index.html in your text editor**

2. **In your browser, open developers.facebook.com/docs/plugins, explore the page that opens, then click the Like Button link**

3. **In the URL to Like box, type facebook.com/cengagebrain, uncheck the Send Button box, change the Layout Style value to button_count, change the Width to 100, uncheck the Show faces box, click the Get Code button, select the contents of the iframe box, copy it to the Clipboard, then click Okay**

4. **In index.html, between the aside tags above the figure element, insert a blank line and indent, then paste the code you copied**

> **QUICK TIP**
> If you have a Twitter account, you can generate custom button code for your account at **twitter .com/about/ resources/buttons**.

5. **Open htmm-2.txt in your text editor, select all the contents and copy them to the Clipboard, then close the file**
   This file contains code that creates a button for following the sample account on Twitter.

6. **In index.html, paste the contents of the Clipboard beneath the code you added in Step 4**
   As Figure M-9 shows, the Web page now contains a tag to create a Facebook button and a set of tags to create a Twitter button.

> **TROUBLE**
> If you're prompted to log into Facebook and you want to complete the remaining steps, enter your specific account information and log in.

7. **Save your work, then open index.html in your browser**
   As Figure M-10 shows, the Web page incorporates a button linked to a profile on Facebook and another button that opens a user page on Twitter.

8. **If you have a personal Facebook account, click the Like button**
   The button changes to the text "You like this," and a box is displayed where you can enter a comment.

> **QUICK TIP**
> If you don't want to permanently like the linked account, click the Unlike link on the right side of the Facebook information.

9. **If you completed Step 8, move the mouse pointer without entering a comment**
   The comment box disappears.

iframe element
containing code
for Facebook
button

Linked img element
for Twitter button

FIGURE M-10: **Social bookmarking icons added to Web page**

Unholy Vault Designs/Shutterstock.com

Twitter
bookmarking
icon

Facebook
bookmarking
icon

HTML5 and CSS3

Creating a Blog

Creating and maintaining a blog is another way to incorporate social media into your online presence. Most blogs are built and edited using a dedicated blogging platform such as WordPress. Blogging platforms simplify content creation and enable users to use a template in order to apply a uniform style to parts of the blog. ▄▀▄▀ Phillip is interested in learning more about blogging platforms. You explore some of the features by setting up a free blog in WordPress.

STEPS

1. **In your browser, go to wordpress.com**

   WordPress offers free hosting for basic blogs.

QUICK TIP

If you prefer not to sign up for a WordPress account, just read through the remaining steps without completing them.

2. **Click the Sign up now button**

   A signup form opens, similar to the one shown in Figure M-11. Because Web sites are regularly updated, the page in your browser may look somewhat different from the one shown in the figure.

3. **Fill in all the form fields, then click the Sign up button**

   Be sure to note the address of your blog, which is a name you provide followed by *.wordpress.com*.

4. **Check the email account you provided in the signup form for an activation email from WordPress, then follow the instructions in the email to activate your account**

5. **In your browser's address bar, type the blog address you created in Step 3 followed by /wp-admin/, then press [Enter]**

   This address opens your blog dashboard, as shown in Figure M-12, which shows you information about your blog and allows you to add content. You may need to log in using the information you provided in Step 3.

6. **Scroll down if necessary to the QuickPress section of the dashboard, in the Title box enter Fall Special, then in the Content box enter Now through August 31, we're offering 15% off September or October bookings of two nights or more.**

7. **In the Tags box enter fall, sale**

   Figure M-12 shows the new content in the QuickPress form.

8. **Click Publish**

TROUBLE

If you don't see the My Blog button, type the blog address you created in Step 3 into your browser's address bar, then press **[Enter]**.

9. **Click the My Blog button at the top of the window to open your blog**

   As Figure M-13 shows, the entry you created is displayed using the default template, along with the tags and other links.

Integrating a blog into your Web site

While the content of some pages on your Web site won't change very often, using a blog as one of your site's pages can be useful for easily including content that changes rapidly. You can include a link to a blog just as you would to a Facebook or Twitter account; however, it's sometimes more effective to incorporate the blog into your site's nav bar and make it appear as a seamless part of your Web site. Using HTML and CSS, you generally create a template that fits the specifications of the blogging platform you've chosen. You then add the blog address as a nav bar link on all your site's pages, including the blog. When you're done, the blog appears to users as just another Web page in the site, but it offers a user interface that non-technical members of your organization can use to add or edit content on the site.

FIGURE M-11: WordPress.com signup page

Your entry here makes your blog's URI unique

FIGURE M-12: WordPress Dashboard

Click My Blog to view your blog

Use the QuickPress section to add new content

New content entered in Step 6

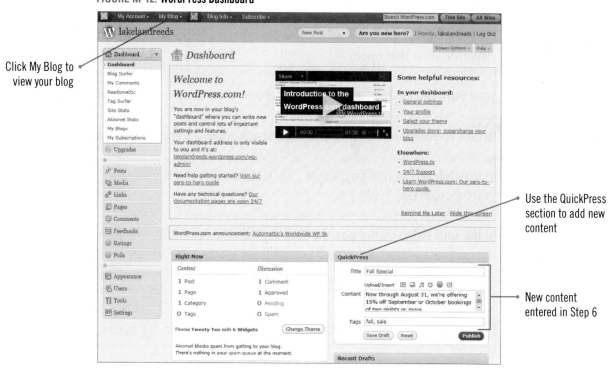

FIGURE M-13: New content in blog

Title

Content

Tags

Links for navigating blog contents

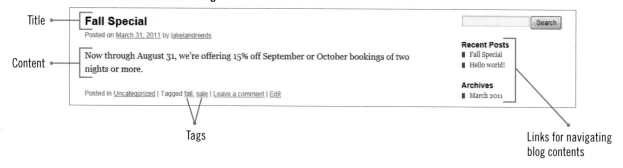

Embedding a YouTube Video

Video hosts such as YouTube can be important tools in social networks. While such sites don't generally incorporate rich interfaces for creating profiles and relationships between users, they excel at making user-generated video available to anyone with Internet access. They're also important complements to social network sites; a Facebook or Twitter user, for example, can incorporate a link to a YouTube video into a status update, and members of that user's network can, in turn, share the original link with members of their networks. Thus, when a business or organization makes a video available on a video hosting site as part of a promotion or campaign, the business or organization can share the link through social networks and invite interested customers or clients to spread the news. ▓▓▓▓ Phillip doesn't have the HTML expertise to add code for video elements into the Lakeland Reeds B&B Web site. However, he's intrigued by the notion of being able to incorporate YouTube videos into a blog. You create a new blog entry containing a sample YouTube video so he can see how the process works.

STEPS

1. **In your browser, go to** youtube.com

2. **In the Search box, type** bed breakfast minnesota, **then press** [Enter]
   A list of search results is displayed, some of which should be related to bed and breakfasts in Minnesota.

QUICK TIP
If you don't want to watch the whole video, click the pause button at any point.

3. **Click the link for a video that seems to be about a bed and breakfast in Minnesota, then view the video that opens**

4. **Select the URI in your browser's address bar, then copy it to the Clipboard**

QUICK TIP
If the dashboard isn't available using your browser's Back button or open in another tab, enter the blog address in your browser's address bar, followed by /**wp-admin**/, then press [**Enter**].

5. **Return to your blog's dashboard, then scroll down if necessary to the QuickPress section**

6. **In the QuickPress Title box, enter** Check out another Minnesota B&B, **then click the** Add Video button 🎞️

7. **In the Add Video dialog box that opens, click the** From URL tab, **click the** URL box, **paste the contents of the Clipboard, then click the** Insert into Post button
   The Add Video dialog box closes. As Figure M-14 shows, the YouTube link is added to the Content box in the QuickPress section.

8. **Click the** Publish button, **then click the** My Blog button **in the upper-left corner of the browser window**
   As Figure M-15 shows, the new entry, containing a preview of the video, is displayed on your blog.

FIGURE M-14: Link to YouTube video added

Add Video button

Formatted link to YouTube video inserted in Content box

FIGURE M-15: Blog containing YouTube video

Title

YouTube video embedded in new blog entry

Video/Sasha Vodnik

Linking to an RSS Feed

Because an active blog is usually updated on a regular, sometimes frequent, basis, people interested in reading your content may not always happen to check your blog when new content is available. In addition, it can be quite a task for anyone interested in keeping up with several blogs to stay on top of the latest writing and links. One solution for users is to use a utility known as a **news aggregator**, also known as a **feed reader**, that lets you bookmark blogs and view the latest headlines and content in a single place. While some news aggregators are available as installable software, the most popular utilities, such as Google Reader, are Web-based. To make blog entries available to aggregators, you need to publish an RSS feed. **RSS**, short for **Rich Site Summary** or **Really Simple Syndication**, is a format for a document that contains feed information for a Web site. Blog platforms such as WordPress generate and update RSS documents automatically; you can copy the link location and add it to a shortcut on a Web page in order to provide users with a shortcut to subscribe to your blog. Because Phillip is interested in creating a blog for the Lakeland Reeds B&B Web site, you add an RSS link for your sample blog to the site's main page to show him what the page would look like with a range of social media options.

1. **In your browser, explore the list of links in the right column of your blog**

   As you can see in Figure M-15 in the previous lesson, the list includes links to both the Entries RSS, which makes blog content that you add available, and the Comments RSS, which syndicates comments that other people might make about your content.

2. **Right-click the Entries RSS link, then in the context menu that opens, click Copy link location, Copy Link, or Copy Shortcut**

   The link address for your blog's RSS document is copied to the Clipboard.

3. **Return to index.html in your text editor**

4. **Just before the closing </aside> tag, insert a blank line, then add opening and closing tags for a div element**

5. **Within the div element, enter opening and closing tags for an a element, then add an href attribute and paste the contents of the Clipboard as the value**

6. **Within the a element, add an img element with a src value of images/feedicon.png, width and height of 28, and an alt attribute with an empty value**

   Figure M-16 shows the completed code.

7. **Save your work, then reload index.html in your browser**

   Figure M-17 shows the orange icon added to the page. This icon is a widely recognized symbol for an RSS feed. Different browsers respond to RSS links in different ways, so clicking the icon might open a dialog box, an aggregator utility, or simply display the raw code for the feed.

8. **Validate the code for index.html, then make changes if necessary to fix any errors**

TROUBLE
You may receive validation errors stemming from widgets you inserted; it's safe to ignore warnings about deprecated attributes, because the layout of your page does not rely on them.

9. **If you have space on a Web server, publish your Web site, then open index.html in your browser from the published location**

```
        <aside class="social">
            <iframe src="http://www.facebook.com/plugins/like.php?href=facebook.com
%2Fcengagebrain&amp;layout=button_count&amp;show_faces=false&amp;width=450&amp;action=like&amp;font&amp;colorscheme=light&amp
;height=21" scrolling="no" frameborder="0" style="border:none; overflow:hidden; width:100px; height:21px;"
allowTransparency="true"></iframe>
            <p><a href="http://www.twitter.com/CengageBrain"><img src="http://twitter-badges.s3.amazonaws.com/twitter-c.png"
alt="Follow CengageBrain on Twitter"/></a></p>
            <div>
                <a href="http://lakelandreeds.wordpress.com/feed/">
                    <img src="images/feedicon.png" width="28" height="28" alt="" />
                </a>
            </div>
        </aside>
```

Code for RSS icon linked to syndicated blog content

FIGURE M-17: **RSS link for blog added to Web page**

RSS icon

Unholy Vault Designs/Shutterstock.com

HTML5 and CSS3

Adding links for specific news readers

While adding a generic RSS link to your Web site makes your feed address available to users of many different aggregators, users who aren't very familiar with RSS may find it difficult to use. To make a feed easier for users to add, some Web developers include separate RSS links formatted for each of the most popular aggregators among their target audiences. Providing such a selection enables a user to click the link for the relevant aggregator and have the feed added automatically. Because many aggregators are available and can vary widely in popularity based on location, you should research the aggregators in widest use among your target market before pursuing this approach. In addition, your link selection should include a generic RSS link to support users of aggregators other than those for which you provide specialized links.

Practice

For current SAM information, including versions and content details, visit SAM Central (http://www.cengage.com/samcentral). If you have a SAM user profile, you may have access to hands-on instruction, practice, and assessment of the skills covered in this unit. Since various versions of SAM are supported throughout the life of this text, check with your instructor for the correct instructions and URL/Web site for accessing assignments.

Concepts Review

Refer to Figure M-18.

FIGURE M-18

Unholy Vault Designs/Shutterstock.com

1. Which item is a hash tag?
2. Which item is used for social bookmarking?
3. Which item is a feed?
4. Which item is a widget?

Match each term with the statement that best describes it.

5. social networking site
6. blog
7. inline frame
8. feed
9. hash tag
10. RSS

a. a searchable term beginning with #

b. a Web page element that acts as a self-contained Web page within the HTML document where it's located

c. a special-purpose Web site that enables one person or a small number of people to post news or updates, usually focused on a narrow topic

d. a format for a document that contains feed information for a Web site

e. a Web site such as Facebook or LinkedIn that enables people to share information about common interests, news, and events with friends, colleagues, and any other people they choose

f. the most recent set of updates created by a user on a social networking site

Select the best answer from the list of choices.

11. Because Twitter limits user updates to 140 characters, it is sometimes referred to as _____.
    - **a.** a hash tag
    - **b.** an RSS feed
    - **c.** a microblog
    - **d.** a social bookmark

12. Which element would you use to present content from another Web site while preserving formatting and presentation that may look quite different from the surrounding Web page?
    - **a.** iframe
    - **b.** figure
    - **c.** html
    - **d.** aside

13. Because social networking sites lend themselves to user updates much more frequently than a static Web page, a widget showing a _____ can be a useful Web site addition.
    - **a.** blog
    - **b.** hash tag
    - **c.** microblog
    - **d.** feed

14. You can more fully engage with current and potential customers by inviting them to connect with you on social media sites, a process known as _____.
    - **a.** social bookmarking
    - **b.** hash tagging
    - **c.** blogging
    - **d.** creating a feed

15. Why are video hosts such as YouTube considered important tools in social networks?
    - **a.** They're a form of microblog.
    - **b.** They generally incorporate rich interfaces for creating profiles and relationships between users.
    - **c.** Their ability to make video widely available is an important complement to social networking sites.
    - **d.** They also serve as feed readers.

16. A utility that lets you bookmark blogs and view the latest headlines and content in a single place is known as _____.
    - **a.** a social network
    - **b.** an inline frame
    - **c.** a hash tag
    - **d.** a news aggregator

Skills Review

1. **Integrate a Facebook account with a Web site.**
   - **a.** In your text editor, open HTM M-3.html from the Unit M/Review folder where you store your Data Files, insert a blank line before the closing body tag, insert a paragraph element containing your first and last name and the text **HTML5 Unit M, Skills Review**, then save it as **index.html**.
   - **b.** In your browser, open **http://developers.facebook.com/docs/plugins**.
   - **c.** Generate code for a Like box using **facebook.com/cengagebrain** as the Facebook Page URL, unchecking the Show stream box, setting the width to 238, and ensuring that the Show faces box is checked, then copy the code to the Clipboard.
   - **d.** In index.html, paste the copied code within the aside element that's part of the *right* class.
   - **e.** Save your work, then open index.html in your browser.
   - **f.** Repeat Steps b–c, unchecking the Show stream box, setting the Color Scheme to **dark**, and ensuring that the Show faces box is checked.
   - **g.** In index.html, delete the contents of the aside element that's part of the *right* class, then paste the code you copied within the element.
   - **h.** Save your work, then reload **index.html** in your browser. If no faces are displayed, change the height values within the src and style attributes in the iframe element to 350, then save your work and reload the page in your browser.

2. **Integrate a Twitter account feed.**
   - **a.** Return to index.html in your text editor.
   - **b.** In your browser, open **twitter.com/about/resources/widgets**, then select My Website.
   - **c.** Generate code for a Profile Widget based on the username **cengagebrain**, then copy the code to the Clipboard.
   - **d.** In index.html, paste the copied code within the aside element that's part of the *left* class.
   - **e.** Save your work, then open index.html in your browser.

3. Add a Twitter hash tag feed.

   a. Return to index.html in your text editor

   b. In your browser, open **twitter.com/about/resources/widgets**, then select My Website.

   c. Generate code for a Search Widget based on the hash tag **#minnesota** with the title **Big J's Pizza** and the caption **Pizza News**, then copy it to the Clipboard.

   d. In index.html, delete the contents of the aside element that's part of the *left* class, then paste the copied code within the element.

   e. Save your work, then open index.html in your browser.

4. Participate in social bookmarking.

   a. Return to index.html in your text editor.

   b. In your browser, open **developers.facebook.com/docs/plugins**. Generate code for a Like button using the URL **facebook.com/cengagebrain**, unchecking the **Send Button box**, changing the Layout Style value to **button_count**, changing the Width to **100**, and unchecking the Show faces box, then copy the code to the Clipboard.

   c. In index.html, beneath the opening tag for the aside element that's part of the *right* class, insert a blank line, then paste the code you copied.

   d. Open htmm-4.txt in your text editor, select all the contents and copy them to the Clipboard, then close the file.

   e. In index.html, then paste the contents of the Clipboard beneath the code you added in Step c.

   f. Save your work, then open index.html in your browser.

   g. If you have a personal Facebook account, click the Like button.

   h. If you completed Step g, move the mouse pointer without entering a comment.

5. Create a blog.

   a. If you have the login information for the blog you created in the unit, skip to Step e.

   b. In your browser, go to **wordpress.com**, then click the Sign up now button.

   c. Fill in all the form fields, then click the Sign up button.

   d. Check the email account you provided in the signup form for an activation email from WordPress, then follow the instructions in the email to activate your account.

   e. In your browser's address bar, type the blog address you created in Step c or in the unit, followed by **/wp-admin/**, then press [Enter]. If necessary, provide your username and password to log in.

   f. Scroll down if necessary to the QuickPress section of the dashboard, in the Title box enter **Oktoberfest Special**, then in the Content box enter **Now through October 31, buy one pizza and get 10% off a second of equal or lesser value**.

   g. In the Tags box enter **October, special**.

   h. Click Publish.

   i. Click the My Blog button at the top of the window to open your blog.

6. Embed a YouTube video.

   a. In your browser, go to **youtube.com**.

   b. In the Search box, type **deep dish pizza**, then press [Enter].

   c. Click the link for a video that seems to be about deep dish pizza, then view the video that opens.

   d. Select the URI in your browser's address bar, then copy it to the Clipboard.

   e. Return to your blog dashboard, then scroll down if necessary to the QuickPress section.

   f. In the QuickPress Title box, enter **Secrets from a deep-dish master**, then click the Add Video button 🖳.

   g. In the Add Video dialog box that opens, click the From URL tab, click the URL box, paste the contents of the Clipboard, then click the Insert into Post button.

   h. Click the Publish button, then click the My Blog button in the upper-left corner of the browser window.

7. Link to an RSS feed.

   a. In your browser, explore the list of links in the right column of your blog.

   b. Right-click the Entries RSS link, then in the context menu that opens, click Copy link location or Copy shortcut.

   c. Return to index.html in your text editor.

d. Just before the second iframe element within the aside element that's part of the *right* class, insert a blank line, then add opening and closing tags for a div element.

e. Within the div element, enter opening and closing tags for an a element, then add an href attribute and paste the contents of the Clipboard as the value.

f. Within the a element, add an img element with a src value of **images/feedicon.png**, width and height of **28**, and an alt attribute with an empty value.

g. Save your work, then reload index.html in your browser. Your Web page should resemble the one shown in Figure M-19.

h. Validate the code for index.html, then make changes if necessary to fix any errors.

i. If you have space on a Web server, publish your Web site, then open **index.html** in your browser from the published location.

FIGURE M-19

Independent Challenge 1

Sarah Nguyen, the manager of the Spotted Wren Garden Center, would like to incorporate social media into the company's Web site. You'll incorporate a sample feed and social bookmarking elements into the site's home page.

a. Open HTM M-5.html from the Unit M/IC1 folder in your text editor. Insert a blank line before the closing body tag, insert a paragraph element containing your first and last name and the text **HTML5 Unit M, Independent Challenge 1**, then save it as **index.html**.

b. Replace the contents of the figure element with the code for a Twitter hash tag search widget. Generate code by going to **twitter.com/about/resources/widgets**, then selecting My Website. Use the hash tag **#garden**, the title **Spotted Wren Garden Center**, and the caption **Gardening News**. In the Appearance section, change the shell background color to **#33b83c**. In the Dimensions section, change the height to **150**. Save your work and preview the page.

c. Before the closing </ul> tag for the nav bar, insert the code for a Facebook button. Generate the code at **developers. facebook.com/docs/plugins** using the Like Button link. Use **facebook.com/cengagebrain** as the URL to Like and uncheck the Show faces box. After you insert the code, mark the iframe element as a list item.

d. After the code for the Facebook button, insert the Twitter button code found in htmm-6.txt. Mark the a element as a list item. Save your work and preview the page, which should resemble the one shown in Figure M-20.

e. Use a search engine to locate three other widgets available for Facebook, Twitter, or another social networking site. In a new document in your text editor, list the name of each widget you find, along with a description of what it does, a description of any customizations you can make to it, and a detailed description of how you'd incorporate it into the Spotted Wren Garden Center Web page.

f. Validate index.html. If you have space on a Web server, publish your Web site, then open index.html in your browser from the published location.

g. Close your browser, then close your text editor.

FIGURE M-20

Maxim Tupikov/Shutterstock.com

Photos/Sasha Vodnik

Independent Challenge 2

As you continue to develop the Web site for the Murfreesboro Recreational Soccer League, you add social media features to help participants stay informed about the league and to assist new member recruitment efforts. You'll add a social network feed, embed a YouTube video, and integrate a blog into the site.

a. Open HTM M-7.html from the Unit M/IC2 folder in your text editor. Insert a blank line before the closing body tag, insert a paragraph element containing your first and last name and the text **HTML5 Unit M, Independent Challenge 2**, then save the file as **index.html**.

b. Before the opening tag for the article element, insert an aside element belonging to the class *right*. Within the aside element, paste code for a Facebook Like box for the profile at **facebook.com/cengagebrain**, showing the stream but not faces. Save your work, then preview the page in your browser and compare it to Figure M-21.

FIGURE M-21

c. Navigate to the dashboard for the blog you created in the unit, or open wordpress.com in your browser, create a new blog, and open the dashboard. Create a new blog entry with the title **Friday 10/3 RAINED OUT** and the content **All games scheduled for Friday 10/3 are canceled, as recent rains have left the fields too wet to play on.** Save the new entry, then view your blog and verify that the new entry is displayed at the top.

d. Open **youtube.com** in your browser, then search on the term **soccer** to find videos related to the sport. Pick one video to view, then copy the URI from the address bar to the Clipboard. Return to the dashboard for your blog, then create a new entry that embeds the YouTube video as the content. Give the entry an appropriate title. Save the new entry, then return to your blog page and verify that the video is displayed as the first entry.

Advanced Challenge Exercise

- Return to the dashboard for your blog. In the menu on the left side of the window, click Appearance. From the submenu that opens, click Header.
- On the Web page that opens, click the Browse button in the Upload Image section, navigate to the location of your Data files, then open the Unit M/IC2/images folder. Click the mrslhead.gif file, click Open, then click Upload.
- When the upload is complete, reopen your blog to view the changes. The MRSL logo should be displayed at the top of the page in place of the default template graphic.
- Return to index.html in your text editor. Add a link to your blog at the right end of the nav bar, using the text **Blog** for the link. Save your work, reload index.html in your browser, then test the link to the blog to verify that it works.

e. Validate index.html. If you have space on a Web server, publish your Web site, then open index.html in your browser from the published location and test the accordion effect.

f. Close your browser, then close your text editor.

Independent Challenge 3

Diego Merckx, the manager of the Hotel Natoma, would like you to add social media elements to the Hotel Natoma Web site. You'll add social bookmarking elements to the main Web page as well as a sample feed to show Diego.

a. Open HTM M-8.html from the Unit M/IC3 folder in your text editor. Insert a blank line before the closing body tag, then insert a paragraph element containing your first and last name and the text **HTML5 Unit M, Independent Challenge 3**, then save the file as **index.html**.

Independent Challenge 3 (continued)

b. Just beneath the opening tag for the article element, add a figure element containing a Facebook Like box for the profile at **facebook.com/cengagebrain**, showing the stream but not faces. Save your work, then preview the page.

c. Just beneath the nav element, add an aside element with the class value **social**. Within the aside element, insert the code for a Facebook button. Generate the code at **developers.facebook.com/docs/ plugins** using the Like Button link. Use **facebook.com/cengagebrain** as the URL to Like. Uncheck the Send Button box, then change the Layout Style to button_count. Change the Width value to 150 and uncheck the Show faces box. Beneath the code you just added, paste the contents of the file htmm-9.txt, save your work, then preview the page in your browser. The browser should display both social bookmarking icons on the right side of the nav bar, as shown in Figure M-22.

FIGURE M-22

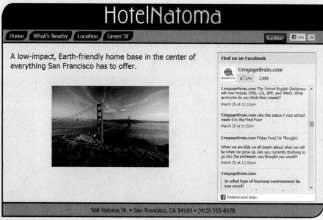

somchaij/Shutterstock.com

Advanced Challenge Exercise

- Use one of the URLs referenced in this unit or a search engine to locate other widgets for a social networking site. If applicable, look for widgets for a site on which you have an account. If you don't have an account on a social networking site, look for widgets for one of the sites used in this unit. (*Note*: Check the URIs to ensure that the widgets you're exploring are on the relevant social network's Web site, rather than a third-party Web site.)

- Explore at least three widgets offered by the Web site. Create widgets for your own account if you have one; otherwise, use the default settings.

- Change default options and examine how the changes affect the appearance of the widgets.

- Choose one widget to customize, generate the code for it, then copy and paste the code into the figure element in the index.html file.

- Save your work, then reload index.html in your browser. If necessary, edit the CSS for the Web site so the widget fits into the page layout.

d. Validate index.html. If you have space on a Web server, publish your Web site, then open index.html in your browser from the published location and verify that the social media features you added display correctly.

e. Close your browser, then close your text editor.

Real Life Independent Challenge

This assignment builds on the personal Web site you have worked on in previous units. You'll add social media features to your site.

a. Copy your Web site files to the Unit M/RLIC folder on the drive and folder where you store your Data Files.

b. Identify social media features you'd like to include in your Web site, including at least two of the following: account feed, hash tag feed, social bookmarking elements, blog, hosted video.

c. Identify where in your Web site you want to include each of the features you'll be incorporating.

d. For social media sites, use a site search or a search engine to locate the site's source of widgets. Identify one you want to use, customize it for your account, then copy and paste the code into your site.

e. If you're creating a blog, add a link to it in your site's navigation bar and an icon linking to its RSS feed.

f. Open your Web page in a browser and test the features you added.

g. Validate your HTML document(s) and make any edits necessary to address any issues.

h. If you have space on a Web server, publish your Web site, then open the pages containing your social media features in your browser from the published location.

i. Close your browser, then close your text editor.

Visual Workshop

Navigate to the dashboard for the blog you created in the unit, or open wordpress.com in your browser, create a new blog, then open the dashboard. Create the two blog entries shown in Figure M-23. Your video does not need to match the one shown in Figure M-23, but you should embed a video that's appropriate for the topic.

FIGURE M-23

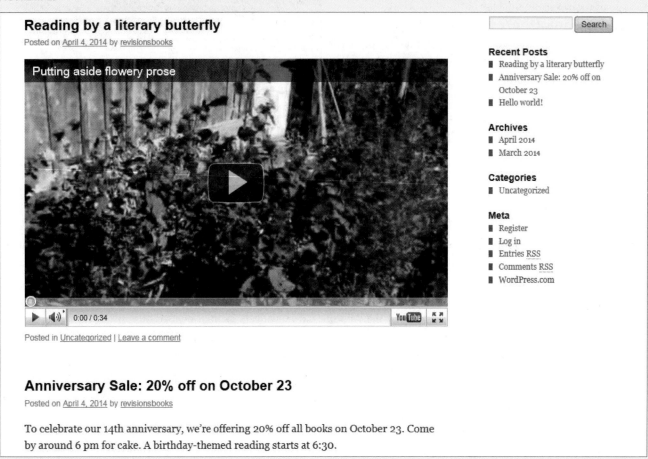

Video/Sasha Vodnik

Optimizing Your Web Site for Search Engines

While we commonly think of people looking for information as the most significant target audience of Web sites we create, Web documents have another important constituency: search engines. Just as you've practiced a number of techniques for making Web sites accessible and usable for people, you can implement techniques that make the content of your pages more understandable to the programs that index and add information to search engine databases. Since the people behind most Web sites want the information they're sharing to be seen by the largest possible audience, optimizing Web sites with search engines in mind is an important practice for creating sites that meet site owners' goals. Philip Blaine, the owner of Lakeland Reeds Bed & Breakfast, has asked if there's anything you can do to give his Web site's pages higher priority in Web searches. In this unit, you'll learn and apply several techniques that can make the pages more likely to be seen in response to relevant searches.

OBJECTIVES

Understand search engine optimization (SEO)

Write indexable content

Add a description with the meta element

Incorporate microdata

Create a Sitemap file

Create a robots.txt file

Preview and finalize your site

Submit your site

Understanding Search Engine Optimization (SEO)

The process of tailoring the structure and content of a Web page with search engines in mind is known as **search engine optimization (SEO)**. Common SEO techniques are often implemented to increase the likelihood that people searching on a relevant query will be presented with a link to your Web site. These practices often increase usability for human users and also provide a side benefit: in addition to their potential effects on search results, SEO techniques enable you to make more of the existing information in your Web pages available for inclusion in search results and for use with other applications that might interpret the data on your Web site. 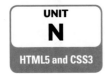 Before you begin implementing SEO practices on the Lakeland Reeds B&B Web site, you review what SEO can accomplish.

SEO brings two main benefits to your Web pages:

- **Increasing your site's priority in search results**

  Search engines balance many factors to decide the priority of search results; these factors are combined into a set of instructions known as an **algorithm**. SEO methods focus on clarifying the overall topic of a Web page as well as the subject of each section. By making the most accurate and specific information about a Web page available to search engines in a format that they can easily use, you increase the likelihood of potential users reaching your site through a search engine query. Figure N-1 compares the link to a Web page in sample search results before and after applying SEO techniques.

- **Giving Web applications useful semantic information about your site**

  Appropriate HTML5 elements incorporated into your Web pages describe the types of content that parts of the pages represent. You can further mark up Web page elements using **microdata**, which is covered in a working draft created by the W3C for adding more types of semantic data to Web page content. Search engines can use microdata to present and format relevant Web page content in search results. In addition, other Web applications can use microdata to group and present marked data in ways that make it easier to understand or to connect with data from other places. In Figure N-1, the lower sample search result illustrates the effects of microdata in the date information shown for specific events.

Creating a title element specific to the Web page avoids a generic heading in the search result

before SEO

Lakeland Reeds Bed & Breakfast
Explore seasonal experiences and special events you won't want to miss! Butterfly Season …
www.example.com

Adding a page description enables the search result to display a concise page summary, rather than simply a random passage from the Web page

after SEO

Events at Lakeland Reeds Bed & Breakfast
Enjoy a comfortable stay and local goings-on year round at Lakeland Reeds B&B.
Butterfly Season   Jun 1 –Jul 31
Accordion Festival   Sep 27 –Sep 29
www.example.com

Incorporating microdata into Web page elements allows search engines to summarize information

Recognizing the limits of SEO techniques

Fundamentally, SEO is about providing search engines with as clear an idea as possible of the focus of your Web pages and relying on the search engines themselves to decide how relevant each page is to a given query. Each search engine continuously adjusts its algorithm to keep it up to date and fine-tune its accuracy. Some people who work with Web technologies approach SEO as a way to provide search engines with a Web site description that's calculated to score a higher position in search results, but which doesn't necessarily accurately represent the site presented to human users. While these techniques may work for limited periods of time, search engine algorithms grow over time to accommodate these techiques and lessen their impact. In addition, some of the coding required for these techniques can negatively impact the experience of human users on your Web pages. Instead of trying to push the limits of SEO in pursuit of higher search rankings, your time will likely be better spent on creating great Web pages and complementing search engine results with other ways of spreading the word about them, such as through social media.

Writing Indexable Content

Making a Web site search engine friendly starts with one of the most basic components: your content. Making even small adjustments to the content you're presenting to users can improve the accuracy of search engines when they index your pages. Title elements, heading elements, image elements, and linked text play important roles in indexing, so you should pay special attention to them in your Web documents. In addition, elements such as the title element play unique roles in results for some search engines, as Figure N-2 illustrates. Table N-1 outlines guidelines for increasing the effectiveness of these elements for SEO. You begin optimizing the Lakeland Reeds B&B Web site by maximizing the effectiveness of the title, link, and img elements.

STEPS

1. **In your text editor, open** HTM N-1.html **from the** Unit N/Unit folder **where you store your Data Files, insert a blank line before the closing body tag, insert a paragraph element containing your first and last name and the text** HTML5 Unit N, **then save it as** rooms.html

2. **In the head section, edit the text of the title element to read** Room selection at Lakeland Reeds Bed & Breakfast

   A clear title helps search engine users recognize when your Web page contains the information they're seeking. Figure N-3 shows the edited title element.

3. **Near the bottom of the** section **element with the id** sunroom, **change the link text** Contact **to** Ask a question, **then change the link text** Book **to** Make a reservation

   Search engines can use link text to help them understand the content of the target page. Replacing these single words with phrases makes them more descriptive without making them cumbersome.

4. **Repeat Step 3 for the section elements with the ids** reedroom, treehouse, **and** gardenroom

5. **In the file manager for your operating system, navigate to the** Unit N/Unit/images folder **where you store your Data Files, then rename** sun.jpg **to** sun-room.jpg, reed.jpg **to** reed-room.jpg, tree.jpg **to** treehouse.jpg, **and** garden.jpg **to** garden-room.jpg

   Giving your images short, descriptive names adds to the information that search engines can collect about your Web pages.

6. **Return to** rooms.html **in your text editor, edit the img element in the** sunroom **section to change the src value to** images/sun-room.jpg, **then edit the src values for the remaining three room images to** images/reed-room.jpg, images/treehouse.jpg, **and** images/garden-room.jpg, **respectively**

   Figure N-3 shows the changed code for the sunroom section.

7. **Save your work, then open** rooms.html **in your browser**

   In your browser, the changed button text may be the only visible sign of your content optimization. However, all the changes you made will be available to search engines when indexing the page once it's published.

FIGURE N-2: Text of title element in sample search result

Search engines often use content of title element as heading of search result

> Events at Lakeland Reeds Bed & Breakfast
> Explore seasonal experiences and special events you won't want to miss! Butterfly Season …
> www.example.com

FIGURE N-3: Completed code for indexable text

Title content edited to clearly indicate the page topic

```
<!DOCTYPE html>
<html class="no-js">
  <head>
    <meta charset="utf-8" />
    <title>Room selection at Lakeland Reeds Bed &amp; Breakfast</title>
    <link rel="stylesheet" type="text/css" media="screen" href="lakeland.css" />
    <link rel="stylesheet" type="text/css" media="print" href="llprint.css" />
    <link rel="shortcut icon" href="favicon.ico" />
```

Image names edited to multi-word phrases

```
        <section id="sunroom" class="roominfo">
          <h3 id="sun">Sun Room</h3>
          <figure>
            <img src="images/sun-room.jpg" width="369" height="268" alt="the Sun Room has large windows and a desk, dresser,
and queen bed" title="" />
            <figcaption>The Sun Room</figcaption>
          </figure>
          <p class="desc">With windows on three sides, the sunlight in this second-floor room supports a large selection of
houseplants.</p>
          <p class="beds">1 queen bed.</p>
          <p class="roomlinks">
            <a class="questionlink" href="contact.html">Ask a question</a>
            <a class="reservelink" href="contact.html">Make a reservation</a>
          </p>
          <p class="toplink"><a href="#skipnav">Back to top</a></p>
        </section>
```

Link text changed from words to phrases for clarity

TABLE N-1: Guidelines for creating indexable content

element(s)	do	don't
title	create short, descriptive titles customize the title text to accurately describe the current page	use generic or long titles copy the same title text for every page in a Web site
h1–h6	add headings to major subdivisions of the page	mark text with a heading element merely for visual formatting
img	give image files short, descriptive names supply alternative text using the alt attribute	give image files long or nondescriptive names rely primarily on images for site navigation links
a	make links concise use text that describes the link target	add links to long sections of text link generic text such as "click here"

Adding a Description with the meta Element

Along with fine-tuning the content of your site to increase comprehension by search engines, you can add several types of code to your Web pages to provide information specifically for search engines. Among the easiest types to implement is a page summary using an attribute of the meta element. You've already used this element, which can specify a number of types of information about a Web page, to indicate the character encoding of your Web documents with the *charset* attribute. You can also add a summary of your page content by creating a new meta element with the *description* attribute. While search engines aren't likely to use your description text to decide which user queries match a page, they may display it as summary text in search results, similar to the example in Figure N-4. ▓▓▒▒▒ Phillip has provided you with a summary of each page in the Lakeland Reeds B&B Web site. You add the description for the Rooms page using a meta element.

1. **Return to rooms.html in your text editor**

2. **In the head section, insert a blank line beneath the meta tag with the charset attribute, then type** <meta />

QUICK TIP

While a few other values are allowed for the *name* attribute, *description* is the most useful for SEO.

3. **In the tag you just entered, add a space after the word meta, then type** name="description"

   Unlike the meta element for indicating the character encoding of a Web page, which uses the *charset* attribute, you specify a description using two attributes. The value of the name attribute indicates the type of data provided in the element. This attribute must always be paired with a content attribute, which contains the actual value.

4. **Add a space, then type** content="Lakeland Reeds Bed & Breakfast offers 4 comfortable rooms that accommodate from 2 to 5 people. All have private baths and views of Twin Lakes."

   Figure N-5 shows the completed meta tag for the page description.

5. **Save your work**

   Because browsers don't display the content of meta elements, there's no need to refresh your Web page.

FIGURE N-4: **Text of description meta element in sample search result**

Search engines often use the content of the description meta element as the summary for the search result, rather than guessing at relevant page text to show

> Events at Lakeland Reeds Bed & Breakfast
> Enjoy a comfortable stay and local goings-on year round at Lakeland Reeds B&B.
> www.example.com

FIGURE N-5: **Code for description meta element**

```
<!DOCTYPE html>
<html class="no-js">
  <head>
    <meta charset="utf-8" />
    <meta name="description" content="Lakeland Reeds Bed & Breakfast offers 4 comfortable rooms that accommodate from 2 to 5
people. All have private baths and views of Twin Lakes." />
    <title>Room selection at Lakeland Reeds Bed &amp; Breakfast</title>
    <link rel="stylesheet" type="text/css" media="screen" href="lakeland.css" />
    <link rel="stylesheet" type="text/css" media="print" href="llprint.css" />
    <link rel="shortcut icon" href="favicon.ico" />
    <script src="scripts/modernizr-1.6.min.js"></script>
    <!--[if lt IE 7]>
      <style type="text/css">
        #mainnav {left: 0px;}
        li img {left: -42px;}
      </style>
    <![endif]-->
  </head>
```

New meta element provides page description

Adding keywords with the meta element

In addition to *description*, another of the accepted values for the name attribute is *keywords*. In a keyword meta tag, the value of the content attribute is a list of words or terms that describe the page content, separated by commas. Generally, you want to list keywords that you'd expect to be search terms entered by someone who is using a search engine to look for your site. Thus, a keyword meta element for a bed and breakfast in Minnesota with lake access might look like

```
<meta name="keywords" content="bed and
breakfast, lake, boating, fishing,
minnesota" />
```

Because the algorithms used by many major search engines have become quite sophisticated, keyword meta elements have greatly decreased in importance in recent years. Some search engine providers have announced that they disregard keyword meta elements totally when indexing a page. In addition, for search engines that do still use these elements, it's possible to negatively impact the ranking of your page in search results by entering keywords that a search engine doesn't see as closely related to your actual page content; for instance, while developers might enter terms such as `hotel`, `motel`, and the names of neighboring states to direct searchers for these terms to a site for a Minnesota bed and breakfast, these terms are not clearly related to the page content. For these reasons, it's best to research whether the most popular search engines used by your target audience make use of keyword meta elements, and if so, to implement them with care.

Incorporating Microdata

While meta elements enable you to describe the overall content of a page for search engines, HTML5 introduced a system known as microdata that enables you to add semantic information to specific Web page elements. Microdata is based on sets of **vocabularies** that define keyword values for specific types of information; vocabularies serve as a common language for referencing various kinds of data. Although anyone can define and use a custom vocabulary, implementing an established and widely used one increases the usability of the data in your Web pages. You reference a vocabulary in your code using the URI where a machine-readable description of the vocabulary is located; several popular vocabularies for widely used information are available at data-vocabulary.org. Phillip would like you to mark up the address of Lakeland Reeds in the page footer using microdata to make it easier for search engines and other Web applications to index.

STEPS

1. **In the footer element near the bottom of the document, add the attribute–value pair itemtype="http://www.data-vocabulary.org/Organization"**

   You use the itemtype attribute to specify the URI of the vocabulary you're using.

2. **Add a space, then type itemscope="itemscope"**

   The itemscope attribute signifies that the vocabulary specified using the itemtype attribute applies to all descendent elements of the element in which it is declared, unless a descendent element declares a different vocabulary; this is known as the scope of the vocabulary.

3. **In your browser, open www.data-vocabulary.org/Organization**

   The Web page lists the keywords and corresponding values that are part of the vocabulary you specified.

4. **Return to your text editor, then enclose the first line of text in the footer paragraph, Lakeland Reeds Bed & Breakfast, in a span element with the attribute–value pair itemprop="name"**

   This code signifies that the value of the span element corresponds to the *name* property in the vocabulary you declared in Step 1. For most Web page elements, the microdata value is the text an element contains.

5. **Enclose the remaining address information in a span element with the attribute–value pairs itemprop="address", itemtype="http://www.data-vocabulary.org/Address" and itemscope="itemscope"**

   All the contents of this element are address information in the vocabulary specified in Step 1. You use a vocabulary for address data to mark each item that's part of the address.

6. **Repeat Step 4 to add span elements with itemprop values of street-address for 45 Marsh Grass Ln., locality for Marble, region for MN, postal-code for 55764, and tel for (218) 555-5253**

   Figure N-6 shows the completed code. Table N-2 shows the microdata name–value pairs based on the code you added, along with their corresponding vocabularies.

7. **Save your work, reload rooms.html in your browser, then scroll down to view the footer text**

   As with other SEO optimizations you've performed, the microdata you added has no effect on the appearance of the footer text. Figure N-7 shows an example of how a search engine might take advantage of the microdata in a business listing.

FIGURE N-6: Code for microdata in footer section

```
<footer itemtype="http://www.data-vocabulary.org/organization" itemscope="itemscope">
  <p id="contact">
    <span itemprop="name">Lakeland Reeds Bed &amp; Breakfast</span>
    <img src="images/flourish.gif" width="16" height="16" alt="" />
    <span  itemprop="address" itemscope="itemscope"
itemtype="http://data-vocabulary.org/Address">
      <span itemprop="street-address">45 Marsh Grass Ln.</span>
      <img src="images/flourish.gif" width="16" height="16" alt="" />
      <span itemprop="locality">Marble</span>,
      <span itemprop="region">MN</span>
      <span itemprop="postal-code">55764</span>
      <img src="images/flourish.gif" width="16" height="16" alt="" />
      <span itemprop="tel">(218) 555-5253</span>
    </span>
  </p>
</footer>
```

itemprop attribute specifies vocabulary property that corresponds to value of current element

itemtype value specifies URL of vocabulary definition

itemscope attribute specifies the vocabulary as the scope

FIGURE N-7: Microdata in sample search result

Room selection at Lakeland Reeds Bed & Breakfast
Marble, MN -(218) 555-5253
Lakeland Reeds Bed & Breakfast offers 4 comfortable rooms that accommodate from 2 to 5 people. All have private baths and views of Twin Lakes.
www.example.com

A search engine could show a summary in search results of Web page content marked with microdata, such as selected contact information

TABLE N-2: Microdata marked in Rooms Web page

vocabulary	property	value
http://data-vocabulary.org/Organization	name	Lakeland Reeds Bed & Breakfast
	address	45 Marsh Grass Ln., Marble, MN 55764, (218) 555-5253
http://data-vocabulary.org/Address	street-address	45 Marsh Grass Ln.
	locality	Marble
	region	MN
	postal-code	55764
	tel	(218) 555-5253

Using RDFa and microformats

At the time this book was written, microdata was a working draft of the W3C; however, other specifications for adding semantic data to Web page elements are in use as well. **RDFa** is a specialized version of the resource description framework (RDF) language; RDFa is specifically focused on marking semantic data in Web pages. For organizations that use RDF, RDFa carries the advantage of connecting with existing systems. **Microformats** are predecessors to microdata that have been developed and used by some organizations for several years. The developers of the microdata standard are working to make it compatible with the code of existing microformats. While microdata has the weight of the W3C behind it, some organizations choose to work with RDFa or microformats instead for various reasons, and you may encounter these languages in Web sites that you work on.

Creating a Sitemap File

Ensuring that the relationships between pages on your Web site are easy to understand is an important part of making your site usable for visitors. Users should be able to get to any page on the site using links from other pages, and links should be organized in such a way that it's clear to users how to navigate to desired content. Especially in a large Web site, however, it can be beneficial to ensure that search engines see and index all the Web pages on the site. You can accomplish this by creating and publishing a **Sitemap** file, which is a file in a specific format that lists all the pages in a Web site, and may include information about content such as images or video in the pages as well. ▧▧▧▧ Even though the Lakeland Reeds B&B Web site is currently small, Phillip would like you create a Sitemap file for the site as a starting point.

STEPS

1. **In your text editor, create a new document**

2. **Type** http://www.example.com/index.html, **then press [Enter]**
   The simplest version of a Sitemap file contains only text. You list the full published URI for each page in your Web site on a separate line. For demonstration purposes, you use the sample domain name example.com.

3. **Add the following URIs on separate lines:**
   http://www.example.com/aboutus.html
   http://www.example.com/rooms.html
   http://www.example.com/reserve.html
   Figure N-8 shows the completed code for the Sitemap file.

4. **If you're using TextEdit on a Mac, click** Format, **then, if necessary, click** Make Plain Text

5. **Click** File, **click** Save, **navigate to the** Unit N/Unit **directory where you store your Data Files, type** sitemap.txt, **click the** Encoding list arrow **if necessary and click** UTF-8, **then click** Save
   A plain-text Sitemap file must use UTF-8 encoding for compatibility with major search engines.

6. **Close** sitemap.txt

FIGURE N-8: Content of Sitemap file

```
http://www.example.com/index.html
http://www.example.com/aboutus.html
http://www.example.com/rooms.html
http://www.example.com/reserve.html
```

Creating an XML Sitemap file

While a plain-text Sitemap file can meet the needs of a small, simple Web site, larger sites and sites with a lot of content can benefit from Sitemap files that provide more information. You can add more data about your Web pages and their contents by creating a file using XML with the Sitemap protocol, which is detailed at sitemaps.org. XML is a markup language like HTML and uses similar rules for tags and attributes; however, XML files require some elements that HTML files don't and have their own specific rules. To facilitate the creation of XML Sitemap files like the one shown in Figure N-9, many free utilities are available. In addition, many blog platforms generate Sitemap files automatically for blog content.

FIGURE N-9: An XML Sitemap file

```xml
<?xml version="1.0" encoding="UTF-8"?>
<urlset
      xmlns="http://www.sitemaps.org/schemas/sitemap/0.9"
      xmlns:xsi="http://www.w3.org/2001/XMLSchema-instance"
      xsi:schemaLocation="http://www.sitemaps.org/schemas/sitemap/0.9
            http://www.sitemaps.org/schemas/sitemap/0.9/sitemap.xsd">

<url>
  <loc>http://example.com/</loc>
  <lastmod>2010-10-06T01:39:16+00:00</lastmod>
</url>
<url>
  <loc>http://example.com/compatibility.html</loc>
  <lastmod>2011-03-18T10:53:03+00:00</lastmod>
</url>
<url>
  <loc>http://example.com/blog/</loc>
  <lastmod>2011-04-06T16:35:05+00:00</lastmod>
</url>
<url>
  <loc>http://example.com/mobile/</loc>
  <lastmod>2011-02-17T19:09:25+00:00</lastmod>
</url>
<url>
  <loc>http://example.com/about/</loc>
  <lastmod>2011-01-13T22:33:35+00:00</lastmod>
</url>
<url>
  <loc>http://example.com/blog/index.html</loc>
  <lastmod>2011-04-06T16:35:05+00:00</lastmod>
</url>
<url>
  <loc>http://example.com/sitemap.html</loc>
```

Creating a robots.txt File

Sometimes your Web site may contain pages or folders that you don't want indexed by search engines. Search engines index Web pages using programs known as **bots** or **crawlers**. By convention, bots look for a file named robots.txt in the root directory of a Web site for instructions on any files or folders to exclude from indexing. Because any publicly available document on the Web can be viewed by anyone with Internet access, you can't rely on a robots.txt file to keep a document on your Web server hidden; if restricting access is your goal, you'll likely want to implement a password-based system to restrict access. However, for influencing which pages are indexed by major search engines, a robots.txt file is an invaluable tool. ▄▄▄▄▄▄ Phillip wants to publish only a subset of the Web pages you've created on the Lakeland Reeds B&B Web site to start. However, he'd like to put all the pages up on the Web server so he can continue to test that pages that aren't yet part of the main site structure. You create a robots.txt file to prevent these extra Web pages from being indexed by search engines.

STEPS

1. **In your text editor, create a new document**

QUICK TIP

The Web site at robotstxt.org includes a database that lists the names of robots for different search engines, which you can use to apply rules selectively.

2. **Type User-agent: *, then press [Enter]**
   Before listing specific pages to include or exclude from indexing, you use a User-agent entry to specify which bots the rules apply to. The * wildcard indicates that all bots should respect the rule or rules that follow.

3. **Type Disallow: /contact.html, then press [Enter]**
   Every value should begin with a slash (/). In addition to listing a specific file, you can specify filename patterns to exclude all files with given characteristics in their names; Table N-3 lists some common patterns.

QUICK TIP

After specifying a group of files to exclude from indexing, you can create one or more *Allow* entries to specify files that should be indexed.

4. **Type Disallow: /events.html**
   Figure N-10 shows the completed code for the robots.txt file.

5. **Click File, click Save, navigate to the Unit N/Unit directory where you store your Data Files, type robots.txt, click the Encoding list arrow if necessary and click UTF-8, then click Save**

6. **Close robots.txt**

```
User-agent: *
Disallow: /contact.html
Disallow: /events.html
```

TABLE N-3

pattern	matches	example
/	entire Web site	Disallow: /
/*directory-name*	all the contents of the *directory-name* directory	Disallow: /test
/*.extension$	all files in the site with an extension matching *extension*	Disallow: /*.ppt$

Excluding pages from indexing with the noindex meta element

Even if you exclude a Web page from indexing in your robots.txt file and other pages in your site don't link to the excluded page, search engines may index the page anyway if another Web site links to it. To avoid this, you can add the following meta element to the excluded page:

`<meta name="robots" content="noindex" />`

You can select a specific bot to which the element should apply by using a name from the robots database at robotstxt.org in place of the value robots for the name attribute.

Previewing and Finalizing Your Site

In addition to previewing and validating your Web pages from usability and accessibility standpoints, it can be useful to give your documents a final check from the point of view of a bot. Search engines index mainly text, as well as selected attribute values such as alt values for img elements. In addition, style sheets don't influence what bots encounter. Thus, viewing text-only versions of your Web pages can help you identify missing or hidden content and ensure that your pages are ready for search engine indexing. You can install a program such as the free, open-source Lynx browser, or an extension to another browser to let you view only the text of a Web page. You can also approximate this view without installing any additional software by changing some settings in your Web browser. ▗▖▝▘▖ As you prepare to finalize the optimized version of the Lakeland Reeds B&B Web site, you review it in text-only mode in your browser to double-check the content that bots will encounter.

STEPS

QUICK TIP

For Safari, open the **Preferences** window, click **Advanced**, and check **Show Develop menu in menu bar**. On the **Develop** menu, select **Disable Images** and **Disable Styles**.

TROUBLE

If the Developer Tools bar opens in its own window, press **[Ctrl][P]** to pin the toolbar to the bottom of the main browser window.

CSS and image settings vary across browsers; the following steps are for Internet Explorer 9

1. **With rooms.html open in your browser, click the Tools button ⚙, then click Internet options**
   The Internet Options dialog box opens.

2. **Click the Advanced tab, scroll down to the Multimedia section in the list, uncheck the Show pictures box, click OK, then click the Refresh button ⟳**
   The Web page reloads, displaying alt text in place of images.

3. **Press [F12], then on the Developer Tools bar at the bottom of the window, click Disable and click CSS**
   The Web page is displayed without images and with only browser default styling, as shown in Figure N-11. For comparison, Figure N-12 shows part of the page as viewed in the text-only Lynx browser.

4. **Scroll through the Web page to view the content as a bot is likely to encounter it**
   Text-only view is especially useful for noticing when site content is available only through technologies such as JavaScript or Flash, which are not accessible by most bots. Because the content of the rooms.html page is made up only of text and graphics, all of the content remains visible in the current view.

5. **Repeat Steps 1 and 2, rechecking the Show pictures box**

6. **On the Developer Tools bar, click Disable, click CSS, then press [F12]**
   The display of CSS is re-enabled, and the Developer Tools bar is hidden.

Skip navigation

☐ Lakeland Reeds Bed and Breakfast

- ☐ Home
- ☐ About Us
- ☐ Rooms
- ☐ Reservations
- ☐ Local Weather
- ☐ Directions

Rooms

All rooms include down comforters, air conditioning, and DVD players, and each can accommodate an additional twin fold-out bed.

Sun Room | Reed Room | Treehouse | Garden Room

Sun Room

☐ the Sun Room has large windows and a desk, dresser, and queen bed

The Sun Room

With windows on three sides, the sunlight in this second-floor room supports a large selection of houseplants.

1 queen bed.

Ask a question Make a reservation

Back to top

FIGURE N-12: rooms.html displayed in a text-only browser

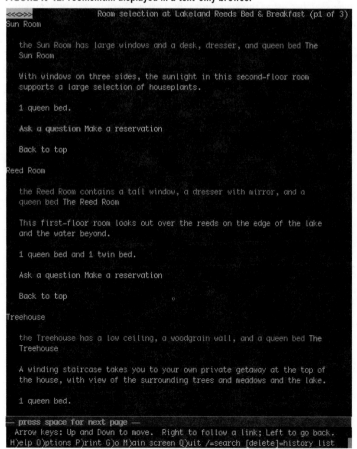

Optimizing Your Web Site for Search Engines

HTML5 and CSS3

Submitting Your Site

When you are finished optimizing your Web site, you can simply publish it to the Web to make it available to potential users as well as to search engine bots. However, you can take other measures as well to increase the chances that search engines that are popular among your target audience index your pages accurately. ▨▩▧ As Phillip prepares to publish his site, you review with him some additional steps he can take to submit information about the site to search engines.

STEPS

QUICK TIP

Because Web page designs and content change regularly, your screen may not match exactly the pages shown in these steps.

1. **In your browser, open the page** www.google.com/addurl

   Major search engines, as well as some smaller ones, provide Web forms where you can submit the address of a Web site for indexing. As Figure N-13 shows, this Web page enables you to submit your Web site to Google.

2. **Read the instructions on the submission page**

   Note that when submitting a Web site, you need to submit only the link to the main page. Because Phillip's site is not yet published, you won't submit a URL right now.

3. **Open the Web page** www.bing.com/toolbox/webmasters

   Some search engines offer tools to help **webmasters**, the people in charge of Web sites, administer sites. You can use pages like this one at Bing, shown in Figure N-14, to accomplish tasks such as uploading Sitemaps.

4. **Explore the options available on the Webmaster Tools page**

5. **Use a search engine to display results based on the keywords** bed and breakfast Minnesota

   The first page of results likely includes links to one or two major sites that list and rate bed and breakfasts. Because search engines use links to your site both for indexing and to set the priority of your site in search results, it's important to let owners of relevant Web sites know when your site is up. In addition to using your professional and/or personal contacts to identify other sites where links to your pages make sense, conducting your own searches using the keywords you'd expect people seeking your site to use, as you did in this step, is an invaluable research tool.

FIGURE N-13: Site submission page at google.com

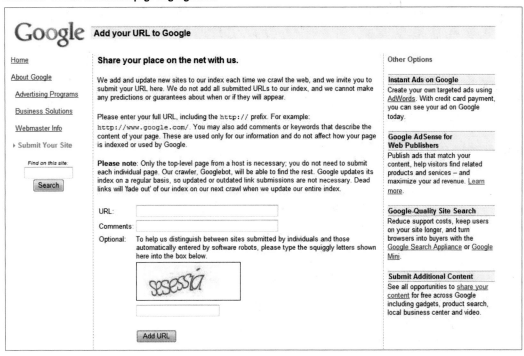

FIGURE N-14: Webmaster toolbox page at bing.com

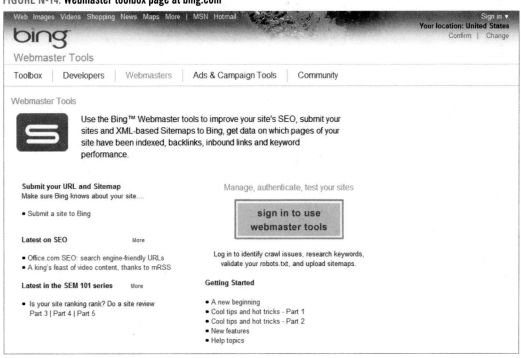

Practice

Concepts Review

Refer to the sample search result in Figure N-15.

FIGURE N-15

1. Which content is based on microdata?
2. Which content is based on the title element?
3. Which content is based on a description meta element?

Match each term with the statement that best describes it.

4. **search engine optimization (SEO)**
5. **algorithm**
6. **microdata**
7. **vocabulary**
8. **bot**
9. **webmaster**

a. a set of definitions of keyword values for specific types of information
b. a set of instructions used by search engines to decide the priority of search results
c. a person in charge of a Web site
d. a part of the HTML5 specification for adding more types of semantic data to Web page content
e. the process of tailoring the structure and content of a Web page with search engines in mind
f. a program used by a search engine to index Web pages

Select the best answer from the list of choices.

10. Which of the following is a working draft of the W3C?

  a. microdata

  b. microformats

  c. RDF

  d. RDFa

11. Which of the following is a strategy for making the content of a title element more indexable?

  a. make it generic

  b. make it long

  c. customize it to accurately describe the current page

  d. copy the same title text from another page on the site

12. Which of the following is a strategy for making an image element more indexable?

  a. give the image file a generic name

  b. give the image file a long name

  c. remove the alt attribute and its value

  d. give the image file a descriptive name

13. To create a meta element that provides site summary text, what value do you specify for the name attribute?

  a. description

  b. robots

  c. keywords

  d. charset

14. Which attribute signifies that a specified microdata vocabulary applies to all descendent elements of the element in which it is declared?

  a. itemdata

  b. itemtype

  c. itemprop

  d. itemscope

15. By convention, what is the name of the file that bots look for in the root directory of a Web site for instructions on any files or folders to exclude from indexing?

  a. sitemap.txt

  b. robots.txt

  c. index.html

  d. sitemap.xml

Skills Review

1. Write indexable content.

  a. In your text editor, open HTM N-2.html from the Unit N/Unit folder where you store your Data Files, insert a blank line before the closing body tag, insert a paragraph element containing your first and last name and the text **HTML5 Unit N, Skills Review**, then save it as **location.html**.

  b. In the head section, edit the text of the title element to read **Big J's Pizza Toronto Locations**.

  c. In the first section, in the paragraph beneath the h3 heading Queen's Park/UT, change the link text **Map** to **Map Big J's Queen's Park/UT**. Repeat for the second and third sections, changing the link text to **Map Big J's St. Clair** and **Map Big J's Dundas** respectively.

  d. In the file manager for your operating system, navigate to the Unit N/Review/images folder where you store your Data Files, then rename bigjs.gif to **big-js-pizza.gif**.

  e. Return to location.html in your text editor, then edit the img element in the h1 element near the top of the head section to change the src value to **images/big-js-pizza.gif**.

  f. Save your work, then open location.html in your browser. Figure N-16 shows the updated page.

FIGURE N-16

Skills Review (continued)

2. Add a description with the meta element.

  a. Return to location.html in your text editor.

  b. In the head section, add a meta tag with a name value of **description** and a content value of **Get Big J's Pizza at Queen's Park/UT, St. Clair, or Dundas**.

  c. Save your work

3. Incorporate microdata.

  a. In the footer element near the bottom of the document, add an attribute–value pair referencing the microdata vocabulary described at **http://www.data-vocabulary.org/Organization**. Add another attribute–value pair setting the specified vocabulary as the scope.

  b. Enclose the text Big J's Queen's Park/UT in a span element with an attribute–value pair marking the content as corresponding to the **name** property in the current vocabulary.

  c. Enclose the remaining address information in the same paragraph within a span element. Add an attribute–value pair referencing the microdata vocabulary described at **http://www.data-vocabulary.org/Address** and another attribute–value pair setting the specified vocabulary as the scope.

  d. Enclose the text 150 St. Joseph St. in a span element with an attribute–value pair marking the content as corresponding to the **street-address** property in the current vocabulary. Add an attribute–value pair to the span element enclosing the text (416) 555-3337 marking the content as corresponding to the **tel** property.

  e. Repeat Steps b–d to mark the contents of the remaining two div elements.

  f. Save your work, reload location.html in your browser, then scroll down to verify that the display of the footer text is unchanged.

4. Create a Sitemap file.

  a. In your text editor, create a new document.

  b. On separate lines, enter the following URLs:

    http://www.example.com/index.html
    http://www.example.com/location.html

  c. If you're using TextEdit on a Mac, click **Format**, then, if necessary, click **Make Plain Text**.

  d. Save the file as **sitemap.txt** with the **UTF-8** encoding in the Unit N/Review directory where you store your Data Files.

  e. Close sitemap.txt.

5. Create a robots.txt file.

  a. In your text editor, create a new document.

  b. Add code specifying that the file applies to all bots.

  c. Add code specifying that order.html should not be indexed.

  d. Save the file using UTF-8 encoding as **robots.txt** in the Unit N/Review directory where you store your Data Files.

  e. Close robots.txt.

6. Preview and finalize your site.

  a. With location.html open in your browser, set your browser to ignore images, then reload the Web page.

  b. Disable CSS within the current Web page, then scroll through the Web page to view the content as a bot is likely to encounter it.

  c. Reenable the display of images and the use of CSS code within the page.

Independent Challenge 1

Sarah Nguyen, the manager of the Spotted Wren Garden Center, is preparing to publish the Web site you've been working on. She'd like you to implement some search engine optimization measures before the site goes live.

a. Open HTM N-3.html from the Unit N/IC1 folder in your text editor. Insert a blank line before the closing body tag, insert a paragraph element containing your first and last name and the text **HTML5 Unit N, Independent Challenge 1**, then save it as **resource.html**.

b. Change the text of the title element to **Gardening Resources from Spotted Wren Garden Center**.

c. In your file manager, navigate to the Unit N/IC1/images folder, then rename the file flowers.jpg to **prairie-coneflower.jpg**. In your text editor, change the img element referencing this file to match the new name.

d. Change the text for the weather link to **Gardening weather forecast for Omaha, NE**. Open resource. html in your browser and compare it to Figure N-17.

e. Mark the contents of the footer element using microdata. Use the vocabulary described at **http://www.data-vocabulary.org/Organization** for the business name, marking the text Spotted Wren Garden Center as corresponding to the **name** property. Use the vocabulary described at **http://www.data-vocabulary.org/Address** for the rest of the text, marking 548 N. 58th St. as **street-address** data, Omaha as **locality** data, NE as **region** data, 68132 as **postal-code** data, and (402) 555-9736 as **tel** data.

f. Create a Sitemap file listing the files **index.html**, **resource.html**, and **hours.html** at the sample domain **http://www.example.com**. Save the file with the name **sitemap.txt**.

g. Create a **robots.txt** file that applies to all user agents and excludes the file **quote.html** from indexing.

h. Close your browser, then close your text editor.

FIGURE N-17

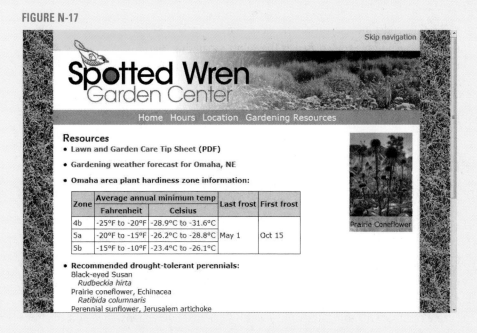

Independent Challenge 2

As you prepare to publish the Web site for the Murfreesboro Recreational Soccer League, you add some search engine optimizations.

a. Open HTM N-4.html from the Unit N/IC2 folder in your text editor. Insert a blank line before the closing body tag, insert a paragraph element containing your first and last name and the text **HTML5 Unit N, Independent Challenge 2**, then save the file as **schedule.html**.

b. Change the text of the title element to include the name of the organization as well as the phrase **Team Schedules**.

c. In your file manager, navigate to the Unit N/IC2/images folder, then rename the file jump.jpg to **soccer-players. jpg**. In your text editor, change the img element referencing this file to match the new name.

d. Mark the contents of the footer element using microdata. Use the vocabulary at **http://www.data-vocabulary.org/Organization** for the organization name, marking the organization name with the **name** property. Use the vocabulary at **http://www.data-vocabulary.org/Address** for the rest of the text, marking c/o Davies Sporting Goods
418 N. Sartoris St. as **street-address** data, Murfreesboro as **locality** data, TN as **region** data, 37130 as **postal-code** data, and (615) 555-2255 as **tel** data.

e. Create a Sitemap file listing the files **index.html**, **started.html**, and **schedule.html** at the sample domain **http://www.example.com**. Save the file with the name **sitemap.txt**.

f. Create a **robots.txt** file that applies to all user agents and excludes the file **signup.html** from indexing.

g. Write a concise description of the page contents, then add it to your HTML file using a description meta element.

Advanced Challenge Exercise

- Create a list of terms that you might enter into a search engine if you were trying to find the information on the current Web page.
- In your HTML file, add a meta tag using the value **keywords** for the *name* attribute. Add a *content* attribute and enter the list of search terms you created as the value, separating each word or phrase with a comma. If necessary, refer to the sample code in the "Adding keywords with the meta element" box in the *Adding a Description with the meta Element* lesson.

h. Close your browser, then close your text editor.

Independent Challenge 3

As you continue your work on the Web site for the Hotel Natoma, you add search engine optimizations to the site, starting with the Local Events page.

a. Open HTM N-5.html from the Unit N/IC3 folder in your text editor. Insert a blank line before the closing body tag, then insert a paragraph element containing your first and last name and the text **HTML5 Unit N, Independent Challenge 3**, then save the file as **streetfair.html**.

b. Edit the text of the title element so it appropriately reflects the page content.

c. Rename the cable car image file using descriptive words separated by hyphens, then edit the img element in the document to match.

d. Mark the contents of the footer element using microdata. Use the vocabulary at **http://www.data-vocabulary.org/Organization** for the organization name, marking the hotel name with the **name** property. Use the vocabulary at **http://www.data-vocabulary.org/Address** for the rest of the text, marking the street address as **street-address** data, the city as **locality** data, the state abbreviation as **region** data, the postal (ZIP) code as **postal-code** data, and the phone number as **tel** data.

e. Create a Sitemap file listing the files **index.html**, **nearby.html**, **museums.html**, and **streetfair.html** at the sample domain **http://www.example.com**. Save the file with the name **sitemap.txt**.

f. Create a **robots.txt** file that applies to all user agents and excludes the file **reserve.html** from indexing.

g. Write a concise description of the page contents, then add it to your HTML file using a description meta element.

Independent Challenge 3 (continued)

Advanced Challenge Exercise

- In your browser, open **data-vocabulary.org/Event**. Read through the property names and descriptions for this event vocabulary.
- In your text editor, add a reference to the event vocabulary in the opening tag for the dl element. Add an attribute–value pair that specifies the new vocabulary as the current scope.
- In the opening tag for each dt element, add an attribute–value pair specifying the element content as **summary** data.
- In the opening tag for each dd element, add an attribute–value pair specifying the **startDate** data type.
- In the opening tag for each dd element, add the **datetime** attribute. For the datetime value, enter the four-digit year the event starts, a hyphen, the two-digit month the event starts, a hyphen, and the two-digit date the event starts; for example, the attribute–value pair for the starting date April 9, 2014, would be datetime="2014-04-09". (*Note:* Because text representations of dates can vary, you add this attribute to provide the date in an international standard format known as ISO 8601.)

h. Close your browser, then close your text editor.

Real Life Independent Challenge

This assignment builds on the personal Web site you have worked on in previous units. You'll add search engine optimizations to your Web site.

a. Copy your Web site files to the Unit N/RLIC folder on the drive and folder where you store your Data Files.

b. Starting with your main Web page, identify and edit content to make it more indexable, including at least two of the following:
- title element content
- image file names
- link text

c. Create a description meta element for your main Web page.

d. If your main Web page includes address information, mark all the elements with microdata. If your Web page includes other types of content that you can describe with microdata, mark them up using the reference pages at data-vocabulary.org as guides.

e. Create a plain-text Sitemap file listing all the Web pages in your site.

f. If you want to exclude one or more Web pages from indexing by search engines, create a robots.txt file with appropriate code.

g. Preview your main Web page using a text-only browser or in a standard browser with images and CSS disabled. If you notice content that wouldn't be clear to a bot, make appropriate edits to the HTML file, then reload the file in text-only mode.

h. If your site includes more than one Web page, repeat the above steps for each file.

i. Close your browser, then close your text editor.

Visual Workshop

In your text editor, open the file HTM N-6.html from the Unit N/VW directory on the drive and folder where you store your Data Files, add a paragraph before the closing body tag that contains your first and last name and the text **HTML5 Unit N, Visual Workshop**, then save the file as **upcoming.html**. Edit the file such that indexing by a search engine could create the search result shown in Figure N-18. Save your work, then close your browser and text editor.

FIGURE N-18

Upcoming Events at Revisions Bookstore/Cafe
Join us for readings, discussions, and other
activities for a variety of ages.
www.example.com

Adapting Your Web Site for Mobile Devices

Mobile Web access is growing quickly in many parts of the world, making support for such devices an increasingly central piece of Web development. Although many smartphones and other mobile devices enable users to view and navigate standard Web sites, optimizing Web pages for mobile users can make those pages much more usable on smaller screens.  In this unit, you'll implement several techniques to adapt the Lakeland Reeds B&B Web site for use on mobile devices.

OBJECTIVES

Evaluate design for mobile devices

Apply @media rules

Implement conditional style sheets

Create a mobile-specific layout

Decrease page load time

Incorporate sprites

Implement geolocation

Optimize a mobile site for search engines

Evaluating Design for Mobile Devices

The growth of mobile device use has increased situations where the potential audience of a Web site can access its content. In tandem, the growing capacity of handheld devices, including mobile phones, to access the Web has made the Web available to people who were previously unable to access it using a computer. While access on more devices enables all sorts of Web sites to be accessed by more people, the use of mobile devices as Web interfaces brings its own set of challenges for Web developers.  Philip Blaine, the owner of Lakeland Reeds Bed & Breakfast, would like to ensure that the Web site for his establishment is optimized for viewing by customers and potential clients on mobile phones and tablet computers. As you prepare to refine the site for mobile use, you review the special requirements that mobile devices bring to Web browsing.

DETAILS

Web pages for mobile devices have several unique needs:

- **Viewability on small screens at a variety of sizes and resolutions**

  While most mobile devices are small enough to hold in one hand, the exact dimensions of mobile screens vary. In addition, even screens of the same size can use displays of different resolutions, meaning that the available pixel count in each dimension can vary greatly, as Figure O-1 illustrates. In addition, new devices are released constantly, sometimes using new, custom screen resolutions. While the browser built into a given mobile device generally tailors Web content as appropriate for the display of the device, browsers can go only so far in making such adjustments. Thus, creating Web page design that's flexible at small screen sizes and resolutions is an important step in making a Web site mobile-compatible.

- **Navigation features that can be manipulated on a touchscreen**

  Even after you ensure that a Web page is viewable on small screens, it's important to include design elements that enable users to interact with the page on handheld devices. On a desktop or notebook computer, users select navigation elements such as links and buttons by using a mouse, which enables them to point to and click small screen elements. Handheld devices, by contrast, increasingly use touch interfaces that users manipulate with blunt fingertips. Figure O-2 illustrates the difference between these two approaches. Because it's more challenging to reliably select small Web page elements with a finger press, navigation elements for mobile users need to be larger.

- **Minimal download size**

  In general, mobile users can access the Web from anywhere their devices receive signals. However, because many mobile networks are slower than home and office Internet connections, a mobile device may load a given Web page much more slowly than the page would open on a desktop computer. In addition, some mobile users pay for downloaded data, including Web documents, based on the amount they use, while others are limited to a fixed amount each month. Thus, to ensure that mobile users can view your pages as quickly as possible and don't experience your site as a drain on their data allowances, it's important to minimize the file sizes of Web pages delivered to mobile users, including minimizing the use and file sizes of images and other related elements.

Devices in portrait orientation

Devices render Web page content at a range of different resolutions and orientations

Devices in landscape orientation

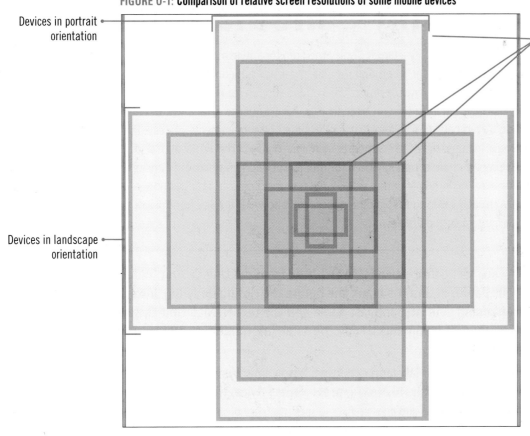

FIGURE O-2: **Mouse pointer vs. touch selection**

The tip of the mouse pointer identifies the Web page element hovered over or clicked

A fingertip touches an area of the Web page, and the operating system must calculate the most likely target of the touch

How touchscreen devices interpret touches

On a computer system that uses a mouse pointer, you can use a mouse or other device to maneuver the pointer to hover over or click even a very small page element. On Windows and Mac computers, the object at the tip of the mouse pointer is the one selected. While early touchscreen devices relied on the use of a pencil-like tool known as a stylus for interacting with the screen, modifying touchscreen interfaces for use with fingers required some adaptations. Because a finger has no discernable point, a single touch on a touchscreen can cover a relatively large area. The creators of operating systems for mobile devices include code to calculate the most likely point on the screen that a user meant to touch, and then to execute events based on that touch. The best systems do a good, but not perfect, job at guessing what a user means to touch when small page elements are involved. Modern touchscreen interface guidelines call for icons and other touchable page elements to be displayed at least one centimeter square, a size that minimizes any disjuncture between a user's intention and an operating system's ability to interpret touch input.

Applying @media Rules

CSS enables you to specify a target display medium for a style rule or style sheet using the media types listed on p. 91. Style rules that incorporate media types are sometimes known as **@media rules** because the selectors start with the @media prefix. CSS3 added support for **media queries**, which are conditional statements that you can include in an @media rule. Media queries enable you to check features of the browser opening a Web page and to apply style rules based on requirements you set. Table O-1 describes some of the media features that CSS3 supports in media queries. The *width* and *device-width* features and their related properties are commonly used for mobile-specific styles because dimensions are good indicators of whether a device is mobile or not. ▰▰▱ On handheld devices, you want figure elements on the Lakeland Reeds Web site hidden to simplify the pages. You also want the site to display a smaller logo. Add @media rules to implement these styles.

1. **In your text editor, open HTM O-1.html from the Unit O/Unit folder where you store your Data Files, insert a blank line before the closing body tag, insert a paragraph element containing your first and last name and the text HTML5 Unit O, save it as index.html, then use CSS comments to add the same information to HTM O-2.css and save it as lakeland.css**

QUICK TIP

The *only* keyword prevents older browsers from mistakenly implementing a rule but isn't otherwise required in an @media rule.

2. **At the bottom of lakeland.css, insert a new line, type @media only screen and (max-device-width: 1024px) {, press [Enter] twice, then indent and type }**

   You can use the *min-* and *max-* prefixes to specify a range of sizes. The styles within this @media rule will be applied when a page is rendered on a screen with a width of 1024 px or less.

3. **Within the braces of the @media rule, create a style rule based on the figure selector with the name–value pair display: none;**

4. **Below the rule you just added, create a style rule based on the #content selector with the name–value pair margin: 0.25em;**

5. **Create another rule based on the #mainnav selector that sets padding to 0.25 em, width to 100%, position to static, and left to 0**

   This rule changes the nav bar to a horizontal arrangement at the top of the Web page. Figure O-3 shows the code for the @media rule and the style rules it contains.

6. **In index.html locate the h1 element near the top of the body section, then add class="desktop" to the opening tag**

7. **Create a new h1 element beneath the existing one, specify a class of mobile, then within the new element, enter the following code:**
   `<img src="images/llrlogo.gif" width="131" height="115" alt="" title="" />`
   Lakeland Reeds Bed & Breakfast

   Figure O-4 shows the updated HTML for index.html.

8. **Save your work, return to lakeland.css, insert a blank line below the .firstcol rule, then create a rule based on the .mobile selector with the style display: none;**

TROUBLE

If you don't have a mobile device for viewing your published page, search on *mobile phone emulator* for sites where you can test it on software that mimics the performance of mobile devices.

9. **Beneath the existing rules in the @media rule, add a rule based on the .desktop selector with the style display: none, add a second rule based on the .mobile selector with the style display: block, then save your work**

   Figure O-3 shows the completed style rules.

10. **If possible, publish the Web page along with its supporting files, then open it with a mobile device**

    Figure O-5 shows the page on a handheld device with a display width of 480 px.

Adapting Your Web Site for Mobile Devices

FIGURE O-3: @media rule in style sheet

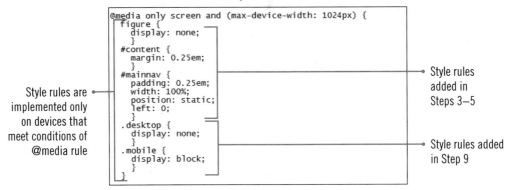

Style rules are implemented only on devices that meet conditions of @media rule

```
@media only screen and (max-device-width: 1024px) {
    figure {
        display: none;
    }
    #content {
        margin: 0.25em;
    }
    #mainnav {
        padding: 0.25em;
        width: 100%;
        position: static;
        left: 0;
    }
    .desktop {
        display: none;
    }
    .mobile {
        display: block;
    }
}
```

Style rules added in Steps 3–5

Style rules added in Step 9

FIGURE O-4: Alternate desktop and mobile page headings

Style rule will ensure that the standard logo is displayed only on a desktop display

```
<body>
    <div id="box">
        <p id="skipnav"><a href="#main">Skip navigation</a></p>
        <h1 class="desktop">
            <a href="index.html"><img src="images/lakeland.gif" width="664" height="180"
            alt="Lakeland Reeds Bed and Breakfast" title="" /></a>
        </h1>
        <h1 class="mobile">
            <img src="images/llrlogo.gif" width="131" height="115" alt="" title="" />
            Lakeland Reeds Bed &amp; Breakfast
        </h1>
        <nav id="mainnav">
```

Style rule will enable text-based heading with smaller graphic on mobile screens

FIGURE O-5: Mobile display using @media rule

Photo/Sasha Vodnik

TABLE O-1: Commonly used media rule features

feature	min/max variations*	description
width	✔	width of area displaying the content
height	✔	height of area displaying the content
device-width	✔	width of screen or other content area
device-height	✔	height of screen or other content area
orientation		whether height value is greater than width value (*portrait*), or width value is greater than height value (*landscape*)
aspect-ratio	✔	ratio of width value to height value
device-aspect-ratio	✔	ratio of device-width value to device-height value
resolution	✔	density of pixels of output device

*For checked items, -min or -max can be added to the end of the feature name to check minimum and maximum values, respectively; for instance, *width-min* checks the minimum width of the area displaying the content and *device-width-max* checks the maximum width of the screen or other content area.

Implementing Conditional Style Sheets

You can specify the *handheld* media type in the link element for a style sheet to specify that only mobile browsers should implement it; however, in practice this media type is implemented inconsistently on mobile devices and thus produces unreliable results. However, you can achieve a similar result using **conditional style sheets**, which are style sheets specified using media queries within link elements to indicate which style sheet browsers should load in a given situation. ░░░░ You've created an alternative style sheet for the Lakeland Reeds Web site to be used by mobile browsers. You test it by linking it to the index.html page.

1. **In your text editor, reopen HTM O-2.css from the Unit O/Unit folder, add a CSS comment containing your first and last name and the text HTML5 Unit O, save the file as lakeland2.css, repeat to save HTM O-3.css as llmobile.css, then examine the contents of llmobile.css**

   The lakeland2.css file is a clean copy of the main style sheet without mobile-specific styles. The llmobile.css file integrates the changes you made in the previous lesson without using an @media rule and adds a few additional tweaks to the presentation of the Web page.

2. **In index.html, edit the link element for lakeland.css so it references lakeland2.css instead, then change the value of the media attribute to only screen and (min-device-width: 1025px)**

3. **Below the link element for lakeland2.css, add a link element referencing llmobile.css with a media value of only screen and (max-device-width: 1024px)**

4. **Beneath the meta element containing description content, insert**
   <meta name="viewport" content="width=device-width" />

   This viewport meta element instructs browsers to assume that the width of the content matches the width of the device; otherwise, many browsers assume a page is meant for desktop browsers and scale content to the smaller size required to fit a large page.

Older versions of Firefox also don't support media queries; if this browser is important to your target audience, research JavaScript methods for making style sheets available.

5. **Below the final link element, enter the following conditional comment for IE users:**
   <!--[if lt IE 9]>
   <link rel="stylesheet" type="text/css" media="screen" href="lakeland2.css" />
   <![endif]-->

   Versions of Internet Explorer prior to 9 don't support media queries. This conditional comment provides a generic link to the main style sheet for users of these browsers. Figure O-6 shows the revised code for the document's head section.

6. **Save your work, then if possible, publish the Web page and open it with a mobile device**

   Figure O-7 shows the page on a handheld device with a display width of 480 px.

viewport element
ensures browser
window size
is correctly
identified

```
<meta name="viewport" content="width=device-width" />
<title>Lakeland Reeds Bed &amp; Breakfast</title>
<link rel="stylesheet" type="text/css" media="only screen and (min-device-width: 1025px)" href="lakeland2.css" />
<link rel="stylesheet" type="text/css" media="only screen and (max-device-width: 1024px)" href="llmobile.css" />
<link rel="stylesheet" type="text/css" media="print" href="llprint.css" />
<link rel="shortcut icon" href="favicon.ico" />
<!--[if lt IE 9]>
  <link rel="stylesheet" type="text/css" media="screen" href="lakeland2.css" />
<![endif]-->
<style type="text/css">
```

lakeland2.
css style
sheet is
loaded when
device width
is at least
1025 px

lakeland2.css style sheet is
loaded automatically for
older versions of IE

llmobile.css style sheet is
loaded when device width
is no greater than 1024 px

FIGURE O-7: **Mobile display using conditional style sheet**

Implementing style sheets for other types of displays

Media queries are widely used to create alternate layouts for small screens. However, this is not their only application. At the same time that the use of handheld devices to access the Web is exploding, users of desktop computers have access to increasingly large monitors. You can also use media queries to change the way your Web pages are displayed in browser windows over a certain size, accommodating the capabilities and limits of these dimensions. For instance, you may reduce a standard three-column layout to a single column for handheld devices but progressively enhance it to create a four-column layout for larger displays.

Creating a Mobile-Specific Layout

Adapting the layout of your Web site for mobile devices is usually the quickest, easiest way to make your site available in a mobile-friendly format. However, creating a separate set of HTML and CSS documents specifically for mobile users is the best way to account for the unique limitations and special capabilities of mobile devices. ▓▓▓▓▓ While your conditional styles hide the large image on the index.html page for mobile users, the file is still downloaded, slowing page loading time. You create a mobile-optimized version of the page that excludes this image and incorporates a hideable nav bar to free up space on small screens.

STEPS

QUICK TIP

The files for mobile pages are located separately from their main Web sites and often have their own URLs.

1. **Return to** index.html **in your text editor, save a copy of the file to the** Unit O/Unit/mobile **directory, then repeat for** llmobile.css

2. **In** index.html, **delete the** figure **element and its contents, then in** llmobile.css, **delete the** figcaption **and** figure **style rules**

   The figure element and related styles will not be downloaded for this version of the site.

3. **In** index.html, **delete the** h1 **element that belongs to the** desktop **class along with its contents, remove the code** class=mobile **from the remaining** h1 **element, then cut and paste the** nav **element and its contents so they are directly above the** h1 **element**

4. **Remove the conditional styles for IE from the head section, then remove the embedded style sheet from the head section**

   This code is unnecessary for users of mobile browsers.

5. **In the** link **element that references** llmobile.css, **change the value for the** media **attribute to "screen", delete the** link **element that references** lakeland2.css, **then add a link to the JavaScript file** scripts/llmobile.js

   Any user viewing this page will be a mobile user, so the conditional style sheet code is unnecessary. The JavaScript file contains a function to enhance the nav bar for mobile use.

6. **In the** p **element with the id** skipnav, **replace the** id **attribute and its value with the code** class="shownav", **change the value of the** href **attribute for the** a **element to** #, **add the attribute–value pair** onclick="showHideNav()" **to the** a **element, then change the paragraph text to** Show/Hide navigation

   Figure O-8 shows the completed code for index.html.

7. **In** llmobile.css, **add** display: none;, **position: absolute;, and** background: white; **to the** #mainnav **style rule**

QUICK TIP

If you've published the site and viewed it on a mobile device in previous lessons, do so here as well.

8. **Save your work, open** index.html **from the** Unit O/Unit/mobile **directory in a Web browser, narrow the browser window to approximate the size of a mobile device, then click** Show/Hide navigation

   As Figure O-9 shows, the nav bar is hidden by default and displayed when you click the link. Hiding the nav bar initially makes more room on small screens for page content users are seeking.

Embedded style
sheet and IE
conditional
comments
removed

script element
added

```
<meta name="viewport" content="width=device-width" />
<title>Lakeland Reeds Bed &amp; Breakfast</title>
<link rel="stylesheet" type="text/css" media="screen" href="llmobile.css" />
<link rel="stylesheet" type="text/css" media="print" href="llprint.css" />
<link rel="shortcut icon" href="favicon.ico" />
<script src="scripts/modernizr-1.6.min.js"></script>
<script src="scripts/llmobile.js"></script>
</head>
<body>
    <div id="box">
        <p class="shownav"><a href="#" onclick="showHideNav()">Show/Hide navigation</a></p>
        <nav id="mainnav">
```

link element
for desktop
style sheet
removed,
along with
conditional
code

Skip
navigation
element
edited

Desktop-specific
h1 element
removed and
nav element
repositioned
before h1
element

```
    </nav>
    <h1>
        <img src="images/llrlogo.gif" width="131" height="115" alt="" title="" />
        Lakeland Reeds Bed &amp; Breakfast
    </h1>
    <article id="content">
```

FIGURE O-9: Mobile-specific page with hideable nav bar

Nav bar hidden
by default

Clicking link
opens nav
bar only
when needed

HTML5 and CSS3

Planning compatibility for mobile Web pages

Due to the popularity of mobile phones, most of which can access Web content in some way, mobile devices vastly outnumber computers as platforms for viewing Web pages. However, in addition to screen size variations, mobile devices vary greatly in the Web content they can access and present. While current smartphones can render images and current CSS properties, they represent a tiny percentage of total mobile devices. More common are basic phones that can display basic text and enable users to select links by navigating through pages by pressing keys. If it's important that your Web pages be accessible to a wide range of mobile devices, you can create additional style sheets to target even smaller screens, removing code that's not interpreted by more basic phones in order to further reduce file size. As for any device, it's also important to test on as many phones or emulators as possible.

Decreasing Page Load Time

Ensuring that your Web pages load as quickly as possible in your users' browsers makes your site more useful to potential customers or other visitors. While many factors that affect the rate of loading, such as the speed of a user's Internet connection, are not within your control, you can optimize your Web pages in several ways to make things quicker. Speed optimization is valuable for all users of your site, but it's especially important to consider for mobile users, who are often accessing your site over slower connections. Web developers agree on many best practices for decreasing page load time; Table O-2 details a few that apply equally to larger and smaller Web sites. You've already eliminated the hidden image in the figure element from index.html. You incorporate compressed CSS and JavaScript files and delay the loading of one of your scripts to enable the page to load more efficiently.

STEPS

QUICK TIP

In addition to automated minification, you can also reduce the size of a style sheet by reviewing its content and removing any unused styles.

1. **In your text editor, open HTM O-4.css from the Unit O/Unit/mobile directory, add a CSS comment containing your first and last name and the text HTML5 Unit O, save the file as llmobile.min.css, then review its contents**

   This file is a compressed, or **minified**, version of the mobile style sheet you created. Minifying removes comments, spaces, and other characters that are useful for human readability but that don't affect the meaning of the code; the process preserves all style information from the original document. Many free programs that minify CSS and JavaScript are available to download.

2. **Return to index.html in your text editor**

3. **Locate the link element for the llmobile.css style sheet, then change the value for the href attribute to llmobile.min.css**

4. **In the script element for the llmobile.js file, change the value for the src attribute to scripts/llmobile.min.js**

   The llmobile.min.js file is a minified version of the script for hiding and showing the nav bar. Figure O-10 shows the edited elements.

5. **Select the script element for the modernizr-1.6.min.js file, then cut and paste it immediately before the closing </body> tag**

   Figure O-11 shows the new location of the Modernizr script reference. Moving the Modernizr script to the bottom of the body section enables a user's browser to render the page content before loading and applying the results of the Modernizr script. Because the Modernizr script only enhances the page contents, moving the script reference doesn't affect the functionality of your Web page. However, if you moved the llmobile.min.js reference to the bottom of the page, users would be able to click the *Show/Hide navigation* link before the script loaded, breaking its functionality; thus, that script reference needs to stay in the head section.

6. **Save your work, then if possible, publish the Web page and open it with a mobile device**

   If you have a particularly slow data connection, you may notice that the page loads more quickly.

7. **Return to index.html in your text editor, locate the link element for the llmobile.min.css style sheet, then change the value for the href attribute back to llmobile.css**

   Because minified files can be harder for humans to read, developers generally edit the original version of a file, then reminify after all changes are done.

FIGURE O-10: Links to minified files

```
    <meta name="viewport" content="width=device-width" />
    <title>Lakeland Reeds Bed &amp; Breakfast</title>
    <link rel="stylesheet" type="text/css" media="screen" href="llmobile.min.css" />
    <link rel="stylesheet" type="text/css" media="print" href="llprint.css" />
    <link rel="shortcut icon" href="favicon.ico" />
    <script src="scripts/modernizr-1.6.min.js"></script>
    <script src="scripts/llmobile.min.js"></script>
</head>
```

link and script elements changed to reference minified versions of files

FIGURE O-11: Modernizr script element moved to bottom of body section

```
    <footer>
        <p id="contact">45 Marsh Grass Ln. <img src="images/flourish.gif" width="16" height="16" alt="" /> Marble, MN 55764
<img src="images/flourish.gif" width="16" height="16" alt="" /> (218) 555-5253</p>
    </footer>
    </div>
    <script src="scripts/modernizr-1.6.min.js"></script>
</body>
</html>
```

TABLE O-2: Selected best practices for decreasing page load time

best practice	effect
minimize number of server requests	eliminates some of the time required for negotiation between user agent and Web host
minimize sizes of HTML documents and related files	reduces amount of data user must download over a potentially slow or expensive connection
compress CSS and JavaScript files	
remove hidden page components that aren't used	
implement image sprites	downloads all images in a single server request
move JavaScript to bottom of page	prioritizes page content downloading first, allowing user to view the page while enhancements are added

Testing Web page load time

Once your Web site is available on the Internet, several tools are available for testing the time it takes to load. These resources include online utilities such as Google Page Speed, as well as downloadable toolkits like Yahoo! YSlow. After you provide the URL of a page to test, these utilities provide a detailed analysis of the amount of time each page component takes to download and recommendations on how to improve the loading time of the Web page.

UNIT
O
HTML5 and CSS3

Incorporating Sprites

In addition to the steps you took in the previous lesson, one of the most commonly used methods for reducing the time it takes for your pages to load over mobile connections is to incorporate sprites. A **sprite** is a combination of simple image editing and CSS code that enables you to load multiple background images for a Web page with a single request to the server. To use sprites on a Web page, you combine all the background images into a single image, then use CSS background-image properties to control which part of the compound image is displayed in each instance. In the nav bar for the Lakeland Reeds B&B mobile site, a background image is displayed before the text for each link; the image is dark for the current page and light for each remaining link. You've been provided a file that combines these two images, and you replace the current code for the background images on the nav bar buttons with sprites.

STEPS

QUICK TIP
You can view the sprite images used on any Web page by opening the page in your browser and then disabling style sheets.

1. **In your file manager, navigate to the** Unit O/Unit/mobile/images folder, **then double-click the** fl_comb.gif **file to open it in your default image viewer**

   As Figure O-12 shows, the file combines the dark and light versions of the image.

2. **Close your image viewer, then return to** llmobile.css **in your text editor**

3. **In the** #mainnav li **style rule, change the filename in the** background-image **value to** fl_comb.gif

4. **In the** #mainnav li.currentpage **style rule, delete the** background-image **name–value pair, then add the** background-position **property with the value** –7px –52px

   Figure O-13 shows the completed code for the changed style rules.

5. **Save your work, then reload the Web page in your browser or, if possible, publish the Web site and open** index.html **with a mobile device**

6. **Click the** Show/Hide navigation **link**

   Although the navigation icons appear just as they did before, the light and dark icons are different parts of the same image file, fl_comb.gif. Incorporating this sprite decreases the number of server requests for nav bar images from two to one, further reducing the amount of time it takes for your Web page to load.

FIGURE O-13: **Nav bar style rules incorporating sprites**

```
#mainnav li {
    display: inline-block;
    list-style-type: none;
    padding: 0.25em 0.25em 0.25em 1.5em;
    margin: 0.25em 0;
    background: #B8944D;
    background-image: url(images/fl_comb.gif);
    background-position: -7px -4px;
    background-repeat: no-repeat;
    position: relative;
    -webkit-border-radius: 10px;
    -moz-border-radius: 10px;
    border-radius: 10px;
    border-bottom: 2px solid #666;
    border-right: 2px solid #777;
    }
#mainnav li.currentpage {
    background-position: -7px -52px;
    background-repeat: no-repeat;
    }
```

Filename changed to name of combined image

background-position added to show icon at bottom of combined image file

Compressing and resizing images

While sprites work only for background images, you can implement other techniques to optimize the balance between image size and download speed for other images in your Web pages. It can be tempting to use the largest available size for an image and scale it down to fit the browser window using @media rules or style sheets; however, this technique requires all browsers, even those using mobile connections, to download huge files. A more efficient solution is to create multiple versions of an image at the sizes and resolutions that your Web page targets and load only the appropriate image for each device. Online services are also available that resize images for you on the fly as users load your pages.

HTML5 and CSS3

Implementing Geolocation

Mobile devices can be used in a wide range of places. Some of the most exciting mobile-specific code takes advantage of this fact to provide information relevant to a user's current location. These features rely on the HTML5 **geolocation** objects and methods, which enable you to obtain and work with a user's precise location. You can use geolocation information to calculate distances, display relevant maps, or provide other information that pertains to a user's location. You add a function for mobile users that calculates and displays their current distance from the B&B.

STEPS

1. **Return to index.html in your text editor, then just above the** footer **element, add opening and closing tags for an** aside **element with the id** visitus

2. **Within the** aside **element, enter** <p>You're <span id="distance">0</span> mi from Lakeland Reeds. Come visit!</p>

   You'll use a script to change the text of the *distance* element based on the user's location.

3. **Return to** llmobile.css **in your text editor, then create a style rule based on the id** visitus **that sets** display **to** none

   As a result of this rule, the aside element you created will not be displayed by default. You'll use a script to make it visible only if you're able to collect geolocation data from a user's browser.

4. **Open the file** HTM O-5.js **from the** Unit O/Unit/mobile/scripts **folder**

   This file contains a function that calculates distance in miles between two sets of geographic coordinates.

QUICK TIP

As in a CSS file, text following /* and preceding */ is treated as a comment in a JavaScript file.

5. **At the top of the file, type** /*, **type your name followed by** HTML Illustrated, Unit O, **type** */, **then save the file with the name** distancecalc.js **to the same folder**

6. **At the bottom of the document, insert a blank line, enter the code shown in Figure O-14, then save your work**

   In the second line of code, the *getCurrentPosition* method of the *geolocation* object tries to get location information for the current device; if successful, it returns that information as a *position* object. The next line makes the *visitus* element visible only if a position is returned. The code that follows calls the *calculateDistance* function, passing along the *latitude* and *longitude* coordinate attributes from the *position* object.

7. **Return to** index.html **in your text editor, insert a blank line just above the closing** </body> **tag, then enter the script reference**
   <script src="scripts/distancecalc.js"></script>

   This script doesn't immediately affect your content, so you reference it at the bottom of the page to enable the rest of the page to load first. Figure O-15 shows the new HTML code.

8. **Save your work, then reload the Web page in your browser or, if possible, publish the Web site and open** index.html **with a mobile device**

TROUBLE

You may need to wait several seconds for the text containing the calculated distance to be displayed.

9. **If necessary, click the OK or Allow button to allow access to your location**

   As Figure O-16 shows, in a browser that supports geolocation a line of text containing your calculated distance from Marble, MN is displayed above the footer.

FIGURE O-14: Code using geolocation objects and methods

```
window.onload = function() {
  navigator.geolocation.getCurrentPosition (function (position) {
    document.getElementById ('visitus').style.display = 'block';
    document.getElementById ('distance').innerHTML =
      calculateDistance(position.coords.latitude, position.coords.longitude);
  });
};
```

FIGURE O-15: Reference to geolocation script added to bottom of file

Inserted script
element loads
distancecalc.js

```
      </footer>
    </div>
    <script src="scripts/modernizr-1.6.min.js"></script>
    <script src="scripts/distancecalc.js"></script>
  </body>
</html>
```

FIGURE O-16: Distance calculated based on user's current position

Calculated value
varies based on
user's distance
from fixed
geographical point

Show/Hide navigation

Lakeland Reeds Bed & Breakfast

Lakeland Reeds is a rustic bed and breakfast on Twin Lakes near rural Marble, Minnesota. Convenient to US 2 and 169, the fresh air and quiet make for an ideal weekend escape from the rush of city life.

You're 1612 mi from Lakeland Reeds. Come visit!

45 Marsh Grass Ln. ⚘ Marble, MN 55764 ⚘ (218) 555-5253

Displaying maps based on geolocation data

In addition to calculating distance, you can put geolocation data to many other uses. One of the most common is to embed a map showing the user's current location, with the option of providing directions to a destination. Adding an interactive map to a Web page requires first selecting a third party map provider, such as Google or MapQuest. Before you start generating content, most providers require you to create an account and obtain an **API key**, which is a unique string that links the map-related requests from your Web site to your account with the provider. After obtaining this key, you can use the resources on the provider's Web site to create and integrate your interactive content.

Optimizing a Mobile Site for Search Engines

As with a standard Web site for desktop users, you can take steps to optimize a mobile Web site for search engines. Many aspects of search engine optimization (SEO) for mobile sites mirror those you've already learned, including making your pages indexable and submitting a sitemap to relevant search engines. SEO for mobile also includes a few unique practices, including setting server configuration options that vary depending on your Web server setup and ensuring that mobile and non-mobile pages link to each other. ████ As you prepare to finalize your first mobile page for the Lakeland Reeds Web site, you add links that enable mobile users to open the non-mobile version of the page and vice versa.

1. **Return to index.html in your text editor**

2. **Below the footer element, add a paragraph element with the id mobilelink, containing the text Switch to desktop site**

3. **Link the text in the mobilelink element using the href value ../index.html**

   In a relative path, .. indicates the parent directory; thus, this link points to the desktop version of index.html, which is located in the parent directory.

4. **Save your work, then in llmobile.css, add a style rule based on the mobilelink id selector that aligns text on the right and sets padding to 0.25 em on all sides**

   Figure O-17 shows the completed code for index.html and llmobile.css.

5. **Save your work, close all open files in your text editor, then open index.html and lakeland2.css from the Unit O/Unit folder**

   These are the non-mobile versions of the Web site that you worked on earlier in the unit.

6. **In index.html, repeat Step 2 to add the text Switch to mobile site, then link the text in the mobilelink element using the href value mobile/index.html**

7. **Save your work, then in lakeland2.css, add a style rule based on the mobilelink id selector that aligns text on the right and sets padding to 0.25 em on all sides**

   Because the mobile and desktop versions of the site use different style sheets, you've added this rule to both. Figure O-18 shows the completed code for the desktop version of index.html and for lakeland2.css.

8. **Save your work, reload the desktop version in your browser or, if possible, publish the mobile Web site and open index.html with a mobile device, then if necessary, click the OK or Allow button to allow access to your location**

   Figure O-19 shows the *Switch to desktop site* link in a mobile browser.

A print style sheet for a mobile site can be the same as the desktop version, because standard-size printer paper doesn't require the same small layout as a mobile device.

9. **Scroll to the bottom of the Web page, then click the Switch to desktop site or Switch to mobile site link**

   The version of the site that's not optimized for your device size opens.

```
        </footer>
        <p id="mobilelink"><a href="../index.html">Switch to desktop site</a></p>
    </div>
    <script src="scripts/modernizr-1.6.min.js"></script>
```

```
#mobilelink {
  text-align: right;
  padding: 0.25em;
  }
```

FIGURE O-18: **HTML and CSS code for mobile site link**

```
        </footer>
        <p id="mobilelink"><a href="mobile/index.html">Switch to mobile site</a></p>
    </div>
```

```
#mobilelink {
  text-align: right;
  padding: 0.25em;
  }
```

FIGURE O-19: **Switch to desktop site link**

Show/Hide navigation

Lakeland Reeds Bed & Breakfast

Lakeland Reeds is a rustic bed and breakfast on Twin Lakes near rural Marble, Minnesota. Convenient to US 2 and 169, the fresh air and quiet make for an ideal weekend escape from the rush of city life.

You're 1612 mi from Lakeland Reeds. Come visit!

45 Marsh Grass Ln. ⚜ Marble, MN 55764 ⚜ (218) 555-5253

Switch to desktop site

Link gives users option to view full version of site and lets search engines know how the current page corresponds to the desktop site

Avoiding the appearance of cloaking

To ensure that you're not trying to artificially influence the placement of your pages in search results, search engines such as Google take extra steps when crawling a site to verify that the content shown to a crawler is the same as that made available to a browser. Configuring a site so different content goes to crawlers and to browsers is known as cloaking; if detected, this practice can get a page or site excluded totally from search engine results. Some search engines use different bots to index mobile and non-mobile sites; because servers can be configured to make mobile pages available to mobile devices and desktop pages available to non-mobile devices, it's possible to mistakenly create the impression of cloaking if, for example, all bots are automatically directed to the desktop pages. To ensure that your site doesn't appear to be cloaked, research the crawler names for search engines that you want to index your content and ensure that your robots.txt file directs mobile bots to mobile content and desktop bots to desktop content.

Practice

Concepts Review

For current SAM information, including versions and content details, visit SAM Central (http://www.cengage.com/samcentral). If you have a SAM user profile, you may have access to hands-on instruction, practice, and assessment of the skills covered in this unit. Since various versions of SAM are supported throughout the life of this text, check with your instructor for the correct instructions and URL/Web site for accessing assignments.

Refer to the code shown in Figure O-20.

FIGURE O-20

a

```
<meta name="viewport" content="width=device-width" />
<title>Lakeland Reeds Bed &amp; Breakfast</title>
<link rel="stylesheet" type="text/css" media="only screen and (min-device-width: 1025px)" href="lakeland2.css" />
<link rel="stylesheet" type="text/css" media="only screen and (max-device-width: 1024px)" href="llmobile.css" />
<link rel="stylesheet" type="text/css" media="print" href="llprint.css" />
<link rel="shortcut icon" href="favicon.ico" />
```

e

```
<h1 class="desktop">
    <a href="index.html"><img src="images/lakeland.gif" width="664" height="180"
       alt="Lakeland Reeds Bed and Breakfast" title="" /></a>
</h1>
<h1 class="mobile">
    <img src="images/llrlogo.gif" width="131" height="115" alt="" title="" />
    Lakeland Reeds Bed & Breakfast
</h1>
```

d

```
    </footer>
    <p id="mobilelink"><a href="../index.html">Switch to desktop site</a></p>
</div>
<script src="scripts/modernizr-1.6.min.js"></script>
<script src="scripts/distancecalc.js"></script>
</body>
</html>
```

c

b

1. Which item is positioned to allow main page content to load more quickly?
2. Which item reduces overall page load time for mobile users?
3. Which item makes different style sheets available depending on the device opening the page?
4. Which item provides important information for search engine optimization?
5. Which item specifies that the width of the content should match the width of the device?

Match each term with the statement that best describes it.

6. minified
7. media query
8. sprite
9. @media rule
10. geolocation
11. conditional style sheet

a. a style rule that incorporates one or more media types

b. a conditional statement that you can include in an @media rule

c. style sheets specified using media queries within link elements to indicate which style sheet browsers should load in a given situation

d. term that describes a style sheet or script file from which comments, spaces, and other characters that don't affect the meaning of the code have been removed

e. a combination of simple image editing and CSS code that enables you to load multiple background images for a Web page with a single request to the server

f. the type of objects and methods that enable you to obtain and work with a user's precise location

Select the best answer from the list of choices.

12. Why do navigation elements for mobile users need to be larger than those for desktop users?

- **a.** Because mobile data connections are slower
- **b.** To replace larger desktop images
- **c.** Because mobile data is more expensive
- **d.** Because touchscreen users interact using blunt fingertips

13. Why is it important to minimize the file sizes and use of images on mobile Web pages?

- **a.** To ensure page content fits on different size screens
- **b.** Because it's more challenging to reliably select small Web page elements with a finger press
- **c.** Because mobile data connections are generally slower and more expensive
- **d.** Because the browser built into a given mobile device generally cannot adjust Web content for the display of the device

14. Which of the following enables you to check features of the browser opening a Web page and to apply style rules based on requirements you set?

- **a.** media queries
- **b.** sprites
- **c.** geolocation
- **d.** touchscreens

15. Which of the following is the best way to account for the unique limitations and special capabilities of mobile devices?

- **a.** creating a single Web page that adapts to multiple devices
- **b.** creating a mobile-specific layout
- **c.** making all Web pages as simple as possible
- **d.** removing all images from your Web pages

16. What's the advantage of moving presentational script elements to the bottom of a Web page?

- **a.** avoids script errors
- **b.** makes page compatible with browsers that don't support scripts
- **c.** prioritizes page content downloading first, allowing users to view the page while enhancements are added
- **d.** optimizes the Web page for search engines

17. What's the advantage of implementing sprites in a Web page?

- **a.** downloads all images in a single server request
- **b.** reduces amount of data users must download
- **c.** prioritizes page content downloading first
- **d.** optimizes the Web page for search engines

Skills Review

1. Apply @media rules

- **a.** In your text editor, open HTM O-6.html from the Unit O/Review folder where you store your Data Files, insert a blank line before the closing body tag, insert a paragraph element containing your first and last name and the text **HTML5 Unit O, Skills Review**, save it as **location.html**, use CSS comments to add the same information to HTM O-7.css, then save it as **bigj.css**.
- **b.** In location.html, locate the h1 element near the top of the body section, change the id value to **desktoplogo**, then create a new h1 element beneath the existing one and specify an id of **mobilelogo**. Within the new element, add an image element that references **images/big-js-pizza-sm.gif**, set width and height to **84 px**, and set the alt and title attributes to empty values. Link the image to the file **index.html**, then following the closing </a> tag but before the closing </h1> tag, add the text **Big J's Deep Dish Pizza**.
- **c.** Save your work, return to bigj.css, then create a rule for the mobilelogo element that sets **display** to **none** and **padding** to **20px 0 50px**. Add an @media rule to the bottom of the file for devices with screens no wider than 1024 px that sets display to **none** for the desktoplogo element and that sets display to block for the mobilelogo element.
- **d.** In the h1 style rule, add code to set the color of h1 text to **red**.
- **e.** If possible, publish the Web page along with its supporting files, then preview it on a mobile device.

2. Implement conditional style sheets

- **a.** In your text editor, reopen HTM O-7.css from the Unit O/Review folder, add a CSS comment containing your first and last name and the text **HTML5 Unit O**, save the file as **bigj2.css**, repeat to save HTM O-8.css as **bjmobile.css**, then examine the contents of bjmobile.css.

...on.html, edit the link element for bigj.css so it references **bigj2.css** instead, then change the value of the ...attribute to apply to devices with screens and with minimum device widths of **1025 px**.

...below the link element for bigj2.css, add a link element that loads **bjmobile.css** for devices that have screens and maximum device widths of **1024 px**.

d. Add a viewport meta element that sets the width of content equal to the **device width**.

e. Below the final link element, enter the following conditional comment for IE users:

```
<!--[if lt IE 9]>
<link rel="stylesheet" type="text/css" media="screen" href="bigj2.css" />
<![endif]-->
```

f. In bigj2.css, add a style rule for the mobilelogo element that sets display to **none**.

g. Save your work, then if possible, publish the Web page and open it with a mobile device.

3. **Create a mobile-specific layout**

a. Return to location.html in your text editor, save a copy of the file to the Unit O/Review/mobile directory, then repeat for bjmobile.css.

b. In location.html, delete the h1 element with the id desktoplogo along with its contents. Remove the conditional styles for IE from the head section.

c. In the link element that references bjmobile.css, change the value for the media attribute to **"screen"**, delete the link element that references bigj2.css, then add a link to the JavaScript file **scripts/bjmobile.js**.

d. In the p element with the id skipnav, change the id value to **shownav**, change the value of the href attribute for the a element to **#**, add the attribute–value pair **onclick="showHideNav()"** to the a element, then change the paragraph text to **Show/Hide navigation**.

e. In bjmobile.css, add **display: none;**, **position: absolute;**, and **background: black;** to the #mainnav style rule. Change the #skipnav selector to **#shownav**.

f. Save your work, open location.html from the Unit O/Review/mobile directory in a Web browser, narrow the browser window to approximate the size of a mobile device, then click Show/Hide navigation.

4. **Decrease page load time**

a. In your text editor, open HTM O-9.css from the Unit O/Review/mobile directory, add a CSS comment containing your first and last name and the text **HTML5 Unit O, Skills Review**, save the file as **bjmobile.min.css**, then review its contents.

b. Return to location.html in your text editor.

c. Locate the link element for the bjmobile.css style sheet, then change the value for the href attribute to **bjmobile.min.css**.

d. In the script element for the bjmobile.js file, change the value for the src attribute to **scripts/bjmobile.min.js**.

e. Select the script element for the modernizr-1.6.min.js file, then cut and paste it immediately before the closing </body> tag.

f. Save your work, then if possible, publish the Web page and open it with a mobile device.

g. Return to location.html in your text editor, locate the link element for the bjmobile.min.css style sheet, then change the value for the href attribute back to **bjmobile.css**.

5. **Incorporate sprites**

a. In your file manager, navigate to the Unit O/Review/mobile/images folder, then double-click the stars.png file to open it in your default image viewer. Close your image viewer, then return to bjmobile.css in your text editor.

b. In the #mainnav li style rule, change the filename in the background-image value to **stars.png**.

c. In the #mainnav li.currentpage style rule, delete the background-image name–value pair, then add the **background-position** property with the value **2px -187px**.

d. Save your work, then reload the Web page in your browser or, if possible, publish the Web page and open it with a mobile device.

e. Click the Show/Hide navigation link and verify that the stars appear as they did before implementing the sprite.

Skills Review (continued)

6. Implement geolocation

a. Return to location.html in your text editor, then beneath the Queen's Park h3 element, insert a blank line beneath the line containing the city and province. Add opening and closing tags for a span element with the id **geo1**. Within the span element, insert a line break element followed by the text **0 km away**. Enclose the number 0 within another span element with the id **distance1**.

b. Repeat Step a to add elements with the ids **geo2** and **distance 2** beneath the St. Clair heading, and **geo3** and **distance3** beneath the Dundas heading.

c. Return to bjmobile.css in your text editor, then create a style rule for the geo1, geo2, and geo3 elements that sets display to **none** and font weight to **bold**.

d. Open the file distancecalc.js from the Unit O/Review/mobile/scripts folder and examine the code. (*Note*: The script code has been provided for you.)

e. Return to location.html in your text editor, insert a blank line just above the closing </body> tag, then enter a script reference to the **scripts/distancecalc.js** file.

f. Save your work, then reload the Web page in your browser or, if possible, publish the Web page and open it with a mobile device.

g. If necessary, click the OK or Allow button to allow access to your location and verify that the calculated distance to each of the three locations is displayed on the Web page.

7. Optimize a mobile site for search engines

a. Return to location.html in your text editor.

b. Below the footer element, add a paragraph element with the id **mobilelink** and containing the text **Switch to desktop site**.

c. Link the text in the mobilelink element to the desktop version of the location.html file. (*Hint*: Use .. to move to the parent directory in the path to the linked page.)

d. Save your work, then in bjmobile.css, add a style rule based on the mobilelink id selector that aligns text on the **right** and sets padding to **0.25 em** on all sides.

e. Save your work, close all open files in your text editor, then open location.html and bigj2.css from the Unit O/Review folder.

f. In location.html, repeat Step b to add the text **Switch to mobile site**, then link the text in the mobilelink element to the location.html file in the mobile folder.

g. Save your work, then in bigj2.css, add a style rule based on the mobilelink id selector that aligns text on the **right** and sets padding to **0.25 em** on all sides.

h. Save your work, reload the desktop version in your browser or, if possible, publish the mobile Web page and open it with a mobile device, then if necessary, click the OK or Allow button to allow access to your location. Figure O-21 shows the completed mobile site on a handheld device.

i. Scroll to the bottom of the Web page, then click the Switch to desktop site or Switch to mobile site link.

FIGURE O-21

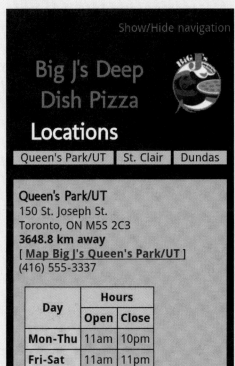

HTML5 and CSS3

ndent Challenge 1

the Spotted Wren Garden Center, Sarah Nguyen, would like you to adapt the current content of the store's separate mobile site. She'd like you to start by creating a mobile version of the home page.

a. In your text editor, open HTM O-10.html from the Unit O/IC1 folder where you store your Data Files. Insert a blank line before the closing body tag, insert a paragraph element containing your first and last name and the text **HTML5 Unit O, Independent Challenge 1**, then save it as **index.html**. Repeat to use CSS comments to add the same information to HTM O-11.css and save it as **spotwren.css**. Open index.html in your browser and review the layout of the page. Save a copy of index.html and spotwren.css to the Unit O/IC1/mobile folder; these are the files you'll edit in this Independent Challenge.

b. In index.html, add a viewport meta element that sets the width of content equal to the **device width**. Delete the div element containing the img element that references swlogo_r.jpg. Edit the remaining img element in the h1 element to reference **swlogo_mob.gif**, which measures 87px × 68px. Add the text **Spotted Wren Garden Center** after the img element within the h1 element, then in the style sheet set the h1 background to **yellow** and add a style rule that floats images within h1 elements on the left.

c. Within the article element, delete the figure element and its contents. Edit spotwren.css to remove the background image from the body element. Save your work, then open index.html from the mobile folder in your browser and note the effect of your changes.

d. Edit spotwren.css to remove the width property from the element with the id box. From the article and aside elements, remove the width, position, and left properties, along with any border properties. For the element with the id tagline and elements in the class taglinesub, remove text alignment settings.

e. Edit index.html to move the nav bar above the logo. Edit the text of the element with the id skipnav to read **Show/Hide navigation**. Change the id value to **shownav**. Change the link target to #. Add the event handler **onclick="showHideNav()"** to the a element. Above the closing head tag, add a reference to the JavaScript file **scripts/swmobile.js**.

f. In spotwren.css, change the selector for the #skipnav style rule to **#shownav**. Remove the position, right, and z-index values, then add a property to right-align text. Edit the rule for the mainnav element to set display to **none**, position to **absolute**, and z-index to **6**. Save your work, reload the page in your browser, then test the Show/Hide navigation link to verify that it displays and hides the nav bar.

g. In index.html, below the footer element, add a paragraph with the id **mobilelink** containing the text **Switch to desktop site**. Link the text to the desktop version of index.html file. Add a style rule to spotwren.css that aligns text on the **right** and sets **padding** to **0.25 em** on all sides. Save your work, then repeat to add a **Switch to mobile site** link to the desktop version of index.html and assign it the same styles.

h. Save your work, reload the desktop version in your browser or, if possible, publish the mobile Web page and open it with a mobile device, then test the Switch to desktop site and Switch to mobile site links. Figure O-22 shows the completed mobile site on a handheld device.

i. Close your browser, then close your text editor.

FIGURE O-22

Adapting Your Web Site for Mobile Devices

Independent Challenge 2

As you continue your work on the Web site for the Murfreesboro Recreational Soccer League, you want to adapt the site for mobile devices. You create an alternative style sheet for handheld devices and implement a sprite to minimize server requests for the nav bar images.

a. Open HTM O-12.html from the Unit O/IC2 folder in your text editor. Insert a blank line before the closing body tag, insert a paragraph element containing your first and last name and the text **HTML5 Unit O, Independent Challenge 2**, then save the file as **index.html**. Repeat to save HTM O-13.html as **started.html** and HTM O-14.html as **schedule.html**. Use a CSS comment to add the same information to HTM O-15.css and save it as **mrsl.css**.

b. Open index.html in your browser, then use the nav bar links to view all the pages in the site. Create a copy of mrsl.css and name it **mrslmob.css**. In the new style sheet, remove the fixed width from the elements with the ids box and skipnav, remove the background image from the body element, and prevent figure elements and the element with the id skipnav from being displayed. Remove the div#red div#blue style rule. Create a rule for h3 elements that center-aligns text. Add code to the table style rule that center-aligns these elements.

c. In index.html, edit the media attribute of the link element for mrsl.css to apply to devices with screens and with minimum device widths of **1025 px**. Add a link element that loads **mrslmob.css** for devices that have **screens** and **maximum device widths** of 1024 px. In index.html, add the same media rule to the embedded style sheet. Add a viewport meta element that sets the width of content equal to the **device width**. Add a conditional comment for users of Internet Explorer versions previous to 9 that sets mrsl.css as the style sheet for all devices with screens. Copy your changes to started.html and schedule.html.

d. Change the display of #mainnav li elements to **inline-block** and increase the top and bottom padding to **0.5 em**. Change the display for the skipnav element to **none**.

e. In index.html, add the class **desktop** to the aside element containing the logo. (*Hint:* You can give an element multiple classes by separating the class names with spaces.) Add a style to the mobile style sheet so elements within the desktop class aren't displayed.

f. Replace the red and green soccer ball images in the nav bar with a sprite using **images/soccer-balls.gif**, experimenting as necessary to find the correct background position. Figure O-23 shows the Getting Started page on a mobile device.

Advanced Challenge Exercise

- Use a search engine to locate a free online CSS minifier. Select and copy the contents of your mobile style sheet, paste them into the input box on the minifier page, then follow the instructions to minify your content, exploring any available options.
- Copy the resulting code, replace your existing style sheet code with the minified code, then save your style sheet as **mrslmob.min.css**.
- Edit the code in all three Web documents to reference the minified style sheet file you created.

g. Save your work, then, if possible, publish the mobile Web page and open it with a mobile device. View all the pages and make any necessary edits to the files.

h. Close your browser, then close your text editor.

FIGURE O-23

Murfreesboro Recreational Soccer League

Part of the North American Recreational Soccer Association

Getting Started

The MRSL is open to players of all levels who want to play soccer in a relaxed, friendly environment. Even if you've never played soccer before, the MRSL is a great place to start.

To get a feel for our league, we recommend you call us at the number below or stop by Davies Sporting Goods to talk to one or our coordinators and get the details on our next all-team practice or workshop day. Then come kick around the ball with us and meet

Xtremer/Shutterstock

Independent Challenge 3

Many of the clients of the Hotel Natoma navigate during their stays using smartphones. You create a mobile version of the hotel's Web site and incorporate geolocation information to calculate distances to local destinations.

a. Open HTM O-16.html from the Unit O/IC3 folder in your text editor. Insert a blank line before the closing body tag, insert a paragraph element containing your first and last name and the text **HTML5 Unit O, Independent Challenge 3**, then save the file as **nearby.html**. Use a CSS comment to add the same information to HTM O-17. css and save it as **natoma.css**. Save copies of nearby.html and natoma.css to the Unit O/IC3/mobile folder, then rename natoma.css in the mobile folder as **hnmobile.css**.

b. Change the style sheet link in the mobile version of the Web page from natoma.css to **hnmobile.css**. Delete the figure element and its content from the Web page. Add a viewport meta element that sets the width of content equal to the **device width**.

c. In hnmobile.css, remove the fixed width from the body element. Change the display of list items in the nav bar to **inline-block** and add a bottom margin of **5px**. Change the selector for the #skipnav style rule to **#shownav**, then change the selector for the #skipnav a style rule to **#shownav a**. Replace all properties in the #shownav style rule with properties that align text on the **right** and set padding to **5px**. Remove all #skipnav selectors and associated pseudo-classes from the link-related rules at the bottom of the style sheet. Remove the borders and rounded corners from the #box and footer elements.

d. In nearby.html, change the id for the skipnav element to **shownav**. Replace the logo image with the file **images/hn.gif** accompanied by the text **Hotel Natoma**. Move the nav bar above the h1 element. Incorporate the show-HideNav() function in the file scripts/hnmobile.js to show and hide the nav bar when clicking a link, and modify the text and code of the Skip Navigation link for this purpose. Add a style property that keeps the nav bar from being displayed when the page is first loaded.

e. Immediately before the closing </li> tag for the first item in the What's Nearby list, add a span element with the id **geo1** containing a space; an opening parenthesis; a span element with the id **distance1** containing the number 0; a space; the text **mi**; and a closing parenthesis. Repeat for the remaining three list items, using the span ids **geo2** and **distance2**, etc. Add a style rule to the style sheet that turns off display of #geo1 through #geo4 when the page loads. Add a link to the file **scripts/distancecalc.js** in the head section of the Web document. Save your work and test in a browser or by publishing and opening on a mobile device. As shown in Figure O-24, the distance to each attraction should appear in parentheses after its name.

Advanced Challenge Exercise

- If you're able to publish your work to the Web, publish the mobile version of the Hotel Natoma Web site.
- In your browser, open **http://code.google.com/speed/page-speed/**. Read the overview and instructions for using Google Page Speed.
- Click the Page Speed Online link or open **http://pagespeed.googlelabs.com/**. Enter the URL for your mobile version of nearby.html. Click the arrow adjacent to the Analyze Performance button, click Get Mobile Suggestions if present, then click the button.
- Explore the page that opens and note any bottlenecks in your site's performance.
- In nearby.html, move the script element for scripts/distancecalc.js from the head section to immediately before the closing body tag. Save your work, republish your Web site, open Google Page Speed in another tab, then repeat the Google Page Speed test. Compare the results of the two tests and notice the effect, if any, of loading the script after the page content.

f. Close your browser, then close your text editor.

FIGURE O-24

Show/Hide navigation

HN Hotel Natoma

What's Nearby

- Asian Art Museum (4334.2 mi)
- City Hall (4333.6 mi)
- Heart of the City Farmer's Market (4333.2 mi)
- Cable Car turnaround (4332.6 mi)

568 Natoma St. • San Francisco, CA 94103
• (415) 555-8378

Real Life Independent Challenge

This assignment builds on the personal Web site you have worked on in previous units. You'll create a mobile version of your Web site.

a. Copy your Web site files to the Unit O/RLIC folder on the drive and folder where you store your Data Files.

b. Add a viewport meta element to each of your Web pages to set the width of content equal to device width, then if possible, publish your Web site and view each page using a mobile device. Note any elements that don't fit or barely fit on the screen, as well as any large images or other elements.

c. Decide whether to use conditional style sheets or to create a separate mobile site. Create the folders, files, and links necessary to set up the approach you choose.

d. Make at least two changes to your site to improve load time and performance for mobile users; changes may include replacing images with smaller versions, minifying CSS files, moving script links to the ends of HTML files, or incorporating sprites for background images.

e. If your site incorporates location information and the site is already published with its own domain name, use a search engine to explore the process of incorporating maps from a provider such as Google or MapQuest. For instance, the instructions for obtaining an API key for Google Maps are available at http://code.google.com/apis/maps/signup.html. If appropriate, incorporate a relevant map in your Web page based on each user's location. (*Hint*: You can use a search engine to find JavaScript code that's free to reuse to accomplish different geolocation tasks.)

f. If you created a separate mobile site, add links between the mobile and desktop versions of each page.

g. Close your browser, then close your text editor.

Visual Workshop

In your text editor, open the file HTM O-18.html from the Unit O/VW directory on the drive and folder where you store your Data Files, add a paragraph before the closing body tag that contains your first and last name and the text **HTML5 Unit O, Visual Workshop**, then save the file as **events.html**. Use a CSS comment to add the same information to HTM O-19.css and save it as **revision.css**. Edit the files so that a mobile device displays the Web page, as shown in Figure O-25. Save your work, then close your browser and text editor.

FIGURE O-25

Home Store History Upcoming Events
Location Readers Read

Upcoming Events

Date	Time	Description
Oct. 31	6:00pm-8:00pm	Spooky stories read aloud (for kids 2-12)
Nov. 2	12:30p-1:30p 7:00p-8:00p	Sam Miller reads from *Lunchtime Chronicles*
Nov. 3	5:30p-7:00p	Cookbook Reading Club monthly discussion
Nov. 4	5:30am-6:45am	"Fitness in the Stacks" Pilates class

412 N. 25th St.
Richmond, VA 23223
(804) 555-2565

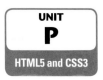

Testing and Finalizing Your Web Site

Once you finalize the content for a Web site and finish its code, you're almost ready to release it to your client or to the general public. However, before doing so, it's important to reserve some time at the end of the development process to test the site for usability, check for potential unnoticed bugs, and clean up the code. While it can be tempting to skip these steps, including them in your Web development cycle can distinguish both the Web sites you create and your work as a developer as high quality, increasing both potential visitors to your sites and referrals to you as a Web developer. As you prepare to finalize the Web site you've developed for Lakeland Reeds Bed & Breakfast, you test it and finalize the code.

OBJECTIVES

Prepare to go live with your Web site

Use HTML and CSS debugging tools

Plan usability tests

Perform browser tests

Measure performance and modeling changes

Remove unused styles

Tidy your HTML

Publish with a domain name

Preparing to Go Live with Your Web Site

Once you and your client, if relevant, are satisfied with the appearance and functionality of a Web site you've created, the final step is to publish it to a Web server in order to make it available to anyone with Web access, a step sometimes known as **going live**. Before you publish a Web site, though, it can be useful to perform a few final checks and optimizations to maximize the site's performance and to ensure that the code is as intelligible as possible, both for future revisions and for anyone who wants to understand how your design works.  As you prepare to finalize the Web site you've designed for Lakeland Reeds B&B, you review some common techniques for testing and finalizing a Web site.

The process of testing and finalizing a Web site may include the following:

- **Publishing to a testing server**

  Viewing pages directly from your local computer is sometimes the easiest way to quickly test and make changes while developing a Web site. However, it's important to transfer all the files in your Web site to a Web server and test them from a published location in order to catch any server-related problems before the site goes live. Because you don't want potential users to stumble upon the unfinished site and be frustrated by any remaining glitches, you should use a testing server, which is a Web server that's available only to you, not to all Web users, as illustrated in Figure P-1. Some large organizations have Web servers set aside for this purpose; however, for smaller-scale development, creating a password-protected folder on your main Web server can suffice. You can then publish your site to this folder and view the pages in your browser after entering the password; once you've worked out any remaining issues, you can simply transfer the files to the main directory.

- **Performing browser tests and usability tests**

  Just as you've done at each stage of development, it's important to test your final Web site using the browsers that are most common among your target audience. As Table P-1 shows, browser use can vary widely by geography; differences can also show up based on many other factors, so it's important to identify your target audience and research which browsers potential clients are most likely to be using to access your site. In addition, it's important to verify that each aspect of the site is functioning by testing all links to ensure that they open the correct targets or pages and by testing any interactive content, such as scripts and CSS pseudo-classes, to verify that it works as expected.

  In addition to doing your own testing, it can be invaluable to bring members of your target audience into the testing process. Conducting usability tests in which you ask potential users to complete common tasks and locate information on a prototype of your Web site can give you important insight into the structure and function of your site, and help you understand what, if anything, could use tweaking before you publish the site.

- **Checking for errors using Web development tools**

  A number of software tools are available to help you identify and fix errors in your Web pages. Major browsers include features that let you view the HTML and CSS code for any element on a page, as well as debug scripts. Utilities, both downloadable and online, can also help you clean up your HTML and CSS code and, if desired, minify your style sheets and scripts to reduce download times.

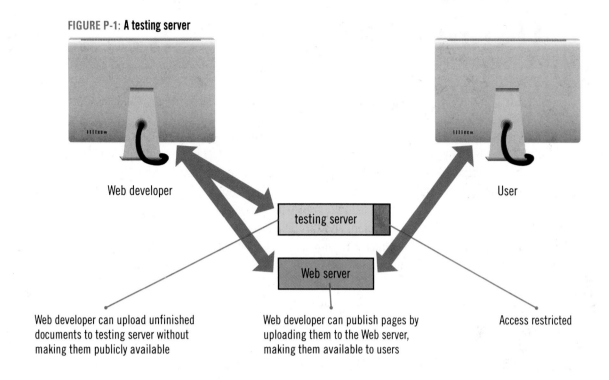

Web developer

User

testing server

Web server

Web developer can upload unfinished documents to testing server without making them publicly available

Web developer can publish pages by uploading them to the Web server, making them available to users

Access restricted

TABLE P-1: Sample browser usage statistics by percentage, July 2011

Browser	Brazil	China	United States	Worldwide
Internet Explorer	41.88	86.38	44.86	42.62
IE9	5.41	3.96	10.11	6.96
IE8	30.95	37.55	27.97	26.50
IE7	3.79	5.10	5.35	5.59
IE6	1.72	39.67	1.39	3.57
Firefox	25.94	3.19	24.71	28.07
Chrome	30.81	5.26	16.84	21.79
Safari	0.81	0.79	12.26	5.18
Opera	0.41	0.42	0.54	1.71

Source: http://gs.statcounter.com

Using HTML and CSS Debugging Tools

As you examine more closely a Web site you've been developing, you may notice errors that hadn't been obvious earlier. As you've already seen, the process of fixing errors involves identifying the element that is being displayed incorrectly, checking the HTML and/or CSS code relating to that element, making changes to the code, refreshing the page in your browser, and repeating this if necessary. Debugging tools are available for all major browsers, and these tools simplify the process of identifying bugs. These tools are built into current versions of Chrome and Safari, and can be added to Firefox by downloading an installing the free Firebug extension. Internet Explorer 9 includes a more limited set of tools. ▓▓▓▓ As you examine your Web pages, you notice a couple of small errors. You use browser debugging tools to identify the code that needs changing.

STEPS

These steps are written for Chrome, Safari, or Firefox (with Firebug extension).

1. **In your text editor, open HTM P-1.html from the Unit P/Unit folder where you store your Data Files, insert a blank line before the closing body tag, insert a paragraph element containing your first and last name and the text HTML5 Unit P, save it as index.html, repeat to save HTM P-2.html as aboutus.html, HTM P-3.html as rooms.html, and HTM P-4.html as reserve.html, then use CSS comments to add the same information to HTM P-5.css and save it as lakeland.css**

> **QUICK TIP**
>
> If you're using Firefox, you can download the free Firebug extension from getfirebug.com.

2. **Open index.html in your browser, examine the page, then use the nav bar to open each of the remaining pages and examine them**

3. **Return to reserve.html in your browser, then examine the numbered list**

   As Figure P-2 shows, the second item in the list isn't numbered.

> **QUICK TIP**
>
> In IE9, press the **F12** key, then navigate through the code tree displayed at the bottom of the browser window to the desired element; if the code tree is in a separate window, press **[Ctrl]+P** to pin it below the Web page.

4. **Right-click the second item in the numbered list, click Inspect element, then if necessary navigate through the tree to see the li elements**

   The developer tools are displayed at the bottom of the browser window with the selected element, highlighted in the code, as shown in Figure P-2. The opening <li> tag is missing before the text *Memorial Day*.

5. **Return to reserve.html in your text editor, locate the second item in the ol element, add an <li> tag before the word Memorial, save your work, then reload reserve.html in your browser**

   All the list items are now numbered.

6. **Near the bottom of the page, right-click the word Phone in the Questions section, then click Inspect element**

7. **Click the triangle before the p element preceding the one you selected**

   As Figure P-3 shows, the code for the preceding p element becomes visible. By comparing the two, you can see that the class name for the span element containing the text *Phone* is misspelled.

8. **Return to reserve.html in your text editor, locate the span element in the Questions section containing the text Phone, change the class to bold, save your work, then reload reserve.html in your browser**

   The word *Phone* is now displayed in bold.

FIGURE P-2: Using Inspect element option in Chrome

Second item in list isn't numbered

ol element highlighted in code

Second list item is not within an li element

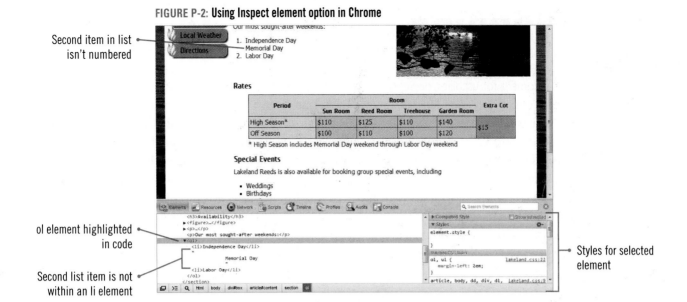

Styles for selected element

FIGURE P-3: Inspecting a span elemen

Phone label is not displayed in bold

span element highlighted in code

Second class name is misspelled

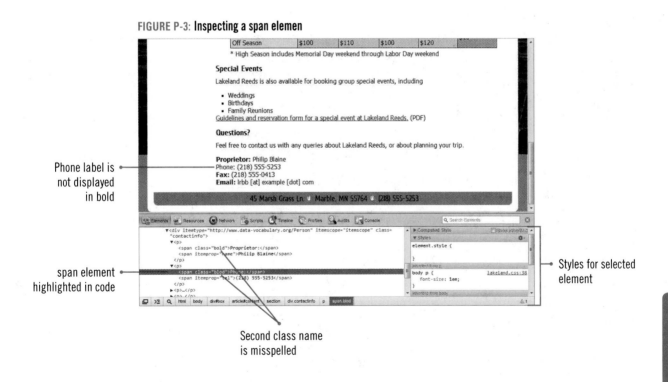

Styles for selected element

Planning Usability Tests

Planning and structuring your Web site logically is an important aspect of making it usable. The most important judgment for usability, however, is that of the site's users themselves. While the process of collecting feedback from likely users can require significant planning and energy, the information these users provide can be invaluable in making your site one that people want to use and in ensuring that the information you're publishing is as widely available as possible. To collect the best information possible from usability tests, it's important to identify questions you want all testers to answer. To ensure that your questions don't vary between testers, it's considered a good practice to create a script and to use it consistently throughout the process. Philip Blaine wants to check that the Web site conveys the impression the he is responsible and treats guests with respect, and that the business is a midrange B&B. He also wants to ensure that users can easily locate contact information, descriptions of rooms, and rates. You create a usability testing plan and script to address these questions.

STEPS

1. **Open HTM P-6.txt in your text editor, enter your first and last name on the first line, then save the file as Lakeland Test Plan.txt**
   The document includes *Feedback* and *Tasks* sections, along with two additional questions. The *Feedback* section already includes two questions asking users for general impressions.

2. **On the line for question 1b, type "Would you expect the owner of this business to be responsible?"**

3. **On the line for question 1c, type "Would you expect to be treated respectfully at this bed & breakfast?"**

4. **On the line for question 1d, type "Compared to other bed & breakfast establishments that you're familiar with, would you rank this one as low end, midrange, or high end?"**
   These questions cover Philip's queries about the impression conveyed by the site. In the Tasks section, you'll ask users to locate certain information on the site and watch whether they're able to do so, and how easily.

5. **On the line for question 2a, type "contact information", repeat for question 2b to enter "descriptions of rooms", then repeat for question 2c to enter "rates"**
   Figure P-4 shows the completed test plan.

6. **Save your work, then close Lakeland Test Plan.txt**

```
Lakeland Reeds Bed & Breakfast
Web site Testing Plan

1. Feedback
    With user viewing index.html, ask
    a. "Based only on this Web page, please give me three words that describe
this business."
    b. "Would you expect the owner of this business to be responsible?"
    c. "Would you expect to be treated respectfully at this bed & breakfast?"
    d. "Compared to other bed & breakfast establishments that you're familiar
with, would you rank this one as low end, midrange, or high end?"
    e. "Do you have any other impressions of this bed & breakfast based on
this Web page?" [If yes: "Please describe them."]

2. Tasks
    "Now, using the Web site, please locate
    a. "contact information"
    b. "descriptions of rooms"
    c. "rates"

3. "Based on this Web site, if you were looking to make a reservation at a
bed & breakfast, how likely would you be to consider Lakeland Reeds?
Definitely not, unlikely, likely, or definitely?"

4. "Do you have any other feedback about this Web site?"

"Thank you for your time and your help."
```

Performing usability tests

You can choose from several methods of performing usability tests based on your testing budget and the equipment available to you. On the high end, some larger organizations have dedicated testing facilities that may include rooms with two-way mirrors for observing testers unobtrusively, as well as computer systems configured to record and play back the keystrokes and mouse movements of testers. In a more modest testing setup, you may simply sit next to a user and write down as accurately as possible what the user does; positioning a video camera with a clear view of the screen and recording the tester's activities for later scrutiny can be a useful addition to this setup. When testing a user's ability to navigate a Web site, some developers find it easiest to print out all the pages involved in the tasks at hand, ask testers to point to the location on the page where they'd click to find certain information, then show the testers a printout of the page that would open and ask questions about it.

Performing Browser Tests

When you're preparing to publish a Web site, scrutinizing your pages on different browsers one more time is especially important. While you may not always find errors, testing your pages exhaustively on the most common user agents among your target audience helps ensure that you don't publish Web pages that display obvious errors or that don't work as expected for some of your audience members. No matter what your audience, the majority of users are likely to be using Windows; thus, if you are developing on a Mac, it's important to ensure that you have access to a Windows system for testing. ▰▰▰▰ Based on discussions with patrons over the past year, Philip believes that over 80% of his clients use Windows, and most use Internet Explorer 7 or 8 or Firefox. The remaining 20% of his clients are largely on Macs and use Safari or Firefox for Mac. You test the links and functionality on each Web page.

STEPS

These steps are written for Windows users with IE9 and Firefox, and Mac users with Safari and Firefox.

> **TROUBLE**
> IE9 is available for Windows Vista and Windows 7 but not for older versions of Windows.

1. **In Windows, open index.html in IE9, press F12 to display the developer tools, then if necessary, click Browser Mode and click Internet Explorer 9**

2. **Click the Skip navigation link, verify that it moves the browser view to the appropriate section of the page, then click your browser's Back button**

   If the visible area of the Web page remains unchanged, verify that the URL in the Address Bar shows #main at the end.

3. **Repeat Step 2 to test all the links on the Web page, then repeat this process for each of the remaining Web pages, verifying that the content of each page is displayed as expected**

   Clicking each link lets you verify that all the links work and point to the appropriate pages.

4. **Compare the nav bar buttons on rooms.html with those on other pages**

   As Figure P-5 shows, the drop shadow for the nav bar buttons is different on this Web page.

5. **Return to rooms.html in your text editor, in the head section add a script element linking to the file scripts/modernizr-1.6.min.js, then add the class no-js to the opening html tag**

   The drop shadow is different because the modernizr script hadn't been implemented on this page. Figure P-6 shows the edited code.

6. **Reload rooms.html in IE9 and verify that the nav bar drop shadows match those on other Web pages**

7. **If necessary, press F12 to display the developer tools, click Browser Mode, then click Internet Explorer 8**

   IE9 enables you to view the results of rendering a Web page in IE8 and IE7.

8. **View each page on the Web site, repeat Step 7 to change the browser mode to Internet Explorer 7, then view each page again**

> **TROUBLE**
> If necessary, explore trading computer time with a friend or colleague who has a different operating system than yours.

9. **View each page on the Web site in Firefox, then repeat on a Mac using Safari and Firefox**

FIGURE P-5: Nonstandard box shadows on Rooms page

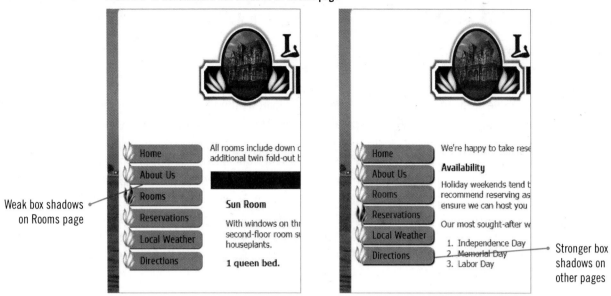

Weak box shadows
on Rooms page

Stronger box
shadows on
other pages

FIGURE P-6: Updated code for Rooms page

```
<!DOCTYPE html>
<html class="no-js">
  <head>
    <meta charset="utf-8" />
    <meta name="description" content="Lakeland Reeds Bed & Breakfast offers 4 comfortable rooms that accommodate from 2 to 5
people. All have private baths and views of Twin Lakes." />
    <title>Room selection at Lakeland Reeds Bed &amp; Breakfast</title>
    <link rel="stylesheet" type="text/css" media="screen" href="lakeland.css" />
    <link rel="stylesheet" type="text/css" media="print" href="llprint.css" />
    <link rel="shortcut icon" href="favicon.ico" />
    <!--[if lt IE 7]>
      <style type="text/css">
        #mainnav {left: 0px;}
        li img {left: -42px;}
      </style>
    <![endif]-->
    <script src="scripts/modernizr-1.6.min.js"></script>
  </head>
  <body>
    <div id="box">
      <p id="skipnav"><a href="#main">Skip navigation</a></p>
      <h1>
```

Script element referencing
Modernizr script added

no-js class added
to html element

Using automated test suites

The manual testing method used in this lesson is most realistic for smaller Web sites with few Web pages. As a site grows in size and complexity, however, you can save time and catch more errors through **automated testing**, which is a set of testing measures performed by specialized software. Some free testing services are available online, such as the W3's link checker at http://validator.w3.org/checklink. In addition, professional Web development software such

as Adobe Dreamweaver and Microsoft Expression Web include link checking options. These options check for **dead links**, which are links whose targets don't exist. For more advanced testing, you can use a configurable testing suite such as Opera Watir. Testing suites enable you to set up a series of actions that a user might take and have them executed automatically by the software, which then provides the results.

Testing and Finalizing Your Web Site

Measuring Performance and Modeling Changes

As you've seen, ensuring that your Web pages load as quickly as possible is especially important for mobile users. However, optimizing page load time improves the experience of desktop or notebook users as well. Any improvements that cause your pages to load more quickly can help avoid users becoming impatient with your site as it loads and those users then going to a different site instead. Some of the most popular browsers include tools for measuring the download speed of published Web pages and identifying bottlenecks, such as large images or objects being downloaded from remote servers. Chrome and Safari include such tools, while you can download and install extensions for Firefox and IE9 to perform these tasks. Some tools also enable you to delete, add, and edit code to preview the effects of potential changes in a browser window. You publish the Lakeland Reeds Web site to a nonpublic test server and use browser tools to access downloading and rendering statistics. You also explore possible changes by editing code in the browser.

STEPS

These steps are written for Internet Explorer and Safari (with Develop menu enabled).

QUICK TIP

Table O-2 on p. 373 details some best practices, which apply equally to desktop and to mobile Web pages, for decreasing page load time.

1. **If you have Web space available, publish the Web site, then if you're using Safari, skip to Step 3**

2. **In Internet Explorer, press F12 if necessary to open the Developer Tools, click the Network tab, click Start capturing, open or reload rooms.html in your browser from the published location, click Stop capturing, then examine the results**
   Figure P-7 shows sample page loading data for Internet Explorer.

TROUBLE

To enable the Safari Develop menu, click **Safari**, click **Preferences**, click the **Advanced** tab, then check **Show Develop menu in the menu bar**.

3. **In Safari, click Develop, click Show Web Inspector, click the Timeline tab, click the Record button ●, reload the page, then when the page is done reloading, click the Stop button ● and examine the results**
   Figure P-8 shows sample page loading data for Safari.

4. **In IE, click the CSS tab, click the list arrow next to the filename, click lakeland.css, then scroll down to the body style rule; in Safari, click Elements, then click the \<body> tag in the Web page hierarchy**
   Both browsers display all the styles for the current page. In IE, a check box is displayed next to each name–value pair; in Safari, a check box is displayed when you move the mouse pointer over a name–value pair.

5. **Uncheck the background-image name–value pair that references the background image file**
   The background image is removed from the Web page in the browser window.

QUICK TIP

CSS changes in the browser are only temporary; to make a change permanently, you must edit the style sheet in your text editor.

6. **In IE, scroll down to the background-color property; in Safari, recheck the background property**

7. **Double-click the value, delete the existing value, type steelblue;, then press [Enter]**
   As Figure P-9 shows, both browsers display the background color in place of the background image. Editing CSS in the browser gives you a quick way to explore potential changes without switching back and forth between your editor and browser.

8. **Click the Close button X for the Developer Tools or Web Inspector**

FIGURE P-7: Page loading data in IE9

Network tab lists files downloaded as part of Web page loading

Timings section shows when each item began loading and when it finished

FIGURE P-8: Page loading data in Safari

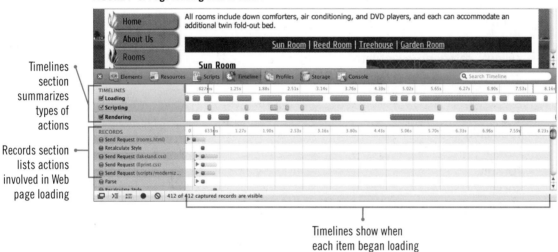

Timelines section summarizes types of actions

Records section lists actions involved in Web page loading

Timelines show when each item began loading and when it finished

FIGURE P-9: Background color changed in browser

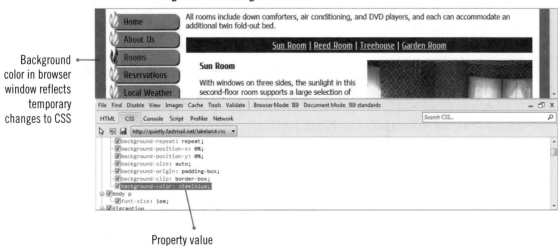

Background color in browser window reflects temporary changes to CSS

Property value changed in browser

Removing Unused Styles

While you are finalizing a Web site for publishing is a good opportunity to remove unused styles from your style sheets. As you add, change, and remove features and formatting while developing a site, you can end up with **orphaned styles**, which are style rules based on selectors that no longer apply to any elements in your Web pages. Removing orphaned styles reduces the amount of code users have to download, shrinking download time. In addition, ensuring that published code is as streamlined as possible makes it easier to work with for other developers who may perform future work on the site. ▰▰▰▰ You've identified several orphaned styles in lakeland.css left over from features and pages that Philip decided not to include in the published site. You remove these style rules and minify the style sheet to reduce the amount of time it takes for users' browser to download the CSS file.

STEPS

1. **In your text editor, return to** lakeland.css

2. **Delete the style rules based on the following selectors:**
   #instructions
   #message
   #name
   #title
   .callout, .category, .eventdate
   .contact
   .contactinfo div, .contactinfo p
   .req
   .roomlinks
   .row
   .row div
   .social
   .social img, .social iframe, .social p
   Figure P-10 shows the rules based on class selectors in the edited style sheet.

3. **Save your work, then save a copy of the file as** lakeland.min.css

QUICK TIP

To locate an online minifier, search on the phrase *free css minifier* and explore the results; once you identify a minifier to use, follow the instructions on its Web page.

4. **Use an online minifier to minify your CSS code, or minify it manually by deleting all line breaks from the file and deleting all spaces between curly braces**
   Figure P-11 shows minified code. Some minifiers make other tweaks in addition to those described, but removing spaces and line breaks is an easy way to manually minify a CSS file. While spaces aren't important in name–value pairs, deleting spaces in a selector can change its meaning.

5. **Save your work, edit the style sheet link in** rooms.html **to reference** lakeland.min.css, **publish the updated Web site if possible, then reload** rooms.html **in your browser**
   The difference in page loading time as a result of your changes may not be noticeable, but it can make a large different in a larger Web site and in conjunction with other optimizations.

TROUBLE

If the appearance of one or more pages changes significantly, use the Inspect Element option in your browser to research the applicable CSS code and make changes as necessary.

6. **Edit the style sheet link in the remaining pages, then view all Web pages in the browser and verify that the changes you made to the style sheet don't impact the appearance of the pages**

```css
.beds {
  font-weight: bold;
}
.bold {
  font-weight: bold;
}
.boxshadow #mainnav li {
  border: none;
  -webkit-box-shadow: 2px 2px 4px #000000;
  -moz-box-shadow: 2px 2px 4px #000000;
  box-shadow: 2px 2px 4px #000000;
}
.clearright {
  clear: right;
}
.cotcol {
  background: #9daecd;
  width: 15%;
}
.desc, .beds, .roomlinks {
  padding: 0;
  margin: 1em 0 0 30px;
}
.firstcol {
  background: #f1eace;
  width: 25%;
}
.rates td {
  text-align: center;
}
.rates td.season {
  text-align: left;
}
.roomcols {
  background: #aecdf4;
  width: 15%;
}
.roominfo {
  padding: 1em 0;
  clear: right;
}
.roominfo h3 {
  float: left;
  margin: 0 0 15px 30px;
}
.roominfo p {
  clear: left;
}
.roominfo p.toplink {
  clear: right;
}
.tablenote {
  width: 90%;
  margin: 0.25em auto;
}
.toplink {
  text-align: right;
  padding: 0;
  margin: 0;
}
```

FIGURE P-11: Minified CSS code

```css
@font-face{font-family:CuprumFFURegular;src:local(☺), url(fonts/Cuprum-webfont.woff) format(woff), url(fonts/Cuprum-
webfont.ttf) format(truetype), url(fonts/Cuprum-webfont.svg#webfontKLktnwy4) format(svg);font-weight:400;font-style:normal}
article,body,dd,div,dl,dt,figcaption,figure,footer,h1,h2,h3,li,nav,object,ol,p,section,table,th,td,ul{margin:0;padding:0}
article,figure,figcaption,footer,nav,section{display:block}dt,h1,h2,h3,nav,footer,th{font-family:CuprumFFURegular, georgia,
"times new roman", times, serif}ol,ul{margin-left:2em}body{width:960px;font-family:tahoma, arial, helvetica, sans-
serif;background:url(images/lake.jpg);margin:0 auto}body p{font-size:1em}figcaption
{position:absolute;bottom:0;left:0;width:100%;background:rgba(255,255,255,0.6);padding:.5em 0}figure{float:right;text-
align:center;position:relative;margin:0 0 .5em 1em}footer{clear:both;font-size:1.25em;margin-top:.5em}footer p
{background:#B8944D;text-align:center;-webkit-border-bottom-right-radius:10px;-webkit-border-bottom-left-radius:10px;-moz-
border-radius-bottomright:10px;-moz-border-radius-bottomleft:10px;border-bottom-right-radius:10px;border-bottom-left-
radius:10px;padding:.25em}h1{font-size:2.25em}h2{font-size:1.75em;margin-bottom:.5em}h3{font-size:1.25em;clear:both;margin-
bottom:.5em}img{border:none;margin:0 auto}li img{position:absolute;left:-22px;top:-8px}nav{font-size:1.25em}nav ul{margin-
left:0}table{width:90%;border-collapse:collapse;margin:0 auto}td{border:1px solid #000}th{border-bottom:1px
solid #000;background:#f1eace;padding:.25em}thead{border:1px solid #000}ul{list-style-type:square}#box
{position:relative;background:#FFF;-webkit-border-radius:10px;-moz-border-radius:10px;border-radius:10px;margin:0
auto;padding:1em}#content{display:block;margin-left:10em}#mainnav{text-
align:left;width:7em;position:absolute;left:10px;padding:.25em .25em .25em .5em}#mainnav a{text-decoration:none}#mainnav li
{list-style-type:none;background:#B8944D;position:relative;-webkit-border-top-right-radius:10px;-webkit-border-bottom-right-
radius:10px;-moz-border-radius-topright:10px;-moz-border-radius-bottomright:10px;border-top-right-radius:10px;border-bottom-
right-radius:10px;border-bottom:2px solid #666;border-right:2px solid #777;margin:.25em 0;padding:.25em .25em .25em 1em}
#mainnav ul{position:relative;top:2em;z-index:2;margin:0;padding:0}#pagenav
{color:#FFF;background:#422100;margin:0;padding:.25em}#skipnav{text-align:right;position:absolute;right:15px;z-
index:10;margin:0 auto;padding:.25em}.boxshadow #mainnav li{border:none;-webkit-box-shadow:2px 2px 4px #000;-moz-box-
shadow:2px 2px 4px #000;box-shadow:2px 2px 4px #000}.cotcol{background:#9daecd;width:15%}.desc,.beds,.roomlinks{margin:1em 0
0 30px;padding:0}.firstcol{background:#f1eace;width:25%}.rates td.season{text-align:left}.roomcols
{background:#aecdf4;width:15%}.roominfo{clear:right;padding:1em 0}.roominfo h3{float:left;margin:0 0 15px 30px}.roominfo p
{clear:left}.tablenote{width:90%;margin:.25em auto}.toplink{text-align:right;margin:0;padding:0}#pagenav a:visited
{color:#D7C39C}#pagenav a:hover{color:#C6A971}#mainnav a:hover{color:#FFF;text-shadow:1px 1px 1px #000}a.reservelink:link
{background-color:#ffe5b2;border:1px solid #000;text-decoration:none;padding:5px}a.questionlink:link{background-
color:#c7e3ff;border:1px solid #000;text-decoration:none;padding:5px}a.reservelink:hover{background-color:#ffd073}
a.questionlink:hover{background-color:#9cf}h1,h2,footer,nav p,.rates td{text-align:center}article p,article section{margin-
bottom:1em}.beds,.bold{font-weight:700}.clearright,.roominfo p.toplink{clear:right}a:link,a:visited,a:active,#mainnav
a:visited,#mainnav a:active{color:#422100}a:hover,#mainnav a:link{color:#000}#pagenav a:link,#pagenav a:active{color:#FFF}
```

Using tools to identify orphaned styles

You can do a Web search to find tools for identifying orphaned styles. A few free tools are available that can pinpoint styles that aren't used on a specific page. To do so site-wide usually requires that your site be published on the Web.

Identifying orphaned styles can be an involved and error-prone process, especially on a project with multiple developers. Adding detailed comments to each style rule can help you track effectively where styles are used, and help you and other developers understand when a style can be deleted.

Tidying Your HTML

In addition to removing unused styles, you can take a few other steps to streamline your HTML code. You can use a utility to standardize the indents and line breaks in your code, as well as ensuring the code conforms to some basic rules. This process is known as **tidying** or **prettifying** your code, and developers often use the free tool HTML Tidy, originally created by Dave Raggett, for this purpose. You run your HTML files through an online tidying service to standardize them.

STEPS

TROUBLE

If this Web site is unavailable, search on *online html tidy* to locate an alternative, then follow the instructions on that site.

1. **In your browser, open** http://infohound.net/tidy/

   This is an online implementation of the HTML Tidy tool. The site is provided and maintained by Jonathan Hedley.

2. **If you published your Web site in the previous lesson, enter the URL for rooms.html in the URL box, then skip to Step 4**

   The site enables you to tidy published code or code that you copy and paste.

3. **Return to rooms.html in your text editor, select the entire contents of the document, copy the selection to the Clipboard, return to your browser, click in the HTML box, then paste the contents of the Clipboard**

QUICK TIP

Move the mouse pointer over any option without clicking to see a tooltip that explains the option's function.

4. **Explore the available options in the HTML/XHTML, Pretty printing, and Encoding sections, ensure only Drop empty paras and Indent Attributes are checked, then change Char encoding to utf8**

5. **Click Advanced, in the New blocklevel tags box, type nav article figure figcaption section footer, then click Tidy!**

   Because HTML Tidy doesn't recognize HTML5 elements, you specify elements in use on the page that shouldn't be treated as errors. A new page opens that displays the tidied code along with any errors or warnings generated.

6. **Click anywhere in the tidied code, select the entire contents of the code box, copy the selection to the Clipboard, return to rooms.html in your text editor, delete the contents of the document, paste the contents of the Clipboard, then save your work**

   Figures P-12 and P-13 compare a section of the original and the tidied HTML code.

7. **Reload rooms.html in your browser**

   While the code itself is easier to read, the contents of the Web page are unchanged.

8. **Repeat Steps 1–7 for index.html, aboutus.html, and reserve.html**

FIGURE P-12: Original code for rooms.html

```
<!DOCTYPE html>
<html class="no-js">
  <head>
    <meta charset="utf-8" />
    <meta name="description" content="Lakeland Reeds Bed & Breakfast offers 4 comfortable rooms that accommodate from 2 to 5
people. All have private baths and views of Twin Lakes." />
    <title>Room selection at Lakeland Reeds Bed &amp; Breakfast</title>
    <link rel="stylesheet" type="text/css" media="screen" href="lakeland.min.css" />
    <link rel="stylesheet" type="text/css" media="print" href="llprint.css" />
    <link rel="shortcut icon" href="favicon.ico" />
    <!--[if lt IE 7]>
      <style type="text/css">
        #mainnav {left: 0px;}
        li img {left: -42px;}
      </style>
    <![endif]-->
    <script src="scripts/modernizr-1.6.min.js"></script>
  </head>
  <body>
    <div id="box">
      <p id="skipnav"><a href="#main">Skip navigation</a></p>
      <h1>
        <a href="index.html"><img src="images/lakeland.gif" width="664" height="180" alt="Lakeland Reeds Bed and Breakfast"
title="" /></a>
      </h1>
      <nav id="mainnav">
        <ul>
          <li>
            <img src="images/fl_light.gif" width="45" height="45" alt="" title="" />
            <a href="index.html">Home</a>
          </li>
          <li>
            <img src="images/fl_light.gif" width="45" height="45" alt="" title="" />
            <a href="aboutus.html">About Us</a>
          </li>
          <li>
            <img src="images/fl_dark.gif" width="45" height="45" alt="" title="" />
            <a href="rooms.html">Rooms</a>
          </li>
          <li>
            <img src="images/fl_light.gif" width="45" height="45" alt="" title="" />
            <a href="reserve.html">Reservations</a>
          </li>
          <li>
            <img src="images/fl_light.gif" width="45" height="45" alt="" title="" />
            <a href="http://bit.ly/dl8xGc" target="_blank">Local weather</a>
          </li>
          <li>
            <img src="images/fl_light.gif" width="45" height="45" alt="" title="" />
            <a href="http://bit.ly/co7Vcs" target="_blank">Directions</a>
          </li>
        </ul>
```

FIGURE P-13: Tidied code for rooms.html

meta element added describing the program that generated the code

Each attribute is indented beneath the tag for readability

```
<!DOCTYPE html>

<html class="no-js">
<head>
<meta name="generator"
      content="HTML Tidy for Linux/x86 (vers 11 February 2007), see www.w3.org">
<meta charset="utf-8">
<meta name="description"
      content=
      "Lakeland Reeds Bed &amp; Breakfast offers 4 comfortable rooms that accommodate from 2 to 5 people. All have private
baths and views of Twin Lakes.">

<title>Room selection at Lakeland Reeds Bed &amp; Breakfast</title>
<link rel="stylesheet"
      type="text/css"
      media="screen"
      href="lakeland.min.css">
<link rel="stylesheet"
      type="text/css"
      media="print"
      href="llprint.css">
<link rel="shortcut icon"
      href="favicon.ico"><!--[if lt IE 7]>
      <style type="text/css">
        #mainnav {left: 0px;}
        li img {left: -42px;}
      </style>
    <![endif]-->

<script src="scripts/modernizr-1.6.min.js"
        type="text/javascript">
</script>
</head>

<body>
<div id="box">
  <p id="skipnav"><a href="#main">Skip navigation</a></p>

  <h1><a href="index.html"><img src="images/lakeland.gif"
          width="664"
          height="180"
          alt="Lakeland Reeds Bed and Breakfast"
          title=""></a></h1>

  <nav id="mainnav">
    <ul>
      <li><img src="images/fl_light.gif"
          width="45"
          height="45"
          alt=""
          title=""> <a href="index.html">Home</a></li>
```

Tidying your CSS

If you choose not to publish minified CSS, you can tidy your CSS as well. CSS Tidy, a free tool similar to HTML Tidy, was originally created by Florian Schmitz and is available both for download and for online use.

Publishing with a Domain Name

Even for small businesses and personal pages, it's common to publish Web sites using domain names. Securing a domain name and using it is a multi-step process involving different services that may be provided by multiple entities, as illustrated in Figure P-14. As you prepare to go live with the Lakeland Reeds B&B Web site, you review the roles involved in reserving and using a domain name.

Obtaining and publishing to a domain name requires three different services:

- ### Registrar

  Domain names worldwide are controlled by an international body called the Internet Corporation for Assigned Names and Numbers (ICANN). ICANN authorizes people and organizations to act as **domain name registrars** through which domain names can be reserved. Hundreds of registrars are currently in business. You pay a registrar for the rights to use a domain name for a specified period of time, and the period can be extended. Any changes you wish to make in your domain name registration, including changing your contact info or transferring the domain to another party, must be done through this registrar.

- ### Web host

  To make your pages available on the Web, they need to be located on a Web server, which is a computer that's always connected to the Internet and is running software to listen for and respond to requests for Web pages. While it's possible to run a Web server over a home broadband connection, the vast majority of Web sites are hosted on machines in facilities known as **server farms** that are specially designed to provide a constant flow of electricity and uninterrupted Internet access. For a monthly or yearly fee, you can rent space on a server through a **Web host**, which is one of thousands of companies worldwide that provide access to these machines.

- ### DNS host

  Web resources are accessed using a four-part address known as an **IP address**. This address is made up of four numbers, each of which can have a value from 0 to 255, separated by periods; for example, 74.125.224.72 is an IP address for google.com. Once you rent space on a Web server, your Web hosting provider will give you an IP address that points to your Web space. The final step in connecting your domain name with your Web server is to ensure that the two are connected in the **domain name service (DNS)**, which is a central directory for the Web, similar to a phone book. A Web client sends a request based on a domain name to a **DNS server**, which maintains a copy of the current directory; a DNS server looks up the IP address that corresponds to a given domain name and passes that information to the client, which then uses it to access the Web site. Many registrars offer DNS hosting for free as part of their registry services; likewise, Web hosts generally offer this service as well. You can pick one of these organizations, but not both, to be your DNS host, thereby finalizing the link between your hosted Web site and your domain name.

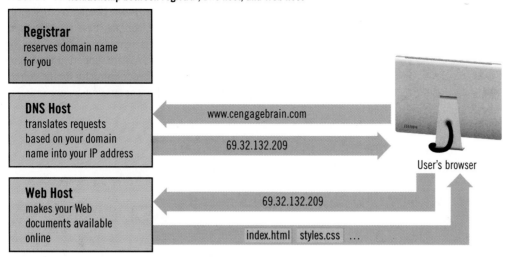

Choosing domain service providers

The roles involved in using a domain name for a Web site can be served by three different entities, combined into a single one, or shared among two. For a small Web site to be maintained by someone without a lot of technological expertise, using a single provider may make sense, because there would be only one organization to contact in case of problems. For instance, a blog host is by definition a Web host; many blog hosts also offer the option to register a domain through them, and they offer to host your DNS as well. For more complex Web sites, however, or for users who have specific technological needs, splitting these roles up among different agencies can maximize the possibility of customized services and can reduce the overall cost.

Practice

For current SAM information, including versions and content details, visit SAM Central (http://www.cengage.com/samcentral). If you have a SAM user profile, you may have access to hands-on instruction, practice, and assessment of the skills covered in this unit. Since various versions of SAM are supported throughout the life of this text, check with your instructor for the correct instructions and URL/Web site for accessing assignments.

Concepts Review

Refer to the code shown in Figure P-15.

FIGURE P-15

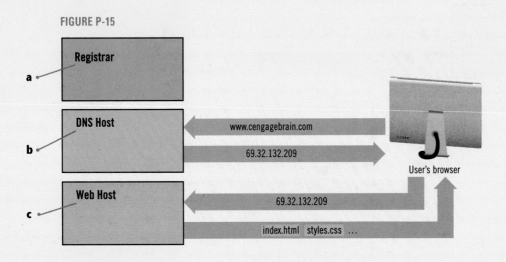

1. Which entity translates requests based on your domain name into your IP address?
2. Which entity reserves your domain name for you?
3. Which entity makes your Web documents available online?

Match each term with the statement that best describes it.

4. testing server
5. automated testing
6. dead links
7. orphaned styles
8. tidying
9. domain name service (DNS)

a. links whose targets don't exist
b. style rules based on selectors that no longer apply to any elements in your Web pages
c. a set of browser testing measures performed by specialized software
d. a central directory for the Web, similar to a phone book
e. a Web server that's available only to you, not to all Web users
f. standardizing the indents and line breaks in your code and ensuring the code conforms to some basic rules

Select the best answer from the list of choices.

10. **Which is an advantage of using a testing server?**
    a. It makes your Web pages available to all Web users.
    b. It identifies orphaned styles.
    c. It tidies your code.
    d. It helps you catch server-related problems before the site goes live.

11. **On which browsers should you be sure to test your final Web site?**
    a. those that are most prevalent in your geographic area
    b. those that are most common among your target audience
    c. those that include the most useful tools
    d. all available browsers

12. **To collect the best information possible from usability tests, it's important to**
    a. have access to a testing facility.
    b. purchase specialized testing software.
    c. identify questions you want all testers to answer.
    d. skip such testing if you don't really have time for it.

13. **Which of the following is a reasonable alternative to performing manual browser testing on your entire Web site?**
    a. automated browser testing
    b. testing on only one operating system
    c. testing on only a single browser
    d. skipping browser testing altogether

14. **Which of the following is an advantage of removing unused styles?**
    a. it ensures that your code is valid
    b. it eliminates large images from your site
    c. it makes your code more likely to work on different browsers
    d. it makes your code easier for other developers to work with

Skills Review

1. **Use HTML and CSS debugging tools**
   a. In your text editor, open HTM P-7.html from the Unit P/Review folder where you store your Data Files, insert a blank line before the closing body tag, insert a paragraph element containing your first and last name and the text **HTML5 Unit P, Skills Review**, save it as **index.html**, repeat to save HTM P-8.html as **history.html**, and HTM P-9.html as **location.html**, then use CSS comments to add the same information to HTM P-10.css and save it as **bigj.css**.
   b. Scrutinize all three Web pages in your browser for errors.
   c. In location.html, use the Inspect element feature of your browser to identify the errors in the code responsible for the mispositioned cell content near the top of the page and the misaligned address information in the footer.
   d. In your text editor, add the missing **<td>** tag to fix the cell contents near the top of the page. Fix the misspelled **id** in the footer. Save your work, then refresh location.html in your browser and verify that the errors have been fixed.

2. **Plan usability tests**
   a. Open HTM P-11.txt in your text editor, enter your first and last name on the first line, then save the file as **Big J Test Plan.txt**.
   b. In section 1, add questions asking if testers would expect to have fun at the restaurant, if they'd expect the restaurant to be kid friendly, and if it's a restaurant where they'd take a date.
   c. In section 2, add instructions for testers to locate a menu and the phone number for the Dundas location.
   d. Save your work, then close Big J Test Plan.txt.

3. **Perform browser tests**
   a. Open index.html in IE9, display the Developer Tools, then ensure that the browser mode is set to **Internet Explorer 9**.
   b. Test the functionality of all the links on the Web page, then repeat this process for each of the remaining Web pages, verifying that the content of each page is displayed as expected.

Skills Review (continued)

c. Change the browser mode to **Internet Explorer 8**, view each page on the Web site, then repeat with the browser mode set to **Internet Explorer 7**.

d. View each page on the Web site in Chrome, then repeat on a Mac using **Safari** and **Firefox**.

4. Measure performance

a. If you have Web space available, publish the Web site.

b. Use the Internet Explorer Developer Tools or the Safari Web Inspector to display the loading times for the contents of location.html.

c. In the browser, view the styles for the first **section** element, then use the browser tools to temporarily change the background color to **tan**, as shown in Figure P-16.

d. Close the Developer Tools or Web Inspector.

FIGURE P-16

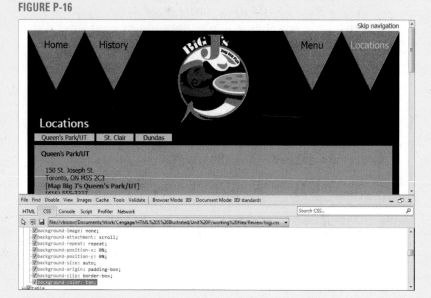

5. Remove unused styles

a. In your text editor, return to **bigj.css**.

b. Delete the style rules based on the following selectors:
#message
#reqinstr
.hours
.req
.row
.row div

c. Save your work, then create a minified version of the file with the name **bigj.min.css**. Link each Web page to the minified style sheet, publish your Web site if available, then verify in a browser that the appearance of each Web page is unchanged.

6. Tidy your HTML

a. In your browser, open **http://infohound.net/tidy/**.

b. Enter the published URL for **index.html** or cut and paste the code for index.html into the appropriate box in the form.

c. Ensure only Drop empty paras and Indent Attributes are checked, then change **Char encoding** to **utf8**.

d. Click Advanced, in the New blocklevel tags box, type **nav article aside figure figcaption section footer**, then click **Tidy!**

e. Replace the contents of your index.html file with the tidied code, then save your work.

f. Repeat Steps b–e for history.html and location.html.

Independent Challenge 1

As you prepare to publish the Web site for the Spotted Wren Garden Center, you test and finalize your code.

a. In your text editor, open HTM P-12.html from the Unit P/IC1 folder where you store your Data Files. Insert a blank line before the closing body tag, insert a paragraph element containing your first and last name and the text **HTML5 Unit P, Independent Challenge 1**, then save it as **index.html**. Repeat to save HTM P-13.html as **hours.html** and HTM P-14.html as **resource.html**. Use CSS comments to add the same information to HTM P-15.css and save it as **spotwren.css**.

b. Examine all three Web pages in the browser of your choice. The resource.html page contains an error in the table as well as a missing image; use a built-in browser tool or a browser extension to examine the code for the elements that are being displayed incorrectly. Correct the errors in your text editor, save your changes, then reload the page in your browser and verify that you have fixed the errors. The Web page should match Figure P-17.

FIGURE P-17

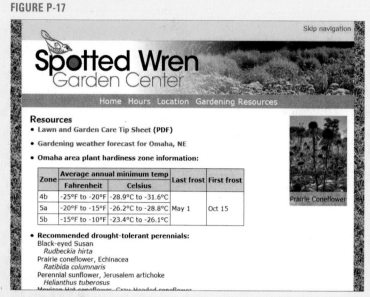

c. Test all links in all three pages. Preview all pages in Internet Explorer 9, 8, and 7, Firefox for Windows and Mac, and Safari for Mac.

d. Tidy the HTML for all three Web pages. Minify spotwren.css, saving the minified code to a new filename **spotwren.min.css**. Change the first style sheet link in each Web page to reference the minified style sheet. Publish the site if possible, then view all pages from the published location.

e. Close your browser, then close your text editor.

Xtremer/Shutterstock.com
Jim Gitzlaff/Shutterstock.com
Maxim Tupikov/Shutterstock.com

Independent Challenge 2

As you prepare to publish the Web site for the Murfreesboro Recreational Soccer League, you test and finalize your code.

a. In your text editor, open HTM P-16.html from the Unit P/IC1 folder where you store your Data Files. Insert a blank line before the closing body tag, insert a paragraph element containing your first and last name and the text **HTML5 Unit P, Independent Challenge 2**, then save it as **index.html**. Repeat to save HTM P-17.html as **started.html** and HTM P-18.html as **schedule.html**. Use CSS comments to add the same information to HTM P-19.css and save it as **mrsl.css**.

FIGURE P-18

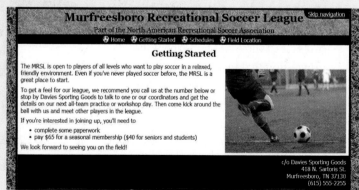

b. Examine all three Web pages in the browser of your choice. For the misplaced image in the started.html page, use a built-in browser tool or a browser extension to examine the code for the image and identify the error. Correct the error in your text editor, save your changes, then reload the page in your browser and verify that you have fixed the errors. The Web page should match Figure P-18.

Lario Tus/Shutterstock.com
Xtremer/Shutterstock.com

HTML5 and CSS3

Independent Challenge 2 (continued)

c. Test all links in all three pages. Preview all pages in Internet Explorer 9 and 8, Chrome for Windows and Mac, and Safari for Mac.

d. Tidy the HTML for all three Web pages.

Advanced Challenge Exercise

- In your browser, open **http://procssor.com**, which is an online implementation of the CSS Tidy program.
- Follow the instructions on the Web site to tidy your CSS, then replace the contents of mrsl.css with the tidied code.
- Save your work, then reload all Web pages in the site in your browser and verify that their appearance has not been altered.

e. Publish the site if possible, then view all pages from the published location.

f. Close your browser, then close your text editor.

Independent Challenge 3

As you prepare to publish the Web site for the Hotel Natoma, you test and finalize your code.

a. In your text editor, open HTM P-20.html from the Unit P/IC3 folder where you store your Data Files. Insert a blank line before the closing body tag, insert a paragraph element containing your first and last name and the text **HTML5 Unit P, Independent Challenge 3**, then save it as **index.html**. Repeat to save HTM P-21.html as **nearby.html** and HTM P-22.html as **greensf.html**. Use CSS comments to add the same information to HTM P-23.css and save it as **natoma.css**.

b. Examine all three Web pages in the browser of your choice. Use a built-in browser tool or a browser extension to examine the code on the What's Nearby and Green SF pages for the images that have extra space to the right. Correct the errors in your text editor, save your changes, then reload the page in your browser and verify that you have fixed the errors. The Web pages should match Figures P-19 and P-20.

c. Test all links in all three pages. Preview all pages in Internet Explorer 9, 8, and 7, Firefox for Windows and Mac, and Safari for Mac.

d. Tidy the HTML for all three Web pages.

e. Create a new text document containing a usability test plan for the Web site, including at least three questions about the impression that the site conveys, and asking users to locate at least three pieces of information on the Web site. Include your name and the text **HTML Illustrated Unit P, IC3** at the top of the document. Save your test plan with the name **Hotel Natoma Test Plan.txt**.

FIGURE P-19

Photo/Sasha Vodnik

FIGURE P-20

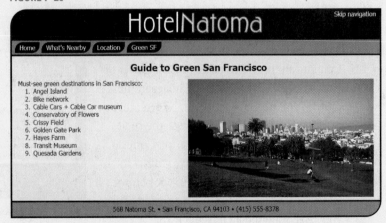

Photo/Sasha Vodnik

Independent Challenge 3 (continued)

Advanced Challenge Exercise

- Use a software tool, such as the free Dust-Me Selectors add-on for Firefox, to identify orphaned styles in your code.
- Remove the orphaned styles from natoma.css, then save your work.
- Reload all Web pages in the site in your browser and verify that their appearance has not been altered.

f. Minify natoma.css, saving the minified code to a new file named **natoma.min.css**. Change the first style sheet link in each Web page to reference the minified style sheet.

g. Publish the site if possible, then view all pages from the published location.

h. Close your browser, then close your text editor.

Real Life Independent Challenge

This assignment builds on the personal Web site you have worked on in previous units. You'll finalize and publish your Web site.

a. Copy your Web site files to the Unit P/RLIC folder on the drive and folder where you store your Data Files.

b. Examine all of your Web pages in the browser of your choice. If you notice errors or display issues, use a built-in browser tool or a browser extension to examine the code for the affected elements. If appropriate, edit the CSS in the browser to model the changes you are considering. Correct the errors in your text editor, save your changes, then reload the page in your browser and verify that you have fixed the errors.

c. Test all links in all of your pages.

d. Research which browsers are most likely used by your target audience. Preview all pages of your Web site in each of the browsers used by more than 5% of your potential users. Make any changes to your code necessary to ensure that pages are displayed appropriately in all of these browsers.

e. Create a usability test plan for the Web site, including at least three questions about the impression that the site conveys, and asking users to locate at least three pieces of information on the Web site. Include your name and the text **HTML Illustrated Unit P, RLIC** at the top of the document.

f. Tidy the HTML for of your Web pages. Minify your css.

g. If you have purchased a domain name and Web hosting services, follow the instructions from your service providers to point the DNS records for your domain name to your Web host. Publish your Web site to a password-protected test directory on your Web server. Verify that you can access your Web pages using your domain name with the directory at the end. Verify that your pages are rendered as expected.

h. Publish your Web site to the public directory on your Web server. Enter your domain name in the address bar of a browser and verify that the main page of your Web site is displayed. View all the pages from the public directory and verify that the site is displayed as expected.

i. Close your browser, then close your text editor.

Visual Workshop

In your text editor, open the file HTM P-24.html from the Unit P/VW directory on the drive and folder where you store your Data Files, add a paragraph before the closing body tag that contains your first and last name and the text **HTML5 Unit P, Visual Workshop**, then save the file as **upcoming.html**. Use a CSS comment to add the same information to HTM P-25.css and save it as **revision.css**. Open upcoming.html in your browser, then use browser tools or add-ons to edit the code so the page appears as shown in Figure P-21. In your text editor, make the same changes. Save your work, then close your browser and text editor.

FIGURE P-21

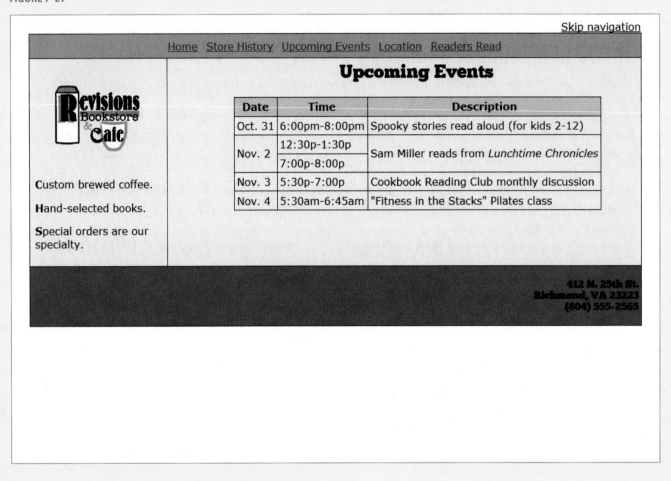

HTML Elements

This table includes all HTML elements covered in this text, along with selected attributes.

element	content/function	new in HTML5
global attributes that apply to all HTML elements		
id="*id*"	a unique identifier for the current element	
title="*title*"	information about an element; displayed in many browsers as floating text when the mouse pointer is over the element	
lang="*keyword*"	the primary language of the element contents, from a standard list of abbreviations	
dir="ltr | rtl | auto"	the direction of text in the element; "ltr" specifies left to right, while "rtl" indicates right to left	
class="*class*"	one or more classes that the element is part of, separated by spaces	
style="*style*"	one or more CSS name-value pairs that apply only to the current element	
!	contains comment text within the <!-- --> tag pair	
a	links enclosed text or elements to another Web page or other resource	
href="*filename | uri*"	address of Web page or other resource that opens when the link is clicked or activated	
target="*name* | _blank | _self"	the name or a keyword for the window or tab in which the linked resource opens	
rel="*keyword*"	keyword describing the relationship between the linked resource and the current Web page	
media="*media*"	media for which the linked resource is intended (default: "all")	
type="*type*"	MIME type of the linked resource	
article	contains a standalone piece of work, such as a single entry in a blog	✔
aside	contains a part of a page that's tangential to the main page content	✔
audio	inserts an audio clip	✔
audio="muted"	mutes audio	
autoplay="autoplay | none"	specifies that video should begin playing immediately when page is loaded	
controls="controls | none"	requests that the browser display its default playback controls	
height="*height*"	specifies the height of the element in pixels	
loop="loop | none"	indicates that the browser should restart playback each time it reaches the end of the clip	
preload="auto | metadata | none"	indicates whether the browser should download the audio file when opening the Web page (auto), download only the metadata related to the video file (metadata), or wait to download until the video is played (none)	
src="*path/filename*"	specifies the path and filename of the video file	
type='*MIME*; codecs="*codecs*"'	specifies the container format and codecs used to encode the file referenced by the src attribute, where *MIME* is the MIME type of the container format and *codecs* is a comma-separated list of codecs used to encode the file	
width="*width*"	specifies the width of the element in pixels	
body	contains the contents visible in the main window of a Web browser	
br	inserts a line break	
caption	contains the title of a table	
col	encloses one or more table columns to treat as a unit	
span="*value*"	specifies the number of columns to include in the element	
colgroup	encloses the col elements for a table	
span="*value*"	specifies the number of columns to include in the element when no col elements are specified	
dd	marks a description associated with a dt element in a description list	
div	marks block-level content with no specific semantic meaning	
dl	marks a list in which each item is comprised of a name-value pair (a description list)	
dt	marks a term or item being described in a description list	

element	content/function	new in HTML5
fieldset	marks a group of related form fields and associated labels	
figcaption	mark caption text associated with an img element; always enclosed within a figure element	✔
figure	contains an image that adds information to a Web page; a user agent should be able to link the contents of a figure element and move them to another location without affecting the information conveyed by the Web page	✔
footer	contains information about a section or document that usually appears at the end of a Web page, such as attributions and/or footnotes	✔
form	marks all the elements that are part of a form	
h1, h2, h3, h4, h5, h6	mark heading text; h1 is the highest level heading on a Web page, and h6 is the lowest	
head	contains information about a Web page, including elements that are not visible within the browser window	
header	contains information about a section or document that usually appears at the beginning, such as a heading, logo, and/or table of contents	✔
hgroup	contains a group of related elements that include a heading; enables user agents to recognize content such as a tagline as related to a heading	✔
html	encloses all the code for a Web page	
iframe	creates an inline frame, which acts as a self- contained Web page within the HTML document where it's located	

img
  alt="*text*"
  src="*uri* | *filename*"
  width="*value*"
  height="*value*"
	inserts an image
	text to display or be read aloud in place of the image
	path and filename for the image file to display
	native width of the image in pixels
	native height of the image in pixels	

input
  checked="checked"
  maxlength="*value*"
  name="*name*"
  placeholder="*text*"
  type="button"
  type="checkbox"
  type="color"
  type="date | month | week |
    time | datetime |
    datetime-local"
  type="email"
 	
  type="file"
  type="image"
  type="number"
  type="password"
 	
  type="radio"
  type="range"
  type="reset"
  type="search"
  type="submit"
  type="tel"
 	
  type="text"
  type="url"
 	
  value="*value*"
  width="*value*"
	marks an individual item of data that users can enter
	marks an option button or a check box as selected by default
	specifies the maxiumum number of characters a user can enter
	specifies the group name that all option buttons in a group must share
	text that appears in input box until user is ready to type
	creates a generic button that can be programmed using a script
	creates a check box, which allows users to select a single item
	supports input of hexadecimal color values
	enables you to accept dates, times, and related values using a standard format
	
	newer browsers may validate to ensure that entries are valid email addresses; touchscreen devices with on-screen keyboards may display customized buttons for email input, such as an @ key or a .com key
	accepts the path and filename for a file to upload from a user's device
	creates a submit button using an image
	enables you to specify a range of valid numbers that users can input
	most browsers display text entered by users as bullets or asterisks rather than showing the actual characters
	creates an option button, which lets users select one option from a set of choices
	enables you to specify a range of valid numbers that users can input
	creates a button that clears all user input and resets all form fields to defaults
	browsers may style input to match styling of search boxes in other parts of the user interface
	creates a submit button, which users can click to send the data they have provided to the server
	can be used in conjunction with style sheet or script code to verify that entries are valid telephone numbers
	creates a text box into which users can type a single line of text
	newer browsers may validate to ensure that entries are valid Web addresses; touchscreen devices with on-screen keyboards may display customized buttons for input, such as a .com key
	specifies the text to be submitted if an element is selected, or the text to appear on a button
	width of the text box	

element	content/function	new in HTML5
label **for=**"*id*"	marks a heading describing the associated input element specifies the id of the input element being labeled	
legend	marks a heading describing the topic of the fieldset	

li
  link
  href="*filename | uri*"
  rel="*keyword*"
  media="*media*"
  type="*type*"
	marks list item content in an ordered list or unordered list
	makes the contents of an external file available in an HTML document
	specifies the destination
	keyword specifying the type of link
	media for which the linked resource is intended (default: "all")
	MIME type of the linked resource	

meta
  name="*name*"
  http-equiv="*keyword*"
  content="*content*"
  charset="*charset*"
	enables you to pass information about a Web page to user agents that open it
	the type of metadata being provided, from list of standard metadata names
	directions to the user agent on handling the Web page
	the content of the metadata described by the "name" value
	the character encoding that the document uses	

nav	contains site or page navigation elements	✔

object
  data="*path/filename*"
  height="*height*"
  type="*MIME*"
  width="*width*"
	includes the content of an external resource in the current Web page
	specifies the path and filename of the external resource
	specifies the height of the element in pixels
	specifies the container format used to encode the file referenced by the data attribute
	specifies the width of the element in pixels	

ol	marks a list in which items are numbered or lettered sequentially (an ordered list)	
optgroup	marks a group of option elements	

option
  selected="*selected*"
  value="*value*"
	marks a single entry in a drop-down list
	marks an entry as selected by default
	specifies the text to be submitted if an element is selected	

p	marks a paragraph of text	

param
  name="*name*"
  value="*value*"
	defines one or more parameters related to the external resource in the containing object element
	parameter name
	parameter value	

script
  src="*filename*"
  type="*type*"
	contains script code or a link to an external file containing script code
	path and filename for the external script file
	the script language or data format	

section	encloses a section of content focused on a common theme, such as a chapter of a larger work	✔
select	marks a set of entries to display as a drop-down list	

source
  src="*path/filename*"
  type='*MIME*; codecs="*codecs*"'
	specifies the location and encoding of an audio or video file
	specifies the path and filename of the audio or video file
	specifies the container format and codecs used to encode the file referenced by the src attribute, where *MIME* is the MIME type of the container format and *codecs* is a comma-separated list of codecs used to encode the file
		✔

span	contains inline text or elements; enables you to style inline elements	
style **type=**"*type*"	encloses style sheet code the styling language	
table	marks content to present as a table	
tbody	encloses table body rows	

td
  colspan="*value*"
  rowspan="*value*"
	marks the content of a table data cell
	the number of columns that the cell spans
	the number of rows that the cell spans	

textarea
  cols="*value*"
  rows="*value*"
	marks a multiline area where users can enter text
	approximates how many characters in a monospace font should fit across the box
	specifies how many rows of input are visible	

tfoot	encloses table footer rows	

element	content/function	new in HTML5

th
   colspan="*value*"
   rowspan="*value*"
	marks the content of a table header cell
	the number of columns that the cell spans
	the number of rows that the cell spans	

thead	encloses table header rows	
title	specifies text that appears in the title bar or tab of a Web browser opening the page	
tr	encloses table cell elements that make up a single table row	
ul	marks a list in which the order of items doesn't matter (an unordered list)	

video
   audio="muted"
   autoplay="autoplay | none"
   controls="controls | none"
   height="*height*"
   loop="loop | none"
   poster="*path/filename*"
   preload="auto | metadata | none"
 	
   src="*path/filename*"
   type='*MIME*; codecs="*codecs*"'
 	
   width="*width*"
	inserts a video
	mutes audio
	specified that video should begin playing immediately when page is loaded
	requests that the browser display its default playback controls
	specifies the height of the element in pixels
	indicates that the browser should restart playback each time it reaches the end of the video
	specifies a path and filename for an image to display before video playback starts
	indicates whether the browser should download the video file when opening the Web page (auto), download only the metadata related to the video file (metadata), or wait to download until the video is played (none)
	specifies the path and filename of the video file
	specifies the container format and codecs used to encode the file referenced by the src attribute, where *MIME* is the MIME type of the container format and *codecs* is a comma-separated list of codecs used to encode the file
	specifies the width of the element in pixels
		✔

CSS Properties

This table includes all CSS properties covered in this text, along with selected values.

property	values	affects
background	**color** as a name from cross-browser compatibility list; **rgb triplet** in the format rgb(*rrr,ggg,bbb*); **rgba value** in the format rgba(*rr,gg,bb,a*); **hexadecimal triplet** in the format #*rrggbb*; **url('path/filename')**; **transparent**; **inherit**	the background color or image for an element
border	**width style color**	combined attribute for all settings for the border around an element
border-color border-top-color border-right-color border-bottom-color border-left-color	**color** as a name from cross-browser compatibility list; **rgb triplet** in the format rgb(*rrr,ggg,bbb*); **rgba value** in the format rgba(*rr,gg,bb,a*); **hexadecimal triplet** in the format #*rrggbb*; **transparent**; **inherit**	the color of an element border on one or more sides
border-radius border-top-left-radius border-top-right-radius border-bottom-left-radius border-bottom-right-radius -webkit-border-radius -webkit-border-top-left-radius -webkit-border-top-right-radius -webkit-border-bottom-left-radius -webkit-border-bottom-right-radius -moz-border-radius-topleft -moz-border-radius-topright -moz-border-radius-bottomleft -moz-border-radius-bottomright	**value** in em, pixels, or another supported unit; **percent** of the height of the parent element	the roundness of specified corner(s) of element
border-style border-top-style border-right-style border-bottom-style border-left-style	**dotted**; **dashed**; **solid**; **double**; **groove**; **ridge**; **inset**; **outset**	the style of an element border on one or more sides
border-width border-top-width border-right-width border-bottom-width border-left-width	**thin**; **medium**; **thick**; **value** in em, pixels, or another supported unit	the thickness of an element border on one or more sides
border-collapse	**separate**; **collapse**	whether adjacent table cell borders are displayed separately or merged
bottom	**value** in em, pixels, or another supported unit; **percent** of the height of the parent element	amount the bottom edge of an element is offset from the bottom edge of the closest ancestor element that is also positioned
box-shadow -webkit-box-shadow -moz-box-shadow	**horizontal vertical blur color**, where **horizontal** is the horizontal offset (required), **vertical** is the vertical offset (required), **blur** is the shadow width and lightness (optional), and **color** is the shadow color (optional)	a shadow behind a block element

property	values	affects
clear	**left**; **right**; **both**	element position, preventing a floated element from being displayed to the left, right, or either side of an element
color	*color* as a name from cross-browser compatibility list; *rgb triplet* in the format rgb(*rrr,ggg,bbb*); *rgba value* in the format rgba(*rr,gg,bb,a*); *hexadecimal triplet* in the format #*rrggbb*; **transparent**; **inherit**	the foreground color of an element, most often affecting text
display	**block**; **inline**; **table**; **table-row**; **table-cell**; **none**; **inherit**	the type of box that user agents create for an element; "none" removes an element from the page flow
float	**left**; **right**	element position, aligning the top of an element with the top of the next element, and horizontally with the specified edge of the parent element
font-family	*family-name*	the font family in which the text of an element is displayed
font-size	*size* in em, pixels, or another supported unit	the relative or absolute size of text
font-style	**normal**; **italic**; **oblique**	whether characters are displayed slanted or in standard orientation
font-weight	**normal**; **bold**; **100**; **200**; **300**; **400**; **500**; **600**; **700**; **800**; **900**	whether text is displayed in boldface, normal, or somewhere in between
height	*value* in em, pixels, or another supported unit; *percent* of the parent element; **inherit**; **auto**	the height of an element, excluding, padding, border, and margin
left	*value* in em, pixels, or another supported unit; *percent* of the width of the parent element	amount the left edge of an element is offset from the left edge of the closest ancestor element that is also positioned
list-style-image	**url('***path/filename***')**	specifies an image to be used as a list item marker
list-style-type	ordered list: **decimal**; **lower-roman**; **upper-roman**; **lower-alpha**; **upper-alpha**; **none** unordered list: **circle**; **disc**; **square**; **none**	the list item marker for an ordered or unordered list
margin margin-top margin-right margin-bottom margin-left	*value* in em, pixels, or another supported unit; *percent* of the enclosing element; **auto**	buffer space outside of the element border
max-height	*value* in em, pixels, or another supported unit; *percent* of the parent element; **inherit**; **auto**	the maximum height of an element, excluding, padding, border, and margin
max-width	*value* in em, pixels, or another supported unit; *percent* of the parent element; **inherit**; **auto**	the maximum width of an element, excluding, padding, border, and margin
min-height	*value* in em; pixels, or another supported unit; *percent* of the parent element; **inherit**; **auto**	the minimum height of an element, excluding, padding, border, and margin
min-width	*value* in em, pixels, or another supported unit; *percent* of the parent element; **inherit**; **auto**	the minimum width of an element, excluding, padding, border, and margin
padding padding-top padding-right padding-bottom padding-left	*value* in em; pixels, or another supported unit; *percent* of the enclosing element	the space between element contents and border
position	**absolute**; **relative**; **fixed**	the way the position of an element is determined on the page

property	values	affects
right	*value* in em, pixels, or another supported unit; *percent* of the width of the parent element	amount the right edge of an element is offset from the right edge of the closest ancestor element that is also positioned
text-align	**left**; **right**; **center**; **justify**; **inherit**	the horizontal alignment of text
text-shadow	*horizontal vertical blur color*, where *horizontal* is the horizontal offset (required), *vertical* is the vertical offset (required), *blur* is the shadow width and lightness (optional), and *color* is the shadow color (optional)	a shadow behind text
top	*value* in em; pixels, or another supported unit; *percent* of the height of the parent element	amount the top edge of an element is offset from the top edge of the closest ancestor element that is also positioned
vertical-align	**top**; **middle**; **bottom**	the vertical alignment of table cell content
visibility	**hidden**; **visible**	whether element contents are visible on a Web page; "hidden" makes contents invisible while leaving the element as part of the page flow
width	*value* in em; pixels, or another supported unit; *percent* of the parent element; **inherit**; **auto**	the width of an element, excluding, padding, border, and margin
z-index	*integer*	the position of an element in the stacking order

Glossary

@font-face rule A variation of a style rule that indicates the font name and the location of the files necessary for implementing a downloadable font.

@media rules Style rules that incorporate media types.

AAC One of three main audio codecs in wide use on the Web today; developed by a consortium of companies and declared a standard by the Moving Picture Experts Group (MPEG).

Absolute link The full and complete address for a target document on the Web.

Absolute positioning A positioning technique that takes an element out of the page flow entirely and allows other elements to flow into the space it would have occupied.

a element The element that creates a link on any element that it encloses.

Algorithm The set of instructions combining the factors that search engines use to decide the priority of search results.

Alpha channel An aspect of a graphic file that allows creators to specify the level of opacity for areas of a graphic, from totally transparent to totally opaque, or anywhere in between.

Anchors Named locations within the current document to which you can link.

API key A unique string that links the map-related requests from your Web site to your account with a map provider.

Assignment operator The = operator, which enables you to assign a value in JavaScript.

Attribute HTML code that follows the element name in the opening tag, which you can use to provide additional information about the element.

Attribute-value pair The two pieces of information you provide to use an attribute: the attribute name and the value you are assigning to the attribute.

Automated testing A set of testing measures performed by specialized software.

Baseline The bottom of text.

Bitmap image An electronic file that represents an image as a grid of dots and specifies the color of each dot.

Block-level element One of the larger chunks that structure a Web page, such as a heading or a paragraph.

Blog A special-purpose Web site that enables one person or a small number of people to post news or updates, usually focused on a narrow topic.

Body section Web page section whose contents include elements that are visible in the main window of a Web browser, such as paragraphs and headings.

Bot A program used by a search engine to index Web pages.

Box model The way CSS represents the characteristics of Web page elements, treating each element as a rectangular box with several global properties.

Browser sniffing A technique to identify the brand and version of each user's browser by using a script to ask the browser to identify itself.

Cascading The process of determining precedence among inline styles, embedded styles, external styles, and/or browser settings, which results in all available styles coalescing into a single virtual style sheet for the user agent's reference in rendering content.

Cascading Style Sheets (CSS) A companion language to HTML designed for describing the appearance of Web page elements.

Cell The intersection of a row and a column in a table, in which each item of data is displayed.

Character encoding The system user agents should employ to translate the electronic information representing a Web page into human-recognizable symbols, such as letters and numbers.

Character references Specially formatted codes that represent characters in the HTML document character set.

Check box A box that users can click to add or remove a check mark, enabling users to select or deselect it.

Child element An element nested within another element.

class selector A selector that creates a style rule based on values assigned to elements using the HTML class attribute.

Closing tag The tag you place at the end of an element you are marking.

Codec An encoding method for audio or video; short for coder/decoder.

Collapse What happens in the box model when adjacent top and bottom margins combine into a single margin equal to the greater of the two values.

Column A vertical set of cells in a table.

Comments Text elements in your Web page code that are not rendered by user agents and are viewable only by people who examine the HTML code of your Web pages.

Comparison operators JavaScript operators that let you determine whether two values are the same.

Concatenation operator The + sign in JavaScript, which unites multiple literal and/or variable values into a single string.

Conditional statement In JavaScript, a statement in which the result of a comparison in values determines which one of multiple options is executed.

Conditional style sheets Style sheets specified using media queries within link elements to indicate which style sheet browsers should load in a given situation.

Container A file within which a video stream and any accompanying audio are packaged for distribution.

Crawler *See* bot.

CSS *See* Cascading Style Sheets.

Dead links Links whose targets don't exist.

Deprecated Describes HTML features that can still be used, but whose use is no longer recommended.

Descendant selector A compound selector made up of multiple individual selectors, which targets elements based on their nesting.

Description list A list that enables you to specify a name–value pair for each list item.

Design document *See* project plan.

DNS server A specialized Web server that looks up the IP address that corresponds to a given domain name and passes that information to a Web client, which then uses it to access a Web site.

DOCTYPE declaration An element that lets user agents know the language in which document contents are written.

Document Object Model (DOM) A standardized way of referring to the parts of a Web page, using a hierarchical arrangement of the content of an HTML document in a tree-like structure.

DOM *See* Document Object Model.

Domain name registrar A person or organization authorized by ICANN to reserve domain names.

Domain name service (DNS) The central directory for the Web, similar to a phone book, which connects the IP address of a Web resource with its domain name.

DOM tree The hierarchical arrangement of the content of an HTML document into a tree-like structure, which is used in the Document Object Model.

Dot notation The syntax used to identify a specific item within the DOM, in which you list the objects, properties, and methods leading to it in the DOM tree in order, separated by periods.

Dots per inch (DPI) The unit of measurement for image resolution, which specifies how close the dots in the bitmap should appear on the output.

DPI *See* dots per inch.

Drop cap A common visual effect in print media in which the first letter of a paragraph or section is enlarged and drops below the first line of text.

Drop-down menu A form interface for creating a list of options from which users can select, which browsers display as a small text box with a triangle next to it.

Element A specific component of a Web page, such as a paragraph or a heading.

Email harvesters Programs that continually explore Web pages looking for email addresses that in turn receive spam emails.

Embedded style sheet A section of CSS code entered in the head element of an HTML document.

Encoding The process of transforming a moving image and/or sound into a digital file.

Event An action defined for a Web page; an event can trigger a script.

Event handler An HTML attribute that specifies a type of user action, enabling you to indicate code to execute in response to a specific event.

Extensible Hypertext Markup Language (XHTML) A successor to HTML 4.01 intended to make HTML interoperable with XML.

Extensible Markup Language (XML) A more generic markup language than HTML that enables users to describe any kind of document, instead of only Web pages.

External style sheet A standalone CSS document containing style information that multiple Web pages can link to.

Favicon A custom graphic file 16 pixels in width by 16 pixels in height, saved in the .ico format, and named favicon.ico associated with a Web page; browsers display a favicon in the address bar and on the bookmark or favorites menu and bar.

Feature detection A technique for identifying the features that a user's browser supports by running a series of tests.

Feed The most recent set of updates from a person or organization on a blog or social media site.

Feed reader *See* news aggregator.

Field A form element in which users enter or select data.

Fieldset A group of fields that forms a logical unit.

File Transfer Protocol (FTP) A means of communication specifically created for moving files between two networked computers and the most common method of transferring documents to a Web server.

Fixed layout A Web page layout that uses a fixed page width.

Fixed positioning A positioning technique similar to absolute positioning that places an element at the top of the stacking order and positions it relative to the browser window rather than to a Web page element.

Flash Video A container format commonly used to encode various proprietary and public audio and video formats.

Fluid layout A Web page layout that gives a Web page the flexibility to adjust its width based on the width of a user's browser window; *also called* liquid layout.

Font family A collection of a single typeface and its variants.

Font stack A list of font families in order of preference, separated by commas, which is a common format for values of the font-family property.

Form A group of elements that lets users type text, select from lists or check boxes, and/or click buttons to provide information, and then submit that information.

FTP *See* File Transfer Protocol.

FTP client A dedicated program for transferring files via FTP.

Function A chunk of JavaScript code with a name assigned to it; a function enables you to group multiple lines of code and call them as a single unit.

Generic font families Groupings of font families according to shared characteristics.

Geolocation The type of objects and methods in HTML5 that enable you to obtain and work with a user's precise location.

GIF An image format that works best for art containing limited numbers of colors and areas with defined borders between areas; short for Graphics Interchange Format.

Going live Publishing a Web site to a Web server to make it available to anyone with Web access.

Graceful degradation Ensuring that the appearance and usability of a Web site doesn't depend on any advanced features; when the site is viewed in browsers that don't support some features, Web page elements that use those features should nevertheless be displayed in a usable way.

Grandchild element The child element of a child element of the current element.

Grandparent element The parent element of the parent element of the current element.

H.264 One of three main video codecs in wide use on the Web today; developed by the Moving Pictures Experts Group (MPEG).

Hand-coding Creating a Web page by entering HTML directly.

Hash tags Searchable codes that allow users to find postings on a given topic on a Web site such as Twitter.

Head section The section of an HTML document containing elements that are not part of the main Web page, such as the title element.

Helper program A program traditionally required for playing a video or audio file on a computer; the program can both unpack the relevant container and decode the video and audio streams.

Hexadecimal system A system for specifying colors that uses a pound sign (#) followed by six digits, which may include the numbers 0–9 and the letters a–f; the first two digits specify the red

value, the middle two digits indicate the green value, and the final pair of digits represents the blue value.

hsl system A system for specifying colors that uses a set of comma-separated values, each ranging from 0–255 or 0–100%, which represent the amounts of hue, saturation, and light in a color.

HTML *See* Hypertext Markup Language.

http *See* Hypertext Transfer Protocol.

https *See* Hypertext Transfer Protocol Secure.

Hyperlink *See* link.

Hypertext Links in and between text-only documents.

Hypertext Markup Language (HTML) A standardized format for specifying the structure of a Web page.

Hypertext Transfer Protocol (http) One of the schemes that Web servers use to make documents available.

Hypertext Transfer Protocol Secure (https) One of the schemes that Web servers use to make documents available.

Id selector A CSS selector that applies code in its associated style rule to the element with the specified id attribute value.

IETF *See* Internet Engineering Task Force.

Inline element A fine-grained element that appears within a block-level element, such as a word or phrase within a paragraph.

Inline frame A Web page element that acts as a self-contained Web page within the HTML document where it's located; commonly used to present content from other Web sites while preserving formatting and presentation that may look quite different from the surrounding Web page.

Inline style A style rule inserted into the opening tag of an element using the style attribute.

Internet Engineering Task Force (IETF) The organization that defined and published the first two versions of HTML.

IP address The four-part address used to access Web resources; the address is made up of four numbers, each of which can have a value from zero to 255, separated by periods.

JavaScript The most widely supported scripting language among modern Web browsers.

JPEG An image format optimized for images that contain many colors, such as photographs; *also called* JPG; short for Joint Photographic Experts Group, the organization that created it.

JPG *See* JPEG.

Label An element containing descriptive text that is associated with a form element; a label helps make the significance of a field clear to users.

Layer A new level displayed on top of the basic flow of elements on the Web page, into which a positioned element is placed.

Legend A descriptive title for a fieldset.

Library A collection of reusable script code.

Link Text or another Web page element that users can select to open another document containing related content; *also called* hyperlink.

Link shortener A Web-based service that transforms large, unwieldy links into manageable URIs.

Liquid layout *See* fluid layout.

Local root folder The main directory on the computer, USB drive, or shared network drive where you save all of the files for your Web site.

Logical operators JavaScript operators that allow you to logically connect multiple values in a comparison.

Mailto link A link that creates a new email to a specified recipient.

Media queries Conditional statements that you can include in an @media rule.

Method An action that can be performed for a node in the DOM tree.

Microblog A blog that limits the size of posted updates.

Microdata A working draft created by the W3C for adding more types of semantic data to Web page content.

Microformats A predecessor to microdata as a specification for adding semantic data to Web page elements.

MIME types A standardized list of data types used to describe the container format for a file in an audio, video, or source element.

Minify To compress a style sheet or script file by removing comments, spaces, and other characters that are useful for human readability but that don't affect the meaning of the code.

MP3 One of three main audio codecs in wide use on the Web today; developed by the Moving Picture Experts Group (MPEG).

MPEG-4 A container format commonly used to encode H.264 video and AAC audio.

Multicolumn layout A layout that involves columns of text and graphics running parallel to each other down the page.

Name-value pair CSS code that specifies the name of a property to apply to a selector, along with the value to assign that property.

Native For a bitmap image, the native dimensions are the original width and height at which the image was saved.

Nav bar A set of links for moving between Web pages in a Web site; *also called* navigation bar.

Navigation bar *See* nav bar.

Nesting An arrangement of Web page elements in which one element is located entirely within another.

News aggregator A utility that lets you bookmark blogs and view the latest headlines and content in a single place.

Node The representation of each part of an HTML document—including elements, attributes, and text content—in the DOM.

Object An HTML element in the DOM.

Ogg A container format commonly used to encode Theora video and Vorbis audio.

One-sided tags HTML tags that are used by themselves, rather than in pairs.

Opening tag The tag you place at the start of an element you are marking.

Operator A symbol used in JavaScript to compare or change the values of multiple objects or properties.

Option button A type of input that presents users with a circular box for selecting one option from a set of choices.

Ordered list A list in which items are numbered or lettered sequentially.

Orphaned styles Style rules based on selectors that no longer apply to any elements in your Web pages.

Page flow The default order of a Web page in which elements are displayed based on the sequence in which they appear in the HTML code.

Parent element An element with another element nested within it.

Patch *See* shim.

Path The part of a URI composed of the sequence of folders in which the target document is stored on the server.

Pixels The individual dots that make up an image, used to measure the size of a bitmap image.

Plugin *See* helper program.

PNG A graphics format originally designed as an alternative to GIF that also supports an alpha channel; short for Portable Network Graphics.

Presentational Describes a language such as CSS, which is designed to describe the appearance of items.

Prettifying *See* tidying

Preview To open a Web page in one or more user agents and examine the result.

Progressive enhancement The practice of adding additional features as enhancements only for browsers that can render them, rather than making advanced features crucial to the layout of a Web site.

Project plan A summary of the goals, objectives, and target audience of a planned Web site. *Also called* design document.

Property A single piece of information associated with a DOM node.

Pseudo-class A categorization of a Web page element for CSS purposes based on a relationship or condition of the element at a given moment, rather than on a static property.

Pseudo-element A selector that enables you to isolate a piece of a larger element for styling.

Radio button *See* option button.

RDFa A specialized version of the resource description framework (RDF) language; RDFa is another specification for adding semantic data to Web page elements.

Really Simple Syndication (RSS) *See* Rich Site Summary (RSS).

Reflowing The process in which browsers change the locations of elements on a Web page to fit a change in available space.

Relative link A link that gives only the path and filename information necessary to locate the target document based on the location of the current Web page.

Relative positioning A positioning technique that lets you make adjustments to the default position of an element while preserving the space allotted to the element in the default page flow.

Render To display, as when a user agent displays a Web page.

Rendering engine Software that translates Web page elements into visual, auditory, or tactile representations based on Web standards.

Resolution Specifies how close the dots in a bitmap should appear on the output; measured in dots per inch (DPI).

rgb system A system that uses rgb triplets to specify colors.

rgb triplet A set of comma-separated values, each ranging from 0–255 or 0–100%, which represent the amounts of red, green, and blue in a color.

Rich Site Summary (RSS) A format for a document that contains feed information for a Web site.

Rollover effect A change to a Web page element when a user's mouse pointer is over the element but not clicking it.

Row A horizontal set of cells in a table.

RSS *See* Rich Site Summary.

Sans-serif font A font that does not incorporate serifs.

Scalable Vector Graphics (SVG) A graphics format that's optimal for encoding line art and that can be displayed at different dimensions with no decrease in quality.

Scheme The way that computers ask for and communicate about a requested document.

Screen readers Devices that many people with visual impairments use to access the Web, which read aloud Web page text and descriptions that a user selects.

Script More complex Web page code written in another programming language.

Search engine optimization (SEO) The process of tailoring the structure and content of a Web page with search engines in mind.

Selection interface A Web page feature that presents users with allowable options visually or enables them to manipulate values without entering text.

Selectors The parts of a style rule that identify the HTML element or elements to which the rule applies.

Semantic Describes languages such as HTML, which are intended to indicate the meanings of elements such as headings and paragraphs, but not to tell Web browsers how the elements should appear.

SEO *See* Search engine optimization (SEO).

Serif font A font that uses serifs.

Serifs Small finishing strokes at the ends of the lines making up each character in some fonts.

Server farm A specially designed facility for Web servers that provides a constant flow of electricity and uninterrupted Internet access.

Server name The part of a URI that identifies the general location of a target document on the Web.

Shim A script written specifically to bridge the gap between browsers with reduced feature sets and more fully featured browsers.

Sibling elements Two elements that are both children of the same parent element.

Sitemap A file in a specific format that lists all the pages in a Web site and may include information about content such as images or video in the pages as well.

Skip link A link at the top of the body section of a Web page that increases accessibility by targeting an anchor at the start of the main page content, allowing users to bypass navigation.

Social bookmarking The process of connecting with current and potential customers on social media sites.

Social media Web sites and other forums that provide users, customers, and community members with methods for sharing online content and integrating their own comments.

Social network The group of people that a person knows or shares a common interest with.

Social networking site A Web site such as Facebook or LinkedIn that enables people to share information about common interests, news, and events with friends, colleagues, and any other people they choose.

Span element A generic element that allows you to isolate a specific section of a larger element.

Sprite A combination of simple image editing and CSS code that enables you to load multiple background images for a Web page with a single request to the server.

Stack To overlap Web page elements using positioning.

Statement Code for a single instruction in a script.

Storyboard In Web site planning, a sketch that outlines the components of each page and their places in the layout, as well as the links between the pages in the Web site.

Stream An encoded set of video data.

Style rules Lines or blocks of CSS code that specify the presentation of Web page elements.

Submit button A button that users can click to submit the data they've entered in a form.

SVG *See* Scalable Vector Graphics.

Tags HTML codes that specify how user agents should treat each item in a Web document.

Target document The Web page or other document that a link opens.

Template A generic Web site layout that includes a color scheme and element positions, but which uses placeholder images and text.

Testing server A non-publicized Web server used for testing purposes, which may require a password for access.

Text area A field that allows users to enter multiple lines of text.

Text box A single-line text field in which users can type a small amount of text.

Theora One of three main video codecs in wide use on the Web today; developed by the Xiph.org Foundation.

Tidying Standardizing the indents and line breaks in your code, as well as ensuring the code conforms to some basic rules.

Tiling The default behavior of user agents when displaying small background images, meaning that, like tiles on a floor or wall, the images are displayed repeatedly both across and down a page to fill up the browser window.

Tweet A single post on twitter.com.

Type selectors CSS selectors that use the names of HTML elements, such as h1 or p, and apply associated name-value pairs to every instance of the specified element(s).

Uniform resource identifier (URI) A standard format for specifying how and where to access a resource on the Internet; *also known as* Web address.

Unordered list A list in which the order of list items doesn't matter.

URI *See* uniform resource identifier.

Usability A Web site's ease of use.

Usability testing A crucial part of improving a site's usability, in which a developer sits down with potential or actual users of the site, asks them to accomplish a task, notes how they go about it and whether they are successful, and asks for their feedback.

User agents Programs and devices that interpret Web documents.

Validation Putting your code through an automated comparison against Web coding standards.

Variable A means of storing the result of a JavaScript command.

Vector graphic An electronic file that describes a graphic using geometric shapes.

Vocabulary A group of definitions of keyword values for specific types of information; in microdata, vocabularies serve as a common language for referencing kinds of data.

Vorbis One of three main audio codecs in wide use on the Web today; developed by the Xiph.org Foundation.

VP8 One of three main video codecs in wide use on the Web today; developed by On2.

W3C *See* World Wide Web Consortium.

WCAG *See* Web Content Accessibility Guidelines.

Web *See* World Wide Web.

Web address *See* uniform resource identifier.

Web Content Accessibility Guidelines (WCAG) A widely used reference for implementing Web accessibility maintained by the World Wide Web Consortium.

Web host A company that provides access to space on a Web server for a yearly or monthly fee.

Web Hypertext Application Technology Working Group (WHATWG) The organization formed by several major technology companies to begin a process of creating the HTML specification that would become HTML5.

WebM A container format commonly used to encode VP8 video and Vorbis audio.

Webmaster The person in charge of a Web site.

Web pages Documents formatted to be accessible on the Web.

Web server A computer optimized to store and share Web documents and that has an extremely high-speed Internet connection.

Web sites Collections of Web pages that are available to anyone with Web access.

WHATWG *See* Web Hypertext Application Technology Working Group.

World Wide Web A vast collection of publicly accessible, linked documents written in Hypertext Markup Language and related languages. *Also called* Web.

World Wide Web Consortium (W3C) The organization founded to take on the responsibility of maintaining HTML standards after the second version.

XHTML *See* Extensible Hypertext Markup Language.

XML *See* Extensible Markup Language.

Index